Masters of Illusion

American Leadership in the Media Age

The contemporary world is being swept along by a swift current of events that has beguiled many Americans into believing our future will be bright if we extricate ourselves from Iraq and shield ourselves from terror. This path-breaking and provocative book not only debunks such wishful thinking but also identifies a series of impending perils that are more threatening to our nation's survival. They include ambitious thrusts from Russia, China, and, perhaps more surprisingly, the European Union, all driven by the progress of a profound reconfiguration of global wealth and power widely ignored in the international relations literature. The authors' perspective is iconoclastic and eye-opening; and it is not limited to diagnostics. They explain why our political and business leaders, captive to our public culture, are unlikely to see the dangers, and why effective presidents must lead by piercing a veil of partisan distortion blurring our vision. They make a compelling case that America will fall prey to multilateralist "friends" and malevolent foes unless the nation replaces the Cold War doctrine of mutually assured destruction, rendered obsolete by nuclear proliferation, with a new policy of strategic independence.

Steven Rosefielde is Professor of Economics at the University of North Carolina, Chapel Hill, and Adjunct Professor of Defense and Strategic Studies at the Center for Defense and Strategic Studies, Southwest Missouri State University, Springfield. The author or editor of eleven books on Russia and the Soviet Union, including *Russia in the 21st Century* (Cambridge University Press, 2005), he is also a member of the Russian Academy of Natural Science. Professor Rosefielde has served as a consultant to the Office of the Secretary of Defense and advised several directors of the U.S. Central Intelligence Agency and the U.S. National Intelligence Council. Professor Rosefielde has also worked with the Swedish Defense Agency and the Central Economics and Mathematics Institute (Moscow) for more than a quarter century and with the Center for Defense and Foreign Policy (Moscow) for more than a decade.

D. Quinn Mills has held the Albert J. Weatherhead, Jr., Chair in Business Administration at Harvard Business School since 1976. He was previously a professor at the Sloan School of Management at MIT. Professor Mills is the author of more than twenty-five books on leadership and management, including *Human Resources Management* (2006); *Principles of Management* (2005); *Wheel, Deal, and Steal: Deceptive Accounting, Deceitful CEOs, and Ineffective Reforms* (2003); and *Buy, Lie, and Sell High: How Investors Lost Out on Enron and the Internet Bubble* (2002). He has been a corporate or executive education consultant to more than a dozen Fortune 500 companies and in nearly twenty countries, as well as to the U.S. government's Fannie Mae program.

Masters of Illusion

American Leadership in the Media Age

STEVEN ROSEFIELDE

University of North Carolina

D. QUINN MILLS

Harvard University

CAMBRIDGE UNIVERSITY PRESS
Cambridge, New York, Melbourne, Madrid, Cape Town, Singapore, São Paulo

Cambridge University Press
32 Avenue of the Americas, New York, NY 10013-2473, USA

www.cambridge.org
Information on this title: www.cambridge.org/9780521857444

First published 2007

Printed in the United States of America

A catalog record for this publication is available from the British Library.

Library of Congress Cataloging in Publication Data

Rosefielde, Steven.
Masters of illusion : American leadership in the media age /
Steven Rosefielde, D. Quinn Mills.
p.   cm.
Includes bibliographical references.
ISBN 0-521-85744-9 (hardback)
1. Government information – United States.   2. Political culture – United States.
3. National security – United States.   4. United States – Politics and government.
I. Mills, Daniel Quinn.   II. Title.
JK468.S4R58   2006
306.20973–dc22   2006004806

ISBN-13   978-0-521-85744-4 hardback
ISBN-10   0-521-85744-9 hardback

In memory of David Rosefielde

Contents

List of Tables and Figures   *page* xiv

Preface   xvii

Acronyms   xxi

Executive Summary   xxv

Acknowledgments   xxvii

PART I. NATIONAL SECURITY IN THE NEW AGE

1   A World Wounded   3

    The Post–Cold War Security Environment   3
    The Need to Adjust Illusion to Reality   7
    Public Culture Distorts Reality   10
    Antiterrorism Measures Are Not Enough   12
    Mastering the Illusions of the Public Culture   15
    CHAPTER 1: KEY POINTS   17

2   Long-Term Economic Realism   18

    Vortexes of Danger   18
    Why Economic Realism and Scientific Objectivity Are Sorely
        Needed   20
    Our Country Has Changed   22
    The Coming Threats to American Security   23
    Strategic Independence   25
    The Need for the International Order to Adapt to Changes
        among Nations and Regions of the World   28
    Presidential Candor   30
    CHAPTER 2: KEY POINTS   33

PART II. AMERICAN PUBLIC CULTURE AND THE WORLD | 35

3 "Smooth Comforts False" – The Illusions That Confuse Us | 37
Ways in Which Public Culture Influences Thinking about the
    World | 41
Harmonism | 42
Convergence | 47
Unjustified Optimism | 52
The Persistence of Public Culture | 55
Public Culture: A Formal Expression | 58
CHAPTER 3: KEY POINTS | 62

4 Towers of Illusion: Dysfunctional Behaviors | 63
Simplification | 64
Naïve Motivations | 64
Either/Or Choices | 65
Overemphasis on Relationships | 66
How Simplification Misleads | 67
Hype | 68
Distortion | 76
Mastering the Illusions of Public Culture | 80
CHAPTER 4: KEY POINTS | 81

5 Mythomaniacs: The Sources of Our Illusions | 82
The American Public's Wishful Thinking | 83
    A Glaring Dishonesty of Wishful Thinking | 84
The Delusions of Wishful Thinking | 86
Political Partisanship | 88
The Media | 91
Journalists | 93
Commercial Enterprises | 95
Presidents and Media | 96
CHAPTER 5: KEY POINTS | 99

PART III. AMERICAN PUBLIC CULTURE AND OURSELVES

6 Champions of Freedom or Imperialists: How We're Perceived | 103
How We and Others See Us | 103
President Bush's Image of Americans versus the View from
    Abroad | 104
What Polls Say | 106
The Complex Character of America | 108
Self-Deceptive Duplicity | 109
Accusations of Imperialism | 111

America's Changed Message 115
CHAPTER 6: KEY POINTS 116

7 We're Different Now 117

Going Where We Didn't Seek to Go 118
How We Americans Have Changed 119
A Change in Direction 121
After World War I 123
After World War II 124
After the Vietnam War 124
Changes after September 11 124
Iraq – The First Big Test 124
Hidden Motivations 126
Our Fatal Flaw 128
CHAPTER 7: KEY POINTS 130

PART IV. THE RECONFIGURATION OF NATIONAL WEALTH AND
POWER

8 The Economic Roots of American Power 133

American Economic Success 133
The American Economic Culture 135
The American Economic Creed 137
How National Economic Cultures Differ 139
How Different Economic Cultures Yield Different Results 141
The Economic Cultures of the Great Powers 142
China 142
Russia 146
Japan 151
Key Points – Japan's Unique Role 161
European Union 161
CHAPTER 8: KEY POINTS 168

9 Economic Disparities among Nations 170

The Consequences of Differing Economic Cultures 170
The Statistical Record 173
The Increasing Gap between Developed and Underdeveloped
Nations 182
CHAPTER 9: KEY POINTS 183

10 Geopolitical Aspirations of the Nations 185

Nationalist Fervor in China 185
Chinese–American Rivalry 185
The Trend of the Political Climate in China 188

The Growth and Modernization of China's Military   195
   China in the Future   197
Will China Be an Enemy?   199
Reviving Superpower: Russia   204
Rose-Colored Glasses about Russia   205
Why the Soviet Union Imploded: Back to the Future   207
   Russia – A False Democracy   212
   Russia Will Rearm   214
   Rose-Colored Glasses Again   215
   Russia in the Distant Future   217
   The European Union: Nation-Building on a
     Super Scale   218
How Europeans Seek to Bind America   223
Britain's Special Situation   226
The American Response to European Nation-Building   228
CHAPTER 10: KEY POINTS   229

PART V. VORTEXES OF DANGER   233

11   A Witch's Brew of Troubles: The Next Big Wars   235

Present and Looming Dangers   236
Dangers of Many Sorts   237
The Biggest Dangers Facing Us   238
Terrorism   240
   Russian Military Resurgence: Rising from the Ashes – From
     Weakness to Strength Overnight   240
   Chinese Nationalism   244
   European Union Unification and Rivalry   246
Interactions   246
Lessons from Experience   248
   The MAD World – The Risk of Nuclear War   248
   Able Archer – 1983   252
Nuclear Missile Defense (NMD)   254
The Dynamics of World Disorder   257
   What Our Leaders Should Do   259
CHAPTER 11: KEY POINTS   262

12   The Middle East   264

The Crescent of Fire   264
   Ummah   267
   Muslim Terrorism and Autocracy   267
The Causes of Terrorism   270
The Contest in the Middle East   277
Palestine   279
The Israeli–Palestinian Smokescreen   283

The Broader Issues 285
Justifying Terrorism 286
Why We Invaded Iraq 288
How the Administration Confused Us about the Purpose of the
    War in Iraq 291
The Ongoing Battle in Iraq 294
Satans Great and Small 298
Containment 299
CHAPTER 12: KEY POINTS 301

PART VI. THE AMERICAN RESPONSE 303

13 Strategic Independence: An Ounce of Prevention 305

An Alternative to Multilateralism 305
Strategic Independence and Engagement 306
National Missile Defense 308
The Bush Doctrine 316
    Defense Policy Should Not be Tied to an Overreaching
        Foreign Policy 317
    A Window of Opportunity 318
    Preemption: An Ounce of Prevention Is Worth a
        Pound of Cure 320
World War II Was Avoidable 322
    Preemption Could Have Prevented 9/11 323
When to Preempt 325
Calculating the Risk 326
Successful Preemptions 328
    Napoleon 328
    Grenada, 1983 328
    Preemption and Nuclear Weapons 328
    The Soviet Union, 1948 329
Soviet Union, Cuban Missile Crisis, 1962 329
    Soviet Union, President Johnson, 1963 and Beyond 329
    Iraq, President George W. Bush, 2003 329
CHAPTER 13: KEY POINTS 330

14 America as Mature Superpower 332

American Military Effectiveness 332
Revolution in Military Affairs 333
The Myth of War without Casualties 335
A Full-Range Military 336
The Case against Strategic Independence 337
Why Strategic Independence Should Now Displace the Current
    American National Security Strategy 338
CHAPTER 14: KEY POINTS 340

PART VII. LEADING TOWARD PEACE

15 The Dangers of Overreach   343

Overreach   343
    America as a Model for the World   343
    America's System Is Too Good to Transfer   344
    America's System Isn't Good Enough to Transfer   347
Beyond Self-Affirming Sloganeering   350
Democracy as the Wellspring of Peace   352
    The Danger of American Overreach   354
CHAPTER 15: KEY POINTS   357

16 The Transatlantic Trap   359

The Multilateralist Vision   360
Forecasts of a Declining America   362
Collective Security Doesn't Work   363
The Limits to Being a Team Player   366
All the Way via Multilateralism to a World Government   371
Multilateralism as an End   373
Unilateral Partial Disarmament   375
An Independent America   378
CHAPTER 16: KEY POINTS   382

17 The Middle Course   384

Adjusting to Major Changes in the World   384
Finding a Grand Strategy   387
Responding to Russia   390
Responding to China   391
Shoulder or Shed: Are We Suited to Be a Hyperpower?   396
Overreliance on Our Military   398
An Inappropriate Public Culture   400
CHAPTER 17: KEY POINTS   402

PART VIII. AMERICAN PRESIDENTIAL LEADERSHIP   403

18 How Public Culture Inhibits Presidential Leadership   405

Poor Choices for President   405
Weak Presidential Leadership   406
The Geopolitics of Presidential Personalities   409
    Harry Truman   409
    John F. Kennedy as "a Little Boy"   410
    Vietnam   411
The Cuban Missile Crisis   412
Domestic Focus in Leadership Selection   414

Weak Leadership in Foreign Affairs 415
Misjudging Foreign Leaders 416
American Presidents' Questionable Skills at War 418
President Wilson 418
President Franklin Roosevelt 419
President Truman 420
President Kennedy 420
President Johnson 421
President Nixon 421
President Carter 421
President Reagan 421
President Bush, Senior 422
President Clinton 422
Grading President George W. Bush 423
Don't Rely on Advisors 429
The Greatest Presidential Challenges 432
CHAPTER 18: KEY POINTS 435

19 Choosing a Great President 436
A Leadership Deficiency 436
Preparation for the Presidency 439
Qualifications for the Presidency 441
Experience 441
Demonstrated Personal Qualifications 442
CHAPTER 19: KEY POINTS 444

20 Master of Illusions 446
A Strong Tide of Truth 447
Truth Used to Be the First Casualty of War 449
George W. Bush and Our Public Culture 453
A Tactical Response versus a Strategic Objective 456
A Game Played with Other People's Lives 460
The Next Steps 461
The Key Arguments of This Book 465
Brief KEY POINTS of This Book 470

Notes 473
Glossary 503
Bibliography 509
Index 525

List of Tables and Figures

TABLES

9.1 Reconfiguration of Relative Living Standards: China and West Europe, 1–2001 AD (1990 international Geary-Khamis dollars) *page* 174

9.2 Global Economic Divergence 1913–2001 per Capita GDP Growth (Compound annual rates: percent) 175

9.3 Centrally Planned Communist Growth Spurts and Decay (per capita GDP growth: percent) 175

9.4 Inferior Russian Economic Performance 1000–2001 AD(per capita GDP growth: percent) 176

9.5 Comparative Size Estimates USSR and the United States 1917–2001 (billion 1990 international Geary-Khamis dollars and percent) 177

9.6 Comparative Size Estimates Russia and the United States 1973–2001 (billion 1990 international Geary-Khamis dollars and percent) 177

9.7 Comparative Size Estimates per Capita GDP 1913–2001(America = 100) 178

9.8 Reconfiguration of Global Living Standards 2000–2050 (1990 international Geary-Khamis dollars) 178

9.9 Comparative Living Standard Size Projections 2000–2050 (America = 100: percent) 179

9.10 Reconfiguration of Global GDP 2000–2050 (billion 1990 international Geary-Khamis dollars) 180

9.11 Comparative GDP Size Projections 2000–2050 (America = 100: percent) 181

9.12 Comparative GDP Size Estimates USSR and US 1917–1989 (dollar PPP, various bases, percent) 182

12.1 GDP in the Judea/Palestine Region 1950–2002 (million 1990 international Geary-Khamis dollars) 268

12.2 GDP per Capita in Judea/Palestine Region 1950–2002   269
12.3 GDP of the Crescent of Fire 1950–2002 (billion 1990
        international Geary-Khamis dollars)   269
12.4 GDP per Capita in the Crescent of Fire 1950–2002 (1990
        international Geary-Khamis dollars)   270

FIGURES

9.1 Comparative Living Stardard Size Projections 1900–2050
       (America = 100: percent)   179
9.2 Comparative GDP Size Projections 1900–2050 (America =
       100: percent)   181

Preface

The ideological conflicts of the twentieth century have faded. In this book, we find no need to deconstruct competing ideologies. Instead, certain habitual attitudes of our nation – embedded in our public culture (hodgepodge of political beliefs and nonpolitical wishful thinking) – now exercise an influence more powerful than the strongest of the ideologies of the past. The public culture is stronger because there is less opposition to it than there would be to a monolithic ideology because wishful thinking is continually reinforced by all elements of society – political, intellectual, and media. Its hold on our minds is stronger than ever was the hold of an ideology on our hearts. Hence, there is a compelling need to compare public culture to reality, and to point to the dangers of the illusions inherent in our public culture.

America will be confronted with a cascading sequence of military-diplomatic threats in the next four decades. Some are glimpsed by our leaders, but none are adequately understood because our leaders' perceptions are impaired by wishful thinking including a childish faith in the good intentions of others and in the world becoming more and more like America. In this book, we try to slice through this fog of illusion by using various technical economic tools and analytic instruments like deconstruction. The latter has often been a Marxist method of choice, focused on exposing the hidden agenda of the capitalist class. We harness deconstruction to a different purpose. The agendas and stratagems we uncover are those of the makers of public culture – itself a far more heterogeneous, elusive, and powerful phenomenon than ideology.

Our methods allow us to foresee the impending reconfiguration of global wealth and power that which will shape the setting of our security concerns in the half century 2000–2050. The threats that emerge are the consequences of pronounced and persistent economic trends that are in some important cases far different from what we are commonly led to expect.

The deconstruction of public culture permits us to appreciate why our leaders deny what is otherwise evident, and why they are perpetually tilting at windmills with ethereal swords like nation-building and democratization.

Finally, we identify a more effective position for America – strategic independence – addressing not only terrorism but also the next wave of dangers posed by Russia, China, and possibly the European Union. Strategic independence accords preeminence to our country's defense in place of moralistic or utopian visions.

Two Americans born during World War II have written this book, employing five major disciplines – leadership, economics, geopolitics, history, and national security. No single author could cover all these areas effectively, and we, the two authors of this book, draw on each other's strengths to integrate insights from the five disciplines into a coherent whole.

Part of this book discusses the defense and foreign policy positions of the George W. Bush administration from a pragmatic point of view. It has not been possible to do this previously because its principles had not yet been much embodied in foreign policy. But in the late summer of 2002, the Bush administration enunciated important principles in its statement, "The National Security Strategy of the United States," and then applied them in Afghanistan and Iraq. Hence, we can now review the application and execution of Bush's foreign policy and defense principles and comment on their strengths and limitations.

We are critical of mainstream conventional political debate. This is because much of today's political dialogue obscures more issues than it illuminates – it's at best oblique to the major concerns; at worse it completely distorts them. For example, the critical matter of the impact of the American invasion of Iraq in carrying the battle to the terrorists is twisted into a question of whether or not the streets of Iraq are safe. So-called democracy-building in Iraq displaces the battle against Islamic terrorism and insurrection as the key concern of American policy in the Middle East (after all, democracy is a characteristic of states, and if it contributes to peace, it does so by making a nation less likely to go to war; but terrorism and insurrection are a nonstate activity and aren't likely to be much influenced by a shift to democracy). The conventional political debate also settles for labels that don't describe what they're labeling and vague terms that aren't specific. The political dialogue is infused with partisan concerns; much of the popular media pretending to inform the public about the issues is driven by hidden agendas that are both partisan and financial and so by choice of editorial content, by disguise of partisan argument as news, and by selective reporting of events, often mislead the public.

The English economist Alfred Marshall penned our point of view succinctly. "What is most wanted now," he wrote, "is the power of keeping the head cool and clear in tracing and analyzing the combined action of many . . . causes."[1] The duty of responsible commentators is to be certain that their observations are verified, and are not merely projections of their wishes or methods they employ for the manipulation of others.

Sometimes in the following discussion we may sound critical of aspects of our country and its policies. Some of our readers may wonder if a frank discussion that sometimes points to limitations of our presidents in the way they've handled foreign affairs and military conflicts is unpatriotic. We think it is not. All great world leaders have had catastrophic failures; it is how they learn from those debacles and what they do afterward that makes them great. Furthermore, America stands at the threshold of a major shift in our country's role in the world and in our attitude toward it, so that failure to choose leaders who do a better job in foreign relations may be catastrophic. A frank and objective look at our failings as well as our successes is needed and is not unfair to America.

This is one of the first postneoconservative books, critiquing the neoconservative defense and foreign policy positions of the Bush administration from a realist position. We offer neither a liberal nor a neocon point of view, but instead a middle-of-the-road American point of view free of wishful thinking, moderate but strong; not a Europhile and diplomatic (that is, largely conventional and dishonest) expression, but an authentic, thought-out, down-to-earth expression. This book expresses the view of the majority of the American electorate who defend our government while being willing to criticize it in a friendly manner; reject the condescending views offered us by the spokespersons of many of our erstwhile Western European allies; and are prepared to adopt a new strategic posture for our nation in the world – one of Strategic Independence – believing it best in future prospect for ourselves and the world.

In writing this book, we rely much on information from expert sources – the kind that is suppressed or misinterpreted by the public culture. We identify such sources carefully, including our own research. But this book is not a treatise based on factual revelations. Rather, the book is unified by the patterns that emerge from decoding and deconstructing American public culture.

In our research, we used both primary and secondary sources, in large part because the breadth of our approach and our subject matter prohibited reliance on primary sources only. In general, in our economics research we used primary sources; in our leadership and national defense research we used both primary and secondary sources; and in our historical research we used mostly secondary and some primary sources. Wherever we used secondary sources, we've attempted to identify the sources and give their authors full credit for their work.

The two models presented in the book are both of our authorship. The model of the public culture is qualitative; the economic model is both qualitative and quantitative.

We strive for two key elements in our approach:
- Objectivity about situations, based on facts not wishes, opinions, or partisanship; and
- Consistency in our analysis.

We attempt to be fact-driven. We do not start from ideology, first principles or political partisanship. Our models are empirically validated (that is, they are scientific) to be best of our or others' abilities. If facts push in one direction, we go there, recrafting our concepts to fit the facts, not the facts to fit our concepts. That's our basic objection to the public culture – that it continually lets wishful thinking shape its perception of facts. When this happens and our leaders are drawn into its snare, our country is unable to successfully confront challenges to our security.

The book is organized in a way intended to help the reader grasp its content. We first address the public culture of the United States in order that a reader may be assisted in breaking free mentally from predispositions about the other topics of the book. Readers will not be able to appreciate our prioritization of the issues discussed until they have mastered the concept of public culture, and how to decode the American version. This is a very unusual approach to a book on these topics. Most writers start with their worldview, treat it as self-evident, and then never defend their assumptions and convictions. We make ours explicit at the outset, in an attempt to improve understanding of our position.

Acronyms

ABM	antiballistic missile
CCP	Chinese Communist Party
CEO	chief executive officer
CFE	Treaty on Conventional Forces in Europe
CIA	Central Intelligence Agency
DIA	Defense Intelligence Agency
DOD	Department of Defense
FSB	Federal Security Bureau (Federalnaya Sluzhba Bezopasnosti). Russian counterintelligence agency, successor to the KGB
G7	the Group of Seven major industrial nations, including America, Canada, United Kingdom, Germany, France, Italy, and Japan. When the Russian Federation is added, the name shifts to G8
Genshstab	the Russian general staff
Goskomstat	the Soviet state statistical agency; the acronym is still used in the post communist period, together with the alternative Roskomstat (Russian statistical agency)
GDP	Gross domestic product; the aggregate value of all marketable goods and services computed at market or official state prices. This measure of aggregate activity excludes income derived from assets held abroad. GDP is only economically meaningful when prices are competitive (or are shadow equivalents). Otherwise, GDP is a weak indicator of utilities and opportunity costs

GNP	Gross national product; the aggregate value of all marketable goods and services computed at market or official state prices. This measure of aggregate activity includes income derived from assets held abroad
GPS	global positioning system (satellite)
GRU	Soviet state espionage agency (military intelligence)
ICBM	intercontinental ballistic missile
IPO	initial public offering (securities)
IMF	International Monetary Fund
IW	information warfare aimed at influencing enemy perceptions and attitude management
Keidanren	Japanese Federation of Economic Organizations (business policy advocacy group)
KGB	Soviet Committee on State Security (Komitet gosudarstvennoy bezopasnosti), the USSR's foreign intelligence service; renamed FSB (Federal Security Bureau) after 1991
MAD	mutual assured destruction; strategic nuclear doctrine claiming to prevent war by making rivals vulnerable
METI	Ministry of Economy, Trade and Industry (Japan)
Minatom	Ministry of Atomic Energy, responsible for Soviet and Russian nuclear weapons and civilian nuclear activities
MIRV	multiple independently targetable reentry vehicles are pods of nuclear weapons contained in a "bus" that can be directed at more than one target from a single launch vehicle
MVD	Ministry of Internal Affairs (Ministerstvo vnutrennikh del). Soviet and Russian domestic intelligence service. The same acronym also applies to the Ministry of Foreign Affairs, which causes confusion
NATO	North Atlantic Treaty Organization
NGO	nongovernmental organizations (private public policy advocacy groups, often an unofficial form of government outsourcing)

NMD	national missile defense; this is the current term for the American antiballistic missile defense program
OECD	Organization for Economic Cooperation and Development (thirty member countries)
OKP	oboronnyi-promyshennyi kompleks, or defense industrial complex; it is Russia's renamed military industrial complex
PLA	People's Liberation Army (China)
RDT&E	research, development, testing, and evaluation; these are the four core elements of the technological adoption process; mastering new technology is an additional phase in which acquirers learn how to utilitize the technology's full potential
RMA	revolution in military affairs, a term stressing the disjuncture between traditional concepts of warfighting and new ones based on advanced technologies, exemplified in the Iraq War
Rosvooruzheniie	Russian Arms Export Agency
SORT	Strategic Offensive Arms Reduction Treaty
START	Strategic Arms Reduction Talks
TVD	teatry voennykh destvii, theaters of military operations
VPK	voennyi promyshlennyi kompleks, military industrial complex
WMD	weapons of mass destruction (includes nuclear, chemical, and biological arms)

Executive Summary

Since the Soviet Union's collapse, the United States has failed to secure a complete and lasting peace, and we now find ourselves facing as great a nuclear threat as before the end of the Cold War due to nuclear modernization in China and Russia and to nuclear proliferation in India, Pakistan, North Korea, and Iran.

America's most immediate foreign engagement is the war on terror, but it is not the most important challenge we face. Our most important challenge remains what it has been for more than sixty years: to avoid a nuclear exchange between great powers.

However, the international situation is now becoming destabilized by major changes in the fate of the great powers, in particular Russia's decline and China's rise. A major driver of potential conflict among the great powers is the struggle for power and wealth among nations – belying the rhetoric of economic harmonization. Divergent national economic cultures and different rates of economic growth over a long period acerbate tensions – a process that is more likely to end in overt conflict than in peaceful transition.

By 2010, Russia will choose to remilitarize and will be building fifth-generation nuclear capability. Meanwhile, China will be enlarging and modernizing its nuclear missile capability and by 2020 will emerge as a much more effective rival to America and our allies (especially Taiwan and Japan) than it now is.

The leaders of our nation have trouble being objective in identifying threats and responding to them because of the public's wishful thinking, which creates illusions about the world and our role in it. The illusions comprise a public culture that generates inappropriate policy options based on simplistic and distorted understandings about the true threats to America's safety. Wishful thinking causes us to underestimate danger and to overestimate our strength, thereby tempting us to overreach abroad through trying to export, with the help of force, our economic and political culture. We ourselves are the enemy of our survival and we can save ourselves by recognizing it and rectifying our misperceptions.

American foreign policy must be overhauled in order to avoid major wars by abandoning the strategy of balance of power that characterized the Cold War and instead now seeking to attain independence in our strategic positioning. We can't trust our past allies any more because of diverging interests and hidden agendas. It is important that this evolution in our policy be carefully thought through in order that a predictable approach replaces today's confusion of purposes and means.

A new policy of Strategic Independence for America involves enhancing our military power via continuing the revolution in military affairs and adding significant additional defense capabilities.

America needs a transition path to cope with the growing risk of nuclear war – a path that simultaneously places restraints on our aggressiveness in the world's economic and political interplay to mollify our adversaries' fears, while utilizing our technological and economic strength to deter potential breakers of the peace.

From the standpoint of national security, what needs to be done by the United States is:

- Recognize the likely threat sequence – terrorism, Russia, China, Europe – and allocate to each its proper priority as the threats mature.
- Respond to each threat via Strategic Independence. Strategic Independence doesn't require a crash program or crusade. We can do it subtly with discreet persistence.
- Reform our public culture by disavowing wishful thinking and recognizing its distorting influence on our attitudes toward the United Nations, the European Union, and multilateralism.
- Encourage Russia and China to Westernize their economies and governance and to abandon military modernization along an authoritarian trajectory, which is where both – contrary to much reporting and comments by our media and political leadership – are now headed.

Acknowledgments

The scope of *Masters of Illusion* is too large to permit us to thank all those who have contributed to its development, but a special acknowledgment for their insightful comments is due to Mark Benson, Stephen Blank, Kim Davis, Ingemar Doefer, John Gray Evans, Patrick Flynn, Stefan Hedlund, George Hoguet, Rakesh Khurana, Paul Lawrence, Jan Leijonhielm, Bernadette Malone (of Penguin Books), Shirley Mills, Elizabeth Moore, Chris Paige, Ralph William Pfouts, John R. Robinson, Justine Rosefielde, Susan Rosefielde, Jan Rylander, Bruce Scott, Vitaly Shlykov, Wilhelm Unge, William Van Cleave, and Carole Winkler.

Nancy Kocher and Ling Wang provided valuable typing and research assistance. To all again, we offer our sincere thanks.

Our project was largely self-funded, but elements have benefited from funding provided for related research. We therefore gratefully acknowledge the assistance of Harvard Business School's Division of Research, the Earhardt Foundation, Carnegie Foundation, FOI (Swedish Defense Establishment), IREX, the Foundation for the Defense of Democracies, the UNC Institute for the Arts and Humanities, the Grier/Woods Presbyterian Initiative China Travel Award, and the UNC Parr Center for Ethics.

Steven Rosefielde and Quinn Mills

PART ONE

NATIONAL SECURITY IN THE NEW AGE

ONE

A World Wounded

I speak of peace while covert enmity under the smile of safety wounds the world.
Shakespeare, **Henry IV**, part 2, lines 9–10.

THE POST–COLD WAR SECURITY ENVIRONMENT

For a brief moment, after the collapse of the Soviet Union, it seemed that the great powers had agreed on a desired outcome: a world characterized by democratic free enterprise with social justice. And it appeared to follow that this new world order could be speedily achieved by liberalization and disarmament. The objective remains, but the terrorist attack of September 11, 2001, Russia's failed transition to democratic free enterprise, China's military modernization and internal political repression, the persistence of hidden agendas among the great powers that cripples the United Nations and the specter of accelerated nuclear proliferation have undermined the high hopes. The new situation has raised the possibility that the United States will explore the possibility of a very different path to its long run objectives – that is, a different short- and middle-term defense strategy. The different path includes the willingness to fight conventional wars and preemptive attacks. This is a very different agenda than liberalization and disarmament. This change has generated much controversy because many prefer trying to build the new world with the previous methods. Such a preference remains a tenable position insofar as it is based on an objective assessment of the risks, but too often the preference is dogmatic, raising serious problems for responsible leaders.

The issue with which this book is concerned is the defense of America; it is not limited to military response only, but in the broader perspective of our foreign policy – how do we defend ourselves in a world full of current

3

and potential antagonists. We are not focused on public relations (winning hearts and minds abroad) or on crusades for democracy abroad but, rather, on the combination of diplomatic and military activities that constitute a national security strategy.

Our topic is the international relations of America with special emphasis on our defense policy. To discuss the topic adequately, two major concepts are introduced: our nation's *public culture* (the patchwork of beliefs and managed attitudes governing public debate that often allows policymakers to find consensus through trans-partisan wishful thinking), which constitutes the key political context of defense policy; and the concept of *strategic independence* (the ability to protect America without extraneous multilaterallist constraints imposed by others) toward which our defense policy is evolving. Unfortunately the two are in conflict.

In this book, we survey the new security environment including the possibility of a successful change in America's short- and middle-term strategy. At the core of the difficulty of such a shift in strategy is a daunting problem of combating disinformation provided by apparently reliable sources in an effort to distort public perceptions and exploit public cultural wishful thinking for commercial or partisan reasons.

Consequently, there is an urgent need for sophisticated leaders capable of effectively pursuing the new strategy with methods that take account of the ways obstructionists coopt public culture and impair global security for private purposes. While little is entirely new, modern communication technologies and informational warfare tactics seem to mark a quantum change from the past.

The requirements of an American President in international relations are to

- see the big picture objectively;
- appreciate the complex interplay of factors;
- actively and purposefully learn;
- integrate hard and soft information, with the help of intelligence agencies but not relying on them slavishly;
- create novel scenarios and approaches for our policy; and
- set our national goals with imagination and insight.

Logic and decency can prevail in the current international setting, but for this to happen opportunists and those with ulterior motives must be beaten at their own image management game. This is why a president must master the illusions with which the minds of people are filled.

Richard Neustadt and the scholars who follow him make sophisticated excuses for weaknesses in presidential leadership. They describe a president who is captive of others in government and of the limited powers of the presidency. This they describe as due to institutional constraints, and proceed to recommend different methods by which a president might loosen the constraints. Neustadt in particular recommends that presidents master the art of persuasion, not that much different from the view expressed here that effective presidents must master the illusions of those they should lead.[1] But it is proper to have higher expectations of leaders than do these presidential scholars. Leadership is not simply about holding office and developing policy. This is an old view of leadership that confuses office (which is no more than an opportunity to exert leadership) with leadership. Leadership has been much more studied in recent decades in the context of business than of politics, and the insights from that study have yet to be fully applied to the political context. The study of leadership in business has concluded that leadership is not administrative, nor even managerial, in its essence, but is different – leadership involves inspiring others to exertions in a direction that is the leader's vision. Leadership is about managing change. As Jack Welch, then CEO of General Electric, once put it to a group of GE managers, "No matter how good a manager you are, unless you can energize others, you are of no use to our company as a leader." Note that Mr. Welch did not presume that there was only one leader in GE, the CEO, nor did he presume that there could not be leadership demonstrated at many levels of the company. Leadership in his view and that of most management scholars is a function, not a position or office. This basic distinction, which allows clear thinking about leadership and its role in organizations, is currently not common in the literature that studies American presidents.[2]

When the modern managerial concept of leadership is applied to American presidents, then the institutional constraints they face are recognized to be real, but also to be challenges to their effectiveness as leaders – not simply excuses for their failures, as Neustat sees the institutional constraints. This is why mastering illusions is so important – it is crucial to persuading people to loosen the institutional constraints on a president. Loosening constraints is part of the task of a leader, not an excuse for failure. Focusing on institutional constraints is at best only part of the story, and not it's most fundamental part, and is at worst an excuse for ineffective leadership.

Effective presidential leadership involves the loosening of institutional constraints. Examples can be found in American history of this. For example,

Abraham Lincoln rode roughshod over legal and congressional constraints to win the Civil War, including suspending the writ of habeus corpus during much of the war. Harry Truman seized the nation's steel industry during the Korean War to keep production going in the face of a strike. When the Supreme Court told him that was illegal (which he probably already knew), he gave the steel mills back to their owners. About this episode George Taylor quipped, "The President has saved the country, and the Supreme Court has saved the Constitution." That there may be only a few such examples is a comment on the poor quality of presidential leadership in America, not evidence of an intractable situation in which presidents are allegedly placed. Why then does scholarship so often explain away presidential incapacity? First, presidents who try to lead and fail do not like that pointed out. They don't see it that way, and neither do their followers and adherents. Second, our electorate generally is very forgiving, having low expectations of presidential leadership. Third, academics rationalize presidential failures and describe their rationalizations as explanations. It requires much self-discipline of academics to avoid this trap, in presidential studies and other fields.

Samuel Kernal describes an "institutional pluralism" in which president's are successful by meeting the needs of interest groups, to which they appeal via the mass media, and in which public opinion or public pressure has little impact on politics.[3] This is a largely valid model of the functioning of the presidency in day-to-day politics, but it overlooks fundamental elements of the context of public discussion, including most importantly, the public culture, which presidents must either master or to which they must pander. The public culture puts bounds on political action, most important in foreign policy that of the president, in ways that are not inconsistent with Kernal's conception, but have a much greater impact on what happens than he appreciates.

The difficulty of a president mastering the public culture has been noted by researchers who study the presidency. "Even 'great communicators' usually fail to obtain the public's support for their high-priority initiatives," wrote George C. Edwards. As a prime example of his point, Edwards quoted Ronald Reagan about his presidency: "One of my greatest frustrations was my inability to communicate to the American people . . . the seriousness of the threat we faced in Central America."[4] In fact, Reagan was unable to overcome the public culture in this matter, and it left his presidency permanently soiled via the Iran-Contra affair.

It is significant not only that there is a public culture (which is anterior to and helps form public opinion), but also that it is a set of significant propositions that are often factually incorrect. Because they are wrong, a president is not only constrained by them but gets entangled in their unreality – unable to do the things he or she believes are crucial for the country because the public generally does not recognize the problems the president is confronting.

Presidents have potentially more accurate information about developments and dangers in the world than others, but only if certain requirements are met. The information they receive must not be:

- too filtered
- too condensed
- too edited

for the reality of situations to emerge to the president's view; and the President must have a valid framework in which to interpret information.

These are not readily achieved requirements. In fact, many presidents have received overly filtered, overly condensed, overly edited information and have lacked a valid framework, meaning an understanding of the dynamics of international rivalries and interests, to correctly interpret accurate information when they receive it. The result is that more and better information about current events hasn't been enough for them to grasp the reconfiguration of global wealth and power that is evidenced in this book.

THE NEED TO ADJUST ILLUSION TO REALITY

We Americans are making our way through a very difficult period in international affairs, risking conflicts of a major nature because of a basic inability to see the world objectively. We dream of peace while enmity endangers the United States and the world. Ironically, enmity is overt from the least potentially dangerous of our antagonists, Islamic terrorists, and covert from the most potentially dangerous, the Russians and Chinese. At the heart of our danger is a public culture that distorts information and a political process that panders to it. A significant consequence is that the nation's leadership, in particular the President of the United States, must deal with public illusions in order to effectively lead the nation's defense policy.

We need to understand this aspect of the presidency because our survival in the nuclear age depends on correctly identifying the true threats to our national security. In this book the case is made for a revolutionary reconceptualization of American international security policy in which a foreseeable sequence of threats is addressed adaptively without the illusion of a panacea of idealized democratic free enterprise the world over.

This book is an attempt to help our country toward a constructive objectivity about international relations. Attaining objectivity requires these six key elements:

1. The concept of public culture, a key to understanding why America acts as it does in the world arena;
2. A description of the striking disjuncture between the real issues of the day and what is featured in public debate and by the popular media;
3. Empirical findings regarding the limits of attempts to create market democracies, with examples from Russia and Iraq;
4. Examination of the widespread coopting of public needs for private purposes in this country and abroad;
5. A rigorous critique of both neoconservative ideology and current practice and that of their opponents – a critique grounded in a cross-disciplinary collaboration of the study of leadership, national security policy, and economics; and
6. The concept of a peaceful global community accommodating diversity among nations that is reflected in different economic and political systems.

That the great challenge of international policy is to adjust illusion to reality is increasingly evident to observers. "For the past generation and more," wrote political observer Anatol Lieven, "western democracies have been engaged in a great experiment, with unregulated television and the tabloid press as the chief instruments. We are testing how long liberal democracies can survive if their peoples . . . become ever more lazy, ignorant and prone to irrational beliefs . . ."[5]

There are two ways for the experiment of which Lieven speaks to have a good outcome. The first is to weaken the illusions that dominate the mosaic of partisan beliefs and trans-partisan wishful thinking that constitute our public culture. The second is to find presidents who are masters of illusions – who take our country in the right direction despite the confusion of the public.

Public culture is not pop culture, which is primarily entertainment centered. It is a crazy quilt of beliefs, elements of which are shared by a large number of people that is informally managed by the media, governs the content of public debate about national issues (dissenters are ostracized), allowing political leaders (not "policy makers") to build bipartisan support by appealing to popular wishful thinking. Examples of the latter include faith in the miraculous power of democracy, globalization, nation-building, reason, and goodwill. Public culture is a collective public mind, which like the minds of individuals is often divided, carrying on an internal dialogue, but in the end conforms to strong behavior regularities. Pop culture is a parallel culture which is not primarily news- and politics-centered. Public culture is ordinarily expressed in local and national newscasts, newspapers, Sunday morning talk shows, internet blogs, and the statements of pundits and politicians. Pop culture and public culture sometimes overlap, as in Hollywood-produced motion pictures and television series with political settings or in popular music with political messages.

Because illusions play such a great role in the political process there are three major consequences for the citizen who wants to be knowledgeable:

First: People who rely on popular media and cocktail conversations are usually misled, and when they have strong feelings about national security issues, they appear foolish to those who gather information in more sophisticated ways;

Second: People who want to be objectively knowledgeable will be in a more uncomfortable position than adherents of the public culture because the public culture provides refuge from thought and the effort of getting real information; it assures people that they know and understand, when they do not; and

Third: People who want to be really knowledgeable must work at getting information; they must go beneath the public culture and avoid partisanship; this can be done, but only with effort.

Furthermore, the dominant role of illusions in the nation's political process has three major consequences for our presidents:

1. Public culture encourages piecemeal problem solving, disregarding the interrelationships of threats believing its wishful thinking, so that a president almost never gets to the bottom of the problems he or she addresses.
2. The success of a president depends on his or her ability to master the illusions of the public – a very subtle and complex task.
3. A president to be successful has to be almost *schizoid* – he or she must watch the public culture because it's the field in which politics is played out, but must also watch reality to make sense of what's happening in the world and as a basis for actions. A president must take actions that are necessary on an objective basis and simultaneously present them to the public in a form that makes them acceptable.

This is a requirement of the presidency that has sometimes been noted in the past. "If the foreign policy of a state is to be practical," wrote a strategist early in World War II, "it should be defined not in terms of some dream world but in terms of the realities of international relations..."[6] Had his admonition been heeded in the period before the war, there need not have been so great and perilous a struggle as the World War II.

Despite the attention of commentators and academic analysts to the topic, the last thing in the world which is obvious is the state of global play among the nations. The only way to bring sense to our policies addressing the world situation is first to appraise it objectively, and this is almost impossible in the context of our public culture.

PUBLIC CULTURE DISTORTS REALITY

How is objectivity to be attained in a world of illusions driven by wishful thinking and political partisanship, and how is a president to master the illusions of those he or she leads?

Americans are not the only people prone to wishful thinking and illusions, of course. For example, one of the founders of Indian democracy, Jawaharlal Nehru, wrote to his daughter Indira, "Only in one country can it be said that economic freedom has been won by the people generally, and that is Russia, or rather, the Soviet Union."[7] Nehru apparently wanted to find an example of economic freedom somewhere in the world and let himself think wishfully that it was in the Soviet Union. For years, millions of people around the world shared this delusion.

Mass opinion is not something on which objective decisions can be based. It's a hotbed of illusions – whether it's an electorate or a consumer market. Consumer marketers know this (as Charles Revlon is said to have observed about the cosmetics business, "In our factories we make chemicals; in our stores we sell hope"), and so do political consultants. A president knows this as well.

Unless the cultural prejudgments and subtle defense mechanisms that bias presidential action and policy making are identified and corrected, then public discourse cannot deal with the realities confronting the nation.

Public culture is a set of socially approved attitudes, values, analytic procedures and decision-making mechanisms transcending and encompassing partisan diversity that shape and often distort national perceptions of reality and appropriate action.

Public culture, except in ideal circumstances, provides only a semblance of reality; it systematically distorts our comprehension with false presumptions created by certain social, political, and economic characteristics of America and its media to gloss unpalatable realities. The result is poor judgment and dysfunctional behaviors that cause major errors in national policy.

The following diagram presents the sequence of discussion in the chapters that follow.

PUBLIC CULTURE

SOCIAL, POLITICAL AND ECONOMIC CHARACTERISTICS OF AMERICA	yield	DYSFUNCTIONAL BEHAVIORS	yield	ILLUSIONS	yield
Wishful Thinking by the public		Simplification		Convergence	
Partisanship in politics		Hype		Harmonism	
Commercialism in the Media		Distortion			

CONFUSION ABOUT REALITY	yields	LACK OF OBJECTIVITY	yields	POOR JUDGMENT	yields	POLICY ERRORS
Misinformation		Misperception		Wrong Objectives		Mistaken actions
Disinformation		Misapprehension				
		Disproportionality		Wrong Methods		Missed opportunities
				Wrong Priorities		
				Wrong Justifications		

Wishful thinking about the peoples and nations of the world is a long-standing characteristic of the American people. For example, before both world wars of the twentieth century most Americans were convinced that we could keep out of war.

Partisanship in politics that distorts the truth for party gain is almost as old as our republic.

A commercially motivated media that supplies most of our news about the world is now firmly entrenched in our society.

These three factors – wishful thinking, partisanship, and a commercially motivated media – drive dysfunctional behaviors that are a key part of American public culture. Matters are simplified, distorted, and hyped by politicians and the media to serve party and commercial interests by preying on the public's wishful thinking. Dysfunctional behaviors result in deeply held illusions by the public: the notions of harmonism – that most peoples and nations are well-intentioned and fair-minded and that as a result conflict among nations is almost always a result of misunderstandings – and convergence – that all countries of the world are moving toward a form of Western capitalist democracy.

These powerful illusions create a fog of misinformation (mistakes and errors) and disinformation (lies) about the world situation, so that we are confused about the reality in which we live. Confusion yields a lack of objectivity in which we routinely misperceive, misapprehend and are unable to place matters in a proper relationship of importance one to another. Lack of objectivity results in poor judgment – both by the nation and its leaders – so that we frequently develop wrong objectives, methods, priorities and justifications for our actions in the world. Poor judgment leads to major policy errors – including mistaken actions and missed opportunities. In an increasingly complex, changing, and treacherous world, such errors are very dangerous.

There are two forms of lack of objectivity:

1. Failure to perceive reality – that is, wearing a form of blinders; and
2. Failure to devise a solution relevant to a problem – that is, applying a preconceived or all-purpose solution to whatever problem is encountered.

Public culture brings both forms of nonobjectivity to American foreign policy on a large scale.

ANTITERRORISM MEASURES ARE NOT ENOUGH

The most serious lack of objectivity and consequent errors that we are now experiencing involve Islamic terror. The likely troubles of the next few decades are not limited to terrorism but are on a grander scale. In consequence, American national defense strategy must be about more than defending against acts of terrorist violence. There are challenges emerging from major powers that must be addressed, and that are entitled to higher priority.

Terrorism below the nuclear threshold is an awful thing, but nuclear war is a ***mortal threat***. Confusing us about this is one of the greatest disservices which our public culture makes to our national survival. Our most significant potential enemies won't resort to terror – it's a weapon of the weak. While we're spending our time, treasure and blood in Iraq trying to prevent another terrorist attack that could kill thousands of Americans, both Russia and China are modernizing their nuclear weaponry that might kill millions of us.

There is now a consensus that great power warfare is highly unlikely. Both government agencies and private organizations participate, echoing each others' views and pointing to each other as evidence that their views are correct. The United States government tells us this.[8] So do private experts: "The United Nations was founded when the gravest danger facing mankind was aggressive wars by industrialized states marching armies across borders."[9] The implication is that no longer are wars by industrialized states a significant danger. But this is true only in the very short run. In fact, aggressive wars are very much a danger in our not-so-distant future, though the industrialized states likely to be involved are not the same ones as in the mid-twentieth century. Furthermore, and most important, the danger that such wars present to humanity is now enormously increased by the proliferation of atomic weapons.

The challenges we face are the consequences of major, long-term developments in the world economy and demographics, including dramatic shifts in international wealth and power among nations – it is these shifts that are driving both Russia and China and others of our rivals, though in different directions. Projections of national economic growth over the next several decades are the bridge between discussions of the military potential of possible adversaries and the strategy that is best for the United States. Such projections offer measures of the strength of our possible adversaries and of our own ability to counter them.

This book presents economic and military forecasts for world powers and the strategy necessary for America to best confront mounting dangers.

Following are key propositions about America leadership and the world situation:

- American presidential leadership must master a public culture full of illusions about the world;
- Major economic and demographic changes among the nations of the world are certain to generate conflict;
- Adjustment to change is the big new demand on the international order; and
- The international order is full of interdependencies which cannot be objectively assessed in the context of analysis on a country-by-country basis, but must instead be assessed in the context of a limited number of vortexes of danger each involving many countries.

A major reconfiguration of wealth and power among nations is under way. It poses problems that our public culture is preventing most people from facing squarely. Our country's leaders need to do three things:

1. Objectively assess our risks and vulnerabilities;
2. Try to limit the scope of conflict so that as little damage occurs as possible; and
3. Be sure we prevail in any contest.

Today:

- America has the economic and military potential to chart its own strategic path in the future without needing to placate others. We call this approach Strategic Independence (SI) and recommend it as the national defense strategy of the United States.
- The prospects for the economic, technological and political development of the United States are so favorable compared to most other nations that there is little likelihood of the United States entering a period of significant decline in international influence, unless our leadership blunders badly (a possibility that is all too possible, given the context of wishful thinking about global issues in which an American president must act).

William Odom and Robert Dujarric note that the United States has such strengths in its economy, demographics, science, technology, and education that the major threat is not a rival power but ineffective U.S. leadership.[10] We currently have considerable friction with many of our former allies because the end of the Cold War is dividing our interests. The United States is progressing toward a peak in its international leadership, and our former allies are receding in relative economic strength, military power, national resolve, and international influence. Many of our former allies now approach us with an attitude of resentment akin to that of the Greeks in the first century B.C.E. as they contemplated the rising power of Rome and desperately sought to subject it to their leadership. As Polybius, a first century B.C.E. Greek, told his fellows: "As, in other states, a man is rarely found whose hands are pure from public robbery, so, among the Romans, it is no less rare to discover one that is tainted with this crime. But all things are subject to decay and change." Thus, it is that envious rivals await the decay of America.

- The United States will have to adroitly manage two major powers undergoing dramatic transitions in the decades ahead, each in opposite directions. Russia is entering a permanent decline; in the transition we must carefully avoid an occasion in which Russia will employ its still formidable military force against us. The power of China will wax in the next two decades, while resurgent nationalism threatens to turn Chinese economic advances from peaceful trade to military adventure. We must forestall a military confrontation until the long-term disadvantages of the Chinese economic culture begin to negate its current advantages of backwardness (that is, of the relatively easy course of economic catchup), a dynamic that has previously occurred for Russia, Eastern Europe and Japan.

The best way to deal with international discord is a geopolitical strategy in which the United States seeks increasing independence from its erstwhile allies. This is a similar strategy to that which, when employed by the Bush Administration in Iraq, encountered bitter criticism. We do not recommend that America abandon engagement with other nations, but that we refuse to accept foreign control over our security policies and defense expenditures.

If properly informed, Americans are likely to embrace Strategic Independence (and our friends abroad will understand why Americans do so). Such is popular sovereignty – the core value of democracy. Americans are also likely to reject the claims of outsiders to transgress in our elections, or impose their laws or perspectives or interests upon us.

MASTERING THE ILLUSIONS OF THE PUBLIC CULTURE

The American public and its political figures and opinion makers have for more than a century persistently indulged in wishful thinking, and steadfastly refused to learn from their errors. This unfortunate behavior is the result of an indulgent attitude that governs public perceptions, cognition, and policy making. The vibrant partisan rivalry between Democrats and Republicans is not sufficient to alter the situation; instead, the partisan contest is waged within a largely unitary public culture that circumscribes much more narrowly than most Americans realize the content and realism of the political controversy.

Public culture discouraged most people from understanding that there is a system, not merely a discrete set of relationships, among nations – a system involving the economics, rivalries, and power relationships among nations. For a metaphor, think of Robert Penn Warren's description of human life in his novel *All the King's Men* as a spider web that when touched anywhere, vibrates to its furthest corner and alerts the spider. There are connections among all decisions and actions the United States takes regarding the world, and, the proper way to address these situations is as problems in optimization – to choose the best among the set of options available for U.S. international and defense policy.

Furthermore, public comprehension is made almost impossible when media and commentators deny the interrelationships; when the so-called news media is full of disinformation; and when muddled thinking is reinforced continually (for partisan political and commercial purposes) in the public culture. "Supporting opinions we already have is what keeps this mediated [that is, media-driven] culture buzzing, the scribblers scribbling, the talking heads talking, the bloggers blogging."[11]

America should adopt a self-reliant national security policy for the next several decades that doesn't depend on the goodwill of other nations.

The statistics in this book show that the comparative superiority of America's long run economic performance and our willingness to bear the burden of a powerful military make it reasonable to suppose that a strategy of Strategic Independence is viable for us in the long term. But one would be compelled to draw the opposite conclusion, if beguiled by the current rhetoric about globalism and convergence. We present statistics and rely on them to a great extent to avoid the dangers of discussion without quantitative support, so well described by Macaulay when writing about England during the reign of James II. Without a census, Macaulay wrote, "All men were left to conjecture for themselves; and as they generally conjectured without examining facts, and under the influence of strong passions and prejudices, their guesses were often ludicrously absurd."[12] Facts help us to limit the influence of strong passions and prejudices with regard to our topic.

Assessing the objective circumstances of the world situation and its trends is necessary for two reasons:

1. To know the facts in order to identify distortions in the public culture, otherwise there would be no objective standards to measure the media and political partisans against; and because
2. There is significant intrinsic interest in the world situation itself.

The leadership of most American administrations is unwilling to tell us directly, even if it wishes to, what it is doing because most of us are not prepared to understand. We are instead misled by misperceptions grounded in our own wishful thinking. A successful president must become a master of illusions – our illusions, making sure that they do not become his.

This should not surprise us. Product marketing is about illusions; and so is political marketing. In the White House a president makes policy; in the media he responds to wishes. This is not a characteristic of this administration alone; it's likely that any American administration would do much the same. In fact, it's hard to imagine how it could remain in power if it failed to address the public culture in its own terms. The problem is how to rise above the dangerous limitations of the public culture.

The full context of the presidential leadership problem includes public misperceptions, media position-taking, and partisan distortions. Describing the impact of public culture on national security policy formation offers a basis for guidance to our leaders in mastering public illusions.

The myths that populate the American public culture are not peace-making myths; they contribute to war as much as try to avoid it, although not intentionally. For example, the myth that the rest of the world is moving toward and would be made more peaceful by conversion to American style democratic free enterprise (a self-affirming illusion) has helped prolong our involvement in Iraq and the fighting in which we are engaged there.

Other nations have their own public cultures, adding an additional layer of obfuscation that must be penetrated by an effective leader. A president who is able to penetrate the pitfalls of our own and other cultures, and employ his insights in the national interest, is freed from being a prisoner of wishful thinking and is instead a Master of Illusions.

CHAPTER 1: KEY POINTS

1. The American president operates in the context of the public's wishful thinking which creates illusions about the world and our role in it. The illusions are an integral part of a public culture that generates inappropriate policy options based upon simplistic and distorted understandings about the true threats to America's safety.
2. To operate effectively within the public culture, the American president must understand what the real threats to America's security are so that effective defense policy can be developed. The president has a choice about whether to communicate within the public culture or to be more candid with the American people about the motives and methods of defense policy.
3. Strategic Independence is proper defense strategy for America in the current era. It should replace multilateralism and mutual assured destruction(MAD) as our policies. Strategic Independence should play the defense role in a self-reliant, multisystem approach to world politics.

TWO

Long-Term Economic Realism

VORTEXES OF DANGER

World issues are best viewed from the perspective of vortexes of national rivalries, rather than the conventional method focusing on country by country relationships. Conventional analysis and interpretations of international relations are of little use. Nations have interests and rivalries of long standing. Human events are the result of great currents of interest, irrationality, and the will to power. There will always be a struggle among nations and people for power; alliances are temporary and today's friend can be tomorrow's foe; and power politics among the nation's of Europe and Asia are a fact of our world. Applying an objective approach to a framework identifying vortexes where national interests are in conflict best equips a president to lead

A useful example of a long-standing rivalry among nations that are allies has been provided by David Pryce-Jones in his description of French efforts to ally themselves closely with Arab leaders as a counterweight to Anglo-American influence elsewhere in the world. This French policy has its roots in the late eighteenth century and is a continuing theme of French foreign policy which explains much of French opposition to American-led responses to Saddam Hussein's activities, quite independent of any of the controversies of the time, 2003, about Iraqi weapons of mass destruction.[1] As the French pursue this objective in the changing atmosphere of international politics, its fate is determined by economic developments and the quality of their leadership.[2]

Given the long-standing strategies of nations, focusing attention on "relations" among nations as do most commentators and the media is a superficial level of analysis that is usually very misleading. It is as if insight is exhausted on the ripples in a stream and that the underlying currents are ignored, so that floods occur unexpectedly – as, to continue the metaphor, did World War I, World War II and the end of the Cold War.

For example, there is much discussion now of our relationships to rogue states, without an appreciation of their dependencies and hidden agendas. From a more sophisticated perspective, there is no such thing as a rogue state except as a transient aberration – no small state can long exercise power without the protection of a great power, and so it makes little sense to think of American relationships with a rogue state as if they had any existence separate from our relationship to the great power that is the "rogue" state's protector. As another example, Iraq thought it was protected by the European Union (in particular, France and Germany) and to a lesser degree by Russia. It must have been a great surprise to Saddam Hussein to learn that this wasn't the case. Iran is protected by Russia and to some degree by the European Union. Hence its willingness to thumb its nose at efforts of the United Nations to prevent it from building nuclear weapons.

North Korea is protected by China. "Reportedly, China's president Hu Jintao told a party meeting that although China was an economic success, North Korea was *the* model for politics and ideology."[3] Stephen Blank has explained how the United States allowed China to broker a deal in September 2005, with North Korea, which was not advantageous to the United States in either content or process. Focusing on the attempt to avoid nuclear proliferation, the United States apparently lost sight of all other aspects of international politics and presumed that China's interests in the situation were similar to our own. They were not.[4]

Most international reporting is on the level of neighborhood gossip – who's getting along and who isn't, who is out of sorts with whom, who said what about whom, who's helping whom, who's betrayed whom, who has threatened whom?

Commentary based on this sort of reporting isn't worth much. It is the source of much of the weakness in the discussion of international relations and diplomacy. Only when analysis is informed by a deep knowledge of historical context (as, for example, in Henry Kissinger's works) and by in depth-understanding of long-term economic and political processes with their implications for the future, is there value in the analysis.

Analytical and personal relation-ism should be rejected as myopic: too short-term and ignoring critical interconnections. A form of analytical cause-ism based on changes in underlying factors focusing our attention on vortexes of danger is preferable. Long-term economic realism applied to geopolitics provides the greatest insight.

Topics that should be treated together are often considered separate and placed in different compartments for specialists to address them. Specialist deconstruction is built into the structure of our State Department where different desks don't talk to each other. This creates error; but neither should interrelated issues be treated as a grab-bag. The topics of defense and international policy should be treated as

- intimately connected;
- arising from the same underling forces; and
- posing challenges to our country which are often traded off against each other. For example, we might deal differently with North Korea if we were not engaged so deeply in Iraq.

A special concern is the interrelationships among developments in various parts of the world. There are many more commentaries that describe crises in various parts of the world than that survey the broader picture, which is more important and threatening that its parts alone suggest.

WHY ECONOMIC REALISM AND SCIENTIFIC OBJECTIVITY ARE SORELY NEEDED

Objectivity has no hidden agenda. It is scientific in its inspiration – using scientific standards of objectivity to cut through the fog of illusions that surround public perceptions. Robert Laughlin says, "Science cannot be radical or conservative but only faithful to the facts," and that "The great power of science is its ability, through brutal objectivity, to reveal to us truth we did not anticipate."[5] This is what our leaders should strive for in addressing our nation's defense needs.

In general, the American mental landscape about foreign affairs is increasingly dominated by partisan commitments when instead there is a need for continuity of national policy that transcends party lines. Partisanship leads to the distortion of reality in a number of ways, and that creates danger for our national survival. Political advantage to either party isn't worth war – yet American partisan politics contributed considerably to our involvement in many wars, including the Mexican War, the Civil War, World War I, World War II, Korea, Vietnam, and perhaps the current conflict in much of the Islamic region – today a Crescent of Fire. In all these instances, a less partisan political environment might have spared our nation much or all of the loss of life we experienced in those conflicts. Yet we know that nothing is more important to many people than that their preferred party attain or hold the presidency. For our readers who address these issues primarily from a partisan basis, we hope that we might provide a surprise by causing them to recognize that they do agree with certain policies or goals of the other party and therefore that the nation's international relations might benefit from a less partisan treatment in the media and in government.

Even the most experienced of commentators (including, for example, Henry Kissinger and Zbigniew Brzezinski) simply assume that they know how the game is played and play it, without regard to the misapprehensions left with many who are not as sophisticated. In public discussion, scientific objectivity is severely limited by the public culture – the public can stand only so much reality. In fact, in an especially peculiar twist the term "realism" is today assuming a meaning very much its opposite. It's become a staple of the public culture expressed by critics of the Bush Administration that the President isn't "realistic" because he supposedly fails to take note of the "failure" of his policy in the Crescent of Fire (the region of Islamic militance from the southern Philippines to Morocco) and of the "damage" to America's reputation and alliances abroad. It's supposedly terribly unrealistic of him to just ignore these "facts" because he is so stubborn and refuses to acknowledge any errors. This point of view is now so firmly attached to the term "realism" that the term is almost a buzzword for criticism of the Administration. If "realism" has any realism left, it's that of the partisan political contest, not of an objective view of the world situation.

"We need to talk," read the headline of an article by the editor of the *London Times* published in the *Washington Post*, November 7, 2004. We need to talk, he argued, because of the great gulf of misunderstanding now separating Europe from America. "A deepening of the dialogue between the two sides of the Atlantic is imperative," wrote Henry Kissinger.[6] "The exercise of American power may well be the central issue in world politics today," observed Shashi Tharoor, Kofi Annan's deputy at the United Nations.[7]

Abroad there is a hunger for a better understanding of the American political psyche at this time. At a recent conference in Warsaw sponsored by the American Enterprise Institute, commentators about America relied on the principles of our constitution to describe the essence of the American political and economic systems. The analysis of public culture that we present in this book is a far more powerful tool for understanding contemporary America.

OUR COUNTRY HAS CHANGED

Our country has changed to some degree since the attack on the World Trade Center in September, 2001. The attack undermined some of the complacencies that are central to our nation's public culture. Wishful thinking is less extreme. A new realism exists, though it doesn't extend yet to the public culture.

Aspects of the American character altered out of suffering (September 11, 2001) and out of sudden and unexpected (although it should have been foreseen) responsibility for the development of other nations in the context of other cultures – a responsibility that has been undertaken via the conflicts in Afghanistan and Iraq. These events have brought to an end a period of uncertainty, which began with the disillusionment caused by the Vietnam War.

America has been frequently accused of being immature as a people, and some of that persists – crusading, moral arrogance, isolationism – but all these characteristics are somewhat in question. In place of crusading there is the beginning of a new realism about the world; in place of moral arrogance there is a new pragmatism; in place of a retreat into isolationism there is a continuing engagement.

The changes now occurring in the American character and the possibility of their going much further are not fully understood by many – certainly not by the media, and not yet by most politicians and political commentators. Europeans in particular seem nonplussed that the presidential candidates of both parties in 2004 were in substantial agreement about what to do about the Iraqi war, though in controversy about how and why the war began in the first place.

We hope that our people can rise above partisanship in their concern for the national welfare. But because neither party is yet in sync fully with the new attitudes of the electorate, the political consequences of the changes in America are uncertain. The party that first adapts completely to the character of the country will find itself in a most advantageous position.

THE COMING THREATS TO AMERICAN SECURITY

By encouraging rapid technological advances in the world's leading economies, the information revolution is exacerbating existing economic disparities among nations. As nations rise or fall in response to new technologies' unequal distribution of benefits, rising nations (like China) will threaten existing powers and declining nations (like Russia) may resort to aggression.

The current American leadership in the world – what some people pejoratively label American hegemony – exists because rivals are not yet ready to challenge the United States for leadership. Islamic militants must reestablish a national base for their activities (at the moment they are a stateless adversary); the Russians have yet to fully reassert their influence in what was their empire and effectively reenergize their military; the Chinese have yet to fully modernize their forces and build full-range strategic nuclear capability; the Europeans have yet to solidify their union. But unreadiness among our rivals will not always be the case. In the next several decades America will face a series of challenges that will likely reach their points of crisis in a predictable time frame. The order is as follows with likely periods of crisis that overlap one another but fall in a rough sequence as follows:

Terrorism	now to 2015
Russian military resurgence	2010 to 2025
Chinese nationalism	2020 to 2035
European unification and rivalry	2030 to 2045

This sequencing is an accident of history. The points of crisis are determined by economic and political forces – bounded by the speed at which economic growth and military modernization are likely to happen. The periods overlap, and the time estimates are judgmentally derived and not certain. But they are not contrived. For example, Chinese nationalism could surge to a "boiling point" as early as 2015 or as late as two decades later. Russian military resurgence could occur as late as 2025, and European unification might conceivably be cemented earlier than 2030 or else be postponed to after 2045. But the sequence of the crises in challenges and the time dimensions are likely close to the mark. There is a danger that the various countries involved will coordinate in some fashion their activities to challenge the United States simultaneously. This would create a much more difficult situation for us.

If coordination doesn't occur, then for America the likely sequencing of challenges is a piece of good fortune. Rather than a group of crises arriving simultaneously – competing for attention, diverting focus, stretching resources – the country is likely to be given an opportunity to prepare in advance, focus on each crisis in turn, and resolve one before the next is upon us. The future depends on how well American presidents are able to do these things.

Because we point to potential dangers where others prefer to see the likelihood of peace, we expect to be charged with crying wolf. But our thesis doesn't turn on the magnitude of the dangers to which we point. It doesn't matter whether the threat is greater or less than we describe. Whatever the scale, the threats are real. Every well informed American knows that Pakistan is a Muslim country that has the atomic bomb, and that Iran is on the threshold of becoming an atomic power. No one is ignorant of 9/11, and escalating suicide bombing in Iraq, Egypt, and Europe. Everyone should know that Russia retains the world's largest nuclear weapons arsenal, that China possesses a large atomic weapons stock, and that both are rapidly modernizing their armed forces. It is generally recognized that political, business, and academic leaders in the European Union are increasingly disgruntled with America's international agenda, desiring to transform their expanding community into a superpower, though they are having difficulty figuring out how to do so. Each of these threats is driven by the processes described later, and each can be diminished with the policies suggested.

Many Americans are tempted to believe the harmonist fable that if people are left to their own devices, everyone will prosper. For example, in democracies, we are told, citizens preoccupy themselves with commerce, and prefer making love to war.

Engaging in a serious discussion of dangers and defense threatens these idylls. It is condemned as protectionism in economics, and provocative in international relations. Worse still, it is said to precipitate wasteful and destabilizing arms races, so that the attempt to defend ourselves is said to be the cause of the dangers we fear. As a consequence, we Americans are predisposed to preach to the world rather than actively defend ourselves. We will respond militarily to terror if sufficiently provoked, but there is little carry over to other dangers ahead. There is little recognition that at this juncture in history America has the option to cow and defeat would-be adversaries, and that it is in our national interest to do so.

What is required is for us to recognize that the potential for international conflict is embedded in and sustained by aspects of diverse humanity that do not lend themselves to universalist solutions. Osama bin Laden will not reconcile himself with America on Western terms, and differences among the nations in economic cultures are bringing about a reconfiguration of global wealth and power that is widening, not narrowing disparities. The world is not catching up with America in certain key areas; nor is it becoming a social and political copy of America. Instead, we are pulling further out in front of the pack, creating dissonance of all sorts, but also a necessity and an opportunity to defend ourselves. We can and should cooperate with other nations when benefits are mutual, or compassion compels, but we don't have to be dependent for our safety on the kindness of strangers. Instead, at this historic juncture, America can be strategically independent.

STRATEGIC INDEPENDENCE

For nearly a half century, America has been strategically dependent choosing to forgo military superiority needed to act preemptively, or surgically against hostiles, and permitting outsiders to constrain our options for self-defense. Strategic independence is a conscious policy to determine for ourselves the best programs for maximizing our national security without tying our hands with obsolete doctrines such as mutual assured destruction, or needlessly appeasing self-interested third parties. A U.S. policy of Strategic Independence, which is defined and described more fully in Part VI, serves the American interest and the world's necessities by providing a response to proliferation, terrorism, the growing power of China and the erratic path of Russia; and by encouraging the continuing economic advance of Asia.

Strategic independence is about self-defense, not hegemony, imperialism or thwarting economic development as often was the case in the nineteenth century, when European nations and the Japanese sought to be militarily strong. Asian economic advance was held up for many years by European imperialism. The most compelling evidence is the explosive economic growth since the end of colonialism in much of Southeast Asia. To get the European colonists out was necessary and America, because of the strong anticolonial convictions of President Franklin Roosevelt, played a major role in the end of European colonialism.[8] Unfortunately ending colonialism alone wasn't sufficient to set many countries on a successful path, as subsequent history in several countries (including Indonesia, Myanmar, and Vietnam) has demonstrated.

Instead of direct or indirect imperialism, the United States' core traditions encompass multiplicity in social, economic and political systems, and in national cultures. Many critics of globalization complain that America uses democratic free enterprise as an imperializing device. But the American federalist tradition is intrinsically tolerant of diversity abroad, and is opposed to the kind of globalist universalism that currently undergirds much of Western international policy making. Thus, the notion that democratic free enterprise has triumphed in the world and that this has been and is a basic objective of American policy (a notion associated with Francis Fukuyama who popularized it in his 1989 essay in *The National Interest*, "The End of History") is alien to the American tradition. The difference between American policy directed at a universal homogeneity in national political and economic systems versus a desirable diversity in systems is crucially important to a successful foreign policy for America since it expands our options and improves them.

Nor is the antithesis of strategic independence, multilateralism (which is discussed in Chapter 16) a central part of the American tradition. Our country was born hearing the caution of George Washington not to trust to the good will of foreign powers. Independence of action was America's first defense policy. George Washington in his Farewell Address, September 19, 1796, observed that America might form "temporary alliances for extraordinary emergencies," but in general it must pursue its course without alliances. "Isolation?" asks Paul Johnson in describing Washington's speech, "Not at all. Independence – yes."[9]

In his recent biography of Washington, Joseph Ellis explains that Washington's Farewell Address is not a statement of an isolationist stance, as some have said, but a statement of the classical realist position. As such, it is consonant with Strategic Independence. Washington's words, Ellis explains, are "the seminal statement in the realist tradition. . . . It was a vision of international relations formed from experience rather than reading, confirmed by early encounters with hardship and imminent death, rooted in a relentlessly realistic view of human nature." About George Washington, David McCullough commented, "Seeing things as they were and not as he wished them to be was one of his salient strengths."[10] Jefferson also warned against multilateralism; the phrase, "entangling alliances with none," often attributed to Washington, instead appears in Jefferson's first inaugural address.[11]

In a surprisingly modern twist, Washington was also concerned about making his views clear in the public culture of the period.

He requested that it be published, verbatim, in newspapers across America.

Thus, it is in one of the most revered of American traditions that our nation seeks coalitions and alliances with other nations for tactical purposes when at war (as we did with France during our Revolution), and reserves our overall strategy-making to ourselves.

Being engaged in the world and pursuing our strategy independently need not mean that the United States is imperialistic. The traditional core of the American approach to international relations is not imperialistic, directly or indirectly. It doesn't seek long-term control of other nations, in the way that European imperialism did. Nor does it seek ordinarily to dictate the shape of their socioeconomic-political systems, an indirect form of imperialism ("neoimperialism" in the terminology of some commentators) much charged against the United States. In both instances, however, there are incidents and spokespersons who suggest that the United States at one time or another is engaged in either direct or indirect imperial adventures.

During the nineteenth century, our nation once or twice engaged in what appear to be directly imperialist wars – wars for the control of territory. The clearest such examples were the Mexican War of 1846–1848, which involved the direct annexation of large regions of North America to the United States; and the War of the Philippine Insurrection, which involved colonial administration of the Philippines for some fifty years. But these are aberrations; made obviously so by the nation's capacity to have assembled an empire, directly or indirectly, in the way that the Mexican War and the War of the Philippine Insurrection permitted, without it in fact doing so. What America does normally stops well short of empire-building – it pursues its own interests normally by means short of war; it seeks favorable trade relations with other countries; it seeks influence in matters that affect it; and when militarily challenged, will demand more of other countries – specifically, it will cause a change of regimes, as it did in Germany and Austria after World War I; in Germany, Italy and Japan after World War II; and in Afghanistan and Iraq after the attack on the World Trade Center in September, 2001. None of this is imperialistic, and all of it is in the long traditions of our foreign policy. In general the United States is reactive – we responded to German maritime aggression in World War I, to the Japanese attack on Pearl Harbor, to the North Korean invasion of the south, and to the terrorist attack on the World Trade Center.

It is certainly possible to condemn America's efforts at advancing its own interests; but referring to such actions as the creation of an empire is simply to confuse the discussion presumably for political purposes of some sort (as, for example, to tar the United States with the brush of colonialism so appropriate to many European nations).

THE NEED FOR THE INTERNATIONAL ORDER TO ADAPT TO CHANGES AMONG NATIONS AND REGIONS OF THE WORLD

The directions of American foreign policy are changing dramatically as the configurations of wealth and power in the world itself change. For four and one-half decades from the end of World War II until the collapse of the

Soviet Union the world was relatively unchanging on its political surface. The two superpowers and their alliances grappled for advantage with the threat of nuclear annihilation keeping the contest within bounds (although, as we shall see, only barely). But underneath the surface great changes were in the making.

The sudden collapse of the Soviet Union issued in a new world in which the new currents suddenly broke to the surface and flowed more strongly. There is a current of economic advance in east Asia – the Asian economic miracle that is real and of enormous significance, thrusting China to the forefront of geopolitics; there is a current of revolution in the Arab world that has now drawn much of the world into its ferment and to which we refer as terrorism; there is a current of American economic, technological and military leadership that make it the sole superpower; there is a current of moral and economic weakening that suddenly has left Russia fractured but strongly armed; and there is a current of finished business that left the close alliance between the United States and Western Europe against the Soviets obsolete.

These currents, now racing along the surface of the international order, bring with them impatient demands for change. Rising powers insist on recognition; new aspirations demand to be satisfied. Yet there is in international relations an enormous inertia. Change is often accompanied by turmoil; but the international system seeks quietude. It is a principle of today's international community advanced by its primarily European advocates that the avoidance of war is the central objective of the system. But where change is necessary, can peaceful means alone accommodate it; and if there is no risk of war, will any advantage of importance be relinquished to a current have-not? Hence, our focus on avoiding war is coupled with an implicit support for the status quo.

Yet the world is changing very much. Some nations are growing and strengthening; others are declining and weakening. Change is inevitable, but if we provide no mechanism for it, then a cause for war is supplied. Conflict is often not sought for itself, but is a symptom of a change that needs to be made. Despite our attempts to preserve peace and to keep change in the world within narrow boundaries, the untidy globe keeps bubbling.

Of all the states (more than one hundred) in existence in the world in 1914, only eight escaped a violent change of government between then and the early 1990s.[12] Change of a dramatic nature is very common and to anticipate stability in a world in which economics and demographics are rapidly altering is another form of wishful thinking – wishing to escape the hard work of accommodating large scale change among nations.

Order in the world must conform to the realities of economic power that is changing fast. So the world order must change. When the world changes and the world order does not, great conflict ensues. The reason the peace of Versailles after World War I didn't last, but gave way instead to World War II was that the Versailles peace "conformed neither to history, nor to geography, nor to economics."[13]

Strategy and leadership are most important in international relations. For example, the sudden change in the Palestinian situation in the winter of 2005 was due to a change in the strategic setting in the Middle East as a result of the removal of Saddam Hussein from the leadership of Iraq, and the death of Yasser Arafat. Saddam's replacement removed a strong support for the violence in Palestine, and Arafat's death removed a leader who had a personal agenda and a particular political base and commitment to tactics which caused him to support violence. Absent the change in the strategic situation caused by the American invasion of Iraq, and the change in leadership caused by the removal of Saddam and Yasser Arafat from the scene, the prolonged violent stalemate between Israel and the Palestinians would have continued without a new effort for accommodation. It was these two changes that were necessary – in strategic situation and in leadership – and all the commentary focusing on other factors for the four years previously was simply irrelevant verbosity.

But even in the Middle East American leaders seem afraid of dramatic change. The inclination of the United States to support the status quo ante, whatever it may be, is evident in the approach we've taken to Iraq. We have tried to preserve the unity of the country, even though there are strong reasons for not doing so, including that Iraq was cobbled together with little rhyme or reason by colonial powers after World War I. But our leadership lacks the vision to either dismantle Iraq or include it as a whole in some broader unity within the Arab world – either of which might be a better solution than trying to stick the country together again.[14] The United States could have divided Iraq in three; then held oil revenues as incentive for the regions to work out peace – by unity, federation, or peaceful separation. Alternatively, we might have forced Iraq into a wider federation with Saudi Arabia and Kuwait. We did neither. Such actions need boldness of concept as well as of action. Modern American administrations sometime act boldly, but never think boldly.

The challenge to the American president is to lead modifications in the international order that are required by the dramatic changes underway, and in order to do so to gain the support of an electorate mislead by public culture.

PRESIDENTIAL CANDOR

How should a leader deal with a gullible public, largely uninformed about history and about events abroad, and subject to manipulation by partisan opponents?

Plato addressed the issue more than two thousand years ago. He concluded, "If anyone at all is to have the privilege of lying, the rulers of the state should be the persons; and they in their dealings either with enemies or with their own citizens, may be allowed to lie for the public good."[15] We make very different demands on our presidents in the United States today. We ask that they be candid with us about what they are doing and why. This is part of the idealism of our public culture. It is a total denial of the essence of diplomacy (or of cocktail party etiquette), which holds it polite to conceal opinions and motives that might offend another. But there is something to be said for it in a democracy, in which the electorate cannot be properly informed without honest communication from the nation's leadership.

Public trust in America in leaders in all fields continues to drop. In this environment, silence, denial and closed door decision making are almost always interpreted as evidence of bad faith.[16]

The new maturity of the American people, limited though it is, may permit more candor in presidential communication and thereby point a way out of the current morass of distrust. The opportunity offers three key things for American political leadership:

- It may be possible for a president to act militarily with the full support of the American people, quite unlike the situation in Vietnam; Americans are in general savvy enough to understand presidential leadership offered honestly in a cold logic of defense grounded in a necessary geopolitical orientation; and

- It may now be possible for a president to lead Americans in our defense without either the complete cynicism of Old World power politics or the wishful thinking of overly ambitious schemes to remake the world in our own image.

- There may be a role for deception in tactical operations, where surprise is often the difference between life and death for soldiers and between success and failure for the mission. But in matters of basic strategy, what we are doing and why, then deception, especially for momentary political gain, usually is found out and the results – U.S. citizens slowly realizing that they have been betrayed by their country – are both irreversible and unfortunate. At the least, people are confused about objectives and don't know what they should do to support them. At the worst, people cease to trust the government. Fearing distrust, the government goes to increasing lengths to try to salvage falsehoods, and so digs itself into a deeper and deeper hole. In such a circumstance, success can be perceived as failure, and the world turned upside down. The best policy for an American government is that suggested by a father to a daughter in the movie *Moonstruck*: "Tell them the truth, Dear. You might as well. They find out anyway."

- Examples are readily available in recent American history. Lyndon Johnson was bitterly attacked when it was discovered that the Gulf of Tonkin resolution, which played an important part in the initial justification of the Vietnam War, was based on an incident the significance of which had been much exaggerated. And Richard Nixon was as bitterly criticized when he gained support for his presidential bid in 1968 by promising that he had a plan to exit the Vietnam war, and then expanded the fighting into Cambodia in May 1970.

Because of the unwillingness of political leaders to be candid with the public about threats and their objectives in choosing how to meet them, a promising new approach that is well fitted to the new sorts of dangers facing the United States is likely to be discarded with an increasingly unpopular war.

It is naïve to suggest that political leaders can be completely candid; this violates basic norms of diplomacy. The White House must always weigh the value of the truth against its cost, said a high official of the Clinton administration to us. "Often the cost of candor is too great, and the White House can't tell the truth."

The current predilection of American administrations for posturing about moral motives while making plans and taking actions based on more realistic assessments of international situations is certain to create massive distrust in periods longer than a few months. This doesn't mean that we should abandon objectivity, but rather that we should be much more modest about moralizing.

We favor sophisticated candor, in which there is honesty about strategic aims, but not naïve recounting of unnecessary detail. Being a master of illusion entails telling people how things seem, and how we need to cope with imponderables, as a counter to wishful thinking, deceitful or otherwise. At the core of the challenge to American leadership in these times is to address successfully counter arguments that insist that there are no threats other than those posed by misunderstandings or our own actions threatening others. For example, it is argued that because Iraq was apparently not involved in the attack on the World Trade Center, it was not a legitimate target of terrorist activity. By this standard, Nazi Germany – which was never informed by Japan of the attack on Pearl Harbor until after it occurred and played no role in the attack – was not a legitimate target of American arms during World War II. Unless a President can address successfully arguments of this type, he cannot lead effectively in the modern world.

The probability is our country will always have inadequate presidents, partisan media, and citizen misperceptions. The inadequacy of leadership lies in the inability of presidents to either select a proper course or to communicate it persuasively to the public, or both. The roots of the limitations of American presidential leadership lie in the attitude of the electorate toward issues of foreign policy (specifically, the lack of historical knowledge and the emphasis on domestic concerns), the selection process for presidential candidates (which emphasizes partisanship and exaggerates the strength of the extremes in both parties), and the character of the public culture (with its emphasis on the immediate versus the middle and long term, its preference for sensationalism and partisanship rather than accuracy, and its projection of our own values onto other cultures). Each of these factors can be altered, but efforts so far have been largely unavailing and a serious effort to address all three at once is not currently on the horizon. The best that can be hoped for is some advance in each arena, perhaps as a partial result of studies like this one that may raise a bit the consciousness of the public about these issues. Forewarned by studies such as this, the great strength of the American democracy which arises from the energy and commitment of its people may again redress the shortcomings of its leadership.

CHAPTER 2: KEY POINTS

1. America has changed since 9/11; there is a new maturity and objectivity about international threats which is in conflict with our dominant public culture. It is possible that our national leadership can seize the opportunity to be more candid with the American people about the threats we face and the appropriate ways to counter them, wherever our leaders aren't themselves befuddled by our public culture.

2. Country-by-country analysis doesn't work in realistically assessing national security threats. The world is full of interrelations and complexities; so that things are often done indirectly. The public culture has no patience for these complexities, and simplifies to a degree that reality is lost.

3. Instead of country-by-country relationships, there are vortexes of danger in different regions of the world and in the possible alliance of rivals wherever they are located.

4. We seek an approach to international policy that is objective and consistent. We are fact-driven and, as economists, bring quantitative analysis to usually largely qualitative discussions about national security policy in which quantitative information gets muddled in the confusion of our public culture.

5. There are four significant threats to America from abroad at this time. They are, in sequence of crisis over the next three decades: terrorism, Russian remilitarization, Chinese nationalistic ambitions and military modernization, and the distant rivalry of a integrated European state. Since the terrorist attacks on 9/11, we have focused primarily on the first risk: terrorism. Although attention to terror is warranted, we must not lose sight of the fact that terror is a series of tragic incidents, whereas nuclear war with Russia, China and rogue states remains a mortal threat to our national survival. Military skirmishes should they occur with the Eu will be conventional.

PART TWO

AMERICAN PUBLIC CULTURE
AND THE WORLD

Americans have big illusions about the world that keep our nation from countering threats effectively. These illusions are embodied in the nation's public culture. It's national in scope, and extraordinarily resistant to change, despite a changing world. Illusions generated by public culture are very broad in their appeal – reaching across the ideological spectrum and appealing to both conservatives and liberals.

THREE

"Smooth Comforts False" – The Illusions That Confuse Us

Smooth comforts false, worse than true wrongs.
Shakespeare, **Henry IV**, Part II, lines 39–40

We have become accustomed to preconceiving world events. The public culture of a country expresses these preconceptions, and many of us accept them uncritically and are strongly committed to them. Convictions planted in us by our public culture are nearly unshakable because they are reinforced continually. Shakespeare got it right in **Henry IV** when he wrote "smooth comforts false, worse than wrongs" – in part because we recognize wrongs for what they are and try to right them; but smooth comforts that are false, the illusions of public culture, are not recognized as wrong and we do not erect defenses against them or try to correct them.

"Man's general way of behaving," Maimonides wrote, "is to be influenced by his neighbors and friends – letting his customs be like the customs of the people of the country."

America has a very distinct public culture – a set of "socially" approved ideas about what the world ought to be. These 'idols,' as Francis Bacon observed centuries, ago garble public discourse by confusing us as to what is reality and by tempting us to try to make the world like we wish it were.

Every nation has its own "self-evident" values, a popular culture that shapes approved attitudes and establishes rules of permissible partisan debate. The benefits of consensus in a world roiled by contentious private interests, the elusiveness of truth, and ethical ambiguities make some common ground imperative.

Central to our public culture are values involving democracy, economic liberty, social justice, tolerance, diversity, equal opportunity, conflict avoidance, reason and progress. Opinions differ about the application of these concepts. Is balloting in authoritarian states democracy? Is preemption justified against terrorists with weapons of mass destruction? The crucial fine points are normally concealed by focusing on the generalities.

Although we rarely acknowledge it, informal control of attitudes – via our public culture – is very strong in the United States today. This is especially true with respect to issues of history and human relations.

We're all vaguely familiar with the way people's attitudes and behavior are controlled in China and Japan by social pressures. The Chinese system is called Confucian, after the ancient teacher, and its behavioral control mechanism is labeled "preceptive" in formal discussions.

It is a set of ideals expressed as rules and maxims, without deistic moral authority. America's public culture does the same thing, without Confucius's formal codification. Such mechanisms are fundamental to human societies, and have been with us a long time.

Western public culture has been particularly effective in building a centrist consensus in foreign affairs around conflict avoidance and the promotion of free enterprise. We are usually prepared to dismiss concerns about Chinese and Saudi authoritarianism to advance the higher causes of peace and prosperity.

It is the inclusion of misapplicable ideals in the public culture that makes such a significant danger – that transforms from merely mistaken notions that will be abandoned by its advocates as evidence piles up against it, to deeply imbedded elements of our national credo. These axioms of faith that a majority of our people take to be self evidently true, but aren't. Public culture is assumptive – it is composed of the presumptions people make. Our difficulty is that the key preconceptions of American public culture are mistaken; they are illusions.

Culture includes basic attitudes, norms, values, and rules that condition and shape group interrelations, including how people decide about significant matters. Attitudes, norms, values and rules are formal and informal. They may be inconsistent, but this is often handled by group-approved rules of thumb that mask inconsistencies or provide tolerance for them. Because attitudes, norms, values and rules aren't universal, but instead are group specific, culture is heterogeneous – and we present it as such. We point out in the next chapter that the fallacy of expecting national cultures and ethnic group cultures to be the universe is part of an illusion of harmonism; and that expecting national and ethnic cultures to develop toward the American model is part of erroneous belief in convergence. Instead of evolving toward similarity, specific cultures abroad often develop in ways that are in conflict with our country's universalizing idealism – our desire and expectation that everyone everywhere should be more and more like us.

Public culture is not ideology (a comprehensive principle such as socialism or communism used to order social policy) – and a continuing mistake of great significance is made by conservatives who seek an ideological interpretation of the public culture (see Chapter 5 for a discussion of the roots of our public culture) and then critics are frequently seduced by conservative illusions. American public culture encompasses a wide range of ideologies – free market libertarians accept most of our public culture, as do liberals who support social democracy. To both extremes of the ideological spectrum and all in between public culture offers commonly accepted preconceptions about certain critical matters. Public culture isn't an ideology nor a substitute for ideology; it is something different – anterior in some ways, pursuant in others. It is a motley set of beliefs, platitudes, and managed attitudes that conceals latent discord and harnesses idealism to forge consensus on public policy, despite contentious partnership.

It is a system of social norms in which castles of illusion are built. Illusions substitute for information by giving us opinions not grounded in objectivity. For many persons, once public culture has been accepted, the last thing he or she wants is accurate information that might conflict with the convictions of public culture and undermine the comforts it provides.

Modern American public culture was established during World War II when alliances of convenience with dictatorships (especially the USSR) led to the harmonist notion; and in the aftermath of the war when attempts at economic development in the postimperialist third world led to the notion of convergence. The public culture is not perpetuated because of self-interested parties that gain from the content of the culture; it's perpetuated by reinforcement which originates in the desire of media and politicians for an audience.

Ironically, as America's broad culture of values (about life, art, morals, etc.) fragments – "the common culture of widely shared values and knowledge that once helped to unite Americans . . . no longer exists" – our public culture of quasi political convictions seems to become more generally shared within our country.[1] Perhaps the two are related – the nation needs some convictions – such as those offered by the public culture – to bind it together as our broad culture disintegrates. If so, it is doubly unfortunate that the public culture that binds us together is primarily one of illusions, not of objectivity – for a public culture that is full of myths offers us danger, not safety.

Contemporary social psychologists suggest that public culture connects with deep needs for belonging, self-expression and reinforcing ego strength. Yet, illusions in our public culture can drive policy actions that may be wrong if they were or could be examined more thoughtfully. ". . . [N]ational self images and the strong feelings often attached to such images constrain the range of options that policymakers have in dealing with other nations," writes Daniel Druckman. "In some instances they can lead to overly aggressive actions when such are precipitous; in other instances they can prevent action where such may be relevant."[2]

Public culture is more than a set of beliefs; it is also a system of processing routines where shocks of all kinds including 9/11 are addressed conventionally in ways that preserve the status quo more fully than objectivity warrants. This system includes asserting that all is now different, while insuring that only superficial things (such as watchfulness for terrorists, which we were supposed to be doing anyway) are actually different while the major presumptions of public culture, which are very important, continue largely unaltered. How the status quo is continued is exemplified in the following process of thought: wishful thinking holds that those who attack others must have been caused to do so by something, so terrorism is a consequence of mistreatment (that is, terrorism involves attacks of desperation). Hence, because Palestinians are attacking Israelis, Israel must be oppressing the Palestinians. Wishful thinking further insists that terrorism is most likely a result of misunderstandings among men and women of good will and that the problems that allegedly cause terrorism can be resolved by joining heads, hands, and hearts: specifically, by economic development that removes poverty and deprivation, and by a peace agreement in Palestine that will remove oppression as a cause of terror. Because such solutions are thinkable in our culture, reason will drive everyone embrace them. In this view, military preparedness and preemption are to be minimized or rejected as unnecessary and counterproductive, because they don't give reason a chance to deliver peace.

An advantage of popular culture is that it accommodates great differences of opinion about what it actually means. For example, democracy means to some of us a process of free choice of government officials by the people; to others of us it means only voting. The result is that some of us are intolerant of so called elections in authoritarian states, while others accept them as an important step toward democracy. The most important example today of this difference of opinion in American popular culture is whether or not Russia is a democracy in any true sense. There are elections and there are multiple parties, so some say it is a democracy; but there is a president so strong that he is virtually a dictator, and elections do not go against him. Thus, some say it isn't a democracy at all.

There is nothing intrinsically wrong with this public cultural prioritization; but it becomes an encumbrance when it obscures Osama bin Laden's terrorist threat or the looming danger of Chinese nationalism.

It is in the arena of national defense that the public culture can be most dangerous to us. The smooth comforts of public culture cause us to underestimate real threats. To see how our public culture contributes to creating and maintaining dangerous illusions, we need to get inside the architecture of public culture and identify the key illusions and their sources.

WAYS IN WHICH PUBLIC CULTURE INFLUENCES THINKING ABOUT THE WORLD

Our public culture is the key expression of the attitudinal context in which a president must lead.

American public culture offers us two key propositions about the world around us – *harmonism* and *convergence*.

Harmonism is the notion that people and nations ordinarily are well intentioned and fair-minded so conflict is a result of misunderstanding.

Convergence is the notion that all economic and political systems are becoming more alike and that the end result is a Western-style capitalist democracy.

Harmonism and convergence combine to create the conviction that economic progress and trade (globalization) reduce the likelihood of conflict among nations so that war is becoming increasingly unlikely.

Conservatives who deny harmonism (who are cynical about humanity and its governments) accept convergence and accept the combination of the two in idealism.

Liberals who deny convergence (who oppose significant elements of modern capitalism) accept harmonism and accept the combination of the two in idealism.

Both conservatives and liberals in the United States today accept the peculiar idealism that is the result of the combination of the two doctrines and is the capstone of our public culture.

Because these illusions are incorrect and misleading, their general acceptance in our public culture is insidious and dangerous.

Public culture is able to exert an astonishing influence over our perception of events, causing us to react in inappropriate and even dangerous ways. At the start of the 1990s, Russia slipped into a severe economic crisis. The proper reaction was economic crisis management, something we do for ourselves and others frequently. The most recent severe crises we've dealt with were in Southeast Asia at the time of the financial crisis (beginning in 1997) and in Argentina (beginning after the turn of the millennium and leading to default on the country's international debt obligations). But in the context of Russia after the collapse of the Soviet Union, we misinterpreted what was occurring as evidence of convergence – the Russians were changing their system to be like ours. So we set out to liberalize the Russian economy, as if liberalization (a change in the structure of the country's economy) were the same thing as crisis management. It is not. Liberalization is a long-term transition requiring changes in the economic culture of a nation; crisis management is a short-term response to deteriorating economic performance.

Because we interpreted Russia's situation as a transformation of the economy, we were able to convince ourselves that Russia's transition was doing as well as could be expected. We opposed crisis assistance thinking it would restore central planning; we pointed the Russians toward privatization and free markets, and watched as the economy fell further and further into crisis. The convergence notion distorted our response in a way that turned out to be very undesirable. A Russian economy in deep depression undermined a possible transition toward a freer society, resulted in the return of an increasingly authoritarian regime, and played a large role in undoing what progress might have been made in Russia toward a more constructive involvement in the world. The transition of Russia after the collapse of the Soviet Union is one of the main events of our era, and it didn't go well. The control that our public culture exerts over our perceptions of reality, the degree to which it distorts them at all levels of our society (from the local news program to the policy-making offices of the White House) has rarely been more clearly and unfortunately demonstrated.

HARMONISM

As part of our general faith in the good will of most people, many of us embrace rationality. We presume that people are generally of good will, that they measure the costs and benefits, the risks and rewards, of courses of action within the laws of virtuous civil societies, and choose those that are the least threatening. But this doesn't always happen. The illusion that it does, or it should, is harmonism.

Long ago, a harmonist illusion blinded Americans to the possibility of World War II and thereby greatly prolonged and worsened the war. "The wreckage of 1918," wrote the authors of a recent comprehensive history of World War II, "had certainly suggested the possibilities [of another great war]. But the democracies chose to forget the harsh lessons of that war in the comfortable belief that it all had been a terrible mistake; that a proper dose of reasonableness – the League of Nations along with pacifist sentiments – would keep the world safe ... "[3] Reasonableness did not keep the world safe from war then. Today, modern harmonists insist that free trade and economic progress will keep it free from war.

One observer commenting on the end of the Cold War wrote, "The signal error of the American elite after the end of the Cold war was its trust in rationalism, which, it was assured would continually propel the world's societies toward systems based on individual rights and united by American style capitalism and technology."[4]

Those of us in America who insist that people are primarily rational implicitly assume that they are both logical and decent – but many people are in fact unwilling to play fair or to abide by a rule of law (even though they may profess to be just the opposite). Many of today's terrorists, for instance, do think logically, reasoning from one step to another, and in this sense they are rational. But in the broader and more important sense of making logical connections between ends and means, and avoiding behavior that is rash and adventurist and cruel, they are not rational as harmonists would have it. Some people simply prefer to win without regard to any rules. We as a national culture try to deny this, preferring to believe in morally just solutions; but our attitude is immature. It is in the broad sense of what it means to be rational that we should recognize that rational calculations neither motivate nor dissuade people who merely believe. Seneca told us that "Within every man is a god and a beast, chained together." There is the potential for good and evil; and rationality can serve either.

Rationality doesn't guide behavior into benign channels as it's supposed to; even in the absence of rational calculations, most people have little difficulty deciding how to conduct themselves. There are cues that they employ to know how to think and act, switching from one logical paradigm to another as necessary to justify their choices, often inconsistently. This is the reality of human nature. Harmonism tells us something very different.

Harmonism insists that people are basically good and rational. Applied to the international scale, it typically leads to uncritical acceptance of such ideas as:

- Sovereignty and national borders are sacrosanct (in reality they are always changing because economic and demographics are always changing the relative power of nations);
- International law is real (it is in fact very weak, and hardly more than a guise for the politics of the nations); and
- The market is a decision maker instead of a pricer and allocator only, so that there are no geostrategically determined trade flows. (Many of us insist on treating the price of oil, determined largely by a cartel, as if it

were the result of competitive free market transactions; and many of us insist on treating the now rapidly growing trade surpluses of China as the result of the action of Chinese consumers, who apparently prefer to accumulate cash rather than spend it to enhance their living standards. Both are misconceptions deriving from the harmonist illusion.)

The conservative tradition that has emerged in America since the 1950s, gives primacy to moral idealism in international politics and defense, and is not critical of the defects of free enterprise. Today's left will not subordinate their causes – including racial discrimination, gender equality and freedom of sexual orientation – to national security. In this they share an uncomfortable bed, a surprising commonality of view of right and left in the harmonist presumptions of American public culture. The fact that left and right agree largely about the world's democratic destiny (harmonism) should not assure that the proposition is correct, but rather should cause us concern that our country is locked by their agreement into illusions which are not effectively challenged.

Virtues sometimes treated as categorical imperatives like peace, prosperity, universal harmony and social justice should not take precedence over American national security. Rather, survival is the prerequisite for attaining other noble goals, and that it is essential to deal objectively with the threats confronting us, instead of idealizing friends, and demonizing foes.

The defense of America should be separated from the idealistic goals of our political philosophies. It should be salvaged from the hazards introduced by the pietism and illusions of political controversy.

In many policy prescriptions today a foundation based on the harmonist illusion can be discerned. One example is the recommendation that America seek better relations with China, essentially ignoring Chinese creation of missile forces which can hit the continental United States. The short answer to the harmonists is that China should cease to modernize and build long-range nuclear missiles; and were China to do so, then better relations could be more than a facade. One can easily imagine a government of China with which the United States could have open and friendly relations, because that Chinese government was not building nuclear armed ballistic weapons directed against us, threatening Taiwan, and squeezing Japan in the politics of the Far East. But this is not the case.

The harmonist then takes the next step – the suggestion that Taiwan should be returned to China over its objections. This, it will be said by the harmonist, will permit peaceful relations between America and China. But will it? It will place China in a position to strangle Japanese trade, and using that new opportunity, to advance its aspirations for greater control in East Asia generally. It would be nice were this not likely, but that is a leap of faith. The harmonist assumes that it will not happen, and leaves us, if it does, in a much less defensible position. And when their assurances prove to be worthless, they insist against the facts that what is, is always for the best.

Instead of facing the reality of ill will and irrationality, both in terrorists and in some governments abroad, many of us project our own attitudes onto others, assuming that they are of good will and rational, and that the natural state of peoples is to live together in harmony. Liberals hold to this notion despite its inconsistency with what has been happening to America at the hands of its enemies. What may be startling is that conservatives, who reject much optimism about human nature, nonetheless accept harmonism as well, and have done so for decades and in more extreme circumstances than those of today.

A key example involves Wendell Willkie, the Republican candidate for President in 1940, who traveled the world late in 1942 in a military aircraft provided by his victorious election opponent, Franklin Delano Roosevelt, President of the United States, and wrote a hugely popular book about his trip. In it he wrote, "I believe it is possible for Russia and America . . . to work together for the economic welfare and peace of the world. . . . There is nothing I ever wanted more to believe."[5]

Willkie continued to reject the convergence notion now so dear to his party's faithful. He didn't think the USSR and the United States were alike or are becoming more alike and said so explicitly. "No one could be more opposed to the Communist doctrine than I am. . . . The best answer to Communism is a living, vibrant, fearless democracy." So he didn't embrace convergence; he didn't think that Russia and America were becoming alike. But he did think that the USSR and the United States were both of good will and could cooperate to make a better world; a classic expression of harmonism.

Willkie's position was a key step in ushering the transition in the Republican Party from isolationism to today's internationalism.

The world offers many examples of circumstances in which people around the world do not act in the spirit of harmony or "reconciliation," indicating that we should not assume that they will. An interesting and important example involves the Turks destroying in the 1950s Greek and Christian communities that had existed in the Turkish capital, Istanbul, for centuries. "In the end, modern statehood proved more harmful to Greek-Turkish and Christian-Muslim coexistence," wrote a reviewer about a book that described the events, "than traditional theocracy (including Ottoman theocracy) had been. That is thought-provoking for anyone who assumes that over time the world is becoming more secular, and from a secular viewpoint, more 'sensible.'"[6]

Yet harmonism lives on. It is illustrative of the wide acceptance of harmonism across the political spectrum years later that Jeffrey Sachs of Columbia University commented to a reporter, " . . . I've worked in all parts of the world and engaged with people of all faiths and cultures. I know the vast majority of people share common aspirations." There is, he continued, "a belief that the world could achieve peace, that the world could achieve shared prosperity, that reason matters and that technology gives an opportunity for human betterment."[7]

Sachs has impressive company in his harmonist convictions. "For the first time in modern history," wrote Richard Haass, "the major powers of the day – currently, the United States, Europe, China, Russia, Japan, and possibly India – are not engaged in a classic struggle for domination at each other's expense. There are few contests over territory. For the foreseeable future, war between or among them borders on the highly unlikely and, in some instances, the unthinkable."[8]

But, of course, exactly such a classic struggle for domination is underway, with all the other powers accusing the United States of leading the contest and the United States denying that it is initiating any such struggle.

In September 2005, former President Clinton assured the people of the world that "one thing is clear – the vast majority of us, from all religions and races, all political views, all walks of life, want a better world. There is more that unites us than separates us." And from it Clinton drew the conviction that a small group of world leaders could be assembled by him (as the Clinton Global Institute) to successfully address what he called "four critical challenges: poverty, religious strife, climate change and governance."[9] This is a standard procedure derived from the harmonist conviction. And perhaps some good may come of it. But is the basic harmonist conviction justified? The world is full of national, business and religious leaders who do not want what Bill Clinton would view as a "better world." What they would see as a "better world," he would not accept. Because this is the case, and examples are too numerous to require citing, whereas Mr. Clinton seeks on a small private scale to address enormous problems, the American government must operate without the illusion of harmonism to objectively assess the actual intentions of others and defend us from them where necessary. The danger of harmonism arises when our government acts on the assumption of shared values and intentions, or when our electorate is so bemused by harmonism that our government cannot act objectively even though it desires to.

There is even a version of harmonism that seems on its face to be the opposite of harmonism – an antiharmonism. For example, the key message of Andrew Wheatcroft's valuable study of the long relationship of Islam and Christianity is that both sides see the other as barbaric; and that while we see them as awful, and often they are, we are not better, just different.[10] Is this the opposite of harmonism – seeing people as generally bad rather than good – as it seems? Perhaps, except that most westerners reading such a point do not really believe themselves to be as evil as Islamic terrorists, so if they are told that in reality they are really like the terrorists, then they reverse the notion and say to themselves, "If we are like them, then they must be good like us." So what appears the opposite of harmonism twists itself into harmonism itself. So strong is the illusion of harmonism in our society.

Another recent version of harmonism is the notion of reconciliation among peoples of the world. It is a wonderful ideal; but it relies on the harmonist presumption that others want harmony, and will sacrifice their objectives for it. Ideals of this sort are numerous – democracy for all, reason in international affairs, goodwill among all peoples, the peace spirit being embraced by all, the invisible hand running the global economy. What they have in common is the appeal of a better world, and the appropriation of a concept (such as democracy, reason and the invisible hand) by harmonists who make much stronger claims than empirical evidence supports – concepts are exaggerated into utopian ideals.

As a profession of hope, there is nothing to object to in harmonism. Quite the contrary, rationality and good will are what we hope for people over the world. But when converted to an assumption on which a nation's foreign policy is based, harmonism becomes a recipe for disaster. Harmonism assumes away much of the danger in our world. It is therefore not a proper basis for establishing policy. The reality of evil in the world is as pronounced as the reality of good; danger is as real as opportunity. Our nation's approach to the world must include equal measures of safety and harmonistic idealism .

CONVERGENCE

Convergence is the conviction that the world is organizing itself around a particular set of economic and social policies that are much like our own, making us more secure in the long run. Convergence is expected to drive the economies of the world closer in performance so that poverty is ameliorated, the world is tied tightly together with bonds of trade, and thereby peace becomes assured.

The collapse of the Soviet communism and the opening to investment and trade of the Chinese economy cause the world's economic systems to appear more similar, but this supposed convergence of systems in is fact much more superficial than usually thought in our country. The changes in economic structure, including ownership and rights, in Russia and China are less than they appear; the movement toward our system is less than commentators insist; and economic cultures, which are hardly affected at all by the changes in rules and regulations that constitute systems, remain very divergent, yielding very different economic results.

In its simplest and most commonly held form, convergence insists that all countries in the world are moving toward capitalist democracy, and that as a result there will be world prosperity and peace. Put this baldly, the debt of the notion to wishful thinking is apparent. It's a very attractive view – a sort of new utopianism, and has entrenched itself in our public culture.

Thomas Friedman is probably the best known of the reporters and political/economic commentators who promote convergence today. Friedman is convinced that our national security is dependant on the world's increasing convergence to American democratic principles. One of Friedman's most discussed arguments is the so-called McDonald's theory of world peace. Friedman says that it is no coincidence that no two countries have gone to war with each other that have a McDonald's franchise, with McDonald's representing a positive symbol of modern capitalism, democratization, and globalization, rolled into one. He adds to the Golden Arches theory – any country with a big enough middle class to have a network of McDonald's restaurants will never go to war – the Dell theory, that any country that is part of the global supply chain will never go to war.[11] This includes China; it may not include Russia.

Friedman is not alone in seeing the world converging around a commercialism that is a key to peace. " . . . as China becomes stronger and richer," wrote Walter Russell Mead, "it also seems to be developing a deeper appreciation of the value of participating in the kind of system the United States has tried to build. China's growing economic might and diplomatic sophistication enable it to achieve more of its objectives within the kind of international system the Untied States hopes to stabilize in Asia. . . . China and the United States seem closer to a genuine meeting of the minds than ever before."[12] "China's move to the market and opening to the outside world have loosened party controls over everyday life and led to the emergence of ideological diversity," Merle Goldman tells us. She adds that these developments are important as far as they go, but do not guarantee movement toward democracy. Supporters of convergence in the public culture ignore her important caveat.[13]

Globalization of commerce is a positive force in the world for peace, but it cannot be expected to have enough influence to provide peace on its own – not when significant countries and their leaders have objectives involving power-seeking in addition to, or instead of, the welfare of the people of their nations. This is true even if power seeking is subjected to a rigorous economic analysis, with governments behaving in a rational way to maximize both their economic and political objectives, so that optimal amounts of security and power are governed by laws of supply and demand. Then purchases of power imply an intention to violate the rules of the competitive marketplace by influencing, coercing, or compelling others to alter their behavior instead of treating them as arms-length competitors. Nothing precludes authoritarian regimes that are largely indifferent to consumer welfare from building superior military forces when the priority their leaders place on security and power exceeds that of the people in democracies. Democratic free enterprise isn't sufficient to assure protection against an authoritarian foe seeking domination.

Moreover, the notion of convergence is wrong on every point.

- The world is not converging on a particular set of economic policies;
- If it did converge on policies, the result would not be to drive the economies of the world closer in performance (that is, for the poor to catch up with the rich), but quite the opposite; and
- Where there is a catchup of the poor with the rich (as especially with respect to China today), the result is not to make peace more likely, but more likely the opposite – it is to provide fuel for the furnace of nationalist expansionism.

For decades now – despite the apparent tighter linking of world economies through globalization – the action of underlying economic forces has been to drive the world apart, to cause the long-term economic performance of nations to diverge and thereby to impose continual pressures for change in geopolitical relations, continually increasing potential conflict and creating challenges to peace.

The world does not converge toward stability but diverges toward conflict – a result of underlying economic forces and cultural differences among human societies. The high hopes expressed for China hurrying to enter the American system of world economic interdependence ignores the duality of China (liberalizing economic development and tightening authoritarian control) and gives a primacy to economic advancement over political and nationalistic goals that is not merited by the evidence.

Reporting on Pakistan, Robert Kaplan informs us that, "South Asia illustrates that globalization . . . can lead to war and chaos as easily as to prosperity and human rights. . . . The very accumulation of disorder and irrationality . . . was so striking and . . . must be described in detail – not merely stated – to be understood." He goes on to describe the extremes of wealth and poverty in the third world which point to conflict in the future:

Karachi's villas look like embassies, with guards, barbed wire, iron grills, and beautiful bougainvillaea and jacaranda trees adorning stucco ramparts. The villas, with their satellite dishes for watching **CNN**, **MTV** and other international channels symbolize a high-end kind of globalization; . . . the slums . . . a low-end . . . [There were ten days] in succession without water for part of the city. The wealthy have their own private water tanks, water-distribution network, and generators.

Kaplan quotes a high official of the Pakistani government who had read the *Federalist Papers* and John Stuart Mills's *On Liberty*, "Every single ingredient that the authors of those books say is necessary for a civil society – education, a moral code, a sense of nationhood . . . we haven't got ."[14]

What is the record of the past few decades in economic progress? Recent data give a very different picture than general progress. Says a recent review:

While some nations made considerable progress in the last decade or so and there is no gainsaying that globalization was often a help matters are actually worse for many nations and have more or less stagnated for a great swath of them. For many countries, the 1990's were years of despair, the *Human Development Report 2003* of the United Nations Development Program concludes. In 1999 1.2 billion people lived on less than $ 1 per day; 2.8 billion (roughly half the globe's population on less than $ 2 per day. In the decade of the nineties, extreme deprivation decreased substantially in China, but it increased substantially in Africa and in central and Eastern Europe, so that on balance, there was only minor reduction in poverty worldwide.[15]

Even though the dollar a day or two dollars a day measurements are a bit misleading, because a person can live in much of the world on very little, these estimates still reveal a grinding poverty that is inconsistent with general improvements in living standards.

The real story is not economic progress and convergence in the world, but stagnation in many places and divergence of national economies all over the world. Only seven developing countries made persistent progress over the past forty years toward catching up with the west, and they are all Asian. Dozens more fell behind. It's important that one of the countries that made progress is China, with its large population. But there is little evidence that China is becoming a closer friend of the United States as a result of its economic advances.

The thought is deeply imbedded in the American public culture that promotion of a much more rapid advance of living standards outside the developed West is a means of lessening the number and strength of our potential adversaries – poverty and deprivation and economic backwardness are believed to be seedbeds of conflict, so lessening them would be a major contributor to world peace. We are an affluent nation, and think ourselves peacefully inclined; it follows therefore that as the economic circumstances of other nations improves, they will also be more peacefully inclined. Unfortunately, this conviction is often wrong.

Sometimes improving living standards are followed by more peaceful behavior; sometimes by more aggressive behavior. Increasing economic power for a nation has often been used to strengthen it for conflict; this was certainly the case for Germany in the nineteenth and twentieth centuries, for Japan in the twentieth century and for the Soviet Union in the twentieth century. There is good reason to fear that it will be so for China in the twenty-first century. The Chinese leadership are aware of the history of Germany, Japan and the Soviet Union in the twentieth century and have spokespersons who explicitly deny any such grasp for power by China. But other Chinese profess to fear American intentions and urge upon China a much more aggressive stance in the world.[16]

This doesn't mean that we should not assist others in the world in improving their living standards; but we should not naïvely expect that such efforts are a necessary contribution to the likelihood of international peace. They may be and they may not be. It follows that economic advance is not a reliable part of our defense strategy, though it's a moral requirement on its own, and it is even a part of an economic growth policy (richer people abroad are better customers). Promoting economic development abroad is a goal in itself, but it isn't an effective part of national security strategy.

The convergence conviction causes us to promote American business practices abroad, to lavish foreign assistance on actual or potential enemies, including for example, Palestine, Iraq, Egypt, Saudi Arabia, and Pakistan. The schizophrenia that thereby has a grip on us that is never directly addressed because terrorism is subliminally linked in our minds with poverty and antidemocratic orientations. This is a largely mistaken linkage, as we'll see later.

Yet, convergence is in such contradiction to realism about the direction of the modern world that it must have significant implications for what America is doing in the world if its leaders embrace this view. Many conservatives believe that they reject wishful thinking and are aware of its dangers, yet, largely unknowingly, they espouse convergence. Conservatives pretend there is a theory behind their wishing, the economic theory of rational expectations, but it's really only a model of consumer behavior, and isn't enough to carry much weight in understanding global affairs – it's still only wishing. Liberals are also locked into inconsistencies when they embrace harmonism and convergence. Fatalism and determinism are currently unfashionable among liberals; but harmonism is merely fatalism, and convergence is merely determinism, both with an optimistic gloss. Future-oriented harmonists claim that their utopias are inevitable. Fatalism asserts that whatever will be, will be and nothing can be done to change outcomes. So future-oriented harmonisms are a subclass of predetermind states with optimistic outcomes (decreed by fate: hence fatalistic).

UNJUSTIFIED OPTIMISM

The unjustified optimism that accompanies harmonism and convergence is not limited to either side of the political aisle. It is as common among conservatives as liberals, though among conservatives it more often takes the form of the convergence notion. The fact that both sides of the political aisle express a form of wishing makes it harder for people trying to be objective to recognize the danger. Both conservatives and liberals are anxious to not seem to think alike, so they are at considerable effort to disguise this fundamental similarity in their thinking. But it continually reveals itself.

The editors of the *Wall Street Journal* wrote in the summer of 2000:

It is difficult to live in the United States . . . and not be optimistic. The constant threat of annihilation that was part of the Cold War has been eliminated. The once-confident predictions of American economic decline have been thoroughly disproved. And two centuries of dismal predictions about the dehumanizing effects of technology . . . have been discredited.[17]

Journalists joined the chorus. Two writers for *The Economist* have recently given us a vision of our future in a book, the title of which says a great deal: *A Future Perfect.*[18] With markets as a dominant economic ideology the authors expect that – from the economic promise of the markets, and the support they provide for individual liberty – there will emerge a marvelous future.

The fall of communism and a protracted respite from inflation have carried the conviction to new heights. Leaders in Washington and on Wall Street herald the dawn of a golden age of peace and prosperity where war is banished and universal affluence is achieved through global liberalization, privatization and macroeconomic stabilization. The Clinton administration even went so far as to reduce the list of rogue states – delisting North Korea – the spirit of the times is moving toward the position that peace is secure in our time because there are no threats.

A result of this bipartisan commitment to wishing was that most commentators and politicians wear rosy glasses. Will Marshall, President of the Progressive Policy Institute, wrote:

> At the turn of the last decade . . . President [George H. W.] Bush proclaimed a New World Order. In fact, only toward the end of the decade, riding the wave of the information revolution, did a new order begin to assert itself. It is based not on the old balance-of-power equation, but on the key pillars of globalization, democracy, American pre-eminence, and collective problem solving. . . . The Cold War order was organized around the clash of opposing theories about the best way to order human affairs. Its successor is organized increasingly around globalization . . .[19]

Hence, it would seem to follow there is decreasing need for defense concerns because globalization signals the end of war-provoking discord.

A widespread perception seems to be that there is general economic advance in the world except in certain areas of central Africa. This is not the case. There are only a few countries in the world that are growing well economically. They are the United States, China, India, Malaysia, South Korea, Taiwan, Thailand, Singapore, and some of the former communist states of Eastern Europe. All else, particularly virtually all Africa, Latin America and most of Southeast Asia, has been experiencing very weak economic growth or actually declining. The Chinese numbers, especially the announcements in 2006 of increases in GDP estimates and growth estimates, are suspect. So, the growth picture is very mixed, and those that are growing are leaving the others behind.

Some observers appreciated early the continuing risks of conflict. In the spring of 2000 a major foreign policy journal carried three articles on Russia dealing respectively with economic decline, political instability, and the supposed coming breakup of the Russian Federation respectively. There was also an article on Pakistan's instability. Out of instability could come conflict, it was recognized. Both Russia and Pakistan are nuclear powers; so the risk of conflict was much more serious than with nonnuclear powers.

But concerns about coming conflicts are quickly pushed aside by the public culture.

"Clinton managed to engage Russia and China, fight nuclear proliferation, liberalize world trade and save lives in Haiti, Bosnia and Kosovo," wrote Stephen Walt in a Spring 2000 edition of *Foreign Affairs*, suggesting that America build on such a firm foundation for peace.[20]

W. Bowman Cutler, Joan Spero, and Laura D'Andrea Tyson in "New World, New Deal," in the same issue of *Foreign Affairs*, told us:

The next ... president should build on Bill Clinton's legacy of embracing global-ization and easing its downsides. This means developing a new system of global economic relations based on American leadership, open markets, engagement with China and other emerging markets, and stronger multilateral regimes to handle transnational challenges such as the environment, labor rights, and the information economy.[21]

Note the presumption of international order and slow transition in these prescriptive articles even while the descriptive articles paint a picture of increasing instability and risk of conflict.

The arguments that sustain the rosy view of a world order are broadly familiar: free enterprise has swept away its ideological foes: communism, socialism, and the welfare state; free trade has pried open previously closed markets for foreign trade and investment; and privatization and liberaliza-tion are increasing productivity, restraining wage inflation, and encourag-ing entrepreneurs. Of course, everyone recognizes that problems persist, but most experts simply assume that these problems will be overcome. More-over, the new prosperity won't only be bountiful; it will also alleviate the plight of the world's poor. The experts assert that this bounty won't be just for the rich. Since returns on equity are expected to be higher in less devel-oped countries, these nations should outperform their richer peers, and, thus, their living standards should catch up with living standards in the rich countries.

Complementing this optimism is an equally cheerful myth that interna-tional conflicts will end. Allegedly, peace and tranquility will prevail because merchants do not make war on one another and governments understand that trade is better than war. To prove this myth, experts point to a global decline (except in Asia) in defense spending and to reductions in the numbers of weapons of mass destruction. Likewise, increasing political and economic integration are said to have vanquished the scourge of nationalism. Some experts even envision a "global village" of harmonious cooperators building a better world for themselves and their neighbors – just as utopians, like Karl Marx, predicted years ago.

As with all such musings, the rhetoric contains just enough truth to be credible. The Cold War with the Soviet Union is over; global hostilities have abated in some theaters; some nations are disarming; democratic ballot-ing is spreading; an appearance of international cooperation is ascendant; nations are liberalizing; entrepreneurship is spreading; inflation is waning;

labor militancy is declining; many nations' economies are growing; technology is advancing, and living standards have been rising. All this has been justifiable cause for celebration, but it is a mirage to the extent that it ignores powerful economic trends reconfiguring global wealth and power, thereby threatening to unravel much of what has been accomplished in the decade following the collapse of Soviet power.

Academics have been particularly myopic in this regard, invoking the concept of rational expectations – the assertion that people and nations ordinarily do what is in their long-term best interests, as determined by a rational process to indulge their idealism. Rational expectations as they construe it excludes a broad range of human behavior that causes people to advance their interests at the expense of others, miscalculate and overreach, and so presumes that these major causes of past international conflict have disappeared or are confined to certain backwaters such as the Balkans.

Attached to rational expectations is the Western model of the fully competitive economy in which acquisitive individuals are caused by the invisible hand (to use Adam Smith's metaphor) of the marketplace to create the greater good for people generally. Furthermore, the Western model involves market processes by which opposing forces, if driven out of balance, are brought back into equilibrium. Hence, the world is always tending, in economics and politics, toward harmony.

People who expect harmony and presume that others are scrupulously rational find it very difficult to accept that things could be going very wrong, or that there is an urgent need for Strategic Independence. They expect to see peace among national systems and improving economic fortunes. Expecting to see these things, they find evidence of them persuasive – they find what they expect to find. They might be right if markets came to the same thing as Pareto efficient free enterprise, and balloting assured that the people's will determined the supply of public programs, but neither presumption is widely valid, and even where they are there might still be a need for masterful leadership.

In the aftermath of September 11 it is much harder to accept a theory of self-creating harmony or convergence as sufficient explanations of human motivation. Instead, there is evidence of a world increasingly in discord.

THE PERSISTENCE OF PUBLIC CULTURE

The persistence of the illusions of American public culture in the face of widening global inequity, world wars, genocide, terrorism and emerging new great power threats is more than a matter of failed individual intellect.

Wishful thinking about American free enterprise, democracy and globalization is culturally approved. People both know that it is silly, and behave as if it isn't, a contradiction that could not be sustained if it weren't socially convenient to double think. American politicians, the media and the people find it expedient to portray themselves and the nation in flattering hues, and to mobilize idealism, while simultaneously participating in self-seeking partisan rivalries that belie their speech and action. They lie, deny and otherwise selfishly exploit popular delusions. Their conduct is hypocritical, but also more than that because communities need a cultural common ground to provide order, and avoid extremism.

People do not readily let go of comforting illusions, and the American public culture has proven remarkably persistent, even rigid, over generations. Public culture persists, by and large, because it discourages everyone from thinking about it – it is simply there, a set of uncritically accepted beliefs that deny and defy examination. It is continually reinforced by influential institutions – in our country especially our two major political parties and our popular media (television, motion pictures, popular music, etc). In effect, public culture is an admixture of illusions to which many pander in order to manipulate others for commercial or partisan political reasons. From this pandering comes continual reinforcement of the illusions of public culture, which explains why public culture is so difficult to change. Because the media (both news programming and advertising) and politicians appeal to existing beliefs in order to gain audiences and to try to create identification for themselves with the audience, once public culture is established in a certain form, it is self-reinforcing and perpetuating. Furthermore, when people have a fixed idea, they have a tendency to look continually for "facts" that confirm it. In this way, they reassure themselves of its validity and counter those who might challenge the idea. So public culture provides an incentive for its own reinforcement, and is accompanied by a psychological need to find and accept reinforcement.

When people are comfortable in their illusions, they tend not to look beneath the surface of the public culture that sustains those illusions. John Rawls argued that these illusions would persist so long as the validity of the whole castle of illusions seemed secure. Security rests in our wishes – in our concept of a politically just world that is embodied in our illusions. "The public political culture is not unambiguous: it contains a variety of possible organizing ideas that might be used instead, various ideas of liberty and equality, and other ideas of society," wrote Rawls. "Whatever idea we select as the central organizing idea cannot be fully justified by its own intrinsic reasonableness, as its intrinsic reasonableness cannot suffice for that. Such an idea can be fully justified (if at all) only by the conception of political justice to which it eventually leads when worked out, and by how well that conception coheres with our considered convictions of political justice at all levels of generality in what we may call . . . reflective equilibrium."[22]

It's difficult to comprehend how stubborn is our public culture – this form of group think that affects us all – unless we've struggled against it in a particular situation. For example, realists discovered after decades of wrestling with the problem of Soviet despotism that it was futile to try to convince most Americans that the Soviet was the terrible place it really was, when our nation's popular culture insisted that Soviet leaders were instead reasonable people. President Franklin Roosevelt, for example, had insisted that he could trust Stalin, and infamously referred to him as "Uncle Joe." Harry Truman insisted that "Uncle Joe is not such a bad sort, but he is a prisoner of the Politburo." The Politburo was the top committee of the Communist Party of the Soviet Union, and Stalin was anything but its prisoner. Yet the logic of Truman's comment was that America should hope to free Stalin from his supposed controllers so that he could be himself – be the real Stalin. Challenged about referring to a monster like Stalin as "Uncle Joe," Truman defended himself by saying, "I did like him. So did Roosevelt and Churchill. I've seen their private, secret cablegrams. They always referred to him as 'Uncle Joe.'"[23]

Against the overwhelming force of the popular culture with its insistence on romanticizing Stalin, realists found it fruitless to point to a "smoking gun" – all the evidence to the contrary – that would convince skeptics, or to engage in ethical debate. The debate can't be won by showing logical inconsistency or factual error on the part of defenders of wishful thinking. Even if inconsistencies and facts are acknowledged, people challenging the popular culture are asked to explain why they are so obtuse – why they don't understand the subliminal rules by which discussion must take place – why the tenets of the popular culture must be accepted.

Public culture is nearly impervious to change; each news event is interpreted by the opinion makers (commentators, politicians, reporters, and editorialists) in terms of the public culture and so the public culture is always being reinforced. In fact, we might define the public culture as the terms of interpretation used by the media and politicians. Information that might challenge the favored interpretations is usually ignored because the reenforcers of public culture dislikes acknowledging fallibility.

Thus, much that is today coming out of the suddenly open archives of the former Soviet Union is being ignored in America. The reason given is that it is history, not news, and so not suited to the news media. But more important is that it would challenge the interpretation we put on past events. This is why leaders must have a background in history, and why a person isn't educated unless he or she reads both some analysis and some history, because otherwise their knowledge is nothing but the accumulated mess of half-truths that is the public culture, reinforced by its continual repetition in conversation and media reports – a sort of national prejudice.

For example, there was and remains a large crowd of Americans, perhaps the majority, who will admit everything bad about Stalin, and still dissociate his despotism from the communist experience as a whole, or rationalize Soviet brutality as necessary to modernize the nation. In dealing with the strongly embedded convictions of the popular culture, it isn't the facts that count – because the tenets of the popular culture tend to be the final arbiter of people's opinions.

Similarly, there remains a body of opinion in America (and a larger body of such opinion in Britain and on the European continent) that accepts Saddam's crimes, but refuses to accept the notion that he was not a reasonable man who could have been maneuvered out of threatening the west had peace been given a chance. The British Prime Minister, Tony Blair, has openly wondered at the inconsistency by which well-meaning people could maneuver themselves into a position from which they, for all practical purposes (if not for purposes of argument), became supporters of Saddam. It was exactly the same process of logic, or lack of it, by which their predecessors had become, for all practical purposes, supporters of Stalin.

This element of our popular culture – its insistence that most people are rational and peace-seeking with the possible exception of our immediate enemies – and its refusal to acknowledge the opposite in many critical cases, involving in the twentieth century Hitler (for years as he consolidated his power), Lenin, Stalin , Mao, even Saddam for a while – has major ramifications today. This is because evidence is so strong since the World Trade Center attack that there is much in human nature that is not rational and is not peace-seeking, that the insistence to the contrary in our popular culture to the contrary is under great strain.

PUBLIC CULTURE: A FORMAL EXPRESSION

Societies are rational about many matters, but tend to persistently misperceive and misunderstand others. We call the attitudes, rules and rituals which fix the thresholds of perception, the boundaries of permissible cognition, and the priorities of societal conduct public culture. The concept of public culture is connected to the approach adopted by Ludgwig Wittgenstein and

Jacques Derrida on other issues. As with their analytics, it is assumed that what is said and written isn't always consistent, or what is meant. This causes confusion, which can be partially alleviated by close textual scrutiny and scientific testing. Mark Taylor asserts that the essence of Derrida's deconstructionism isn't merely breaking things apart, but lies in the insight that " . . . every structure – be it literary, psychological, social, economic, political or religious – that organizes our experience is constituted and maintained through acts of exclusion. In the process of creating something, something else inevitably gets left out."[24] The term encompasses both nations' credos and their contrary actions, and provides a conceptual framework for understanding key aspects of partisanship, opportunism and policymaking. The impetus for denial arises naturally from conflicts between privilege and idealism, and from challenges to explain inconsistent ideals – it's easier to just deny any inconsistency. All societies fail to adhere to their ideals and actualize their potentials. Although they recognize shortcomings and could learn, they often don't, ignoring problems or offering a million excuses. This can be easily blamed on rational lapses but ignores the pattern. Just as individuals want to have their cake and eat it, societies deny fundamental conflicts, evading hard choices and preferring to believe that what is, is best without concern for the probable consequences of wishful thinking and denial.

Americans are no exception. Most of us are proud of our credo. We believe that the United States is a society where the majority democratically rules, but is mindful of minority rights. We hold that individuals enjoy unfettered personal and economic freedom under a rule of law. We believe ourselves to be rational, sensible, self-reliant, courageous, diverse, tolerant, just, peaceful, compassionate, charitable and willing to help others be the same. We recognize that our nation sometimes falls short of its ideals, but we vigorously debate shortcomings and maintain a strong faith in the system perfectibility. Surveying 240 years of our history, we find ample grounds for believing in progress. We don't expect perfection, but are confident that America's future will be more democratic, prosperous, free and just.[25] When all is said and done the American credo inclines people to wrongly assume that business is free and fair, elected officials are faithful representatives, that conflicting claims for social justice are optimized, that governmental restraints on personal freedom are appropriate, and that most lapses are self-correcting.

The American credo is the core of the nation's "public culture," epitomizing its central values and symbols, but not its operational content. The credo doesn't itself hold elected representatives accountable to constituents instead of special interests. It doesn't create a presumption for or against affirmative action, or for the scope of government intervention in enterprise, especially when taxation, property rights, and health and safety regulations are concerned. Nor does it offer clear guidance as to war or peace. These tasks fall to the implementational dimension of public culture, and are accomplished with a variety of means including passions, attitudes, scales of values, science, debate, political expediency, and ritual which in their entirety are more subtle and potent than ideology. Although the credo and socially approved cannons of social pragmatism are widely accepted, there is ample room for dispute. Partisan activity, government policymaking and public action are battlefields, operating under stable informal rules, and contextual cues that are seldom ideal in form and content, judged from the rigorously logical standards offered by the Pareto -Arrow-Bergson standard.[26] The good society is efficiently consumer sovereign both with respect to private and public goods. Efficiency is Paretian; that is, given a voluntary (as proposed by John Locke) social contract, and a corresponding fair play rule of law, individuals capable of rationally ordering their preferences and acting consistently on them, will seize every opportunity in education, training, employment, entrepreneurship, finance, production and distribution to maximize their utility, without coercing others. A system that generates these outcomes is consumer sovereign in the sense that supplies maximize individual utility, and hence social welfare under the conditions specified. Abram Bergson and Paul Samuelson have shown the "plausible" existence of a Pareto class of social welfare functions, which allows individuals to voluntarily employ the state to acquire public goods, and redistribute income and wealth. The simplest of these welfare functions democratically determines transfers. American public culture doesn't require citizens to be morally scrupulous, judicious, and wise in accordance with their credo, essential for the maximization of their personal and social welfare. Instead, it is notably tolerant of business, political and governmental misconduct, degrading economic and democratic efficiency by stressing facile persuasion (appeals to ideals, emotions, opportunistic self-interest, concepts, and symbols) more than science, reasoned discourse and balanced judgments.

This discrepancy between credo and practice is apparent both in the nation's factionalization (identity politics), and governance, although few fully appreciate the contradictions. They see the faults in their rivals attitudes, symbolisms and loyalties better than their own. Republicans, who perceive themselves as champions of compassionate democratic free enterprise, stressing individual self-reliance over the nanny state, are cast as the party of rich businessmen by Democrats, and Democrats, who view themselves as postmodern guardians of society's oppressed are portrayed as self-serving statists by Republicans.[27] Government policy making follows these cleavages. Republicans press a declaratory agenda of tax and deficit reductions, decentralization, and deregulation that more often than not is countervailed by the contradictory goals of some of its constituencies. The perpetual expansion of business friendly state programs winds up expanding the size of government, ballooning the national debt, and shifting the burden to consumers instead of putting more money in their pockets. Democrats match this by expanding social programs in ways that often benefit government administrators, NGOs, and diverse business interests more than the needy, while continuously shifting the burden onto the middle class. Republicans talk about defense, but their actions are often inconsistent, while Democrats who stress peaceful diplomacy are frequently aggressively interventionist. Both parties pay homage to the American credo, and drape themselves in the flag insisting they are acting in the national interest, but in most instances subordinate public welfare to partisan values, the claims of insiders, motivated constituents, political expediency, and their muddled perceptions of reality. Instead of treating national security and international economic challenges appropriately, an indulgent public culture permits solutions to complex problems to be sought in extraneous causes like feminism.[28] And governmental bureaucracies exacerbate the problem by carrying out their duties more with an eye to avoiding controversy, and padding their budgets than to providing useful services. The CIA's demand for more funds to remedy lapses revealed in its 9/11 and Iraqi intelligence estimates is typical,[29] reaffirming the old adage that nothing succeeds better in Washington than failure. Although there can be no assurance that a Pareto compatible public culture would provide better results in all instances, or narrow divisions, it should almost certainly do so.[30]

The resulting biases aren't easily dispelled in American public culture by enhanced information, science, and public discourse because the body politic is misinformed, addicted to partisan symbolism, superficial,[31] and is easily mislead.[32] What passes for knowledge from private and government sources too often is a pale semblance of the truth;[33] a virtual reality deadened to dangers and opportunities. It is a perverse case of the tail wagging the dog. Free enterprise and democratic theory, the touchstones of the American credo, teach that people are able to see through the public culture snares of wishful thinking, expediency and superficial consensus, maximizing utility in the private and public domains. But as public opinion experts are aware, they cannot do either if their preference functions are warped because they are disinformed, miseducated, deluded, and beguiled.[34] And pretending otherwise doesn't make it true.

CHAPTER 3: KEY POINTS

1. Different expressions of patriotism and concern about how to protect our nation have roots in deep psychological needs of belonging, self-expression, and denial of danger. However, our public culture provides inappropriate ways of expressing these valid human needs, and, helps explain the persistence of the illusions in our public culture. The public culture provides false comforts, and potentially dangerous myths.

2. Harmonism and convergence are the two illusions that dominate national security discussions in our public culture. They make it seem that peace and prosperity are assured by pretending that whatever individual and governmental motives might be, things will always ultimately turn out right. Harmonism is the illusion that all peoples and nations are peace-loving and that conflict is always a result of misunderstandings. Convergence is the illusion that most nations of the world (including most importantly Russia, China, Iran and Iraq) are moving toward our own model of capitalist democracy, and that given time, all nations will adopt our system. When the two illusions are combined, the conviction emerges that improving national economies abroad and increasing international trade will generate peace. The historical evidence is strongly against all three of these propositions; and there is sufficient current evidence that they are mistaken.

3. Public culture provides a framework for most of us to understand what is happening in the world. It is reinforced continually by commercially motivated media, which turns to public culture for a frame of meaning for its news stories; and by political leaders who seek partisan political advantage by identifying with the misperceptions of the electorate.

4. Differing economic cultures among nations and geopolitical power struggles drive international relations. There is no harmonism and no convergence of significance, only changes in the power and ambitions of other countries to which we must adapt.

FOUR

Towers of Illusion

Dysfunctional Behaviors

Yogi Berra is supposed to have cautioned us that it's not what we don't know that will kill us; it's what we do know that ain't right!

The point is very well taken. Public culture encourages us to be certain of things that are not correct and this sort of false certainty can kill us all when it distorts our understanding of significant threats.

We have seen in the previous chapter that American public culture offers us two great illusions – harmonism and convergence. Both are potentially dangerous on a large scale to our country. We will discuss in this chapter how they come to exist, are continually reinforced, and become so rigidly a part of our thinking. But this will be a difficult discussion for many of our readers. Trying to question what we believe to be true is always very challenging and often unpleasant, and so it is when we address the strongly held convictions of our public culture

In private life people are often inconsistent, emotional, passionate, self-indulgent, involved in denial, fantasies, and delusions, and are hypocritical and moralizing about others. It's not surprising that all this is projected into public life as well, and is largely tolerated by an electorate that behaves in the same way. These dysfunctional behaviors can be traced to the false set of choices and ideas provided by our political culture – choices that stifle new ideas and stymie those who want to articulate new ideas to form a more relevant political consensus. The American citizen is one whose intentions are good and information is bad. This is often a recipe for disaster.

Our public culture involves three key categories of dysfunctional behaviors – *simplification, hype,* and *distortion.*

SIMPLIFICATION

One of the most attractive aspects of public culture is that it simplifies otherwise complex matters. By doing so it makes its propositions accessible to the majority of our people, and it conveys a false sense of understanding.

NAÏVE MOTIVATIONS

Public culture makes world events understandable to many by providing naïve motivations – with which anyone can identify – for actions. "The Chinese," wrote a reporter in a major news magazine, "feeling their economic and diplomatic influence on the rise, are doing their best to counter Tokyo. 'They think enough is enough' . . . says Eric Heginbotham," the article continued citing a "senior fellow for Asia Studies at New York's Council on Foreign Relations."[1] This interpretation is presented as a news story, which it is not. Instead, it is a commentary described as a news story. It reflects key elements of the public culture: there is a victim (the Chinese) and a transgressor (the Japanese), and there is an attempt by the victim to set things right. Already a geopolitical contest is placed into a moral framework. Finally, to meet the needs of this morality play, basic facts are simply ignored – that China is an authoritarian state with ambitions in the region, and that Japan is a democracy of sorts without offensive military strength. Ignoring these basics allows the writers to present an authoritarian militaristic regime as the victim of a democratic, antimilitarist state. This is what public culture does.

What is most insidious about this aspect of public culture – for international relations, the most significant aspect because it leads us astray from objectivity – is that treatment as news implies (and almost every story about international relations in American periodicals does the same) that the action of a government which is reported grows out of some potentially remediable circumstance of the moment, usually some ill-considered action of the other government, or some misunderstanding, and not, as is in fact so often the case, out of purposeful determination (whose object is ordinarily not disclosed to the public). In other words, we are given no idea of the real motivation behind an event, so that international relations seems no more than a hodge-podge of messages that have no cipher. Unable to find the code that gives a news report meaning, we must translate it using a sort of generic code which treats all actions as the result of remediable circumstances, often simply misunderstandings – when in fact there are strategies and long-term scripts of many scenes in play. The great value of history is that in the hands of skilled historians the real behind-the-scenes story about great events which result from the interplay of differing strategies can be made evident to a reader; whereas inferring the different strategies and making out their interplay in the current scene requires much more effort and skill than the media can provide, and therefore than most observers can attain. The result is the superficial self-serving misinformation that the public culture offers as news.

There are two secondary points of significance:

First, as well-written history shows us that nations' leaders usually have purposes, if not overt strategies, not just reflective reactions to circumstances, it ought to be surprising that public culture blinds us to what we know – that is, that it has us pretend there are not purposes other than reflective actions, when we know this is unlikely.

Second, among great powers there are long-term scripts concealing hidden agendas in international relations as was made evident by Machiavelli five centuries ago, and also should be no surprise; again it is striking that public culture can blind us to it.

Public culture is by these examples revealed as a set of conventions by which we pretend that the world is not so harsh and threatening as it is.

EITHER/OR CHOICES

Another pervasive simplification is the presentation of policy choices in an "either-or" construct. Public culture prefers simple and direct responses to questions like, "Did or did not Iraq participate directly in the 9/11 attack?" If so, then the US is presumed to be justified in attacking Iraq; if not, it isn't. "Did or did not Iraq have WMD?" If so, the United States might be justified in attacking; if not, not justified at all.

Why is this type of simplification a problem in our public culture? The short answer is that it glosses over true calculations of the national security environment. As you review the questions above, what is missing? Answer: any consideration of Iraq's importance as a strategic key to the Arab world. Realizing the interconnectedness of events reveals many difficult and dangerous problems for us, including, indirectly, terrorism – but all of that complexity is lost on the media.

Here is another example of an important security matter addressed by a simplistic question: "The fundamental paradox of America's technology superiority: How can a small band of men, armed with obsolete weapons, operating in a country devastated by war, pose a direct threat to U.S.

security?"[2] The implication of the question is that a small band of men armed with obsolete weapons, and so on, do in fact constitute a direct threat to U.S. security. This is fully consistent with the hype given terrorism in the American public culture. But, a more accurate answer to their question is, of course, that a small band of men armed with obsolete weapons . . . do not in fact constitute a major threat to U.S. security. They constitute a minor threat composed of a tragic series of incidents from which we are increasingly able to protect ourselves by vigilance of many sorts.

A better question, posed later by the same authors, is "Why do strong countries such as the United States repeatedly fail to intimidate much weaker foes?"[3] Again, there is a implication buried in the question – that the United States does in fact fail repeatedly to intimidate much weaker foes. Perhaps it does so fail; and if so, then why is a good question, but one that has no simple answer.

OVEREMPHASIS ON RELATIONSHIPS

Another simplification applied to our understanding of world politics is the overemphasis on relationships. Just before the 2004 presidential election, a headline in *The Economist* asked, "The End of the Affair? Russia's Relations with the West are Deteriorating."

What is wrong with this headline? The answer is that relations are only part of a much bigger story about the state of play in the world, particularly between the United States and Russia. The other key parts are what is the likely strategy (purpose, objectives) and tactics of each in an increasingly obvious rivalry. Relations are not even the important point. Strategy and tactics are the most important things to understand and analyze. They tell us about the future and its dangers.

Relations are not important because they are superficial. In business, two top executives can have good relations – be civil to one another, even compliment one another, smiling before television cameras during joint appearances – but not be partners at all, but instead bitter rivals, competing and betraying one another. Relations good or bad, tell us nothing about the underlying situation. Relations are matters of press releases; of statements made by leaders at press conferences. The underlying situation may be deteriorating very quickly, but leaders are all smiles for the camera. Superficial issues of trade or cultural relations may be cordial, whereas underneath all is fury. For example, when President Bush visited Russia in May 2005, he took a spin in President Vladimir Putin's classic Volga. Whether the pair enjoyed their road trip is not going to help us understand the geopolitical rivalry between the two nations and where it is taking us.

Journalists, commentators, and editors ordinarily cannot determine the strategy of leaders of our own or other countries, (some wouldn't recognize a strategy if they encountered it), and without a sense of strategy, they can't comprehend tactics, so they focus on the most superficial, undependable, and misleading of all factors – relationships.

HOW SIMPLIFICATION MISLEADS

The simplifications of public culture make it misleading.

Simplifications produce illusions that can have serious consequences. Implicit in the notion that relationships among nations are the important thing for news media to cover is the conviction that conflict arises from misunderstandings, not from more basic conflicts of interest or even aggressive motivations. An example that is very significant involves the question whether peace between Israelis and Palestinians would be automatic if Israel met Palestinian claims for a homeland in the West Bank and Gaza. If one believes this is the only fundamental issue separating these two historic enemies, then he or she should demand that America's political leaders press Israel toward the required concessions. However, if one doubts the origins of today's violence between Israelis and Palestinians lies primarily in the issues of the West Bank, and believes instead that there are no concessions Israel can make that will bring real peace except agreeing to its own extinction, then one cannot ask Israel to make what could well be fatal concessions of land in the West Bank and Gaza. Simplification here – that the only issue is the West Bank and Gaza – leads to naïve conclusions.

Simplification sometimes substitutes for any thinking at all – when people just repeat the canned answers that public culture provides. This kind of simplification is a key source of ire in Anatol Lieven's comments on modern liberal democracies quoted in Chapter 1: that modern democracies are characterized by lazy, ignorant, irrational, and dysfunctional behavior coming in large part from uncritical absorption of information from television and the tabloid press. Another excellent statement of the dangers resulting from this type of simplification comes from sociologist Daniel Bell. "... simplifiers ... make it unnecessary for people to confront issues on their individual merits. One simply turns to the ... vending machine, and out comes the prepared formulae."[4]

A major contributor to the simplifications that fill our public culture is the continuing political contest of our democracy. Simplifications amplify the divisions of the electorate, and politics in a democracy is as much about polarization as anything else (including "the possible," "accommodation," and "alliance building," other favorite objectives of democracy offered by commentators). Every politician understands that in many situations it is necessary to polarize the electorate in order to win an election, and after winning it is sometimes appropriate to try to bring people together to try to govern effectively.

HYPE

Hype is exaggeration so extreme that it significantly distorts reality. "Don't believe the hype" is a popular expression of frustration when we are bombarded with overstatements by hucksters.

Unfortunately, hype is a common occurrence in the news and commentary fed to us in our public culture. Take for example, this opening line from a CNN reporter at the January 2005 World Economic Forum:

World leaders, screen stars, businesspersons have gathered in Davos, Switzerland for the World Economic Forum with the sole objective of making the world a better place.[5]

The sole objective of making the world a better place!! This isn't news; it's public relations-style hype. It can't be taken seriously.

"What is America trying to do in the world, why things have gone so terribly wrong . . . ?" asks an analyst of American national security policy. But of course, they haven't gone so terribly wrong. There are definitely problems, the most important of which we point to in this book; but we are not engaged in a big war; our national existence isn't threatened. The exaggeration "so terribly wrong" is merely hype.

In another place the same analyst writes about "dealing with the menace of a tactically flexible, morally ruthless, fanatical, and heavily armed Arabian fascism that is implacably opposed to everything we value in an age of mass terror . . ."[6] "Implacably opposed to everything we value?" Everything? Good food; family affection; warmth when it is cold; coolness when it is hot; natural beauty – everything? Again, mere exaggeration, but exaggeration intended to demonize an enemy and thereby make it more difficult for us to devise a sensible policy of response.

Our society is permeated with exaggeration, much of it intended to create a climate of fear. Politicians and commercial interests (including the mass media) employ fear to manipulate the public. In consequence the American public exists in a context of continual overstatement bordering on hysteria. Exaggerated fear causes the public to miss the threats we should really be worried about.

The danger of the American system's tendency toward exaggeration is most recently evident in the response of our media, our thought leaders and our politicians to the World Trade Center attack.

We have exaggerated:

- the danger to the United States (it's more immediate, but small compared to the risk of a nuclear exchange with a foreign power);
- the degree of conflict involved (it's not a war but a large scale police action); and
- the requirements for us to respond successfully (we could have minimized the matter, and responded better and without international controversy, rather than maximized it and created hysteria and the consequent expectation of a major reply by us.)

Contrast for example, what how the British reacted when London was attacked on July 7, 2005. The British treated the attack as a crime ("we will find the perpetrators and bring them to justice" said London's police chief), not as an act of war. And the British went about their business, not exaggerating the situation as was done in the United States. There was no hype from them, only stoic determination.

Extreme, unwarranted excitement (hysteria) at events is a continuing theme in American history. For example, John Brown's act in capturing the Federal arsenal at Harper's Ferry and trying to ferment a slave's rebellion transformed the South, in Paul Johnson's words, "into a tremulous and excitable body – a case of collective paranoia – which believed anything was preferable to a continuation of the present tension and fear."[7] Much the same happened to America as a whole as a result of the terrorist attack of September 11, 2001, in New York City.

It's instructive to revisit the commentary of the time, only a few years ago:

No other President has faced anything quite like 9/11. Pearl Harbor was militarily disastrous but not devastating to the economy, or so destructive of civilian life.[8]

This is an example of the hype, and not in a tabloid or on a radio talk show, or even in a television news show ratings contest, but in a respected, allegedly responsible, journal of informed opinion, *The Atlantic Monthly*. The author compares 9/11 with Pearl Harbor, and suggests 9/11 was the greater challenge to presidential leadership. A similar exaggeration is to call the conflict with militant Islam World War IV.

This is a failure of judgment about proportion of such magnitude as to be nothing other than astonishing. Pearl Harbor was the opening of the greatest and most dangerous war America ever experienced – one in which our major allies were almost conquered, a war we could have lost; a war that took us four years to win and cost us some three hundred thousand dead. In contrast, 9/11 put us into conflict with a loose group of terrorists who however frightening their attacks, pose no significant threat at all to America's national existence.

The damage done by 9/11 to the American economy was quickly repaired. To the extent that any significant damage to our economy can be laid at the door of 9/11, it was a result of the hysteria promoted by the media and politicians – by the same excessive rhetoric employed in *The Atlantic Monthly* – which caused many people, not directly affected by 9/11, to alter their economic behavior in unjustified panic. Even then, the American economy was not plunged into recession, but only suffered a reduction in its rate of growth. Pearl Harbor, on the contrary, presaged a diversion of more than one-third of the activity of the American economy from civilian production to the production of weapons of war.

"Does Bush have the imagination to lead a great war?"[9] the same author asks us. But we must ask, what great war? The war on terror? This isn't a great war – a great war is World War II. During World War II, the world lost about sixty million dead and America lost some three hundred thousand killed. World War II was a great war. In terms of treasure, defense expenditures as a percent of our national production were as follows:[10]

World War II	37.9%
Korea	14.1%
Vietnam	9.4%
Gulf War	4.8%
Iraq	4.1%

The war on terror is a large-scale police action at most, even though the danger including suit case nukes makes victory essential. So the question about President Bush's capacity to lead a great war asked in the context of the current conflict is absurd on its face and is part of the lack of proportion that has characterized so much of our response to the World Trade Center attack. It is our public culture in action – exaggerating to such a great extent that we cannot ask the right questions or frame sensible answers to the reality of the challenges we face.

Nor are civilian deaths due to the current cycle of terrorism of great significance when compared to what has happened previously. The most careful estimate of government killings (led by those of Stalin and Mao) in the twentieth century, excluding deaths of combatants in war, is 262,000,000.[11]

This enormous figure dwarfs anything imagined in the wildest dreams about terrorists and is equivalent to the killing that might have been caused by a full-scale nuclear war.

More examples of hyped-up post-9/11 commentary:

Who would have thought that day, who knew that morning, at 8:45 A.M., for instance, three minutes before the first plane struck, that everything in our lives was about to change?[12]

In fact, of course, almost nothing in the lives of most Americans changed, as has been repeatedly pointed out since. There are now more stringent security regulations at airports and public buildings; for some people there are more difficult interactions with security-conscious police, federal agents and prosecutors. These things may be right or not, but they do certainly not merit the assertion that everything in our lives has changed.

... what bin Laden accomplished [in the destruction of the World Trade Center] was truly a new, significant step.... The most successful military strike ever against the richest, most powerful country in the world...[13]

Was the World Trade Center attack really more successful against our country than the Japanese attack on Pearl Harbor in 1941, where much of our Pacific fleet was lost, potentially imperiling the United States itself; or the battle in 1943 at Kasserine Pass where the American Army was almost routed in its first engagement with the Germans? It wouldn't seem that the World Trade Center attack was more successful than those efforts. Was it more successful than the surprise Chinese intervention against us in Korea which reconquered North Korea for the authoritarian world and led, thereby, directly to today's crisis over the nuclear ambitions of the North Korean leadership? The answer again is no. In fact, the attack on the World Trade Center wasn't even a military strike – it wasn't made by soldiers and it wasn't made against a military target. It was an act of terrorism against civilians by civilians – something that rarely serves a military purpose.

Our government is also in the hype business. In Spring 2003, Condoleezza Rice was quoted in French periodicals to the effect that "Iraq is the most serious threat of our time."[14] This is a remarkable statement from someone who at that time headed the National Security Council and now is Secretary of State. What could she have meant? That Iraq was at that specific moment the most serious threat faced by the international community? Possibly, but only if the threat of nuclear attack from North Korea, then widely publicized, was discounted. Or could she have meant that Iraq is the most serious threat of our era? Is it more serious than the Cold War rivalry with the USSR; more serious than a potential conflict with a rapidly strengthening, nuclear-armed China; more serious than the ongoing threat of global terrorism (exclusive of Iraq's contribution thereto)? The notion that Iraq was a more serious threat than any of these is not credible. So what was her statement? It was an example of official hype – a genre of speech that is contributing to the inability of people to perceive and discuss threats in a sensible framework of thought. And it fits well in American public culture.

Allen Weiner has pointed out that the war on terror is not in strict legality a war because it is not waged between states.[15] But the use of the term "war" to describe our conflict with Islamic militants is unfortunate in a number of ways. For one thing, it allows our foes (in Europe as well as the Middle East) to accuse our military of killing civilians. Yes, civilians get killed; the militants are all civilians. They are not members of any legitimate armed force. They are civilian combatants; for example, all the suicide bombers are civilians; people who pose as noncombatants right up to the time they blow themselves up to kill and main others. By calling our conflict with the terrorists a "war" we suggest that there are soldiers against us and civilians standing on the sideline. In fact, all our enemies, armed or not, are civilians. We make every effort to avoid injuring real noncombatants, but sometimes such people get killed, and then a criticism of our killing genuine noncombatants may be justified. But the terminology "war" confuses the whole matter in a way that does us more damage than help.

Furthermore, because the president has exaggerated both the danger from terrorists and the scope of our response, insisting that it is a major war, he is forced continually to exaggerate even more to try to bolster his previous claims. The whole situation thereby becomes increasingly unrealistic, something that many people realize, even some who wish to support the Administration.

Challenged by his top Pentagon officials, who wanted to reduce the level of rhetoric about the response to terror attacks from the word "war," President Bush publicly persisted in retaining the phrase, "War on Terror." "Make no mistake about it," he said, "we are at war."[16]

Beneath what appeared a modest dispute about labels lay in fact a fundamental issue. The military was objecting to being used by the presidential authority, once again, to try to build a nation in our image abroad, something the military cannot do and which imposes on it loses and strains that are unnecessary and to no good purpose. Political leaders so misuse our military in pursuit of the illusions of our public culture. Only the acceptance by the military of its subordination to the political authority prevents military leaders from objecting publicly to their misuse. But Americans should be sensitive to the issue. The media, were it doing its job, would point this out, but it doesn't, preferring to reinforce at every opportunity the public culture.

That the war on terror is hype is suggested by its failure to take actions that would be part of a wartime scenario. For example, the United States has not closed its borders effectively. Estimates are that only one-quarter of the millions entering the United States illegally are actually apprehended. A researcher who has studied the matter tells us that "The main barrier to tightening the border is the absence of political will."[17] With the border leaking people, terrorists can presumably enter our country almost at will.

The hype is that we are engaged in a war that requires extraordinary methods (many of which we do not take), confronting novel tactics. But, in fact, 9/11 wasn't the first time we've confronted suicide bombers. That's exactly what the Japanese kamikaze fighters were at the end of World War II. The kamikazes were used on a greater scale than today's terrorist suicide bombers and kamikazes were used against the core of our military might, damaging it severely, something far more potentially dangerous to us than inflicting damage on civilian targets. There were also German suicide flyers, modeled on the kamikazes, although many fewer and less effective.

Japanese and German suicide bombers during World War II were directed against our military, of course, and not against our civilians. Civilian deaths are tragic, and we wish to completely eliminate them, but for the people of most nations, they do not cause the nations to lose conflicts, but strengthen resolve. They are not, therefore, a threat to the nation itself, as a defeat of its military forces is. For example, when Hitler unleashed the first significant aerial terror bombing of civilians during the Nazi attack on Poland in 1939, it was not the terror that caused the collapse of Polish resistance (as Hitler may have hoped), but the invasion of Poland by German and Soviet ground forces. Similarly, terror bombing by the Nazis of London during World War II on a scale unimagined by Islamic terrorists, failed completely to break the British spirit.

In reality, terrorism is a less dangerous form of conflict than others – especially nuclear exchanges between nuclear powers (as almost occurred several times during Cold War) and conventional war between great powers (as in the two world wars and Korea). Terrorism is directed mainly at civilians and cannot result a military defeat for our nation – the other two forms of conflict can. The danger of nuclear and conventional conflict between great powers has not been eliminated, so it's a mistake to subordinate them in priority to a terrorist threat. Yet hype of the sort described above is intended to put terrorism on the same level as the much more serious risks.

Some normally responsible people imagine terrorists with a biobomb who could thereby destroy mankind. This apocalyptic vision becomes a justification for making terrorism the top priority threat to America – it puts terrorism on a par with nuclear war with Russia or China. It's a new way to say that old time rivalries between nation states are no longer important. Yet there is no real evidence of the possibility of any such bomb, much less of terrorists having it, or being likely to get it. It is important to watch carefully all such possible threats, and if they actually emerge, or are likely to, to raise them on the priority list and deal with them accordingly. But it is merely hype to pretend that such threats exist today and that they should displace the reality of Russian and Chinese nuclear arsenals in our concerns.

Hype about terrorism gets in the way of identifying more serious threats. "By painting doomsday scenarios," Bruce Berkowitz tells us, "government officials lose credibility and over time their ability to influence the public. . . . They simply make it harder to build support for dealing with real threats."[18] In fact a modern nation cannot be defeated by terrorism – it was tried again and again in World War II and since, and has never succeeded. A nation attacked by terrorists is ordinarily angered and energized, just as happened in America as a result of the 9/11 attacks. The notion that terrorism is a threat to the survival of our nation is hype, and it's destructive for the reasons Berkowitz sets forward. First, it causes leaders to lose credibility over time, and second, it distracts from more serious threats.

Americans continually confuse their feelings with facts; and if challenged about it say that feelings are facts; thereby confessing their confusion. Feelings are emotions that are responses to facts; and are facts themselves only in the sphere of psychology and therefore of politics and public relations. Feelings cause other facts – like panic may lead to deaths as when a crowd spills out of a burning nightclub and tramples people. But to assert that the fire, the original cause, was a major thing because of the emotions it engendered and not the results that came from it is a serious confusion. So, the World Trade Center attack was tragic, but not a big thing; the emotional reaction (driven by hype) was dramatic and has had significant results – but it's circular reasoning, and therefore not at all convincing, to argue that the World Trade Center attack was a major fact (and thus justifies the hype) because of the emotional reaction to it. It was a big or little event in itself; its emotional consequences were simply that – they were in fact stoked to fever pitch by the hype, and so to justify the hype on the grounds of the emotion is completely circular.

Hype is always getting America in trouble because it causes us to lack proportion in judgment. Destructive as hype is, it seems a permanent part of the American mental landscape, and is a separate challenge to both clear thinking and political leadership – the challenge is: how to preserve responsible judgment about public issues in an atmosphere of public hysteria?

Winston Churchill warned about this. "True daring in war arises from a . . . sense of proportion, which again can only spring from a wide comprehension."[19] When there is no sense of proportion, then it is not true daring that emerges, but wildly irrational reactions. About the Duke of Marlborough, victor over Louis XIV of France, Winston Churchill wrote, ". . . his unerring sense of proportion and power of assigning to objectives their true priorities . . . mark him for the highest repute."[20] It is exactly these two crucial characteristics – discerning proper proportion and priorities – that the public culture of the United States continually removes from our discussion of international challenges and from the policy of our presidents. This is the danger it causes us.

Had our media and politicians responded differently to the 9/11 attacks, stressing not our supposed vulnerability to more attacks, not the supposed damage to our economy, not the dangers, that is, but instead that we are a great nation that cannot be intimidated by such acts of terror and that will not allow such attacks to cause us to panic and thereby injure ourselves, like a crowd rushing from a crowded theatre because a fire has started, who trample each other in the staircases, and so themselves, by their fear cause the very deaths they are trying to avoid – had we not reacted in panic, that is, fed by the media and political pronouncements, then there would have been almost no economic damage from the attacks. The American economy is simply too large to be significantly affected by what happens to two buildings, even big buildings like the World Trade Center.

Had American leadership responded to 9/11 not with panic but with a calm statement that this was an unusual event, caused because we had let our guard down about threats of terrorism we knew to exist (9/11 was simply a group of plane hijackings – we'd been dealing with them for years and were supposed to have security measures in place to thwart potential hijackers – but our security systems were defective – their people were inattentive); but that we would not be caught napping again, that there would be no more terrorist attacks in America for the next three years and more (as indeed there have not been), that people should simply grieve and return to work feeling safe themselves, that we would hunt down quietly and effectively all over the globe our assailants, then there would have been little of the adverse impact on us that 9/11 supposedly caused.

DISTORTION

Distortion is the result because the illusions of our public culture are usually an ineffective lens for perception. Events in the real world are often complex, and our public culture offers only a few simple categories in which to describe them. Hence, public culture simplifies to good and bad, friends and enemies, chooses sides, and thereby distorts reality in an often dramatic fashion.

In the late fall of 2004, there was a disputed election in Ukraine. One candidate for president leaned to the West; the other to Russia. When the Americans (in the form of Secretary of State Colin Powell) criticized the election and supported the West-leaning candidate (whom we identified with democracy), President Putin of Russia rejected his criticisms. The Russians then attacked publicly the American position on Iraq. There was almost no suggestion that the Russian criticism about American involvement in Iraq had been carefully developed, the situation there assessed, and a considered evaluation made. It was just a Russian reaction to the U.S. criticism of Russia's supporters in Ukraine – a shot at the United States where Russia thought us vulnerable. This is geopolitics: both the exchange of critical statements and the tug of war between the West and Russia over influence in Ukraine.

What motivated this international exchange? Why were Western countries and Russia involved in Ukraine? Why wasn't Ukraine left to itself? How did Ukraine get mixed up with Iraq in international politics?

There are two reasons. The first is that Ukraine and Iraq both play important roles in the domestic politics of each of the major countries. The second is that major powers cannot resist fishing in troubled waters. The first reason finds its continuing expression in mass media news coverage and the posturing of politicians. It is public and can be readily followed by the public. The second reason is ordinarily a hidden agenda, usually denied by spokespersons for the various governments, or so distorted as to real motivation as to be unrecognizable to objective observers. The second reason is not public and cannot be readily followed by the public.

What happened in Ukraine was a political contest between the two geographical regions of the country with both candidates backed by elements of the country's economic oligarchy found its way into a hotly contested election for president. The country's outgoing president had backed one of the two candidates. The election ended in charges of fraud. It was resolved by a deal in which the outgoing president retained considerable power via a change in the country's constitution, and the challenger was given the weakened post of president.

Into this internal mess jumped the European Union, siding with the challenger (who represented the western, more European region of Ukraine). The EU's external relations commissioner, Benita Ferrero-Waldner, promised to do "everything in my powers to keep Ukraine on our side at least." This brought Russia into the conflict on the other side; and the United States sided with the European Union (EU).

The result, "... the whole fight inside Ukraine ended in a compromise that largely suited the interests of the oligarchs ... the political fireworks outside the country were ... pointed and pointless. Both sides – the EU and United States on one hand, Russia on the other – accused the other of interfering in Ukraine's internal affairs to suit their own interests. The only results thus far seem to be twofold: First, relations between Russia and the United States and EU have soured; second, Ukrainian democracy has come off worse, as trust in the electoral process dwindles."[21]

The American media, acting within the constraints of our nation's public culture, provided virtually no understanding of the underlying reality to its audiences. Instead, the media distorted the situation by participating gleefully in taking one side in the Ukrainian contest and interpreting the outcome as a great victory for the west. Specifically, the media:

- Focused on the election process, not the underlying realities, as if the election was itself the most important thing (like focusing on outcome of battle, not what's happening in the war – actually, media often keeps sight of war even when reporting the battle, but not in political discussions, much more subject to public culture).
- Accepted the posturing of Ukrainian politicians at face value – this one is like us; that one is not. This one is honest; that one is not. They simplified the situation into contest between a hero and a devil.[22]
- Willfully disregarded history and the broader context of the Ukraine in geopolitics. Were Ukraine to slip into the orbit of the EU, then Germany (the EU's dominant member) would get access to what used to be Russia's Black Sea ports and its fleet (now in the hands of Ukraine). What the Wehrmacht couldn't achieve in World War II, the EU and Euro might achieve peacefully now. This the Russians would find it very, very hard to accept. Such a threat to Russia and it's possible reaction is far more important to the United States than is the health of Ukrainian democracy – which is what the media focused on.
- Engaged the West's predilection for wishful thinking (the world is becoming more like us) and ignored the reality of the situation, including the real risks involved.

- Adopted the simple convention that there are allies and enemies and they are distinct. Hence, Ukraine with a different government becomes an ally and dangerous tendencies against our interests are ignored. In reality, the rivalries among nations are not ended by alliances. Our allies usually have different interests to a large degree, and hence are in part rivals. Enemies and rivals are not the same, but both are dangerous. In the most dramatic example of recent history Winston Churchill protected the British Empire successfully from its enemies (the Germans, Japanese and Italians) but not from its ally and rival, the United States. The Empire was lost despite victory in World War II largely because Franklin Roosevelt opposed European imperialism and wanted the British Empire dissolved. America accomplished indirectly what the Axis powers could not accomplish directly – the dissolution of the British Empire. An ally who is a rival is not an enemy but can be as dangerous.[23]

In the end, the media and to a large degree the countries of the West treated what was occurring in the Ukraine not as a matter of international relations, though it was that, but as a matter of domestic politics – seizing on it to reinforce patterns of thought for partisan purposes. By projecting domestic politics onto the international scene, and distorting mass media reporting for partisan gain, objectivity was abandoned and the world stumbled closer to conflict – even though the media reports and political pronouncements said exactly the opposite. Yet within a year, the media were acknowledging how much oversimplification there had been in the reporting about the Ukrainian situation.[24]

The hidden geopolitical motives which enticed the major powers into squabbling over Ukraine are straightforward. Simply, Ukraine lies on the borders of both the European Union and Russia. Europe is interested in Ukraine because it would prefer a friendly democracy on its border to a Russian rival, especially because Ukraine possesses what were once the major Russian (in the form of the Soviet Union) naval bases on the Black Sea. With Ukraine oriented to the West, those bases, which were the focus of bloody battles between Germany and the Soviets during World War II, would be under German influence rather than Russian. Russia is interested in Ukraine because its strategy at this point is to reassert influence in the now independent nations that once composed the Soviet Union. America is involved to show support for the Europeans and to further weaken Russia.

In general, nations cannot resist fishing in troubled waters, and Ukraine is much troubled. Geopolitics is about such interactions between nations – it is politics enmeshed in world geography; politics between countries and their leaders.

Geopolitics is dangerous because the major participants are armed with weapons of mass destruction and the risk of their use is always there. It is not at all difficult to recognize that had Russia invaded Ukraine, as it certainly considered doing, there could have been a risk of major war, unless the west had backed down.

Politics was at the heart of the involvement of other countries (including America) in Ukraine: politics of a domestic nature in countries outside Ukraine; and politics of an international nature.

What is most striking about these two reasons for our involvements abroad is that both result in distortions offered to the public. Domestic politics misrepresents situations abroad for domestic political advantage, just as it misrepresents situations at home for partisan political advantage. The geopolitical agendas of nations involves misrepresentations of situations and motives abroad because diplomacy insists on conventions of politeness that generally prevent open and honest discussion.

As interesting as the tussle over Ukraine between Russia and the West is the public culture spin given in reporting by the *New York Times*. The story insists that the underlying problem involves different conceptions of democracy. This is accompanied by a brief comment about "competing economic and political interests," but this isn't stressed at all. In the usual public culture way the conflict is made to rest on misunderstandings about democracy. Presumably the conflict could be resolved by diplomatic dialogue, since its root cause is misunderstanding.[25]

But it's also hard to pin this distortion tightly on the *Times* article. For how can a critic object that there isn't a difference about the meaning of democracy between Russia and the West that is profound and significant? He or she cannot. And so if the article is criticized, the defenders of the public culture simply slip their emphasis a bit and say, "We said that. You agree that differences about democracy are existent and important." Yes, but irrelevant to the real situation – a clash of interest and objectives between strong nations.

In order to make any sense of reporting and commentary, one must have additional information – an interpretative key, so to speak. For some people ideology provides such a key. For others, a thought leader provides the key. This what Pravda used to do for the Soviet Party apparatchiks – tell them the party line. For many of us, public culture provides the key. But it is a key that is full of distortion.

The only way to adjust for the distortion is to do the work of having additional sources of information that provide a reliable interpretative key. The sources to seek are ones that are not primarily partisan or ideological. What complicates this search is that media in our public culture pretend to an open mindedness that they do not possess. Our public culture suggests that freedom of speech and of the press insures breadth and depth of insight. It does not. The public culture restricts breath and depth of insight to a very significant extent.

Economic culture is one of the two drivers that move the world's history – the other is the grasp for power and wealth that is embodied in nation states and nonstate actors. Changes in either of these factors are very infrequent. When they occur in a nation, they are very important. Unfortunately our media have no ability to distinguish a crucial alteration in an underlying source from a press release issued by a government to mislead its rivals (that is, the basic and significant from the self-serving and trivial). Hence, our public culture is full of misinformation and confuses us profoundly.

MASTERING THE ILLUSIONS OF PUBLIC CULTURE

Discerning the national interest behind the confusion created by the illusions of public culture is a feasible task. A master of illusion must start with a deep appreciation of public cultures in America and abroad. He or she can enumerate a short list of pressing issues and inventory the attitudes shaping partisan conceptualization, and errant public policymaking. The data required to appraise their comparative merit, and other more dispassionate alternatives then must be collected, scrutinized and purged of bias enabling the "masters" to construct a road map identifying one or more potential optimal paths, and the public cultural traps blocking their realization. It is essential in creating the road map to appreciate that optimization is multiobjective. Masters of illusion cannot allow themselves to fixate on a single objective like extricating America from Iraq. They are obligated to take account of all collateral factors including the larger security matrix and competing social priorities affecting national, and or global welfare. The piecemeal approach, favored by common law, and partisan self-interest is a recipe for incoherence and the preservation of the status quo.

In an ideal world the truth would make men free. Once masters of illusion had seen the light, and communicated their wisdom the rest of the jigsaw puzzle would fall into place. But this isn't our world. Masters of illusion must appreciate that the truth is seldom self-evident, that they are fallible, and must operate in an arena strewn with public cultural snares. Consequently, all road maps are drafts which should be disclosed for public scrutiny to the fullest extent. This may not always mean complete disclosure due to danger of partisan distortion, but candor otherwise is essential as the foundation for popular sovereign democratic free enterprise. Moreover, recognizing that modern electorates are befuddled by public cultures, masters of illusion should attempt to educate citizens to think independently outside the blinders of partisanship, and harmonist placebos. Nonpartisan NGOs above the fray also could play a valuable role in this endeavor. Moving from an illusion to a knowledge based public culture committed to optimizing national or global social welfare instead of privilege preserving chaos, therefore is achievable with leaders wiser than those presently at hand.[26] Neither the approach, nor the outcomes are utopian. Optimization only means doing the best within the constraints of bounded rationality. It isn't ideal, but is better than self-delusion. Neither Republicans nor Democrats appear to have learned this lesson from the 2004 presidential election. Although both sides grasp that antipostmodernist identity politics have allowed Republicans to gain a growing electoral advantage, neither party has a clear perception of how to translate the new reality into optimal national policy. Republicans aren't looking beyond pressing a few traditional goals like partially privatizing social security and curbing entitlements, whereas the democrats refuse to accept that their postmodernist ethics have diminishing appeal, and aren't even contemplating strategies for suboptimizing as a minority party. The growing divide will have interesting ramifications, including a widening transatlantic identity gulf, but the nation can't harness shifting opportunities until our leaders surmount the confusions of American public culture. A sampling of public commentary substantiates that cognitive dissonance remains the order of the day.[27]

CHAPTER 4: KEY POINTS

1. Public culture is attractive to many people in part because it simplifies otherwise complex matters. It ascribes naïve motivations to others; it provides either/or choices; and it emphasizes relationships as a basic cause of conflict or peace, as if nations were merely families living together in a neighborhood.

2. The public culture is full of extreme exaggeration generated by commentators seeking attention or media companies seeking ratings.

3. Situations and issues are distorted in order to permit them to fit into the lens offered by our public culture.

4. The result of simplification, hype, and distortion is that the public culture prevents people from understanding important matters while causing them to believe that they do understand.

FIVE

Mythomaniacs

The Sources of Our Illusions

Mere facts are worthless except through their interpretation.
Will Durant, **The Life of Greece**, pg. 615

There is never a mere listing of facts, for they are too many and too confusing; they have no meaning without a context. What facts are chosen to be reported, and the interpretation which gives them meaning, are what public culture, the collective public mind decides. When the context is not accurate, as when it's distorted for partisan or commercial aims, then there can be no assurance that people understand what is really happening and that decisions can be made properly in response to events.

Media stories, especially on TV, are often so shallow, so carefully selected, so contrived, so subordinated to a predetermined story line, that they're not news at all, not even infotainment (because there's almost no information in them), but are merely entertainment posing as new reporting. Commentators choose hype instead of balanced reporting because they can't pen compelling headlines when interdependencies create gray zones instead of stark black and whites.

To justify such inferior communications, and to keep people interested, media executives and political activists create myths – stories that are compelling though not true or only partially true. In recent years, our public culture has passed into the hands of people who do this well – who are myth-builders, and many of us, avid consumers of myths in the disguise of information, have become mythomaniacs. What most characterizes the myths of today is that they derive from and embody the wishful thinking in which most of us engage.

THE AMERICAN PUBLIC'S WISHFUL THINKING

Many Americans are optimists about the world, a characteristic often remarked by people from abroad. An expression of our optimism is that we engage in wishful thinking on a grand scale. We see a world in which other people are generally like us, wanting what we want and, if they have freedom and the right laws and the kind of economic system we have, will be our friends, not our adversaries. Some of us believe that all the people of the world are basically like us despite superficial differences of culture, and if given a chance to choose peace will be our friends and allies; others believe that all or most of the nations of the world are converging toward our economic and political system, and that when that occurs, the world will be peaceful at last.

Wishful thinking makes what seems to be a benign assumption: that the people of other nations are like us underneath superficial cultural differences, and if we can only communicate effectively and take their legitimate needs into consideration, there will be peace and harmony in the world.

Today, many Americans presume that the natural laws of economics, politics, and human society necessitate happy endings. Many Americans assume that economies will, if left to their own devices, generate economic growth; that nations prefer peace to war; and that global stability increases with time. These naïve assumptions mischaracterize natural law, which is complex, generates diverse outcomes, and often ends in catastrophe.

Wishful thinking holds that improving living standards is both a good in itself and a contributor to peace. A great illusion is that economic progress is enough in itself – that it can be timely and sufficiently rapid – to make peace in the world. We wish for peace. To support that wish we presume that all the peoples of the world want peace, and all the nations, too. Where aggression exists, it does so primarily because of wrongs, either current or past, that can be righted, or misunderstandings that can be corrected, ending the impulse of anger or despair that generated conflict.

As evidence, wishful thinkers cite what they perceive as the evolution of the world toward peace among all peoples. Here's a statement of that hopeful conviction: "We know from archaeology that the amount of warfare has declined markedly over the course of human history and that peace can prevail under the right circumstances. In spite of the conflict we see around us, we are doing better, and there is less warfare in the world today than there ever has been. Ending it may be a slow process, but we are making headway.... History shows that people with strong animosities stop fighting after adequate resources are established and the benefits of cooperation recognized. . . . Adequate food and opportunity does not instantly translate into peace, but it will, given time."[1] It is in this sort of supposed evidence that the illusion of harmonism finds its roots.

Wishful thinking also results in a convergence view – economic growth along market-oriented principles drives nations in only one direction: toward peace. It holds as well that economic forces are more important than other forces. A report put the matter recently, "Taiwan has invaded Mainland China – with jobs and capital. Politics will adapt to the new reality."[2] This comment is unexceptionable if it means only that where there is a new economic reality, political processes will somehow accommodate to them. But if it has a stronger meaning – that peace will follow trade – then it is patently false. Peace may follow trade, but war may also follow, of which history has given ample evidence.

Because harmonism is an illusion to which liberals are especially inclined, and convergence is an illusion of special attraction to conservatives, we see that wishful thinking is not limited to either side of the political spectrum. Furthermore, and even more unfortunately, wishful thinking causes both left and right in our political spectrum to engage in a particularly virulent form of self-deception.

A Glaring Dishonesty of Wishful Thinking

A glaring dishonesty – a self-deception on an enormous scale – lies at the heart of approaching foreign policy via wishful thinking – a willingness to deny evil, to take monumental hypocrisy (such as the Chinese and Saudi Arabian guarantees of human rights; or the United Nations' acceptance of Colonel Muammar Gaddafi as head of its Human Rights Commission) at face value, to excuse horrors, to blame ourselves and blame the victims in order to exonerate the perpetrators. Accepting these terrible things, in order to preserve a conviction that people are rational and peace-seeking, causes wishers to discount threats that are actually very real. Refusing to acknowledge threats discredits wishers claims to power in America today.

Outlawing war, and other notions that have superficial appeal, are a form of wishful thinking – not because war is inevitable; hopefully it is not. In fa⸱ ꞉eople who accept war in certain situations usually do so not because ·or war or fail to recognize its horrors. But great evils often cannot be ꞏ꞉ without war. In the case of the United States, the Civil War was ꞏ eliminate slavery, and World War II was necessary to eliminate ꞏe people who advocate an end to war thereby signal that they ꞏavery or the genocide practiced by the Nazis? Probably not.

They are simply special pleaders, not willing to acknowledge that there are circumstances in which their proposed cure is worse than the disease.

For those who argue that there never has been a just war, was the war to end slavery in America unjust? Was the war to end the Nazi horror unjust? Even if one can imagine that slavery and Nazism could have been ended without war, does that make the wars to end them unjust, or simply unfortunate?

Wishful thinkers must prove they see the world for what it is – dangerous and treacherous (in which our enemies can hide successfully for years) – and to do so they must repent their first sin, excusing Soviet Communism, and condemn Lenin and Stalin (to recognize the full evil in the world, including the bin Ladens) and must show that they really care about the victims, and don't simply write them off as unfortunate road kill in the race toward a better future. Continued whitewashing of the Soviets disqualifies wishful thinkers on the left for power in today's world.

It has always been a deception: using supposedly idealistic goals to try to justify force and brutality. It could be seen as such by moderate people even in the heart of the great ideological controversies of the twentieth century. Glamorizing the Soviets was a vice of the left, but there is no need to cite conservative to make the point. We can turn instead to John Maynard Keynes – for decades the darling of liberals because of his advocacy of interventionist economic policies – who saw the deception clearly.

Writing in 1926 Keynes said, "We lack more than usual a coherent scheme of progress, a tangible ideal. . . . It is not necessary to debate the subtleties of what justifies a man in promoting his gospel by force; for no one has a gospel" [that is, a compelling explanation of the present and ideal for the future]. Because no one, including the communists, had a real vision, what they claimed was an ideology of progress was concocted to rationalize the use of force. Force was used to gain and hold power, not to promote a vision of a better world.[3] Wishful thinkers rejected Keynes's opinions then, and may do so today, preferring a fantasy that keeps them from seeing the full scope of danger and evil in the world. This isn't a mere ideological fantasy (that is, a fantasy about an ideal – like the conservatives' fantasy about perfect competition), but is a fantasy about history itself and about what the world is. Nor is the fantasy a pardonable exaggeration made for political purposes. There is nothing pardonable about the fantasy because of the great evil it caused us to accept in the world – Communist slave labor camps and mass exterminations of people (in the USSR during Stalin's period and more recently in China during the Cultural Revolution).

But liberals are not alone in such wishful thinking; conservatives defend rightist dictatorships (as some did Hitler's regime and that of Mussolini before World War II). Again, wishful thinking ignores the brutal realities of these regimes.

THE DELUSIONS OF WISHFUL THINKING

Wishful thinking prevents us from perceiving the world as it is. Wishful thinking is expressed by, and can mislead, American politicians, thought leaders and citizens at every level. It is not confined to either end of the political spectrum – liberals do it and so do conservatives, and in surprisingly similar ways. Different ends of the political spectrum take their wishes to opposite conclusions. The liberal argues for a less-well-armed America working closely with other powers; the conservative argues for an American remaking the world in our image.

For example, one of the central themes of the Congressionally mandated report on the failures of intelligence that led up to September 11 is that we weren't ready for September 11 because the intelligence community did not want to see it coming. Over many years, people in the field and analysts in Washington and Langley had seen careers ruined because somebody tried to warn the policy makers that trouble was coming. The policy makers didn't want to hear that sort of thing because they were not prepared to do the unpleasant things that knowledge of the real situation required. The ultimate example was the Clinton White House, where the top people simply refused to even receive information about Osama bin Laden's activities in Sudan. Clinton was hardly unique; the NSC under Bush senior simply refused to believe that Saddam would invade Kuwait, and even ignored seemingly incontrovertible information provided the night of the invasion, when General Brent Scowcroft went home early.[4]

The impact of wishful thinking in our public culture is surprisingly significant.

First, it keeps us from perceiving the world as it really is.

Tolerance, pluralism, and conflict avoidance encourage our political and thought leaders to downplay the deficiencies of our rivals, even though their economic and political systems violate all the axioms of western public culture. This approved contradiction in our beliefs prevented American intelligence agencies from correctly assessing the Soviet Union's performance and potential for years, overestimating its provision of consumer goods, underestimating its military strength, and overestimating its internal political cohesion. Wishful thinking also misled them in dealing with the terrorist threats.

Second, wishing leads to underestimating the risk of conflict. If only there were similarity in government (democracy) and economic structure (capitalist free enterprise), the expectation goes, then there would be geopolitical harmony. But this is also not proven. Because European democracy is pacifist doesn't mean all democracies are similar. In fact, that American democracy today is not pacifist, seems a bitter reproach to the Europeans – something that angers many.

Third, wishing causes us to overreach. For example, in Iraq our highest priority must be that Saddam and his ambitions for weapons of mass destruction and for support of terrorism are gone, and a new Iraqi government doesn't follow him in trying to do those things. Then we've pulled the teeth of the Iraqi demon.

More is not necessary. But more may be desirable. Thus, democracy, capitalism, free markets, liberal attitudes toward women's rights, the love (or the hearts and minds) of the Iraqi people for America – that is, the hopeful agenda – are good things, and we should urge them on the Iraqi people and support them if they seek these things, but all these things are not necessary to our security and if they are rejected by an Iraqi government, we should not press for them.

The danger of wishful thinking is that it causes us to see these good things as required and that in seeking them we overreach ourselves and end up disappointed, disillusioned and perhaps defeated.

Fourth, wishing deflects us from a strong response to threats.

For example, writing in the summer of 2003, Michael Ledeen pointed to two peace initiatives – the Saudi peace plan of 2002 and the roadmap for peace in Palestine in the spring and summer of 2003 – as efforts to stall the American war on terror. Both peace initiatives had been accepted by the Bush Administration and each allowed our enemies in the Mideast and our rivals among the large powers to attempt to frustrate our energetic attacks on terrorism:

Just as the delay after Afghanistan permitted our enemies to organize their political, diplomatic, and terrorist forces against us, so our current defensive stance enables them to intimidate and indoctrinate the Iraqi people, murder our own men and women on the ground, and galvanize the president's critics and opponents, both at home and abroad ... our regional enemies in Iran and Syria had plenty of time to plan their response to our pending occupation of Iraq. As they unhesitatingly and publicly proclaimed to anyone who cared to listen, they organized a terror war against us, accompanied by jihadist propaganda, mass demonstrations, and hostage seizures, just as we experienced in Lebanon in the 1980s. ... The president gave voice to a welcome revolutionary doctrine when he refused to deal with Yasser Arafat: He said that just as only free Middle Eastern countries could be expected to abandon terrorism and join us in fighting it, only a free and democratic Palestinian people could make a durable peace with Israel.[5]

This often perceptive article offers a perfect example of how far hopefulness has penetrated almost all American thinking about combating terrorism in the Middle East. The two peace initiatives Ledeen cites were part of a strategy by our adversaries to delay our response, yet they were accepted by the United States as a result of the notion that the world is made up of wellmeaning people with whom peace can be made by diplomatic initiatives given adequate time and support.

But Ledeen's proposed remedy, to build democracy in the region as a basis for establishing peace, is itself a version of the same fallacy he otherwise condemns. His remedy reflects the conviction that America should try to export democracy (and most likely free enterprise) expecting it to change the complexion of the region. This is as much an illusion as the expectation of many people that dialogue with our adversaries will bring a just peace. Instead, the reality is that our secure defense lies in destroying the leadership of our enemies, then restricting our further involvement to supporting indigenous efforts at democratization and economic reform, but not imposing them.

It's the effort to impose not only regime change, which has been accomplished, but also democracy and free enterprise that have mired us down in a guerilla war in Iraq. Wishing causes us to overreach; it causes us to equivocate; each is disastrous for our security and one or the other is deeply built into the thinking of Americans of both parties. Thus it is very difficult for America to act in ways consistent with our current role in the world – difficult for us to objectively assess the situation and adopt policies that are in our own interest.

POLITICAL PARTISANSHIP

Political parties seek popular support. To gain it, they behave little different than advertisers, seeking to attract an audience, obtain identification with the audience, and then persuade the audience to support them. An effective way of doing this is to associate the party and its candidates with views held by the electorate. The public culture offers those views. For partisan political purposes politicians use and reinforce those views. Partisan politics doesn't create our public culture (the wishful thinking of our electorate is the more basic cause) but it does strongly reinforce our public culture. Thus, political partisanship contributes to the building of the public culture. Without partisanship our public culture would be less significant and different in its context – it might be closer to reality.

For example, President Clinton resonated successfully – but without regard for the truth – with the wishful thinking about a peaceful world which lies at the heart of American popular culture.

"For the first time since the dawn of the nuclear age," Clinton told his audiences, "on this beautiful night, there is not a single nuclear missile pointed at an American child." This was a line in one of President Clinton's stock speeches – a line that always evoked great applause. But it was a lie, as pointed out by the military officer who was at his side carrying the nuclear cipher by which the president could cause the launch of American missiles, should the threat suddenly emerge. Had what the president was saying been true, there would not have been any need for the cipher to be nearby – no need for deterrence. Perhaps Clinton thought his statement was true, because he once lost the cipher completely, so little attention did he pay it.[6] Clinton's misinforming the American people about this danger should remind us that there are two sorts of dishonesty with which a president can deceive the American people – the lie that danger is greater than it actually is, and the lie that danger is not as great as it actually is.

We are indeed somewhat safer now than during the height of the Cold War, because the threat of a large-scale nuclear exchange among the great powers has been reduced. But we are not safer because our enemies have become friends – as our public culture would have it, via the harmonism and convergence illusions – but because our enemies are weaker than they were. The inability of many Americans to accept this – because they hope for a world better than it is – is one of the great limitations in America's ability to defend itself sensibly.

But as utopia – the peaceful world so longed for by our public culture and promised by President Clinton – beckons, up rears the ugly head of national rivalries.

The first presidential debate of 2004 took place strictly within the limitations of the public culture. There was little or no mention of security concerns involving Russia or China, and just a brief mention of in reference to North Korea. Neither candidate discussed where Iraq fits into the overall U.S. world situation, other than Senator John Kerry's assertion that how we've dealt with Iraq has hurt our standing in the world. Instead, the candidates said the following:

Both endorsed preemption.

Both said what they thought what the biggest threat to the US: Kerry said nuclear proliferation, Bush said nuclear weapons in the hands of terrorists.

Each candidate declared that he has a grand vision. For Bush, it is the US championing democracy around the world, especially in the Middle East. For Kerry, it was the US avoiding conflict by acting in concert with other big powers.[7]

The discussion reflected the romanticism about the American position in the world that is embedded in our public culture. Bush stressed romantic crusaderism, championing democracy all over the world, whereas Kerry stressed an equally romantic notion of multilateralism. Neither dared suggest that any other nation, with the possible exception of the North Koreans and the Iranians, were acting in anything but good faith – the type of illusion we have labeled harmonism.

Indeed, by the closing weeks of the 2004 presidential campaign, most of the media was irresponsibly partisan, and everything published had a hidden (or not so hidden) agenda of support of for one candidate or the other. There was little real news – only stories colored to advance a candidate's chances. Nuances of terminology were always partisan. Anything that could be seized and used against a candidate was used, without regard to substantiation; and even, in some instances, in flagrant disregard of a lack of substantiation (e.g., Kerry's charge that Bush had failed in his duty to protect American servicemen when stockpiles of Iraqi high explosives were found to be missing from an Iraqi ammunition dump. It turned out that the munitions had been missing before American troops arrived at the dump in the early weeks of the war).

Presidents sometimes argue for anticipation as a better strategy than reaction or resilience (as did Franklin Roosevelt before World War II), but our nation has historically preferred reaction, despite its enormous cost, because we cannot ever assure ourselves that the danger we anticipated was real since the party out of office cannot resist the temptation to maintain that there was really no danger at all and so no need for action. The twin pillars of today's public culture – harmonism and convergence – reinforce the wishful thought that there is no danger that requires anticipation.

Political partisanship is driving accurate information out of the American system – either because the media are playing the political game themselves and doctoring their reporting to that purpose, or because the intensity of political controversy, involving leaks and demonization of opponents, causes people with information to keep silent. This is rather like how the threat of violence keeps people from informing on criminal activities.

During the antiterrorist campaign, there has been primarily partisan criticism – the content of which is always predictable because it is partisan, and unconvincing because it is predictable.

Our presidents are not fools. They know when they are pandering to the illusions of the public culture; they know that the realities of geopolitics are quite different. They sense the constraints placed on their actions and words by the public culture and reflexively try to loosen them. Their adversaries push in the opposite direction. The resulting tug of war sometimes leads to unpremeditated, gradual, and often unpredictable modifications in public culture.

Alexis de Tocqueville commented that in America some are raised to the common level in human knowledge that drives politics in America and some are lowered to it.[8] We call that common level public culture, and recognize that there is a difference between one who is raised to it versus one who is lowered to it. Those who are raised to the public culture do not fully understand it. They accept it and play by its rules. In contrast, those who lower themselves to it are choosing to play according to the rules of the public culture, though they see other alternative ways of being and thinking outside the public culture construct. Presidents sometimes fall in this category, as do many of their advisors.

There are consequences. As Americans latch on to a sanctioned belief system provided by our public culture they develop an unhealthy fear of honest brokers of information. "One of the worst by-products of our venomously partisan political culture is a growing distrust of anyone who claims to be nonpartisan. Red and blue combatants have systematically attacked the credibility of a wide variety of professionals whose jobs require objectivity: judges, pollsters, economists – and particularly journalists. Many of these same . . . crusaders . . . have simultaneously worked to undermine the very professional standards that all of these occupations have developed . . . to promote neutrality. . . . In the news business, things have gotten so bad that the term 'mainstream media' has actually become an epithet. . . . Problem is, imposing higher standards would drive up the cost of journalism while cutting its dramatic value. . . . The plain truth is that opinionated content . . . is often simpler, snappier, and less expensive to produce than objective content."[9]

THE MEDIA

In general, our media rely on and support the public culture. They draw their interpretation of events from it. Our politicians reference it in order to draw support for their positions. This is often done to the exclusion of truth telling.

Interestingly, the public culture is formed not by the reporting of events as much as by the meaning that an event is given. In this way it is much like the party line of a totalitarian state. We first noticed this surprising similarity several decades ago in the Soviet Union. Our Soviet hosts would listen surreptitiously at night to the English-language radio broadcasts of the Voice of America and the BBC in order to obtain information about developments in the world. (Incidentally, the Russian language broadcasts of the VOA and the BBC were jammed by the Soviets, so that only the intelligentsia who understood English, and were largely Communist Party members, were able to get their news via this illegal but tolerated means.) Then the next morning the intelligentsia would read Pravda – the journal of the Communist Party of the Soviet Union – to find out the meaning given to events by the Party. Often Pravda, printed in Russian and available broadly, didn't report the news, but only the interpretation – relying on its more sophisticated readers to have received news via the English-language broadcasts.

So it was that our Soviet hosts and ourselves, Americans, had the same information as to world events, but gave them dramatically different interpretations.

It is by such a device in America that the public culture persists despite openness about reporting events. That is, a free press is not sufficient to a realistic interpretation of what is happening in the world.

In America events – the "news" – is reported reasonably accurately, often as well as reporters can do it, but then its meaning is often exaggerated or given a twist (when the White House does this, it is called "spin"). The meaning of the event or events is distorted to fit a particular political agenda. In this way, the media and politicians can claim accuracy as to reporting the news, yet be wildly inaccurate as to the significance of the event.

Newspapers direct the meaning of a news story by leaving to editorial directors the headlines on a story. Less commonly do they alter a story itself, and when that happens a reporter often objects that it is a violation of journalistic ethics. TV accomplishes the same objective by what context is given a story in a news broadcast, and by how much of the event is related. It is by such devices that the public culture is manipulated and reinforced continually.

Possibly in America the CIA is best at this game. It documents carefully. It composes a balanced assessment of outside "authoritative" opinion, but then falsifies one or two things. Almost no one catches on, except in extreme situations – as in the case of the weapons of mass destruction not found in Iraq, or in the case of the underestimates in the Cold War of Soviet military capabilities and the overestimates, also in the Cold War, of Soviet economic growth.

JOURNALISTS

News reporters are extremely important in our political life, and they are generally well intentioned in trying to do an honest and professional job. But there are fewer of them; they have less resources with which to work; they are employed for increasingly commercially oriented businesses that try to manipulate their reporting; they are subject to the direction of news directors who have motives that are primarily commercial (including the ratings competitions) rather than professional; and they are subjected to increasingly ham-handed interference in their work by courts – it's no wonder that they are increasingly forced to lean on the public culture for assistance in their work.

Journalists rely on our public culture because it provides a frame for the news and gives it meaning. "In order for an event to reach the public, it must first be viewed by reporters, then related in stories. . . . Journalists help mold public understanding and opinion by deciding what is important and what may be ignored, what is subject to debate and what is beyond question, and what is true and false . . . ," wrote Kathleen Hall Jamieson, Dean of the University of Pennsylvania's Annenberg School of Communication, in a study she coauthored. "The critical variable is usually not the facts themselves but the manner in which they are arranged and interpreted in order to construct narratives. . . . Because the terms we use to describe the world determine the ways we see it, those who control the language control the argument. . . . The language, stories and images . . . become filters through which we make sense of the political world, . . . alter the facts that are deemed important, [and] the ways in which fact is framed and frames come to be assumed . . ."[10]

It is the public culture that provides the framing for most news stories. The facts are framed by the public culture; when they are reported as news stories, the public culture is reinforced; and the frames (that is, the public culture itself) comes to be assumed.

Journalist is a broad term that includes news reporters, and investigative-enterprise reporters, pundits, and analysts. They provide basic information, deciding what is or is not newsworthy. The stories are based on a careful calculation of what fits into the prevailing public culture. ". . . Reporters determine whether a proposal is considered 'reasonable' in public debate in large part by whether it is embraced by elite figures," Jamieson writes.

"Reporters have a bias toward the use of official sources, a bias toward information that can be obtained quickly, a bias toward conflict, a bias toward focusing on discrete events rather than persistent conditions, and a bias toward the simple over the complex . . ."[11]

Much of the public culture has its origins in experts of various sorts who tell us something we want to hear, harmonism or convergence. According to V. O. Key, journalists and the media largely transmit the ideas of others much as a trucking company carries books to a book store. The trucker is not responsible for the books content; nor the media for the ideas it transmits.[12] If this is true, we can dig further into what the experts do and what they read. " . . . If we are interested in the quality of information reaching the public, we must understand how it is manufactured, which is to say, we must understand the politics of expert communities as they relate to the generation and diffusion of knowledge claims, policy recommendations and general frames of reference."[13]

This extensive effort, to understand the politics of expert communities, is beyond the scope of this book, but is admirably addressed in John R. Zaller's, *The Nature and Origins of Mass Opinion.*

The public culture offers reporters an easily accessible frame for individual leaders and confining the leaders within it. In the context of public culture complex national figures become simple. For instance, the media has simplified and distorted the personality of President Bush, so that he is believed by many Americans, especially among the elite, to be a person of limited intelligence. And yet he is one of the two most educated of all our presidents (Andover, Yale, and Harvard, for Bush; Woodrow Wilson had a Ph.D. from John Hopkins), and managed to get himself elected president twice, when the candidates of those who despise his supposed ignorance failed.

The strength of a story frame with journalists is very great – it persists despite evidence to the contrary, or in ambiguous settings. For example, during the 2004 Presidential election Bush's supposed limited intelligence was contrasted unfavorably with the supposedly superior intelligence of the Democratic candidate, John Kerry. When, in the spring of 2005, John Kerry's grades at Yale (which both Kerry and Bush attended as undergraduates) were released to the media, and turned out to be very similar to Bush's, the story could have been that Bush was smarter than had been realized, as smart as Kerry. Instead, the original frame of the story prevailed, and the reports were that Kerry had turned out to be as dumb as Bush.

Furthermore, the public culture seems determined to ignore that Bush has been elected to governorship of Texas, a state in which his credentials of Ivy League education would ordinarily be fatal to a politician. The fact is that he is very smart – smart enough to avoid being labeled an elitist in Texas and smart enough to be twice elected president. But as we point out, he came to the presidency poorly informed about international affairs, as do most American presidents (though not all), and there is much to criticize in his policies. But to do so on the basis of his alleged lack of intelligence is to fall into the simplifying trap of public culture as transmitted to us through the media .

Reporters and political analysts operate in two parallel universes – the public culture and a better informed subculture. Reformers ask that news reporters and pundits aspire to be in the well-informed subculture – fitting "the story to the facts, not the facts to the story."[14]

It would be nice if this were to happen; it is devoutly to be desired. But expecting it to happen is simply more wishful thinking, largely because of the influence of commercial media firms on what the news is.

COMMERCIAL ENTERPRISES

No serious reporter wants to be seen as a propagandist, or a shill. "One of the great attributes of journalists is their almost religious insistence on independence. . . . [But] a major factor determining what media content gets produced is the structure of economic and legal support for the media."[15]

It was in the aftermath of World War II that media businesses began to restrict news operations. William R. Shirer noticed changes at CBS in the early 1950s, especially in connection with the national anticommunist hysteria. Businesses who advertised on CBS news wanted a say in the way the news was presented, and, more significantly, what content was acceptable. "Should a shaving cream company, or any other company that advertises on a network, determine whom the public should hear broadcasting news and comment, and by its selection make certain that the public will hear what the company wishes it to hear – most likely a narrow and conservative view of events? Or does the responsibility belong to the network?"[16] In *The Powers That Be*, David Halberstam reports that Murrow and Fred Friendly, Murrow's producer at "See It Now" on CBS, were limited by certain advertisers in getting the message out quickly on the lies and deceptions of McCarthy in naming communists and other anti-Americans.[17]

Media businesses succeed financially largely as a result of advertising revenue, which is determined by the size of the audiences they attract. In the competition for audience, they hurry stories in order to be first to break them; they simplify content; and they attempt to fit audience predispositions. In all this, they follow most of the time the public culture. Their job is not to educate; nor even to inform their audiences, but to attract audiences with popular programming. If information leads to that result, it may be pursued; if it doesn't, news programming becomes little more than magazine-like features, and newspaper stories become the sensationalism of the tabloids.

The self-interest of the media businesses, therefore, is closely tied to the continuance of public culture, for two reasons:

- Staying within the limits of public culture helps gather an audience, because people are comfortable with the frame of reference; and
- Conforming to the public culture saves the business money because it gives meaning to news reports without the business having to spend money to determine its actual meaning.

Thus, from both the revenue (or audience) side and from the expense side a profit-oriented media business has strong incentives to conform to and reinforce the public culture.

PRESIDENTS AND MEDIA

When President George W. Bush commented that he doesn't read the newspapers, he was condemned for it by some observers. They saw him as ignorant and dumb and evidencing both by ignoring the media. But a more charitable interpretation is that the president receives a lengthy briefing on the international situation each morning, so that he has his information from unusually reliable sources that are quite up -to -date, and what the media provides is so often wrong and dated that it provides not information but disinformation to him. So he ignores it. Also, he has political advisors who read the papers for political spin, so he need not spend his time doing that.

During an earlier but more difficult time in our nation's history President Lincoln walked each day from the White House to the telegraph office in the War Department where he waited by the hour for bulletins from the armies in the field, and looking at newspapers not for information but only to ascertain what the editors were thinking and what the public was being told, no matter how erroneous it was. In capsule, Lincoln read the papers to see what the editors knew; what they invented; and the spin they put on the two. The situation then, 150 years ago, was not much different for the president than now.[18]

The president's access to information and knowledge of events is very different from that of the public. This isn't a great thing for a democracy, but it's what we have. The president, if he wishes to master the illusion fostered by the media, must provide the public with a large and credible body of information. Rarely does an administration do so.

Public culture exerts a very strong influence on American politics. What we call public culture is akin to Stephen Skowronek's concept of a "regime," a particular public philosophy of the role of government at a given time.[19] In fact, Skowronek's regime is a significant part of our concept of the public culture. Skowronek sees presidential success in affiliating and expressing the particular regime of the times. His is a formal expression of the efforts of American presidential candidates (and most of our presidents remain candidates while in office) to follow – not lead – the public by discovering the public culture – convictions, prejudices, and misconceptions included – and identifying closely with them. It reminds one of the old irony: the best way to lead is to find a parade and get in front of it.

Although Skowronek seems to see the changing regimes as benevolent, and so seems to applaud politicians who successfully identify with them and thereby are elected to office, public culture (his "regime") has a darker side. Public culture invites Americans to lose focus; to shift agendas; and in so doing to overreach. It is, fact, a profound flaw in the Western intellect.

Because the public culture is at variance with reality, although it appears to presidents to be a refuge, it is in fact a trap. Its expectations cannot be fulfilled, so that disillusion and disappointment are inevitable for the electorate. When this happens, the protectors of the public culture, including the media, business interests and other politicians will turn on the president, and his popularity will collapse.

Despite the danger, or because they fail to perceive it, American presidents rarely challenge the popular culture no matter what the situation. Thus, President George W. Bush justified intervention in Iraq as necessary to eliminate weapons of mass destruction and to build democracy, being unwilling to discuss the issues of global politics that forced him to act. We will see in later pages that in this he was just like President John Kennedy, President Lyndon Johnson and others.

In searching for a safe political home in the public culture, the Bush Administration brought itself to a substantial overreach. The Administration began the war on terror with a broad, careful, long-term, strategic clarity that was expressed in the National Security Policy Statement of the United States issued in September, 2002. But it saw a short-term political advantage, so it exaggerated the terrorist threat and its own response, won the congressional elections in the fall of 2002, then tripped into the pit of distorted expectations that it had itself dug.

For example, in Iraq we set out to do one thing and ended up doing another. Writing in November, 2003, Zell Miller, a Democratic Senator from Georgia, expressed his support for Republican candidate Bush in the conflict in Iraq. "This is our best chance," said Senator Miller, "to change the course of history in the Middle East."[20] How is the course of history to be changed? The idea is apparently that a democratic, free enterprise Iraq would be built to be a model for the rest of the region; so that Egypt, Saudi Arabia, Syria, and Iran would follow by becoming more democratic and more like us economically. This is a remarkably ambitious agenda!

America started out to deny terrorism shelter in the region and to try to prevent our adversaries from obtaining weapons of mass destruction, and now we're engaged in trying to build a wholly different Middle East.

We overreached because our public culture required that our actions there to be legitimized in moral terms – not only as attacking terrorism, but as trying to build a world of democracy and free enterprise. So partisans on both side of the political aisles sought to twist the agenda into that framework. Yet, it's wishful thinking to believe that we can achieve the goal. After all, we've been preaching democracy since the American Revolution more than two hundred years ago, and its progress in the world is halting and imperfect – driven more by our victory in the three world wars (First, Second, and Cold) than by persuasion, and implemented in much of the world more in pretense than in reality (that is, many of what we today call democracies in the world are not that at all).

The Iraqi situation is a classic and serious example of the application of the public culture to our actions abroad, even when initiated in our defense. Thomas Friedman, classifying himself as a liberal and a leftist, argued for support from the left of President Bush's attempt to build democracy in Iraq in the following terms: ". . . here's why the left needs to get beyond its opposition to the war and start pitching in with its own ideas and moral support to try to make lemons into lemonade in Baghdad. First, even though the Bush team came to this theme late in the day, this war is the most important liberal, revolutionary U.S. democracy-building project since the Marshall Plan. The primary focus of U.S. forces in Iraq today is erecting a decent, legitimate, tolerant, pluralistic representative government from the ground up. I don't know if we can pull this off. We got off to an unnecessarily bad start. But it is one of the noblest things this country has ever attempted abroad and it is a moral and strategic imperative that we give it our best shot."

He then adds a single sentence that sums up the wishful thinking, "Unless we begin the long process of partnering with the Arab world to dig it out of the developmental hole it's in, this angry, frustrated region is going to spew out threats to world peace forever."[21]

Thus, Iraq has become a theater of overreach that threatens to stretch our resources too thin and undercut an effective response to the more significant challenges that are now and will be presented by Russia, China, and nuclear-armed rogue states. We got to this situation via the temptations of public culture. It is the combination of wishful thinking about cause and effect with the desire for a moral imperative to justify actions taken originally in self-defense that characterize the American public culture approach to defense issues today and tempts our president to commit us to extreme goals.

Yet Americans are outgrowing some of the extreme elements in our public culture. We are increasingly aware that it is all right to pursue national security without trying simultaneously to attain other major goals promoted by our public culture; and we are accepting that self-defense is itself a moral imperative. This is a crucial part of the new maturity of the American people, but is not enough appreciated by our political leaders.

CHAPTER 5: KEY POINTS

1. The wishful thinking of the American public projects good motives onto people who lack them, until events prove different. Often that is very late to begin to defend ourselves.
2. Wishful thinking is reinforced by elements of the media and our political activists who invent information or who place on events interpretations which mask their reality. We call these people mythomaniacs because they are addicted to fables for the purpose of personal advantage, commercial or political.
3. The desire for peace is not an element of myth in the public culture alone. Most of us hope for peace. Our criticism of public culture is because we fear it threatens peace with its illusions.
4. Americans need to look at U.S. politics with the harsh objectivity of American moderates – who view with concern extremist tendencies in both our major parties, and yet know they must choose between them at election time.

5. American presidents must deal with the public culture as a key element of the context in which they lead the nation. They must avoid being deceived by it (accepting it as true), and they must fashion explanations of their actions with it constantly in mind. There is a temptation to fashion explanations that are consistent with public culture, even though the explanations are false.

PART THREE

AMERICAN PUBLIC CULTURE
AND OURSELVES

Champions of Freedom or Imperialists

How We're Perceived

Americans see big differences among ourselves; some of us are conservatives, some liberals; some are Republicans, some Democrats. Some are moderates, a few are radicals (of either the left or the right). Looked at from abroad, except among a few people who make it their business to be very familiar with our politics, these distinctions are very hard to perceive. Americans seem a lot alike. There seems little difference among the political parties, and less among the candidates they offer for president. Many, perhaps most, Europeans, for example, were stunned during the 2004 presidential campaign debates when both candidates (Kerry and Bush) endorsed military preemption against threats from abroad. What stand out to others are the things we have in common; and the most evident of these is our public culture – its optimism and its illusions.

HOW WE AND OTHERS SEE US

A most important element of our public culture is our view of ourselves. It's shaped by the same forces (wishful thinking, partisan politics, and media commercialism) as are other elements of our public culture, and it is reflected in misapprehensions and misinformation as well. Our politicians and our media tell us what we want to hear about ourselves. But our self-image is more complex and self-contradictory than other parts of our public culture. This is most easily seen when we contrast our self-image with the perception of America abroad.

Americans are perceived increasingly badly abroad. The reality is complex, because America is still seen as a beacon of liberty and well-being in the world, but American activities abroad are less and less admired. Our own view of ourselves is much more favorable, but has a major contradictory element of self-criticism.

The American self-image is so confused today (part self-worship, part European-style self-hatred) that we need reassurance about our role in the world. So we turn to the positive side of our self-image for rationalizations of our actions abroad that are consistent with our public culture. Because we think ourselves true democrats, we find it easy to rationalize interventions abroad as in pursuit of democracy, rather than objectively as an attempt to defend ourselves aggressively and protect our interests abroad.

We are now told as if it were a profound truth by many Europeans that the American President is hated all over the world, and it is not good for the United States – so we must do something to change our image, and they, of course, have suggestions as how best to accomplish that by accommodating ourselves to their positions. "Yes," we might reply, "but how did this terrible reputation come about?" Bush is in fact their victim, the victim of the corruption of the European leadership by Saddam Hussein via the United Nations Oil for Peace program; and the victim of demonization (extended to our entire country) by the President of France and the Chancellor of Germany in pursuit of their attempt to extend and unite Europe.

Having blackened Bush's name (and that of America), the same Europeans now want to turn the situation to their further advantage by treating it as a fact of life independent of their doing. This is how politics are played in democracies, and how democratic leaders play politics in the international arena.

PRESIDENT BUSH'S IMAGE OF AMERICANS VERSUS THE VIEW FROM ABROAD

We have a place, all of us, in a long story – a story we continue, but whose end we will not see. It is the story of a new world that became a friend and liberator of the old, a story of a slaveholding society that became a servant of freedom, the story of a power that went into the world to protect but not possess, to defend but not to conquer. It is the American story. . . . We are not this story's author, but another who fills time and eternity with his purpose. Yet his purpose is achieved in our duty, and our duty is fulfilled in service to one another. . . . This work continues . . . George W. Bush, First Inaugural Address, January 20, 2001

In the president's eyes, we Americans are participants in a plan the Almighty has for bringing freedom to humanity all over the globe. The president and many other Americans see ourselves this way, while much of the rest of the world sees us differently.

For example, America's traditional culture and much of its domestic politics have a bias toward Puritanism. Our popular culture, in dramatic contrast, has a bias toward commercialism, licentiousness, and exalting violence – no longer excepting sports[1] and art.[2] In consequence, many – some polls say most – Americans think of themselves as religious and ethical, while much of the outside world sees us as amoral and corrupt.

Second, American politics is ordinarily obsessed with domestic issues and ignores foreign policy. Yet increasingly we police the world and are now engaged in at two major military operations that go beyond peace-keeping (Iraq and Afghanistan). So Americans see ourselves as normally detached from matters abroad while the outside world sees us as interventionist.

Third, we Americans see ourselves as champions of a free market economy, but we have lots of regulations and subsidies and protections for particular industries. So we see ourselves as free marketers and others see us protectionists.

How can we reconcile these divergent views? We can't. We have both elements in our character and in our behavior. Our politics is full of arguments over which course to take in every specific situation.

Just like President Bush, most Americans think well of our country and its motives. But many people abroad and some at home have a far more negative view of us. We are viewed not as liberators, but as seeking to control other nations for our own ends, that is, as imperialists; not as bringers of freedom, but as threats to world peace; not as agents of God's truth, but as hypocrites who clothe our real interests in moralisms.

Favorable views of the United States have declined in nearly every country since the invasion of Iraq.[3] Probably the negative opinions that most sting Americans, and that make us wonder if we really are off the track, are those of Western Europeans, to whom we are most closely related by history. But we must remember that Western Europeans are a people consumed by self-dislike. There are numerous examples of this, but a recent one involves the award of the Nobel Prize for Literature in 2003 to a white South African novelist. In its announcement of the award the Royal Swedish Academy of Sciences praised in particular the laureate's "ruthless criticism of the cruel rationalism and cosmetic morality of Western civilization."[4] It is striking that the intellectual leadership of a country that is a member of Western civilization thinks so little of its own civilization. The Swedes do not seem to be unusual in Europe in this regard. It is not surprising, in light of this, that Europeans find Americans, most of whom still believe in the value of Western civilization, fit targets for criticism and contempt.

"States on the European continent regard the English-speaking peoples as 'masters in the art of concealing their selfish national interests in the guise of the general good,' wrote an historian, adding that 'this kind of hypocrisy is a special and characteristic peculiarity of the Anglo-Saxon mind.'"[5]

Is there merit in this view?

WHAT POLLS SAY

Public opinion polling has come to play a very important role in American politics. It is now moving onto the international stage, and will begin to shape our international relations and our view of ourselves. The Pew Foundation, for example, conducted what is probably the largest effort ever to measure public opinion internationally, involving questions asked of some thirty-eight thousand people.

In some ways, enhanced international polling is very good; but it also offers a profound danger. It is good because we will better understand how we are perceived abroad; the danger is that we might shape our policies to affect world public opinion of ourselves, rather than to determine and pursue those policies that are consistent with what is best as we see it.

We must remember that there are serious limitations to polls. First, there is the question as to whether or not the samples (that is the people questioned) are representative of the whole populations of the countries polled. Second, there is the question whether or not in dictatorships, where the media is tightly censored, there is in fact any independent public opinion, or whether poll results are not simply reflecting what the populace has been told by government. Third, poll results reflect the questions asked, and many pollsters design questions with biases. Because in much of the world reliable samples are hard to obtain, public opinion is highly shaped by government propaganda, and questions reflect biases, polls of foreign opinion are subject to considerably greater unreliability than are domestic polls. The Pew polls, for example, are subject to criticism on each of the three grounds given above.

Given their limitations, it's significant that in the polls as America has become increasingly assertive internationally, negative views held abroad of America are increasing. Polls show that many people believe the main reason America went to war in Iraq was to get control of Iraqi oil. And frighteningly, actual majorities in some countries have supported suicide bombings.[6]

"'The war has widened the rift between Americans and Western Europeans, further inflamed the Muslim world, softened support for the war on terrorism, and significantly weakened global public support for the pillars of the post–World War II era – the U.N. and the North Atlantic alliance,' said Andrew Kohut, the Pew center's director .

Here is what is perhaps a moderate view of Americans, a view that is somewhere in between that of President Bush and that of those who despise us abroad. It's a candid account of her perceptions of America by a young woman whose antecedents are in India, is now a Canadian citizen, played in the world's professional tennis tour, and graduated from Harvard College.

"Before I went to the United States for college, I was part of a Canadian society that saw America as a land of more opportunity with fewer constraints on the individual. In America, success is celebrated not discouraged; competition is promoted not hidden; the winner takes all; hard work is rewarded. But in Canada, Americans were seen as generally more ignorant than Canadians. Canadians recounted with pride how Americans would stow a Canadian flag on their nap sacks when backpacking around Europe because Canadians were liked better than Americans abroad. America was seen as a fast-paced consumer-society that didn't care about quality of life or the welfare of its people as much as in Canada.

"In America at first sight it's dazzling to have everything and anything at your disposal. America is, without a doubt, the biggest and best play ground for any young dreamer.

"Perhaps America has been more like Clark Kent all these years and has now been given the opportunity to make a quick telephone booth change to reveal the red cape, stripes, and stars that were always proudly worn underneath, always knowing it was a Superhero, but now events are calling it forth.

"America has become so competent and capable internally that it seems to exist somewhat apart from the rest of the world. In the world, America's like a new kid on the block who never quite fit in with the others who've been around for a while, and decided to become his own best friend. And by the new kid focusing on his own self-sufficiency, there developed a capability that has everyone else in awe."

What are Americans: agents of God's plan for humanity (as President Bush would have us) or violent grasping hypocrites (as many see us abroad)? Or are we simply an independent, vigorous people who care little for each other, as a more moderate but nonetheless critical view has it? The answer is that we are each of the above, but in an orderly way of which a person can make sense.

At the core of the American self-image from the very beginning has been the notion that America is a model for mankind, a place in which humanity could start over, leaving behind the inequities of the old world and building a better new world. Thus it was that the first settlers of New England, the first large-scale migration to what is now the United States, spoke – in an image borrowed from the Bible – of their colony as a city on a hill, built to enlighten mankind. Americans strive at times to live up to this high conception of us and our nation.

But we often fall short, and have from the beginning. Religion and the role of Americans as God's agents is a key element of the character of our nation, but from the beginning there has been also a strong commercial motive and other motives less than admirable. And these cross-currents of the American character continue today.

There is much falling away of America from its highest ideals, and much self-doubts. The highest conception of America's role in the world was that of the Puritans who settled New England, but they too had their limitations. What most Americans know today of the Puritan settlement is limited to the Salem witch trials and to a misconception of them so that the term Puritan today connotes superstitious brutality and hypocritical and sterile moralism. Thus, many Americans are uncomfortable with their heritage as moral leaders for the world – conflicted about the core of our character.

Self-government is a commitment also at the core of our national character. But self-government has always been an imperfect process, full in our country, as in most, with imperfections. Our legislatures and our electorate are very susceptible to enthusiasms, fears, and wild changes of mood. In consequence, we often stray a long way from our better motivations. We often fail to live up to our pretensions .

THE COMPLEX CHARACTER OF AMERICA

It was Winston Churchill, an Englishman half American (on his mother's side) and who knew America well, both from personal visits and as an ally in two world wars, who best caught both strains of the American character, and thereby made sense of the paradox that we are: "You can always trust the United States to do the right thing," Churchill once observed, adding, "after it has exhausted every other possibility."

In this single statement Churchill identified both the utopian and moralistic element of America – "you can always trust the United States to do the right thing . . ." – and the self-aggrandizing, confused and often incompetent means by which we often go about it – "after it has exhausted every other possibility." Also implicit in Churchill's observation is the patience and great resources of America, we have time and strength to do things wrong again and again and yet find the right course and prevail in the end. Churchill captured America as it has always been and remains today – pointing toward the right and lurching from one side to the other as we try to get there.

Following Churchill's line of thought we should ask now, and the question may well serve as a key theme for this book, "We Americans have emerged at this moment as a leading nation in the world, how close are we to finding the right thing to do, and what other things are we trying now in mistaken efforts?"

Thus, the key question isn't one on which the media seems to focus – how does the world regard us – but instead is how well will we play our role – how quickly will we find the right thing to do, and how effectively do it?

A reason why so many people in the world view Americans as hypocrites is that we often recognize only the side of our personality that searches for the right thing to do, and we ignore the side of our personality that is selfish, grasping and often misguided. For example, one of our best sociologists describes Americans this way:

"Americans are utopian moralists who press hard to institutional-ize virtue, to destroy evil people, and eliminate wicked institutions and practices."[7] He has spelled out in modern language the better side of our character, and has implied, by spelling out nothing else, that there is only this side. Americans, he seems to be saying, have no dark side. But this is nonsense. Denying the dark side of our collective personality reflects, in psychoanalytic terms, the need for superego rules to guide what is for us risky emotional choice making.

As this dichotomy in our character plays out in international relations, our people think of our nation as having altruistic motives while our political leaders and diplomats act in a much more self-serving manner. As one commentator says, "Our people think of our nation one way, and our policy makers act another."[8]

Unfortunately, when there is this sort of ambivalence in the national consciousness, there is always the danger that coherence will be lost. Today there is confusion at the top level – with the rapidity and omnipresence of modern communications, it's become difficult to keep the two attitudes apart, their inconsistency becomes blatant, and our politicians get caught in confusion of rhetoric and conviction as they try to cover over their apparent, even obvious, hypocrisy.

SELF-DECEPTIVE DUPLICITY

Americans are not alone in self-delusion that suggests hypocrisy. In the immediate aftermath of the September 2001, attacks, the United States declared our commitment to defending ourselves with all instruments at our disposal including multinational cooperation, but reserving the right to do more if "friends" didn't want to share the effort and risk. At that time, every major power made statements of public support. But in the months that followed, support slipped dramatically until, when America addressed the issue of Iraq, most of it slipped away entirely. Why did this happen?

At the root of the situation was that the United States had been attacked and was a target, and the other major powers were not, at least not in the way and from the same antagonists. America had been attacked, and expected to be attacked again – Europe had not and did not; nor, in the same way did Russia and China. In the immediate aftermath of the September 11 attacks surprise, horror, and sympathy evoked support for America; but as time wore on, national interests reasserted themselves. Other countries were not targets, and so took a different view of what needed to be done than did America. Even where there was a possible identity of danger – where America's enemies might strike others as well – it was easy for other countries to let America carry the load of response. Other countries had their own national interests, and so began to object to American policies that interfered.

Probably China had the least direct potential involvement in American action in Iraq, and so seemed to appreciate America's new realism about the world, though the Western media, ever uncertain how to deal with a fact that seemed inconsistent with a dominant story line, reported the opposite – giving publicity to pro-forma Chinese denunciations of U.S. policy while ignoring Chinese efforts to see that a war did in fact occur.

The Russians focused quickly on what most concerned them – the Bush Doctrine's assertion of a right to preemptive self-defense – exactly what America was pursuing in Iraq. The declaration by the United States, of the right to conduct preventive strikes as an intrinsic extension of the right of a nation to self-defense, has been repeatedly criticized in the Russian press. Yet, here are two quotations: "If anyone tries to use weapons commensurate with weapons of mass destruction against our country, we will respond with measures adequate to the threat. In all locations where the terrorists, or organizers of the crime, or their ideological or financial sponsors are. I underline, no matter where they are." And, "In such cases, and I officially confirm this, we will strike. This includes preventive strikes."

"Who are these hawks," asks a Russian commentator, "preaching a concept of preventive strikes violating the sacred principle of national state sovereignty? Donald Rumsfeld, Paul Wolfowitz, Dick Cheney, Condoleezza Rice?" No, not at all, he observes. The first quote comes from President Vladimir Putin's speech on October 28, 2002. The second is a statement by Defense Minister Sergei Ivanov, made even earlier, on September 22, 2002. "Vladimir Putin's declaration was an official order by the Supreme Commander-in-Chief to the appropriate government agencies to develop a new Russian military doctrine that would include the concept of preventive strikes in response to threats against which the traditional deterrence concept proved ineffective."[9]

Some of the sharpest turns in public opinion took place in Western Europe, where, for example, more than 60 percent of the French and the Germans held a favorable view of the United States before the Iraqi War. After a difficult dispute over whether the United Nations should authorize the Iraq War, follow-up polls showed that positive views of the United States had dwindled to 45 percent in Germany, 43 percent in France, and even 38 percent in Spain, where the government supported the war.

ACCUSATIONS OF IMPERIALISM

Some foreign observers now insist that the United States has actually sought its preeminence in the world – that we are closet imperialists – a nation that is imperialist while denying it. To a large degree, this argument would seem to be based on two sorts of spurious logic. The first is that whatever has occurred must have been intended, or it wouldn't have happened – specifically that the United States is now a superpower with reach across the globe, and must have intended to be so or it couldn't have happened. The error in the logic is of course that there are unintended consequences often, even for nations, and that the United States has in fact gotten where it is without ever intending to be so, a topic to which we return in a different context in the next chapter. The second error of logic is to label the United States' current position in the world as imperialism, when it is in fact something quite different. We'll return to that error later in this chapter.

Imperialism is applied to America because it is a pejorative term, implying some type of unwarranted domination. But ordinarily, our country doesn't' seek dominion. It seeks security through superiority, and through a strategy appropriate for our time. That is not imperialism.

We can become imperialist – seizing the territory of other nations and directly administering it. We can probably get away with this, but it's not something Americans are likely to want to do, despite being charged by some commentators – adversaries and friends alike – with intending to build an empire. But empire building is not our way. Speaking of the positions of the British and French in the peace conferences at the end of World War I, George C. Marshall, then General Pershing's chief aide (Pershing was commanding general of American forces in Europe), said, "We had no thought of colonies; they thought of little else."[10] America doesn't think of colonies any more today than then, and thankfully, neither today do the British or the French.

This is another reason why speaking of "imperialism" today is misleading. Imperialism meant colonies, and today colonies are passé.

There's more to the argument that the United States is imperialist than spurious logic and a desire to do harm; there's also historical evidence offered, especially from the nineteenth century. The new argument points first to the thrust of the United States across the North American continent and calls this imperialism, but the contest America fought with Spain, Mexico, France, and Britain for the north American continent was less an imperial projection of power abroad, than the efforts of a nation to protect and expand its own borders. Expansionist these efforts were; imperialist, not at all.

The new argument points second to America's miserable, limited, half-hearted effort at the end of the nineteenth century to join the European powers in obtaining foreign colonies – an effort that netted for the United States the Philippine Islands, Guam, and Puerto Rico, and no more, whereas otherwise the United States left to the European powers their colonies in Africa and Asia (although we surely could have wrested important colonial properties from several European powers, for we had the strength to do so), and we were satisfied to protect the Americas from European colonization rather than attempt colonizing Latin America ourselves. If this is a record of colonialism and imperialism, as some are now loudly arguing, it is certainly one of the most ineffective records in history and is by far the greatest failure of all when the colonies we actually obtained are compared with the resources potentially available to obtain them. On such a measure, which is the correct one for labeling America either imperial or not, Portugal and Belgium and Italy far outdo the United States, to say nothing of Britain, France, and Germany.

There's further apparent support for the notion of an imperial United States since our leaders have toyed with the idea throughout our history. For example, John Adams, our second president, predicted that the thirteen United States would one day "form the greatest empire in the world."[11] Our context, finding ourselves in a world of imperial powers – in John Adams's early nineteenth century, for example, including not just the European imperial powers but also China – dictated that America would continually ask itself whether or not it should copy them and seek an imperial destiny. But America never acted for more than brief and largely insignificant periods as if it wanted to become an imperial power. Yet the continuing background of discussion about imperialism in our country causes considerable confusion for us today, because as we take an ever more prominent role on the world stage both supporters and detractors label our engagement imperial, while it surely is not, and not intended to be.

Yet neither the existence of logical errors nor the nonexistence of persuasive historical evidence prevents a plethora of loose commentary today insisting that America is imperialist.

"It is already a cliché among historians," insists Richard Rorty, "that the United States emerged from the cold war an empire rather than a republic."[12] A cliché' it may be, but erroneous nonetheless.

Here is a sample of other recent statements that America is imperialist:

- "We pursue global hegemony with single-minded purpose . . . an expression of the United States unadmitted imperial primacy."[13]
- " . . . the unprecedented stature that the United States had acquired at the end of the Cold War as an empire without rival."[14]
- "America today is Rome, committed irreversibly to the maintenance and, where feasible, the expansion of an empire."
- "The question . . . is not whether the United States has become an imperial power . . . [but] what sort of empire . . . ?"[15]
- "We look like an empire to others, even if not to us."[16] Purdy appears to believe that if this is so, and the perception cannot be altered whatever the reality, then we might as well accept the perception as its own form of reality and act as if we are an empire; as we can't avoid the expectation that we will do so and its consequences.
- The American imperial system "has wrecked our society – $ 5 trillion of debt, no proper public education, no health care – and has done the rest of the world incomparable harm."[17]
- America is "trapped within the structures of an empire of its own making . . ."[18]
- "Since the end of the Cold War the United States has in fact adhered to a well-defined grand strategy . . . to preserve . . . and expand an American imperium. Central to this strategy is a commitment to global openness – removing barrier that inhibit the movement of goods, capital, ideals and people. Its ultimate objective is the creation of an open and integrated international order based on the principles of democratic capitalism, with the United States as the ultimate guarantor of order and enforcer of norms . . . a precondition for American prosperity. . . . From the perspective of its architects, this 'strategy of openness' is benign in its intent and enlightened in its impact."[19] "Those policies reflect a single-minded determination to extend and perpetuate American political, economic and cultural hegemony – usually referred to as 'leadership' – on a global scale."[20]
- America is "an empire . . . that dare not speak its name. It is an empire in denial. . . . Americans have taken our old role [that of the British Empire]

without yet facing the fact that an empire comes with it."[21] Yet the author of this statement recognizes that the United States is in fact not an empire, or at least not a traditional empire: "There clearly is a difference between influencing a nominally sovereign state, whether through economic pressure or cultural penetration, and actually ruling a colony. . . . [America's] weapons have a longer range [than those of the British Empire] but not its writ."[22]

Does it matter if we're an empire or not? Or is the controversy simply one of labels?

It matters, because many conclude that as we're an empire and imperialism is a bad thing, it follows that terrorist attacks, including those of September 11, 2001, are somewhat justifiable as provoked responses to American imperialism.[23]

It is not helpful to think of America as an empire; it simply causes us to confuse the present with the past. Yet there is a danger that America will be pulled in the direction of empire. It isn't that we're seeking colonies, but we are tempted by a role that has us seize other countries and then try to help them by implanting democracy and free markets. It isn't imperialism of the old style – captive markets and ethnic prejudice – but it's a lot like imperialism in that it involves direct control of foreign lands. As in Afghanistan and Iraq, the role of free markets and democracy in our public culture, and the appeal of political leaders to public culture in order to gain support for their policies, is pulling us into a quasi – imperialist role.

America's great purpose, given eloquence by many of our presidents, is labeled by international bureaucrats the "Washington Consensus."

It's supposedly a recipe for economic growth. Developed nations with democratic governments are expected to flourish via increasing the scope of free markets: less developed nations with authoritarian governments and restricted economies are expected to prosper via both democracy and free markets.

The key elements of the Consensus are:

- Fiscal and Monetary Rigor
- Appropriate exchange rate (not an overvalued currency)
- Broad based tax regime with moderate rates
- Effective property rights
- Open product and labor markets

But there is an undercurrent of criticism of the Washington Consensus that it isn't a healthy prescription for economic growth in less developed countries.

Further, the criticism goes, the Washington Consensus is culturally specific, and is inappropriate for countries like Russia that endorse the rhetoric and distort the substance. The prescriptions of the Washington Consensus work for America today, the criticism concludes, in America's current setting, but it didn't work for America a century and a half ago when America was an emerging economy, and it won't work for other nations today.

Instead, the argument is, the Washington Consensus isn't about growth but about penetration. When the IMF insists for its financial assistance that a country open its markets, it means only that U.S. firms are likely to take over its banks and big companies and some of the political power in the country that go with them.

If this is true, then America risks a great deal if it presses too hard for the application of the prescriptions of the Washington Consensus abroad. To do so by overturning the governments of other countries (including Iraq and Afghanistan) and then imposing the Washington Consensus, however much we believe and assert that our interest is the welfare of the populations involved, skirts too close to imperialism. We should promote the Washington Consensus so long as we believe it to be useful abroad, but never impose it by force or control of foreign nations. On this separation of end and means lies the difference between successful engagement of America in the world and a form of overreach that could be disastrous for us.

AMERICA'S CHANGED MESSAGE

There has been a change in America's position in the world, and it is natural that people here and abroad should be trying to understand its implications. America's role in the world today is about supremacy, not parity with other nations – not the balance sought in the Cold War. We did not seek this change directly; we sought a peaceful end to the Cold War, but the end came in an unusual way, the collapse of the Soviet Union – a rot from inside that brought down the only other superpower and left us alone with the responsibility of a single dominant power. Our position could be turned into an empire in which we directly control and administer other nations; it most likely will not because we don't want that result. It could be turned into hegemony in which by a preponderance of military power we dictate the policies of other nations; it most likely will not because we don't want that either. Discussing these alternatives is useful, because it helps make clear actual choice and our commitment to it. But insisting that the United States is already an empire, or is bent on hegemony, is not helpful because it is a falsehood and because it confuses the discussion and diverts it into non-productive controversies. Furthermore, trumpeting that the United States has imperial ambitions threatens to send the wrong message to our potential rivals abroad, and therefore increases the risk of conflict in the world.

As an influential historian wrote before World War II, "America is not to be Rome or Britain. It is to be America."[24] That is, America is defining its own reality, not reflecting some "ism" of a past age and different nations.

CHAPTER 6: KEY POINTS

1. According to President George W. Bush, America is the friend and liberator of the rest of the world – a model for emulation.
2. We are not always viewed in so favorable a light abroad. Instead, we are seen as overbearing, militaristic, moralistic, and hypocritical.
3. An increasing body of opinion both in America and outside insists that America is now imperialist. This is not correct.
4. The task for us is to defend ourselves without tripping into imperialist designs; to support democracy and free enterprise abroad, where others want them, but without trying to impose them on others.

SEVEN

We're Different Now

A friend of ours boarded a plane recently in a European city to fly home to New York. The seat beside her was empty. Not long after takeoff she fell asleep, after all other passengers in the row of seats in front of her and in back were already asleep.

Suddenly she was awakened in the middle of the night; flight attendants were putting into the seat next to our friend a woman concealed from head to foot in a chadrah. To our friend's astonishment, the woman was stretched out in the chair, which had been reclined as far as it would go, and the flight attendants were giving her oxygen. Standing behind the woman and gripping her hand was a man dressed in the full regalia of an Afghan – a turban, flowing robes, a wide belt, baggy pants, and wearing a long black beard.

"My God," thought our friend, "that man's the perfect image of a terrorist."

She reached over and grabbed the sleeve of a flight attendant. "Who's that?" she asked, whispering.

"The woman is traveling in back with a group of children" the attendant whispered back, "and she fell ill."

"Who's that with her?"

"That's her son."

Our friend looked closely at the man. Then she studied the woman lying beside her. "They're each about thirty years old," she told herself. "So the man isn't her son at all, but someone else." Fear gripped her – maybe the plane was going to be hijacked!

Suddenly, the door into the flight compartment opened, and the pilot walked out. He came over to the seat in which the woman was stretched out, apparently to check on the situation. To our friend's horror, the pilot left the door to the cockpit wide open.

Our friend gestured vigorously to a flight attendant to close the door.

The attendant ignored her. Our friend slid back in her seat and hoped for the best.

And fortunately, nothing more happened. The attendants provided oxygen to the woman, and the man stood beside her for hours. The pilot went back to the flight compartment, and hours later the plane landed uneventfully.

This is how Americans now travel abroad – alert, suspicious, and fearful. But there's much more than simple insecurity. There's

- a loss of innocence, and;
- a new maturity.

Americans are different than we used to be – we're less secure and increasingly assertive; but the world is much the same as it has always been – dangerous, self-seeking, and hypocritical. The result is a change in our public culture, one in which there is less wishful thinking and the illusions which result from it are somewhat weakened. Another consequence is a different type of engagement of Americans with the world – one that changes the lives of us all, and very much alters the politics of America.

GOING WHERE WE DIDN'T SEEK TO GO

How America became the world's sole superpower and its policeman while having set out to do exactly the opposite, is one of the great ironies of history and would seem to preclude any judgment of American foreign policy over most of the twentieth century as any other than a complete and total failure. That is, we ended up where we didn't want to go. Because we got there in a glorious fashion, winning war after war, it's hard to believe it was all unintended, but it was. Other countries have engaged in conflict for preeminence in the rest of the world, into which we've been drawn. Our country was never prepared for any major war we entered (the Revolution, the Civil War, World War I or II), and that's the most convincing evidence for our lack of design.

Having spent two centuries trying to avoid engagement with the geopolitics of the world, America is now twisting on its heels, making a 180-degree turn in our intentions, abandoning isolationism and instead accepting our engagement with the world and to try to make sense of it. This is the great story of how America is changing. For many of us the shift is made reluctantly, and solely because 9/11 demonstrated so conclusively that we were both a target and vulnerable, and therefore that we had to be more aggressively engaged abroad with our enemies, lest the conflict be fought out on our own streets and in our own backyards. Similarly, the Japanese attack on Pearl Harbor rendered isolation immediately obsolete. So in 1941 the United States abandoned trying to hide from the world (isolationism) and sixty years later the United States abandoned passivity in its global engagement.

It's been said that the British acquired their empire in a fit of absent-mindedness (meaning that the Crown was otherwise occupied and British financial adventurers, seeking gain, conquered lands that became the empire); America has no empire, but it has an imperial-like dominance in much of the world today which it has acquired, not by intent, and not, like Britain in a fit of absent-mindedness, but instead while trying to achieve exactly the opposite – to avoid foreign entanglements.

In the aftermath of the World Trade Center attacks, it seems that Americans may be coming to a more favorable opinion of their nation's involvements abroad – accepting them as a positive necessity, rather than stumbling into them while seeking to avoid them, as has been our practice in the past.

HOW WE AMERICANS HAVE CHANGED

On and after 9/11 America played the role of victim. This is a familiar role to Europeans, and one to which they give much support. American assumption of the victim's role was therefore welcomed and encouraged there. We were in fact victims, but whether or not our leaders should have encouraged us in the role is questionable, and a matter to which we shall return later. Suffice it to say here that Americans today in their private lives frequently tell their family members and friends not to play the role of victims, even in the context of loss, because it is unattractive and usually unavailing, but instead to recognize a degree of their own blame in what happened, and to move on with confidence from the loss. Probably this would have been a good approach for the nation as a whole immediately after 9/11.

But during the subsequent invasions of Afghanistan and Iraq, America transformed overnight from victim to conqueror, and this much of the world did not like. Further, our role as Americans was suddenly to support our military. This was a big shock to many liberals, but most accepted it gracefully.

Events are creating a new national character – one forged in terrorist attack and preemptive war – both of which are new to our nation. This is the most important result of September 11 and of the recent war in Iraq, and the changes in ourselves presage major changes in our future and that of the rest of the world.

Polls show that the trust of the American people in the military is rising strongly and to high levels. "A poll by the Harvard Institute of Politics, based on interviews with 1,200 college undergraduates . . . [taken in April, 2003], found that 75 percent said they trusted the military 'to do the right thing' either 'all of the time' or 'most of the time . . . ' In contrast, in 1975, 20 percent of people ages 18 to 29 said they had a great deal of confidence in those who ran the military, a Harris Poll found."[1]

The growth of confidence in the military is occurring at the same time as a loss of respect for other major institutions of our society. "From 1975 to 2002, the percentage of Americans who expressed a 'great deal' or 'quite a lot' of confidence in the people who ran organized religion fell, to 45 percent from 68. Those expressing a great deal or a lot of confidence in Congress declined, to 29 percent from 40, according to a Gallup Poll. But also in 2002, Americans who expressed a great deal or a lot of confidence in the military rose, to 79 percent from 58 in 1975."[2]

What is our new character? Why do Americans seem to be traveling such a different emotional and political path than the citizens of other wealthy countries?

It appears that the American character has suddenly matured – matured out of the pain of September 11 and matured out of the responsibility for the second Iraqi war and other conflicts abroad. This is the end result of a process that began with the disillusionment caused by the Vietnam War and the decades of confusion that followed, and that has now culminated in a new perception of us and our role in the world.

In the past we've seemed to people abroad to be immature as a people, and some of the immaturity persists – including our tendency to crusading, a certain moral arrogance, our focus on our own concerns to the exclusion of the problems of others – but each of these characteristics are now significantly modified. In place of crusading is a new realism about the world; in place of moral arrogance is a new pragmatism (we do what we have to do). To some observers these things constitute a loss of innocence, but such a coming of age is something that must happen to the people of every nation, as to every individual, at some point, and so is not to be regretted, but to be accepted and understood.

Unfortunately, it is not fully understood – certainly not by the media, and not yet by most American politicians. Before the second Iraqi war many news anchors continually asked why so many people in the Mideast don't love us? But most Americans no longer seek or expect love abroad. We've outgrown that adolescent concern. Instead a new maturity forgoes affection for respect; and asks of allies not love but friendship and support. We accept a new stridency of criticism, when convinced we are right – right as to defending ourselves, right as to our interests, and ashamed of neither.

Yet our old tendencies persist; and they threaten to return to bedevil us. The American desire to cloak all actions in robes of morality; to rebuild the world in our own image; and yet to turn away from obligations abroad and back to our domestic concerns – that is our tendency to crusade, to arrogance and to isolationism – are again reasserting themselves. It sometimes seems as though it's not enough for us simply to defend ourselves: we have to try to remake our adversaries in our own image. In part this approach stems from a confusion created in our public culture by the Freudian revolution. Freud changed our lexicon and attitude from a moral to a psychological focus, but left us confused about which framework is appropriate in international contexts. Americans in our new maturity struggle against this sort of moral recidivism. When our politicians lead in that direction, resistance strengthens.

We're changing in other ways too, of course, and they also reflect a new maturity. Many Americans don't want to narrow their life choices by what they now consider misplaced pieties – such as intolerance for gays, and many other Americans are prepared to extend to them more tolerance than in the past. This is evident, even though the majority of our people haven't yet figured out how to rewrite our nation's social contract. Enhanced personal liberty requires more, not less, discipline in acting cooperatively and productively with others. Essentially, America is moving forward fitfully to a greater maturity both personally and publicly. These important changes accompany and help structure the shifts in our attitude toward the outside world, but changes in our society are not a key topic of this book.

It's not a new approach to foreign challenges that tells us that Americans are becoming more mature but, rather, the opposite. It's because Americans are becoming more mature that we're adopting a new approach to foreign challenges. The new maturity is an attitudinal change that reflects a deeper understanding of reality. We now know that the world is a more dangerous place than we'd thought and that we have to address its dangers differently than in the past.

A CHANGE IN DIRECTION

The greater recognition of danger and of mixed motives abroad that make up new maturity in Americans does not send us back to the cynicism and duplicity that characterize diplomacy abroad. Ours is an intermediate position, between America's traditional simplicity in opinion and action and the jaded cynicism of the old world. It is much better for us to have made such a change, and not worse for the rest of the world.

In part there has been a gradual change in the direction of new American maturity. A most significant example is the dramatic change in attitude toward military preparedness. Before World War II America was perennially unprepared for war, and when wars came upon her, her citizen soldiers suffered grievously. George C Marshall spoke bitterly in the aftermath of World War I about what had happened to the Americans who went to fight in France. "Everywhere on the battlefield individuals were paying the price of long years of national un-preparedness. They paid with their lives and their limbs for the bullheaded obstinacy with which our people had opposed any rational system of training in time of peace, and with which Congress had reflected this attitude."[3]

After World War I, despite Marshall's and others' pleas, America again all but disarmed. Even while Germany and Japan armed, even after World War II began in Europe, America remained woefully weak. As late as the early 1940s, before Pearl Harbor, America's few soldiers often lacked rifles and tanks, and trained in some instances with wooden rifles and with trucks with signs painted on their sides saying "Tank." Even after the start of war in Europe, American military strength ranked about thirty-fifth in the world, just behind Bulgaria.

In fact, America's weakness, born out of a desire to escape foreign wars and to keep national expenses low, was a key reason why Japan and Germany were so willing to declare war on America in 1941.

But all that changed with World War II. Americans took the lesson that unpreparedness invited war, not the opposite. Since the war we've maintained a strong military establishment, one that has evolved into the strongest of all nations.

In no other area of American's interaction with the rest of the world is the ability of the nation to change its basic positions more clear. America's posture toward national defense did not change with the end of the Civil War, nor of the Spanish American War, nor of World War I, after each of which America disarmed. But our stance altered totally at the end of World War II.

From the start of the twentieth century onward, the American peoples' is an especially interesting story. We were first isolationist (but not pacifist), trying to stay out of World Wars I and II. We entered World War II unprepared. Then followed the Cold War; we abandoned isolationism, if reluctantly, and were militarily prepared. We entered the Korean War in a mood of resignation – more war with little desire for it. Vietnam was a disaster that left a strong antimilitary and pacifist element in our character (which mirrors to a degree a similar but more popular attitude in Europe and Japan). Still, we did not disarm after the war in Vietnam, but remained well-armed, rebuilt the capability and morale of our military by a succession of significant reforms, so that the first Iraqi war was a success.

During World War II we built a strong military, and have not dismantled it since. During this long period, despite a substantial setback during the Vietnam War, there has emerged in America a more favorable attitude toward the military than has been the case in the past – fed by successes in Gulf War I and II. Higher favor for the military, almost a sort of militarism, is made possible by the end of conscription – so that large numbers of people and their families are not made angry by being forced into military service – and by a better-led military establishment. Higher favor is a result of our admiration for a winner; our interest in advanced military technology; our hatred of foreign oppressors who are often the target of our military operations; our fascination with efficiency and can-do, virtues not usually associated in our past with our military, but which it possesses to a surprising degree today. Thus, the modern American military resonates deeply with certain of our values and suddenly a new American is emerging – more different from Europeans and Canadians than in the past.

This change of attitude toward our military is historically significant. We're abandoning the somewhat pacifist orientation left by the Vietnam War; we're adding a new link to the long chain of our history – a link which is preemptive, unilateralist, militarist.

We are maturing further now, and will conduct ourselves very differently in the world. In these instances our change was due to external challenges – the challenge of the Japanese and German aggression in the early 1940s, the challenge of Vietnam, and the challenge of the terrorist aggression fifty years later.

These are the big changes in American attitudes with respect to engagement with the rest of the world.

AFTER WORLD WAR I

1. From involvement in an alliance to wage the war to isolationism; and
2. From a strong military to fight the war, to a pared-down military so weak that as World War II neared our military power was lesser than that of several of the small nations in the Balkans.

AFTER WORLD WAR II

1. From avoiding entangling alliances abroad to collective security based on a whole series of treaties; and
2. From military nonpreparedness to militarism and a military-industrial complex that armed the nation.

AFTER THE VIETNAM WAR

1. From overconfidence in our ability to defeat any foe to a recognition that we must be cautious about entering guerilla wars; and
2. From a military built on conscription, poorly led and armed conventionally, to a professional (all volunteer military) with new and improved styles and standards of leadership, and with revolutionary changes in weaponry and tactics.

CHANGES AFTER SEPTEMBER 11

What are the changes after September 11, 2001? The Bush Administration has suggested, and is implementing, two key ones:

1. From reaction after we are attacked to preemption to forestall attacks; and
2. From enough military strength to defend ourselves to sufficient military strength to ensure dominance of any potential adversary.

Iraq – The First Big Test

Iraq became the first big test of the post–Cold War world. The test could have come elsewhere than Iraq – North Korea and Iran were alternative candidates, as was the incident when the Chinese shot down an American surveillance plane – and it could have come at a different time. The American president had the option to choose the time and setting of the test, but not to determine its outcome. Bush chose Iraq in 2003 – knowingly or by accident – so America faced the test at this time and in this place.

The administration told us that the issue was about the existence of weapons of mass destruction in the hands of Saddam Hussein, and about assistance by the Iraqi dictator to terrorists. There was some truth in this, but it was very superficial; perhaps even mostly a rationalization that later turned sour when no weapons of mass destruction were found in Iraq. There was plenty of reason for a second Iraqi War, regardless of weapons of mass destruction or of links to Al Qaeda, and most of the reasons had little to do with Iraq. Specifically, the United States wanted to establish a power base in the Middle East to intimidate Iran, Syria, Saudi Arabia, and other countries that might be hosting terrorists. (We assumed that once we had freed the Iraqis that we could maintain a military base there.) As is common in wars fought in small countries, Iraq had the misfortune to become a cockpit for great power rivalries.

By choice of the president, who felt he could justify it as a response to the terrorist attack on the World Trade Center on September 11, 2001 (this later was cause for significant confusion among Americans as President Bush first said Iraq was part of the September 11 plot, and then admitted there was no evidence of that), the United States chose to assert in an unmistakable way, its global leadership by targeting Iraq. Afghanistan had already been subdued, but that action had not raised the same issues as Iraq because Afghanistan had clearly hosted Al Qaeda, the terrorist group who was responsible for the attack. (There is an argument seemingly given credence by many in Britain, that Al Qaeda does not exist – that it is an imaginative creation of American law enforcement and the American media. In fact, the best information we have indicates that it is real, hostile, and that Osama bin Laden is associated with it.[4])

Iraq is also a more important country, a major oil producer, a more sophisticated society, and involved much more important great power interests and rivalries than did Afghanistan at this time. Iraq also had a leader well able to play the game of global politics, something the Taliban regime in Afghanistan lacked.

When President Bush chose to make the first full test of America's new assertiveness in Iraq in the fall of 2002, every other major power recognized the significance of the occasion. What would the Americans do? Would America consult with its allies? What role would allies receive in the decision about what actions should be taken? What role or influence would nonallies (especially Russia and China, but also Iran) have? How and where would any influence be exercised, or any role be determined – in bilateral discussions with the United States? In the large alliances such as NATO? in the United Nations?

President Bush was criticized by many for allegedly damaging our relations with our European allies by acting unilaterally on Iraq. However, the critics are ignoring the hidden agenda of the Europeans, which is their need to bond, consolidate, and wield their new power as one European Union. Coming together to criticize America's actions was one way for them to unite against a common "enemy," and opposing the war was their way of wielding power, as we shall see in greater depth in later chapters.

Equally important was how America would measure up to the test. If there were war, how would our military perform? Could America win a conventional war in the Middle East? It had done so to a limited extent in the first Iraqi war, but only in the context of a coalition, and only with a confused and muddled result in which its primary foe, Saddam Hussein, was left in power. If America prevailed in a conventional war, how would it perform in a guerilla conflict? The United States had lost a guerilla war in Vietnam twenty-five years earlier; would it do any better this time? A major question was: did America have the strength to be the world's sole superpower – its so-called hyperpower? And if it had the power, did it have the will? Suppose the United States attacked Iraq, would it accept casualties and a long period of conflict or reconstruction – could it do so given its own impatient internal politics? In effect, the question was: did the United States have what it takes to be the world leader?

These questions about America's role in the world are each being answered in the second Iraqi war and its aftermath. America has the military power, and the will, to fight and win a war in the Middle East; it has the capability to conduct a guerrilla war, at least at the beginning. It is able to sustain casualties, at least on a small scale. It is not prepared to listen much to either allies or rivals about its plans, and it is prepared to act without the approval of the UN or other multinational bodies.

These answers to the questions about American power are the greatest significance of the war – not what happened to Iraq, or to Saddam Hussein and his regime, or to Iraqi oil, or to America's stated objective of establishing Iraqi democracy. Yet the press hardly recognized these more significant issues, in part because the Administration hid many of its real motivations, and in part because they do not want to ask the right questions. Only rarely, for example, did one find a discussion in the general media about China's reaction to the war, and then the report was almost always in a very narrow context. Yet China's interest in America's display of military power was intense, and China may well alter her own relations with America in the short run to reflect what happened in Iraq.

Hidden Motivations

Without getting drawn into a long narrative, listed here are the hidden motivations of the other world powers as to how they hoped America's would assert itself with respect to Iraq:

1. The French and Germans didn't really care about Iraq, but used Iraq as a vehicle for other concerns such as the unification of Europe. It was not, as reported in the media, a disagreement over Iraq that led to disruption in the NATO alliance; it was a progressive deterioration of the NATO alliance that led to the disagreement over Iraq. But the media got the causality backward, and so misunderstood the whole thing and asked all the wrong questions.

2. Each major power tried to exploit the Iraqi issue for its own purposes:

France and Germany

The French used the Iraq issue to isolate the Anglo-Saxons (the United States and England – the Canadians refused to be so isolated) from Continental Europe, driving home the point on the Continent that Britain was too close to America to be really European, and thereby increasing the likelihood that France and Germany together would dominate an enlarged and increasingly united Europe.

Russia

The Russians used it to get more leverage in negotiations with the United States over several other things than Iraq – the most important being the increasing reach of American power and military bases into the former republics of the Soviet Union in central Asia.

China

The Chinese played the most sophisticated game of all. Secretly wanting a demonstration of the United States' military capability to compare to its own, China knew that if the Security Council united in favor of war, Iraq would have given in and there would have been no war. Thus, to encourage the war, China threatened to veto a resolution supporting the war. Thus, the UN never supported the war, which forced the United States to wage war on its own, and literally gave China a front row seat with our embedded journalists in viewing U.S. military capability, which was China's goal all along.

In all of this moralistic posturing by the continental Europeans, the Russians and the Chinese, Iraq was only a vehicle for other purposes – not a matter of significant concern in itself.

To each of these powers and its principal concerns we will return later in this book since the attitudes and aspirations of the other great powers are the most significant aspect of the context in which we now live.

Our Fatal Flaw

America is a great nation, but it's vulnerable – not so much to an external adversary, or even many, but to our own limitation – our inconsistency, our possibly fatal flaw.

The Greek concept of the tragic flaw may be defined as the element in the character of a person that brings him or her at a moment of seeming triumph to an unexpected disaster – for example, Oedipus's discovery, after he had seized a kingdom and was at the height of his power, that the man he had killed to achieve the throne and the queen he had married were in fact, his father and mother. His flaw was his overbearing pride that blinded him to the reality of his situation, despite many clues. The fatal flaw in personality that so interested the Greeks is akin in our world to some basic inconsistency in a leader's or a nation's policy that threatens to undermine the nation's security.

Great flaws usually have at their heart an inconsistency. The inconsistency causes different actions to be at cross-purposes – one turning it against another and becoming its own adversary. In that situation, the more effective and efficient the effort, the more it's frustrated by itself, blocking its own every move, and so brought to failure. The holding of mutually inconsistent convictions is a sure source of danger in our international relations – it makes us our own enemy because we tend to act against our own interests.

The notion of a nation's fatal flaw, the inconsistency that undermines it, is very different from that of simply making a mistake. The flaw does lead to mistakes, indeed fatal ones, but mistakes occur for other reasons as well. Britain's victory in World War II was accompanied by many errors – a poor choice of commanders in the desert which prolonged the African war; putting troops ashore in Greece in an attempt to stop the Nazi invasion; the raid on Dieppe; and so on. But none were fatal. What was fatal, as we've pointed out earlier, was the notion that the Empire could be preserved and Hitler overthrown at the same time. The fatal flaw in a nation's approach to its relations with the rest of the world is a basic inconsistency in its objectives that produce repeated errors and ultimately undermines one or another of its most basic purposes.

In the end usually a great nation, with all its prestige and power, defeats itself; it isn't defeated by others, but instead overreaches, or more commonly, undermines its own position by its own actions. Adversaries know this, and often seek to exploit a nation's inconsistencies – it's the same notion that in jujitsu urges the smaller, weaker opponent, to learn moves that will turn the larger, stronger adversaries' strengths against him or herself.

Most nations have strengths that can be turned against them; inconsistencies that are large enough to become fatal flaws; America does. This is why thoughtful, logical analyses of defense and foreign policy is so important, why it is not merely an academic exercise but deserves the most careful attention – because it keeps us from defeating ourselves.

Bin Laden is a peculiarly dangerous adversary for America because he seems to understand our flaws and how they can be turned against us (Saddam did not). Bin Laden knows that our military strength is great enough to prevent him from seizing control of major countries in the Islamic world by overt aggression; just as we prevented Saddam from seizing Kuwait. But he also knows that we have a messianic element in our personality that causes us to overreach – to want to create our own image in the wake of our troops; so we try to change other societies in the wake of military victory. This creates an enormous political opportunity for radicals – who find their greatest opportunity in the chaos that follows the collapse of a regime. What seems a great triumph for America, therefore – the military overthrow of a hostile regime – can be its point of greatest vulnerability.

The fatal flaw of America is an inability to distinguish between the world as it is and the world as we wish it to be, and therefore to overestimate what we can achieve – it's a flaw of perception that prevents us being fully objective about situations in which we find ourselves. Its expression is our public culture.

Americans are becoming more and more realistic in trying to find an accommodation between the two sides of our nature with which we can live. We are becoming more interventionist, unilateralist, and militaristic while remaining excitable, self-centered, only sometimes sensitive to others suffering, prideful, arrogant, without proportion in judgment and reaction but still with a heady dose of idealism and generosity. We are less hypocritical than in our past, not because we are more idealistic, but because we are less so, leaving our idealists more isolated today than in the past. We are trying to come to grips with our role in the world by being more realistic and less idealistic about it, as benefits a country which is now in the action – rather than standing aside in an isolationist position observing and commenting on other powers which are doing most of the acting (which is the posture in which we spent the entire nineteenth century and the first half of the twentieth).

The American people are likely mature enough now to adopt the posture of a mature superpower in the world. Whether or not our political leadership is sufficiently trusting of our people to take us in that direction is a key concern of this book.

CHAPTER 7: KEY POINTS

1. Americans are different since September 11, 2001; there is a loss of innocence and a new maturity forged in terrorist attack and preemptive war.
2. Even before the attack on the World Trade Center we had been shifting dramatically our relation to the world – from isolationism to military strength and deep engagement.
3. The Bush administration is carrying us further – toward military dominance, preemptive war, and the installation of democratic freedom around the world.
4. Our country's public culture has always had a potentially fatal flaw in our approach to the world – a conviction that our system is the best, that it fits anywhere, that we have an obligation to extend it, and that if we extend it successfully, there will be peace and prosperity thereafter. This conviction causes us to overreach periodically – it is likely doing so again.
5. We should instead aim to become a mature superpower, protecting our country, helping others who want to go in our direction, but avoiding overreach. To do this American politicians have to recognize the greater maturity of our people, and be more honest about both our objectives and the limitations of our reach.

PART FOUR

THE RECONFIGURATION OF NATIONAL
WEALTH AND POWER

EIGHT

The Economic Roots of American Power

The American economy provides the sinews of American power in the world. It's not only the world's largest economy, but also the fastest growing among the developed countries. The secret of the American economy's success is not only free enterprise and markets, which could be copied abroad, but an economic culture derived from our history – something it is very hard if not impossible to replicate abroad.

In 1875 the great English economist Alfred Marshall visited the United States for four months, and when he returned to England said that he had been enabled by his trip to "expect the coming supremacy of the United States, to know its causes and the directions it would take."[1] His mission is of no less significance for us now, one hundred and thirty years later, as it was then. During all the discussions, year after year, of the decline of American power, the opposite has been happening and continues to happen.

Like any people we find ourselves where we are because of what has happened in our past. As Americans we are prisoners of our economic success that imposes on us great responsibilities in the world. It is striking that America has not sought global power so much as it has stumbled into it all the while seeking to be left alone behind its ocean barriers. Power has emerged from the richness of our continent, the energy of our people, and the freedom of our economic and political systems. America is a prisoner of its own success in the world; a prisoner because we haven't sought this status and are in some ways ill-equipped to deal with it.

AMERICAN ECONOMIC SUCCESS

The United States is in its current position as sole superpower primarily because it has a unique economic system that is able to support dominant military strength. The economic strength of the United States is long term – an engine of growth from a very high base. The United States is a commercial nation par excellence – so that America's staying power on the world stage is very substantial. What sets America apart from its rivals is its workaholism (especially compared with Europe), its preference for a constituent form of economic governance, its opposition to cartels, and its encouragement of entrepreneurship. These factors explain America's superior quantitative performance, as well as some of our social failings.

Ironically, American politics does not provide a balanced view of our economy, but instead conducts a continual controversy about its supposed failings. A balanced view finds the glass more full than empty. In recent years the American economy has survived the collapse of its stock market, the 9/11 attacks, scandals in business, and wars in Afghanistan and Iraq, and still had only its shortest, shallowest recession in history, and now is growing strongly again. Commented a British writer, "Europe's and most of Asia's . . . best hope . . . is to share in the fruits of the American recovery." He added in admiration of the American economy, "When it comes to economics, there is still only one game in town."[2]

Because of the continual criticism of America's economic performance, it's very easy for noneconomists to underestimate the power of the American economy, so that international relations theorists are continually forecasting the decline of American power. Most recently, and with the most influence, Paul Kennedy of Yale studied the right things but reached the wrong conclusions by comparing the United States to Spain at the height of Spanish power several centuries ago. But Spain had no economic or technological engines, so the comparison was faulty – hence Kennedy forecast America's decline only to repudiate his own conclusions in articles written subsequent to 9/11.[3]

American economic power shows itself in its ability to maintain great military forces without unduly burdening the economy. The proportion of the resources of the United States devoted to defense has risen in the short term due to the Iraq War, but continues on a long-term downward trend. "When we use a variety of statistical measurements, it becomes readily clear that the United States is increasingly devoting its economic, fiscal, technological, and manpower resources to civilian purposes. . . . The record shows that, at its World War II peak, military outlays equaled about 35 percent of GDP; during the Korean War, approximately 15 percent; Vietnam, 10 percent; and the Gulf War, six percent. The current ratio (as of late 2005) is less than 5 percent."[4]

Not only is the United States the world's largest economy, it is the leader in growth among the great powers (with the single exception of China).

Even so, the United States falls far from the competitive ideal and therefore far from its potential growth rate. Even at its current size and growth rate, it has considerable inefficiencies which, if remedied would increase its performance.

The American economy falls substantially short of its potential because market participants consider it legitimate to bend the competitive rules, and government misregulation and abuse are rife. On the one hand, Americans are overworked. On the other, they are misemployed. Oligopoly degrades economic efficiency, and government frequently is more concerned about placating interest groups with public money than promoting effective markets, or providing government services on a cost-effective basis. These shortcomings are not uniquely American. All the nations of the developed west are beset by some of these same problems. By enacting reform, America could increase its own growth rate to pull even further ahead of the pack.

THE AMERICAN ECONOMIC CULTURE

Americans are justly proud of our economic strength, but they tend to underestimate the difficulty others would have in copying it. This is significant because it leads Americans to attempt to export their system when it cannot be effectively done. That is, the naïveté of Americans about our own system's unique qualities tempts us to overreach abroad by trying to export it. This is a serious problem to which we'll return in a later chapter.

America possesses an individualistic culture with collectivistic safeguards in which work and fair competition come first. It epitomizes the ideal of Western civilization, the forging of social compacts empowering individual effort under the rule of law.

The American creed doesn't reject altruism and compassion – as often charged. But it applies them to income creation. Although individualism and democracy imply that people need not be materially self-seeking, American culture is intolerant of idleness and dependency for almost all. Likewise America accepts wide disparities in income and wealth and is averse to compassionate transfers unless they are justified by infirmity or discrimination.

Income creating is equated with success. The more individuals make, the greater their consumption options and social approval. The productive rich are esteemed for their business acumen, even when they bend the rules and live ostentatiously. Oligopolistic profit making is acceptable, and all forms of expenditure are valued because they support production.

Consumer liberalism helps maintain high levels of activity by encouraging the unrestricted pursuit of individual desires, often at the expense of nonproductive leisure.

Few are immune from this cultural pressure. The idle rich are scorned, and the pursuit of quiet is disesteemed. The image of lonely geniuses, poets and artists standing aloof against these temptations may be occasionally extolled, but more often than not they are dismissed as eccentrics unless they are commercially successful. As a consequence most Americans are absorbed in a frenetic spiral of work and market consumption. When those who survive the strain aren't consuming, they busy themselves with charity, or in acquiring skills that will make them better income creators.[5]

America's high level of productivity and enormous economy reflect self-seeking. In the 1950s venture capital was created in America as a financial means of supporting entrepreneurship. Coupled with freedom for consumers to pursue their own desires, venture capitalists and entrepreneurs have pushed ahead technological advance at a rate unequaled in history. It should be recognized that technical progress at this pace will not occur just because science provides opportunities for new products; opportunity must be coupled with incentive and capital. Furthermore, science itself advances only when economic resources are provided; it is a great error to believe that technological progress will occur of its own – it will not. It occurs in America at a very rapid rate and on a large scale today because of a combination of economic factors – of freedom to start businesses for entrepreneurs, of capital for highly risky startup firms provided by venture capital firms, and of large-scale investments by government and large business in research. This combination of economic factors drives the improvement of technology and long-term growth of the American economy. There is nothing on their scale elsewhere in the world.

Social welfare is also high because competition among big firms in many industries makes supply adequately responsive to demand. Of the world's large nations, the United States most closely approximates the liberal ideal by which economic efficiency and growth are maximized. Over long periods the size of the American economy and its growth rate reflect its favorable economic culture.[6]

The American work ethic, openness, and entrepreneurship are proverbial. They are commonly associated with the generally competitive ideal and are routinely invoked as explanations of its economic successes and as proof of the superiority of the liberal model without taking sufficient account of the countervailing factors. From the outset of the revolution, the American economy has been influenced not only by free enterprise, including conspiracies in restraint of trade, but by an activist government that does more than just "neutrally" respond to the popular will. Beginning with the signing of the Magna Carta at Runnymede in 1215 where the English barons forced King John to grant them a charter of liberties, through the gradual development of broad based political democracy in the nineteenth century, rights and collectivist obligations have been stratified in ways that often subvert the logic of free competition. Stratified rights have meant privileges for some to dominate others, and the obligation of the state to restrain socially destabilizing market activities.

This obligation persists. The American government – like its Continental European counterparts though to a somewhat lesser degree – intervenes in the economy on behalf of constituencies clamoring for special protections, but justifies its actions differently. Instead of emphasizing social solidarity, American politicians rationalize state regulation as fair competition. They pretend that granting quotas, preferences, subsidies, specific tax concessions, privileged contracts and transfers is akin to antitrust activities assuring everyone equal market access. Likewise, although America and Continental Europe both have gargantuan welfare states providing the population with imperfectly competitive services like social security, Americans claim this reflects the will of the people, whereas the Continental Europeans see it as social democratic duty.

American collectivism is more pro-competitive, and is less elitist. Political leaders see themselves as stewards of a pluralist open society. But since the high water mark of the New Deal's "fair trade" retail price-fixing they have sought to avoid creating excessive barriers to marketing and entrepreneurship. Our politicians do indulge constituents with very specific tax breaks. Veterans' preferences and comparative worth (wage-fixing across occupations to remedy gender discrimination) are typical but appear to be on the wane.

THE AMERICAN ECONOMIC CREED

The comparative efficiencies of the American economy are bolstered by a frontier spirit that encourages entrepreneurial risk-taking; the remnants of a Puritan ethic that applauds "busy-ness" and a shadow culture that approves aggressive self-seeking. The American creed is frenetic and innovative.

This energy, supported by government financed military and civilian high tech research, partly countervails the chilling effects of substantial taxation, regulatory compliance reporting, bureaucratic waste, and misregulation.

American economic growth accordingly is more robust than might otherwise be expected. The post–World War II rate has generally equaled the long-term historical average of 3.2 percent per annum. New Deal restrictions on retail pricing, distribution, imports, and labor contracting have been pared, and foreign businesses encouraged. These liberalizing initiatives have increased labor mobility, reduced real wage growth, spurred employment, augmented choice and contained inflation. As a consequence, Americans are fully employed, and are enjoying a standard of living well above that of more controlled economies. Further pruning big government would make things better, but politicians are content to bask in their success, delighted that public programs haven't killed the goose that lays the golden egg.

America indeed is doing exceptionally well judged by the usual macroeconomic yardsticks. Growth is higher, and unemployment is lower than in any of the other developed great powers. Inflation and interest rates are low. But these macro criteria mask the fact that American economic performance is drastically below its competitive potential. Other great powers could easily eclipse the United States by more thoroughly embracing laissez-faire, or even finding alternative ways of empowering their managed markets.

The American system today seems invincible because its competitors are more inefficient and stagnating. But America is hardly a paragon of dynamism, life quality, and social justice. This is because the motivations, mechanisms and institutions that govern demand, supply and their equilibration differ importantly from those assumed in the classical tradition (where governance must be in accordance with individual preferences, not those of politicians, bureaucrats and assertive constituents), creating a system where these groups rather than consumers are economically sovereign. Bureaucratic and constituent preferences unduly influence outcomes, superseding those ordinary individuals would otherwise forge for themselves. It is their preferences that warp demand and define the sense in which the American managed market system is micro and macroeconomically distorted by government misadministration, where the well connected unduly prosper at the expense of those abiding by the rules of markets competition.

There is a substantial body of opinion in America that longs for a purer democracy and truer free enterprise. It is much to be desired that America improve in these directions. But the impediments that exist in our public and political cultures are very substantial. Efforts that start out to improve competition are often diverted; efforts to improve democracy are undermined. The notion that our democracy is complete and effective is another illusion of public culture. When well-meaning Americans recognize this, they often take refuge in the observation that even if our system is imperfect, it is better than others.

Informed and powerful segments of American society are content with the rules of the game as they are, and the rest of the community doesn't know better. There is no effective public consensus for restraining oligopolistic competition, constituent advocacy and state administration, and until there is the managed market will endure with unpredictable fluctuations, winners and losers, although within a largely stable macroeconomic context. The American system is stronger now than ever before in history, and is likely to adapt well to shocks and challenges.

It is enlightening to contrast the American experience with that of Rome: Rome was a military machine par excellence, and was able to turn its military strength to economic wealth. America is an economic machine par excellence and turns its economic strength into military power.

But America, despite the ambitions of its current national leadership, is not a dominant power in the world. It's the world's leading economy and the world's strongest military power. But together these don't add up to dominant power because American diplomacy is so weak. Thus it is like Gulliver tied down by the Lilliputians. This was very evident in the debates in the Security Council of the United Nations that preceded the second Iraqi war. The result is that U.S. dominance is only asserted when it can apply its military power, or when the threat of applying military power is real. Thus, American leaders have a temptation to rely almost exclusively on military power, a topic to which we'll return in a later chapter when we ask how suited the United States is to be the world's sole superpower.

Americans often assume that our economic power can be equaled by others who do little more than mimic our economic system's elements. This assumption leads us to promote our economic system in other countries, and even tempts us to impose it, believing that it will generate economic progress and lessen conflict caused by poverty. But this is naïve because it's not our economic system per se that would have to be emulated successfully, but our entire economic culture, and our economic culture grows out of history and cannot be copied completely or effectively. The superiority of the American economic culture lies in entrepreneurial emphasis; flexible labor markets; broad capital markets, and attitudes toward work and invention.

HOW NATIONAL ECONOMIC CULTURES DIFFER

Different cultures forge economic systems that yield different long-term rates of growth, creating winners and losers, adding to the strength of some nations and deducting from that of others, creating turbulence and global instability. There is considerable and growing risk rooted in the predictable consequences of the world's diverse economic and political systems.

A national economic culture is a complex of market, administrative, and legal mechanisms that determine the way national economies and governments shape demand, and connect it with supply. The simplest case is a single individual. We all know from direct observation that styles of demand formation and self-supply differ broadly.

Flaws in the design and operation of personal and national economic systems are the main source of global economic dysfunction. They cause underproductivity, injustice, degeneration, and collapse. Economic performance and social justice are degraded.

This point is often lost on those who view individual and national choices too narrowly by failing to consider the wider ramifications of specific actions. It is also obscured by the imperfection of all human systems. Contrary to what partisans of competition suggest, the world isn't divided into two neat categories: perfect markets and dysfunctional economic planning. All individual and national interest seeking is to some extent flawed, greatly complicating the task of discriminating better from worse systems. Americans aren't all saints, and Russians aren't all sinners. The personal and national systems of economic management are mixes of good and bad, differing both in proportion and content. Nothing needs to be said about proportion. Obviously, the more individual and national behavior depart from the ideal, the worse performance is likely to be. But content is another matter. Systems biased toward entrepreneurship at the expense of consumption are likely to be more affluent than ones where people focus on consumption, but shun work. Economic stability is likely to be lower in nations made up of gamblers than in lands where people are risk-averse.

The distribution of such behavioral traits isn't random. Some personalities are concentrated more in particular nations than others. National economic cultures – that is, the rules and processes chosen by individuals and nations to manage their economic relations – reflect these temperaments and preferences, which also explain the persistence of basic features of national economic cultures. Temperament and culture determine the roles peoples and nations cast for themselves, the romance and artifice that shape the ways in which their behavior deviates from a rationalist ideal.

Players may realize that they would be better off changing parts, but can't because they are ensnared by their values, routines, and obligations. They cannot easily escape their history. People often knowingly act against their personal interest, and the rational ideals that are supposed to govern their behavior.

HOW DIFFERENT ECONOMIC CULTURES YIELD DIFFERENT RESULTS

The divergent performance of the planet's economies since World War II can only be adequately grasped from the perspective of differing economic cultures. Some countries have flourished, whereas others have languished, not because the first were perfectly competitive while the others weren't, but because some culturally driven economic strategies of nations were better suited to generating economic growth, employment and price stability. The human roles preferred in America favor entrepreneurship, competitive profit-seeking, market access, technological emulation, globalism, and liberal governance more than do those preferred in most other countries, allowing comparatively brisk improvements in productivity, and increased exertion of market power.

American preferences collectively constitute a cultural wager on socially orchestrated, individual wealth-building where work and fair competition come before play, spirituality, community traditions, criminal opportunism, and autocratic privilege. The ideal of the West as it has evolved over the centuries is to forge a social compact which commits everyone to regimes of political and economic governance that empower individual effort and constructive labor, kept in bounds by the rule of law. The strategy has not been implemented uniformly. Every Western nation has construed this megastratagem through its own cultural prism, and built unique systems for its implementation. They have not always faired equally well, and some are exhibiting unmistakable signs of degeneration. Still, compared with other countries, the strategy has proven its material merit not because participants have played their roles well maximizing their own advantage, nor because political and economic governing instruments have been ideal, but because constructive forces more often managed to gain the upper hand than else-where. Much indisputably has been accomplished, but it is important to understand that it has been a pale shadow of the potential both in terms of affluence and social equity.

Many nations of the less developed world by contrast have chosen vari-ously to preserve traditional cultures, modify, or revolutionarily transform them in ways that discourage entrepreneurship, competitive profit-seeking, open market access, technological emulation, globalism and liberal state governance, leaving large segments of their populations unempowered. This has in a few instances produced remarkably good results especially in the Chinese cultural bloc. Taiwan, Hong Kong, Singapore, South Korea, Malaysia, Thailand, and, more recently, post-Maoist China have managed to reconcile elements of authoritarian economic regulation with aggres-sive, export-oriented entrepreneurship to propel rapid economic growth, in much the same manner as the Japanese in an earlier epoch. But these countries are the exceptions. The performance of the vast majority of states outside the West has ranged from lackluster to abject, reflecting the par-ticularities of their specific, culturally fashioned systems. This failure has not gone unnoticed, nor have leaders been inert. Many have campaigned for modernization and partially liberalized, but the changes have not been sufficient to significantly overcome resistance, negative adaptations, and too frequently the disorienting effects of foreign economic penetration. Conti-nuity in most instances has triumphed over change.

THE ECONOMIC CULTURES OF THE GREAT POWERS

China

The Growing Economic Power of China
Chinese economic growth has been spectacular for two decades. Not only has its GDP risen briskly, but also unlike Russia China has integrated itself into the global trade system. This achievement is attributable to the Chinese Communist Party's improbable success in combining authoritarian disci-pline of labor, state ownership of enterprise, and wage fixing – all elements of the old command economy – with massive foreign direct investment and significant elements of profit-driven markets. The ability of the Chinese to attract foreign investment is particularly remarkable since private property is not legally protected in China, though an amendment to the Chinese constitution that would protect private property is making its way toward enactment.

China's economic system today precariously balances the incentives for business development provided by low wages and lucrative profit potential against the inefficiencies of state ownership, leasing and control. The Chinese economy has a pronounced bias toward inequitable but rapid development; but this advantage will gradually diminish as export markets mature, labor transfers become more difficult, and accumulated inefficiencies take their toll. The current Chinese system may allow China to overtake America in the next twenty years in terms of the dollar value of its gross domestic product, but inefficiencies will place a low ceiling on living standards. Foreign businessmen in China, and other Chinese insiders urge that outsiders not be deceived by the glitter of Chinese economic development. Chinese government, businesses and workers are inefficient left to their own devices tend to be corrupt. What appears to be rapid economic advance in China's big cities is only partly real. For example, many high-rise buildings in Shanghai are vacant. They are essentially seasonal homes or speculations by the overseas Chinese. Like the former Soviet Union – and this is a great tragedy – China is better positioned to be a great military power than an affluent nation. To global insecurity created by differential growth rates among the great powers, China adds the distinct risk of internal instability caused by corruption – a struggle to control productive assets for private purposes (as has occurred in Russia) – and popular discontent.

China is America's only economic rival in terms of growth now, and only because China is at a particular stage of its development which gives it very great advantages (extremely low labor costs, reasonable political stability, an educated population with strong commercial instincts).

The Advantages of Chinese Economic Culture

China and Japan have shared a strong cultural heritage in religion, governance, literature and architecture from the mid-seventh through the twentieth centuries. Both at various times were profoundly influenced by Confucianism, Buddhism, Tao, and aspirations to regional power, yet in at least one respect they have always been fundamentally different. Chinese social behavior is based on the guilt principle, whereas the Japanese rely on shame. China is a community of individuals acting according to their consciences – with individual guilt as the price paid for failing to abide by conscience; Japan is communally governed with shame – a social stigma – as the price of failure to abide by group norms.

The autonomy associated with guilt culture gives China a significant edge in emulating Western market mechanisms and therefore in economic growth potential. Yet this has been so for a long time. China was better placed than Japan to emerge as the superpower of the East during the last quarter of the nineteenth century. But this never happened. For a host of complex historical reasons, including an insufficiently developed rule of law stemming from a weak system of private property rights, China's transition to a modern market economy foundered, her economic growth potential was unrealized, making her prey first to European and then Japanese imperialism. It was not until the mid-1980s that Deng Xiaoping's liberalizing reforms made gradual integration into the global market system possible. Yet all those lost decades have a heavy cost for China. Per capita GDP in Japan today exceeds China's by a factor of five.

Can China recover this lost ground? Can the Chinese cultural style of individualism be as or more effective than Japanese communalism in generating economic growth? The spectacular postwar successes of the "Asian Tigers," Singapore, Hong Kong, Taiwan, and South Korea suggest that it can, if China rids itself of state ownership of the means of production and jettisons the Communist Party in favor of the rule of law. There are no reasons for supposing that the managed market strategies adopted by ethnic Chinese in Singapore, Hong Kong, and Taiwan couldn't work on the mainland, allowing China to quickly become the world's largest economy, and narrow the living standard gap with the first world.

The contemporary Chinese authoritarian market system is an exotic blend of inconsistent elements, administered by a development minded communist bureaucracy. The state owns the nation's natural resources including land, and most industrial, transportation, and communication assets. This gives the state both the legal and administrative right to directly determine production levels, financial arrangements, monetary policy, and distribution of goods and services. But in accordance with Deng's liberalization strategy, the state has chosen to delegate considerable autonomy to enterprise managers and communes, and to permit the gradual emergence of leasing and private entrepreneurship.

All this however creates two significant internal conflicts. On the one hand, many economic agents are encouraged to maximize profits for the state, although they cannot act on their own behalf because they have no personal ownership. This limits incentives. Why should state agents exert themselves for the state, without adequate compensation? In fact, they are not likely to.

On the other hand, the rise of private entrepreneurship creates a channel through which managers of state-owned enterprises and leaseholds can divert state resources to their own private accumulation, thereby providing an incentive for economic growth. Yet this process jeopardizes the Communist Party's implicit political contract by which it promises to protect workers and peasants against private exploitation. When private entrepreneurs press workers and peasants into activities for the private benefit of entrepreneurs, the party's legitimacy and right to rule is undermined.

Deng's strategy paradoxically strengthens Chinese economic power by leasing state property, decriminalizing business and accelerating entrepreneurship, but subverts the Communist Party's control by undermining state owned enterprises in ways that foster adverse selection including unemployment, misinvestment and inferior technological choice. The Chinese leadership appears to believe that rapid economic growth and the people's deference to state authority will allow it to harness these opposing forces for its benefit whether or not the economy ultimately transitions to a Western market model. It is counting on the deference to authority so deeply rooted in Chinese culture to hold labor in check (as it has done successfully in the smaller economies of southeast Asia), without buying off labor with Continental European style social benefits. Nor does the Chinese Communist Party seem to be prepared to wholly commit to private enterprise under the rule of law. Hence, the Chinese formula is unique and distinguishes the Chinese authoritarian leasing market concept from all rivals upholding the sanctity of private property and the rule of law.

As in America and Japan, but not in Europe, income creation is China's principle success criterion, not social welfare, even though the Communist Party pays lip service to Marxist precepts of social justice. State managers, private entrepreneurs and the party elite assigned to supervise private business initiatives are revered for their productive acumen as long as they don't fall into conflict with state guidelines. The good society from this perspective is one that rapidly creates wealth, empowering the state and the Party elite.

China's economic performance reflects these cultural characteristics. Its productivity and GDP are low due to the deficiencies of state ownership, adverse selection, economic mismanagement, leasing and corruption. But growth is high as a result of increased private initiative, low wages, state-financed modernization, massive foreign capital investment and global marketing of Chinese products. The efficiency of the Chinese economy is low because it flouts the rules of competitive free enterprise, but its growth can exceed that of developed countries because the Chinese regime ignores worker rights and consumer's desires for rising living standards, preferring instead to direct resources to further its own goals.

China's Potential

Thoughtful Western economists don't accept Chinese economic growth figures. "I don't believe China's official eight percent growth figure. It's a politically mandated number, first conjured up in 1988 by Chinese officials. Independent surveys of industrial capacity, energy use, employment, consumer income and spending and farm output imply much slower growth."[7] A more probable figure is about 5 percent.

Yet visiting Shanghai and the cities of Jiangsu (Nanjing, Suzhou, Yangzhou) it's easy to believe higher numbers. The construction boom there puts Russia to shame. There is obviously a new middle class that lives reasonably well because labor costs remain low. The family income of one of our students with two full-time workers is $2,200 per year.

Nonetheless, the bulk of the population remains agrarian, and lives poorly, or in abject poverty. The peasant subsidizes the urban living standard.

What this means, of course, is that China has an almost inexhaustible supply of labor to fuel industrial development. Some Americans expect that there will be a time in the near future when China has siphoned off all the manufacturing jobs it needs, and the transfer of manufacturing to the Far East will slow of its own accord. This is undoubtedly true, but it will not happen in the lifetimes of the authors or most readers of this book. By little more than bringing a few tractors to the agricultural sector in China, government planners say, authorities could release more than a hundred million workers to work in industry – a labor force as large as that of the entire United States in all industries.

In the next decade, the Chinese impact on world economy will grow. It is now beginning to run trade surpluses generally – previously it had imported more than it exported and though it had a positive balance of trade with the United States, it had a negative balance of trade with the nations (particularly in Asia) that supplied it with raw materials. Furthermore, its exports to the United States are going to come increasingly to include not just consumer goods (its WalMart connection) but industrial products, produced in China by U.S. multinationals and exported to America. U.S. multinationals have spent a decade investing in China to build export facilities to the United States and now will begin to use them large scale.

This is not to say that there may not be significant problems in China's economic future caused by the inconsistencies in the Chinese economic culture that we have identified. Financial crises originating in internal weaknesses of the national economies are forecast for both China and India by 2010, and both are expected to lead to political crises in turn.[8] Inflexibility in the

Chinese political system is expected to cause the crisis to be very serious with significant implications for world politics. Whether a short-term crisis in the Chinese economy will set off a military conflict is something about which we must be concerned.

Russia

The Economy of the Soviet Union

Many Americans have yet, even today, to face the reality of what the Soviet Union was, blurring their understanding of what Russia has become today.

The USSR was the embodiment of what all democratically oriented westerners abhorred. It was a authoritarian state, committed to burying the freedom of the west, run by a self-anointed vanguard of an initially largely nonexistent proletariat. It criminalized private property, business, and entrepreneurship. It outlawed rival political parties, and used its secret police to repress dissent, terrorize and kill tens of millions, consigning similar numbers to gulag (concentration camps). It maintained a huge army equipped and spread its control across much of the world. The Soviet economy was a physical management system, not a value added maximizing economy, where government bureaus determined the amounts of goods and services to be produced and allocated by assigning the resources necessary to produce them. Resources were mobilized, engineered and fabricated into goods without a market mechanism or consumer guidance. Managers, administrators, and workers were motivated with traditional western incentives: bonuses, perks, career rewards, wages, piecework incentives, and also a host of punitive sanctions for failure to meet established targets. Workers and managers were closely monitored and supervised, but carrots, sticks, and supervision were not enough to assure that factors were rationally allocated and technology wisely chosen. Optimal planning was a myth. Gosplan, as new archival research shows, only planned 150 composite goods, leaving the supply of twenty-five million goods to a haphazard assortment of decision makers, a phenomenon Friedrich von Hayek aptly called "planned chaos."

This was all very different from the propaganda, accepted by many in the west, that the Soviet Union was an optimally planned, nano-administrated, command economy designed to maximize the welfare of the Soviet population according to socialist conceptions. Instead, in a Soviet variant of the Muscovite tsarist model, the Kremlin granted economic rights to ministerial overlords and enterprises, guided by ruler-approved bureaucrats who tried to control the overall economy. Physical management, uninformed by competitive supply and demand processes, misgoverned the actions of Gosplan (the State Planning agency), ministries and enterprises alike.

The system didn't work well for consumers. Direct state-mandated allocation of production targets and resources was the principal cause of Soviet blight. As market theorists tirelessly insisted the separation of demand from supply prevents consumers from receiving goods and services with the characteristics they desire, in the preferred assortments. It also prevents optimal investment, and warps scientific and technological progress, transfer, and diffusion. Yet in an authoritarian political environment in which the public has insignificant power, it makes little difference that the system doesn't work well for consumers. Americans, who are used to both consumer sovereignty and of voter sovereignty (albeit both imperfect) always overestimate the importance of public opinion in Russia.

During the Soviet period, most American scholars and intelligence experts insisted that the Soviet Union was providing improving living standards for its people. During the 1960s and 1970s the CIA contended that Soviet living standards were growing more rapidly than our own. Yet how could a country that criminalized business, entrepreneurship and private property, fixed prices and shouldered a double-digit defense burden have increased per capita consumption more rapidly than the United States and Europe for most of the postwar period as the CIA's series indicated? The answer is, of course, that it couldn't, and American intelligence personnel should have seen that clearly and early. They didn't. Their data were corrupt; it was wrong.[9]

However inept at improving living standards for the population, the Soviet's system of direct state-mandated allocation of production and resources permitted the Kremlin to mobilize resources for defense without competition from consumer needs. The system involved great waste, but the Soviets limited themselves to a relatively small number of mass-produced military products benefiting from economies of scale so that the General Staff of the Red Army was able to emulate foreign weapons, and by borrowing or stealing military technologies, obtained the necessary weapons. Both aspects of the Soviet system – direct allocation of resources and a limited line of weapons – worked fairly well for military purposes. During both world wars, for example, America had to resort to direct allocation of resources to the military in order to prosecute the wars successfully. That is, we did not use a market system exclusively to run our wartime economy.[10] And during World War II, for example, while the Germans had some 175 sorts of vehicles in use in the war against the Soviets, with enormous maintenance and repair problems, the Soviets used only a small fraction of that number of different vehicles, mass-produced, and with minimal maintenance and repair issues. The result was that Soviet equipment was in greater supply than the Germans and a greater proportion of it was working at any given time. As a result, the Soviets had as good a system of wartime production as we did, and a better system of keeping weapons and equipment operating effectively than did the Germans.

The Soviet economy was mobilized for war, all the time. It was very effective in that capacity. It was not mobilized for consumer welfare, and it was a disaster in that regard.

The Russian Economy Today

The contemporary Russian economy is a pre-Soviet type, "Muscovite" authoritarian rent-granting, mixed market system with roots traceable to Ivan the Terrible, displaying weakly developed competitive institutions unregulated by the rule of law, and destabilized by politically connected individuals who seek privileges on a large scale. As such it cannot narrow the gap with the West, even though a partial, oil windfall driven recovery from hyperdepression is being trumpeted as sustainable rapid growth.

Important segments of Russia's economy remain under the thrall of something very like the Soviet system. Structural militarization persists, renationalization is on the rise especially in the natural resource and military industrial sectors, and most of the population continues to be impoverished by Western standards. For a time, some hoped that Russia's oligarchs would rid Russia of this poisoned legacy, but Putin's destruction of Mikhail Khodorkovsky and the ascendence of the *siloviki* (power sources) suggests that this won't happen. There is now a market economy in luxury consumer goods, generally imported, and some revival in domestic production for ordinary people, but it is overregulated, undercapitalized, and corrupt. Industrial modernization is tepid, foreign investment discouraged and markets are anticompetitive.

Today's Russian economy is somewhat like China's, reflecting their common evolution. Both started at the beginning of the twentieth century as imperial/semifeudal market regimes, flirting with democracy, only to succumb to authoritarian communism that replaced markets with administrative command planning, until the nineties when much of their directive control apparatuses were dismantled and replaced by more market-oriented forms of state regulation. Nonetheless, the Russian economy during the nineties sank into hyperdepression, whereas the Chinese economy grew spectacularly. What explains this divergence? Is it China's communism, private ownership, foreign investments, a willingness to accept qualitatively inferior growth, or some conjunctural factor?

The answer is all of the above. Russia's scuttling of the Communist Party-state control apparatus in 1991 combined with a predilection for revenue misappropriation and asset-grabbing prevented the emergence of full employment preserving competitive markets, and Boris Yeltsin refused to devise new state institutions to foster growth. Deng Xiaoping stood ready to support the state industrial sector until it became competitively viable, provided strong incentives for private investment and severely punished those who misappropriated or misused state assets. Russian leaders, in contrast, instead of transferring ownership equitably to the most competent managerial hands, and creating an environment in which investors could be reasonably certain of their claims on future incomes, crafted a hodge-podge Muscovite regime that misdistributed property rights, pitted co-owners against each other, encouraged fraud, and repressed production, encouraged capital flight and discouraged export-led development.

These destructive policies were compounded by hyperinflation, capital flight, and endless schemes to swindle investors that precluded any possibility of mimicking China's strategy of using foreign capital to lead development and global integration. After fifteen years of this style of Muscovite authoritarian mixed economy, Russia is not only materially worse off than before, but has made little headway in constructing a better market system. Although, most of the population has suffered, the elites have flourished beyond their wildest dreams, and are more interested in consolidating their gains than making improvements that jeopardize their wealth and privilege. The authoritarian martial police state they have crafted, which is reminiscent of tsarism during its epochs of weak leadership, is the one they prefer. They want a state which allows them to pilfer public revenues and assets, institutionalize their privileges, legalize their property claims, and suppress incipient competition.

Russia's contemporary Muscovite system, both the Yeltsin and post-Khodorkovsky variants, is best perceived as a set of rules, attitudes, contingent property rights, and agency mechanisms that permits members of a small elite to vie among themselves for power, privilege, and wealth, living off the nation's mineral riches, and cheap labor. The Yeltsin version made few concessions to defense; the post-Khodorkovsky world will be more deferential to the governmental services that possess real power – police, intelligence and defense.

Russia's economic performance reflects these cultural proclivities. Its productivity and total output are low, on some measures lower than China's. Its growth was sharply negative for the decade 1989–1998. It has rebounded back to ninety percent of the Soviet level since then if official statistics are true, but Gregory Khanin cautions that they are substantially inflated. The system's potential after the achieved level of the eighties is regained isn't likely to be any better than the long term, inferior Muscovite norm. President Putin in his State of the Federation speech July 8, 2000, warned that Russia was in danger of becoming a third world nation (which it already is), with a population shrinking at the rate of 990,000 per year.[11]

Nothing prevents President Putin from abandoning indulgent Muscovite patrimonialism except his addiction to it. The Kremlin can act responsibly, but seems disinclined to do so.

These problems can be various remedied including by rewriting corporate governance statutes to protect workers and outside shareholder property rights. But the issue isn't being seriously discussed. President Putin has proposed guaranteeing that managers won't be prosecuted for past embezzlement, misappropriations, fraudulent borrowing, divestitures, and asset acquisition, and hasn't taken any concrete steps to deter future abuses. There is no prospect of progressive change. It's just the old Soviet "treadmill of reforms."

Putin speaks effusively about creating a level playing field under the rule of law, but isn't doing anything about it. There is no substantive discussion about transforming Russian business ethics, or creating statutes and institutions that stringently punish business misconduct and conspiracies in restraint of trade, clearly signaling businessmen to anticipate no fundamental change.[12] Unlike China, the Putin administration shows no desire to subordinate rent-seeking to the higher goals of growth and development.

Russia's economic system doesn't function as market theory implies, not because markets don't exist, but because political control of Muscovite business administrators – operating in lieu of property rights as in Western systems – ensures that politics is more important than rule of law abiding markets or free enterprise. In effect, Russia's economy was during the tsarist period, during the communist period, and is now one of Kremlin political intrigue – not free enterprise market forces in command. This is the most important feature of Russia's economic culture, one that discourages the kind of direct foreign investment propelling Chinese growth, and the key determinant of the potential and lack thereof of its economy .

Japan

A Crisis of Direction

Japan has the second largest economy on the planet, but is often overlooked in discussions of possible international conflict. This is because Japan's military is designed for home defense, not external power projection. Yet to overlook Japan is a mistake; as it is an error to underestimate her potential in geopolitical contests. Japan wields powerful economic weapons and can create a substantial defense capability, including   nuclear weapons, very quickly if it should decide to do so.

Economic Performance

Japanese postwar economic performance after 1995 has been disappointing but not perplexing. During the 1960s and 1970s, it was the world's fastest growing developed nation; in the 1990s, it fell into a long stagnation that has prompted the vice minister of METI to privately worry about the possibility of a protracted malaise lasting until 2050, driven by an aging and shrinking population. This fear is warranted. Japanese economic growth has been in protracted decline for four decades.

The problem has two distinct sources. The first, might be called the Krugman effect after the MIT economist who first boldly called attention to it in his famous article "The Myth of Asia's Miracle" in 1994.[13] Krugman contends that Asian economies generally, and Japan in particular enjoyed rapid growth after WWII due to "perspiration," which he defines as working harder rather than smarter. These nations harnessed opportunities latent in the global market place by reequipping with the latest technologies from abroad, by capital deepening (increasing the capital labor ratio), by augmenting labor force participation, improving education, and availing themselves of international trading opportunities. Japan in particular was also attentive to foreign taste, and committed to quality manufacturing (the "ichiban" mindset). As a consequence, it was able to add value by penetrating lucrative markets abroad (especially the United States), while simultaneously increasing factor productivity. But the gains from "perspiration," as the dismal science always predicted soon began to wane. Capital deepening was accompanied by diminishing incremental capital productivity. The growth generating effect of ever higher capital labor ratios declined. Likewise, the payoff to education fell, and labor force participation reached its natural limit (given the prevailing social structure), and due to aging has started to drop. Although growth is a much more complicated phenomenon than economists usually let on, influenced by shifting tastes, and fortune, nonetheless, the burden has conspicuously shifted from "perspiration" to "inspiration." Japan's future growth prospects now hinge on its ability to continuously develop, borrow, and diffuse high value added technologies to offset diminished labor force participation, and intensifying export competition from China and South Korea. No one doubts the Japanese engineering and adaptive skills, but the record is plain. Despite, mighty and well designed efforts to arrest growth retardation, and escape the jaws of stagnation, neither improved innovation, nor smarter management has gotten the job done.

Blame for this failure has understandably fallen on Japan's peculiar cultural style of doing business, which until the late nineties had been touted as the secret of its extraordinary success.

Japan is a communally focused, shame-based culture. Group interest and welfare usually take precedence over individual concerns. Instead of organizing economic activity on an individualistic basis, where everyone tries to maximize his or her utility at work and play, the Japanese are inclined to rein their personal aspirations for the collective good. This altruism is laudable in many respects. It explains why Japanese are willing to work longer hours, and perform more conscientiously than westerners, but can be economically disorienting. Individualistically organized economies with private ownership of the means of production, maximize shareholders' returns on equity. But in Japan there is an inherent conflict between the group within enterprises, and outside shareholders. Managers', supervisors', and workers' loyalties are to their internal group, not to owners. The organization of work, compensation structures, and investments all reflect these insider priorities to the detriment of optimal capital allocation. Likewise, firms in Japan typically are affiliates of larger entities, orchestrated by main banks, and obligated in various ways to associations linked to the Keidanren, and government authorities. This chills competition in favor of the establishment of mutually tolerated preserves. Clearly, "inspiration" both in the forms of improved management and innovation might be enhanced, and growth reinvigorated by discarding communalism and switching to a competitive, individualistically organized economic mechanism.

This isn't a secret. Americans have been preaching liberalization, since 1945, and a large segment of Japanese elite culture has been persuaded, even though some distinguished academics like Masahiko Aoki aren't convinced. The problem for all concerned is that the medicine appears to have worsened the patients health. The more Japan has liberalized – and it has made very bold strides indeed during the last decade – the more its aggregate economic performance has deteriorated.[14] Not only has growth ceased, but also unemployment has risen sharply, accompanied by deflation, suggesting that one shoe may not fit all feet. There is a distinct possibility that individualistic solutions may not be curative, and could be dangerous to Japan's communalist health without significant modifications of the matrix culture. As matters currently stand, while increased competition has lowered prices, it has also diminished worker loyalty, and the effort mobilization with which it has long been associated.

The nurturing of a leisure society intended to stimulate aggregate effective demand, likewise has had the counterproductive effect of subverting Japan's communalist work ethic.

"Liberalization" may ultimately prove its mettle, but unfortunately there seems to be an equal likelihood that the Japanese will have to pioneer an alternative communalist solution more compatible with their cultural reflexes. Japan remains prosperous, but its ability to meet mounting external challenges is being called increasingly into doubt.

For this reason, Japanese leaders would be well advised to follow a two track policy, experimenting further with liberalization, but also being more attentive to cultural reengineering with the aim of turbo-charging its future.

Cultural Roots Create a Different Kind of Economy

Japan is the only advanced industrial great power culturally rooted in the East. Because Japan is a member of G-7, it is often presumed that Tokyo's market system is like that of its Western neighbors, but this is misleading. For at least a millennium, since Heian times, Japanese culture has disesteemed Western egoism and individual self-seeking. The notion that the good society is one in which people are pitted against each other through competition to better their own position even at the expense of others is viewed by Japanese as absurd. In traditional Japanese values loyalty to the group and the well-being of members takes precedence over personal self-interest. In consequence, individual advantage – which motivates economic activity in Western economic theory – and the market practices of the West don't apply in the same ways in Japan. Instead, market behavior is governed by communal goals and governance that seem effective to the Japanese even though they flout Western principles governing market behavior. Japan is therefore an exception to Western economic principles.

Japan possesses a consensus building, communally orchestrated economic system that esteems work and places the welfare of the group above member self-interest. Both competition and leisure time are subordinated to this goal. The welfare of the group is also important in Continental Europe, but in Europe group members are individualists first instead of team players as in Japan. Communal compacts in Japan don't commit everyone to political and economic regimes empowering personal effort under the rule of law. Consensus takes precedence over the law, and individual initiative, especially entrepreneurship is restrained whenever it conflicts with group goals. The culture also discourages free-riding and disloyalty. It is risk averse and inclined toward egalitarianism. The priority given to group welfare makes consensus coordination preferable to competition, even though the efficiency costs of oligopoly are well understood. Likewise, communal solidarity predisposes consumers to buy Japanese products, whatever the merits of foreign substitutes, prestige brand names aside.

Westerners tend to confuse pressure for conformity in Japan and Japanese organizations with consensus, and there is much less consensus-seeking and building in Japanese organizations than Westerners believe and the Japanese say. Even though consensus-building in Japan is not as important as most Westerners have been led to believe, it is much greater than in America, and it is an important dimension of the Japanese economic model.

The subtleties of these issues are significant. Japanese leaders often act in a very authoritarian fashion (certainly they did before World War II), but they are concerned that their young people will take matters into their own hands because of energy, idealism, and impatience. Much of the search for consensus comes out of this concern. On the factory floor the Japanese did pick up and improve U.S. ideas (not practice) of extensive worker participation via quality circles, and so on. There are elements of what is consensus in the Japanese practice, but there also are strongly top-down directive elements that really aren't consensus but rely on the pressure to conform – which is probably stronger than in any other society.

Consensus building in Japan is top-down, not bottom-up. The group knows what the authority believes, and this sets the framework of the discussion. But the conventions of consensus building protract dialogue and provide a vehicle for considering qualifications and opposing viewpoints. This is the way the Japanese reconcile opposites: respect for hierarchy and participation.

Success in Japan is strongly associated with group income creation. The business acumen of the rich is only valued when it advances group welfare. This attitude reflects Japan's Buddhist and Confucian traditions. The good society promotes national harmony through elite guided consensus building. As in the West, coordination is hierarchical. Elites are able to sway opinion. But unlike Continental Europe, where policy is often shaped by ideology, consensus building makes Japan's elites more broadly attentive to the needs of all constituencies.

Few are immune from this cultural pressure. Deviance is severely sanctioned and self-promoting individualism is perceived as a Western illness. People are encouraged to pursue a balanced existence for the group's greater good.

Japan's economic performance reflects these cultural influences. Team work, group accountability, self-sacrifice, hard work, and diligence have enabled it to achieve a high standard of living, but communally managed competition has taken its toll on growth. The spread of Western attitudes is also diminishing the satisfaction that Japanese derive from team self-sacrifice. Unsurprisingly, outcomes in Japan fall far short of the competitive ideal, even though government misregulation and abuse are lower than in the West. Workers labor more and consume less than if they optimized their individual utility. And they are competitively misemployed. The culture drives them to disregard market pressures more than they should, causing Japan material losses partly compensated by other aspects of its lifestyle.

Japanese Economic Culture Today

The Japanese economy today is a communally managed market system. Its uniqueness doesn't lie in what is often loosely termed "Asian values," but in the specific way Japan's culture combines Shinto, Buddhist, and Confucian values with Western market principles to communally mobilize effort for the production and sale of high quality goods. Unlike the individualist West, where people are encouraged to form and assert their own preferences within bounds set by universal precepts of right and wrong (guilt culture), more than group opinion, the Japanese operate the other way round. They form and inculcate "situational" team values through consensus building with peers and superiors. This profoundly affects the Japanese approach to economic activity. The market isn't a mechanism for personal utility maximizing. It is a device realizing team goals.

The communality of Japanese market activities is often misunderstood. Many equate it with Continental European corporatism in which professional and business groups promote their interests. Some even confuse the Japanese communality with welfare states. But the Japanese are not primarily concerned with using groups for personal advancement, or the state for assisting the needy. They are more interested in protecting and preserving their community and national culture. This is clearly reflected in the Japanese policy of employment for life, which rejects unemployment cushioned by relief. Member's problems in Japan are addressed directly; not delegated anonymously to "society," or advocacy groups. Consequently, employees consider themselves team players. They work overtime without complaint or extra compensation, whereas in the West the length of the workday and overtime compensation are an integral part of labor market processes.

These distinctions are matters of degree. The Japanese aren't completely codependent, deferential, self-sacrificing, hardworking, consultative, or antientrepreneurial; they just exhibit these traits more strongly than others. Japanese economic activity isn't exclusively communal; it is only skewed toward group market management, group leisure, communitarian administration and even communally influenced organized crime (Yakuza).

Japanese communalism is often misunderstood because it is founded on the shame principle, instead of guilt more common in the West. Shame cultures do not have clearly defined universal ethical systems. Right and wrong; good and evil are matters of transitory group attitudes. The commandments read "Thou shall not shame the group by openly committing adultery," not "Thou shall not commit adultery."

When group members violate communal norms or let the group down, they are criticized, censured, and punished for disloyalty, not for committing sins against god or reason. The pain felt from transgressing is the sting of shame, and its social purpose is to make the group's goals, not universal precepts, the arbiter of conscience. This profoundly affects autonomy. Individuals in Western cultures can function autonomously in accordance with their notions of right and wrong. But personal behavior in shame societies is more circumscribed. People can act independently as they believe the group desires, but they are reluctant to challenge communal authority. They lack a moral compass independent of group attitudes.

Western individualists, who bristle at the idea of surrendering their autonomy to group attitudes, often assume that everyone feels the same way. But the Japanese don't mind curtailment of freedom for other benefits.

This doesn't mean that the Japanese are drones. Their "shadow culture" permits a rich variety of "deviant" behavior under well-defined circumstances. It is as if Japanese society recognizes that its strict social control can be too much for some people, and provides an informal release valve. Outsiders may see this approved deviancy as a contradiction; the Japanese understand that it is not.

In Japan it is impolite to undermine the self esteem of others by calling public attention to inadequacies, yet the Japanese from Heian times to the present have always coveted badges of distinction in dress, manners and speech that set them apart from those of lesser stature in certain contexts. Rank and obligation that might seem to contradict communality are inextricable elements of the culture. Modesty, loyalty and respect for others are prized, but this doesn't deter the avid pursuit of *ukiyo-e* (floating world) pleasures in Yoshiwara and Gion. And of course although it is essential to conceal personal emotion on most occasions, and to avoid offense by telling others only what they want to hear (tatemae), not what is true, the Japanese can be exuberant and candid as any other people in the appropriate business, social and personal circumstances.

Safety Valves

This flexibility within the culture provides safety valves that soften the burden of Japanese communalism and facilitate adherence to group norms. The secret of personal success and adaptation in Japanese culture is to master the rules that apply to each situation, and to adjust effortlessly – as does bamboo (strong, yet pliable) – to the requirements of the moment. This skill isn't easily acquired. People don't always succeed and are often anxiety ridden fearing that they will misread subtle cues. But these difficulties – which tend to make the Japanese cautious – are at least partly compensated by an unusual ability to take pleasure in things that Westerners might find distasteful. The Japanese know how to enjoy work, its social context, and the sacrifices made for collective welfare. Activities and associations that others might find distasteful provide substantial gratification and strengthen the system's appeal.

It is therefore reasonable to conclude that Japan's market economy – which is at most a part of Japanese society, not its master – has not, and is not soon likely to operate according to the individualistic principles of the Western competitive market ideal. In Japan motivation, mechanisms and institutions that govern demand, supply and transaction terms all differ importantly from those assumed in the Western model, being embedded in a system in which groups rather than individuals are sovereign. The Japanese system can be conceptualized as graduated concentric rings, like a Buddhist stupa where the widest element forming the base represents individuals who perceive themselves as integral members of a family-nation, upwardly linked with neighborhoods, communities, teams, firms, keiretsu, keidanren, the state administrative bureaucracy, parliament, and the emperor. This arrangement shapes people's attitudes in every ring and harmonizes behavior throughout the hierarchy. Control rests in the consultative process that sets group values and agendas, rather than in the hands of specific individuals.

The mechanisms employed to realize group objectives have a strong communalist character. The organization of markets, the rules of entry and participation, and the rituals of merchandising are all group-determined. "Time isn't money" in Japan. It is the welfare of the group that counts most.

The practical consequences of Japan's motives, mechanisms, and institutions are most evident in the special properties of its markets. As in most national economic systems the transfer of economic sovereignty from individual consumers to others doesn't scuttle the laws of demand, supply, and transactions. Individual Japanese consumers appear to conduct themselves like everyone else. They decide what they want; and how much they buy seems to fall and rise with price. The assortments they purchase are price-sensitive, given their budget constraints. Their preferences appear consistent, and they try to minimize the cost of their purchases. But their consumption behavior departs from the standard practice in Western economies in three ways. Japanese consumers are prone to substitute group-approved choices for their own. They find pleasure in things they might otherwise dislike except for group approval, and they place a remarkably low value on personal leisure, attitudes which have frustrated G-7 policy makers seeking to open Japan's markets to foreign imports.

The situation regarding supply is similar. Most Japanese firms disregard the law of labor supply, and seldom profit maximize. Wage differentials in Japan are unusually narrow, and unpaid overtime work is ubiquitous. Labor supply is only weakly associated with wages, and instead reflects personal obligation. This is why statistics on annual person-hours worked place Japan at the top of the list of industrialized nations.

Japanese firms do not maximize profits in the sense expected by Western theory because communal obligations deter individual proprietors and corporations from placing personal gain ahead of group welfare. Business isn't a device for doing what it is in the West: allowing individuals to optimize their lifetime consumption including leisure, detached from communal obligation. In Japan doing business is a social process requiring compromise. Entrepreneurial ambition, innovation, and modernization must be tempered to accommodate the risk profile of the group; RDT&E and corporate growth must be pursued beyond the point at which profits are maximized in order to provide members with opportunities denied them outside the firm by the limitations on labor mobility in the Japanese economy. Levels of employment cannot be determined by the forces of supply and demand in markets because group values require that members be protected from the impact of market forces. Whether firms hold on to workers long after cost minimization dictates their dismissal, or employment is granted for life, group obligation thwarts any possibility of maximizing shareholders' profits by adjusting labor employed as business situations change.

The Uniquely Japanese Way

Another perspective is to recognize that the Japanese economic system has its own distinct method for determining the terms of transactions in addition to those familiar in the West: consensus building. It sacrifices competitive efficiency for group security. Input and output prices are prevented from optimally allocating labor and other inputs to alternative use among occupations and firms due to barriers like lifetime employment, whereas surplus inventories aren't rapidly liquidated because of collusive price fixing. As the international community frequently alleges, Japanese firms sell their excess inventories abroad at excessive discounts.

Japanese firms create jobs that shouldn't exist, and resist dismissals by making internal accommodations. Japanese enterprises expect the state to do whatever is required to bolster aggregate effective demand, and promote steady long-term growth. But the institutionalization of these practices has costs. It erodes national financial stability, perpetuates anticompetitive inefficiencies and encourages their intensification, transforming problems of cyclical adaptation into ones of gradual system degeneration.

The main features of Japan's communalist brand of managed market are that the system is work intensive, accommodative, administratively regulated, macro-economically stable, and moderately egalitarian, creating a high standard of living and social welfare with little crime. Insofar as people take pleasure in their excessive labor, and are content with the obligations imposed by group consensus, the system is successful. Many Japanese scholars argue that their economy is as, or more efficient than the Western competitive ideal because it harnesses the power of communalism to mobilize effort, mitigate labor management conflict, and class antagonisms; to nurture and accumulate team knowledge, concentrate team attention on quality, modernization and innovation; to coordinate and plan in an environment of trust (in teams, associations of keiretsu cross shareholding firms, other business associations like the keidanren, and the government; to take stakeholder interests directly into account; to risk share, and to regulate specific and aggregate effective demand.

But this exaggerates its benefits. Communalism makes the Japanese under-productive, compels them to overwork, and imposes group obligations that diminish the quality of their existence. It perpetuates anticompetitive inefficiencies and saps the economy's long-term vigor.

The Future

The costs of Japan's communally managed markets in terms of the nation's economic growth rate are not small. This is evident from Japan's waning economic vitality. Communal consensus building at all levels isn't enough to assure efficiency because the consultative process doesn't take methodical account of competitive alternatives, and insider control frees decision makers from competitive market discipline. Although Japan does have many commonalities with the American and Continental European managed market systems, it is unique. Communalism enables the Japanese to work harder, and enjoy it more, with lower moral hazard, less crime and greater egalitarianism and social welfare than its Western rivals. These are formidable advantages. But it also shelters economic activity of all types from market competition, diminishing efficiency. Japan's economic culture seems coded to underperform the growth potential of the American system, even though it provides greater communal well-being.

This is Japan, and Japan's future is tied to what it is. There is currently little likelihood that Japan will experience again the sort of rapid economic growth of the post–World War II period. Instead, in the late 1980s, the dynamism went out of the Japanese economy as a whole and it is not likely to reemerge.

Liberalization of the Japanese economy in the direction of the Western model might change this for the better, but that is not certain. It would make matters worse should aggressive individualism disorient communal coordination and erode the work ethic. There are signs that today's limited Americanization in Japan is generating both these disadvantages, and is therefore provoking a backlash. Should transformation occur in the Japanese economic culture, it will be slow and rocky.

European Union

How Europe's Economic Culture Keeps It Behind

If economic culture didn't matter, there should be little difference in the economic performance of America and Western Europe. Both continents share common values, aspirations, and market institutions. But the economic performance of the European Community has lagged that of America for a decade, and is almost certain to continue to do so. The reasons lie deep in the economic culture of the major European nations.

Europe and America are much alike; America is Europe's renegade child. Of course, the vagaries of history greatly affect the details, but the factors that divide Europe and America are on the wane. And although Europe for a time was enthralled by socialism, liberalization is eroding many of the protectionist institutions that still pervade the Continent. To many observers, the economic systems of America and Europe seem destined to converge ever more closely.

The discordant element is postwar economic performance. West European per capita GDP growth, particularly in Continental Europe (excluding the United Kingdom which has a very different economic culture and to which we will turn later) has been decelerating for decades, despite ample opportunities for technological catchup. Real living standards in Europe have doubled since 1970, but are less than two-thirds of the U.S. level and are falling further behind.[15] Instead of converging, they are diverging.

Despite numerous formal similarities, the market systems on the opposite shores of the Atlantic are generating strikingly different outcomes. This is due to two factors. Western Europe is more collectivist and leisure-oriented than the United States. Its managed market system places greater emphasis on social economic activity and communitarian traditions that often take precedence over work effort and competition. In the Continental European version of the idea of the West personal effort, especially entrepreneurship is restricted whenever it conflicts with collective welfare, and the law is intended to protect society more than individual initiative. Compared to the United States, the dominant European economic culture indulges idleness and dependency, and favors egalitarianism.

Income creation is less firmly equated with success than in America. Social approval isn't correlated as strongly with affluence, and the rich are esteemed for their business acumen only when their activities are harmonized with social welfare. This attitude reflects Europe's elitist traditions, both aristocratic and socialist, which require the benevolent state to suppress excessive individualism and competitive market access. Competition and self-seeking aren't ends in themselves, and need to be subordinated to cartels and corporatist management for the greater good. Consumer liberalism is encouraged insofar as it helps maintain high levels of activity, but compared with America is bounded both by social concerns and the priority of leisure.

Few are immune from this cultural pressure. Materialism is derided, and work for its own sake is viewed as an American disease. Creativity is prized above commercialism; life quality is prized above consumerism.

In this economic culture, management behaves differently than it would in America. "The European way of managing is different," Philippe Camus, head of the European Aeronautics Defense and Space Co. told a reporter. "We have to pay much more to reduce headcount so we are careful when hiring and do more subcontracting."[16] Similarly, there are fewer layoffs, and little outsourcing to cut headcount – to avoid hiring yes, but to cut staff, no. European companies rely less on the flexibility of the labor market, and thereby relinquish certain efficiencies in the interest of social harmony. Despite much speculation in the Anglo-Saxon press that European companies are about to become more like American firms, pursuing near-term efficiencies at the cost of social destabilization, less of this is occurring than might be expected, even today.

Europe's economic performance reflects these cultural restraints. Its productivity and GDP are high due to individualistic self-seeking, social altruism, and the state's successes in economic management. But it is lower than in America because of collectivist restrictions placed on personal and business economic freedom, strong demand for leisure, impediments to entrepreneurship, cartels and egalitarian disincentives. Continental European economic performance thus falls far short of the generally competitive ideal because democratic socialist management warps people's choices, encourages them to bend competitive rules, and government misregulation and abuse are endemic. Continental Europeans labor and consume less than if they thoughtfully optimized, and they are misemployed. The culture drives them to overestimate the utility of social democratic programs. Cartels degrade economic efficiency, and government frequently is more concerned about placating broad ideological constituencies with public money than promoting effective markets, or cost effectively providing state services. These factors explain the weakness of Continental Europe's performance compared with the competitive market ideal and the American managed market system. They illuminate some of its social failings, as well as attractive aspects of its lifestyle.

The Continental European economic system today is a social democratically managed market model which arose in the late 19th century and evolved as an attempt to reconcile private property-based individualistic business traditions with state social protection, professional alliances, managed commerce, public ownership and socialism. Individualism makes Europeans autonomous, often aggressively self-seeking, materialist, and sometimes anarchistic in the spirit of 19th century radicals like Pierre-Joseph Proudhon. Collectivism makes them dependent, security-minded, and submissive to group authority and obligation. These contradictory tendencies have been partially harmonized over the centuries through the evolution of corporatism, a managed market system regulated by state elites in cooperation with various private associations referred to generically as "corporations. They include guilds, professional organizations, trade unions, business corporations, and affiliated cartels. Their role is to discipline those under their jurisdiction, while promoting mutual interest through the political process. Members do not submerge their identities in these associations, but are self interestedly loyal. Group solidarity diminishes fractiousness, promotes order, skill, enhances authority, and facilitates societal accommodation, whereas reverence for state authority allows the elites to tax the population more heavily than in America; to disregard some constituencies in favor of others, and to meddle in the marketplace. The term statist is used to describe the elite's use of state authority to control social behavior.

State elites and corporatist interest groups intervene in every aspect of economic activity. The labor market is made inefficient by government mandates, regulations, wage/price controls, and transfers that force employers to mis-hire and needlessly retain workers, fostering laxness, apathy, and early retirement. These policies are supposed to benefit everyone. Improved labor motivation, protective legislation, state contracts, and government macroeconomic regulation, including qualitative barriers to foreign competition, improve corporate profits. Enhanced job security, conditions of labor, compensation (including social transfers), and stakeholder participation benefit workers.

All is give and take. In return for state assistance, Continental European firms agree to hiring quotas, restrictions on hours of employment, jurisdictional and seniority preferences. They provide generous paid vacations, maternity, sickness, and compassionate leaves. They shun layoffs, dismissals, and offer early retirements. They accept affirmative action programs, and partially surrender managerial autonomy to worker participation. They tolerate the excess labor costs imposed by state wage fixing; heavy medical and other social insurance costs, as well as bearing the expense of fringe benefits, mandated conditions of employment, and compulsory overtime payments. In return for these benefits, and direct state social transfers, workers are supposed to loyally, skillfully, and unstintingly exert themselves for their employers, the state and society.

Continental European social democrats and corporatists recognize that these concessions may be costly. Shortened work years reduce output. Occupational, gender, and age restrictions impair efficiency. And of course excess unemployment benefits, transfers, and disciplinary restrictions depress effort and encourage free-riding. But advocates believe that corporatist solidarity, professional pride and a profound sense of civic responsibility offset these disincentives.

The same reasoning justifies state elite and corporatist intervention in other factor markets. Capital and land are all subject to rationing and regulation. New capital formation and the reallocation of existing equipment are discouraged when they threaten corporations, professions, and workers, even though this diminishes production potential and efficiency.

Likewise, corporatism subverts profit maximizing. Corporatist enterprises deploy their assets to benefit the community, not particular subgroups like shareholders, managers, unions, and the government. Members feel entitled and obliged to influence corporate policies to the detriment of outside shareholders. They subordinate returns to equity to other purposes, overcompensating themselves, and can be extremely corrupt. These distortions diminish productivity. Supply costs aren't minimized, demand isn't optimally satisfied, and new capital formation is depressed by pessimistic investor expectations.

Corporatists partially mitigate these losses by forming cartels, or using large industrial banks to manage intercorporate competition. Markets are segmented, and wages and prices regulated to benefit affiliated groups. These actions, it is claimed, promote stability and planning, creating healthy companies with deep pockets which fuel economic growth, despite the high costs of corporatist innovation, and barriers to individual entrepreneurship. Strong corporatist firms, it is said, are better positioned to finance research, develop new products, and deliver them to the market, enhancing Continental European growth prospects.

This belief is central to the corporatist vision because it implies that violations of competitive market principles are mitigated by rapid economic development. Corporations, cartels, professional associations and trade unions are able to enjoy oligopoly rents, economic security, and generous welfare benefits, without sacrificing future prosperity.

No wonder then that Continental European politicians don't fret about improved entrepreneurship, work incentives and the curtailment of the welfare state as much as they should. The elites remain convinced that they can beat rival economic systems and expand the scope of social democratic management through the European Union because corporatist managed competition allows them to excel in the long run.

The early postwar economic performance of Continental Europe surprised doubting Thomases. Whereas the continental elites talked glowingly about collectivism, the population was extremely individualistic and self-seeking, making it difficult to believe that members, and contending groups would really sacrifice for the greater good. Liberals anticipated that corporatism would diminish employment flexibility, severely impair labor productivity, reduce work participation, cause acute unemployment, and restrict exports.

They expected similar constraints on variable and fixed capital and new asset formation to impair production potential, and anticipated that inter-corporate collusion and state indicative planning would cause complacency, laziness, misinvestment and corruption. And of course, some believed that state ownership of the means of production, accounting for more than 20 percent of assets in countries like Italy in the 1950s would depress productivity, or worried that denationalization might lead to a spate of asset grabbing and asset stripping behavior of the kind which later destabilized Russia in the nineties.

Continental Europe's initial postwar successes relieved these anxieties, but despite favorable developments like the emergence of the European Union and the burgeoning of global free trade, things began to deteriorate with growth decelerating, converging toward stagnation. According to one observer, "Ironically, Germany prospered mightily by looking to the US for entrepreneurial inspiration. . . . For the last quarter century it has fallen increasingly under the spell of France and the French fantasy of a European superstate that will rival America. Precisely during this period of French hegemony, Germany has entered upon an accelerating economic decline, already relative and soon to be absolute."[17] In the transition out of the immediate post- World War II recovery, corporatist duty withered and free-riding increased as people discovered that the state would pay them not to work if they were dismissed, couldn't find a job, or chose early retirement. Unemployment rose into the double digits, persistently exceeding 20 percent in Spain for these reasons and because corporate costs of dismissal became so high that it was prohibitively expensive to keep positions staffed.

Statesmen have responded by curbing the growth of public expenditures, cutting marginal tax rates, encouraging trade union accommodation to liberalized work rules, paring some nonfunded benefits, denationalizing most industries, welcoming investment from abroad and pushing ahead with European integration, including monetary union. This triggered merger mania driving equities to astronomical heights, but failed to reaccelerate aggregate economic growth, spur entrepreneurship, establish Continental European technological leadership, reduce open and concealed involuntary unemployment, or improve rates of labor participation.

Continental Europe's leftward EU drift suggests that the elite will adhere to its established social democratic course, pro-competitive rhetoric notwithstanding. The motivations, mechanisms and institutions that govern economic action will all continue to differ importantly from those assumed in the classical tradition, creating a system where the government elite and private corporatist institutions are economically sovereign. Statist-corporatist preferences govern demand and define the sense in which the Continental European system is micro- and macro-economically controlled, providing government and corporatist elites a life of opulent privilege, with everyone striving for a secure niche.

The main effects of Continental Europe's brand of elite-guided corporatism – reconciling individualism with collectivism are evident. It has created a highly productive, but increasing effort-discouraging, pro-leisure and free-riding ethic that is not only debilitating, but is encouraging immigration by free-riders, including significant numbers of easily disgruntled Muslims.

This differs strikingly from Japan where shame-based communalism counteracts these particular growth-inhibiting tendencies. The Continental Europeans system also has a bloated public sector. Nonetheless social democracy in Continental Europe has stabilized macroeconomic fluctuations, promoted modest growth, and provided its people with a high standard of living. Insofar as Continental Europeans feel that their sacrifices are justified, the system must be considered successful. Most Continental European intellectuals argue that social democracy is more efficient than the competitive market ideal because it harnesses the power of collectivism to inspire competent effort without oppressive discipline, mitigates labor management conflict and class antagonisms. They contend that it nurtures group knowledge, concentrates corporatist attention on quality, modernization, and innovation; that it coordinates and plans in an environment of trust, takes stakeholder interests including those of the community directly into account, risk shares, regulates specific and aggregate effective demand, fostering attitudes of civic and social responsibility that promote cost-efficient delivery of private and public services.

Social Democracy is compatible with capitalism – the European experience demonstrates that. But Social Democracy isn't compatible with the American version of capitalism, one in which shareholder value maximization is the rule; a rule which forecloses balancing among the interests of stakeholder groups. In the United States, there is a primary class (shareholders) and every other interest is secondary. Out of this difference, among a few others, have emerged in recent years the more vibrant economy of America.

From a liberal perspective, statist corporatism, like Soviet communism, is inferior. It makes the Continental Europeans underproductive, encourages dependency, free-riding, and an antiwork ethic; imposes deeply resented group obligations that diminish the quality of their existence.

Moreover, they blame Continental Europe's pronounced growth retardation, and intractable double-digit unemployment and underemployment on the cumulating effects of statist-corporatist inefficiencies, including disguised protectionism, and have been urging them to abandon all anticompetitive corporatist restraints on profit seeking.

Just as in the American case, insofar as the Continental European system departs from the consumer sovereign ideals for the private and state sectors, they are largely right. Government and business collusion in both America and Continental Europe lack the capacity to socially optimize and so are more likely to harm than help. The main differences between the two are matters of emphasis. The American-managed market system stresses dynamic efficiency over social stability. It encourages labor over leisure, risk taking and entrepreneurship over security, competition over cartels, and growth over egalitarianism. As a consequence, although economic efficiency on both sides of the Atlantic is less than it could be, the Continental Europeans prefer leisure and security to affluence and sustained, rapid growth. They could abandon their system for America's, but are unlikely to do so anytime soon.

CHAPTER 8: KEY POINTS

1. The various economic cultures of nations are crucial to determining each nation's economic trajectory and they establish a framework for international cooperation and discord.
2. Unlike governmental policies, the elements of economic culture cannot be quickly altered or discarded.
3. Because no economy is fully competitive, all are "managed" and give up growth potential. But inefficiencies differ widely. Broadly speaking, the first world has mastered the art of prosperity creation, and the third world hasn't.
4. The foundations of economic advance are insecure – even in the first world – and threaten to draw every nation into crisis. The Russian debacle graphically illustrates the point, but China, Europe, Japan are also at serious risk. Even the United States isn't immune, but the likelihood of a self-defeating economic calamity is far less in America than elsewhere.
5. American economic leadership is driven by American vitality, and emerges out of the confusion and hubbub of our society. It is full of good and full of bad but always vital.

6. America possesses an income-creating economic culture in which work and fair competition come first. It epitomizes the idea of the West, the forging of social compacts that commit everyone to political and economic regimes that empower individual effort under the rule of law.

7. Of the world's large nations, the United States most closely approximates the liberal ideal by which economic efficiency and growth are maximized. Over long periods, the size of the American economy and its growth rate reflect its favorable economic culture.

8. Technology transfer makes it possible for systems of all kinds to "modernize," that is, adopt the appearance of the West . They can "walk the walk" and "talk the talk" but their cultures prevent them from being efficient. There are tall buildings in Russia, but that doesn't mean that the gap between America and Russia will narrow, not increase, in the coming decades.

NINE

Economic Disparities among Nations

THE CONSEQUENCES OF DIFFERING ECONOMIC CULTURES

Why do divergences of economic outcomes matter? They matter in three distinct areas: capabilities, exploitable grievances, and governance. Relatively affluent nations can afford stronger militaries, and have greater economic clout. Relatively poor and vulnerable states can be drawn to weapons of mass destruction, and provide fertile ground for terrorism. And authoritarian societies on the rise often are predisposed to excessive coercion because they are either intoxicated with power, or use compulsion to compensate for their inefficiency. Liberal economic theory teaches that widening inequality shouldn't cause discord because rich and poor alike can benefit from democratic free enterprise. However, divergence creates inflammatory grievances, providing incentives to alter the rules of games, played out through the fog of partisan public cultural engagement.

There are too many imponderable forces at work to precisely forecast when, where and how divergence will generate this or that conflict. However, as we said in Chapter 2, we see four coming threats to American security that are a product of these divergences. These threats are ones we can foresee and it is imperative for an American president to make the effort to see the economic component of driving each of these threats. We recognize that differing economic cultures mean considerably different economic experiences among America, Europe, Japan, China, and Russia and the rest of the world. We also include Japan here due its strong economy, military potential, and its historic animosity with China.

America and Europe are representative of the West. Japan has a unique blend of West and East that has found its way into the first world. China and Russia haven't. All five systems rely largely on markets rather than coercive central plans, but the influence of consumer demand on supply, what is called "consumer sovereignty," is much stronger in the two Western powers. Liberalization notwithstanding, China and Russia remain authoritarian-managed economies, where leaders retain control by substituting partial state ownership, government contracting and regulation for Soviet era edicts and plan directives. The efficiency of self-regulating market systems like those of America and Europe in achieving consumer sovereignty depend heavily on a well-functioning mechanism for the legal enforcement of contracts. The partially marketized authoritarian-managed systems of China and Russia by contrast subordinate the rule of contract law to the goals of the ruling elite.

The European economic system is similar to ours, differing primarily in the attitude of communities and the state toward individual economic freedom and egalitarianism. Elites in the aristocratic tradition perceive themselves as guardians of corporatist interests (workers, peasants, artisan, professionals, and business). They conceive their task as private and governmental leaders to fashion customs and laws that provide secure employment and stable income for all, even if this bridles competition. These cultural preferences have the effect of depressing labor effort, repressing entrepreneurship, impairing factor mobility, degrading the responsiveness of supply to consumer demand through the rationing of public services, and tilting the distribution of privilege toward the governing elites; all infringements of the competitive ideal incurred in the pursuit of social justice and egalitarianism. The economic growth of the European welfare state system has been gradually deteriorating, raising the possibility that it will fall further and further behind the American standard, and be eclipsed by the second world power – China.

Japan departs still further from the Western paradigm. Although it can be argued that the Japanese economy is more open than Europe's and America's because government programs, regulations, and transfers as shares of GDP are half theirs, lean government in Japan only means that restrictions on the economic freedom of the individual imposed elsewhere by government is done in Japan by communal consensus building. The first priority for Japanese of all walks of life isn't what it is in America: individualistic self-seeking, entrepreneurship, equal opportunity, fair competition, and wealth building under the rule of law. In Japan first priority is given to doing whatever is required to assure the well-being of the group to which an individual belongs. One way to appreciate the chasm between individualistic and Japanese communal rules and processes is to compare how they respond to external shocks. Americans and Europeans react first and foremost to price and profit signals, using custom and state regulations in varying degrees to cushion these adjustments. The Japanese by contrast won't do anything until the group reaches a consensus, placing insider harmony over outsider market responsiveness. This thousand-year-old strategy of the Japanese is hazardous today because it insulates insiders from the challenges of progress-generating competition. The Japanese compensate for their insularity with a strategy of aggressive exporting, domestic price and market share-fixing, and insider obligation and burden sharing. As in Europe, their version of managed competition performed better than advocates of free enterprise imagined likely, but the stresses are beginning to take their toll, partly due to intrinsic communalist inefficiency, and partly to the disorienting onslaught of American inspired liberalization.

The waning of the Japanese economic miracle stands strikingly in contrast to China's recent meteoric success. The Chinese system is an exotic blend combining elements of Western market-based wealth building, but without a rule of law; and with socialist ownership of the means of production, indigenous authoritarianism, Communist regulation, and a segmented development strategy similar to Japan's in that it is externally competitive, and internally protectionist but different in welcoming direct foreign investment. The model is more closed than the first world; more open than many third world rivals, and its concentration of market activities in the export sector makes it asymmetric. Generically, it is a partially marketized variant of a Soviet style command system where rulers' preferences take precedence over consumer sovereignty. The Communist Party through its control over state-owned enterprises, resources, especially land, and the instruments of state programming, leasing and regulation, micro- and macro-economically directs and shapes most aspects of employment, production, finance, distribution, and income transfers. But it also allows peasants, small private businesses, professionals, managers, and foreign joint venturers more autonomy than previously in China when most activities were tightly regulated and more restrictively planned. At this point, it is difficult to assess whether Deng Xiaoping's authoritarian leasing market system will fare any better than the Soviet model in the very long run because of intrinsic problems of authoritarian inefficiency, incentives, and moral hazards. As long as the Communist Party directs market competition and state ownership and leasing persist, Chinese managers will be less effectively incentivized to seek profits for their firms than their Western counterparts, and will be more tempted by corruption in a country that rejects a rule of law. They will underperform and be enticed into a myriad of schemes that enrich them at the expense of the nation. The danger is widely recognized in China, but no solution is in sight without radical transitions that neither the leadership nor the population as a whole seems to desire.

The potential for catastrophe that the Chinese have thus far avoided is vividly illustrated by Boris Yeltsin's experience in Russia. Because China reorganized its economy after the Communist conquest on the Soviet model, and before that both relied on imperial rent-granting, many elements of the Chinese and Russian models are virtually the same. They share in common a legacy of state ownership of the means of production, rule by executive decree, a socialist heritage, an elaborate administrative regulatory mechanism, and more recently partial marketization including partial privatization, negotiated price and wage setting, managerial autonomy and the encouragement of entrepreneurship, all without a rule of law. They differ in only three respects. The Chinese have (1) retained the monopoly of Communist Party power, and with it a commitment to rapid, state-led economic development; (2) preserved state industrial ownership, and Communist Party supervision of individual enterprises; and (3) adopted a strategy using industrial exports to expedite its integration into the global economy.

Yeltsin did the opposite in Russia. By destroying Communist Party power without installing an alternative disciplinary mechanism, privatizing helter-skelter, and shunning globalization, he opened up a Pandora's box of antiproductive corruption. Managers, the Russian Mafia, and the political and security elites turned their energies away from production to predatory self-enrichment. As a consequence, Russian markets lack financial and distributive efficiency, suppress productive activity, and thwart any constructive commands issued by the leadership. The economic mechanism established during the Yeltsin years and continuing under Putin exemplifies an authoritarian market system run amok.

THE STATISTICAL RECORD

Tracking the comparative performance of the world economy is a dark art. Data are often dubious, incomplete, and contradictory. Adjustments are required, but they are contestable, and difficult to independently scrutinize. And even if these concerns are set aside, results are sensitive to weights employed for valuation and index aggregation. As a consequence, there is no single truth, only a multitude of competing estimates. Nonetheless, a new study undertaken by Angus Maddison at the OECD, pricing GDP in 1990 American dollars for most of the planet from the year 1 A.D. to the present provides a valuable framework for parsing past and future reconfigurations of global wealth and power.

Table 9.1. *Reconfiguration of Relative Living
Standards: China and West Europe, 1–2001 AD
(1990 international Geary-Khamis dollars)*

Year	China	West Europe
1	450	450
1000	450	400
1300	600	593
1400	600	676
1500	600	771
1820	600	1,204
1913	552	3,458
1950	439	4,579
2001	3,583	19,256

Source: Angus Maddison, ***The World Economy: Historical Statistics***, OECD, Paris, 2003, p. 249.

Maddison's bimillennial estimates of Chinese and West European living
standards illustrates the principle. Table 9.1 reveals that per capita income
was identical in both areas at the dawn of the Christian era. The figure
in 1 A.D. was $450, slightly higher than Chad in 2001.[1] There was little
change for the next thirteen-hundred years either in parities or levels. But
the West began to gradually advance, while China languished during the
next half millennium. By 1820, living standards in West Europe were double
those in China, reflecting the gains reaped during the first phase of the
industrial revolution. Thereafter, the disparity accelerated, peaking in 1950
at more than 10 to 1. Living standards had dectupled in West Europe over
the millennia, but actually declined absolutely in China, culminating in an
epochal reconfiguration of global wealth and power. The process of reversal,
recovering lost ground only appears to have begun with the installation of
a radically new economic system. During the communist era, the disparity
narrowed to 5 to 1, mostly in the post-Mao period (Table 9.3)

Of course, it can be argued that credit for China's reversal of fortune under
the communists is attributable to its relative backwardness rather than the
market communist mechanism crafted by Deng Xiaoping, but not only had
the Middle Kingdom failed to capitalize on this factor for the preceding 650
years, much of the less developed world languished or lost ground 1913–
2001. Table 9.2 presents the evidence. It shows American per capita income
pacing the world average, while Latin America and Africa fall increasingly
behind. Clearly, Communist China after Mao found a formula that many

Table 9.2. *Global Economic Divergence 1913–2001 Per Capita GDP Growth (compound annual rates: percent)*

	1913–50	1950–73	1973–2001
World	0.9	2.9	1.4
United States	1.6	2.5	1.9
Latin America	1.4	2.6	0.9
Africa	0.9	2.9	1.4

Source: Angus Maddison, **The World Economy: Historical Statistics**, OECD, Paris, 2003, p. 263.

Table 9.3. *Centrally Planned Communist Growth Spurts and Decay (Per capita GDP growth, percent)*

	1928–40	1950–73	1973–1991	1991–1998
USSR	3.8	3.3	0	−7.5
Eastern Europe	–	3.8	−0.2	1.8
China	–	2.9	4.8	7.0

Source: Angus Maddison, **The World Economy: Historical Statistics**, OECD, Paris, 2003, pp. 100–1, 184.

other similarly situated less developed nations growing at or below the global average did not.

The positive Chinese communist growth experience up to the start of Mao's "cultural revolution," 1950–1966 also deserves attention because it wasn't unique. Other communist regimes relying on natural economic, command planning principles displayed similar surges, which ultimately petered out. What makes the Chinese case distinctive, is a silver lining. The revulsion occasioned by the horrors of the cultural revolution enabled Deng Xiaoping to gradually dismantle the Stalinist model, and transition to Beijing's variant of market socialism.[2] The statistics in Table 9.3 tell the tale. Both the USSR and Eastern Europe start with a bang and end with a whimper. Rapid growth in the initial phase is followed by stagnation, and in the case of the USSR culminates in hyper depression. China alone escapes the Soviet Union's grim fate by adopting an alternative non-Western strategy for economic modernization.

The USSR's failure goes well beyond the deficiencies of Stalin's natural economic system. It is rooted in Russia's history. Per capita GDP growth not only lagged America's and West Europe's 1917–2001 but was subpar for a

Table 9.4. *Inferior Russian Economic Performance 1000–2001 AD (Per capita GDP growth, percent)*

YEARS	Former USSR	United States	West Europe	Japan
1000–1500	0.04	–	0.13	0.03
1500–1820	0.10	0.36	0.14	0.09
1820–1870	0.63	1.34	0.98	0.19
1870–1913	1.06	1.82	1.33	1.48
1913–1950	1.76	1.61	0.76	0.88
1950–1973	3.35	2.45	4.05	8.06
1973–2001	−0.96	1.86	1.88	2.14

Source: Angus Maddison, ***The World Economy: Historical Statistics***, OECD, Paris, 2003, p. 263.

thousand years. Table 9.4 offers evidence. It reveals that except for the mixed results 1913–1973, which were soon disastrously reversed, the former USSR operating in the tsarist-like mode has been persistently inferior. The cost of this deficiency is manifested dramatically in the measures of comparative size reported in Tables 9.5 and 9.6. They show the USSR living standard falling from 28.4 to 16.6 percent of America's from 1917 to 2001, despite the purported advantages of backwardness. The corresponding decline for Russia 1973 to 2001 is from 39.4 to 19.4 percent. These figures probably overstate Russia's standing throughout because the numbers don't capture data falsification, the qualitative inferiority of Russia's goods and services, and forced substitution.[3] Nonetheless, the trends themselves are sufficiently powerful to demonstrate the deficiency of the Russian model, and serve as harbingers of more bad times to come.

The Japanese experience is edifying in a different way. It suggests that even excellent non-Western systems which outshine democratic free enterprise in hard work, team play, growth, and social justice don't have staying power in the global rivalry for wealth and power. Table 9.4 shows Japan's living standard gaining on West Europe throughout the period 1870 to 2001, and the United States 1950–2001. But the devitalization after 1973 is pronounced, worsening after 1990. Japanese living standards improved 0.9 percent per annum 1990–2001; only 0.2 percent per annum 1996–2001, and have virtually ceased growing thereafter. Top Japanese policy makers and academics moreover are pessimistic. Tadakatsu Sano, former vice chairman of METI, for example, has voiced his concern that living standards in Japan might not improve until population growth revives around 2050.[4] The same pattern moreover has arisen in advanced Sino systems like Hong Kong and

Table 9.5. *Comparative Size Estimates USSR and the United States 1917–2001 (billion 1990 international Geary-Khamis dollars and percent)*

	GDP			Per Capita GDP		
	US	USSR	USSR/US	US	USSR	USSR/US
1917	544.8	232.4	42.6	5,248	1,458	28.4
1928	794.7	231.9	29.9	6,569	1,370	20.9
1955	1,898.1	648.0	35.8	10,897	2,841	26.1
1970	3,801.9	1,351.8	43.9	15,030	5,575	37.1
1989	5,703.5	2,037.5	35.7	23,059	7,098	30.8
1991	5,775.9	1,863.5	32.3	22,785	6,409	28.1
1998	7,349.9	1,124.9	15.3	26,619	3,861	14.5
2001	7,965.8	1,343.2	16.9	27,948	4,626	16.6

Note: The Geary-Khamis approach (named for R. S. Geary and S. H. Khamis) is a method for multilateralizing (multi-national index weighting) that exhibits transitivity and other desirable properties. It was used by Kravis, Heston and Summers as a method for aggregating ICP results available at the basic heading level. Maddison uses PPPs of this type for seventy countries, representing 93.7 percent of world GDP in 1990. Also, the figure for USSR per capita GDP for 1917, actually refers to 1913, and figures 1992–2001 pertain as indicated to the former USSR. Data on Russia are also available but don't alter the big picture.

Sources: Angus Maddison, **The World Economy: Historical Statistics**, OECD, Paris, 2003, pp. 84–89, 98–101.

Table 9.6. *Comparative Size Estimates Russia and the United States 1973–2001 (billion 1990 international Geary-Khamis dollars and percent)*

	GDP			Per Capita GDP		
	US	Russia	Russia/US	US	Russia	Russia/US
1973	3,536.6	872.5	24.6	16,689	6,582	39.4
1991	5,775.9	1,094.0	18.9	22,785	7,370	32.3
1998	7,349.9	655.4	8.9	26,619	4,459	16.8
2001	7,965.8	790.6	9.9	27,948	5,435	19.4

Source: Angus Maddison, **The World Economy: Historical Statistics**, OECD, Paris, 2003, pp. 89, and 111.

Singapore, where per capita GDP 1996–2001 rose 0.2 and 1.0 percent per annum respectively, with persistent sluggishness through 2004.[5] The Asian financial crisis of 1998, and Hong Kong reversion to China are contributory factors, but the possibility of a systemic climacteric cannot be excluded on either theoretical or statistical grounds.

Table 9.7. *Comparative Size Estimates Per Capita GDP 1913–2001*
(America = 100)

	West Europe	USSR	Japan	China	World
1913	65.2	28.1	26.2	10.4	28.8
1950	47.9	29.7	20.1	4.6	22.1
1973	68.4	36.3	68.5	5.0	24.5
1990	68.8	29.6	80.9	8.0	22.2
2001	68.8	16.6	74.0	12.8	21.6

Note: West Europe includes twenty-nine nations in Maddison's classification.
Source: Angus Maddison, **The World Economy: Historical Statistics**, OECD,
Paris, 2003, pp. 69, 89, 101, 184, 234, and 262.

Table 9.8. *Reconfiguration of Global Living Standards 2000–2050 (1990*
international Geary-Khamis dollars)

	America	West Europe	Russia	Japan	China
2000	28,129	19,002	5,157	20,683	3,425
2010	33,821	20,845	7,135	22,689	6,221
2020	40,666	22,867	8,011	24,890	11,300
2030	48,895	25,085	8,788	27,304	20,525
2040	58,789	27,518	9,640	29,952	24,679
2050	70,687	30,187	10,575	32,857	29,679

Sources: Angus Maddison, **The World Economy: Historical Statistics**, OECD, Paris,
2003, pp. 89, 111, 184, 234, 263.
Assumed growth rates: America 1.86 (2000–2050); West Europe and Japan 0.93 (2000–
2050); Russia 3.3 (2000–2011) and 0.93 (2011–2050); and China 6.15 (2000–2030) and
1.86 (2030–2050).

Likewise, the evidence supports the hypothesis that the rate of advance
of EU area living standards is decelerating despite liberalization, monetary
union, and the advantages of relative backwardness. America has outpaced
the EU, particularly Germany, France and Italy during the past fifteen years
as the benefits of postwar reconstruction waned, and momentum suggests a
continuation of the trend.[6] Not only have the antientrepreneurial and anticompetitive aspects of West European social democracy caused America's
lead in living standards to be maintained 1913–2001, but that advantage seems poised to significantly widen. The comparative size statistics in
Table 9.7 show that West Europe has been unable to gain ground on America
since 1973. And if the United Kingdom and Ireland are excluded because
they are better classified as part of the Anglo-American model, then the
position of Continental Europe has eroded. The deterioration of the former

Table 9.9. *Comparative Living Standard Size Projections 2000–2050 (America = 100; percent)*

	West Europe	Russia	Japan	China
2000	67.6	18.3	73.5	12.2
2010	61.6	21.1	67.1	18.4
2020	56.2	19.7	61.2	27.8
2030	51.3	17.8	55.8	42.0
2040	46.8	16.4	50.9	42.0
2050	42.7	15.0	46.5	42.0

Source: Table 9.8.

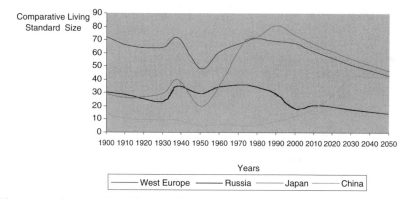

Figure 9.1. Comparative Living Standard Size Projections 1900–2050 (America = 100: percent)

USSR and Japan is unmistakable, as is the long term trend for the world as a whole. Apparently, when all is said and done, systems really matter and their impact is about to become more pronounced.

Projections from 2000 to 2050 displayed in Tables 9.8 and 9.9 (Figure 9.1) provide some guidance about how the reconfiguration of wealth and power in the first half of the twenty-first century are likely to unfold. These estimates are theory-normed extrapolations, informed by historical trends. The priors that drive the results are as follows. We assume that American per capita income grows to mid century at the 1973–2001 mean; and that West Europe and Japan grow at half this rate, as they have in recent years. We assume further that Russia grows at the robust postwar USSR rate 1950–1973 until it reattains the Soviet living standard in 1991, and then paces West Europe and Japan, yielding better long term results than those achieved by the USSR. Finally, we assume that China chugs along at the stellar rates

Table 9.10. *Reconfiguration of Global GDP 2000–2050 (billion 1990 international Geary-Khamis dollars)*

	America	West Europe	Russia	Japan	China
2000	7,941	7,430	791	2,669	4,330
2010	10,265	8,708	1,063	2,970	8,614
2020	13,269	10,206	1,163	3,322	17,136
2030	17,151	11,962	1,232	3,708	34,088
2040	22,170	14,029	1,329	4,136	44,842
2050	28,658	16,431	1,421	4,614	58,989

Source: Angus Maddison, *The World Economy: Historical Statistics*, OECD, Paris, 2003, pp. 45, 57, 83, 86, 109, 111, 164, 174.

Assumed growth rates: GDP per capita: America 1.86 (2000–2050); West Europe and Japan 0.93 (2000–2005); Russia 3.3 (2000–2011) and 0.93 (2011–2050); and China 6.15 (2000–2030) and 1.86 (2030–2050) Population growth (extrapolated rates 1994–2003): America 0.98 (2000–2050); West Europe 0.23 (2000–2050); Russia −0.25 (2000–2050); Japan 0.17 (2000–2050); and China 0.91 (2000–2050).

Composite: America 2.6 (2000–2050); West Europe 1.16 (2000–2050); Russia 3.0 (2000–2011) and 0.67 (2011–2050); Japan 1.1 (2000–2050), and China 7.12 (2000–2030) and 2.78 (2030–2050).

recorded 1990–2001 for another three decades, when diminishing returns to its asymmetric overtrading strategy forestall further catch up. After 2021, China moves forward stride for stride with America.

At the outset of the third millennium America's GDP is 6 percent greater than the EU's, dectuple Russia's, treble Japan's and double China's. Although, China's living standard is only 12 percent of America's, its enormous population generates GDP half America's and Europe's and 50 percent higher than Japan's, making Beijing an important economic and geostrategic player despite its low per capita income. In just 10 years from now (2015), China's GDP overtakes America's, becoming twice as large in 2030. Its output at this date is dectuple Japan's and twenty times larger that Russia's, making it the dominant actor in the Asia Pacific. By assumption, China paces America thereafter, but the EU, Russia and Japan continue losing ground to both, so that midway through the twenty-first century there are only two global economic superpowers, America and China. Europe's GDP in 2050 is a distant third, with America and China between them accounting for more than 60 percent of global GDP, assuming the persistence of the long growth trend 1973–2001 in other countries (Tables 9.10, 9.11, and Figure 9.2).

Needless to say, these results are driven by systemic assumptions, and historical trends drawn from the OECD's series. They may be misleading on both accounts, and are subject to chaos theoretic shocks. Wars,

Table 9.11. *Comparative GDP Size Projections 2000–2050*
(America = 100; percent)

	West Europe	Russia	Japan	China
2000	93.6	10.0	33.6	54.5
2010	84.8	10.4	28.9	83.9
2020	76.9	8.8	25.0	129.1
2030	69.7	7.1	21.6	198.8
2040	63.2	5.8	18.7	202.3
2050	57.3	5.0	16.1	205.8

Source: Table 9.10.

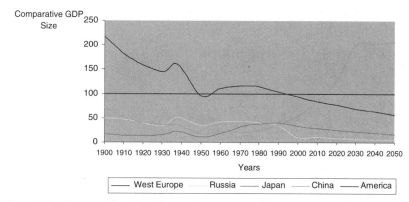

Figure 9.2. Comparative GDP Size Projections 1900–2050 (America = 100: percent)

pestilence, reform, and cultural change could all affect outcomes, and it should be stressed that aspects of Maddison's series are sensitive to opaque and controversial adjustments. Table 9.12 contrasts comparative dollars purchasing power parity GDP size estimates compiled by Abram Bergson, the doyen of Soviet studies, and the CIA derived from official Soviet statistics with Maddison's estimates. The former indicate that the USSR improved its position vis-à-vis America by nearly a factor of three under communism, judged from the benchmark of GDP, while Maddison's statistics imply a 16 percent deterioration. Because all estimates are ultimately grounded in official Soviet statistics (there are no alternatives), it is apparent that discretionary adjustments made are anything but trivial.[7] The same miasma affects Chinese GDP statistics. Maddison's numbers greatly discount Maoist data, which remain official, but current data are largely accepted, as are contemporary Russian statistics that continue to be strewn with contradictions.

Table 9.12. *Comparative GDP Size Estimates USSR and US: 1917–89 (dollar PPP, various bases, percent)*

	Bergson/CIA	Maddison
1917	23.4	44.9
1928	20.9	30.0
1955	45.2	35.8
1970	62.9	43.9
1989	67.0	37.7

Source: Steven Rosefielde and Stefan Hedlund, *Russia After 1984: Wrestling with Westernization*, Cambridge University Press, London, 2007, Chapter 5, note 15. The underlying sources are Abram Bergson, *Productivity and the Social System – The USSR and the West*, Harvard University Press, Cambridge, 1978, Table 8.1, pp. 120–21, and Steven Rosefielde, *Efficiency and the Economic Recovery Potential of Russia*, Ashgate, Aldershot, 1998, Table S.1. Also see Angus Maddison, *The World Economy: Historical Statistics*, OECD, Paris, 2003, pp. 85–86, 98–99.

These adjustments explain why Maddison's results and similar independent long term historical calculations by the World Bank, United Nations, and the U.S. government[8] differ from common perceptions. The annual data that inform (misinform?) contemporaneous policy debates seldom look anything like the reconstructed series. Close analysis indicates that Bergson's calculations for the early period are more nearly correct, and that Maddison's postwar figures are better, but whatever the truth, caution is clearly in order when trying to gauge the future through the fog of biased authoritarian state statistics, and public cultural influenced long terms adjustments. Masters of illusion must operate with the best data at their disposal, warts and all, but remain wary.

THE INCREASING GAP BETWEEN DEVELOPED AND UNDERDEVELOPED NATIONS

Many people hope that today's technological revolution will raise productivity and living standards all over the globe, and it would be wonderful if that would happen. But it isn't likely because some cultures and systems are more receptive than others and can make disproportionate gains by exerting market power. The United States with its strong entrepreneurial tradition will fare best, and more advanced countries will benefit much more than Russia and the Third World. Only China and other states in its orbit appear to be capable of rapidly catching up to the developed west. As a consequence while today's rich get richer and poor poorer, China will emerge as a new superpower. Since countries are growing at different long-term rates with major impacts on national power, the United States and China seem destined to be tomorrow's dominant superpowers, whereas other nations underperform. From different economic performance is emerging bitter rivalries among the nations for influence and power.

President Kennedy told us that a rising tide lifts all boats – the point being that in an improving economy some will do better than others, but if all are doing somewhat better, then resentments and deprivation will be muted. Many observers presume that this is what is happening in today's world. But it is not. In fact, the rise of the tide is slowing – that is the economic growth rate of the world has been steadily slowing for decades – and for many nations the tide is already running out – that is, absolute economic declines are significant. In this environment, turbulence in international relations is increasing rapidly.

During the past forty years as global economic growth has decelerated, the gap between rich and poor has widened generally, with China and the tigers of southeast Asia being a major exception. China has emerged as a potential future nuclear superpower, the Soviet Union's nuclear arsenal has been vested in less stable hands, and economic and political rivalries remain as intense as ever, partly concealed behind a veil of diplomatic smiles. These developments, together with nuclear proliferation, have called into question the adequacy of MAD and arms control as multinational nuclear deterrents, raising the specter that reliance on MAD and arms control won't be enough to deter nuclear war, and establishing the need for Strategic Independence.

Why does the gap between rich and poor widen? Because the rich have very complex socioeconomic systems (economic cultures) that operate with enough effectiveness that economic development can proceed. If this weren't so, globalism would have spurred economic convergence (as the mythology of our public culture insists), not the divergence that shows itself in economic data and that reflects itself in the political controversies of the world.

The first quarter of the twenty-first century is most likely to be a period of global destabilization characterized by slow economic growth and a radical reconfiguration of wealth and power as some nations fare better than others.

CHAPTER 9: KEY POINTS

1. The world's overall rate of economic growth has long been declining and has not been reversed by the technological revolution.

2. The worldwide triumph of the ideology of markets has not resulted in improving living standards for much of the world's population, nor in improving growth rates for many nations.
3. In consequence, those nations that can't keep up are not merely falling behind, they are in real decline into increasing misery, creating a world environment which is not conducive to peace.
4. The last decade has shown us the operation of the world's economies in the context of an ideology of free markets and the information era. Because this is the likely context of the next two to three decades, we are able to forecast economic performance for major nations for twenty-five years ahead.
5. The United States will grow moderately; Japan, Europe, and Russia will crawl ahead as well; China will grow rapidly.
6. By 2025, China's economy will exceed that of the United States in size.
7. Today's underdeveloped countries including Russia will generally fall further and further behind.
8. The changes forecast here are certain to roil international relations, especially in the Asia Pacific, where the interests of Russia, China, America, Japan, and Korea clash.

TEN

Geopolitical Aspirations of the Nations

We watch today the military buildups of the great powers and wonder: What are the aspirations which the buildups are intended to further? National leaders explain them as necessary to their defense, but neither Russia nor China is directly threatened (though the declared geopolitical interests of both, particularly the Russians are being steadily infringed by the western powers and China).

NATIONALIST FERVOR IN CHINA

China's economy is improving rapidly and it is more and more our trade partner. But it is also highly nationalistic and is arming steadily. China need not be our enemy, but it is not entirely in our power to avoid a conflict should Chinese intentions or the flow of events so determine. China already can target our West Coast cities with nuclear missiles, and is modernizing and enlarging its strategic missile capability so that in a few years Chinese missiles will be able to hit all of our country. Then the military situation between America and China will be very different than it is today, and to our detriment.

CHINESE–AMERICAN RIVALRY

"Now, it could happen that China becomes our enemy," Henry Kissinger told a reporter. "But it is not foreordained. And it should not happen as a result of our actions."[1] This seemingly innocuous principle is in fact potentially misleading, because it implies that we may have the ability to avoid a conflict with China if only we act in a friendly matter toward it. But China is certain to become our enemy if China retains an authoritarian government with its current ambitions for Taiwan and control of the South China

Sea. And in this situation we risk much by treating a likely enemy as a friend.

There is much more going on with regard to China – repeated military incidents, military discussions on and off, U.S. discussions with India about "destabilization" in Asia, which means what to do about China – than the press is reporting.

China's previous foreign policy (beginning in 1954) was "the five principles of peaceful coexistence." Now the five principles have been quietly abandoned in favor of asserting Chinese interests.[2]

"Beijing perceived," according to David Shambaugh, one of America's most careful students of Chinese military affairs, ". . . a new propensity on the part of the United States . . . to intervene in regional conflicts, under the pretext of 'humanitarian intervention' for the purposes of extending and consolidating American global 'hegemony' and domination."[3]

China dismisses as not worthy of discussion the notion that the United States is intervening for humanitarian purposes in any regional conflict including those in Africa and Eastern Europe. President Bush's shift to self-defense of America instead of humanitarianism – although it's also still cited – as a justification for American intervention in Afghanistan and Iraq is not accepted by China either. Whether for defense or aggrandizement, the US is attempting to dominate the globe, in the Chinese view. All non-geopolitical explanations offered by the United States are treated as subterfuges, and given no publicity or discussion in China. Facing this, the United States is engaged in a geopolitical contest with China no matter what our real motives might be. They are irrelevant – dismissed by our rival as meaningless.

Looking at current events through Chinese eyes gives a very different perception to an American of what is going on. Interestingly, Shambaugh calls the Chinese refusal to accord any motivations to the United States except geo-political ones "simplicity" on the part of the Chinese.[4] But in ascribing other motives to the United States than geopolitical ones, he is possibly the simple one and is merely caught up in our own propaganda.

The current perception of U.S. motives represents a major change from China's previous perception – the late Deng Xiaoping's "1985 pronouncement that the threat of war was on the decline, that the global system was moving toward multipolarity, and that all countries sought 'peace and development.'"[5] China now perceives itself to be "facing a United States bent on global dominance and the permanent separation of Taiwan from China."[6] China sees the U.S. presence in Central Asia "as an American strategy of encircling China."[7] Perhaps the Chinese really feel threatened by America; perhaps they find it convenient now to pretend as if they feel threatened.

Whether in response to fear of the United States or in support of its own ambitions, or as a result of both, China is enlarging its already substantial conventional military forces. "Military training has become mandatory for all Chinese middle school, high school and university students."[8] This is not the action of a country fully committed to peace; nor is the modernization of its nuclear missile capability, which we will examine later in this chapter.

"That the PLA [People's Liberation Army] will grow more powerful is not in question . . . the consequences . . . truly involve questions of the global balance of power, war and peace."[9]

China's growing apprehensiveness (whether real or pretense in the minds of its leaders) need not be a threat to America. But it may be, and we are not able to control which way it turns. We can influence it, but we can't determine it, and the impact of any influence we attempt to exert on the Chinese may be difficult to predict. For example, if we are assertive, the Chinese will find their fears confirmed. If, in contrast, we are accommodative, the Chinese government may view that as evidence of weakness rather than a desire to avoid conflict. So the controversy now beginning in America about how to deal with China is somewhat off the mark. We must both be friendly and cautious.

The author of a history of the emergence of American expansion at the turn of the twentieth century has referred the "American nationalism that had grown from the rich soil of economic success."[10] The same phrase could as appropriately be applied to the growth of British and German imperialism in the nineteenth century – both had grown from the rich soil of economic success, and is likely to be applicable to China as well.

This issue has been at the center of the discussion in the west about China for about a decade. Those who pay attention to history worry about Chinese nationalism and about China seeking a return to its dominance in the Far East of centuries ago. Others who are more in tune to our public culture dismiss the notion that China's increasing economic success could be anything less than a blessing for all humanity. They are convinced that China is no threat so long as we do not offend or frighten it. They are sure that China's government is now stable; they explain away China's bloody past by saying that China has always had an emperor; that Mao was merely a bloody one; and they conclude that the Chinese don't want another. It follows that the current government will liberalize to avoid the emergence of another bloody "emperor." The current government is firm but not frenzied, they insist, so it will be tolerated if not loved by the Chinese people. And China is gaining greatly in the peaceful expansion of world trade. It's already a magnet for manufacturing from the world over. China therefore is making rapid economic and political progress and has no reason to resort to militarism or to provoke us.

So all that is needed for peace, in this view, is that America find a way to coexist with China. We should not try to stand between China and Taiwan, we are told, because that position is certain to be a loser for us. So we have to get Taiwan off the table lest we fall into conflict with China over it.

This might be a convincing argument, except for Japan. Taiwan lies across Japanese shipping lanes, especially for oil, and if China controls it, China has her hands on Japan's throat. In 1941 Japan went to war with America over something akin to this when we embargoed oil to Japan in support of telling it to stop their aggression against China and French Indo-China. To give China control of Japan's key shipping lanes is to invite a struggle between Japan and China, something we would find it hard to stay out of.

"China's many outside boosters have become confident that, in a decade or two, economic and social progress will automatically lead to a more open political system," wrote a reviewer of Ross Terrill's book that asserts Chinese imperial pretensions. "Don't be fooled . . . ," the reviewer continues. "Over the years . . . China has used its moments of strength to grab neighboring territory . . . China remains . . . an 'empire of theatre and presumption,' a country that is 'deeply corrupt, politically unstable, yet extremely ambitious.'"[11]

We have to do our best to try to avoid conflict with China, but despite all that we do, it might come. And this is the possibility that must most engage our attention; peace will take care of itself, but conflict could mean disaster.

THE TREND OF THE POLITICAL CLIMATE IN CHINA

The Western press continues to wear rose-colored glasses about China. Our media and politicians pretend, wrote Arthur Waldron, "that a dictatorship is a normal country, and that an economy having a closed capital account, government allocation of credit, and a vast state-owned sector is somehow capitalist or free market. We pretend that Hong Kong really is not part of China and that Taiwan is."[12] Furthermore, when the first Chinese man-spaced flight went up, an editorial in *The Financial Times* correctly stated that it was a triumph of Chinese nationalism, and that space had military applications, but went on to ignore the threatening connection of these two points to say, with much more hope than conviction, "China's manned space flight is for show, but the world may benefit." And how was the world to benefit? "If even one Chinese taikonaut contemplates the fragile earth from his capsule – and thinks for a moment not just of his country but of the planet – the world will be a better place,"[13] Perhaps, but not much, and certainly not in comparison to the risk for the world of the intersection of Chinese nationalism, increasing technological sophistication and military development. The predilection of the West for wearing rose-colored glasses when looking at China is evident here.

In part, this is because most Americans are both ignorant about China and opinionated. A series of rather commonly expressed views about China, which can be heard frequently among American businesspersons, especially those from Wall Street, follow. The errors inherent in the views expressed are identified:

- *I don't think capitalism can coexist with a totalitarian government, and I also believe China has been too successful with its experiments with a market economy to turn back to the old command economy. My guess is that that the economic miracle in China will lead to political change, although the changes will probably happen much slower than they did in the USSR and Eastern Europe.*

But just such a transition has happened before. In the 1920s, the Soviets under Lenin introduced capitalism labeling it "The New Economic Policy." The reform worked well for a few years, but a consequence was Stalin's dictatorship and a big shift toward authoritarianism. There is nothing certain about the evolution of China toward political liberalism – the expectation is the fallacy of convergence .

- *I think China is in a great position – it's perfectly clear that one can pursue capitalism while still being communist. Look at its great neighbour India which tries very hard to be capitalist in its development policies but is severely hamstrung in its efforts precisely because its a democracy. I think the cost of democracy can be slow GDP growth.*

There is a big difference in economic experience between a country catching up to the economic status of leading countries, which China has been doing, and a country generating sustainable long-term economic progress, which China has not yet done.

- *China tends to take a middle or mixture position on many fronts, economically and politically. Most people understand that the economy in China is not completely free market driven, which is still under the influence of goverment position/policy. What outsiders don't fully appreciate is that actually there is democracy in China, but it resides only within the Communist Party. Democracy within the Party ensures that the party wouldn't make severe mistakes such as Cultural Revolution that was initiated by the single individual power, Chairman Mao. What isn't there is democracy outside the Party. Regardless, the path China is on right now is a mixed model that nobody else has taken. Only time can judge how effective it is.*

Democracy is not democracy when it is limited to the membership of one political party; it is instead a form of consensus-making within a ruling elite. Confusing the two is a rather serious error of intellect.

- *In order for democracy to work in a country, there needs to be at least $6,000 GDP per capita, which is well below China's GDP per capita of $1,200. High income ensures democratic stability. Therefore, the world's richest democracies also appear to be the most stable. China may be politically unstable if its move into a democratic state.*

The argument is not persuasive. Not the United States, nor the European democracies, nor India had a GDP per capita of $6,000 (adjusted for inflation), when they became democracies.

- *China is made of more than fifty different groups which includes Han, Mongolian, Tibetan and others. And it's only recently that China was united under one government and covered the wide area that it does now.*

The Chinese population is more than 90 percent Han. It's unity in much the same region as now dates back thousands of years; the inclusion of Tibet is more recent, as is the inclusion of much of Turkestan. But these areas, although large, are thinly populated.

As these comments illustrate, the harmonist notion that is part of our public culture is very strong with respect to China. Commentators refer to China's recent leaders as "pragmatic nationalists," and insist that they are focused on economic growth and are so concerned with political stability and national unity. In other words, nationalism is a means to national unity which is a means to economic growth. China's national leaders are rather like corporate CEOs in the West, with a focus on the success of their enterprises. This is the core of the assertion that Chinese economic growth means peace.[14] Bill Gates has described China as a brand new form of capitalism with the consumer at its center. He was contradicted in print by a Chinese-born and raised American academic who pointed out that China's consumption to GDP ratio has consistently fallen for years – hardly a consumer-centered economy (but rather an investment-centered economy). The same Chinese-born American academic reported having been told, when he criticized China, "by a senior professor who had visited China only once and spoke no Chinese," that the criticism proved that someone with his critical view of China simply didn't understand China.[15] In fact, the tentacles of the Chinese Communist Party reach into the United States – to students, professionals, business people and politicians.

Wishful thinking with respect to China isn't justified. It relies on three key propositions: the Chinese government isn't ideological but is instead pragmatic; the freedoms granted to Hong Kong point the direction to greater freedoms in all China; and that as China liberalizes, it will accomplish a peaceful absorption of Taiwan. "These comfortable assumptions," writes an American observer of China, ". . . have been completely overturned by the mass pro-democracy demonstrations in Hong Kong in July, 2003.[16]

If China is liberalizing in any way, it is not as a result of a weakening Communist Party. Quite the contrary. In 2003 the Communist Party of China enrolled as new members a record seven hundred thousand college students, a full 8 percent of all the nation's students. This is a sharp increase from 1990, when about 1 percent of college students joined the party.[17] Both authors of this book have had students in courses that they taught in China. Chinese students are intensely nationalistic, reflecting the effectiveness of propaganda directed against nineteenth-century foreign imperialists. The Communist Party has made itself inseparable from Chinese nationalism, and won't fade any time soon.

Hence, all reports of the imminent demise of the Communist Party in China[18] would seem to be significantly premature, and any evolution toward democracy would appear to have to take place within the context of what is now an authoritarian government with a single party. Stranger things may have happened in history, but an evolution of this sort is not likely. Here again the convergence theory seems to be very much off the mark – China is not converging toward a Western-style democracy. It's on a very different path – toward a nationalist, not ideological (that is, not communist) authoritarianism. This is the dominant trend. There may well be within this tide some subcurrents of increasing liberalization and localized democracy as the government attempts to modernize and defuse substantial popular discontent.

China wears two faces. It is both liberalizing and repressive. The regime has granted more scope to private initiative, but it also operates some three hundred special prisons that are actually concentration camps, housing some three hundred thousand inmates, operating outside the civilian legal system, despite China assuring all that it is a society based on rule of law.[19]

"This item should not contain forbidden speech. . . . Please enter a different word for this item." This is an error message appearing on the mainland Chinese version of a Microsoft Web site when the words "democracy,"
"freedom," or "human rights," are typed in. Microsoft has put it there at
the behest of the Chinese government.[20]

In China, repression continues unabated. Among the groups most persecuted by the Chinese government is the spiritual society, Falun Gong. As
described in the newsletter of the society,

The African slave trade, Hitler's concentration camps, and the Soviet gulags, all
added together, are not enough to describe the sinister nature of the Chinese communist regime's "laogai" system – the system of "education and rectification through
forced labor." This evil system is by far the most-employed apparatus in the PRC government's persecution of Falun Gong. What Falun Gong practitioners have further
revealed is the absolute cruelty in the Chinese "laogai" system that had previously
evaded academic description. Hundreds of thousands of Falun Gong practitioners have been incarcerated in labor camps and detention centers since the start of
the Chinese government's persecution of Falun Gong. At great risk to their lives,
these practitioners continue to send firsthand information on the torture, killing,
and slave exploitation of prisoners throughout China. Their tear and blood-stained
reports add "texture" and "content" to what we know about the Chinese "laogai"
system, a most cruel system against humanity.[21]

In October 2005, the Chinese government issued its first white paper on
democracy, entitled "Building of Political Democracy in China," and concluded that the continued rule of the Communist Party is "the most important and fundamental principle for developing socialist political democracy
in China." By what slight of logic can it be argued that authoritarianism is
required for democracy? The answer is that the party is said to provide social
stability and economic progress that are essential to setting the conditions
for sustainable democracy; and that there is democracy in the party.

According to national governance indicators compiled by the World Bank,
China has slipped in comparison to other countries in all the dimensions
of liberty and human rights (among them: voice and accountability, rule of
law, control of corruption) in the years between 1998 and 2004. Far from
economic progress bringing about political liberalization – the opposite has
been the case in recent years.

This is the side of China that is so willingly disregarded by much of the
American community. When forced to confront the police state practices of
the Chinese government, outside as well as inside China, many Americans
express disapproval, but insist that these practices will change as China progresses economically. This is, of course, the convergence fallacy – the notion

that economic progress always turns a society in the direction of American-style democracy. Yet the evidence is persuasive that far from liberalizing, China, since it's economic growth spurt began almost twenty years ago, has become significantly less liberal, not more so.

It was revealed at a conference initiated by former President Clinton in New York City on September 16, 2005, that Yahoo had led Chinese authorities to the identity of a leading dissident who was thereafter jailed for a ten-year sentence. Google excludes from its links sites blocked by the Chinese government; MSN banned the words "democracy" and "freedom" from its site at the behest of the Chinese government. Challenged about these actions, the American companies defend themselves by saying that they have to obey the Chinese government to operate in China, and that their influence in China is, in the long term, liberalizing. That argument is certainly disputable. If the Chinese government thought as the companies say they do, then it would not permit their activity in China, as the government is tightening, not loosening, its control. Cooperation with the agents of dictatorship by American companies has a long history in this century and is exactly the sort of short-sightedness that periodically convinces dictators that the West will be an easy mark.[22]

China has some successful leasehold entrepreneurs; but the state continues to own most of Chinese industry. Corruption is so deep that virtually every decision in the country must be bought. Its top leaders seem very effective in international relations, good salespeople for the regime, and most of the top five went through American Universities. But they are at top of a one-party system that preserves their power and they aren't about to change it. When American commentators say "the senior Chinese leadership is very good," we must ask, "What do they mean?" Do they mean good enough to hold on to power? Good enough to be dangerous adversaries? It is very unlikely that they mean good enough to liberalize the political system into a multi-party democracy.

Chinese culture is very status conscious; very hierarchical; very bureaucratic – much more so than Western cultures generally. This acts as a major drag on economic liberalism. But the Chinese are very good at bringing an organization to essentials: at keeping costs down by operating efficiently. They are very pragmatic; resourceful; and can operate on little resource (which the United States generally cannot).

The whole course of Chinese history is somewhat different than we in the West have been taught. The standard history is that China entered eclipse with the advent of Western naval incursions on a sizeable basis in the seventeenth and eighteenth centuries. But this is likely wrong on three counts:

first, it ignores a more important historical development of the same period; second, it continues the Western penchant for seeing importance only in developments that involve western powers; and, third, it accepts uncritically the claim made by China for current political purposes that it was a great victim of western aggression, of colonialism, just like India and Africa. However, it was in the same era that China bested other challengers (including Russia) for control of central Asia. Russia's presence in Tibet, Xinjiang, and Inner Mongolia was negligible in the seventeenth and eighteenth centuries. It was more successful in modern Uzbekistan, Tajikistan, and Turkmenistan. It is a victory that casts a longer shadow into the present than does the residue, if any, of European incursions in China in the same period.[23] The general direction – the trend and tide – of Chinese history and politics is not at all favorable to a future of peaceful relations with America. Instead, China will be nationalist and authoritarian in the next decades, and both fit ill with an America concerned about its own defense and sponsoring democracy around the globe. That the Western press continually reports greater liberalization in China and suggests that China is evolving toward democracy is merely the continuing influence of the wishful thinking attitude on what the media tells our people. China remains an authoritarian state in which there is censorship, police oversight of political activities, persecution of small religious sects and union activists, and in which political expression is subdued due to the threat of physical repression. A military base exists in each city and near each university – a continuing reminder of the strength and willingness of the political authorities to repress dissent.

The essence of China's challenge to us is that it seems able to combine two features that are considered by the West to be incompatible: economic freedom and political authoritarianism. Either China is unique, and can do what no other authoritarian state has done, or there is an internal inconsistency that will ultimately put a brake on China's growth. Yet many American observers fail to make the connection. Instead, they write commentary such as: "China, economists and Asia experts say, does not face some of the inherent limitations that ultimately stymied Japan and led to economic stagnation there over the last 14 years. With its giant population, China is developing a large and diverse economy, creating an almost Darwinian competition for a domestic market that has extremely low-cost companies ready to export inexpensive goods around the globe." "The economy is much more flexible, adaptable than Japan's," said Liang Hong, an economist in Hong Kong for an American investment bank. "Being a continental economy is an advantage because it has competition within." That Japan is a democracy and so should not be subject to the internal contradiction of combining political repression with free enterprise is ignored. Implicitly, the notion in such commentary is that China has somehow mastered the internal contradiction and given the world a new model, a great endorsement for the effectiveness of authoritarianism. This would indeed be a remarkable economic culture – an authoritarian growth machine that could rival and then overtake the United States.[24]

Faced with a challenge to the inconsistency of their opinions, many Western commentators simply insist that China will evolve toward a Western-type liberal democracy as its economy improves. But this is not certain – as China's military modernization suggests. Its growing economy supports military enhancement that increasingly threatens the West, and that strengthens its dictatorship in power by giving expression to the nation's nationalism.

China's policy seems to be to profess peaceful intentions, build warmaking capacity, especially nuclear arms, rapidly, and if challenged on its military buildup to say that it's entirely defensive and to denounce whomever challenged it. It helps to give credibility to the effort if the American president can be made to seem aggressive.[25]

China's course isn't set. Things could go well for China and for America. But the risks of confrontation are familiar: Taiwan, the Luzon straits, trade conflicts, and the likelihood that China will drift toward reasserting suzerainty in the Far East.

THE GROWTH AND MODERNIZATION OF CHINA'S MILITARY

It is possible for Americans to be quite complacent about Chinese military capability – but it is also an error to do so. The Council on Foreign Relations in mid-2003 released a study saying that China is far from becoming a global military power and that the United States could prevail even in a conflict over Taiwan. The conclusion rests on a comparison of the military arsenals of the two countries, and the judgment that China is at least twenty years behind the United States in military technology. But the conclusions are subject to challenge. American dominance depends on effective leadership, intelligent, and timely use of American resources, and the freedom of the Americans to focus on a Chinese challenge. Absent these things, China could prevail in a conflict. In the early 1950s, America would have been judged to have a similar preponderance of strength against China, yet China fought us to a standstill in Korea.

If China remains no threat to the United States for years ahead, it will not be for lack of effort. China has the positive motivation of nationalism to build a strong military, and the negative motivation of fear.

"The breadth, the quantity, the quality, and level and sophistication of the modernization [of the Chinese military is an increasing concern," a reporter quoting what he called a "senior US defense official." The official continued, ". . . we have a very broad [Chinese] modernization that continues in every year to outstrip our projections as to where they will be in the year ahead'" Furthermore, ". . . Admiral William Fallon, new head of the U.S. Pacific Command, told the Senate armed services committee last month that he was particularly concerned about the strength of the Chinese navy, including its expanding fleet of submarines. . . . Men Honghua, an expert on strategic studies at the . . . Central Party School for Communist party cadres, noted in a recent essay that China's 'lifeline' ran through the Taiwan Strait, South China Sea, Malacca Strait and Indian Ocean all the way to the Arabian Sea. China has to strengthen its naval forces to guarantee the security of its access to shipped resources and should actively develop a large shipping fleet capable of operating in distant ocean."[26]

China is a nuclear power with a full range of capability for designing and building nuclear weapons. "China currently has the capability to strike U.S. cities with a force of approximately 20 long-range Dong Feng-5 missiles, each armed with a single 4- to 5-megaton warhead." The 20 Dong Feng-4 missiles "are almost certainly intended as a retaliatory deterrent against targets in Russia and Asia, according to U.S. intelligence assessments, but the missiles could strike parts of Alaska and the Hawaiian island chain. China has 80 to 100 other missiles that could strike targets in Eurasia."

The time needed to launch these liquid-fueled ICBMs, a lack of hardened missile silos, and a lack of missile mobility have raised concern in the Chinese leadership about survivability of these forces. In addition, China's sea-based force (one *Xia* submarine armed with twelve medium-range ballistic missiles) does not pose a credible threat to either Moscow or Washington. The *Xia* has never sailed outside China s territorial waters, is considered vulnerable to modern anti-submarine warfare techniques and is not currently operational. To overcome these concerns, China has been pursuing the development of smaller, mobile missiles.[27]

The Chinese see a new type of warfare prosecuted from great distance in which the Chinese might not "see, hear or reach their attackers."[28] This is America's Revolution in Military Affairs, which is discussed in Chapter 14.

In response, China is developing an increasingly modernized military that will be able to increasingly project force on all of its borders. Its modernization is based on a thorough study of recent conflicts around the globe,[29] and will affect the balance of power in east Asia and in the world.

China's "steady program to modernize and deploy more nuclear-capable intercontinental ballistic missiles is in large part driven by the need to have a bona fide second-strike minimum deterrent against the United States."[30]

The roots of Chinese ambitions to be a full-scale nuclear power with a strike capability against America go deep in history. The ambitions are not the result of recent distrust of America, of any actions we might have taken or not have taken, but instead are part of a long-standing Chinese ambition that in the past has had marked impact on Chinese foreign relations. The most dramatic example involved the Soviets.

"In August, 1957, Nikita Khrushchev reneged on a secret agreement and refused to supply . . . [atomic and hydrogen weapons]. Sino-Soviet relations never recovered, eventually rupturing fully in 1962." Thus, it was nuclear proliferation over which China and USSR fell out.[31] "After 1980, China achieved the capability to hit the continental United States with ICBMs."[32]

". . . [A]t least at some levels, the PLA's Second Artillery [China's nuclear missile force] most likely operates on the presumption of offensive nuclear war-fighting, albeit always couched in terms of a . . . counterattack . . ."[33]

"Most western analysts place the PLA's conventional capabilities at least twenty years behind the state of the art, with the gap widening. . . . In the area of ballistic missiles, however, China's capabilities are considerably better – and improving."[34]

". . . China's accelerated development and deployment of ballistic missiles is a real source of concern . . . the PLA now has in service a full range of ballistic missile systems."[35]

China in the Future

There are areas, however, like information warfare, in which "China's ambitions . . . should not be confused with capability."[36] This suggests complacency based on what is likely only a momentary weakness. The Chinese are working hard to remove this deficiency in their military strength.

Soon after the September 11 attack, in the fall of 2001, the Chinese government approached two Australian universities with a proposition. Both schools were developing significant capability in software engineering instruction. One was about to build a $50 million software center. The dean of engineering at the Australian School learned from the Chinese about the plans to build the expensive center at his school. "Their intelligence was unbelievable," he said to us.

The proposition was that the universities would work with the Chinese government to train software engineers. The purpose, the Chinese were willing to state, was to develop for the Chinese the top software design capability in the military sphere. Because the Americans could not be trusted – they're warmongers, the Chinese explained – the Chinese would guarantee not to share the technology with America.

The Chinese described their strategy for developing world leadership in military applications of computer technology. They already had the hardware capability for military applications, the Chinese explained, but not the software. By lucrative offers, they were now attracting back to China software engineers who were working in America. They had brought to China from India a few software engineers. But they needed to train many more, and wanted Australian help to school the new engineers in China.

The Chinese had come to the Australians by a process of elimination. They had been relying on American universities to train their software engineers, but in the aftermath of the September 11 attacks, they thought that the United States was going to be much harder for foreign students to get into; so the Chinese were seeking alternate sources of education. The English were not much interested in China, the Chinese explained; their students knew English, but not French or German, so those countries were not desirable partners; India was a strategic enemy, ever since the Chinese had defeated India in a military conflict on the slopes of the Himalayas, decades before, and would not help China now. Of the countries with significant software capability, only Australia remained.

The Australians temporized. First, they proposed a price for such training more than double what they would ordinarily charge. The Chinese accepted it. Then the Australians demurred about doing the training in China but suggested that Chinese students be sent to Australian universities instead. The Chinese did so. With Chinese students pouring into the country, and Indians following, Australia has become a major force in the foreign student market, eclipsing the United States and Britain.[37]

It would appear from such intense efforts to train more software engineers that China is way behind in obtaining such skills. But this would be incorrect. According to the chief executive of Microsoft, China is already first in the world in the number of computer science graduates, followed by India and then by the United States.[38] Marcus Franda, who has contributed value studies of Chinese and Indian efforts online, points out that the rivalry among the world's two largest nations increases the appetite of both for international power.[39]

The Chinese also seek via less direct methods to obtain technology for military purposes. The Chinese apparently sought during the Clinton administration to obtain benefit by a disguised contribution to the president's campaign funds. A respected former federal judge was selected to investigate the matter, and accepted the position, but the investigation was never funded.

There are continuing reports of Chinese efforts to obtain licenses for export from America to China of parts of supercomputers, presumably to be used at some point for missile targeting.

Meanwhile, the Chinese are moving ahead rapidly in computer hardware manufacturing. "Huawei's [a Chinese created and owned router manufacturer for telecoms, like Cisco] rapid expansion has brought it plaudits from China's top leaders, who are eager for the country to establish itself as a high-technology power and not just a factory floor for the world."[40]

WILL CHINA BE AN ENEMY?

It would be a great tragedy if America and China stumbled into an armed conflict. Today the Chinese are at long last making significant economic progress and there is at least some greater degree of personal freedom than before. To see all this lost would be extremely unfortunate. At the start of this chapter, we quoted Henry Kissinger to the point that China need not be America's enemy – that such a result is not foreordained. Then we discussed the trends in Chinese politics and economics and concluded that they point to a high likelihood of enmity between the two powers as Chinese strength grows. Now we turn to the issue of overt conflict – how might it occur?

Essentially the Chinese are likely to view America as strong but lacking the will to use force with a will to win, if losses are imposed on America.

They may consider us unlikely to use force to support an ally, but willing to use force to support our economic interest. In this case, their strategy at this stage is clear: to acquiescence in trade agreements that embody America's major economic aims; and to press us to hard choices in the geopolitical realm.

The pressing has already started.

Today in the Far East there is unceasing elbowing between China and the United States. Hardly a day goes by that some Chinese civilian or military official does not warn the United States and its allies about their supposed hostility toward China, and hardly a day passes without a response from the American military or civilian leadership. In 2001, for example, the Secretaries of State and Defense of the United States invited Japan, South Korea, the Philippines, and Australia to join in a more formal military alliance; and China quickly warned the four Asian countries not to toe the American line. China then began the largest military maneuvers in its history, directly opposite Taiwan. A defector from the Chinese embassy in Australia reported knowing of a thousand Chinese spies in Australia.

China conducts tests of long-range ballistic missiles frequently. It recently fired from a submarine a missile believed to have a range of about six thousand miles, which could reach U.S. territory from the western Pacific. The system isn't yet operational, but may be in a few years. It marks a major advance of China's strategic weaponry.[41]

In Asia and Australia papers follow the almost daily elbowing of the Americans and the Chinese – statements by the civilian governments, or by military leadership, directed at the other and at other countries; the Americans proposing new security discussions and arrangements by China's neighbors; China warning those so contacted not to follow the American line. The America media rarely report such matters, since they do not fit in with the general story – the development of trade between America and China, the loss of American jobs to China, and the increasing liberalization (it is said) of Chinese politics. The elbowing between China and America can be followed in specialized reporting services both in print and online), however.

The Chinese interest in Taiwan goes beyond nationalism, though it is nationalism that excites the Chinese public. In fact, Taiwan is today one of the world's most strategic spots, equivalent to what Gibraltar used to be. This is because Taiwan sits astride the sea routes by which Japan receives almost all its raw materials, including oil from the Middle East and coal and iron ore from Australia. Whoever controls Taiwan has a stranglehold on Japan's economy, and were China to obtain that, the balance of world power would shift. This the United States cannot permit.

The current great game in east Asia (including, for example, the elbowing between China and the United States over the Straits of Malacca, and the public relations furor in east Asia about Japan's prime minister visiting war cemeteries) is in large part about who has a solid grip on Japan's throat. But, we might ask, why does that matter? Japan isn't armed. Why is China so interested?

The broad answer is power. Strangleholds can be used for a spectrum of goals from influence, to intimidation and extortion. The Chinese Communist leadership may not have thought the matter through, and it might not have an endgame in mind, but the party will test the possibilities.

Taiwan is a key to strategic power. It's like a huge unsinkable airfield, army base and missile station which overlooks the connection between the South China Sea and the Sea of Japan – through which much of Japan's trade, including especially its oil, must pass. So it's the key to domination of Japan.

Even with Chinese missiles that can reach over Formosa to the ocean beyond, Formosa in other hands than those of the Chinese communist government, provides a base from which the missiles can be shot down or their bases destroyed. It follows that Formosa may be the single most important strategic spot in the world today. Hence the rivalry between China and America over it.

In February 2005, the United States and Japan signed an agreement asserting that Taiwan and the Taiwan straits were a mutual concern between both countries. China expressed displeasure at the agreement but met with Japan in April 2005 to discuss Taiwan.

China and the United States might at any moment stumble into a confrontation over Taiwan. China is arming for this by building nuclear-armed missiles able to reach the United States. Already China has some twenty-five such missiles operational, and Chinese military officials have threatened to use them to hit American cities.

Major General Zhu Chenghu of China spoke at a function for foreign journalists organized by the Chinese Foreign Affairs Ministry on July 14, 2005. During the function Zhu said: "We . . . will prepare ourselves for the destruction of all of the [Chinese] cities east of Xian. Of course, the Americans will also have to expect that hundreds . . . of cities will be destroyed by the Chinese." Zhu has previously said that China has the capability to attack the United States with long-range missiles. The general is a professor and dean in China's National Defense University Strategic Defense Institute which is under the direct leadership of the CCP's Central Military Committee.

The American House of Representatives called for his dismissal, but the Chinese Communist Party did not reject Zhu's speech nor dismiss him and a spokesperson from the Foreign Affairs Ministry said Zhu's speech was his own personal opinion. This spokesperson declined to comment on whether or not the speech represented the government's view.

"Although General Zhu emphasized that what he said was his own opinion, a Pentagon official, speaking to a reporter at the Washington Times, said that Chinese generals normally express only official positions and that Zhu's comments represent the views of senior Chinese military officers. 'These comments are a signal to all of Asia that China does not fear US forces,' this official said. Professor Tang Ben of the Claremont Institute's Asian Studies Center published an article in Singapore's Lianhe Zaobao on July 20, in which he asserted that what General Zhu alluded to was actually Beijing's strategy to deal with current world circumstances, even though Beijing labeled his remarks as "personal opinion." Professor Tang wrote that people aware of the CCP's diplomatic history would know that Zhu's speech was purposely arranged by Beijing and not written by him."[42]

A likely scenario that would lead to a very tough decision for the United States goes as follows:

> *China asserts sovereignty over Taiwan and a determination to occupy the island. Nationalist fervor rises to a boil in China.*
> *The United States says no.*
> *China asserts a determination to attack and occupy the island.*
> *The United States replies, "We'll stop you."*
> *China replies, "If you intervene against our invasion, we'll take out your west coast cities with nuclear missiles."*
> *The United States then replies in accordance with the Mutual Assured Destruction Doctrine of the Cold War, "Then we'll take out all your cities." Stability during the Cold War between the United States and the USSR rested on the near certainty that neither side would risk destruction to upset the status quo. This was deterrence.*
> *But now there is a difference. For, unlike Russia, China is likely to reply, "We'll risk that. We don't think the American government and/or the American people will trade Los Angeles, San Francisco, and Seattle even for all our cities."*
> *Faced with this challenge, the United States is likely to back down. China then invades Taiwan, occupies it, and whole strategic position in Far East is altered against the United States and U.S. allies in favor of China.*
> *It's to avoid this result that the United States seeks to build a missile defense shield.*

This is classic big power politics, and it can happen even in today's world: China, in pursuit of national unification, or under the cover of nationalism, seeking to obtain Taiwan and thereby strategic control of the connection of north Pacific to south, and thereby the lifeline of Japan; the Americans determined to prevent this; the Japanese becoming very nervous about seeing their fate possibly pass from the control of the Americans to that of China. To defend Taiwan, the United States must be able to intervene against a Chinese invasion, and to do so must be able to protect U.S. cities from Chinese attack. Against China, unlike against the Soviet Union before 1991, or Russia today, deterrence alone, the threat of mutual assured destruction, is not at all certain to work. Hence the need for a new American defense strategy with which to urge the Chinese toward peaceful integration into the world community.

But not all American commentators see it that way. Instead, some limit themselves to urging restraint on the Chinese. Working within the public culture, there is a complete failure to see the broader (or systems) aspect (the interrelationships) of the Formosa situation. "To lock in today's fragile status quo, Taipei should forgo full independence and Beijing should stop threatening to use force."[43] Yes, that is all to the good, but largely off the point. China has strategic motives for wanting direct control of Taiwan that goes much beyond national reunification – to get better control of the sea lanes from the middle east to Japan; and to remove what it must consider an American arrow aimed at its heart. These motives cannot be satisfied by better relations within today's status quo.

John Mearsheimer has studied the emerging rivalry between America and China and comes to a very different conclusion. "American policy," he writes, "has sought to integrate China into the world economy and facilitate its rapid economic development, so that it becomes wealthy . . . and content with its present position in the international system. This . . . policy . . . is misguided. . . . wealthy China would not be a status quo power but an aggressive state . . ." In consequence, "a policy of engagement [by the United States with China] is doomed to fail. . . . China and the United States are destined to be adversaries." Instead of engagement and support for Chinese growth, the United States should "do what it can to slow the rise of China."[44]

We think this an unnecessary conclusion at this time, and therefore too risky a policy. America should continue to seek China's integration into the world community through engagement via trade, investment, cultural exchanges – that is, through a policy of positive engagement. But America must also adopt a defense policy that has two objectives:

- to protect our country if the effort at peaceful engagement fails; and
- to persuade the Chinese that there is little or no gain from military aggression against us or our allies.

MAD is not a viable way to do so. Strategic Independence , including a national missile shield is.

The American government has been reluctant to reveal the strategic purpose of the missile shield, and has so bungled the matter that it sometimes seems to urge the Chinese to faster construction of missiles able to hit our cities. This is the perverse result of dishonesty about our objectives combined with the topsy-turvy logic of MAD.

The best American policy with respect to China is a vigorous effort to persuade it to further integration into the world economic community, coupled with a strong defensive posture to persuade China against military adventures.

REVIVING SUPERPOWER: RUSSIA

On April 25, 2005, President Putin said to the Russian Parliament: "The greatest geopolitical catastrophe of the twentieth century was the break up of the Soviet Union. It left millions of Russians outside their homeland."[45] The first of his two sentences shows the direction of Putin's thinking; the second begins setting stage for reassembling the USSR. One can almost hear Hitler speaking of the Germans outside Germany before World War II.

American public culture has great difficulty adjusting to the fact that Putin has created an authoritarian martial police state (although it is only euphemistically acknowledged) with nationalist ambitions. Martial denotes a reinvigorated structural militarization; police, the central role of the FSB, and siloviki. People in the United States thinking within the public culture seem to believe their mischaracterizations of the Russian situation. It is very dangerous. Russia is still locked in imperial ways, trying to restore its empire, neutralize NATO, and return to a rivalry with the United States, according to a study by Janusz Bugajski.[46]

The odds are very high that America is going to have to deal with a resurgent and militaristic Russia. Already the country is far better armed than we admit, and it has announced its intention to move toward the fifth generation of nuclear weaponry. It intends to launch a weapons modernization drive at the end of 2005, which seems to be sputtering, but Vitaly Shlykov, former co-chairman of Yeltsin's defense council, is vetting a scheme that would solve the problem. That Russia has a weak consumer economy matters very little for its military potential in the next two decades. Western leaders have to stop pretending that Russia is a democracy with peaceful intentions, and a market-oriented free enterprise economy operating in accordance with the rule of law. Instead, we must face the possibility of a resurgent Russian superpower and attempt to deal with it openly before it's too late.

There is no other country about which Americans have more misconceptions than Russia – and about which they've been more misinformed for decades. It isn't that the truth about what was happening in Russia isn't from time to time slipping out via visitors and the news media, it is that opinion makers in America and western Europe were always interpreting Russian and Soviet reality to fit their preconceptions. Basically, most Americans don't know how the Soviet Union operated, don't understand why it collapsed, and don't have a realistic perception of Russia today. Hence, in order to discuss the future of Russia and its potential for becoming again a serious danger to our country, we must briefly (for that's all the space we have) revisit the past.

ROSE-COLORED GLASSES ABOUT RUSSIA

When our society is fundamentally ignorant of foreign nations (as we certainly are of Russia, China, and Japan), we project our own experience onto them. It is a great paradox that we think Russia, China, and Japan are more like us (though we never say so directly, but our commentary and listen to our media suggest that exactly) than is, for example, Mexico – this is wrong, and occurs because we know enough of Mexico to know how it is different, and know so little of Russia and China and Japan that we presume they are like us. Thus, we defend the Russian oligarchs from their government on the presumption that they are like our businesspeople (which they are not). Russia, China and Japan have always been treated as exotic, yet this is flawlessly juxtaposed in public culture with the idea that they are at bottom the same as us. This is a perfect example of the essence of public culture. People have to be preconditioned to be so purblind.

There is a long history of rose-colored projection that leaps without difficulty over hurdles of paradox. Western public cultures driven by a mix of liberal sympathy and conservative expediency made Moscow over according to their idealist requirements after 1929. The insurrection of a few conspirators in St. Petersburg in 1917 became a revolutionary upheaval. The proletariat of the future substituted for the small number of Russian workers lost in a sea of peasants. Authoritarianism became a vehicle of social progress. Servitude became economic justice; military aggression became national liberation; forced concentration camp labor became progressive reeducation; terror became self-defense (a euphemism that today has been reborn in trying to justify terrorist attacks in Palestine and America); and aggressive militarism became an expression of Kremlin fears of attack from the west.

The rationalizations continued. Yes, it was argued, Bolsheviks sometimes were unjust, but they were maturing, and a fair society would evolve. "And to be fair," went the discussion in the West, "there were commendable successes." The Soviets were said to have proven that planning could generate rapid industrialization, allowing them to partly close the economic gap with the west, while simultaneously achieving egalitarian objectives. Authoritarianism, economic illiberality, human rights abuses and obsession with defense were regrettable, but Soviet leaders were reasonable and reason was propelling them to liberalize, democratize, reduce their arsenals, and as Gorbachev put it as the USSR began to come apart, to return to its common European home.

This exercise in a Western equivalent to Soviet speak, calling red white, and white red, overlaid with pious justifications, was embraced by many

American leaders from Franklin Roosevelt to Jimmy Carter. In retrospect it should be truly astonishing to us, and hasn't been substantially altered since the emergence of the new Russia. Western public culture hasn't recharacterized the Soviet experience. It has just developed selective amnesia about the Soviet period, and true to form, opinion makers of various types are now busily sanitizing Putin's authoritarianism, his media monopoly, and Russia's reemerging militarization just as for decades previously they disregarded the horrors of Soviet Russia.

Why did so many Western governments and leaders so mislead themselves and others about the Soviet Union? Briefly, at the outset of the Soviet government, Western leaders had to decide how to deal with Lenin and his successors. For a time they chose confrontation, but once they reversed field it became counterproductive to harp on all the negatives, and expedient to defer to Soviet sensibilities. Later, at the time of World War II, there was little to be gained by doggedly calling the Bolshevik coup d'état an insurrection when Moscow insisted on characterizing it as a proletarian revolution, or labeling Stalin a despot while he was an comrade in arms against the Nazis. Still later, during the Cold War, there was no mileage in insisting that the Soviet economy was structurally militarized while lobbying the Kremlin for arms controls, reductions and disarmament. Nor could Moscow be prodded to cooperate on a spectrum of confidence building initiatives, if its purported economic accomplishments were denigrated. And no American administration could develop a coherent engagement policy with the USSR if it allowed other branches of government including the CIA, and DIA to stray far from the party line. Western public culture in this way became biased toward coloring Soviet realities more brightly than they deserved, and for historical reasons this distortion was exacerbated by liberal democratic sentiment in America, and social democratic partisanship on the continent.

American policy toward the Soviet Union and its successor states has been surprisingly and disturbingly consistent across administrations since Roosevelt recognized the USSR. Nixon's science and technology agreement, Reagan's embrace of Gorbachev shortly after Reagan's "evil empire" speech, George W. Bush's looking Putin in the eye and proclaiming that he can trust him (recall Roosevelt's infamous assertion about Stalin that "I think we can trust Uncle Joe"), and Bush's reference in the late summer of 2005 to Putin as "My friend Vladimir," adding "every time I visit and talk with President Putin, our relationship becomes stronger,"[47] are examples of a failure to recognize an ongoing threat to America and to deal with it realistically.

In the fall of 2003, President George W. Bush referred to Russia as "A country in which democracy and freedom and rule of law thrive." The editorial writers of *The Economist* magazine quoted the President, then went on to ask, "Was the American president out of his mind?"[48] Russia today is anything but a country in which democracy and freedom and rule of law thrive. It's instead a new political reality, one which may spread, and which is currently dangerous for Americans because we mistake it for something more familiar. It looks like a democracy, but isn't. It looks like an open market economy, but isn't. It looks as though there is private property protected by a rule of law, but there is not. What there is is more freedom in political discussion. In effect, Russian autocrats, elected by spurious means, have developed a tolerance for pluralistic discussion and debate. The system is a nonrepresentative electoral sham providing a democratic semblance. About Putin's Russia, Nikita Khruschev's daughter has written: "Russia's split personality – symbolized by its tsarist coat of arms, a two-headed eagle – has been on open display recently. . . . Despite his insistence on rubbing shoulders with world leaders, and portraying himself as a modernizer, Putin, like his predecessors, is in fact a ruler who believes that only authoritarian rule can protect his country from anarchy and disintegration."[49]

Americans seem to presume that diversity of opinion (which exists in Russia) means that popular will determines political governance. This is incorrect. Modern authoritarians are willing to tolerate diversity of opinion because debate provides information to their policy monopoly. The willingness to tolerate diverse opinion also reflects a new maturity in authoritarian regimes. Until recently, authoritarian regimes were so insecure that they felt it necessary to squash all dissent and to win fake elections by 99 percent majorities. Now more sophisticated authoritarian regimes (we should no longer call them totalitarian since they do not suppress all dissent, and they hold elections which they win by comfortable but not near unanimous majorities) recognize that they can retain power securely via dominance of modern mass media and of election processes without heavy-handed resort to authoritarian measures.

It's dangerous that we Americans mistake this new political form for our own type of democracy, and apply the same term, "democracy" to it. Democracy should be used to apply only to a system of government in which dissent can lead to changes in political control .

WHY THE SOVIET UNION IMPLODED: BACK TO THE FUTURE

What is probably the most intriguing historical question of our time is what caused the Soviet Union to come apart? This is one of the most unusual and significant events of our time – a superpower destroyed, not by losing a war, but by dissolving from within! No matter how bad the economic troubles of the USSR, knowledgeable people did not expect it to dissolve. Paul Kennedy, in his book on the rise and fall of great powers, made only one direct prediction: that no great power ever simply collapsed – they all overreached in conflict abroad and only then disintegrated. Yet the USSR did the opposite. How did it happen – and why?

Fascinating as the question is, we can only comment on it briefly. The Soviet elite – the apparatachiks and second economy opportunists – gradually began to crave affluence, and grew tired of martial regimentation. Mikhail Gorbachev introduced some elements of a market economy. So-called privatization allowed the Kremlin to steer government assets into carefully chosen private hands without safeguards to prevent diverting resources from productive use in conformance with established goals and incentives. It disorganized the planning and control system, causing the economy to plunge.

The USSR's dissolution was expedited by the conflict of Mikhail Gorbachev and Boris Yeltsin for power. Yeltsin promoted secession of the various republics of the Soviet Union during the late 1980s as a tactic to oust Gorbachev. The Commonwealth of Independent States (the loose alliance of former Soviet republics that still exists) began in November 1991 as the alliance of the Ukraine, Russia (one of the constituent republics of the USSR) and Belorussia against the sovereign authority of the Soviet Union. Then the Soviet economy declined about 9 percent in 1991. A consequence was that Gorbachev decided to abdicate. When Gorbachev resigned, he passed the scepter to this new "union," which really meant the dissolution of the Soviet empire. Gorbachev had no intention of allowing disunion, but his political position had been so undermined that when he departed, he was unable to keep the USSR together.

It is important that had Gobarchev and Yeltsin not destroyed the Soviet Union, and had the Kremlin maintained its armed forces (as it almost certainly would have, with GDP growth being officially registered at 3–4 percent annually), then today it would be the EU, not Russia, that looks in bad shape. Europe's left would have pressed for EU Sovietization to combat stagnating economies and double-digit unemployment, while pressing for reducing military spending. Instead of posturing as an emergent superpower rival of the United States, the EU today would be falling increasingly under the Soviet Union's sway and appear vulnerable to Soviet expansionism. The Cold War would have intensified. That history took the direction it did beginning in the early 1990s is one of its great surprises.

Russian leaders could have executed an orderly transition from the Soviet period, even under conditions of structural militarization by preventing resources from falling into the wrong hands, redirecting physical systems management toward civilian needs, transforming physical into value-added based systems management, adopting market facilitating cultural reforms, building market institutions, establishing the rule of contract law, initiating self-purchase privatization, applying lump sum compensatory dividends for those unable to participate in self-purchase privatization, and creating competitive asset markets.

They chose instead, to revert to the tradition Russian patrimonial strategy of reparceling out administrative usage rights in the guise of property rights through "spontaneous privatization," unsupervised managerial empowerment over state assets, poaching and shock therapy, understood as the abolition of coercive state planning, and productive administration, together with the cancellation of all state contracts. Producers, distributors, and workers were left to fend for themselves, and given the opportunity to "legally" misappropriate state assets.

In the aftermath of the Soviet collapse it has become fashionable to blame the USSR's demise on its excessive defense burden and the deficiencies of central planning. Militarization was a burden because it inhibited systemic change, but the Soviet Union's massive defense spending wasn't primarily responsible for the USSR's low living standards. The CIA gave this a different spin, claiming that Gorbachev's disarmament had been too abrupt.

Central planning was unresponsive to consumer demand by design and this defect couldn't be overcome because resources couldn't have been effectively reallocated to consumption under the Kremlin's central planning regime. Instead of collapsing due to a too-heavy military burden, the Soviet Union was undone by a wave of insider plunder precipitated by the green light Gorbachev gave to spontaneous privatization, managerial misappropriation, asset-stripping, and entrepreneurial fraud, all under the guise of economic liberalization.

Yeltsin could have done better, but both didn't want to, and was mislead by western advocates of so-called shock therapy, the notion that the Soviet economy could be transformed into a Western-type market economy overnight. It couldn't have been; and wasn't.

Putin is fashioning a new order to his liking, combining a bureaucracy dominated by the security and military services with . . . state agents running businesses. Today's Russian government is autocratic with a democratic veneer, just as it was under the last tsar (Nicholas II). The "commanding heights," as the Bolsheviks used to say, of the economy are managed and controlled by insiders who are beholden to the president, who at his discretion can confiscate the assets they administer. Authoritarian politics is in command, not markets, and the state apparatus strongly reflects the aspirations of the security service. Putin appears to believe that markets and democracy without the rule of law will provide his administration with the best of both worlds: free enterprise driven prosperity and natural resource funded superpower. This won't happen.

Few western observers are prepared to accept the possibility that Yeltsin has placed Russia in a quagmire from which it may not emerge during our lifetime. They have been well indoctrinated by their own cultural premises, believing that departures from the competitive ideal everywhere are much the same. But Russians have seldom operated this way. With the exception of a few brief interludes associated with powerful leaders like Ivan the Terrible, Peter the Great, Catherine the Great, and Joseph Stalin, Russian culture has favored weak forms of authoritarianism in which a small, extravagantly wealthy elite has been able to unproductively idle away its time in personal intrigues by keeping most of the population in bondage. This preference has been refined over the centuries, but it still seems determinative. Russia is not converging toward Western-style free market capitalism, and is not going to do so.

Western harmonism predisposes our leaders and publics alike to believe that non-Western economic systems can be abruptly and radically changed. Lenin's Bolshevik insurrection was interpreted as a break with authoritarian tsarism, where most of the nation's wealth was owned or controlled by the emperor, and parliament was a rubber stamp. This was mistaken – there was no such complete break. There was regime change and a new ideology, but under Soviet communism the people remained disenfranchised, and were subjugated by the Kremlin, just as before. It therefore comes as no surprise, that Yeltsin's usurpation of power was misconstrued as a revolutionary transition to democratic free enterprise. But, as is now widely admitted after fourteen years of Western self-deception, the regime change was anything but revolutionary. The one-party communist state is gone, replaced by a no-party autocracy as in the bad old tsarist days. The Duma is back, just as it was before the revolution – a rubber stamp. Markets are back, as before the revolution, but with only a very limited role.

Before 1917 a handful of noble landowners, and entrepreneurs closely allied to the state created and used malleable markets to their and the tsar's advantage, while the vast majority of the people were straitjacketed in communes, and oppressed by a parasitic bureaucracy. The costumes and demographics have now changed, but the economic mechanism adheres to the traditional mold. It is best described as a tsarist or Muscovite model, a style of rule that emerged under Ivan the Terrible in the sixteenth century. As Grand Prince of "all the Rus" from 1533, and later as Russia's first tsar, he perfected a regime where he as nominal owner of all he surveyed, turned over the administration of his domains to favorites who did not own property, but were permitted to enrich themselves, so long as they paid rents and collected taxes for the sovereign, their methods being unquestioned by the tsar.

Noble recipients of surplus-generating administrative grants in turn subcontracted on the same principle, each layer exploiting those subjugated to them, creating a society with a handful of haves and a myriad of have nots, without the benefit of a rule of law. The system had markets, but bore no resemblence to democratic free enterprise. It was the tsar and his grandees who were sovereign, not consumers, and the system had none of the desirable efficiency characteristics associated with Adam Smith's notion of the invisible hand.

There is no analogue for this in American history. In English history, it is akin to the period of William the Conqueror when William had just defeated King Harold at Hasting and suddenly owned the entire realm of England. He then divided the country among his knights and over time, most of the country became their property, controlled by the monarchy only via an unwritten constitution.

This is what much of English history is about – the limitations and qualifications put on the crown with respect to subject's rights. This is what we mean in the West by the rule of law. Over time, in England the government came to belong to the people, not to the monarch, and private individuals were protected in their property by law. This was also the case in America. Similar developments occurred all over western Europe and this is the heart of the Western legal/economic system. This is how we in the West think things should be. This is what we want the rest of the world to be like. This is the framework in which we interpret events. This is what Americans understand, and so this is how the story of Russia is told to them. But it is wrong.

Putin's Russia is no different than earlier versions of Muscovy. It neither walks nor talks like a democratic free enterprise duck, and isn't. It is a creature of Russian culture, that sometimes pretends to adhere to Enlightenment norms, like Putin's advocacy of the "dictatorship of law," but is the same old Kremlin succinctly conceptualized as an authoritarian martial police state. It is authoritarian because Putin is above the law, ruling by edict, implemented by an executive bureaucracy, just as under the tsar. It is martial, because the army is a central instrument of authoritarian power. And it is a police state because the FSB (old KGB) is the eyes, ears, and shield of the "president" with immense power, including oversight of the military. FSB officers still have the right to shoot any military official suspected of treason, no questions asked. The oppressiveness and predatory nature of the tsarist-like model fluctuates. There are periods of conservativism and liberalism, but Russia isn't normal in the Western sense, and wishful thinking continues to bemuse those who insist that it is.

Just as in Soviet times, its preferred economic model won't allow the Kremlin to have it all. If Putin manages to mobilize society for a super-power agenda, he can restore Russia's military might, and insiders can live extravagantly, but general prosperity will always remain elusive.

Russia – A False Democracy

Contemporary Russian democracy differs from the Soviet pretense at democracy in several ways, but not enough to make the contemporary version real. Under the old regime, there was a single party, the communists, with a nonelected leader, who effectively appointed representatives to the Supreme Soviet (equivalent to today's Duma). The Chairman of the Communist Party ruled both the party and the state. The Communist Party periodically held balloted elections for all positions, including "supreme leader," which 98 percent of voters usually supported the appointees, not too dissimilar to balloting for judgeships in the United States. Legislative representatives were powerless, and the electorate effectively disenfranchised. Under Gorbachev, the title for the head of state was changed to "president."

Yeltsin was elected to the "presidency" of the Russian version of the Supreme Soviet in the heady days of 1996 without even the fiction of party endorsement. President Putin, who as head of the secret police acquired incremenating evidence against Yeltsin's daughter, Tatyana Dyachenko, was essentially designated by Yeltsin. The President appoints a large portion of legislators and governors. The rest of the positions are usually obtained by people supported by the most wealthy, the so-called oligarchs. As before, balloting occurs, but not only is it rigged, the president ignores the Duma at his discretion. The people's preferences simply don't count.

All this is consistent with the main theme of Russian politics through the ages. As described by the Gorbachev era insider Alexander Yakovlev:

"The land of Rus accepted Christianity from Constantinople in A.D. 988. Characteristics of Byzantine rule of that era – baseness, cowardliness, venality, treachery, over-centralization, apotheosis of the ruler's personality – dominate in Russia's social and political life to this day. In the twelfth century the various fragmented Russian principalities . . . were conquered by the Mongols, Asian traditions and customs, with their disregard for the individual and for human rights and their cult of might, violence, despotic power, and lawlessness became part of the Russian people's way of life.

"The tragedy of Russia lay first and foremost in this: that for a thousand years it was ruled by men and not by laws. . . . They ruled ineptly, bloodily. The people existed for the government, not the government for the people. Russia avoided classical slavery. But it has not yet emerged from feudalism; it is still enslaved by an official imperial ideology, the essence of which is that the state is everything and the individual nothing."[50]

The post-Soviet order wasn't planned. Its form and content were determined by a process in which Gorbachev's "authoritarian, martial police state" was partially marketized.[51] In the initial phase opportunists, or "roving bandits" in Mancur Olson's colorful terminology,[52] misappropriated state revenues and assets precipitating a series of political events which culminated in the destruction of communist power, but not state authority. The unscrupulous plundered Russia, masquerading as free enterprise democrats, but deferred to Boris Yeltsin's and now Vladimir Putin's autocracy.

The postcommunist model is traditional. Oligarchs and their retinues are granted privileges at the people's expense in return for taxes, tribute and fealty to the national leader. They can assert claims to property, engage in business, act as entrepreneurs, buy positions in the Duma, the Federal Security Service (FSB) and bureaucracy, grab state assets (privatization), exert power, and misbehave (from the standpoint of Western norms) as long as they refrain from challenging the leader.[53] The constitution and precedent allow the president to command without a party, and control, as it has always been in Russia, is mostly informal.[54]

The characteristics displayed by the Russian system depend significantly on circumstances. When the state is vulnerable as it was during War Communism, NEP, and for diverse reasons throughout much of Stalin's reign, it turns to the secret police to subdue enemies and sometimes to mobilize productive effort. But when it is courting new oligarchs, when candidates are submissive, when defense isn't pressing and the people are quiescent, autocrats are more permissive. This adaptability has allowed authoritarianism to survive over the centuries. Of course, because Russian autocracy is incompatible with an authentic rule of law, there is always the danger of oppression when oligarchs run amok, or the people are driven to insurrection.

Autocracy remains the gravitational center of politics in Russia, but because our public culture prefers to ignore it, it is valuable to have an authority like Yevgeniy Primakov, a former prime minister and now president of the Russian Chamber of Commerce and Industry admit it. He disagreed with the criticism of Russia drifting toward authoritarianism expressed by Human Rights Watch in its 2005 annual report. "I have absolutely nothing against authoritarianism," Primakov said in an exclusive interview with Ekho Moskvy radio on January 20, 2006. "Authoritarianism should not always be associated with Stalin's practice. For me it does not necessarily mean party leadership or throwing people to jail," he went on to say. "Authoritarianism should not affect freedom of speech. But a state cannot exist without fulfilment of the orders and administrative discipline," he added.[55]

Today, Russia is a vulnerable and brittle autocracy; a system in which oligarchs and siloviki tirelessly scheme to place their private agendas above the ruler's. At the current juncture the nation appears to be simultaneously beset by three perils: obstreperous servitors, poverty, and an oppressive regime.

Russia Will Rearm

The strategy of the Soviet regime was to impose Spartan living standards on its population in order to maximize military preparedness. Since the end of the Soviet period, Russia has continued to economically subjugate its people, but for a decade or so the Russian leadership gave precedence to greed over martial power.

An economy structured to provide maximum military strength (the Spartans of our time) has lost sight of its raison d'etre – military strength. We must expect that it will regain it. This is the path of least resistance for the Russians. To try to become a Western-style consumer society is proving to be very difficult, and it's increasingly clear that Russia won't ever be very good at it – the West and even the Chinese will always exceed it. Hence, Russia is likely to go where it has been before and where it has historically been quite effective – a structurally militarized state. In fact, the CIA's analysis to the contrary not withstanding – the Soviets have since the 1930s never led the United States in the rate of increase in living standards; rather, the only economic success the Kremlin has ever achieved is mass weapons production.

Russia must be expected to find a security strategy keyed to its economic potential. Markets which were supposed to have been vehicles for serving consumers, are being gradually harnessed for the development of a fifth-generation, full spectrum military capable of contesting with America by

2010.[56] The potential of Russia's economic system is large enough to support the full spectrum, fifth generation rearmament scheduled 2005–2010, if Putin restores the Genshtab's and Ministry of Defense's control over the Federation's natural resources as is currently happening, because the Soviet era military industrial complex is largely intact, and missing pieces can be reassembled with funds from the natural resource sector that the Yukos affair and the subsequent Gasprom-Sibneft merger will ultimately provide.

The armed forces sought by President Putin greatly exceed the size required for optimum security. They will be sufficient to restore the Russian Federation's undisputed status as a superpower, but only a junior one that provides little tangible benefit because the economic model lacks the commercial base to compete technologically with America. Moreover, full spectrum rearmament will strengthen authoritarianism, nail the coffin shut on democratic free enterprise, starve civilian investment, hamper global integration and bind Russia to Soviet-style impoverishment, after the oil bubble bursts.

"For Russian President Vladimir Putin and Defense Minister Sergei Ivanov," writes Stephen Blank, "modernization, not reform characterizes defense policy. Ivanov defines modernization as policies that strengthen the armed forces' combat capacity, particularly its command and control structures."[57]

At the moment, this trend is somewhat obscured because high natural resource prices, particularly petroleum, have allowed the Kremlin to temporize, believing it has the financial resources to provide both guns and butter. But as weapons production ramps up in 2005, Putin will be compelled to choose one or the other.

Rose-Colored Glasses Again

Western public culture provides a long list of cogent economic and political reasons for believing the Russian will jettison militarization, assuming that Putin's policies are guided by enlightened rationality. Rapid fire shifts in Putin's foreign policy, together with the usual chatter about prosperity being just around the corner help to keep hope alive in the West. Our public culture strongly inclines us toward nonconfrontational engagement in which we attempt to promote democratic free enterprise, emphasizing economic assistance and sanctions to the Russians for going where we'd like them to go. Our president goes to Moscow and chides the Russians for slipping back from democracy. But although democratic free enterprise is probably Moscow's best long-range solution, the Kremlin almost certainly doesn't have either the insight or the resolve to extricate itself from remilitarization. The ceaseless effort to portray the economy as self-healing or self-transforming into democratic free enterprise is unconvincing.

The counterlogic of the Russian economic system, and the Kremlin's unwillingness to relinquish targets of opportunity to countervailing American power, and a variety of other security concerns, including the potential Chinese threat, further diminish the likelihood that Russia will abandon remilitarization. Putin probably won't overtly choose between remilitarization and today's attempt to have guns and butter, but his authoritarian instincts will lead him to gradually ally with the forces of remilitarization.

In the fall of 2005 Russia conducted at least six successful strategic missle launches. About these launches Martin Sieff wrote, "American analysts tend to discount the value of such weapons and such tests.... But such confidence, or arrogance, may well be misplaced. Over the past century Russian military, space and missile and technology have repeatedly astonished and confounded the world by getting impressively reliable results from unassuming, simple or supposedly obsolescent technology.... For the key point about all six major missile tests that the Russian armed forces conducted in late September and early October is that the weapons actually worked. The rocket engines fired and the missiles went where they were supposed to..."[58]

Many Western security analysts like Keir Leiber and Daryl Press, largely under the thrall of the public culture and ignorant of the disinformative purposes of Russia's official arms control statistics erroneously imagine that Russia's nuclear forces are inadequate,[59] and don't believe that Russia will implement a full spectrum fifth generation rearmament by 2010, or any time soon thereafter. There is always the possibility that they could be right about rearmament, but they are missing the drama, and underestimating the risks.

Thus, contrary to all that is being said in the American and European press and by Western governments, the Soviet Union didn't disappear – it simply reorganized, changed its name to Russia, dropped its ideological orientation, embarked on a publicity campaign to persuade the rest of the world that the tiger had changed its stripes, and set out on a course of expediency in a changing world.

Seen in this way, it can be argued that the Cold War has never really ended; it merely entered a new phase with the collapse of the USSR. Western harmonists denied this, of course, but today even those in the European Union are being made to face the unpleasant reality. "The future of Europe's relations with Russia is all but settled," wrote an astute European commentator in 2006. "Official communiques on relations between Russia and the European Union are generally tuned to the requirements of positive thinking and the designs of strategic planners in European big business . . . but multilateral cooperation is characterised by discrete discontent on the side of European diplomacy. The Council of Europe blames Russia of non-compliance with a whole range of European standards and multilateral treaties. As the 1997 Cooperation and Partnership Treaty between the European Union and Russia is up for renewal in 2007 the EU commission is filing a whole range of alterations. Russian foreign policy, however, remains quite content with the current situation, i.e. the practical irrelevance of these agreements."[60]

Russia in the Distant Future

In the longer term, the reconfiguration of global wealth and power among the nations is making Russia more and more vulnerable. Its GDP will probably be only 2 percent of the global total by 2025, leaving it in the dust behind America, China, the European Union, and Japan.

Russia's declining population will sharply curtail the Kremlin's ability to field the armed forces needed to defend its borders, and a parallel fall in scientists and engineers hampers its economic and military potential.

The Genshtab response to these concerns following past precedent is likely to be an exaggerated perception of the threat (which the Soviet's did before them – for example, overestimating American tank production capacity during the Cold War by a factor of twenty-five), and a massive arms accumulation drive to make up for Russia's manpower and technological deficiencies.

A resurgent Russia will be very different in global politics than the Soviet Union. Most important, it will no longer have the messianic conviction of communism, with its drive to create fifth columns in all the nations of the world and to advance its ideology whenever possible. Instead, Russia will be more like the tsarist empire, a major power with its own interests; always expansionist, but not ordinarily adventuresome. It will seek to dominate a large region around its borders, and will probably seek to restore some of the direct control that its predecessors (tsarist Russia and the Soviet Union) had over its near neighbors. There is not likely to be a declared new Cold War (the ideological fervor and global reach of communism are gone) between Russia and the United States, but there is likely to be something quite similar, a constant elbowing for geopolitical advantage with the risk of stumbling into overt conflict. The elbowing will be especially risky of nuclear war were the United States to have no national missile defense. Furthermore, elbowing may sometimes take what are from the perspective of the Cold War astonishing forms. For example, Russia may be permitted by a Europe increasingly distant from America in geopolitics to join European military alliances, perhaps even a strangely modified NATO. It would be an error to see in new arrangements of this sort a continuing lessening of rivalry between Russia and us; they will be evidence of the opposite.

We will not have an arms race with a remilitarizing Russia, but we will have a military rivalry. Surprisingly, strictly speaking there was no arms race during the cold war! The Soviets increased their weapons at a double-digit clip, and we responded with mutually assured deterrence and high-tech intimidation.

We won't respond directly to counter their buildup weapon for weapon and soldier for soldier next time either, unless Russia threatens the European Union. Instead, we are going to rely on high technology weaponry with some sort of missile defense.

This means that America will concede to Russia World War II–type land wars outside Europe, and will hope that other threats can be won by mobility and high-tech. We will have a doctrinal rivalry (what is the best way to wage a war) with Russia while we have asymmetric arsenals to match. Superpower will mean for us properly understood what it meant during the Cold War – making the world free for different kinds of conventional war; RMA for us, mass armies for Russia.

In the long term, if we can get there, when China challenges all others for world power, in the period 2020 to 2030 in our expectation, Russia may become a natural ally of the West. Even Putin hasn't grasped this yet, and may not. (The suggestion comes from the civilian head of the Swedish defense intelligence establishment.)

The European Union: Nation-Building on a Super Scale

The European Union is involved in the world's most important effort in nation building – far exceeding the significance of anything being done in Iraq or elsewhere. The French and German governments are driving a federalist agenda. The significance of European unity for the world of the future is enormous, and how America reacts to it is of the utmost importance. In the spring of 2005 there were significant setbacks to the pan-European agenda, but they are most likely only setbacks. Some Europeans express a desire to become a rival of the United States by expanding and integrating until a superpower can be created. This would present a significant challenge to America.

The Treaty of Rome has "evolved from a set of legal arrangements binding sovereign states into a vertically integrated legal regime conferring judicially enforceable rights and obligations on legal persons and entities, public and private."[61] Since World War II, Western Europe has been our close ally and simultaneously has been seeking closer unity among its national components. Until recently, the two were closely connected and ran in parallel lines. Because of the Soviet threat, increasing European unity required American protection. But now they are diverging – Europe is looking for a way to take a very large step toward a federal union, the Soviet threat is gone, and America is the most likely candidate for an external danger around which European unity can be forged. This was the underlying reason for the dispute between America and Europe (especially France and Germany as the leaders of Europe) over Iraq, and it's the harbinger of increasingly difficult political conflicts to come. It may be hard to think of Europe as a potential antagonist, but in the future, once the Europeans have achieved a larger measure of unity and turn the focus of their attention outward, it is a likely development. Europe has the population, economic potential and geopolitical orientation to be a major rival of the United States – what it currently lacks is the unity – and that it may achieve in the next few decades.

No political path is perfectly straight, and the nation-building of the European Union has its setbacks. But at each setback its proponents learn, and return to the effort. In the aftermath of the rejection of the proposed European Constitution by voters in France and the Netherlands, defenders of the EU as a nascent nation state began to express themselves more clearly. "A common market is not enough . . . a common market inspires no solidarity."[62]

Because Europeans are engaged in building their own nation, for their top leaders (especially France and Germany) this must take precedence to other issues. They are not free to be simply allies of the United States as in the past. Hence, long-repressed resentments and rivalries are now allowed to bubble to the surface of global politics. Europe must be distinguished from the United States if it's to be strong and united.

There's a problem building the strong, unified European nation. ". . . forging a 'common destiny' for the diverse peoples of Europe, after . . . years of conflict and suspicion, is a monumental task. The drafters [of the new European constitution] envisioned a Europe 'united in diversity,' but diversity has seldom been a unifying force in the affairs of mankind."[63]

The European elite's mindset is committed to promoting EU expansion and integration in a social democratic framework. Thus the dominant European lens for viewing geopolitical developments suggests that Russia isn't

European yet because its security thinking is based on great power rivalries instead of the concepts of "societies and integration," the European way. It is intriguing that in this point of view what makes a country European or not is a mind-set. For the United States, what is most important is to avoid this mind-set, lest we become European in essence and susceptible to integration into the Europe de facto if not de jure. Joe Nye got it backward when he saw America with soft power and Europe as its victim; more likely the opposite is the case.[64]

The bitter controversy about Iraq between the our government and those of France and Germany was not primarily about Iraq itself; nor even about our acting unilaterally, as even the more sophisticated analysts insist; it is rather about nation building in Europe, and we are the adversary around which cohesion is being built by those who will lead Europe in the future and must create a national identity. We are chosen for that role because in the age of the single superpower there is no other candidate.

The controversy over invading Iraq was also the first significant collision in global politics between a uniting Europe and a more assertive United States. In the national elbowing which is global diplomacy, Europe (that is, its most important leaders, Chirac of France and Schroder of Germany) opposed our initiative for a coalition to bring down Saddam Hussein in part because Europe didn't want America learning to be better practitioners of real politik, foreseeing a shift in the correlation of global forces against Europe – one that is in fact occurring. France and Germany understood that they could not build a military counterforce to the United States and its new allies because of the pronounced tilt of European public opinion toward pacifism. Instead, therefore, Europe sought to contain American initiative by seeking to get us included in a multinational decision-making context. That they failed is of great significance for the future.

Unifying Europe requires separation from the United States, and so France and Germany opposed us on Iraq and will oppose us elsewhere. The grounds on which they oppose us are secondary, though they must be so chosen and expressed that they command considerable public support in Europe. Iraq was a perfect issue from this point of view; the United States could be made to appear warmongering and unilateralist, uninterested in Europe's opinions, preferring war to peaceful solutions. The European public was all too ready to believe all this, and European political leaders to offer it to them. Many Americans get upset by this, but it's a mistake for Americans to get too deeply involved in the details of European objections to our policy, for that's not the core of the opposition. And because we don't oppose increasing integration of Europe, we should be prepared to let the Europeans use us as a foil, if they think it necessary.

Carrying European unification forward is not going to be easy for its proponents; and major difficulties are now occurring. There are forces tending to prevent closer unity as well as those favoring it. Central to the forces against increasing unity are ancient rivalries and hatreds and the enlargement of the union to more and more members, which creates more difficulties in getting agreement on a federalist agenda. Swimming against this current are European federalists who are promoting a full Constitution for Europe. It is rather like the period through which the American colonies passed immediately after we'd won our independence from Britain and had created Articles of Confederation between the thirteen colonies, but did not yet have a federal union. It was not certain then that thirteen colonies would combine to create a single nation – certainly not a strong, centralized federal government. It is not at all certain today that some twenty-two different nations that now compose the European Union will establish a strong, centralized federal government with its own foreign policy and military force, as the federalists desire. If the federalists are successful, it's going to take considerable time to enhance the union and make it work.

Thus, as the pro-American former Spanish prime minister, José María Aznar, ruefully notes, the fashion in central Europe is to be "leftist, federalist and anti-American."[65] He doesn't seem to understand that this is much more than simply a fashion.

This conjunction of elements in Europe is very important:

- leftist – and therefore anticapitalist,
- federalist – and therefore committed to building a single entity of the European nations, and
- anti-American – as a focus around which to unite.

Europe has gone as far as it can in the direction of unity via the rather technical elements of economic union, which has been driven by the business and political elites. It now must engage the masses and get their support for the next big step toward European federalism. As an observer of the European process notes, "The elitist character of European integration has been rapidly reaching its limits. The European project needs to become more democratic and hence more explicitly political."[66] The stage is set for federalists in Europe to wage a political battle to unify the Continent, and a political battle without a positive goal requires an opponent around which to unite – and we are being chosen for that role.

Americans must expect to hear Europeans offer impassioned statements of how intensely they loathe America's Iraq foray, and then go on to lament the Muslim menace in Europe, without seeing that the situation in Europe would be even worse if America weren't standing up to Islamic fundamentalist aggression.

Europe is captive to its social democratic romanticism, and deeply resentful of those who won't buy into the dream. As a consequence, American/European relations are bound to become more and more rancorous, even though this is irrational for both sides.

In the midst of a constitutional crisis and stagnating economies, EU leaders are mounting a campaign against long vacations and other social perks under the banner of globalist necessity, but the population is deeply resistive. Judging by the Swedish experience, if the social democratic benefit package is pruned, the anticipated economic effect will be swallowed up in political corruption. If this is right, we should expect EU leaders to become increasingly strident against America as they try to deflect blame abroad.

HOW EUROPEANS SEEK TO BIND AMERICA

According to a recent interpretation that has received much comment, Europe and the United States do not share the same sense of danger and their common interest is weakening, partly because the "rogue" states are located outside Europe and are a lesser threat to Europe than to America, and largely because that Europe is militarily weak today and America strong. In effect, this view attributes Europe's preference for appeasement to Europe's weakness. A gap in military power is said to generate a difference in strategic perceptions between Europe and the United States. Because the United States is stronger, it sees the world differently than Europe.

The result, so goes the argument, is a very different choice of tactics in the international sphere. The Europeans now endorse negotiation, diplomacy and commercial ties, and multilateral action (preferably via the United Nations). They opt for international law over the use of force, for seduction over coercion, and for multilateralism over unilateralism. In contrast, America is said to favor military dominance and overt conflict to resolve issues because America possesses military power.[67]

The analysis is provocative because it gives a plausible explanation of an important political difference between Europe and America, but it weakens on close examination. This statement by its leading proponent is troubling, for example, "The United States, meanwhile, remains mired in history, exercising power in the anarchic Hobbesian world where international laws and rules are unreliable and where true security and the defense and promotion of a liberal order still depend on the possession and use of military might." Yes, but why the verb "mired" when the author seems to support the American position? In fact, his argument is carefully couched to walk both sides of a political street. It seeks approval from Europeans by suggesting the United States is out of date and Neanderthal (not naïve, interestingly, which used to be the European charge against the United States); and yet the argument seeks support from the Americans by suggesting that the European view is nothing more than the political resort of weakness.

Neither is convincing. As we've seen, currently Europe is inward-focused in a stage of nation-building, and it seeks not to be distracted by outside matters, and so it looks to international order, multilateralism, and so on to limit outside diversions and also to restrain its great rival, the United States. In fact, Europe is today in much the position of the United States during the American Civil War – it wants to be left alone to work out its own fate. Europe will at some point emerge from its inner direction, and be more assertive in the world, and at that time – its geopolitical strategy having changed – it will begin to rebuild its military strength. This is two decades off, but is one of the most important factors on the long-term international scene.

Although, as we've said, there's a superficial plausibility to the view that Europe wants multilateralism and international law because it is weak, unfortunately, the argument has the actual direction of causality backward. It's because of a difference in strategic perception that the Europeans are content to be weaker than America; not the other way round. Lack of military preparedness is not an act of God; it's not something that just happens to a country or a continent; especially when underlying economic and technical strength is as great as that of Europe. Lack of preparedness is a choice. Military weakness reflects a deep strategic perception – that there isn't great danger of attack or invasion and that more is to be gained by other methods than military force.

For Europe to now be weak, and America militarily strong, is a major reversal of roles. Until World War II, the opposite was more commonly the case. It was America, not Europe, that invented multilateralism (an attempt to bring order and a form of law to international relations) in opposition to competing alliances among the European powers, as a response to America having been dragged into World War I. It was an American response to the European system of alliances intended to form a balance of power; a system that had lead to the disaster that was the World War I. That war was hoped to be a war to end wars, and to make it so, America proposed a multinational mechanism to keep the peace – the League of Nations. And America proposed this at a time of its strength, not weakness – at the end of World War I, with the European powers either collapsed (Germany, Austria, and Russia), or exhausted (France and Britain and Italy), America was the strongest power in the world; a million American troops were on the borders of Germany. So the proposal for multilateralism and international law reflected not America's weakness, but America's strength and strategy – to keep out of foreign wars by preventing them, while itself disarmed again. It was not that America was weak that caused it to propose the League. So, today, it's not that Europe is weak that causes it to embrace multilateralism but, rather, that it wants to keep out of foreign entanglements while it continues its efforts at unification. The full panoply of multilateralism, diplomacy, weak military, and so on now fits the needs of European leaders so it is being nurtured in the politics of Europe. Britain's Tony Blair seems sometimes not to understand this and is being entangled in a political web that is being woven on the Continent.

Additionally, since World War II, Europe has become adept at biting politically the American hand that has so long protected it, while simultaneously congratulating itself on its moral superiority. "Western Europeans wanted the United States to involve itself in European affairs after 1945 – but they also resented that involvement," writes a major historian of modern Europe.[68] During the Cold War, secure because of American defense, the European nations learned to enjoy taking aid while denying the Soviet threat and sparring with us over trade and tariffs. The Europeans became convinced wishful thinkers, abandoning their centuries long penchant for real politik, because being hopeful played to their vanity and filled their pocket books. Now they are hopelessly addicted to wishful thinking, and aggrieved because a more mature and sophisticated America is much less easy to manipulate.

Europe's lack of military strength and its preference for multilateralism are simply tactical choices to support its current strategic aims. Europe may be said to have reversed Theodore Roosevelt's dictum for American foreign policy, "Speak softly and carry a big stick." Today in the hands of European leaders the dictum would seem to be instead, "Speak loudly, and carry a match stick!"

What some observers want to identify as two very different paradigms of international behavior (those of Europe and America – that of multilateralism and that of the Bush Doctrine's unilateralism) are in reality merely different strategies within the arena of geopolitics. That is, the Europeans still play the geopolitical game as vigorously as ever, but they have changed tactics, preferring not to compete with America in the military sphere, because they are now inward focused and have more to gain, they think, by a strategy of multilateralism (even pacificism and it's handmaiden, appeasement). By such devices the key European leaders seek to bind the American Gulliver. Again the reversal of roles is ironic and instructive. Before to World War II America was inward-focused and isolationist, hoping for peace from multilateralism (via the League of Nations, though we ultimately rejected close involvement ourselves), whereas European nations continued to vie for position in the world via huge armaments. Today, it is Europe that is isolationist and seeks peace via multilateral arrangements and America that vies in the world for position via huge armaments. Europe is weak because its strategy has it so; and America is strong because its strategy has it so.

The European Union is not simply an ally of the United States – instead, it is both an ally and increasingly a rival. Certainly not our enemy, Europe is none the less dangerous because its interests are so different from our own. An example can be helpful, drawn from what is probably the closest military and political alliance of great powers in modern times – that of the United States and Britain. Winston Churchill, who more than any other individual was parent to the alliance, protected the British Empire successfully from its enemies (including the Germans and Japanese) but not from its ally and rival (the United States). Britain lost the empire despite victories in two world wars. Franklin Roosevelt didn't like the European colonial empires, would not support them, and in the end brought about their demise. It was Roosevelt's role in bringing about the collapse of the French colonial empire that was at the heart of de Gaulle's mistrust of the Americans.

France remains a dangerous ally for the United States. Generally posturing for peace in order to embarrass America when it is defending itself, France sometimes saber-rattles in ways that are so irresponsible as to cause concern even to American hard-liners. For example, early in 2006, French President Jacques Chirac rattled a nuclear sword, going beyond anything the United States has threatened as a response to terrorism. He warned that France could respond with nuclear weapons against a nation that sponsored a terrorist attack against France.[69] Chirac's threat was a dangerous assertion of an intention to make a nuclear first strike.

BRITAIN'S SPECIAL SITUATION

Britain is unique and important, but its special situation may not last. Its economy is much more vibrant than that of Continental Europe, with which it shares few defining features. Its economic growth is quicker; reforms that are very difficult on the continent were achieved a decade or more ago in Britain. Furthermore, Britain has a special relationship with the United States that often gives it far more influence than the rest of Europe with Washington.

But Britain is also part of the European Union. As Europe unifies, Britain will be forced into joining or becoming increasingly separate. That decision is not yet made – Britain is still on the periphery and being courted by the makers of the new Europe, especially France and Germany. This is why meetings between the heads of state of Britain, France, and Germany attract so much media attention in Europe. There is the sense of something important in process. But Britain cannot keep its special economic and geopolitical advantages if it enters Europe. All of the countries entering the new Europe have much to gain, though some may think not, but Britain alone has a great deal to lose. What will it do?

A Tory Member of Parliament has argued in a recent book that a struggle has already begun between Asia (especially China) and the United States for supremacy in the world, and that Britain should ally itself closely with America, not with Europe.[70]

What should America's position be? The issue is tied to the issue of our reaction to the federalist agenda in Europe. We are probably not going to be able to derail the further unification of Europe, even were we to try. What then of Britain? We are best advantaged if Britain seeks closer ties to us, in an enhanced Atlantic alliance, rather than if Britain enters a federalized Europe.

The reasons are several:

1. The close ties to Britain in our history;
2. A close tie in our language and culture;
3. A century of close alliance in several wars; and
4. Britain's support for us in the war on terror and the Second Gulf War.

The decision about the direction of its future belongs not to us, of course, but to the English. But so long as the United Kingdom wants a special relationship with America, it should have it, and we should be prepared to make the relationship even closer should that be in ours and Britain's interest as Europe unifies.

Britain in fact has good reasons for wanting to keep some distance from the European Union:

1. It's growing faster, with better economic performance since the 1980s. It has made a remarkable economic advance: from 65 percent of French

economic output (GDP) in 1980 to 110 percent in 2002; from per capita economic output at 95 percent of the French in 1980 to 104 percent in 2002. From 1990 to 2001 the British economy grew at 1.9 percent per annum; that of the French at 1.4 percent per annum.[71]

2. It has stayed out of the European common monetary system (the Euro) and may not want into the tighter European Union now being forged for fear its economy will join that of the major continental powers in ongoing stagnation.

If so, America should support Britain in keeping some independence of the European Union. This would be Britain's form of Strategic Independence, and we should endorse it.

THE AMERICAN RESPONSE TO EUROPEAN NATION-BUILDING

The American government seems ambivalent about what to do about European unification. Our formal policy has long been to support it, believing that a divided Europe could somehow, someday, repeat the internecine wars that enveloped the globe for centuries past, and into which we were so often dragged unwillingly. But the exigencies of the moment cause us to see our advantage elsewhere. As a British commentator observed, "Some of the Administration (Rumsfeld and Cheney) seem to believe American interests "can best be served by a fractured Europe from which they can select 'coalitions of the willing.' "[72]

This is a very important issue – what does America want for Europe – now and in the future? To what will we give support? What will we oppose – whether publicly or in private? Do we want Europe united in the long term but divided now? If so, how is that to be achieved? Won't the short-term interest in division prevent the long-term objective of unity from being achieved? And if Europe were somehow to bring off unification over our efforts to prevent it, are we not likely to have sown a harvest of resentment and hostility?

A former leader of the European Union has this to say about our policy. ". . . the United States shows little interest in a Europe united behind a common foreign policy, and today often seems to work against it. . . . Mr. Prodi, 64, has come to Tuscany to relax and reflect before beginning the final year of his five-year term as president of the union's European Commission."

". . . In this complex world, nobody alone is able to dictate a policy, even a country so strong and so powerful like the United States," he said, his voice alternately gruff and purring. "The great risk of great powers is overstretching." A unified

Europe as America's partner would only increase global stability, he argues. But Mr. Prodi worries that Americans understand neither the value of a united Europe nor the difficulty in securing that unity. "Their prevalent doctrine today is to have a divided Europe," Mr. Prodi said of the United States. . . . Meanwhile, Mr. Prodi says, Europeans are building something new and different. That may suit the United States just fine, he acknowledged, because internal bickering keeps Europe from presenting a unified challenge to Washington's foreign policy, as in the months before the recent Iraq war. But Mr. Prodi argues that it is in the Americans' long-term interest to have a united Europe that can share the political and economic costs of world affairs. "Look how difficult it is to invent a new policy for the postwar Iraq." In any case, Mr. Prodi said, it will be "decades, not years" before Europe has a totally united foreign policy because "it will be the last piece of sovereignty the member states will pool together."[73]

It's the delay in uniting Europe around a single foreign policy that gives America such a long time to prepare its attitude toward European integration and to pursue it. There will be a strong body of opinion in America that will want to let Europe tell us what our policy should be. Via wishful thinking, Europe has a strong fifth column in America. Believers in wishful thinking are not viewed as fifth columnists because we don't think of Europe as an adversary. But as it unifies, and uses America as an opponent around which to unite, then Americans who espouse the European viewpoint, a perspective intended to keep America in its place, will become suspect.

There is no greater need for presidential leadership in American foreign policy than here. In our view American policy should be that we want the European nations to pursue their own welfare as they see it, so long as they cross no adversarial threshold with us. We should not care whether they prefer a loose confederation or a strong federation. Should they choose the latter, we prefer that they not select us as the ogre against whom the Continent will unite, lest this course unintentionally cross a threshold of antagonism that cannot be reclaimed. Furthermore, we should support Britain in staying outside, should it so wish. And we should prepare, while endeavoring to avoid it, for a long-term rivalry that at some point might worsen into the possibility of overt conflict.

CHAPTER 10: KEY POINTS

China

1. Chinese economic growth has been spectacular for two decades and China is integrating itself into the global economic system.

2. This achievement is attributable to the Chinese Communist Party's improbable success in combining authoritarian discipline of labor, state ownership of enterprise – elements of the old command economy – with massive foreign direct investment and significant elements of leasehold profit-driven markets.

3. The Chinese economy has a pronounced bias toward inequitable but rapid development.

4. The current Chinese system will allow China to overtake America in the next twenty years in terms of the dollar value of its gross domestic product, but inefficiencies or other state priorities will place a low ceiling on living standards.

5. As is the Soviet Union, China is better positioned to be a great military power than an affluent nation.

6. To global insecurity caused by its momentum toward becoming a great power, China adds the distinct risk of internal instability.

7. The Chinese already have scores of nuclear missiles that they assert can hit America's West Coast cities.

8. The Chinese are rapidly modernizing their nuclear missile capability with the objective of bringing the entire United States into their targeting range.

9. America must respond to this increasing Chinese threat.

Russia

1. In the period of the early 1990s, there was a major geopolitical change (the USSR broke up), but there was little or no change in Russia's economic and governance systems. The required qualification is that economic and political control is less heavy handed than before.

2. Individuals have far greater autonomy over economic and political matters that the leadership deems inessential.

3. The contemporary Russian economy is a Muscovite authoritarian mixed system with weakly developed competitive institutions that invite corruption.

4. Russia's scuttling of the Communist Party–state control apparatus in 1991 combined with Boris Yeltsin's predilection for revenue misappropriation and asset-grabbing by his favorites, prevented the emergence of the rule of law and competitive markets, which might have preserved full employment; furthermore, Yeltsin refused to devise new state institutions to foster growth.

5. The consequence is that Russia has been stuck in an incomplete transition from communism to free enterprise, which has resulted in 17 years of hyperdepression.

6. There is now little likelihood that the Russian economy will successfully manage a free enterprise transition, so that Russia will continue to decline economically relative to the other major powers.

7. What Russia has done well in the past is to harness its economy to military preparedness, while providing only very weak consumer welfare. It is very likely to do this again.

8. Already the Russians have announced their intent to fully modernize their nuclear weapons systems complemented by full spectrum military modernization, something that should be at full speed by 2010.

9. In the longer term, the Russians are being left in the economic and technological dust by America and even China.

10. In consequence, from 2010 to 2020, there is a window of great risk for an American confrontation with a militarily resurgent Russia.

European Union

1. The most important effort at nation building in the world today is going on in Europe. Lacking a strong positive reason for unification, European federalists are making the United States an opponent around which a European nationalism can be forged. This is the underlying motivation behind French and German opposition to America's war in Iraq.

2. Despite numerous formal similarities, the market systems on the opposite shores of the Atlantic are generating strikingly different outcomes.

3. This is due to two factors. Western Europe is more collectivist and leisure-oriented than the United States. Compared to the United States, the dominant European economic culture indulges idleness and dependency, and favors egalitarianism.

4. In the European economic culture management behaves differently than in America, and the result is a lesser level of economic performance.

5. In consequence, Europe is likely to continue to grow more slowly than America for the next twenty to thirty years. In that period America will have further lengthened its economic and military lead, and China

will have established itself as a great power. Europe will have fallen behind.

6. Because European economic growth is and will be weak, Europe seeks to develop economic and military strength through enlargement rather than internal growth.

7. America must decide how to react to European unification. We should not oppose it, because it will occur anyway; we should accept with good grace our role as an ogre around which federalists will unite Europe; and we should prepare for a challenge in the geopolitical world from Europe in the middle of this century.

8. Britain faces an especially difficult choice between Europe and America. Should Britain choose to remain outside a federal Europe, we should support it as fully as possible.

PART FIVE

VORTEXES OF DANGER

The United States faces several threats of equal reality but of different magnitude. The concept of vortexes of danger is valuable in giving clarity to an objective assessment of the threats.

ELEVEN

A Witch's Brew of Troubles

The Next Big Wars

A great power can be constrained only by another great power or potent coalition. When a great power is surrounded by weak states (as are both China and Russia today, with the exception of each other), the result is often aggrandizement by the great power, if not open aggression. And conflict of the great powers, when it comes, is the greatest danger mankind faces. For this reason it is essential always to keep our eye first and foremost on the great powers.

Woodrow Wilson made this basic mistake at the end of World War I and thereby contributed to the making of World War II. He believed that the dissatisfaction of minorities within polygot empires was the basic cause of the war (after all, didn't a Serbian nationalist assassinate the heir to the throne of the Austrian Empire and thereby occasion the war?). So he worked for the dissolution of the Austrian and European parts of the Russian empire; but left the German empire (made up of a single nationality) intact. Thus, he surrounded Germany with weak states, providing the temptation and opportunity for Hitler.

We are in danger of doing the same now. We are taking our eyes off the great powers, and looking instead at issues like terrorism.

We rationalize this to ourselves by three devices:

1. We pretend to ourselves that the atomic arsenals of the great powers are somehow no longer dangerous. We tell ourselves there will be no conflict of the great powers, insisting again, as before World War I, that increasing trade and improving economies make war impossible (harmonism); we tells ourselves that Russia and China are becoming like ourselves, so the likelihood of war disappears (convergence); thus the harmonist and convergence illusions mislead us.

2. We insist to ourselves that terrorism is somehow as great a potential threat as great power conflict (which it is definitely not – the United States in four years of terrorist conflict since September 11, 2001, has lost about forty-five hundred dead – including those killed in the World Trade Center bombing; during World War II the United States lost in four years of war some 330,000 dead, and this was before atomic weapons and before today's vulnerability of our homeland to direct attack).

3. We mislead ourselves about the causes of international conflict, deciding now that it is dictatorship (the absence of democracy) that is the root cause of war. Before that it was economic deprivation; and before that, thwarted nationalism was the root cause of war (Woodrow Wilson's view). Unfortunately, dictatorship is not the root cause of war, and so we ignore again the rivalries and changing economic situation of the great powers and pursue instead another will-o'-the-wisp.

4. The terrorist threat needs to be upgraded by emphasizing the vortex effects of the Crescent of Fire (crescent shape swath of Muslim fundamentalist agitation from Morocco through Indonesia). Terrorism itself is a small direct threat to the United States, but it is a potential catalyst for great power conflict, especially multilaterally ballistic missile exchanges.

PRESENT AND LOOMING DANGERS

America faces a sequence of challenges – from terrorism, Russian remilitarization, Chinese nationalism and military modernization, and possibly even in the distant future from a united Europe.

It is crucial that we keep the differing magnitudes of these dangers in perspective, and prepare to meet each with an imaginative and effective response.

Terrorism is at the top of the agenda of American defense concerns today, including the threat of small scale weapons of mass destruction. But it is the least significant of the dangers facing us over the next several decades. We will confront a series of challenges from major powers well armed with nuclear weapons. Fortunately, there will be a sequence of these challenges, rather than their all coming at once. Thus far our policy for dealing with nuclear rivalry has been deterrence via Mutual Assured Destruction. MAD has always worked (though only at great risk) before. But in a world of many nuclear powers (great and small) and of shifting challengers, MAD is unlikely to be at all effective. Hence, we need a new approach to our security.

DANGERS OF MANY SORTS

The terrorist attack on the World Trade Center on September 11, 2001, was so traumatic that in its aftermath many Americans have ceased to think clearly about our nation's place in the world. Blindsided by the emotional impact of September 11, our leaders lost perspective and proportion. (See the discussion in Chapter 12.) They seem to have adopted the view that terrorism is the greatest threat to our country, and have forgotten that far greater threats exist. They argue that the war on terror is our greatest priority; but this is both short-sighted and potentially fatal.

The danger in America today is that, traumatized by September 11, our leaders confuse secondary threats with great ones. Terrorists, even armed with atomic bombs in suitcases and biological weapons, can do us harm, but cannot destroy us. We are a continental nation of almost three hundred million people. We can be hurt, but not destroyed by terrorism. But we might be obliterated by a major nuclear or biological exchange with another great power.

This point can be illustrated by recalling that the September 11 attacks killed fewer than three thousand people, and in the Second Gulf War we've lost several hundred soldiers and killed several thousand Iraqis. Yet during World War II, killing was on a different scale. For example, on Okinawa in 1945 of the four hundred thousand civilians when the Japanese island was invaded by Americans, despite efforts to keep them out of the fire, 150,000 were killed. In addition, tens of thousands of Japanese and American soldiers died in the fighting. During World War II, in the world as a whole, counting combatants and civilians, for two thousand days, comprising six years of war, some twenty-eight thousand people died on average per day, totaling some fifty-six million dead. (The fifty-six million figure includes ten million killed by Stalin in the 1930s and 1940s, concealed as war heroes.) During the war about ninety million men and women were inducted into the armed services of their countries (sixty million by the Allied Powers and thirty million by the Axis powers). Fourteen million Americans served in our armed forces during the war.[1]

That was a war. Our leaders have chosen to call our response to terrorist attacks a "war" also; but if antiterrorism is a war, what word should we use for something as different in scale as World War II? To call each by the same label confuses our thinking. In America because of our tendency to exaggerate concerns and responses, we've had "wars" on poverty and drugs and terrorism, and are in danger of forgetting what a real war is and how much more dangerous it is in our nuclear age than any of the other threats we now label "wars."

The most important threat we face is another conflict on the scale of World War II, or as is perfectly possible with today's weapons, on a greater scale.

In particular, trends in our world are increasingly destabilizing, rather in the fashion of a geological fault line that may suddenly split, causing earthquakes and even tidal waves.

1. Nuclear proliferation;
2. The growing national ambitions of powers, great and small
3. Economic success and economic failure for different nations;
4. Distress of those nations falling behind economically;
5. Power seeking by all nations, especially those with the fastest growing economies; and
6. Increasing nonnuclear conflict.

THE BIGGEST DANGERS FACING US

For exactly the opposite reasons, the seeds of the most dangerous future conflicts for America lie in Russia and China, not in terrorist states. Both are proud nations driven by nationalist aspirations. In China, the danger stems from economic success; in Russia, from economic failure. Both China and Russia seem destined to continue on their current paths: the one to growth, the other to economic stagnation – and both will grow increasingly uncomfortable in a world dominated by the United States.

A possibility that should concern our country is that other great powers combine against us. Yale's Paul Kennedy has argued that the decline of great powers in the past has often been associated with successful combinations against them. Our policy of preemption, if not executed properly, will increase the temptation because it will allow other countries to paint us as overly aggressive.

But the sequencing of the national peaks of Russia, China, and the European Union limits the likelihood of a successful coalition of our rivals challenging us successfully. Rather, the internal dynamics of Russia, China, and the European Union, and the rivalries among them, will likely prevent a tight coordination of them to challenge us (although it will not prevent tactical combinations against us, as in the case of the political controversy over the Second Gulf War). The danger that the other great powers will align themselves against us successfully is therefore not acute –unless the speed of economic growth and military modernization decreases for Russia or increases for China. It is imperative that the American president consistently monitor the speed of developments in these nations, for it could mean survival or not for the United States. All economic decisions about what to import and export, allowing U.S. companies to manufacture goods abroad (thus training foreign workers in technology), whether we let China get ahead of our own manned space program, and many other economic and political decisions should be made with the goal of maintaining the speed of development abroad at a level that will spread out the timing of the major potential threats to the United States.

Many factors could significantly change the speed of these developments, thus altering the sequence for the worse. If our leaders can prevent it from happening, there is unlikely to be any combined military challenge in the next thirty years or so.

Certainly we are being ganged up on politically by coalitions of other countries. This occurred during the political disputes leading up to the Iraqi war. It is likely to continue to happen in the longer term. Our best means of avoiding being seriously discomfited by coalitions against us is to prevent the coalitions from becoming alliances via our diplomacy and economic persuasiveness.

The broad geopolitics of the next decade are already fairly clear. The United States will be attacked repeatedly by terrorists or rogue states. Terrorism will become a sort of continuing guerilla war. Our European friends – avoid becoming targets themselves – will urge so moderate a response upon us that it will be almost no response at all. They will find willing supporters in Russia and China. In the extreme, we may find Russia or China attacking us in the guise of terrorism by working clandestinely with the terrorists. The Europeans will either be or pretend to be unawares of the combination against us. We should listen to the Europeans carefully, but resist the pressure they will exert on us to act only with their agreement. Instead, we should determine our own defense strategy independently. In a real sense our most dangerous political rival today is the European Union. Our most dangerous military adversary is now Islamic terrorism, but it is a weak adversary with limited capability to damage us. But it will be quickly displaced as our major military adversary by Russia and then by China. The developments that will cause this to happen are underway; there is virtually no likelihood of their being derailed; and so the issue for us is how to cope with the sequence of challenges facing us.

TERRORISM

The one significant regional threat is the Crescent of Fire, and hence the inclusion of terrorism in a list of strategic threats, as we do here, is appropriate. A disruption occurring in the Middle East of the world's oil supply would likely plunge the world into economic depression with significant consequences for international peace, and must therefore be avoided if at all possible. Thus, a terrorist attack on Saudi oil production or shipping, for example, if on a sufficient scale, becomes a strategic threat to the world that must be addressed.

The reconfiguration of global wealth and power is likely to have a pernicious effect on out-of-theater low intensity conflicts that could provoke great power intervention, and escalation. Genocidal aggression on the scale witnessed in Cambodia, the Congo, Bosnia, Albania, and Dafur, spawned by poverty, political opportunism and despotism seem destined to erupt, together with guerrilla insurgencies in Nepal and Latin America. Similar forces make the Crescent of Fire an ongoing powder keg, and there will be zones of confrontation elsewhere between China and India over Myanmar and the Himalaya region; India and Pakistan, Japan and North Korea. And, of course, further economic divergence provides fertile ground for proliferators like Iran and North Korea to buildup nuclear arsenals, and aids terrorists in recruiting troops, and acquiring weapons of mass destruction. Summit talks were first held between the two Koreas in June 2000. The North Koreans were supposed to set aside their plans for becoming a nuclear power. They didn't. Instead, by 2005 they were announcing that they had obtained nuclear weapons. But the South Koreans by then had modified their hostility toward the North. It was a set back for us because North Korea got atomic weapons and greater acceptability simultaneously.

Russian Military Resurgence: Rising from the Ashes – From Weakness to Strength Overnight

Russia presents the most imminent danger. Its economy declined by about half in the 1990s, but it has recovered much lost ground. Military outlays fell 90 percent, and remain about a third beneath the Soviet high, although these figures should be viewed with considerable skepticism. Consequently, Russia remains vulnerable to both internal disintegration and foreign exploitation. Sparring in anticipation of the succession struggle of 2008 is also roiling the waters. Yet, its nuclear arsenal is second to none (the peculiar accounting done for arms control and disarmament to the contrary notwithstanding).

On an on-again, off-again basis (at least as described in President Putin's statements), Russia has adopted a first-use policy for nuclear arms and announced an ambitious military modernization program that, if undertaken, will almost certainly provoke an arms race with its Asian neighbors that are already modernizing their forces (most importantly China). Russia has also directly threatened to use force against the United States should we place weapons in space (which may include our missile defense initiative.)[2] Because Russia's first-use policy is one of nuclear brinksmanship, any nuclear arms race will be all the more dangerous.

With respect to Russia it cannot be stressed enough for an American audience that a large nation with modern technological capabilities and an educated workforce can be weak and demoralized one day, and yet become – with effective leadership – a great power at alarming speed.

In 1932, for example, Germany was disarmed and disillusioned by the loss of World War I and street clashes between communists and fascists roiled its politics. Germany posed a military threat to no one. In that same year, however, Hitler came into power as the choice for Chancellor of a plurality – but less than a majority – of the German electorate. Just seven years later, in 1939, Germany was strong enough to launch World War II. And less than one year after the start of the war, Germany crushed France to emerge as one of the strongest and probably the most aggressive power (Germany's rivals for this dubious distinction were Japan and Italy) in the world. In sum, Germany progressed from weakling to deadly world threat in just eight years under Hitler's leadership.

Russia is able to pursue a similar course from weakness to strength. It has done so in the past. Russia lost World War I to Germany, signing a treaty of what was, in effect, surrender at Brest Litovsk March 3, 1918. During the war, Russia lost battle after battle to the Germans, including one of the great catastrophes of history at Tannenberg. Observers concluded that Russia was economically hopelessly backward and militarily inept – certainly not a power to be feared. Yet, writing about this period in Russia's military history, a foremost historian concluded "the Tsarist army was not crippled by its inferiority in artillery or men; it was crippled by its inability to use its superiority. . . . Tannenberg did not illustrate Russia's economic backwardness. It merely proved that armies will lose battles if they are led badly enough."[3]

Little more than twenty years later, Russia's successor, the Soviet Union, seemed remarkably weak. Stalin's purge of the top military leadership had thoroughly demoralized the army. In 1940 Russia was barely able to win a war against Finland. Russia had lost World War I to Germany; it appeared vulnerable again. It was this apparent weakness that persuaded Hitler to attack. So on June 22, 1941, Germany invaded Russia, unleashing the greatest war in history. Yet within two years, despite constant Nazi attack and having sustained the loss of most of its territory in Europe and about one third of its population, the Soviet Union emerged as the strongest land power on earth. It then, with America and Britain as allies, crushed the Nazi regime. (Americans should recall that just thirty percent of German military strength was devoted to its conflict with the United States and Britain during World War II. Fully 70 percent of the German's military was dedicated throughout the war to its conflict with the Soviet Union.)

Apparent weakness in a great nation can be very deceiving. It can change to strength in an instant. Today, all Russia needs to become an effective world power is aggressive and capable leadership. If that leadership were to emerge in the Kremlin – as may now be happening under Sergei lvanov – Russia's current weakness would quickly disappear.

The Russian defense situation is immensely complex and we are not able to discuss it here with all the nuances and qualifications appropriate to a fuller treatment. However, the sinking of a Russian nuclear submarine in the Arctic a few years ago is illustrative. The Kursk went down with the loss of its entire crew. On the surface, the sinking highlighted the internal decay of the Russian military, but more significantly, it showed that Russia is still building new ships. The submarine was built in 1995,[4] and Russia launched a new nuclear submarine in 2000.

In another example, President Putin announced that Russia was willing to pare nuclear outlays with a goal of reducing Russia's strategic nuclear missiles to only 1500 in number. Yet this is probably disinformation, an untruth offered to mislead Western opinion about the merit of national missile defense. Rather than curtailing its nuclear development programs, Russia is maintaining them at high levels (ironically with U.S. assistance, offered in the belief that the Russians are demobilizing when they are actually modernizing nuclear forces and discarding obsolete systems) . Finally, we must recognize that Russia can, with sufficient political resolve, reverse its current military weakness even if it cannot successfully transform its economy into one that provides a high standard of living for consumers. Indeed, the process may already have begun. Weapons production in 1999 and 2000 grew respectively at 36.7 and 29.5 percent, and the defense budget for 2001 was doubled.[5] In 2006, it will increase 50 percent over 2005.[6]

The likely reassertion of Russian military strength will add to the world's growing disorder – to the dangers we face in the years ahead. But in the longer term, Russia's military strength will decline because Russia's economic system cannot keep pace with the United States' and China's rate of economic growth and technological innovation. The result is that Putin's Russia may well emerge from its current weakness only to fall into third class status.

But, in the foreground, how will the world respond to Russia's sudden reemergence as a strong power? The danger from Russia's instability could be far greater than the danger we faced during the Cold War from a comparatively stable Soviet Union – yet those dangers, as we'll see later, were severe in the extreme.

The Cold War is over, but not rivalry with Russia. This is peace, but a peculiar kind of peace. It is a "peace that is war by other means."[7]

Yet few Americans believe Russia is still a threat. We have forgotten that it is still heavily armed. When told, we discount the fact because Russia remains an economic weakling and doesn't appear on the surface to be aggressive; further, historically Russia is said to be dangerous only when attacked (as Napoleon and Hitler discovered to their discomfiture); and since we have no intention of attacking Russia, there would appear to be no threat.

And, probably, for the next few years Russia won't be a problem for America. And it will also fade in the long run.

But there will be a Cold War – type spike of danger between 2010 and 2020. It is this Russia of tomorrow that is the serious problem. The Russian government is taking actions that suggest it is trying to reassemble the former Soviet Union, something that would, in the words of an independent defense analyst, "will be adamantly opposed by the West, as well as by most of the former Soviet countries themselves." He adds, "Russia could become completely isolated. The post-Soviet landmass could turn into a bloody mess just as the former Yugoslavia did."[8]

The period 2010–2020 is important because the first phase of Russia's fifth weapons generation remilitarization is scheduled for completion by President Putin in 2010. The Russians can and are returning to structural militarization. They are opting for full spectrum fifth generation weapons modernization, and a market-assisted variant of the old, but proven Soviet military industrial production model. As these initiatives take effect, by 2010, the Genshtab (Russian general staff and MOD) will become emboldened. The threat array to America has not yet crystallized, but unquestionably we will be transformed into an adversary.

For ten years, there will be great danger of an overt conflict with Russia. But if we survive that period, then by 2020 the population of Russia should have fallen from 2005's roughly 143 million (it was some 293 million as the Soviet Union) to only 110 million, and China's economic and military progress will be daunting (China's population will then be some 1.4 billion). It will then be clear to everyone that the jig for Russia is up. Russia will become increasing vulnerable to dismemberment, should any of its potential enemies choose to act.

Chinese Nationalism

Today Asia is the scene of great power rivalries and jostling of the type we used to associate with Europe, which led to a whole series of great wars but which is mercifully gone at the moment. As expressed by an American reporter, "In the decade since the Cold War ended, Asia has largely failed at the task Europe has fairly well mastered – defusing many of its geopolitical land mines.... The major capitals – Moscow, Beijing, Tokyo and Seoul – have never overcome the centuries of distrust, competition for dominance, and open conflict that sucked the United States into three Asian wars in the twentieth century."[9]

China's growing power is destabilizing the Far East and must be somehow countered or accommodated.

Japan is the target of immense continuing animosity in China, Korea and much of Southeast Asia. Its relationship with Russia is difficult, and there are contentious territorial issues about seeming trivial islands, but really about seabed minerals.

The Japanese could easily rearm, and go nuclear if they feel imperiled.

Their culture is such, that abrupt changes are commonplace. Japan may become a rival of China; it may stir up antagonisms with North Korea. It may struggle with Russia over oil.

Thus, China and Japan can be drawn into the Asian vortex of danger, and both can become sources of its intensification.

Unfortunately, power rivalries are rife in Asia, and it is not possible for America to end them. China is asserting itself in ways that challenge America and our allies; challenges we cannot avoid. There is no reason to believe that any miscommunication or misunderstanding underlies the rivalries; it is instead a blunt contest for preeminence in the region. "Like it or not all of Asia, albeit to varying degrees," writes a careful student of the region, "is now fully swept up in a series of revolutions and conflicts to which no end can yet be envisaged but from which there is no disengagement possible." [10]

There is a special danger in the Chinese situation that is hard to assess properly from the outside. How independent is the Chinese military from the civilian administration of the government? It is a crucial question, because there is historic precedent for conflict started by the military of countries without civilian approval. In the most important case, the Japanese army in

Southern Manchuria in the early 1930s fabricated an incident at Mukden as an excuse for invading China and began a war that was to be a major forerunner and cause of World War II in the Pacific, and it did so without informing the Japanese civilian government and without its approval or direction. The Japanese army at that time was largely independent of the civilian government, and later took over the civilian government to prosecute World War II. Similarly in China, the army is an institution in itself, possessing large economic interests and what is most likely a substantial degree of influence with the civilian government, and perhaps considerable independence of action. Our relations with China, therefore, take place with both the civilian government and the military, and without our having a clear concept of what is the relative power of either.

Chinese nationalism may run away with the nation's caution. "National self-images and the strong feelings often attached to such images . . . can lead to overly aggressive actions. . . . In the world of international relations, . . . they can be manipulated by groups or their leaders . . ."[11] Facing an environment of weak states, China is becoming more and more assertive. It is now putting a very effective squeeze on Japan via:

1. Oil – threatening Japan's oil pipeline deal with Russia by a side deal of China's own with Russia to get a spur to China off the new trans-Siberian pipeline and get oil before Japan does; and by beginning a process with the Kuomintang to get a peaceful reassociation of Formosa with the mainland, cutting across Japan's oil shipping lines from the Middle East and Europe;
2. Direct military threat – North Korea's missiles and nuclear programs;
3. Political isolation – the demonstrations against Japan in China; forcing Japan to apologize to other Asian countries for World War II, and so on, which serve both to isolate and estrange Japan from other countries in the region and to give evidence of Chinese influence and power.

China is a potential menace, and is playing with fire with Japan. Hu is also playing a clever game by joining forces with the Taiwanese ruling party against the independence party. He could force the United States out of the Formosa straits, and limit our naval presence to Japan. This would leave the sea-lines to the Middle East and Europe unprotected, and be a great victory, which would create a combustible situation with Japan, as China reaches for hegemony in the region before taking the United States on in the broader world. There is a chance that China will emerge as an unopposed hegemon, without having to engage in combat. This is likely the Chinese calculation, tempting them to more self-assertion. China is therefore a major emerging crisis if it continues to shed its self-restraint.

European Union Unification and Rivalry

America has been allied so long with Western Europe that it is hard to imagine open conflict between America and Europe. But it is possible, and its earliest stages may already be occurring. It is a commonplace of history that when a threat lessens or disappears, or seems to disappear, then the alliance that combated the threat tends to dissolve. The close alliance between the United States and Western Europe that lasted throughout the Cold War was predicated on the Soviet threat, and with the extinction, or apparent extinction of that threat, the close alliance no longer has a reason to exist. Instead, we see increasing evidence of rivalry (for example, the dispute over the second war with Iraq; the establishment of a European self-defense force outside NATO; the increasing differences over policy toward Palestine).

Nationalism doesn't require that other nations be viewed with hostility; but it often happens that a country defines itself by hostile reference to another. Over the next several decades, if Europe successfully builds nationhood, it should surprise no one if tensions develop with America and if those at some point risk turning to overt conflict. This will not necessarily occur, but if it does, it will look in retrospect to have been inevitable given the size and strength of the two powers (the European Union and the United States), the rivalry in economic and political interests, and the deep differences of attitude about world affairs that distinguish the two.

A particular danger is likely to arise over Ukraine, about which Russia has long-standing interests, and which the EU seems bent on drawing into its own sphere of influence. Should rivalry sharpen between the EU and Russia over Ukraine, we could be drawn into a complex and difficult conflict.

INTERACTIONS

We have stressed before that American international relations are part of an interconnected global system. We've been told ad nauseam about the interconnectivity of the global economy, but it is as true about the relations among nations. We now turn to the major interactions between the challenges we face.

The terrorist challenge to the West allows our rivals to assess our willingness to protect ourselves. Enemies of the Western democracies have always had a tendency to underestimate their determination. Hitler thought that

Britain would collapse under the bombing of London; the Japanese thought that the United States would not pay the price in blood of expelling Japan from its empire in East Asia; Stalin and the North Koreans were sure that the United States would not spend American lives to defend South Korea. All were wrong. So when Islamic terrorists attacked the World Trade Center, China and Russia watched carefully to see how we responded.

When the United States attacked Iraq in 2003, the Russians and the Chinese were given an opportunity to measure the truth of American claims for its new weaponry – the smart weapons we have labeled the Revolution in Military Affairs (RMA) . Furthermore, they were able to assess the professionalism and effectiveness of our Army, Marines, and Air Force. The more effective our weapons and soldiers, the less likely is a challenge from our rivals. It may be crass to say so, but the most important aspect of our invasion of Iraq may be the demonstration it gave of our military competence to potential adversaries.

But it is also true that our involvement in Iraq stretches our military capability and so lessens our own ability to intervene in other parts of the world.

Crises such as that over the World Trade Center attack and afterward over Afghanistan and then Iraq, when the United States wishes to take action, offer other powers an opportunity to support us or oppose us for reasons that have nothing to do with the issue at hand. The same is true of more recent crises over Iranian and North Korean nuclear weapons programs. The Chinese, who most likely have the influence to determine North Korean policy, are able to use North Korean actions to threaten Japan, frustrate the United States, and cause Japan to doubt American willingness to defend Japan. Thus, what appears an issue of nuclear proliferation is also an issue of the great power rivalries involving China, Japan, and the United States.

There is a real danger, which we shall discuss later, of the United States being drawn into a war with China over Taiwan. Our position has been that we do not oppose the reunification of China with Taiwan, so long as it is accomplished peacefully. Yet, a peaceful reunification would be very threatening to Japan (because it would strengthen the stranglehold that China is attempting to gain over Japan's oil supply), and therefore would also call into question our commitment to defend Japan.

Seeking to gain a more secure oil supply, Japan is attempting to get the Russians to build a pipeline across Siberia to Russian ports from which oil can be shipped to Japan. China is attempting to have a spur from the pipeline built to China. Japan opposes this. Oil is necessary not only for industry and consumer use, but also for military use. Hence, this confrontation involves two of the world's current nuclear powers and a third power which is the world's most significant potential nuclear power. America's involvement in the oil-rich Middle East impacts directly its relationship with Japan, China and Russia about oil. To the extent that the security of Japan's oil supply from the Middle East is in question for any of a number of reasons, tensions over a future Russian pipeline to East Asia will increase.

Thus, apparently separate issues of international relations such as the Middle East, China, Japan, and Russia are in fact not at all separate, but are intimately intertwined. There are possible solutions to tensions in our relationships with the Arab world, Russia, and China that are not acceptable because of their impact on Japan; and vice versa. Similarly, there are possible solutions to tensions in our relationship with China that are not possible because of their impact on Japan.

LESSONS FROM EXPERIENCE

The MAD World – The Risk of Nuclear War

How should America respond to China's growing strategic nuclear capability? Should we help China develop its strategic nuclear capability on the theory that the current period, in which China lacks strategic parity with America, is too unstable and that we should reach for Mutual Assured Destruction (MAD) – the balance of terror – quickly to avoid risking war? MAD requires that each side be subject to destruction by the other, but our destruction is not assured as long as the Chinese lack abundant and reliable ballistic missiles. To make MAD feasible, therefore, China must have the capacity to destroy us. Does the logic of MAD require us to support Chinese missile building? Rather than prosecute the Americans who gave nuclear secrets to China, should we praise them as patriots working to ensure our survival through creating conditions in which MAD can succeed?

Does the notion that we would actively seek to expand China's strategic missile capability sound insane? It is in the logic of MAD. Unless we espouse some other policy about potential nuclear conflict, then we are driven to embrace China's increasing nuclear strength.

But no administration could seriously advance such a policy. The American public doesn't want to help China build ballistic missiles that are aimed at us. But with MAD as our policy, then our government must fear a period of disproportionate nuclear strength because it tempts both sides to a pre-emptive strike; and our government must welcome an emerging balance of nuclear strength – the balance of terror that lies behind MAD and makes it viable.

Hence, an American government that remains committed to MAD – either because it believes in it (as the Clinton administration did) or because it hasn't thought the alternatives through clearly (as the Bush administration hasn't) – will most likely sit quietly on its hands as the Chinese rapidly build the capability to hit all of America with nuclear missiles. By inaction the American government's policy will be revealed. If it sits still as China builds its long-range nuclear capability, then we will know that our leaders remain committed to MAD. If this happens, we may each want to pack our bags and move to another country.

What are the alternatives to MAD? There are three:

1. Arms control, so that a balance of terror (MAD) is not necessary;
2. Dissuading the Chinese from pushing forward their nuclear missile program; or
3. Preemption, exactly what MAD proponents fear from an imbalance of nuclear power.

Arms control is the most attractive alternative to MAD. But finding the right balance with potentially untrustworthy adversaries is always difficult, and has become much more so with nuclear proliferation.

Nuclear containment is now unglued and proliferation is unleashed. With Russia protecting the Iranians and China the North Koreans, there is little left of the nuclear nonproliferation effort. Having failed to get any restriction on North Korea's nuclear weapons program, the administration spread the word that it wasn't sure North Korea had nuclear weapons. Then it made an agreement with India, which allows India greater flexibility and secrecy in developing its nuclear forces.[12] It is possible that strategic intentions that are myopic led to the arrangement with India. Indian nuclear weapons aren't likely to be used against the United States. Instead they are aimed at the Pakistanis and the Chinese. We have potential problems with both – Pakistan if it falls into the hands of radical Islamists, and China under a variety of possible scenarios.

There are two problems with this approach:

1. India, Pakistan, North Korea, and Iran are pushing the envelope creating the precedent that any nation that wants nuclear weapons has a right to them. In the abstract, they are justified, but from the standpoint of survival it has always been best for the United States to bully unstable states into desisting. This is the precedent that is now eroding.
2. When nuclear-tipped ballistic missiles start flying in Asia, there is a high risk of Russia being drawn into the fray, with escalation to Japan and America not far behind.

These are reasons to regret the administration's timidity in addressing nuclear proliferation.

The result is that today any state moving toward nuclear weapons will simply find a great-power protector (we are the protector of both Israel and India, for example) and thereby be insulated from effective international pressure. The campaign for international sanctions to avoid nuclear proliferation is apparently in ruins. It's another example of the seemingly irrational in international politics, which seems much more pronounced since the collapse of the Soviet Union. The Russians seem to be very foolish in protecting Iran, as they are a potential target of an Iranian bomb; and the Chinese appear to be calculating far too finely the game they are playing on behalf of the North Koreans. With the international effort to limit nuclear proliferation in ruins, there is no reliable answer to the threat of nuclear weapons in the hands of terrorists, and the best America can do is to address the coming crisis via strategic independence and moral suasion.

Effective arms control requires the consent of America, Russia, and China, and soon may require that of India and Pakistan and possibly Iran and North Korea. Given that any one of these countries could veto an arms control treaty, multilateral arms control treaties may prove impossible to attain. Another problem is that all such treaties invite cheating. After World War I, the great powers signed various treaties designed to prevent a naval arms race, but they merely encouraged the great powers to build unregulated weapons. In effect, the incentives ran amok. The Russian nuclear-armed submarine Kursk – which sank unexpectedly – wasn't regulated by an arms control treaty. There is no way to avoid the risk of unintended consequences, so even what is desirable arms control must be supplemented or hedged with an alternative of some sort.

This is the world we used to live in – the world of MAD. Somehow the notion has gotten around that it was a stable world, a relatively safe world, and so that if we go back to it, that won't be so bad. This gives credence to the idea that if the Russians move to the next generation of nuclear weaponry and we do the same, a type of new world of MAD is established, a situation that we at least dealt without disaster for decades during the Cold War, and we could do it again. And if the Chinese achieve a major nuclear capability vis-à-vis us, then that, too, is manageable and preferable to a world of a single superpower, our world today.

These notions constitute a terrible illusion – the world of MAD was a dreadfully dangerous world. One reason there is such a strong misconception about the world of MAD is that Americans weren't informed of its dangers at the time. In a few following pages, we revisit some of the most dangerous moments in the world of MAD.

A recent biography of Nikita Khrushchev, Soviet premier during the Cuban missile crisis, demonstrates how, in the words of a former Secretary of State, "even in this supposedly planned venture, and with the possibility of worldwide destruction, a remarkable level of incompetence prevailed. The general who was chosen to be in charge [of Soviet weaponry during the Cuban Missile Crisis] Issa Pliyev, was distinguished only for having put down a rebellion of Soviet workers in the southern city of Novocherkassk earlier that year. Described as knowing more about horses than missiles, Pliyev impressed no one in the Soviet hierarchy but, nevertheless, was given authority to launch tactical nuclear missiles. It is clear . . . that of the three parties involved the Cubans were the most reckless."

There exists a remarkable letter, quoted in the biography of Khrushchev, from Castro to Moscow in effect arguing that the USSR must use a first strike against the United States in the expected final crisis. The author suggests that Castro's attitude was due, in part, to his belief that the Soviets held nuclear superiority over the United States and that they could destroy it even if they suffered great damage themselves (after all, John F. Kennedy had told the world during the 1960 presidential campaign that there was a missile gap in which America was behind the Soviet Union – apparently Castro believed this disinformation). Castro was, in turn, enraged by the Soviet withdrawal, calling Khrushchev a "son of a bitch . . . bastard. . . . "[13]

This incident raises a significant question: where is rationality in the actions of Khrushchev and Castro, each of whom took steps that almost plunged the world into nuclear war? The answer, of course, is that there is no rationality – at least not above the level of tactics – so that even with MAD there was enormous risk of nuclear war.

The risk of a nuclear exchange during the Cold War came in two forms – by challenge and by error. For the most part, American historians prefer to ignore the former and emphasize the other. There seem to be two reasons for this somewhat peculiar predilection. First, the paper trail of historical evidence for mistakes is often far clearer than for the more personal matters of direct personal challenges – leader to leader – mano e mano; and second, most historians seem to shy away from the sort of immature and volatile machismo that accompanies personal rivalries among leaders of nations.

But where a paper trail does exist, it offers insight into what is a far more common and dangerous a set of personal rivalries than most of us realize.

America almost stumbled into war with the USSR several times during the Cold War. At least twice it was by challenge – the first when Stalin prepared a strike in the early 1950s during a time that he thought Soviet power was at its peak and that his own life was ebbing, causing him to worry that his successors' personalities were too weak to challenge the West. The second time was when Khrushchev spotted weakness in John Kennedy and sought to exploit it via placing Soviet nuclear missiles in Cuba. And at least once more, it was by accident.

Able Archer – 1983

On an otherwise ordinary day in November 1983, the world stumbled to the brink of nuclear war. At that time and for years thereafter, these events went virtually unnoticed outside the top officials of the American government and a few senior officers inside the Soviet Rocket Command.

Armageddon almost began with Able Archer, the code name for the largest military exercise in NATO's history. To forestall any potential misunderstanding, President Reagan's Administration explained Able Archer's benign intent to the Soviet Union's leadership, but American military intelligence should have warned him that his efforts would prove inadequate. Western intelligence had access to *Voennaia Mysl'*, the Soviet High Command's journal of military tactics and doctrine. It contained numerous articles warning that NATO would disguise any surprise attack on the Warsaw Pact as a military exercise and that NATO would accompany its surprise attack with a preemptive nuclear strike designed to destroy the Soviet Union's nuclear arsenal. To some extent, the Soviet Union's thinking on military exercises like Able Archer reflected its disastrous experiences during World War II, in which the Germans had partially disguised their preparations for invasion as military exercises.

The politburo's anxieties were heightened further because, as part of the exercise, President Reagan and Defense Secretary Caspar Weinberger dropped out of public sight. Unbeknown to them, Yuri Andropov, Chairman of the KGB, had launched operation "RYAN" in 1981 designed to give the Kremlin seven to ten 10 days' warning of a US/NATO surprise nuclear attack. When these key American leaders disappeared from the KGB's radar it sounded an alarm bell that could not be quieted by American verbal assurances. Consequently, the Soviet Union initiated a phased response. As part of this phased response, the Kremlin ordered a partial conventional mobilization and placed its ballistic missiles on ready alert, permitting the Commander of Soviet Strategic Rocket Forces to order the preprogramming of launch authorization codes into the Soviet Union's ballistic missiles. Pre-programming enabled the Commander to launch a nuclear strike against NATO without a final "go" order from the political leadership. Unlike his American counterpart, the Soviet Union's missile commander did not need a final "go" order because the Soviet nuclear weapons had only one "key." In contrast, American nuclear weapons required two keys. Even today, Russia's missile commander can launch a nuclear strike without the authorization of Russia's President. Photo reconnaissance from NATO satellites soon detected the Soviet Union's response to Able Archer. Recognizing the danger, President Reagan and Weinberger publicly surfaced, and cut Able Archer short, defusing the situation. Sensors and good sense seemed to have saved the day. But there is a less reassuring version of the tale. On this recounting, the world's survival may have owed more to old-fashioned incompetence than space age satellites. The Commander of Soviet Strategic Rocket forces didn't take America's cancellation of Able Archer any more seriously than he accepted President Reagan's initial assurances of Able Archer's benign intent; he dismissed both as maskirovka (deception). Consequently, he ordered Colonel Brezhnev – no relation to the former leader of the Soviet Union – to continue entering the launch authorization codes. As a result, any mistake – including a simple misidentification of a bird as a missile – could have precipitated a global nuclear holocaust. According to Vitaly Shlykov, former deputy chairman of Russia's Defense Committee under Boris Yeltsin and a GRU Colonel at the time, the world survived unscathed because the Soviet Union's missile system malfunctioned! Colonel Brezhnev had entered defective codes, which acted like a virus, shutting down the Soviet Union's entire command-and-control system. The episode ended with a whimper, not a bang.

The Soviets blamed Colonel Brezhnev, whom they shot as a CIA saboteur. Neither Colonel Brezhnev's loyalties nor Shlykov's story have ever been independently confirmed. There are other variants of the Colonel Brezhnev story in circulation, and Colonel-General Valery Mironov, former chief of the Leningrad TVD (theater of military operations), former Deputy Minister of State for Military Reform, and formerly, in 2000, Russia's defense minister, disputes Shlykov's account. The CIA has released one of two special National Estimates on the crisis written in 1984 and an expanded assessment in 1998, but still downplays the danger. Our account is disputed also by Fritz Ermarth who was involved on America's side during the incident and concludes that it showed American intelligence at its best because a war was avoided.[14] It doesn't appear that Ermarth is aware of Shlykov's version.

Unfortunately, Able Archer wasn't the first or last time that the superpowers flirted with nuclear Armageddon. Peter Vincent Pry[15] has documented seven other occasions in the 1990s when, for various reasons, America and Russia approached the brink of nuclear war.

What lessons should we draw from the closeness of nuclear war during the Cuban Missile Crisis and Able Archer? First and foremost, we should recognize that nuclear conflict is more unpredictable than we would like to admit. And our ability to foresee and manage crises is poor, a point underscored at the CIA-sponsored conference, "CIA's Analysis of the Soviet Union 1947–1991," March 6, 2001, where panelists gave the agency's Cold War political analysis a grade of D.

Second, we are likely to confront similar challenges in the near future. Able Archer almost ignited a nuclear war because rivalries and suspicion between the great powers generated a colossal misunderstanding. With the end of the Cold War, we hoped that such rivalries and suspicions had disappeared, but they persist.[16] Moreover, where once we lived in a world with only two great powers, we will soon live in a world with at least three: the United States, Russia, and China.

NUCLEAR MISSILE DEFENSE (NMD)

It is this strategic role for the missile defense shield that the United States government has been unwilling to discuss publicly. The formal American position is that the defense shield is aimed at terrorist attacks by rogue states (Iran, Iraq, and Syria in particular). Were that the case, then the shield would be tactical only – another mode of defense against potential terrorist acts – and would be vulnerable to the criticisms made against it – that it is potentially grossly expensive, uncertain to work, and threatening to the current balance of the great powers. It would be, in short, an error.

But when it is admitted that the missile defense shield is, in fact, strategic in nature, and necessary to preserve our current position in Asia, and likely to be an important factor in avoiding a large war, then the shield is subject to none of these criticisms, for reasons which will be given in detail later. It is, in fact, a central element of a great shift in American strategy for the twenty-first century made necessary by an enormous shift in the relative economic strength and military power of the great nations.

As Russia again suddenly flames into superpower status, then burns out like a supernova, China will be building its economic power and dramatically expanding its arsenal of ballistic missiles. As it builds its nuclear arsenal, China's missiles will threaten directly Japan and Taiwan; soon afterward, its missiles will threaten the entire United States. Even if we were to assume that China's rationality and economic self-interest preclude aggression, there will be the increasing risk of an unintended nuclear war. We cannot simply assume that China will act rationally. China's growing nationalism, for example, may preclude rational decisions about Taiwan, the Luzon Straits, the Spratley Islands, the Senkaku Islands, India, Siberia, and the Russian Far East.

Most important to us, China's strategic nuclear capability will increasingly threaten the United States. The Chinese tested a solid-fuel road-mobile, 8000-kilometer range missile Dong Feng 31 in August 1999, and an even longer range Dong Feng 41 is under development. In the spring of 2001 *The Economist* referred to, as if it were general knowledge in America, China's "own limited nuclear arsenal of about 25 missiles which, it has hinted, it could use against Los Angeles."[17] The authors' impression is that the American public is unaware of the Chinese missile threat to our west coast even today.

China's continuing development of a strategic nuclear capability will escalate tensions between the United States and China. After all, China's increasing ability to kill American civilians via long-range nuclear missiles does nothing to assuage our fears about what might happen. A more nuclear China does not help better secure trade, or indicate peaceful intentions, so we must ask why it is being done. When the German Kaiser built his new battleships at the start of the last century, the British knew Germany's navy endangered Britain even though Germany's Kaiser and Britain's Queen were close relatives and the two nations were also seeking peaceful accommodation. Just as the Kaiser's navy provoked an arms race with an otherwise friendly Britain, China's strategic nuclear capability will provoke an arms race with the United States, unless China can be persuaded that nuclear competition with us is futile and drops its missile development and building effort.

The danger of nuclear war has increased dramatically in the last few years due to nuclear proliferation and Russia's doctrine of limited nuclear war. There's no way to sugarcoat this. Ten years ago, most of the world believed that the collapse of the Soviet Union meant that the threat of nuclear war, which had hung over the world for decades, would finally recede. Yet, since the Soviet Union's collapse, we have not only failed to secure a complete and lasting peace, we have also found ourselves confronting another potential nuclear threat. Compared to a full-scale nuclear war involving the Russians, Chinese, Indians, Pakistanis, and North Koreans, acts of nuclear terrorism are almost insignificant.

Meanwhile, and equally important, the American government is going to have to decide how to respond to China's growing arsenal of ballistic missiles. In the 1960s, when Presidents Kennedy and Johnson faced such a decision, the Soviet Union's ballistic missiles were a unique and unprecedented threat to the United States. Even today, only Russian missiles present a similar threat. China, however, may soon acquire a similar strategic nuclear capability, and we are going to have to decide what to do about it.

Most of us thought the risk of global nuclear war had disappeared with the end of the Cold War. Of course, we recognized the risk of nuclear terrorism, but we thought that global nuclear war could never happen because the United States is, and seems likely to remain, the world's only conventional military superpower. Will we confront more Able Archers in the future? Will other American presidents be confronted with nuclear brinksmanship over Taiwan, or the collateral risks of nuclear exchange stemming from hostilities among other nuclear states? Unfortunately, the answer most likely is "yes."

The reality is that the end of the Cold War has not ended the risk of nuclear war, and that what was at one time a snake with one head is now a hydra-headed monster. We had planned at first for a general reduction in the risk of nuclear war, but this hasn't happened and we are now attempting to rely on the old methods of balance of forces and mutual assured destruction. But there is no possible balance among the many nations now building nuclear strength, and there is no formula like MAD on which we can rely to avoid war – though our leaders may wish to try. In today's situation, we can only strive unceasingly to eliminate nuclear weapons, while trying to protect ourselves if arms control falls apart.

Both courses involve significant and considerable risk. We could find ourselves eliminating our own nuclear arsenals on the promise that others will do the same, when in fact our potential adversaries have deceived us. Deception about arms reduction happened on a large scale before World War II, and could happen again. Further, governments could disarm, while terrorists do not. The risks do not make a persuasive argument against arms control efforts, but do constitute reasons to conducting them very carefully. This illustrates exactly why we need to dominate every inch of space – so that our satellites can see both underground and evaluate enemy satellites' technical capabilities. The quickest way to shut a country down is to destroy its satellites! China is most likely developing a strategy to do this. Destroying enemy satellites would be a good preemptive tactic, where one is required.

We must recognize that nuclear arms remain attractive to many governments in today's world. They are often cheaper than conventional forces to acquire and maintain. For states that aspire to be major powers – especially

Russia and China – nuclear weapons are available, affordable, and credible counters to American power.[18] They are not likely to give them up. Hence, there are significant limitations on what may be achieved by disarmament in the nuclear arena.

Defense against nuclear attack has its risks as well. We may be unable to build an effective defense, and may delude ourselves into a false security. This could lead us into aggressive behavior that could bring on war. These risks again are no argument against efforts to build a missile defense, but constitute an argument to be very careful about being sure that it will work. We return to this topic when we discuss the important role of national missile defense in ensuring the Strategic Independence of the United States in Chapter 14.

THE DYNAMICS OF WORLD DISORDER

Suddenly and without warning, in the past decades, growth in Europe, Russia and Japan began to decelerate, all converging asymptotically toward zero. China alone marched to its own drummer. For a time these recuperating states continued to close the gap, but by the nineties the tide turned, with America pulling ahead of Europe, Russia and Japan, despite their widely vaunted liberalizations. For proponents of convergence this was merely the pause that refreshed. Time however hasn't validated the surmise.

Masters of Illusion need to be resolute on this point because contemporary patterns of reconfiguring global wealth and power are promoting both high- and low-intensity conflicts by shifting perceptions of capabilities, vulnerabilities, national interest, rights, prerogatives, and redressable grievances. China's rapid economic, technological and military modernizations challenge established relations in Asia, including vital American interests in Japan, Taiwan and the sea-lanes of the Pacific. It is easy to see how Beijing's leaders might conclude with the passing years that Japan could be intimidated and enticed into surrendering its claims to the Senkoku Islands and surrounding petroleum rich seabeds. Similar tactics could be applied in other seabed territorial disputes off the coast of Indonesia, and America could be cowed into accepting an invasion of Taiwan. The reactions of Japan, Indonesia, Malaysia, Taiwan, and the United States however might not follow Beijing's script, and could heighten tensions. China's rivals in the Asia Pacific region could dig in their heels, enhancing their offensive and defensive capabilities, forming economic and military anti-Chinese alliances, and engaging in brinksmanship. The struggle for shrinking petroleum supplies could be particularly combustible, as it was in the years preceding the Second World War II.

China's ascendance and Japan's relative decline don't necessitate American embroilment in an Asian Pacific cold or hot war, but they do raise risks that won't be countervailed by balloting and globalized markets. The turbulence caused by the reconfiguration of global wealth and power given systemic realities are likely to outweigh latent forces of enlightened democratic free enterprise.

America also could be reluctantly drawn into territorial tussles between China and Russia. Regardless of the positive tone of recent Sino-Soviet relations, as China discovers its new found powers it could lay claim to vast tracks of Siberia and the Russian Far East which were under its sway during the Yuan dynasty. These lands have enormous natural resource reserves, and are only sparsely populated. The Kremlin has powerful nuclear forces targeted on the Sino-Russian border, but their effectiveness is being degraded by illegal Chinese settlement some claim abetted by complicit Russian border guards selling forged citizenship papers. It has been alleged that there already are millions of Chinese "Russian" immigrants in Siberia and Primoriya, and that the situation will worsen as Russia's population diminishes from 143 million today to 80 million in 2050, as Soviet era residents return to Moscow and Saint Petersburg, and more of the 120 million Chinese along the Sino-Russian border infiltrate. Moreover, this demographic asymmetry is exacerbated by gapping disparities in GDPs and living standards. Although Japan, China's other regional rival will remain a great economic power during the next half century, Russia won't. Starting from a humble level in 1989, per capita Chinese GDP will soon eclipse Russia's, and its GDP could surpass it by a factor of twenty by 2050, allowing Beijing to modernize its armed forces beyond Russia's means, and to build a credible nuclear deterrent that will reduce the credibility of Moscow's border defense. The Kremlin is aware of the problem, and is in denial, continuing to perceive itself as the superior power in command, hoping that China will be self-restrained.

Russia's unfavorable position in the reconfiguration of global wealth and power also may prove destabilizing along its western and southern borders. The Kremlin's addiction to economic-favoritism and martial police state authoritarianism is a constant source of friction with America and the EU. Both not only periodically chide Russia for its tsarist-like vices, but compete for influence in the former Soviet Republics known as the near abroad, including Central Asia, the Ukraine, Georgia, Moldova, and Azerbaijan. The EU has talked about discussing Ukrainian membership, and America the possibility of the near abroad joining NATO. Moscow has responded by alternatively declaring its version of the Monroe doctrine for the near abroad, and acknowledging these states' autonomy, while harboring ambitions for their formal reincorporation into the Russian Federation, superceding the Commonwealth of Independent States (CIS) political, economic and military alliance. The stakes from the Kremlin's viewpoint are high. Central Asia has enormous reserves of petroleum and natural gas, while the Ukraine provides important access to the Black Sea. Both are also geostrategic assets. Defection from Moscow's orbit could bring China, Turkey, and NATO to its southern and western flanks, as has already occurred in the Baltics, and in the Ukrainian case thwart ambitions for projecting forces into the Middle East, if and when the oil sheikdoms collapse, precipitating a great power free for all. Russia's economic and military weakness compels Moscow to bide its time until the full spectrum military modernization program commencing in 2006 comes up to speed in 2010. Putin chose to turn the other cheek at Vladimir Yushchenko's EU leaning antics November-December 2004, but hasn't accepted Ukrainian defection. As Russia reemerges as a military superpower 2010–2050, the Kremlin is apt to be more tenacious, creating the possibility of a war no one wants, but like World War I could happen.

What Our Leaders Should Do

The threats we face are not commensurate with each other. One sort of threat is to the lives of thousands or tens of thousands of our citizens; another is to the lives of tens of millions or even hundreds of millions of us. They are both terrible, but they are not of equal size. This is a horrible calculus. The moralist in us wishes to say that the death of one person is as important as the death of many. But this is an illusion itself. It confuses our sense of proportion and our decisions. It leads to thinking in which we are prepared to sacrifice millions of people to save a few. In the current situation, it causes us to focus our attention on the risk of terrorist attacks while ignoring the risk of nuclear exchanges. Terrorist attacks would kill thousands; nuclear exchanges would kill tens or hundreds of millions. The worst conceivable terrorist attack would be a small fraction of the horror of a nuclear exchange. Islamic fundamentalism threatens us with terrorist attacks; Russia with nuclear exchange, and China is racing to be able to do the same. To allow ourselves to neglect the danger of great power nuclear war in preference for a focus on terrorism is one of the most serious errors into which we could fall.

Effective leadership of America in these times requires that this crucial sense of priorities and proportion not be lost. A war with another great power is the most significant danger we face and it must not be placed on a back burner because of a much less significant threat now.

In no way does this attempt to clarify our priorities mean that we should ignore the smaller threats now to focus on the larger. It means instead that we must not lose sight of greater dangers as we focus on eliminating smaller ones. We must undertake a strong response to terrorism and do all we can to stamp it out. But we must not take our eye off the bigger threats that lie just beyond the horizon, despite the fact that we have become unwisely complacent about them.

Yet, ask our leadership today what is the most important threat which Americans face, and they will almost uniformly reply, terrorist attack. This sudden confusion of proportion, and thus priorities, and the lack of good judgment that results, is a great danger to us.

The developments among the great powers are an unprecedented challenge to American presidential leadership. The current administration is able to draft a coherent shift of our national defense strategy; and it is able to take decisive action, as in Iraq. These are major strengths. But it seems unable to explain to the American people convincingly the necessity for its new doctrine and its course of action; it has allowed domestic affairs to get completely out of control, diverting national attention and energy away foreign affairs just when it is most needed;[19] it's unable to generate sufficient confidence in its ability to lead the nation in these times; and it's allowing itself to be drawn into damaging and unnecessary controversies with our erstwhile allies. In effect, the end of the Cold War is now permitting the allies of that conflict to separate and regroup; and we in America, the leader of the coalition that was successful in the cold war, are unable to glimpse the world beyond the old coalitions. To our disadvantage, European leadership has seized upon America as a useful rival around which European solidarity can be built.

American defense analysis is surprisingly unsophisticated about the threats we face, possibly because a focus on military capabilities of potential adversaries is too narrow a focus – economic capabilities now and in the future and geopolitical objectives are crucial to longer-term threat assessments. "Who might . . . future threats be? [Defense Department] analysts predicted they would include warlords, tribal chiefs, drug traffickers, international criminal cartels, terrorists, and cyber-bandits . . ."[20] General

Kennedy headed the analysts studying future threats for the Defense Department during the early 1990s.

Yet this is not the best way to view the future. It stresses not the challenge, but its form, especially as it diverges from the sort of military preparations we've made. Implicit in this formulation, which has great currency outside as well as inside the military, is the presumption for a military response (that is, defense means military defense), and whereas if challenged this way on the matter, even military planners will acknowledge that presuming a military response is too narrow, yet this is how Americans tend to look at the future.

American leaders must learn to look over the horizon, to see the dangers possibly facing us, and suggest how they can be addressed now.

John Mearsheimer is a perceptive American writer who presents himself as a realist about international affairs, and though he is critical of what he sees as his countrymen's aversion to realism (preferring he says their optimism and moralism), he still reassures Americans that "Behind closed doors, however, the elites who make national security policy speak mostly the language of power, not that of principle, and the United States acts in the international system according to the dictates of realist logic."[21] Unfortunately, he's too optimistic. The thinking of Americans – politicians and bureaucrats alike – who make national security policy is blurred by wishful thinking. During the Cold War, they were badly confused about Soviet economic and military capabilities; they were confused about the full extent of the terrorist threat before 9/11, and in both instances actually faked intelligence data to support their presuppositions, examples of which are provided later. America needs unfiltered realism, not wishful thinking. Our people are mature enough for truth in how we look at the world and honesty from our government about it. Furthermore, presidents today risk a mixed success at best by acting militarily without the full support of Americans. We face serious challenges in the world not based exclusively on economic deprivation, but rooted in different cultures, religions, and the ongoing human rivalry for power and dominance.

Our leaders should provide us with a cold logic of defense, grounded in a geopolitical orientation but without the cynicism of Old World power politics. The perspective of our leaders should be American and their intent should be to defend America and to pursue American interests, but in an enlightened fashion, with due regard to the interests of others in the world. We examine how to meet these requirements in the different threats that face us in the chapters that follow.

An American defense policy that follows from the considerations set forward in this chapter would involve:

- Recognition that "elbowing" among the great powers makes deep and continuing engagement a poor peg on which to hang our foreign policy. This is especially true with regard to the European Union.
- The demotion of peaceful engagement from a major element of our defense strategy to a less important role requires us to upgrade military preparedness.
- This means first and foremost that we should pursue Strategic Independence with respect to all threats.
- We should restructure our national missile defense initiative to meet large-scale threats from major powers, and upgrade our defense against tactical missiles.
- Resources being spent on Iraqi democratization should be transferred to these other purposes.
- Counterterrorism should be funded for the rest of this decade, but funding should be reduced thereafter.
- The American public must be informed about the continuing need for a robust defense.
- We should inform the world that our policies can be adjusted, if others become more cooperative. This involves directly a challenge to our president to master the illusions of our public culture which insist that the world is already becoming more like us and safer of its own volition.

CHAPTER 11: KEY POINTS

American opinion leaders have been lulled into complacency by an unwarranted faith in international harmony, and fail to see that the world is becoming unstable.

Contrary to a vision of peace and prosperity, the world is once again drifting back toward sharp economic and political rivalries and the danger of thermonuclear war.

Five major trends are driving the world toward the brink:

1. Nuclear proliferation;
2. Economic success and economic failure for different nations;
3. Distress of those nations falling behind economically;

4. Power seeking by all nations, especially those with the fastest growing economies; and

5. Increasing nonnuclear conflict.

The West has won an ideological struggle, but not the economic and geopolitical contests, which continue. Ideology was merely a weapon in the other struggles, so all that has really happened is that our adversaries have been partially, and temporarily, disarmed in one aspect of the conflict.

Our leaders often dismiss such concerns. Their advisors demand to know the causal sequence which links the reconfiguration of global wealth and power – which they recognize – with nuclear risk before treating the dangers seriously. There is such a sequence, and this book describes it.

1. Russia is rearming and by hook or crook the United States will be transformed into an adversary. The Russian threat will peak in 2010 to 2020.

2. China is currently enlarging its nuclear missile capability with the intent of targeting the entire United States. It is building economic strength, developing superior space capabilities and modernizing its entire military establishment. The Chinese threat will peak in 2020 to 2030.

3. The current U.S. military dominance is certain to be challenged in the next decade. Russia will regain superpower status in weaponry by 2010 and China by 2020.

4. Each adversary will have a different strategy. The Russians on mass force; the Chinese on economic growth supplemented by growing missile capability and space dominance.

5. For forty years, we have relied on Mutual Assured Destruction to prevent nuclear war. Yet during this time, the world has several times stumbled to the brink of nuclear war. Furthermore, the logic of MAD requires us to either strengthen our adversaries to parity with us or to wait uncertainly in a risky situation until they on their own reach parity. Either course seems fraught with danger.

6. Because MAD is no longer viable in a world of many nuclear powers, the United States should pursue a policy of Strategic Independence.

TWELVE

The Middle East

THE CRESCENT OF FIRE

When the World Trade Center was attacked, the threats potentially posed by Russia and China were subordinated to the more immediate terrorist menace, even though the contours of the danger were obscure. Terrorism isn't an end in itself. It is a means to ends like victory or retribution, and can take many forms from sabotage to mass annihilation.[1] Moreover, whereas terrorism, like crime and war, involves unlawful coercion, it occupies a middle ground in international jurisprudence between them.[2] States are permitted to suppress terrorism more vigorously than crime, but cannot act with the impunity permissible under a formal declaration of war.[3] In this sense, war on terrorism is an acknowledgment that terror should be combated with counterterrorist methods, and a warning that America will escalate beyond this boundary to full-scale state to state war if necessary.

The dimensions of the terrorist threat are correspondingly elastic. At one end of the spectrum, demented individuals could bring about the "end of days" with weapons of mass destruction for no rational purpose,[4] but this is a remote possibility. At the other extreme, these same individuals like Hamas could seize the reins of state, transforming themselves from outlaws like Yasser Arafat into statesmen subject to standard rules of international engagement. And, of course, terrorism could persist somewhere in the middle, circumscribed but deadly. All perils deserve attention. It is in America's interest to deter and contain. But the expected benefits don't warrant unlimited expense. No amount of effort can preclude doomsday, and like the Cold War it is unwise to spend prodigally on defense, as the Soviets ruefully discovered. Terror that cannot get beyond sabotage doesn't threaten America's survival, and terrorists who seize national power become vulnerable to conventional counterstrikes.

We're in conflict with a militant branch of Islam that uses terrorism as a major tactic;[5] so our government has defined us as at war with terrorism. But we have also been at war with governments who aide the terrorists, and we have used military force to overthrow governments that had not themselves attacked us, but who were in league with terrorists who either had attacked us (Afghanistan) or were sympathizers and allies of those who had attacked us (Iraq). In late 2005, President Bush apparently changed our enemy from the tactic of terrorism to people who seek to create a radical Islamic empire from Spain to Indonesia.

Dangerous and heartbreaking as is this conflict, it must be kept in perspective. Terrorists do not threaten the existence of our country – not the way a major conflict with a nuclear-armed rival threatens our country. So we must be sure that what we do in the war on terrorism does not endanger other important concerns of our country. Yet already we have stretched ourselves in Iraq, trying to fashion a new future for the country in the mold of western capitalist democracy.

Our public culture results in dramatic reversals of political stance. Thus, many of those who most strongly opposed our entry into Iraq now oppose our exit. They argue that since we are there, we've assumed a responsibility for it. Hence, if we leave Iraq, even if our initial objectives have been met, then we'd lose the moral high ground, which they consider crucial. In this view, it's not enough for us to defend America. We must do more.

It is worth asking "Why?" We got into our current involvement in the Middle East because of the attack on the World Trade Center. It's quite a stretch to move from the attempt to defend our country by eliminating hostile regimes in Iraq and Afghanistan – in order to deny refuge to terrorists and prevent weapons of mass destruction from falling into our adversaries hands – to bringing Western style democracy to the Middle East. Asserting that only if there is democracy will we be safe from terrorist attack doesn't lessen the stretch. Initially, we sought a regime change and a guarantee there were no weapons of mass destruction. We changed the regime and we discovered no weapons of mass destruction. Why should we now remain in Iraq? Shouldn't we go, having fulfilled our stated obligations? Shouldn't we let the Iraqis run their own country? If it becomes a terrorist center, we will have to respond to that – we've intervened in Iraq twice and we can do it again, if necessary. As for the broader context of the Iraqi war, we can retain bases in the area from which to protect ourselves from militants, Syrians and Iranians.

"For 60 years, my country, the United States, pursued stability at the expense of democracy in this region here in the Middle East, and we achieved neither," Secretary of State Rice declared at the American University in Cairo. "Now we are taking a different course. We are supporting the democratic aspirations of all people."[6]

Stability was never a proper goal of policy. It reeks of preservation of the status quo for its own sake. Stability is fine when it comes naturally, but our national security must be protected whether or not there is stability. We could have achieved our own security had we but kept reasonable diligence about our defense from airline hijackings (hardly a new terrorist tactic even in 2001). But we did not; so now we are involved to a greater degree than before in the turmoil of the Middle East. We sought to avoid military involvement in Iraq, but Saddam Hussein continually violated the armistice that had ended the first Gulf War, the food for oil program, and obstructed inspections for weapons of mass destruction. Indeed, we offered him a peaceful solution up to the bitter end, but he refused, presumably because he expected his friends in the Security Council of the United Nations to prevent American military action against him.

We were not able to impose stability on the Middle East no matter how hard we try, since that is in the hands of those who live there; and we will probably be unable to impose democracy. Both stability and democracy for others are simply the wishes of our public culture. Both are illusions in the context of the Middle East today. They are not proper goals for an objective American foreign policy.

Democracy has become America's party line, supported by Republican and Democrat alike. It finds strong support in the public culture, but is very dangerous because it reflects wishful thinking and not objectivity about the world. We are trying to export American mores to other countries. For example, we have required that thirty percent of the seats in the new Iraqi parliament must go to women. This contributes to making our faux democracy the laughing stock of the Middle East and hardens negative attitudes to us. Rather than master the illusions of the public culture, we seem to have political leaders who are fully self-deluded.

It isn't terror itself that should command full attention, but the possibility that terror in specific contexts could spark conflict in vortexes of global instability. The war on terrorism as defined at this point by the Administration includes Basques, Irish, Peruvians, and Om Shin Rikyo in Japan,[7] but they are peripheral to American security. The primary target is the Islamic "Crescent of Fire," a geographical region connecting fifty countries with at least a 40 percent Muslim presence, containing 1.3 billion people.[8] The flames are fanned by the Arab-Israeli conflict, and the great game of petro-politics,[9] but the enmity runs deeper, rooted in history,[10] culture, tribalism, and religion, frequently exacerbated by state oppression and failure. Despite oil wealth and substantial foreign assistance, the incendiary potential of the crescent of fire has intensified during the last decade, and seems destined to worsen due to sectarian struggle, fanaticism, the increasing lethality of conventional ordnance and proliferation of weapons of mass destruction.[11]

Ummah

The Islamic fundamentalist dream of a pan-Muslim theocracy spanning the Crescent of Fire (which is based in significant part on an utopian reading of the first caliphate) is called "Ummah."[12] Advocates contend that it is the Muslim world's manifest destiny to reconstitute a transnational Islamic theopolitical order, tolerant of minorities, but free of western contamination. Like Bolshevik communism it rhetorically aspires to be just, prosperous and magnificent, but allows itself to employ "emergency" methods, including waging jihad (holy war) to "liquidate" infidels as "vragy naroda" (enemies of the true faith).[13] The details of this messianic musing, like Marx's idyll of communist bliss, are sophomoric and can be safely disregarded.[14] The possibility of cobbling a transnational theocratic empire akin to a fifties-type communist bloc sustained by guns and oil however is a more disturbing prospect. Although, it probably would suffer from the antidemocratic, and antifree enterprise shortcomings of its secular predecessor, the Crescent of Fire could imperil peace. The likelihood that the Ummah movement will metamorphosize into a superpower bloc may seem slight, but is thinkable. Communism too was rife with intense internal rivalries, and riddled with inefficiencies. Nonetheless, the Soviet Union, and China, following their own idiosyncratic interpretations of Marxist scripture were able to mount a credible threat when first Russia and then China acquired nuclear weapons. With Pakistan already nuclearized, and Iran on the cusp,[15] it doesn't require fevered imagination to appreciate the destabilizing possibilities of Ummah.

Muslim Terrorism and Autocracy

Imperial Ummah however isn't an immediate threat. A fragmented Crescent of Fire battered by the crosswinds of Muslin terrorism, rival autocracies, and sectarianism is now more incendiary than a united Islamic fundamentalist caliphate.[16] Muslim culture across the globe during the past sixty years hasn't transitioned to western democratic free enterprise.[17] It sometimes displays a veneer of balloting, and traditional markets abound,

Table 12.1. *GDP in the Judea/Palestine Region 1950–2002 (million 1990 international Geary-Khamis dollars)*

	Israel	Muslim	West Bank and Gaza	Lebanon	Jordan	Syria	Egypt
1950	3,623	32,917	965	3,313	933	8,418	19,288
1960	9,986	48,106	1,534	4,274	1,977	13,704	26,617
1970	23,520	76,854	2,044	6,950	3,600	22,155	42,105
1980	41,053	169,620	3,732	10,879	9,689	57,097	88,223
1990	58,511	239,586	7,222	6,099	12,371	70,894	143,000
2000	94,408	376,472	16,153	12,198	20,288	121,988	205,845
2002	92,155	399,659	10,338	12,753	21,732	130,046	224,790
Growth							
1950–02	6.4	4.9	4.7	2.6	6.2	5.4	4.8

Source: Angus Maddison, *The World Economy: Historical Statistics*, OECD, Paris, 2003, Table 5b, pp. 176–7; Table 6b, p. 211.

but sovereignty is mostly autocratic, relying on Arabic/Ottoman style traditional economic organization without a social contract for the equitable distribution of income and wealth and without a rule of contract law to permit entrepreneurship. Corruption is endemic; income and wealth are inegalitarian; and society unjust despite injunctions in the Koran against such a situation. Therefore it isn't surprising that technological innovation, global integration, and economic growth have been deficient in the Islamic world, despite the potential benefits of vast petro wealth and the possibilities of economic catch up. Per capita income has lagged the global average since 1950, and is especially poor in comparison with China and India.[18] Performance in some countries has been horrendous. Chad's per capita GDP is the same as the West's in 1 A.D.,[19] whereas living standards in 2002 were lower than in 1973 in Iran, Iraq, Kuwait, Qatar, Saudi Arabia, and the UAE.[20] Similar declines for the subperiods 1980–2002 and 1985–2002 were recorded in Lebanon, and Israel's Palestinian territories (West Bank and Gaza).[21] However, the economic performance of an important sector of the Muslim world, that which excludes African states other than those bordering the Mediterranean, has been good enough to permit the Ummah to continue to exert influence in world affairs. Its GDP in 2001 was more than 60 percent of China's, and more than a third larger than India's[22] (Table 12.3). Despite notable ups and downs for individual states, GDP growth has been a respectable 4.7 percent per annum 1950–2002, if one believes the numbers. But, per capita GDP is unimpressive (Table 12.4). It was 20 percent below China's in 2001, and is much worse with the inclusion of Africa's Muslim communities.

Table 12.2. *GDP per Capita in Judea/Palestine Region 1950–2002*

Year	Israel	Muslim	West Bank and Gaza	Lebanon	Jordan	Syria	Egypt
1950	2,817	1,672	949	2,429	1,663	2,409	910
1960	4,663	2,023	1,378	2,393	2,330	3,023	991
1970	8,101	2,417	1,980	2,917	2,395	3,540	1,254
1980	10,948	3,865	2,744	3,526	4,480	6,508	2,069
1990	12,968	3,552	3,806	1,938	3,792	5,701	2,522
2000	16,159	4,599	5,124	3,409	4,059	7,481	2,920
2001	15,756	4,395	3,953	3,430	4,055	7,547	2,992
2002	15,284	4,251	3,050	3,468	4,095	7,580	–
Growth 1950–02	3.3	1.8	2.3	0.7	1.7	2.2	2.4

Note: Figures for Israel's Muslim neighbors are unweighted averages. Also, the Muslim composite for 2002 extrapolates the Egyptian growth rate in 2001 to 2002.
Source: Angus Maddison, *The World Economy: Historical Statistics*, OECD, Paris, 2003, Table 5c, pp. 186–7, Table 6c, p. 219.

Table 12.3. *GDP of the Crescent of Fire 1950–2002 (billion 1990 international Geary-Khamis dollars)*

Year	West Asia	Indonesia	Bangladesh	Pakistan	Algeria	Egypt	Morocco	Total
1950	103	66	25	25	12	19	14	264
1960	186	97	30	33	23	27	17	413
1970	390	139	42	63	31	42	26	733
1980	716	276	48	99	59	88	44	1,330
1990	874	451	70	182	74	143	64	1,858
2000	1,252	676	114	272	87	206	80	2,687
2001	1,249	698	119	282	89	215	85	2,737
2002	1,297	721	124	292	91	225	90	2,840
Growth 1950–02	5.0	4.7	3.1	4.8	4.0	4.8	3.6	4.7

Note: The 15 West Asia nations are Bahrain, Iran, Iraq, Jordan, Kuwait Lebanon, Oman, Qatar, Saudi Arabia, Syria, Turkey, UAE, Yemen, West Bank and Gaza. Also the Indonesian, Bangladesh, Pakistan, Algeria, Egypt, and Morocco figures for 2002 are estimated from the 2001 growth rate.
Source: Angus Maddison, *The World Economy: Historical Statistics*, OECD, Paris, 2003, Table 5b, pp. 174–5, 177; Table 6b, pp. 210–13.

Nonetheless, per capita GDP growth was an adequate 2 percent per annum 1950–2002. This is well below potential, and inferior to the performance of some developing regions, but should be enough to keep it from losing ground to the EU and Japan.[23]

Table 12.4. *GDP per Capita in the Crescent of Fire 1950–2002 (1990 international Geary-Khamis dollars)*

Year	West Asia	Indonesia	Bangladesh	Pakistan	Algeria	Egypt	Morocco	Total
1950	1,776	840	540	643	1,365	910	1,455	1,076
1960	2,492	1,019	544	647	2,088	991	1,329	1,301
1970	3,998	1,194	629	952	2,249	1,254	1,616	1,699
1980	5,397	1,870	548	1,161	3,143	2,069	2,272	2,351
1990	4,856	2,516	640	1,597	2,918	2,522	2,596	2,521
2000	5,706	3,203	873	1,920	2,792	2,920	2,658	2,867
2001	5,580	3,256	897	1,947	2,813	9,292	2,782	2,895
2002	5,664	3,310	922	1,974	2,834	3,066	2,912	2,955
Growth 1950–02	2.3	2.7	1.0	2.2	1.4	2.4	1.4	2.0

Note: West Asia covers Bahrain, Iran, Iraq, Israel, Jordan, Kuwait Lebanon, Oman, Qatar, Saudi Arabia, Syria, Turkey, UAE, Yemen, West Bank, and Gaza. The 2002 estimates for Indonesia, Bangladesh, Pakistan, Algeria, Egypt and Morocco have been extrapolated from 2001.
Source: Angus Maddison, *The World Economy: Historical Statistics*, OECD, Paris, 2003, Table 5c, pp. 184–5, 187; Table 6c pp. 218–21.

These failures compounded by political repression, intrigue, and virulent anti-western sentiment make the Crescent of Fire explosive. Muslim nations like Iran, Iraq, Kuwait, Syria, Lebanon, Egypt, Sudan, Libya, Somalia, Ethiopia, Yemen, and Pakistan wage wars of conquest and plunder against each other directly, or indirectly via proxies, under the banner of high principle. Domestic opponents plot coup d'etats in Algeria, Iraq, Saudi Arabia, and Indonesia, resorting to insurrection, pitched battles, guerrilla war and terrorism. And often groups like Hamas, Hezbollah, and Fatah conduct terrorist attacks against Israel and Russia (regarding Chechnya) not just to harm enemies, but to muster support for internecine struggles at home. All is fair in love, terror, putsches, and war. Treachery is ubiquitous.

THE CAUSES OF TERRORISM

We point here to an attempt to rebuild Iraq in America's image as an example of overreach that we are unlikely to be able to accomplish. But it also is not likely to eliminate terrorism, even were we successful in changing Iraq. The reason for this lies in the deep causality of terrorism.

The basic point is that people can violently oppose America, and do it by terrorism, with other motivations than poverty. In fact, America has never been brought to war by an adversary driven by poverty and deprivation.

By nationalism, by ambition, by contempt for us, yes – but by desperation caused by deprivation, no. Not Germany, not Japan, not the Southerners who fought against the Union in our Civil War, not Spain, not Vietnam, not North Korea, not China (in the Korean War). There is no reason to think that our adversaries in the war on terror are any different, and many reasons to think they are like our other adversaries – well-to-do but our adversaries.

Well-to-do people can oppose America and as they and their sympathizers become richer, they can do it more effectively. It's a great illusion to think that opposition to us grows only in the soil of deprivation and oppression – such a conviction is a form of arrogance that lies at the heart of wishful thinking. The arrogance lies in the notion that if people anywhere were well off, they'd admire and support what we are and what we do. This simply isn't the case now, never has been, and won't be in the future.

Why would some people make themselves our adversaries even if they themselves were well off? They might oppose our values, or what they believe to be our values. America is complex – there is a traditional side to our culture and a side dedicated to destroying what is traditional. Here, for example, is a young American writing about the positive changes he sees in American life since the counterculture began in the 1960s.

"... [T]he 60s rid us of certain aesthetic and stylistic inhibitions. Ladies will never again be required to wear white gloves. The notion of 'Sunday best' clothes becomes more antiquated every year. The conventions of rock 'n' roll, rap, and even country music now permit profanity, and they forever will." This he believes is all to the good – thus there are people actively trying to achieve these things, and glorying in them.[24]

Thus, whether it's modesty or manners, there's a strong force in American culture trying to undermine it, and people abroad who support the old verities are likely to find themselves antagonists of America.

America has allies and supporters in other nations in the world; their opponents are natural adversaries of America. The most dramatic such example today is America's support for Israel against a host of those who are ill-wishers to the Jewish state.

However, rich might be another country, it could find itself envying and seeking to rival America's global might. The most dramatic examples today involve Russia and China; in the future the most dramatic example may be a united Europe.

In the case of terrorism directed today at America, each of these factors plays a key role – cultural antipathy, America's support for enemies, and envy of American power. What role does poverty play?

What is the connection between terrorism and poverty? This is an important question because a particularly strong variant of wishful thinking holds that the terrorist threat to America is caused by economic deprivation and can best be answered by economic improvements.

For example, a reporter for the *Washington Post* writes, "... terrorism ... the seeds of that problem were planted in the soil of despair, isolation and zealotry."[25]

In such a view, terrorists are people whom despair and isolation have led to zealotry. But there is little evidence for this. Instead, an increasing body of evidence and analysis shows that those who point to poverty as a cause of terrorism are mistaken, at least to the extent that poverty usually exists without giving birth to terrorism, and terrorism sometimes exists without poverty and deprivation (for example, America's Unabomber, who was a graduate of Harvard College). Yet people who take this point of view often have an admirable motive. They wish to eliminate poverty since it is an evil in the world, and if they can only interest others in their objective by insisting that addressing poverty will also reduce terrorism, then they'll use that method of getting support. This isn't the most reputable approach, but neither is it the worst thing that happens in our world, and at least the goal is admirable.

This analysis is a sophisticated way of blaming Americans for the attacks on the United States – again blaming the victims for their victimization. Amy Chua of Yale argues that Americans are hated abroad because we're rich (in her words, we're a "market dominant minority"), and therefore the disadvantaged attack us.[26] So it turns out that terror is rooted in understandable resentment – not ethnic hatred (or if it is, we're fueling that by our insistence on democracy), not lust for power or wealth, but just resentment. She thus attempts to transfer envy to the level of geopolitical activism. Although envy plays its role, it won't carry this much weight as a cause of global conflict.

We must be careful not to be misled into a response to terrorism that is wholly economic and ameliorative.

What have we learned about terrorism and its causes in recent years?

- Terrorists are rarely the completely deprived, but instead are usually well-educated people. "Mass and indiscriminate murder is the crime of educated people ... " They believe they have the right to decide for others what is important and to impose it on them; they are convinced that their ends justify their means. [27] Terrorists are not, in their own minds and to outside observers, irrational. "... Someone whose rational insights produce apparently irrational behavior ... doesn't fit the usual psychiatric categories. ... Rather than being irrational, he takes ideas more seriously than most. He suffers from an excess of reason."[28]

- Any connection between poverty and terrorism "is at best indirect, complicated and probably quite weak."[29]
- Poverty is usually a pretext, not a cause, of mass murder. "Don't fall for the hypothesis that poverty is the cause of mass murder. It is just a pretext used by people with other agendas. If poverty were eliminated, then the same people would find another pretext. ... As logical as the poverty-breeds terrorism argument may seem, study after study shows that suicide attackers and their supporters are rarely ignorant or impoverished. Nor are they crazed, cowardly, apathetic or asocial."[30]

The causes of terrorism lie as much or more in a political culture of violence and fanaticism as in poverty.[31]

- Research dating back decades and updated frequently shows that most terrorists do not come from backgrounds of deprivation. For example, only some 13 percent of Palestinian suicide bombers are from impoverished families.[32]
- Rather, poverty seems to become an excuse for efforts to take political power; it is seen as a way to rally the masses and a justification for direct and violent action. Poverty is not a cause of violence or terrorism, it is rationale for it; and absent poverty, the impulse of terrorists trying to gain political power would simply seek another justification. Terror is a weapon – sometimes used by the weak (as by Arab militants); sometimes used by the strong (as by Hitler at the height of Nazi Germany's power and Stalin always). It is a weapon of choice, and employed in different ways. It is neither the result of poverty; nor is it the peculiar weapon of the desperate instead of the strong.

Finally, in the indirect connection between poverty and terrorism, the nexus lies in comparative poverty, not absolute deprivation. The Middle East is not one of the poorest regions of the globe. But it has some of the world's greatest extremes of wealth and poverty. Oil wealth in the Middle East has greatly increased the difference between haves and have-nots, enormously increasing social tensions. This is the cauldron from which hatred and terrorism bubble, not from the differences between the United States and the Islamic countries, and it is in the bubbling of this cauldron that we are now caught.

The problem, from the point of view of wishful thinking and its prescriptions for economic development as a cure for terrorism, is that economic progress in these countries will first acerbate the differences within, not decrease them, and so progress will make things worse. Wishful thinking is again shown to be an illusion.

"The poor in Muslim states may be the popular base of terrorist support, but they have neither the money nor the votes (who votes doesn't count, who counts them does, in Stalin's words) the privileged do. Ultimately, Islamic terrorism, just as its Marxist or secessionist version in the West and Latin America was, is a matter of power – who has it and how to get it – not of poverty. Accepting this as a fundamental aspect of terrorism does not suggest any immediate solutions, but can direct further study toward better explanations of terrorism and theories with some potential predictive value."[33]

A sea of poverty and disappointment is necessary for middle class revolutionaries to get any foothold. They can exist in Germany or the United States, but only at the margin and with little or no chance of success. If they are, as Michael Radu says, concerned primarily about power, they are completely marginal in Germany and the United States, for example, because there is no likely context in which they can achieve power. But in the Arab world, for example, the context is there (as it was in Russia at the time of the Bolshevik coup d'état) and so they are a real threat because they could gain power. A terrorist group in a context in which they could achieve power is a very different thing than a terrorist group in a context in which they cannot achieve power, and little is gained by talking about "terrorism," which is only a method.

Examples are offered continually by secular dictatorships in the region, including Egypt, Saudi Arabia, and Syria. The governments never cease to repress middle-class revolutionaries looking for a foothold among the poor. For instance, in May 2005, some forty students at Tishreen University in Syria were arrested and tortured by Syrian police because of their involvement in Islamic fundamentalist movements. "Syria's emergency laws, adopted some 40 years ago as a national security measure" wrote a reporter for *The Chronicle of Higher Education*, an American publication, "forbid the formation of any group without explicit government approval. Thus, merely forming an illegal student group, let alone an Islamist one, is grounds for arrest in Syria."[34] Syria also conducts an equally brutal campaign against its better established political rivals. In Lebanon, a car bomb killed anti-Syrian political leader George Hawi, just weeks after the similar murder of anti-Syrian journalist Samir Kassir. There is little doubt about the instigators of the murders.[35] The murder of political leaders of an opposition is an old Communist and fascist tactic and is very effective.

It is possible that the attachment of Osama bin Laden and other middle-class radical leaders to Islamic fundamentalism is no deeper than necessary to mobilize warriors against their chosen enemies. We must always keep in mind that their most direct enemies are other Muslims, in particular those governing Saudi Arabia. "The fight against the enemy nearest to you has precedence over the fight against the enemy farther away," said Muhammad Abd al-Salam Faraj, tried and hanged in connection with the 1981 assassination of Anwar al-Sadat of Egypt. ". . . In all Muslim countries the enemy has the reins of power," he continued. "The enemy is the present rulers." And bin Laden's deputy Ayman al-Zawahiri is reported to have said, "Victory for the Islamic movements . . . cannot be attained unless these movements possess an Islamic base in the heart of the Arab region," a clear statement of geopolitical objectives.[36] Islamic radicalism undergirds the movement as communist ideology undergirded the foreign policy of the USSR. Osama bin Laden, like the leaders of the Soviet Union, may or may not have believed in their own demagoguery, but the movement itself was powerful.

In August 1996, Osama bin Laden published a fatwa, though technically he is not a cleric, he may have had no authority to do so, but the document is certainly a statement of hostility (if not a declaration of war, as he represents no state), entitled "Declaration of War against the Americans Occupying the Land of the Two Holy Places." (Osama bin Laden, first published in *Al Quds Al Arabi*, a London-based newspaper, in August 1996; obtained from the PBS *News Hour* Web site.) It is 24 pages long. We quote a significant excerpt that we believe to be representative from it here because it demonstrates the focus of our adversaries; and because so few Americans have read it. It is not a denunciation of Christianity or Judaism. It is not a polemic against the American way of life. It is something much more nationalistic in nature.

Praise be to Allah, we seek His help and ask for his pardon. . . . It should not be hidden from you that the people of Islam had suffered from aggression, iniquity and injustice imposed on them by the Zionist-Crusaders alliance and their collaborators; to the extent that the Muslims blood became the cheapest and their wealth as loot in the hands of the enemies. . . . The people of Islam awakened and realized that they are the main target for the aggression of the Zionist-Crusaders alliance. All false claims and propaganda about "Human Rights" were hammered down and exposed by the massacres that took place against the Muslims in every part of the world.

The latest and the greatest of these aggressions, incurred by the Muslims since the death of the Prophet (ALLAH'S BLESSING AND SALUTATIONS ON HIM) is the occupation of the land of the two Holy Places – the foundation of the house of Islam, the place of the revelation, the source of the message and the place of the noble Ka'ba, the Qiblah of all Muslims – by the armies of the American Crusaders and their allies. (We bemoan this . . . iniquitous crusaders movement under the leadership of the USA; who fears that . . . the scholars and callers of Islam, will instigate the Ummah of Islam against its' enemies. . . . We, myself and my group, have suffered some of this injustice ourselves; we have been prevented from addressing the Muslims. We have been pursued in Pakistan, Sudan and Afghanistan, hence this long absence on my part. But by the Grace of Allah, a safe base is now available in the high Hindukush mountains. . . . From here, today we begin the work, talking and discussing the ways of correcting what had happened to the Islamic world in general, and the Land of the two Holy Places in particular. We wish to study the means that we could follow to return the situation to its normal path.

. . . The inability of the [Saudi] regime to protect the country, and allowing the enemy of the Ummah – the American crusader forces – to occupy the land for the longest of years. The crusader forces became the main cause of our disastrous condition, particularly in the economical aspect of it due to the unjustified heavy spending on these forces. As a result of the policy imposed on the country, especially in the field of oil industry where production is restricted or expanded and prices are fixed to suit the American economy ignoring the economy of the country. Expensive deals were imposed on the country to purchase arms. People asking what is the justification for the very existence of the regime then? . . . the regime refused to listen to the people accusing them of being ridiculous and imbecile. The matter got worse as previous wrong doings were followed by mischief's of greater magnitudes. All of this taking place in the land of the two Holy Places! It is no longer possible to be quiet. It is not acceptable to give a blind eye to this matter. . . . The financial and the economical situation of the country and the frightening future in the view of the enormous amount of debts and interest owed by the government; this is at the time when the wealth of the Ummah being wasted to satisfy personal desires of certain individuals!! while imposing more custom duties and taxes on the nation.

. . . The miserable situation of the social services and infra-structure especially the water service and supply, the basic requirement of life. . . . The state of the ill-trained and ill-prepared army and the impotence of its commander in chief despite the incredible amount of money that has been spent on the army. The gulf war clearly exposed the situation. Therefore every one agreed that the situation can not be rectified . . . unless the root of the problem is tackled. Hence it is essential to hit the main enemy who divided the Ummah into small and little countries and pushed it, for the last few decades, into a state of confusion. The Zionist-Crusader alliance moves quickly to contain and abort any "corrective movement" appearing in the Islamic countries. Different means and methods are used to achieve their target. . . . If there are more than one duty to be carried out, then the most important one should receive priority. Clearly after Belief (Imaan) there is no more important duty than pushing the American enemy out of the holy land.

The Mujahideen, your brothers and sons, requesting that you support them in every possible way by supplying them with the necessary information, materials and arms. Security men are especially asked to cover up for the Mujahideen and to assist them as much as possible against the occupying enemy; and to spread rumors, fear and discouragement among the members of the enemy forces . . .

I say to you William (Cohen, Defense Secretary of the United States) that: These youths love death as you love life. They inherit dignity, pride, courage, generosity, truthfulness and sacrifice from father to father. They are most delivering and steadfast at war. They inherit these values from their ancestors (even from the time of the Jaheliyyah, before Islam).... Our youths believe in paradise after death.... Those youths.. have no intention except to enter paradise by killing you.... Those youths are different from your soldiers. Your problem will be how to convince your troops to fight, while our problem will be how to restrain our youths to wait for their turn in fighting and in operations.

...I rejected all the critics, who chose the wrong way; I rejected those who enjoy fireplaces in clubs discussing eternally;I rejected those, who inspire being lost, think they are at the goal;I respect those who carried on not asking or bothering about the difficulties.... The walls of oppression and humiliation cannot be demolished except in a rain of bullets. The freeman does not surrender leadership to infidels and sinners.... Our Lord, guide this Ummah, and make the right conditions (by which) the people of your obedience will be in dignity and the people of disobedience in humiliation, and by which the good deeds are enjoined and the bad deeds are forebode.

There is not much in this document about denying to Americans our way of life. For a document that is supposedly a religious manifesto, there is a surprising amount about the finances of the Kingdom of Saudi Arabia. There is a great deal of a rather nationalist concern – overcast with pan-Arabic and religious rhetoric – about the alleged occupation of a home country (Saudi Arabia) by foreign troops (America's) and an allegedly corrupt regime (the Saudi monarchy) that permits this. There is, that is, much about power and wealth and about the government of a particular nation.[37] And there is much threat and bluster.

Rather like the Cold War, there is the sense of a battle between nations (or the self-anointed leaders of nations) played out in part in an ideological or religious context in which the emotions of all sides can be more easily aroused, even if the ideological or religious concerns are not at the root of the controversies. That is to say, the Cold War was not about Communism, and the War on Terror is not about Islam, except insofar as leaders of each side needed ideology or religion to rally supporters. It is the public culture that makes the conflict seem to be about ideology or religion. To accept as fact the illusions of the public culture about the basic cause of the conflict is to lose objectivity about the contest and therefore – via wrong objectives, wrong methods, wrong priorities, and wrong justifications – to become prey to mistaken actions and missed opportunities.

THE CONTEST IN THE MIDDLE EAST

Americans had been attacked by Islamic terrorists several times before September 11, 2001. For example, more than two hundred of our Marines had been killed in a bombing of their barracks in Beirut, Lebanon, in 1983.[38] In response, we chose not to declare war on terrorism, but to withdraw from Lebanon, leaving it ultimately in control of Syria for more than twenty years – a continuing haven for terrorists. About the American reaction to the Beirut bombing Osama bin Laden remarked in an interview with John Miller of ABC News on May 28, 1998, "We have seen in the last decade the decline of the American government and the weakness of the American soldier, who is . . . unprepared to fight long wars. This was proven in Beirut when the Marines fled after two explosions . . . "[39]

It is sometimes argued that the beginning of the Islamists' use of terror bombing as a tactic against the West was the bombing of the U.S. Marine barracks in Beirut in 1984. That bombing caused the American superpower to withdraw from Lebanon in just six weeks or so, and is alleged to have proved to Islamic radicals the value of terror bombing. Thus, the increasing use of terrorism was the Reagan administration's fault. However, terrorism was a part of the Islamist response to the West in the nineteen century. It was used throughout the war for Israeli independence. It use against Americans can be dated to Beirut in 1984, but even had Reagan been more vigorous in response, matters would likely not have unfolded very differently.

Bin Laden's comment is consistent with a radical Islamic interpretation of recent history. According to this interpretation, Muslim fighters defeated the stronger superpower – the Soviet Union – in Afghanistan, precipitating its dissolution, and have now turned to what they apparently consider the weaker superpower – America – and believe they will soon force its collapse. In their view the United States is further away, less well armed, less ruthless, more morally corrupt, socially degenerate, and therefore "politically and militarily enfeebled."[40] It seemed to bin Laden that there was a pattern in the behavior of the United States. The terrorists attacked and we denounced them and threatened retaliation and withdrew. We were all talk and no action.

Yet after the attack on the World Trade Center in September 2001, we sprung on them. Perhaps it was because the attack had been on American soil; perhaps it was because so many lives had been lost; perhaps it was because the victims were civilians not marines. Whatever the reason, America responded very differently than it had eighteen years before.

We defined ourselves as at war. We need not have done this. We'd been attacked before by the same group several times, and we hadn't responded by saying we were at war. We could have treated the terrorist attacks as rather more a crime than an act of war – and we need not have chosen to include foreign governments in our list of enemies – we could have restricted ourselves to the terrorists who are nongovernmental entities. But once the World Trade Center had been destroyed, we chose to declare war and include in our adversaries certain foreign governments. We thereby threw ourselves into the middle of the Middle Eastern political cauldron.

The Islamic terrorists' threat to us is not primarily religious in its motivation; it is political. The motivation of suicide bombers is not primarily religious either, except insofar as Islam promises paradise to those who die in its behalf. When we define the conflict as one of cultures or religions, we give it a depth it does not deserve, misidentify our enemies in a way that makes them far more numerous than they really are, and makes the problem of countering them even more difficult than it is. Those "who carefully parse the statements of Osama bin Laden . . . find them completely secular," writes Louise Richardson of the Radcliffe Institute at Harvard. The World Trade Center towers "were hit not as icons of blasphemy, but of arrogant power" (our power). Al-Queda is fighting to get the West out of the Middle East and it is our involvement there in support of rich and repressive regimes that is the cause of their actions toward us (the Palestinian cause is not a real source of al-Queda's animosity toward us). Suicide bombing, the weapon of our adversaries that gets the most attention from the media, is the result of "a desire for glory, coupled with strong group ties . . . and often more interest in the dying than the killing."[41] There is underway a political battle for control of the Middle East, in which the prizes are the oil of the Persian Gulf and the nuclear war capability of Pakistan.[42] The contest involves Islamic traditionalists who use terrorism as a weapon, established governments that use police repression as a weapon, and outside powers who covet the oil of the Middle East. "One could easily do a revisionist history of 9/11," wrote Thomas Friedman, "and show how it was simply the opening salvo in an attempted coup within Saudi Arabia – with the attack on America meant only as a bank shot to undermine one of the main supports of the Saudi ruling family."[43]

PALESTINE

What is most striking about Friedman's comment is that he labels this view, which is almost certainly the accurate one, "revisionist" and therefore outside the mainstream. What then is the mainstream view? It is that terrorists are attacking America because they hate our values and way of life, and because of our support for Israel in its alleged repression of the Palestinian people. For example, according to a British writer, the United States has been stuck in a largely unchanging mess in the Mideast for four decades. He adds,

"Yet all routes in the maze lead back to the Israel-Palestinian conflict. The perception of the Arab world – and, it should be said, of most Europeans – is that America's enduring support for Israel now amounts to a blank check for a government led by Ariel Sharon that will never make an enduring peace. Mr. Sharon builds settlements and walls in the occupied territories that guarantee such an outcome is impossible. The most he can expect from the White House is a mild rebuke."[44]

However, the view that the Palestinian dispute is at the bottom of the turmoil in the Middle East is mistaken. Quite the contrary. The dispute over political control in the Islamic world is at the bottom of the Palestinian conflict. The Israeli-Palestinian conflict is a sideshow to the greater conflict in the Crescent of Fire. The clash of civilizations is one reason for the conflict in the Crescent of Fire, if for no other reason that the differences between American traditional values and Muslim values is exploited by demagogues and intriguers.

The clash of civilizations is only menacing when there is a specific alignment of forces with opposing societies. Civilization is a conditioning factor, not an enduring cause taken in isolation. At this historical junction, civilization factors have been pushed to the forefront.

A key element is the clash of moralities – with radical Islam representing a radicalized Puritanism and the West an extreme cosmopolitanism represented by U.S. popular (not public) culture. Puritanism is patriarchical, religious, moral; cosmopolitanism is egalitarian, tolerant, amoral. There is a strong cosmopolitan element in Islam (the governing powers in most Islamic states, especially Saudi Arabia, Kuwait, and the Emirates are cosmopolitan): and there is a strong puritan element in the West (in America there is the religious right and orthodox Judaism). But Puritanism is resurgent in Islam and cosmopolitanism dominates the United States and reaches around the world via our popular culture with its glorification of sex, drugs, pornography, relativism, and so on.

The Bush administration sees America as puritan (which is the administration's political orientation), but America is really cosmopolitan. So the administration fails to comprehend the puritan/cosmopolitan division in the world.

The puritan/cosmopolitan divide is much older than the religious divide (especially Christianity/Islam, which is only about fourteen hundred years old). Abraham was puritan; the Mesopotamians and the Egyptians were cosmopolitan. The Hebrews were puritan; the Phillistines were cosmopolitan. The Persians were puritan; the Babylonians were cosmopolitan. The Persians became cosmopolitan; the Greeks were puritan. The Greeks became cosmopolitan; the Romans were puritan. The Romans became cosmopolitan; the Germanic tribes were puritan. The Byzantines were cosmopolitan; the Arabs were puritan. The Chinese were cosmopolitan; the Mongols were puritan. The Catholic Church was cosmopolitan; the Protestants were puritan. The Cavaliers were cosmopolitan; the Roundheads were puritan. The English were cosmopolitan; the Americans were puritan. Today, America is cosmopolitan (the dynamic of history is that successful puritan societies evolve into cosmopolitan societies); its Islamic radical antagonists are puritan.

Thus, there is not so much a clash of civilizations as a clash of moralities. Or, put differently, a clash of civilizations occurs only when there is a clash of moralities beneath it.

In this context, Palestine is a cockpit in a conflict that is much wider than Palestine.

The real conflict is not over Palestine, but over the efforts of Islamic radicals to seize control of the most financially viable and militarily powerful elements of the Muslim world (today Saudi Arabia and Pakistan, respectively) and Palestine is a tool in these efforts.

The disproportion of cause and effect supports this view. How could it be that the prime minister of Israel proposes to build a wall separating Israelis from Palestinian Arabs, and as a result the World Trade Center is destroyed and thousands die in New York City? Yet this is what those who attribute terrorism to a Palestinian cause assert. Sharon's settlements in Palestinian lands and his defensive walls neither justify nor explain the broader conflict in the region in which we have become entangled.

The challenge from Muslim radicals is not a clash of civilizations nor a shout of rage by the disadvantaged, but is instead rooted in political ambition, intrigue and self-preservation. The usually cited causes –Israeli actions and poverty—are primarily pretexts for terrorism the purpose of which is much broader than support for the Palestinians. Hence, the challenge cannot be eliminated by resolving the dispute in Palestine.

There's a great struggle for political power going on in the Arab world occasioned in part by the economic developments of the past fifty years (oil revenues, population growth, nonoil economic stagnation, emergence of fundamentalist Islam, etc). The struggle is exported to the rest of the world via two routes – oil which interests the great powers, and Islam which overlaps into non-Arab regions. Oil entices non-Arab powers to get involved in the Arab power struggle for their own purposes; and Islam carries the rhetoric and violent methods of the struggle into non-Arab communities.

It was Israel's misfortune to emerge at this point in Arab history. Israel is largely a consequence of European politics and war (of the Zionist impulse of the late nineteenth century and of the Nazis and World War II). In the setting of the internal conflict in the Arab world, Israel became a pawn in the Arab conflict. It is thus absurd to suggest that a full reconciliation in Palestine can be achieved while the Arab struggle continues; and it is a greater absurdity to suppose that if a peace could somehow be crafted in Palestine, it would lead to a broader peace in the Arab world. Turmoil in the Arab world is not a result of turmoil in Palestine; rather the reverse. The tail (Palestine) is too tiny (about four million people in Palestine, the total population for United Palestine nine million) to wag the dog (an Arab world of some 165 to 235 million – depending on how much of north Africa is included). To insist that the tail does wag the dog is a fundamental misconception that leads to all sorts of errors of strategy and tactics for America – and it is an element of the dominance of illusion over reality in our public culture.

If Israel did not exist, and there were no conflict in Palestine between Jews and Muslims, there would remain conflict in the Muslim world between modernizers and traditionalists, it would be violent, and we would be drawn into the conflict, given oil and the geographic significance of much of the region. The Palestinian issue is only a small part of the whole conflict, and we'd be as involved were there no Israel. In consequence, Israel is a benefit to us in the Middle East, not a cause of our difficulties.

Israel has little margin of error for survival. The country has a population of only about five million Jews, and it is only about eight thousand square miles in area (smaller than Massachusetts). At its narrowest point, it is only about fifty miles across; and it has many neighbors sworn to its extinction. Israel has fought four wars with its Arab neighbors; it need lose only one to be eliminated.

This is difficult for Americans to comprehend. We are a nation of almost three hundred million; residing on much of a continent (3.7 million square miles); protected by two great oceans; with friendly neighbors, both of which we dominate in population, economics and military strength. We have a huge margin for error; and in fact, as Churchill said, we Americans make mistake after mistake in international affairs, but ultimately have the resources, leadership, and determination to correct them and win the victory. Israel is not in this position.

When one combines the two facts: that the conflict in the Middle East is not driven by economic deprivation, and that Israel is almost indefensible and has no margin of error, then it is understandable why many Israelis, including the government, do not accept our illusion – that if they treat the Palestinians as the Palestinians say they wish to be treated, then the result will be a secure peace and an end to Arab aggression toward Israel. It might, but it might not. Israeli has no margin of error to see which it is. So it's no surprise that the Israelis' do not rush into a peace that may be flawed, and may be a fatal trap for them. The issues of "right of return" and the unwillingness of Palestinians to settle for anything less than a united Palestine under Muslim control could block the path to peace.

American opinion has been shifting toward the notion that Israeli mistreatment of the Palestinians is causing the Arab world to be anti-American because we are supporting Israel. In giving credence to this point of view, we are accepting the position of bin Laden and his allies, who have adopted this position as a justification for their terror tactics against us. But the politics of money and oil that underlie the turmoil in the Arab world would be there regardless of Israel; and we would be involved in the turmoil regardless of Palestine.

THE ISRAELI–PALESTINIAN SMOKESCREEN

The Crescent of Fire's engagement across and beyond its borders is often reduced by commentators to a single source of dispute: the Israel-Palestine conflict. Politicians of diverse persuasions contend that it is the key to the whole dangerous puzzle.[45] If Israel and the Palestinian authorities in Gaza and the West Bank follow President Bush's "road map" to a two-state solution in which land is exchanged for peace, and Palestinians are permitted to return to their ancestral homes, so goes this proposition, then all other grievances will recede into obscurity.[46] Islamic fundamentalism, insurgency, terror, war, political intervention, and occupation will recede into insignificance.

For nearly sixty years, it has seemed wise to many people to engage in this wishful thinking,[47] even though bundling issues has circumscribed options, and the linkage has grown increasingly implausible. With the stakes rising, including the possibility of an Iranian Islamic fundamentalist nuclear weapon,[48] it behooves scholars and politicians to acknowledge the nonlikelihood of the "roadmap" culminating in a durable peace for Israel and Palestine, and in an armistice across the Crescent of Fire.

There are two reasons for this unpleasant conclusion. First, there are no terms that can resolve the Israel-Palestine conflict to the satisfaction of both parties. Second, even if there were, those terms would not resolve the ambitions of Islamic fundamentalism, Muslim imperial aspirations, intrastate and intra-Ummah opportunism, and petro rivalries.[49]

The intractability of the Israeli-Palestinian conundrum is exposed in Palestinian insistence on the right of return and restitution for Palestinian refugees in Israel, and on the eventual attainment of a unified Muslim Palestinian state in which infidels are allowed to exist only within limits of toleration acknowledged by the fundamentalist majority. The Arab's concept of a two-state solution not only permits displaced Palestinians and other Muslims to settle in a new Gaza-West Bank homeland, but requires Israel to accept all returnees and their descendants to their ancestral properties.[50] Israel under this scheme is obligated to evict Jewish tenants, transfer forfeited assets, and make room for millions within traditional precincts, rather than merely permitting refugees to resettle as they can throughout the country. And of course, it must accept a concommitant shift in electoral politics which in short order, under international pressure, is apt to result in a transfer of power to a Muslim dominated Palestinian state.[51] Some Israelis are willing to "give peace a chance" under these adverse terms, but the Oslo accords, Taba discussions of 2001, and the second intifada of 2000 have inclined the majority of Israelis to a different attitude.[52]

Interim Prime Minister Ehud Olmert recognizing the impasse is seeking to circumvent protracted negotiations with the Palestinians on the right of return, and the character of a new Muslin state in Israel's territories (which the Arabs tendentiously call occupied lands) by unilaterally withdrawing from much of the West Bank, after Ariel Sharon unilaterally withdrew from Gaza in August 2005. Their actions comply with the roadmap by creating some kind of Muslim Palestinian state in accordance with the UN resolution of 1948,[53] but is unlikely to produce a final solution to the controversy.[54]

Relatedly, fertility rates in Gaza and West Bank have fallen precipitously during the last seven years; ameliorating another destabilizing element of the Israeli-Palestine comflict. A study done by a team of American and Israeli demographic researchers concluded that the UN and Palestine Bureau of Statistics have greatly over-counted the Arab population in Yesha (West Bank and Gaza) which is not 3.8 million but closer to 2.4 million, and the growth rates are not as high as previously stated.[55] The factors explaining the new estimates are fewer births, lower fertility rates, net emigration, double counting, inclusion of nonresidents, migration to Israel, alterations of birth data, and miscounting population regarding themselves as Israeli such as Palestinian Arabs (including, for example, Druze, Bedouins).

President Bush's and Natan Sharansky's faith in a roadmap leading to democratic free enterprise in Palestine is no more realistic than the plan being pursued by the Israeli government.[56]

They suppose that Muslim Palestinians will accept a two-state solution with a token right of return for refugees to Israel as soon as Arab residents of Gaza and the West bank embrace democratic free enterprise, or that Israel will abandon its Jewish state for an open multicultural society eventuating in a minority Jewish presence. Olmert is keenly aware of the possible demographic time bomb if Arab fertility rates return to past norms, and isn't going to make any concessions that exacerbate the risks. He realizes that by 2050, according to moderate projections, Jews and other non Muslims will be a minority of every age cohort except the elderly in what might be a unified state, and will have a dwindling majority (from 81.4 to 73.7) within Israel proper.[57] Counting on Israel's superior economic performance (displayed in Tables 12.1 and 12.2), they believe Israel's best chance for survival is within a separate Jewish state.[58]

The controversy in Palestine thus has only two probable futures, both of which preclude the kind of settlement that some imagine would extinguish all flames in the Crescent of Fire. Either there will be seesaw confrontation, perhaps with periods akin to the Battle for Britain during Word War II where England painfully survived V-1 and V-2 terror bombing, or one side will subdue the other. Hope notwithstanding, an open, multicultural, democratic free enterprise united Israel-Palestine is inconceivable. This being the case, the illusion of such an outcome provides a pretext for terrorist attacks against infidels everywhere, and for insurgencies and xenophobia within the Ummah hologram. Because spokespersons for Muslim fundamentalism continue to insist on a resolution of the conflict in Palestine that they know is not feasible, it should be evident that their purpose is something else – an attempted justification for violence directed widely and with purposes that go beyond the issues in Palestine.

THE BROADER ISSUES

Because the conflict in the Middle East is at its core a political contest over control of a vast region, it's a mistake for our President to formulate for the American people one aspect of it – terrorism – as a military challenge: a war. It is especially dangerous to mischaracterize the contest as a war as large-scale and very widely publicized military successes may in fact be counterproductive in the political struggle (our military successes may permit our adversaries to strengthen their political position by making us seem intent on conquering the region). Should our adversaries succeed in overthrowing the governments of Saudi Arabia or Pakistan, or both, then despite military successes in Afghanistan and Iraq, we should have been soundly defeated in the broader and more important contest.

Hence, it was probably a mistake to have characterized our response to the World Trade Center attack on September 11, 2001, as a war. We would have done better to respond in the very way we did in action, but less provocatively in words. A different label would have been better in the political battle. We are in fact pursuing an antiterrorist campaign as a sort of international police action, working with local allies and with small units of American military and with limited numbers of air strikes. In this sort of engagement with terrorists, the political and the clandestine should always take precedence over the military and it is an error to confuse the two by the use of the term war as a label. This is exactly the kind of error that our leadership is prone to make because of the pressure of a media that tends to magnify everything into a national hysteria.

JUSTIFYING TERRORISM

Terrorists employ bombs; but not every bombing is a terrorist attack – not when done by combatants and not when directed at combatants. We know that the members of Islamist military organizations are at war with us, they so declare themselves, and they are armed and are combatants, even though they do not wear the uniform of a recognized national state. When they attack our military – as in the attack on the USS *Cole,* or on the Marine barracks in Lebanon , or in Iraq – these actions are acts of war, not terrorist attacks. When however, they attack civilians (as in the case of the attack on the World Trade Center) these are clearly terrorist attacks. International law (going back to the Hague Conventions of 1898 and 1907, and reaffirmed by Additional Protocol 1 to the 1977 Geneva Convention) makes a crucial distinction between combatants and civilians. It calls on warring parties to make that distinction and not to target civilians.

Terrorism involves an attack made on civilians by whatever methods – bombs, artillery, rifles, pistols, bioagents, nuclear bombs, and so on. Our media commonly talk about "innocent civilians" as if all civilians were innocent. But there are civilians who are not innocent – such as those who aid and abet terrorists, and others who are terrorists. The young women who carry suicide bombs into Israel to attack civilian targets are themselves civilians, but they are not innocent, and they are legitimate targets of the Israeli military – they may be considered combatants because they are both armed and also intend to attack others.

According to the Declaration of the World Islamic Front for Jihad against the Jews and the Crusaders, published in London in February 23, 1998, " . . . to kill Americans . . . is an individual duty of every Muslim . . . "[59] This sort of statement could have been dismissed as bluster until the destruction of the World Trade Center in September 2001, at which time it became clear that America faced a determined and sometimes effective enemy.

That the tactics of this enemy were directed at the civilian population also became clear.

It is ordinary for people engaged in a political conflict to try to justify even their most reprehensible tactics. In the nineteenth and twentieth centuries, a common defense was that nations were trying to reunite with others of their nationalities who were under the sway of a different power. Hitler used this ruse to justify his aggression against Austria and Czechoslovakia and even Poland – he was only trying to free Germans who were citizens of those countries, he said, and who were being persecuted. Today, a more common ruse is to maintain that violence is justified to help liberate those who are oppressed. Thus, terrorism against the Israelis is justified because they are said to be occupying Palestine. Because many people have apparently given credence to this argument, a similar argument is now being crafted to justify terrorist attacks against Americans.

It's important that Americans know that there are westerners who are part of the effort to give moral justification to terrorist attacks against our civilian population. If terror is likely to succeed in righting a political wrong, some argue, it is justifiable. And they endorse it.

Ted Honderich, a Canadian-born philosopher who taught at University College London has published a book entitled *After the Terror* in which he tries to justify terrorist attacks (though not that on the World Trade Center) by citizens of third world countries on civilians in first world countries because, in his view, first world countries are responsible for poverty in third world countries. He argues that terrorism is morally justifiable if it is likely to lead to better conditions in the third world. In other words, it is morally right to kill civilians as part of an effort to better the lives of the poor. But if terrorism isn't likely to be successful in this ultimate aim, it's not justifiable – and as in his view the World Trade Center attack only served to provoke American retaliation without bettering the lives of the Arab poor, it was unjustifiable. This is a distinction the moral validity of which may well be lost on the victims of terrorist attacks. It seems to argue that killing civilians with the likelihood of political gain is morally justifiable, but that killing them without that likelihood is not. But surely the terrorists who attacked the World Trade Center thought they were advancing their cause, not merely killing to kill, and so by Honderich's criterion they were justified.

A Rutgers University (State University of New Jersey)–based group, New Jersey Solidarity, opposes the existence of Israel and defends suicide bombings of civilians with the argument that "Palestinians have a right to resist occupation. It is not our place to dictate the forms and practices the Palestinians must use."[60] Thus, the old argument that the ends justify the means is extended by Honderich and New Jersey Solidarity and probably many other groups to suicide bombings of civilians in our country.

In fact, not even resistance to occupation justifies targeting civilians for maiming or death. The famous resistance groups in France during World War II did not target German civilians. Communist groups in eastern Europe did target civilians, not so much German occupiers, as people of their own nationality who they intimidated as part of an expected struggle for control after the Germans were driven out.

Perhaps a state of war, if one exists between the Palestinians and Israelis, justifies attacks by bombs or other devices by Palestinians on Israeli military targets, or even on our own troops to the extent we're identified as allies of the Israelis and are notified that we are going to be attacked by Israel's enemies. But attacks on Israeli civilians who are not combatants are not justifiable, nor are attacks on our own civilians. That is, suicide attacks on military targets may be justified as acts of war; but not attacks on civilians who are not somehow directly involved in the combat.

The terrorists who declare themselves our enemies also insist that it is their right to target for death all Americans and all Jews – men, women, and children, civilians and combatants alike. They espouse genocide and regret only that they lack the resources to achieve it. We have seen this effort made by a more efficient and effective enemy – the Nazis – and we should not let it happen again. Attacks that are retributive or preemptive are both justified in self-defense against such an enemy.

WHY WE INVADED IRAQ

The notion that because the Saddam regime may not have been directly involved in the 9/11 attack, Iraq constituted no threat to us is akin to believing that because Hitler's Germany was not involved in the Pearl Harbor attack (it had not even been informed by Japan about the attack before to its happening), then Germany was not a threat to us in the war that followed. That would have been an error of judgment, and it's an error to think similarly about Iraq.

Bush initiated the Iraqi conflict adequately by making it part of the battle against terror and pointing to the risk of weapons of mass destruction if Iraq had them. He continued it adequately by telling the truth about not finding the weapons. It is now doctrine in the mass media that Saddam Hussein had no weapons of mass destruction, and that the administration either erred or intentionally misled the American people when it asserted in justification of the second Iraq War to the contrary. Yet, beneath the canopy of the mass media is a body of evidence suggesting that Saddam had such weapons but had them removed to Syria by the Russians before the American attack.[61] The logic of his intervention then required withdrawal. But instead, the president went off base by shifting the grounds of the intervention to nation-building and democracy spreading. In taking this course President Bush succumbed to the public culture and abandoned the objective requirements of our defense.

Saddam Hussein was a supporter and sympathizer with the terrorists who had repeatedly attacked Americans, and he was continually challenging our efforts to protect the world from violence conducted by states against states. President Bush expressed these reasons well. "By supporting terrorist groups, repressing its own people and pursuing weapons of mass destruction in defiance of a decade of U.N. resolutions, Saddam Hussein's regime has proven itself a grave and gathering danger. To suggest otherwise is to hope against the evidence. To assume this regime's good faith is to bet the lives of millions and the peace of the world in a reckless gamble. And this is a risk we must not take."[62]

Moreover, Osama bin Laden and Saddam Hussein had an operational relationship from the early 1990s to 2003 that involved training in explosives and weapons of mass destruction, logistical support for terrorist attacks, Al Qaeda training camps and safe haven in Iraq, and Iraqi financial support for Al Qaeda – perhaps even for Mohamed Atta, who led the attack on the World Trade Center.[63] Whether or not he was immediately armed to do great damage was never a critical issue, but the administration chose to insist that it was. The WMD emerged as a critical security issue, more so because of Saddam's unwillingness to cooperate with weapons inspectors.

However, that was only the first of the two great confusions that the administration has interposed in our strategy toward Iraq – that weapons of mass destruction were the primary justification for our invasion of Iraq. The second great confusion is to suggest that we have as a primary objective the creation in Iraq of a Western-style capitalist democracy.

Neither of these objectives was at the core of our decision to invade. There were many reasons – a coalition of political forces that permitted the president to act. A majority of the American people, who were not tied to any particular of the following political objectives, was brought along in support of the war by the supposed threat of weapons of mass destruction. Among the other reasons were: that the Israeli government, in particular prime minister Sharon would not agree to revive the peace process, in the form of the administration's roadmap, unless Saddam were removed from power – Israel's fear was that the Palestinians, Saddam and Syria would combine more effectively, threatening Israel's security. Furthermore, "Secretary of Defense Donald Rumsfeld wanted an arena in which to test and display new defense methods and theories. A group of active neo-conservatives had an ideological motive: they saw an opportunity to export democracy to the Arab world."[64] Another group of people hoped to create a new alliance for a free market in the Middle East – involving a newly Western-oriented Iraq, Israel and Turkey.

One of the more provocative justifications for our invasion of Iraq was penned by Thomas Friedman of the *New York Times*. It got around the Muslim world, he said, "that plowing airplanes into the World Trade Center was O. K., having Muslim preachers say it was O.K., having state-run newspapers call people who did such things 'martyrs' was O.K. . . . Not only was all this seen as O.K., there was a feeling among radical Muslims that suicide bombing would level the balance of power between the Arab world and the West, because we had gone soft and their activists were ready to die. The only way to puncture that bubble was for American soldiers . . . to go into the heart of the Arab-Muslim world, house to house, and make clear that we are ready to kill, and to die, to prevent our open society from being undermined by this terrorism bubble. . . . We hit Saddam for one simple reason: because we could . . ."[65]

Our invasion of Iraq was first and foremost a matter of defending ourselves, and we chose to do it when we thought it necessary and convenient for us. That other nations that had not been attacked opposed our action should and was not binding on us.

But there were geopolitical reasons as well to invade Iraq, although they were secondary in this matter. We needed to demonstrate the RMA to potential antagonists – in an environment in which we've scaled down the size of our military, but in which challenges are increasing – Iraq, North Korea. The value of the Second Gulf War in this regard was immense – it helped make a settlement with North Korea possible by showing both North Korea and China that the American power is today substantial, and not to be lightly challenged.

To argue that the recent conflict in Iraq has its roots not only in terrorism but in great power politics is only to bring into the present a significant cause that has acted before. The legacy of great power politics in the Arab world is more than the much publicized one of anti-imperialism and economic backwardness; it's sometimes much more directly connected to the present. For example, Saddam Hussein's political party in Iraq is a direct descendant of Nazi efforts in the Middle East before and during World War II. As another example, the Soviet Union served for most of the period of the Cold War as a counterweight to Western influence in the Middle East, supported in that capacity by many Arabs despite its own atheistic ideology and oppression of its Muslim population. Now, with the Soviet Union gone, and Russia weakened and not so strong a counterweight, and with America dominant, there is a clear opportunity for Europe to consider the role of counter-weight, rather than ally, to the United States in the Islamic world. This was a secondary motivation for the opposition of France and Germany to the American intervention in Iraq.[66] There was nothing wrong with the geopolitical objectives that the Administration pursued in the Iraqi invasion. As described by one commentator, an invasion of Iraq by the Americans made Osama bin Laden not only the man who humbled America in the World Trade Center attack, but also the man who lost Baghdad thereafter to the Americans. "A violent tyrant who had applauded the September 11 attacks would be removed before the acquisition of WMD . . . and progress would be made towards defusing various pretexts for terrorist violence. . . . This geopolitical logic has been spectacularly vindicated by events."[67]

HOW THE ADMINISTRATION CONFUSED US ABOUT THE PURPOSE OF THE WAR IN IRAQ

The administration erred in trying to justify the invasion of Iraq to our rivals and opponents. It wasn't enough that America had dealt a significant setback to the terrorists in the Middle East and had strengthened its hands in the geopolitical rivalries that are always continuing. Instead, the Administration announced that it was going to build a new nation on the Western model in Iraq. No longer was the motive of defending America sufficient; now we added aggrandizement to it – increasing the reach of the American culture in the world.

The media immediately got confused. "History will judge the second Gulf war on a number of criteria," opined the editors of *The Economist*, "including how the war itself went . . . how the reconstruction effort progresses . . . what sort of democracy (if any) emerges in Iraq; and how the security of the region and the world are affected."[68]

This interpretation, widely shared in the media and apparently even accepted by the Administration, was deficient in several respects. First, it focuses primarily on Iraq and not the wider reasons for which the war occurred – the war on terrorism and the geopolitical rivalry of major states. Second, it implies that the war was fought for multiple and highly idealistic objectives: to build a democracy in Iraq, to increase the security of the region, and so on. But the primary reason was to inflict a defeat on terrorism and those seeking to use terrorism as a cudgel to create a new insurrectionary order in the Middle East and spawn discord along the periphery of the Crescent of Fire. This has been accomplished. All else is nonessential. But if our objectives include building a different society in Iraq, then we are once again thrown into the morass of a battle for "hearts and minds" in a different society. We lost that battle in Vietnam, and we'll probably lose it in Iraq. "How successful has the United States been in making its policies and values better understood among Muslims in the Middle East and Southeast Asia?" asks a visitor to the Muslim world. "Based on my experience last summer as a Fulbright senior specialist in Indonesia, the answer is: hardly at all. During May and June, I spent three weeks giving a series of lectures on American history and the global impact of American culture to students and faculty members at several universities in central Java. I was based in Yogyakarta, which the guidebooks describe as the "intellectual" capital of Indonesia. . . . The disparity between my expectations and my experiences could not have been greater. Since 1978 I have been a visiting professor abroad on many occasions – not just in relatively tranquil places like Western Europe, Scandinavia, or Australia, but also in Eastern Europe during the Communist era, Turkey, Thailand, Malaysia, and Brazil. But never have I had as difficult a time communicating with audiences, or deciphering what they were saying to me, as I did in Indonesia. . . . What I encountered in Indonesia was mutual incomprehension."[69]

But we can win enough of a military victory to defend ourselves – that is, we can suppress the terrorists, severely compromising their ability to attack us successfully, and we can keep Saddam out of power, thereby depriving our terrorist enemies of an effective (though brutal) ally. We need not occupy Iraq to do this.

We should remember that World War II was won without winning a battle for the hearts and minds of the German and Japanese populations. They both fought us to a bitter end. Instead, the victory for hearts and minds followed the military victory by years. In Vietnam, we got confused and told ourselves that a battle for hearts and minds (that is the allegiance of the indigenous population) had to be won to permit a military victory, and we fought the war that way. We lost it that way – we didn't win the hearts and minds of the Vietnamese population and we limited our military force, and the result was a fiasco. We will do the same, probably, in Iraq if we define our goals and objectives in Iraq in a similar fashion to the way we defined them in Vietnam – as a battle for hearts and minds that will lead to pacification of the country and the defeat of our adversaries. We seem to be doing so. It's almost as if we have a death wish in these situations – but it's really more a result of mental confusion about means and ends and the overreach of ambition as we try to remake the world in our own image.

We have seriously compromised our situation in Iraq by the confusion of objectives. How did this happen? Once again we fell prey to the nonsense of our public calture.

In order to obtain public support for the war in Iraq, President Bush wrapped his objectives up in the terms most acceptable to the American people. He talked about weapons of mass destruction, and never said that our primary goal was to prevent terrorists and their closet sponsors an opportunity to further harm our national security. Instead, he suggested that a primary goal was transforming Iraq into a state like our own, featuring democratic free enterprise. It cannot be done. The "rest" (of the world) would have transformed itself or been transformed into the "West" long ago, if that goal were achievable.

The United States has a right of self-defense in the aftermath of 9/11 that justifies certain actions. Yet the Bush administration, following the public culture, has tried to shift to other lines of justification for its war in Iraq, including ridding Iraq of a tyrant, freeing the Iraqi people, building democracy – which are moral affirmations urged on U.S. foreign policy by the harmonists. Probably this wasn't necessary. The new maturity for the American people after 9/11 was the perception of great evil in the world and of right to defend ourselves against it. Yet the years since the attack on the World Trade Center have dulled our politicians' perceptions and instead we have an aggressive return to harmonism by both the administration and its critics.

The administration seems sometimes to suggest that it wishes to reorder the entire Middle East. In a speech to the American Enterprise Institute on March 1, 2003, in the immediate aftermath of the success of the invasion of Iraq, the president seemed to set forth that expansive an agenda.[70]

The smarter policy would be to leave Iraq as soon as we have done as much damage to the terrorists as we can, and so long as the Saddam regime is not restored. Some observers are now accusing (that is, they think it an accusation) Secretary of Defense Donald Rumsfeld of secretly desiring to leave Iraq unreconstructed. It would be good if that were right; and if it were the president's intent also. America needs control and deterrence in Iraq; everything else should be peripheral. This doesn't mean unimportant, just secondary. Iraq is a piece of the Middle East equation, not the key to its solution.

THE ONGOING BATTLE IN IRAQ

The American intent was to overthrow the Iraqi regime and stamp out Saddam's control. The method was to insert sufficient American force into Iraq to do so. Hence, we staged a full-scale invasion. The Iraqis could have fought our forces directly in a conventional manner, soldier-to-soldier, tank to tank, platoon to platoon, company to company, division to division – or they could have chosen a guerrilla war, or both. By choice or by force of circumstances the old Iraqi regime seems to have been driven from the field of conventional warfare and into guerrilla and terrorist tactics. This should have pleased us but not surprised us. It's testimony to our overwhelming strength in conventional arms.

The guerrilla war which is now occurring in Iraq is what would have happened in our own Civil War or in Germany at the end of World War II, had not years of full-scale conventional war preceded occupation of the defeated land (the American South and Germany), so that the zealots of the South and of the Nazi regime had been largely slaughtered in combat before the occupation. Had they not been killed in conventional war, there would almost certainly have followed a guerilla conflict.

In Iraq, we did not kill enough of the regime's stalwarts in open battle to eliminate their taste for a continuing conflict. There was not a large-scale conventional engagement of coalition and Iraqi troops, so that the zealots of the Saddam regime were left alive and under his leadership to carry the fight into the streets in a guerrilla action. Guerrilla war is the price we paid for almost bloodless victory in the conventional conflict. It was, therefore, inevitable.

It seemed that the administration was surprised at this – had the president had a better knowledge of history, he would not have been. Surprised, or anxious for a good day with the media, President Bush made his second great public information error of the Iraqi war (the first was to justify the invasion on the grounds of weapons of mass destruction, not as a response to terrorism) when he announced that major ground actions had ceased in the Iraqi war. The statement was correct – the conventional war had been won, and won well and with few casualties – but only the conventional war was over – the rest of the war in Iraq was only beginning. Hence, the media was invited to treat the president's comments as if he were saying that Iraq had been pacified, when it had not.

Had the president merely recognized this (he did say it by saying that we still had a long way to go in the war against terrorism), the American people in their new maturity would have understood. The number of our soldiers who've died in all the Iraq combat is still fewer than those killed in the World Trade Center attack, and we must defend ourselves from other terrorist instigated losses of American lives.

We are a large country. Some 125 Americans die each day in traffic accidents in our country; some 44 Americans are murdered each day. The loss of American soldiers in Iraq, tragic though it is, should be considered in this context.

Nor should it be a surprise, though it is much to be regretted, that we were initially unable to locate bin Laden. We've had the same sort of difficulty before in our history. For years, the New England colonists were unable to locate King Philip of the Wampanoags, and almost lost the first major war with Native Americans in our history as a result, only to have an allied Native American find and kill our adversary. During the Seminole Wars in Florida in the mid-nineteenth century, we were unable for years to locate Osceola, chief of the Seminoles. We never were able to capture Geronimo, despite giving defeat after defeat to Apache bands in Arizona, until Apache scouts captured him and brought him to General Nelson A. Miles. At the turn of the nineteenth century into the twentieth, we were unable for two years to locate Aguinaldo, leader of the Philippines resistance to American occupation after the Spanish-American War. Finally, we never found Poncho Villa in Mexico, despite sending an army under General Pershing to chase him. Thus, it should not surprise any American that today we find it difficult to apprehend bin Laden; our history is full of similar frustrations. In the case of bin Laden, it is likely that a nation state is giving him protection and that our intelligence people are aware of it. If this is the case, it makes capturing him more difficult. But difficulties of this nature have never been fatal to our overall objectives and need not be now.

Strategically, we should not be seeking pacification in Iraq for the purpose of rebuilding Iraq. We're at war with terrorist insurrectionaries, and they are now streaming into Iraq to fight us. This is a good thing for a while in the overall conflict, though it is a bad thing for pacification in Iraq.

It's difficult to discus a war that's in progress because of the loss of life, and because everyone wants it to end. But objectivity requires overcoming to a large degree these emotional response. Iraq's importance doesn't lie in Iraq but in the global context in which the Iraq situation is playing itself out. Of itself, Iraq matters little, except to the Iraqis, who ultimately will decide its fate. The real significance of the Iraqi conflict lies in the broader conflicts of which Iraq is only a theatre. There are two such conflicts – one is the struggle with Islamic radicalism (which President Bush has labeled the War on Terror); the other is the ongoing rivalries – not yet and hopefully never actual wars, but cold wars of a sort – involving the great powers, the United States, Russia, China, and, perhaps, in the future, the Europeans Union. Russia is involved because it is fully armed; China because it is aggressively nationalist and of growing economic and military strength; and the European Union because it aspires to have weight in the world and, should it ever get its act together, it has the potential to be a great power. So the significant question is: how does the ongoing conflict in Iraq fit into this global context? The answer is that Iraq's role is important but not a all critical. The United States could suffer a setback in Iraq, like we did in Vietnam, and not much would be lost except face. But a success in Iraq can be of help to us in the world context by helping to strengthen our position and by lessening the potential for overt conflict elsewhere in the world. And already the Iraq conflict is doing that – in Iraq the United States has demonstrated that the RMA is not merely Madison Avenue hype; and it also has demonstrated that the United States can now fight urban guerillas without undue casualties. These lessons are not at all lost on China, in particular, and have caused an important shift in Chinese military thinking.

We've been in a conflict with them for years. Now we are fighting them in those countries – where we have strong forces and few American civilians and those are closely protected. We finally have the initiative in the war and are fighting on grounds chosen and dominated by us, where we have our military ready and able to destroy terrorists.

But we've confused ourselves and the world by premature talk of rebuilding Iraq and of full pacification. We have told the world that our objective is a peaceful Iraq with improving living standards for its people and a democratic regime. Iraq has become an objective in itself, not simply an element of the war on terror insurrection; our objectives have become not merely to defend ourselves but to build a new type of Iraq. And we are being judged on how well these purposes are going. Yet the difficulties for the United States as a foreign power to bring real democracy to Iraq have been graphically described.[71] Trying to do all this is a mistake and it is confusing and frustrating our strategy in the battle against terror.[72]

The only way to legitimize a new democracy in Iraq is to get endorsement from the religious authorities who are respected by much of the population; but the price of endorsement is the institution of Islamic law with clerics as judges, and this is profoundly nondemocratic (as we Americans see democracy – with a separation of church and state) – nor does it put the choice of instituting Islamic law to a democratic process. So the attempt to build democracy has put us in a box – real democracy cannot be legitimatized. At best we will be able to paper this glaring inconsistency over and hope that what is called democracy in Iraq will develop in ways that lessen the contradiction. This is a glaring example of why the American system of democracy cannot be readily transferred abroad.

The conflict among our objectives gets worse. In the effort to transfer our system of democracy to Iraq, we need to pacify the country, to provide security for the population in which a democracy might take root. But we need to bring terrorists out into the open in the face of our military to destroy them. This is required because during the invasion of Iraq many loyal to Saddam simply went underground and our military forces didn't crush them. It's as if rather than fight to the death in Germany, the Nazis had gone underground and we then faced a long guerrilla campaign. It would have had to be fought or the world wouldn't have been cleansed of Nazism. So it is in Iraq – our invasion didn't dispose of enough of the Saddam loyalists, so now we have to fight it out with them. That should be our objective at this point. But as an American reporter in Baghdad put it on American television news reflecting the confusion of our government's objectives: "Every day spent fighting Iraqi terrorist insurrectionaries is a day lost in our objective of building a new democratic Iraq." Somehow, in this formulation, the reason we invaded Iraq, to fight terrorism, has come to be seen not as an objective in itself, but as an impediment to building a new Iraq.

Building democracy is very premature; conflicts with our current objectives; and is never likely to be very successful. Hence, it is a diversion of effort, a distortion of focus, and a route to frustration.

The first priority of the Bush administration should be to recognize our involvement in Iraq as part of our struggle with terrorism and Middle Eastern insurrectionaries more broadly, rather than as part of the Palestinian issue or of a goal democratizing Iraq. Unless this is done, and the larger array of threats accurately assessed we will not only lose in Iraq, but in the Crescent of Fire, and place our survival in jeopardy with Russia, China, and the European Union. It is the job of a president to enlightened the public, in large part by fighting the public culture, to insure support for the long haul for objective defense policies.

Iraq is a battlefield in the large struggle, not a place for us to begin to remake the Arab world in our own image. It is the responsibility of Iraqis to choose what sort of society they want and to go about building it, with such aid as they can obtain from the outside world. We should help them, as we would any nation trying to develop itself.

"When we do leave . . . we are absolutely quit of responsibility for them of every kind and description," insisted President Theodore Roosevelt discussing American withdrawal from the Philippines after the islands had been an American protectorate.[73] This is what the U.S. position should be on Iraq; and we should get out as soon as possible.

SATANS GREAT AND SMALL

America cannot escape being public enemy number one for Islamists and demagogues in the crescent of fire. America has permitted itself to be drawn into the Palestinian morass on impractical bases – promoting an unworkable roadmap, and failing to pressure Arab governments to resettle Palestinian refugees outside Gaza decades ago when relocation would have facilitated accommodation. It has thereby become the scapegoat of choice in much of the world. Groups like the PLO are willing to accept American financial assistance for dealing with Gaza's refugees, and participate in constructing an independent Palestinian state, in the same spirit in which Lenin bought "rope" from the capitalist West in order to "to hang the capitalists," but otherwise are implacably opposed to U.S. influence. Insurrectionaries and Islamists despise America for their own parochial reasons, and even sheiks in the petro patch are only fair weather friends. The attack against the United States on September 11, 2001, wasn't about the Israel-Palestine conflict. It was a violent expression of a more consuming hostility.

This is why American counterterrorism should be focused on the Crescent of Fire, and not limited to Palestine. The broader threat is neither speculative nor transitory, and cannot be easily placated. Nor is it a matter of absorbing some casualties and turning the other cheek. Like the Israeli-Palestine conflict, pinpricks have a nasty way of escalating into full fledged war, including the looming possibility of a nuclear exchange with Iran in the possibly not-so-distant future. America cannot relinquish the petro patch to its rivals in the EU, Russia, and elsewhere, because our national interests prevent such an action; nor can we idly accept Al Qaeda control over the sheikdoms of the Persian Gulf because fundamentalist ambitions go even further. And now that Islamists have joined the battle for Iraq, we cannot simply step aside, whether or not intervention was predicated on a mis-assessment of Saddam Hussein's WMD capabilities.[74] Demagogic terrorist insurrectionaries are bent on making Iraq an American graveyard, and cannot be permitted to prevail without raising the risk of even more general conflict. The United States must play a masterful game of engagement, mindful of the broader interplay.

Islamic fundamentalist terrorism, insurrection, aggression, and intimidation are also aimed at other infidels in ways that could affect vital American interests, or even spawn another world war. Osama Bin Laden, for example, has made no secret of his desire to drive Russia from Muslin lands acquired by Russia since the seventeenth century, and to end its hegemony over the independent Central Asian states of the former Soviet Union.[75] This would not only allow him to secure enormous petroleum and natural gas reserves, but to capture strategic sections of Russia's oil and natural gas pipelines, increasing America's dependence on the fuels of Ummah. Fundamentalist victories here would also involve China, which is looking to Russia as a prime fuel supplier,[76] and of course Islamists seek to "liberate" Xinjiang and challenge Chinese interests in Malaysia, and Indonesia.[77] Islam has grievances with India over Kashmir, and, as the crisis in Dafur illustrates, is adopting an increasingly belligerent posture in Africa.[78] Its attitude toward Europe is provocative.[79] On the one hand, it wishes to use the EU as a safe base for organizing international terrorist operations in part as a result of building bridgehead Muslim communities. On the other, it brazenly employs terror against European states to affect their policies. Although America may be able to stand aside from some of these conflicts, the danger of inveiglement is real.

Islam poses a serious challenge to America in part because our public culture prefers to gloss over the distinction between religious tolerance and Muslim fundamentalist enmity by pretending that a resolution of the Arab-Israeli conflict, acceptance of international legal norms, and democratization will Westernize the Ummah. There is no basis other than wishful thinking for these premises. The good points of the Koran don't expunge 9/11, and economic progress in some limited areas hasn't dampened terrorism.[80]

CONTAINMENT

America's post-9/11 counterterrorist operations in Afghanistan and Iraq constitute an initial effort to cope with the challenge posed by Islamic radicalism. Defining our actions as counterterrorism allows them to be presented as religiously and politically neutral, doesn't require a declaration of war against states, and provides a legal framework for dealing with the problem. It permits America to muster its forces against all aspects of Islamic terror and demagoguery without being stymied by accusations of crusader imperialism. But the posture is excessively confining. It places too many trammels on policy, and undermines the sustainability of our counterterrorist operations. The Islamic terrorist inurrectionary threat in the Crescent of Fire is in all significant modalities akin to international communist aggression during the twentieth century. True believers and opportunists are prepared to employ nearly every means at their disposal including state to state aggression inside and beyond the Ummah to have their way while simultaneously proclaiming beneficent and peaceful intent. American policymakers therefore cannot permit adversaries safe haven. They must inform the public about the durable challenge, and the necessity of staying the course to deter potentially greater catastrophes.

This requires a frank acknowledgment that history may not be on our side. The internal and external dynamics in the Crescent of Fire are very unlikely to eventuate in western democratic free enterprise; instead, they threaten our security even if the Ummah is ultimately secularized. It is also essential to dispense with the delusion that anti-Western enmity in the Muslim world stems from the Arab-Israeli conflict and can be appeased by forcing Jerusalem to accept a unified Palestinian state for the greater good. America should modify the roadmap by substituting the concept of survivable, nonbelligerent Israeli and Palestinian states for the land for peace formula. Land wasn't enough for Arafat, and should not be believed to be a sufficient quid pro quo. Instead of encouraging treaties that are stepping stones to the annihilation of one state or the other, our emphasis should be on achieving an enduring armistice that allows America to get on with the business of containing the broader threat posed by Islamic fundamentalism.[81]

In this regard, it is especially important to face up to the threat of nuclear, biological, and chemical weapons, including ballistic missile attack.[82] Saddam Hussein didn't hesitate to launch Scud missiles against Israel during the First Gulf War, and Iran has threatened to follow suit – building missiles that can reach the EU, Russia, and eventually the United States. American nuclear capabilities will probably serve as an effective deterrent against Iranian initiation, but it might not – actors in the crescent of fire may prove less rational than the Soviets were. Consequently, prudence dictates that the United States accelerate its tactical and strategic anti-weapons capabilities.[83]

The War on Terrorism is a euphemism for dealing with the clash of interests between the West and fundamentalist Islam. The threat differs from that posed by established great powers to the United States. It is apt to persist and intensify regardless of whether material conditions in the Crescent of Fire improve or deteriorate compared with the international norm. The challenge is reminiscent of international communism in its formative phase, and seems likely to mature in the direction of an Ummah-based conflict, with all the instability this implies. Presidential leadership is needed to candidly apprise the public about the true nature of the threat so that our hands aren't tied by escapist double think of the type so common in our public culture. Although China and Russia are likely to be more formidable military adversaries in the coming decades, the Crescent of Fire is certain to be explosive.

CHAPTER 12: KEY POINTS

1. Islamic terrorism does not have its roots in the conflict in Palestine but, rather, in the contest for power in the Islamic world generally – a three-way contest between traditionalists, reformers, and those currently in power, in which the spoils include oil revenue and nuclear arms.
2. Terrorism involves the killing of civilians for political objectives. Yet, a surprising number of people try to justify its use against us.
3. Dangerous and heartbreaking as is this conflict, it must be kept in perspective. Terrorists do not threaten the existence of our country – not the way a major conflict with a nuclear-armed rival threatens our country.

Formulating our defense against terrorism as a "war" instead of an effort to foil would-be insurrectionaries in the Middle East and Crescent of Fire is an exaggeration that threatens to divert our focus from other more serious dangers in the international environment.

PART SIX

THE AMERICAN RESPONSE

There is an interrelated world system that presents us many dangers, and the proper way to address it is through a comprehensive strategy that is ours alone. This is made necessary after the end of the Cold War because of a divergence of interests with our former allies, and it is made possible by our increasing economic, technological, and military strength.

THIRTEEN

Strategic Independence

An Ounce of Prevention

Strategic Independence is a new American strategy that can be integrated into America's engagement with the world. Strategic Independence means independence of today's weakened alliances in determining our geopolitical strategy and of overdependence on nuclear deterrence in defending our country.

Recent administrations have been groping toward this strategy, and the Bush administration has taken a long step toward it, though it has not yet completely embraced the strategy. Strategic Independence is a comprehensive approach to defending America without the dangers inherent in deterrence and the excesses involved in trying to remake the world in the interests of our security. Strategic Independence is modest in scope, effective in action. Strategic Independence is the means; pluralism in the world is the end, as we cannot effectively reengineer other cultures into our image of democratic free enterprise.

AN ALTERNATIVE TO MULTILATERALISM

Strategic Independence is an alternative to multilateralism (which is discussed in Chapter 16). Strategic Independence and multilateralism are both tactics, not absolutes, and are not preferable for themselves but, rather, as means to an end – the safety of our country. It is possible to combine them to a degree – advocates of Strategic Independence expect our country to seek allies in carrying out specific missions.

Since the end of World War II, U.S. Strategy has been dependent on both allies and enemies. It had been dependent on allies because of alliances against the Soviets; it has been dependent on the Soviets because in a bipolar world we had to measure each of our actions against Soviet reactions. Ironically, Mao Zedong complained to French representative Andre Malraux about how the United States let the Russians determine its strategy – that is, how reactive our country appeared to him to be.[1]

Today, the United States can't let allies determine our strategy because of too wide a divergence in interests (including attacks on our people and territory, such as the attack on the World Trade Center, cause an immediacy of concern to us that is not felt by our allies). Nor can we let our enemies determine our strategy because nuclear proliferation and the emergence of nonstate threats has created an unstable situation. So we are driven to independence of policy, although not to action alone.

STRATEGIC INDEPENDENCE AND ENGAGEMENT

The case for Strategic Independence, whether in Washington's time or now, is essentially the same. It is that we should avoid being drawn into others' conflicts, and we should be able to defend ourselves without the permission of others. Only if we have this sort of independence can we be free to pursue our domestic concerns. It is therefore a reversal of the truth to argue that defense needs come at the expense of domestic concerns. Quite the opposite. An effective and efficient defense sustains and empowers our broad domestic agenda. We can't get there without Strategic Independence, because as September 11 reminded us, attacks that kill our citizens take first priority, and the purpose of Strategic Independence is to make them less frequent and less damaging.

Strategic Independence means the military deterrence of potential adversaries achieved by a combination of superior offensive capabilities, arms control, and national missile defense.

At the core of Strategic Independence are four things:

1. A focus on the defense of the United States;
2. Independence in timing; that is, determining when and how to defend ourselves;
3. Avoidance of an arms race with a rival power or powers via a combination of:
   • arms control agreements;
   • strategic missile capability to damage an aggressor;
   • flexible conventional forces; and
   • national missile defense;
4. Preemption to deal with real threats, from wherever they originate, especially the threat of attacks on us or our allies using weapons of mass destruction; and

5. Sufficient conventional forces to allow us to decide and act on our own behalf.

Fundamental to Strategic Independence is the conviction that America needs to place self-defense above other objectives abroad. Strategic Independence – including national missile defense – means that we have the freedom to pursue both conventional and nuclear self-defense because we aren't stopped by the threat of nuclear escalation, whether by terrorists or by a great power.

This situation won't continue after 2010 when (and if) Russia completes its military modernization. MAD will come back into play, and we may not be able to take significant action abroad without a national missile defense because of Russian objections to American initiatives such as Iraq.

Thus national missile defense may become critical to defeating terrorism and Muslim fundamentalist expansionism.

Today, Islamic war on terrorism is the principal cause of our concern with self-defense, but this is going to become increasingly outdated as Russia and China militarize.

Russia and China in this way aren't separate problems, they are each elements of a nested self-defense requirement, including each other and the battle against terrorism.

Finally, NMD can be funded and scaled flexibly as the threats unfold.

Strategic Independence may sound isolationist but is not. It's not a turning of our back on the world – as was isolationism before World War II – nor does it require us to forego the benefits of free trade and alliances of the willing, but instead it's the means by which we intend to manage our continuing close engagement with the rest of the world. Strategic independence is a method of self-protection from an overt attack and from political entrapment in which we are made to bear the costs of helping other nations achieve their objectives, not ours.

Yet, there might be a circumstance in which non-intervention abroad (isolationism) would make sense; when it would become a useful version of strategic independence. It should not be ruled out. But Fortress America isn't apt to work today because at the very least the Middle East is likely to be seized first by radicals, then by other major powers, creating a very dangerous situation for us.

The United States has earned its independence in strategy via its persistence in building a strong economy and a strong defense; by its victory over overt enemies; and by its repulse of challengers. It has achieved the potential for Strategic Independence via World War I, World War II, Korea, and the Cold War and numerous other smaller conflicts and interventions.

It has achieved the potential for Strategic Independence via the failures of its antagonists, and the unwillingness of its allies to sacrifice their present enjoyment of life under American military protection for building their own strength. It is as if the American people at great effort and sacrifice have competed in a contest and have outdistanced all rivals. So we arrive at a position in which we still have antagonists – some new, some old – and we still have rivals, but they've fallen behind and we are now free to set our own course. And at this time, the only way we can be compelled to look to others for their permission, the only way we can allow others to share in our success, the only way we can bring our competitors who lost the race up to the finish line even with us, is to stop, turn around and hoist them forward. Unfortunately, that is exactly what many Americans seem to prefer.

On February 24, 1990, President George Herbert Walker Bush wrote in his diary: "I don't want to move to isolation, but I don't want to see us fettered by a lot of multi-lateral decisions. We've got to stand, and sometimes we'll be together with them; but sometimes we'll say we differ, and we've got to lead, so we should not be just kind of watered down, picking up the bill, and acquiescing in a lot of decisions that might hurt us. . . . I've got to look after the U.S. interest in all of this without reverting to a kind of isolationist or stupid peace-nik view on where we stand in the world."[2]

Here was a clear early statement of the situation facing the United States in the aftermath of the collapse of the Soviet Union. How was our country to behave – how design its policies. Was it to return to a isolationist orientation, perhaps in an understandable quest for peace in withdrawal from the world stage? Was it to accept multilateral restraints? Or was it to define some as yet uncertain role in between the two. Twelve years later his son tried to spell out that middle course – which we call Strategic Independence.

NATIONAL MISSILE DEFENSE

The central premise of Strategic Independence is that technology and entrepreneurship allow America to better defend its people and achieve its peace-keeping and peace-making goals – without completely scrapping MAD or turning our back on arms control – in three ways:

1. We can develop and deploy a national ballistic missile defense or space-based missile defense that fully utilizes our technological potential since we have repudiated the US-USSR ABM treaty.
2. We can fully incorporate the best technologies in our weaponry, and deploy them in sufficient numbers to chasten aggressors; and

3. We can build robust crisis production capabilities so that if a need suddenly arises, we can put a surge into our production of weaponry.

We require conventional forces to fight Iraq type wars, and an adequate missile defense shield to intimidate everyone from trying to compete with our strategic missile forces. The Europeans won't spend the money. The Russians will screw up trying to build a missile defense system. The Chinese are the only wild card.

It also can be argued that an effective space-based defense could be a reasonable alternative to NMD, as from space other countries' communications satellites can be disabled or reconfigured, reconnaissance and GPS positioning capabilities can be disabled (thus "blinding" an adversary), and low-earth orbit satellites or modified space shuttles could make the perfect launching pads for a space-based missile defense.

The fundamental purpose of the Antiballistic Missile Treaty is to prevent either Russia or the United States from nullifying the other's missile deterrent. This is the primary concern – and to meet it several American defense commentators have proposed building a missile defense so limited that Russia's missile deterrent is not nullified, or make a deal with the Russians for a joint effort or other approach which also will not nullify our vulnerability to Russian missiles (for after all, that's what the Russian deterrent is, our vulnerability to it, otherwise Russian missiles are not a deterrent). But the flaw in this approach is that we now face missile capability from other countries than Russia, and in a multipolar world there is no advantage to keeping ourselves vulnerable to other powers, for if we remain vulnerable to the Russians, we do to the Chinese, and possibly, later, other powers.

It is unfortunate that this key fact was not communicated clearly to the American people at the time the Bush Administration canceled the ABM treaty. Instead, the impression was left that the United States was purposely starting a new arms race, which isn't the case at all.

Instead, in this new multidimensional, multithreat situation, logic calls for Strategic Independence, which means we set out to nullify the missile attack capabilities of all major powers, including that of the Russians.

The core of the matter is that the United States is in process of making a fundamental shift in its nuclear defense policy from a focus on the Russian threat to a situation in which nuclear threats can come from a variety of nations – that is, from a bi-polar nuclear world to one of nuclear proliferation. We wouldn't build a national missile defense against the Russians – MAD would still handle the situation. But MAD is impossible in the context of multiple nuclear powers. Hence, we require a national missile defense or a new space-based missile defense as a response to the widening threat – but we will also achieve a certain level of defense in the process from a Russian attack.

National missile defense by whatever technology is a centerpiece of Strategic Independence because it increases our degrees of freedom in managing crises in the many theatres which are outside Russia's vital interests, all the while providing our population with valuable protection from a broad array of nuclear and conventional threats, including those from Russia. The independence afforded isn't complete.

What is crucial about national missile defense is that it not be unreasonably expensive and that the system must actually work.

The purpose of Strategic Independence is not to achieve geopolitical dominance, or hegemony. We will not have hegemonic capabilities, but we will be able to operate responsibly without undue concern that every act of conventional self-defense is precluded by the danger of nuclear escalation. Should China threaten Taiwan with a ballistic missile attack, we won't have to flinch.

Upgrading, deploying, and building new capabilities for our advanced weapons complement NMD by expanding our range of responses to the burgeoning array of threats we will be facing (see Chapter 16). As the Second Gulf War demonstrated, an ample supply of advanced weaponry can nullify the large conventional armies of powerful aggressors without provoking a wider war. This was of the greatest importance in demonstrating the advisability and practicality of Strategic Independence. The substantial virtues of Strategic Independence are compatible with many arms control objectives. Effective NMD permits America to accept large cuts in its strategic nuclear forces. Advanced technologies allow us to negotiate reductions in more indiscriminately lethal systems such as land mines. Strategic Independence in this regard isn't a mindless quest for unlimited superiority and rearmament, but a flexible national security optimization strategy which harnesses our superior technological prowess to cost effectively attain our traditional strategic goals. If external threats diminish, our defense effort can be reduced, and vice versa. If China becomes a superpower, the doctrine can be revised to reflect this situation when it arises.

In some ways, of course, the resurrection of Strategic Independence as the cornerstone of U.S. security policy isn't new. Defense officials always claim to provide as much security as possible with the resources at their disposal. During the Cold War, when MAD seemed better than a preemptive first strike or a destabilizing arms race, it allowed us to realize acceptable levels of security even though the realities of Soviet military power severely constrained our room for maneuver. But MAD is no longer adequate. It cannot serve as a rational basis for our international security agenda outside the periphery of Russia's vital interests, and doesn't apply in the same sense as before in Russia because the Kremlin's strategic options have changed. Russia cannot engage the United States in a nuclear arms race, and no longer needs us to be as vulnerable as we were during the cold war to pursue its new security agenda. Strategic Independence in its contemporary guise thus isn't provocative. It is simply a matter of taking the opportunities created by the global reconfiguration of wealth and power, instead of foolishly preserving vulnerabilities that no longer serve valid security purposes.

The Clinton administration's argument for a limited national missile defense directed at the states in the Crescent of Fire took the following form. When Reagan proposed NMD, it was to protect us from the Soviet's many missiles, but it wasn't possible technically. In addition, the Soviets could have countered our effort by building more missiles, overwhelming whatever defensive shield we could erect. But when the Clinton administration proposed NMD a decade later, the situation had changed.

North Korea was obtaining nuclear ballistic missiles (its Taepedong 1 missile has a range of almost five thousand miles) and to fail to construct a shield would make the United States vulnerable to North Korean nuclear attack. This is unthinkable. Technology today probably permits a shield to be built either from the ground or from space against North Korean missiles, so it ought to be built.

Yet today's situation offers even greater opportunity. A shield can be built which would go beyond protecting us against Crescent of Fire states, and would provide partial protection against Russia and China as well. Further, although the Russians are modernizing their strategic weapons, they are so much weakened that they lack the option to build so many additional missiles that they will simply overwhelm our defenses. In addition, many of the current Russian missiles have passed beyond their service life, reducing further Russia's ability to overcome an American NMD. With nuclear proliferation, we even risk getting caught in an exchange of missiles not intended for us. From this an NMD could help protect us. NMD will not be perfect overnight; it may not be perfect ever. It doesn't have to be perfect to be very useful; it only has to provide superior defense capabilities for the amount invested than any other option that costs the same amount. The goal isn't a fail-safe system, but it must be a system that is reasonably functional. Otherwise, in the age of tiny cameras on cell phones, advanced spying technologies, more accurate satellite surveillance capabilities, and the internet, the Russians and the Chinese will be quite educated as to NMD's actual ability to shoot down enemy missiles, so they won't be intimidated unless it is technologically superior. A technically successful system placed on earth or in space will be positive protection against the irrationality of Crescent of Fire states, and intimidation against the Russians and Chinese who would be pressed for different reasons to build so many missiles and decoys that they can overcome the system in the foreseeable future. In this regard it is important to appreciate that NMD has no downside other than cost. It cannot increase the Russian threat, and could deter China from trying to become a nuclear superpower, if China can be brought to recognize that the effort will be futile.

NMD is not a panacea. As with all new systems it can be degraded if needlessly constrained by obsolete arms control treaties designed for a bipolar environment, but the diversity of the risks we now face makes it essential for leaders to extricate themselves from the Cold War mindset, and the utopianism of those gullible enough to believe that universal disarmament is an effective antidote for national aggression.

The editors of *The Economist* expressed reservations about NMD, saying that if Bush handled the diplomacy wrong, Americans could end up with "the worst of all worlds: one in which suspicion and rivalry, not security and stability, were the name of the game."[3] But, of course, that is where we already are, and so the NMD is necessary.

Criticism is strong, especially from the Chinese, that putting weapons in space as part of a missile defense system is actually an offensive system intended to intimidate other countries (especially China) and will lead to an arms race in space. Instead, there should be an agreement among the nations to demilitarize space, it is asserted.[4]

The two major arguments against NMD are:

- it won't work, and
- it is destabilizing.

Often, these are cited simultaneously. But they are inconsistent. If it won't work, it won't destabilize. The objections ought to be: if it won't work, it's a waste of money; if it does work, it's destabilizing. So opposition should be reformulated: it won't work, or it's destabilizing. These are legitimate arguments; though they are not persuasive. Our answer is that NMD's potential benefits are worth trying to make it work, and it's not destabilizing if it works because the current situation is so unstable with nuclear proliferation and unstable governments in Russia and China that in this very dangerous setting NMD will be stabilizing instead.

The secret of the American missile defense shield proposal is that it's aimed at China and Russia and that it's part of a major shift in overall U.S. defense policy. Reagan introduced the concept this way, but each president since has found it expedient to mislead the public about the shield, insisting that it is aimed at terrorist states and that it is a minor part of existing U.S. strategy. Whatever the reasons for the deception, the media and the public have been smart enough to recognize that the implications of the shield go far beyond terrorism, and that if the shield is to be justified, it must be on another basis. Honesty about this has become crucial because the clumsy deception is now so confusing the international security environment that America's attempt to build the shield and change it's defense strategy may cause us to stumble into a serious war. The secret is becoming dangerous in itself.

Nuclear arms control and national missile defense are the joint response to the emerging dangers of nuclear war. But we must recognize that the nuclear non-proliferation effort is in tatters. According to the Director General of the International Atomic Energy Agency, nearly forty countries are now familiar enough with nuclear technology to make bombs (although only about nine are thought to have done so), and the non-proliferation treaty itself is fundamentally flawed in its provisions because it permits countries to enrich uranium to make reactor fuel and to reprocess fuel rods once they've been used – both techniques being not essential for an electric power program, but both essential to bomb making.[5]

We have been relying on Mutual Assured Destruction to deter nuclear war. But this is a strategy best suited to a bipolar confrontation – like the Cold War – and increasingly risky in today's different environment. Nuclear proliferation diminishes the credibility of MAD because we cannot be sure whom to counter-attack, and credibility is the essence of MAD – otherwise a potential aggressor is not deterred. That Russia continues to modernize its nuclear striking forces despite national hardship demonstrates that it has no intention of relying instead on conventional weapons and the abolition of weapons of mass destruction. China makes no bones about its commitment to becoming a nuclear superpower and has devised a market communist economic system that can support its ambitions. With even less of a foundation than Russia's or China's, other nations are building nuclear weapons. There are certain to be more nuclear weapons in more unstable hands tomorrow than today and our past reliance on MAD is no longer credible in deterring their employment.

In the summer of 2001, Secretary of Defense Donald Rumsfeld justified the building of an American national missile defense shield as follows:

"Imagine what would happen if a rogue state were to demonstrate the capability to strike U.S. or European populations with . . . weapons of mass destruction. A policy of intentional vulnerability . . . could give this state the power to hold us hostage."[6]

The Bush administration here followed the same path of political least resistance that its predecessor did, tying a national missile defense shield to a rogue-state justification. In doing so it risked the same appearance of inconsistency that bedeviled the Clinton approach. For a national defense shield cannot be justified on rogue-state grounds.

Why, then, is it done? Clinton may have had adopted this justification knowing that it was inadequate, and in the ill-disguised hope that the shield would be discredited and abandoned.

This was not Bush's motivation, however. Probably the administration feared that it could not win enough liberal support for the shield if China and Russia were revealed as the targets of the shield, and hoped that conservatives would see the intended threat while liberals could be won over by the rogue state argument.

But the weakness of the justification for the shield was quickly perceived. For example, commentators abroad objected to the junking of the Anti-Ballistics Missile Treaty (ABM) that necessarily accompanied the plan to build an antiballistics missile shield. "The ABM Treaty . . . has been the settled policy of the US for nearly 30 years . . ." wrote an Australian commentator, adding, "One US commentator likens the US to a 'blind Samson, tearing down the very arms-control temple it built."[7] The argument was well made – why should a treaty with Russia, a cornerstone of MAD, be junked just to build a defense against a possible attack by a few missiles from rogue states in the Crescent of Fire? Where was the evidence of capability by North Korea, Iraq, or Iran to make such an attack on the United States or Europe? There was little or none. And if there was so little threat, why junk MAD, a policy designed to prevent a really big threat – that of a nuclear exchange between Russia and America?

The rogue state argument was disingenuous, hinted the press. For example, an editorial in *The Economist*, appears to accept the rogue state argument, speaking of "rogue rockets . . . ," but then adds that "America's hopes . . . must rest on preferring honest arguments . . . over specious ones." The editorialist suspects that the rogue state argument is specious, and says so.[8] The story then became more bizarre. The Bush administration, stung by criticisms of its justification of NMD as a response to rogue states, sought to shore up support for NMD by the strangest of political tactics. It seems to have gotten turned around on its basic strategy. According to a report in

The New York Times, "The Bush administration, seeking to overcome Chinese opposition to its missile defense program, intends to tell leaders in Beijing that it has no objections to the country's plans to build up its small fleet of nuclear missiles, according to senior administration officials."[9]

One senior official said that in the future, the United States and China might also discuss resuming underground nuclear tests if they are needed to assure the safety and reliability of their arsenals. Such a move, however, might allow China to improve its nuclear warheads and lead to the end of a worldwide moratorium on nuclear testing. Both messages appear to mark a significant change in American policy. For years the United States has discouraged China and all other nations from increasing the size or quality of their nuclear arsenals, and from nuclear tests of any kind. The purpose of the new approach, some administration officials say, is to convince China that the administration's plans for a missile shield are not aimed at undercutting China's arsenal, but rather at countering threats from so-called rogue states." Soon thereafter, still trying to salvage its justification of NMD as aimed at rogue states, American officials told reporters "that once China has more missiles in its arsenal, it should be less concerned about Mr. Bush's missile defense system – because China would have a sufficient number of missiles to overwhelm any American missile defense now being contemplated."[10]

This is the topsy-turvy world of political diplomacy. The American government, seeking to avoid the increasing Chinese buildup of nuclear missile capability, sets out to dissuade the Chinese from this course by building a national missile defense. But out government fears it will not gather enough political support and so it disguises the intent of NMD as being directed at rogue states.

When commentators challenge this fairly obvious deception, the American government refuses to admit its subterfuge, but instead tries to shore it up by, of all things, encouraging the Chinese to build their nuclear missile arsenal better and faster in order that our missile shield would not be a deterrent to them! Somehow, from trying to deter the Chinese from building more missiles aimed at us, our government found itself doing exactly the opposite.

Here, in a witches' brew, two factors combined to put our government in a backwards posture – first, the political necessity of defending a falsehood tempted our political leaders to abandon our own real purposes; and second, the logic of MAD – to strengthen your enemies to parity of weaponry with you – reasserted itself in the ensuring confusion about the real aims of our NMD policy.

This was not the first time that politically motivated deception about strategic purposes tripped up our government; and it was not to be the last, as we saw in our discussion of the confusion of objectives in the aftermath of the Second Gulf War. But stumbling into urging China to increase more rapidly its ability to attack America with nuclear missiles must be a high point of confusion into which deception has led our government.

The vibrant and much-needed debate – over national missile defense and its advisability as part of a strategy to displace MAD in dealing with the changing nuclear arms balance – that was occurring in the summer of 2001 in the press, in the halls of Congress and in the recesses of the defense agencies of Washington was ended suddenly on September 11, 2001, and has not been resumed. Thus, terrorist attacks derailed for years the most important public discussion being conducted in the world.

Meanwhile, the need for a missile defense shield is rapidly growing. Without a missile defense shield the United States has no effective means of persuading China to direct its rising aspirations into peaceful channels. Without a shield, we have only MAD – an increasingly flawed policy ill-suited to changing conditions in the world and therefore likely to result in an unwanted war.

THE BUSH DOCTRINE

In September 2002, the White House issued a document entitled " The National Security Strategy of the United States."[11] It expressed in simple and direct language what has come to be called the Bush Doctrine – preemption and military supremacy:

- "To forestall or prevent such hostile acts by our adversaries the United States will, if necessary, act pre-emptively . . .
- "Our forces will be strong enough to dissuade potential adversaries from pursuing a military buildup in hopes of surpassing, or equaling, the power of the United States."[12]

National Security Adviser Condoleezza Rice has elaborated on the document several times, saying at the time of its issuance, "if it comes to allowing another adversary to reach military parity with the United States in the way that the Soviet Union did, no, the United States does not intend to allow that to happen."

But military supremacy and preemptive war are not the only very significant elements of this document. In fact, it is not a national security strategy at all, but rather an entire statement of American foreign policy.

For example, its first section is not titled " The National Security Strategy of the United States," as a reader would expect from the title of the document, but rather, "Overview of America's International Strategy. The second and third sections discuss defense policy, but the following sections go much further. Section VI is titled "Ignite a New Era of Global Economic Growth through Free Markets and Free Trade." Section VII is titled "Expand the Circle of Development by Opening Societies and Building the Infrastructure of Democracy."

Here we have the full Bush Doctrine, the full foreign policy of America:

- to defend our country via military superiority and preemptive war, when necessary, and
- to rebuild the world, or as much of it as we can, in our own image – as a free enterprise democracy.

Defense Policy Should Not Be Tied to an Overreaching Foreign Policy

In a very significant way, the Bush Doctrine is a mistaken policy. It's a dangerous overreach, as we demonstrate in later chapters. America has the opportunity to adopt Strategic Independence – a coherent, forward-looking, sensible defense policy stressing military strength and independence of action. But it is important is that we not let a poorly developed, inconsistent and utopian foreign policy interfere. We recognize that this is the opposite of what most specialists and analysts argue should be the case. The position they advocate has a distinguished lineage, since the Renaissance, and is that the geopolitical strategy of the nation should direct its defense strategy – that war should be an instrument of foreign policy. In our view, in the instance of America today, this is clearly wrong.[13] When a country has the sort of foreign policy our leaders ordinarily articulate – full of high-sounding phrases and impractical objectives drawn from our public culture, then foreign policy cannot be a secure guide to anything. But at least we can defend ourselves effectively, so long as we don't let the confusions of our foreign policy disrupt our thinking about defense.

A better response than the administration's would be to focus on our defense alone, leaving broader goals to persuasion and support, rather than to force and direction – we call this approach Strategic Independence, a return to a policy followed successfully for two decades by our country between the end of World War II and the development by the Soviet Union of a full-range nuclear missile capability in the mid-1960s. A special issue arises with respect to the administration's call for preemptive war; something that fits within the framework of Strategic Independence, but must be exercised with extreme caution. Another special issue involves the value of national missile defense, which plays a significant role in Strategic Independence.

The formalization of the Administration's posture in the Bush Doctrine is a milepost indicating how far America has come since September 11, 2001. Before that time, in the Clinton Administration, we were down sizing our military quickly. The Bush Administration planned to slow or even reverse the build down, but 9/11 precipitated the Bush Doctrine that provides a policy strikingly different from even that proposed by Secretary of Defense Donald Rumsfeld earlier in 2002. At that time, Rumsfeld gave no hint of the military superiority goal in the Bush Doctrine. He described preemption as only an inexpensive tactic to deal with terrorists and rogue states while the United States was building down its military, not building up to military supremacy.[14]

The Bush Doctrine is a huge shift from the policies with which many of us grew up – isolationism until we were forced into World War II, and then containment of the Soviets that we achieved as part of an alliance. The shift appears to have been brought about by the threat of terrorists using weapons of mass destruction, but in reality has been promoted for more than a decade by several experts.[15] It has major implications for our relations to Russia and China also, as we'll see in later chapters.

The Bush Doctrine is a step in the right direction for America, but it is also a significant overstep – two steps too far. It is a costly error to assert that our country will seek clear military superiority over any potential rival; and it is an even more costly error to attempt to remake much of the world in our own image. If the Administration has gone too far in these two ways, then what is the alternative? In our view the best alternative is to return to a strategic posture of the United States in the first two decades of the Cold War – a period of our Strategic Independence – in the search for peace in coming decades.

A Window of Opportunity

The information revolution, Russia's failed transition to a more productive economic culture, and China's current backwardness have created a window of opportunity for shifting the terms of engagement in our favor. America should be responding to this changed reality because at this historic juncture America might have it all: deterrence with Russia, a defense against Chinese missiles, arms reductions of many kinds, and independence in our choice of actions. Given such a rare opportunity, it is prudent to try.

Changing priorities can be accomplished without appearing to alter our core policy. Current management of the terms of engagement can be tweaked by shifting priorities, not by junking the terms and starting over. Giving a much higher priority among the terms to Strategic Independence doesn't require that we scrap ballistic missile ceilings nor foreswear arms reductions; it doesn't even require that we abandon MAD. But it does cancel what has been our primary reliance on MAD; substituting for it greater reliance on Strategic Independence. MAD wasn't a strategy for all seasons. It arose from the conjunction of a specific set of historical circumstances that have irreversibly changed with nuclear proliferation.

What is required for America now to successfully assert Strategic Independence is:

At the military level, a counterterrorism capability and a missile defense capability to join our current conventional and nuclear capabilities; and, at the broader level, the

- economic strength to pay for these things;
- technological superiority to enable them; and
- political will to maintain Strategic Independence.

Although Strategic Independence may seem inconsistent with military supremacy in theory, it's very much like it in practice. This is because to have real independence of action, we must not have a rival of equal strength. If we do, then we must have allies, and we lose our independence of action. But this does not mean that we must match the strategic capability of each rival item by item – a danger in the concept of military supremacy; instead, we should oppose large numbers of missiles in an adversary's hands with a combination of weaponry that will frustrate and overcome our adversary's strength. To define our goal, as does the Bush administration, as having so much military power that an adversary cannot equal or surpass it is to confuse our proper objective and to suggest that we will participate in an arms race. This is unnecessary and potentially very costly .

An objection to Strategic Independence is that it seeks absolute security for the United States and that absolute security for one party is absolute insecurity for others – because the secure party can act with impunity. Thus, in seeking absolute security for itself, the United States undermines security everywhere else and destabilizes the international scene. Certainly, many countries in the world assert today that the United States does whatever it wishes, regardless of others, and that freedom of action can be attributed to the supposed security it feels as the world's sole superpower.

But this objection, though sophisticated and with a superficial plausibility, is without merit.

First, the United States should seek Strategic Independence not because it is currently invulnerable as the world's sole superpower, but for precisely the opposite reason – that it is very vulnerable, as the events of September 11, 2001, made distressingly clear.

Second, Strategic Independence does not seek absolute security for the United States, only sufficient security to provide freedom of action in our defense.

The objection would have merit, however, if, as is a dangerous possibility, American leadership overreaches and seeks not reliable defense, but the capability of remaking the world.

Preemption: An Ounce of Prevention Is Worth a Pound of Cure

On May 12, 2003, a group of bombings killed some twenty-one persons, including seven Americans in Riad, Saudi Arabia. Said a Saudi spokesman to a television reporter soon thereafter, "We knew something was brewing. We had raised our terror alert. We had them under surveillance. It's just a question of how do you know when they will strike?"

Well, they did strike.

Did the Saudi official have to wait for the damage to be done? Or should he have arrested them first?

Sadly, the Saudi official omitted a crucial step: Recording the incidents and observations that led him to conclude, "We knew something was brewing." He likely believed that the evidence wasn't specific enough to warrant such rigorous treatment; which, in the end proved to be a fatal error.

Ordinary everyday traffic provides a simple analogy here. How many of us, while driving on a crowded highway, sense that a car in the lane next to us is about to change lanes even though no turn signal is displayed? How often is such "intuition" correct? Almost always.

The reason is that our brains record imperceptible clues about the world around us that we aren't even aware of such as the driver's expression, a slight turn of head, a minor change in speed, a split second swerve and correction to the left. It is no different in war – but lives depend on being able to recognize, record, and analyze these changes to our environment and enemy behavior.

How did this individual conclude "something was brewing"? Most likely small changes in behavior occurred that, if compared to historic clues before similar attacks in the past, would have been shown to be strikingly similar. The official's lack of discipline and awareness of his environment should surely have cost him his position.

This is the key issue of preemption; it applies on both the personal and the national basis.

It seems to us that the Saudi security services should have acted in advance, saved the people's lives, and borne the criticism from civil rights activists – which would have been rendered far less damaging in light of a thorough analysis of environmental clues. Also it seems to us that our nation must do the same in the world; act, save our people, and bear the criticism.

Preemption is an element of Strategic Independence – an uncommon policy, to be used only infrequently. The currently popular notion that war should always be a last resort seems self-evident to many who don't think it through carefully. In fact, the opposite is often the case – that is, some kinds of war should be not a last resort but an early one. Force, applied at the right time – early, before the attacker is prepared – is often both effective and inexpensive. Exhausting other means of attaining an objective can mean, ironically in certain cases, that ultimately a war results that is much longer, harder, more expensive, less certain, and more horrible for combatants and noncombatants alike, than otherwise. Preemptive war has significant promise if used correctly.

Preemption extends to other dangers to American lives than those of terrorism only. For example, Donald S. Burke of the Johns Hopkins Bloomberg School of Public Health wrote about preparing for a pandemic as follows: " . . . it may be possible to identify a . . . outbreak at the earliest stage. . . . The new mindset should be one that focuses upstream on the earliest events, emphasizing prediction and prevention before a pandemic begins." Although we don't usually think about terrorism or warfare as a kind of pandemic, it is just as much a public health problem as bird flu, and can be responded to in the same way.

Had the Western powers acted preemptively against Hitler in 1936, then the conflict would have been very small and quickly ended. World War II, as we shall see below, would not have been necessary. But preemption is also subject to the risk of serious misuse, and so must be employed rarely and only when a significant danger looms – and by presidents of our country who are experienced in foreign affairs and able to make the proper judgments. By employing preemption in the invasion of Iraq in 2003, President Bush put the question of preemption at the top of political discussion in America.

WORLD WAR II WAS AVOIDABLE

World War II was almost certainly avoidable, had we acted in a preemptive way as the danger became apparent. Hitler took power in Germany in 1933 and soon after began to rearm. The Western democracies knew of this soon thereafter. The persecution of the Jews by the Nazis was soon underway and was well known in the United States in the late 1930s. In 1936, in defiance of the Versailles treaty that had ended World War I, Hitler occupied the German Rhineland. The Rhineland was German territory adjacent to France that was demilitarized after World War I. Hitler's first use of Germany's expanded army was to enter the Rhineland and reabsorb it into Germany. French, and British leaders debated what response to make; possibly they discussed the matter with the Americans. They decided to make none. It was learned after the war that Germany military leaders were so convinced that they couldn't have handled French and British opposition, to say nothing of American, that they were preparing to depose Hitler. But when Hitler got away with the gamble; when the British and French and Americans did nothing; then Hitler's hold on Germany tightened; the opposition in Germany was demoralized, and World War II became virtually certain.

In the Pacific, the Japanese fired on a U.S. gunboat, the Panay, in Chinese waters in December 1937, and we chose not to respond strongly. Four years later, with Japan increasingly aggressive, and Germany triumphant in Europe, we embargoed oil to Japan, forcing Japan to decide on war or peace. They chose war, and somehow surprised us with an attack at Pearl Harbor.

Now it should be said that we were not armed for war in 1936 or 1937. So in a sense, we couldn't have successfully preempted either Germany or Japan alone. But we could have preempted both Germany and Japan if we had been armed, and we should have been; and we could have done so with allies (France and Britain), had we exerted leadership at the time.

Had we preempted Nazi Germany in 1936 and Hitler had been deposed, so that World War II never occurred, then there would never have been a great war, France would not have been overrun, the battles of Britain and the Atlantic would not have been fought, the Soviet Union would not have been invaded, the Holocaust would not have occurred. Pearl Harbor would not have been attacked; there would have been no Bataan death march; and no atomic bomb. None of these events, the clear evidence of the value of having prevented the war, would have occurred. Had the German invasion of the Soviet Union not occurred, few today would have believed that something so brutal would have been possible; had the Holocaust not have occurred, few would have believed today that something so horrible had been averted. Had there been no world war, few would have thought that some three hundred thousand American lives were saved by preemption.

Instead, in preventing World War II by some military action, some few American soldiers might have died in the Rhineland, and there would have been those political opponents of the president who insisted that Hitler would never have actually unleashed a great war. In fact, so strong was the spirit of denial in the western democracies that even in 1938 British prime minister Chamberlain was still insisting that he had obtained from Hitler at the Munich conference "peace in our time . . . peace with honor."[16]

Either action would have either prevented World War II, or caused it to occur prematurely from the point of view of Germany and Japan when our victory would have been more certain, faster and less costly.

Would action by the American military to stop Germany in the Rhineland or Japan in China have been preemption? Yes, because in the case of the Rhineland, there was no attack on American forces and Hitler made no threat against the United States; and in the case of the Panay, where there was an overt attack on an American naval vessel and two American sailors were killed, the Japanese government quickly apologized and paid compensation.[17] So for us to have embarked on a military response was to have preempted the aggressors, not responded to an assault on our forces.

Preemption Could Have Prevented 9/11

There is another more recent example. During President Clinton's term in office, years before the September 11, 2001, attack on the World Trade Center, the president was apprised of an opportunity to kill Osama bin Laden by an attack by our covert operations people. Osama bin Laden was associated with the first World Trade Center bombing, then with the bombings of our embassies in east Africa, then with the bombing of the USS *Cole*, but we made no effective response to any of these events. Here was an opportunity to get the man before he did more damage to us. Generally, when our country has enemies, and knowing about them, still allows them to gather strength, then we suffer for it. But President Clinton failed to approve the request and the opportunity passed. Had the opportunity been seized and bin Laden killed, there would probably have been no 9/11 attack, and thousands of our fellow citizens would be with us still.

Another opportunity was offered just before September 11, 2001. Richard Miniter reports that "By the end of August, a plan was hammered out to give the CIA some $200 million to arm the Northern Alliance, a rebel group that opposed the Taliban and bin Laden. . . . The boldest part of the plan was an elaborate effort to arm the Predator, a small, unmanned, remotely controlled plane . . . that (Richard) Clarke had long hoped to persuade the Air Force to equip with Hellfire missiles. . . . Now, with intelligence reports of pending attacks on Americans – one intelligence analyst, citing intercepts from Afghanistan, believed that Al Qaeda could strike over the July 4 holiday – and threats to his own life, President Bush was determined to bypass the usual objections."[18] On September 4, 2001, the National Security Council approved the plan to strike bin Laden. It had been in the works for months. The National Security agency called on the Secretary of Defense to plan for military options "against Taliban targets in Afghanistan, including leadership, command-control, air and air defense, ground forces, and logistics." The NSA also called for plans "against Al Qaeda and associated terrorist facilities in Afghanistan, including leadership, command-control-communications, training, and logistics facilities." President Bush was expected to review the plan on September 10, but he was out of the White House that day. The meeting was rescheduled for the afternoon of September 11.[19]

The point, of course, is that we failed to preempt the bin Laden attack, and perhaps in anger at this, President Bush seized on the World Trade Center attack to declare "war" on terrorists.

Do lost opportunities and successful preemptions in history suggest that preemption should be a part of our response to a dangerous world? There are strong arguments against it – including that preemption can be misused or mistaken with possibly tragic results. And there is a special dilemma that any president who proposes preemption must resolve. Like any preventative measure, preemption, if it is successful, can never be proven to have been 100 percent necessary. This means that in order to employ it, the president must engage in a highly rigorous analysis of the situation that makes it clear that the probability of a future threat from this source is very high (see our risk analysis later in this chapter). This makes it a highly risky tactic politically – but the American people are now mature enough to understand the tactic if explained properly and intuitive enough to recognize when certain warning signs ring true. Nonetheless, the potential for political suicide remains; and we predict that only the truly great and the truly reckless presidents will attempt to harness its power.

To understand where the minefields are in such a tactic, we should recognize that ordinarily in politics a pound of cure is always preferable to an ounce of prevention. This is because the pound of cure is offered only when the need is apparent, while the need for the ounce of prevention can only be argued for. People who don't want to make any expenditure or effort on prevention need only deny the need; and if preventive measures are taken anyway, and are effective, opponents will insist that there was never any danger in the first place. Fair-minded people won't be certain, and since the danger didn't actually materialize, can't be convinced of the need for prevention. The result is that a successful campaign of prevention is likely to have few friends and some strong enemies. Most politicians will prefer to wait until the need is evident – to opt for the pound of cure.

Preemption is prevention in geopolitics and subject to the same dynamic.

WHEN TO PREEMPT

For preemption to be fully accepted, it's not enough to have a foreign leader who declares that America is his enemy; who arms to be able to fight us; who slaughters his people (Hitler began by murdering German citizens who were Jewish; Saddam killed Kurds and Shiites by the thousands). None of this is enough for many people. They argue in effect that there is no justification for resort to force until force has been used against us. In the case of all the Jews and other people of Europe who died at the hands of the Nazis before Hitler declared war on us in December 1941, does this mean that those who oppose our use of force accept some responsibility for their deaths?

Suppose that President Clinton had approved the effort to kill Osama bin Laden in the 1990s and it had been successful. We know now that a result would likely have been to avoid the disaster of 9/11, but that's hindsight. Before the tragedy occurred, who imagined it? Not even Hollywood fantasized such an event. How would President Clinton have justified to critics the murder of a man only suspected, not tried and convicted, of involvement in terrorist attacks on us? He couldn't have pointed to the World Trade Center disaster as the reason because no one would have imagined it, or believed him if he had foreseen it. Critics would have demanded evidence that the attack was likely, that it was imminent, that it would be successful, that there were not other, less violent ways to avoid its occurring. We would have searched among the rubble in which bin Laden's body lay to find the plans for some horrid attack in order to justify our action. Would we have found them? Not likely. Then the president would have been subject to criticism for using deadly force where it was not needed.

Where does the critic's string of logic – which many people in our country and the rest of the world espouse – lead? It begins by arguing that we should never resort to force first; that we must always be attacked, and only then defend ourselves. Suppose that in 1941 we were attacked by Japan, then as our response gathered force, Japan had offered to cease fighting and make some reparations to us alone, would we then have been required by this rule of moral action to abandon our allies and cease the war – leaving China, Britain, France, and the Netherlands to their fate? Probably, because by the standards of those who oppose conflict at nearly all costs we could not help those who later became our allies until we were attacked by our allies' enemies. It was this string of logic that led America to stay so long out of the international conflicts that became the two world wars that we created great losses for ourselves in ultimately winning them.

CALCULATING THE RISK

There has been discussion over the centuries about the circumstances under which preemptive war should be permissible. They stress the immediacy of an attack by the adversary, clear evidence of the intent to attack, the lack of any other alternative, and that the force used should be proportional to the threat. In effect, the notion is that a nation can defend itself by preemption only at the time that the attack is imminent and that only to the extent necessary to deflect the attack.

These standards, although plausible, would not have prevented the horror of World War II or the Holocaust. By the time that the Western powers would have been authorized by these standards to preempt Hitler, the Nazi state would have been so strong that only the full rigor of World War II would have been sufficient to destroy Nazism. Similarly, in the Pacific America could not have acted, according to these standards, until the Japan fleet was on its way to Pearl Harbor in December 1941 – a time sufficient – had we had proper intelligence about the coming attack and so ourselves attacked the Japanese fleet en route to Hawaii – to prevent our naval disaster at Pearl Harbor, but certainly far too late to have avoided the Pacific War with Japan. In effect, the standards proposed for preemptive war make preemption solely a tactical resort – all strategic consequence is removed from it. The nation acting preemptively must let its adversary arm itself fully, chose its time and method of attack, and even then can only parry the blow (the rule is that the preemptive action must be directly proportional to the attack anticipated).

Today, when states are vigorously seeking to build nuclear arsenals, and perhaps biological weapons as well, to wait for the potential adversary to fully arm itself before responding could and is likely to be suicidal. Hence, there is a strong argument for strategic preemption – to avoid a great conflict in the future.

Preemption is the method by which a strong power can protect itself from the rise of enemies who are likely at some point to attack it. It is a way to reduce the losses ultimately sustained.

The analysis is extremely difficult because enemies both disclose and deny simultaneously (as did Hitler, Stalin, Saddam, and others) their aggressive intentions. They disclose their intended attacks to rally their supporters; they deny them to mislead us, knowing that there is a strong opposition in our country and among our allies to any act of preemption.

This is the paradox of preemption – that if it is successful, it can never be proven beyond doubt to have been necessary and is always subject to criticism that it wasn't really necessary. However, truly great presidents who are dutiful students of history will use their worldly knowledge to describe other situations that shared important characteristics (that might not be obvious on first glance) as well as other risk factors that heighten the danger to convince Americans that there is a huge risk in doing nothing. That is all that need be proved. Americans are coming of age. They are now mature enough to accept that as long as they don't feel they are being oversold. This is also true of the war in Iraq, for which it might seem that weapons of mass destruction in Saddam's hands might have justified preemptive war. Certainly President Bush said so. But if we found them, it wouldn't prove that preemption was necessary, for our critics insist that they could have been found and eliminated by peaceful means – by UN inspection teams and the weight of world opinion.

In fact, the question of finding weapons of mass destruction in Iraq is not about the justifiability of preemptive war, but is instead about the honesty of the president. Finding weapons of mass destruction will not persuade the opponents of preemptive war, who will simply argue that the weapons would not have been used by Saddam. But finding such weapons would restore credibility to President Bush, who cited them as a key reason for war.

Thus it is that accepting a doctrine of preemptive or preventive war requires a very high degree of political maturity in a democracy and a very high degree of trust between the citizens and the president. For any resort to force is unfortunate and likely to be decried, especially where even if it is successful, it can never be afterwards shown that it had been needed.

SUCCESSFUL PREEMPTIONS

There are successful examples of preemption in global political history.

Napoleon

In 1807 when Napoleon was at the height of his power, and England stood alone against him, "an English secret agent reported that an arrangement had been reached whereby Napoleon was to seize the Danish fleet..." thereby challenging England's control of the seas. Only a few years earlier Napoleon had made extensive preparations to invade England but was prevented from doing so by the English fleet. Now, again he was preparing to challenge England on the seas; the seizure of the Danish fleet "was to be a preliminary to a joint invasion of England with the help of the Russians." The British government sent a fleet into Danish waters to compel the surrender of the Danish fleet. "This act of aggression against a neutral state (Denmark)," Churchill wrote, "aroused a storm against the Government.... But events vindicated the promptitude and excused the violence of their action.... Had the British Government not acted with speed the French would have been in possession of the Danish Navy within a few weeks."[20]

Grenada, 1983

Perhaps the most successful episode of preemptive action by America in recent years, until the Second Gulf War whose ultimate success is yet to be demonstrated, occurred in the Caribbean island of Grenada. In 1979, a pro-Soviet self-styled Revolutionary Military Council, overthrew the government of Grenada. The Cubans sent in soldiers, and the Russians advisors. America was again faced with a Soviet and Cuban attempt to extend Soviet reach in the Americas. Six days later, President Ronald Reagan sent in six thousand marines and overthrew the Council. In hours of fighting, nineteen Americans died and unknown numbers of Cubans and Grenadians. The American invasion was condemned around the world as preemptive unilateralism, but a year later an election was held, a centrist coalition won, and government was returned to the hands of the hundred thousand islanders.

Preemption and Nuclear Weapons

Preemption has been especially problematical in the arena of nuclear weapons. In general, America has repeatedly failed to employ preemption to protect itself from nuclear threats from abroad.

The Soviet Union, 1948

First, in 1948 as the Soviets were about to get the atomic bomb: " . . . when America was on the point of losing her monopoly of the atomic bomb, as leader of the opposition in the British Parliament, Churchill was gravely alarmed . . . and in 1948 favored the threat and – if need be the reality – of a pre-emptive strike to safeguard the interests of the Free World."[21] We decided against preemption; the result was a long Cold War and nuclear standoff that appears today to have had a favorable result, but as we shall in a later chapter, the issue is not yet fully resolved.

Even in the late 1940s and early 1950s, a nuclear attack by the Russians was much closer than most Americans realize, since revelations from members of Stalins circle in recent years now suggest that in 1953, armed with nuclear weapons, Stalin was preparing to attack the west, but died or was murdered before the attack commenced. His motivation was clear. At a meeting of the top officials of the Soviet Union just before his death in 1953, Stalin commented with contempt in his voice – "when I'm gone the imperialists (the Americans) will eat you up like blind kittens."[22] Stalin died before he could rectify the situation, and what he predicted is exactly what happened, although it took until 1990 for the Soviet Union to collapse.

SOVIET UNION, CUBAN MISSILE CRISIS, 1962

Second, in 1962, when the Soviets put nuclear tipped missiles in Cuba and Kennedy threatened a preemptive war, the Soviets backed down. We discuss this dramatic incident in more detail later.

Soviet Union, President Johnson, 1963 and Beyond

Third, in 1963 when the USSR was about to get intercontinental delivery systems so that it could hit the United States with nuclear arms (without having to base them in Cuba, on our doorstep), Presidents Kennedy and Johnson both refused to make a preemptive strike, and thereafter we narrowly avoided nuclear war on several occasions.

Iraq, President George W. Bush, 2003

The final results of the invasion of Iraq in the spring of 2003 await the passage of time. It was originally justified as an effort to prevent Iraq from building nuclear weapons, something that turned our not to be correct. But judged purely as an act of preemption (it was much more than that strategically) the president's action had strengths and weaknesses:

- It was successful in overthrowing the Iraqi government which was the object of our concern; and
- It eliminated any risk of attack on us or our allies by that Iraqi government.

But there were also significant limitations, including

Inadequate explanation and justification for our actions (including inventing justifications)

Exaggerated Iraq's involvement in the 9/11 attack;

Falsely claimed that Iraq possessed weapons of mass destruction that were a danger to the global community;

Confused our intentions – were they to conduct a quasi-judicial process of investigation, indictment, trial and punishment, involving only those directly involved in the attack; or to engage in a military campaign to drive our enemies from safe-havens?

Also, the Administration switched strategic purpose in midstream: from regime change to changing the world by bringing democracy to the Arab world. But we weren't well prepared for the new mission – our military is not an appropriate instrument for nation-building abroad.

In general, in Pericles' formulation: Bush knew what needed to be done, but not how to explain and justify it satisfactorily.

Preemption is one of the most difficult topics in thinking about how to defend our country. Used properly, preemption can be enormously valuable in protecting ourselves; used wrongly it can bring about great tragedies. Because of the risk, should our country simply eschew preemption? We've been doing that in general, but it would have been a good thing to have avoided World War II and the holocaust; and a good thing to have avoided the World Trade Center tragedy; and both could have been avoided by preemptive actions.

CHAPTER 13: KEY POINTS

1. The best approach for America in today's world of very divergent threats is to return to our defense policy in the early years of our country, and again in the early years of the Cold War – a policy of Strategic Independence.
2. Strategic Independence consists of:
   - a focus on the defense of the United States without being drawn into broader goals;
   - avoidance of an arms race with a rival power (s) via a flexible strategic response;

- preemption to deal with terrorists and states in the Crescent of Fire, especially the threat of attacks on us or our allies using weapons of mass destruction; and
- sufficient conventional forces to allow us to decide and act on our own behalf.

3. Preemption could have avoided World War II; and it can help us defend ourselves now; but it must be used with great caution because it is subject to dangers of misuse and it is easily misunderstood as to motives.

4. The Bush Doctrine is a major step toward Strategic Independence but departs from it in important ways.

FOURTEEN

America as Mature Superpower

AMERICAN MILITARY EFFECTIVENESS

The major lesson for other countries from America's changed attitude toward its defense strategy, and specifically from the Second Gulf War and its aftermath is that the United States is able to defend itself effectively – it is no paper tiger. We have however developed an extremely effective military; one of which Americans are increasingly proud.

A few years ago, in the period between the two Iraqi wars, the Minister of Defense of a major European power at a dinner conversation commented on his meetings with the American military leadership and his assessment of their performance in Iraq in the early 1990s. "You'd be amazed at how good these Americans really are these days," he said. "They're committed, hard-working, very professional. There's nothing else to match them in the world today. I'm just amazed. It's a totally different situation from the American military in the Vietnam War."

He was right, and his judgment has been confirmed again in the second Iraqi War. That a significant outcome of the Iraq engagement was to demonstrate American military effectiveness is confirmed by the now revealed desire of the French military forces to participate in the invasion (although they were refused the opportunity by French political leaders for reasons that had much to do with the political rivalry between France/EC on one side and the United States on the other). French military officials were interested in joining in an attack because they felt that not participating with the United States in a major war would leave French forces unprepared for future conflicts. A French general, Jean Patrick Gaviard, visited the Pentagon to meet with Central Command staff on December 16, 2002 – three months before the war began-to discuss a French contribution of ten thousand to fifteen thousand troops and to negotiate landing and docking rights for French jets and ships.[1] The initial demonstrations of American military prowess were in smart weaponry, fire power and speed of action. Later demonstration was of the ability to wage urban warfare with limited casualties. The demonstrations are a warning to potential adversaries from small to large (from Syria and Iran to Russia and China).

Much happened between the Vietnam War and the First Iraqi War, between 1974 and 1990, to improve the effectiveness of our military, particularly in the Army. Briefly, we abandoned conscription and went to an all volunteer force; in so doing, we largely rid our military of drugs (in dramatic contrast to our civilian society); we changed the general orders of the Army to stress individual initiative by officers in combat situations – for example, the general orders now provide that the primary responsibility of a subordinate officer is to carry out the INTENT of his commanding officer's instructions – not the letter of the orders, but their intent. And we began a new regime of leadership training intended to forge tight bonds between officers and soldiers – no more of the sort of fragging (when soldiers shot their officers) that occurred in Vietnam. In addition, somehow we managed to establish a culture in our military leadership of flexibility and innovation. This is remarkable.

REVOLUTION IN MILITARY AFFAIRS

In the concluding stages of the Cold War Secretaries of Defense Harold Brown and Bill Perry decided that America shouldn't try to compete with the Warsaw Pact in quantity of force but should try instead to master them by greater quality. This gave impetus to the technological revolution that became the Revolution in Military Affairs (RMA). "... the US military is entering one of those periods of technological advance that come along every few generations, when there is a quantum leap in the family of technologies and operational concepts that push warfare into completely new realms."[2]

RMA involves not only smart missiles that can find their targets, but the information and communication revolution with its big impact on the organization of the military. It's another weakness of the media that it focuses on the new technology of warfare, and not the much more important issues of the capability of command and execution. Americans are thereby encouraged to believe that if we continue to introduce technological innovations in warfare, we will remain effective militarily, although this is only part of the story. Another part of the story is the difficult process of modernizing command and control. For example, when a sergeant in Afghanistan calls in a B-52 from Omaha for a strike, what do each of the layers of command in between do – are they all redundant now? If so, they will resist the change in how battles are directed. Not only is the technology of the RMA a challenge, but modernizing the culture of the military as well.

The public culture is beginning to recognize the RMA, driven in part by the gee-whiz impact of the new technology of warfare as illustrated for the American people by television. But again, public culture both simplifies and exaggerates. "Geared to fight traditional wars against conventional enemies," writes a pundit, "our military must make significant, and in some cases, radical changes in the way it organizes, equips and operates its forces if we are to win the war on terrorism."[3]

This observation simplifies the battle against terrorism by suggesting that a primary part of our response is military. This isn't the case; much of our response to terrorism involves security, diplomacy, and geopolitics. Furthermore, the observation exaggerates what needs to be done – it is not at all necessary to make radical changes in the way we organize, equip and operate all or most of our forces simply in order to suppress terrorism. In fact, large-scale conventional war continues to be a major concern in the future, in part because of the crucial importance of denying state support to terrorist groups. This was, of course, a motive for our invasion of Iraq.

The observation is within the classic pattern of our public culture – it is an overstatement, making the point that we need more terror-fighting capability, which is accurate, but combining it with the implication that we should give up our traditional defenses (leaving ourselves vulnerable, though this is not admitted) through the presumption that the new threat, terrorism, is the only, or the most important threat. Instead, we require multiple capabilities in our military: to fight nuclear wars; conventional wars; guerrrilla wars, insurrections, and terrorist provocations.

Stephen Biddle informs us that material factors (weaponry and its amounts) "are only weakly related to historical patterns of victory and defeat. . . . A particular nonmaterial variable – force employment or the doctrine and tactics by which forces are actually used in combat – is centrally important . . ."[4]

He continues: "A particular pattern of force employment – the modern system – has been pivotal in the twentieth century and is likely to remain so . . ."[5] "The modern system is a tightly interrelated complex of cover, concealment, dispersion, suppression, small unit independent maneuver, and combined arms at the tactical level, and depth, reserves and differential concentration at the operational level of war. . . . The modern system . . . insulates its users from the full lethality of their opponent's weapons. Militaries that fail to implement the modern system have been fully exposed to the firepower of modern weapons. . . . The net result has been a growing gap in the real military power of states that can and cannot implement the modern system."[6]

In essence, the key elements of what Biddle calls the modern system are the ability to protect one's own forces from today's overwhelming fire power while permitting mobility to one's forces, all the while either pinning down or destroying the enemy's forces with fire concentration.

Because quantities of material are not determinative in warfare, one must be careful of projecting effective military strength of nations based on size of economy alone. It is not the size of the American economy that makes us a global superpower. It is the enhanced (since Vietnam) capability of our military leadership at all levels, including our ability to employ in expert fashion modern systems of force employment that combined with our ability to arm and supply materially our forces (a function of the large size of our economy) that gives us our military strength.

A significant danger is a bureaucratic rigidity in the American forces. Historically, we are susceptible to this. It is a political struggle to close bases and open new ones. It is difficult to redeploy forces on a permanent basis. For example, U.S. Army forces are being redeployed with fewer left in Europe but better configured for rapid redeployment.[7]

There is, however, considerable opposition to this. We have already pointed above to the likely resistance within the multiple links of the chain of command in our military to direct communications between combat-level leadership and support units.

THE MYTH OF WAR WITHOUT CASUALTIES

"Effectively prosecuted, modern war [offers] the opportunity for decisive success without having to use decisive force."[8] This is because of smart weapons, and is the flawed notion behind the start of the Iraqi war with "shock and awe." We were awed by our weapons and expected them to have been equally awe-inspiring to our adversaries. The insurgents found a way to neutralize them by adopting what are classic guerrilla tactics; forcing us into a form of conflict in which we much take casualties. The notion of a war without casualties is, of course, another expression of the wishful thinking that pervades our public culture.

A word is necessary here about the Kosovo conflict, from which the most commonly drawn conclusion is that Western air power virtually alone forced a recalcitrant Serbia to withdraw from Kosovo. Thus, the argument is that

America can via airpower maintain stability in much of the world. This is a very attractive proposition because both costs and casualties can thereby be kept low.

However, this conclusion has now been convincingly challenged by Pentagon studies of the effectiveness of the western bombing of Kosovo and Serbia itself. The damage done from the air, even with smart bombs, to the Serbian military on the ground was in fact very limited, due to Serbian use of dummy weapons and installations and concealment of actual weapons.

What actually caused the Serbian withdrawal from Kosovo is still concealed by the governments involved, but it appears to have been the combination of the threat of Western ground attack and Russian pressure on Serbia due to commitments made by the West to the Russians, which Russia didn't want to imperil by supporting Serbia. The solution was not gained by air power, but by great power intervention and by the threat of ground attack. The air campaign provided the ostensible cause needed by the politicians involved on all sides – the apparent reason for Serbian withdrawal and for western victory. Had the West had to drive the Serbs out of Kosovo on the ground, casualties would have been substantial and the American will sorely tested.

What we can achieve with military power that does not risk our taking casualties is not sufficient to deter or deflect opponents in many situations that matter to us, and there is no strong evidence to the contrary. Iraq is a very good example. The deposition of Saddam's regime was by ground attack.

A FULL-RANGE MILITARY

An effective military that permits us flexibility in response to various sorts and combinations of threats is critical to our defense. Today, we distinguish between nuclear, conventional and terrorist threats as if they were distinct, requiring different types of force configurations, and certain to remain separate in the future. This is unrealistic. A combination of all will probably confront us in the future, and in many permutations:

- A conflict with a major power in which our adversary uses nuclear weapons, large-scale conventional forces and irregular (guerrilla or terrorist) units; or
- A conflict with a nonstate network of terrorists, in which small-scale nuclear weapons are used and the conventional forces of supporting states.

A military with full-range capability and modernized command and control is essential for the flexibility of response that Strategic Independence requires.

THE CASE AGAINST STRATEGIC INDEPENDENCE

Opponents of Strategic Independence claim:

1. Strategic Independence, with its reliance on military force to deter war, only increases the risk of war;
2. Potential adversaries are more likely deterred by peaceful expressions than threatening ones;
3. A less bellicose method – to wit, MAD – is more effective.

It would be wonderful if we lived in the sort of world in which our disarming increased the likelihood of peace; in which MAD could deal with nuclear proliferation; and in which turning the other cheek dissuaded adversaries – but we do not, and can't afford the pretense of our public culture that we do. Hence, a more proactive defense strategy is necessary, and Strategic Independence is preferable to our current posture.

Strategic Independence has no hidden agenda. It's not a vehicle for American imperialism. In fact, Strategic Independence as a grand strategy requires us to disengage from conflicts only distantly related to major power challenges. We should not, in the context of Strategic Independence, be involved in many of the world's flash points. The only purpose of Strategic Independence is the defense of the United States.

"The only defense against [modern warfare] is the ability to attack," General Marshall told Americans in his review of World War II.[9] This is equally true half a century later and applies today as much to terrorist threats as to those of the great powers. But it is now outdated. The ability to attack is not stopping nuclear proliferation, and, as every country in the world recognizes, once a country has nuclear weapons no one else dare attack. The ability to attack was, of course, deterrence, which Marshall sponsored. It worked for fifty years, haphazardly, as we demonstrate in this book. But it worked. Now it's past its day, and Strategic Independence must replace it – that is, a real defense against nuclear weapons.

Nor is Strategic Independence a military strategy only. To be successful it should be supplemented by addressing the great problems of economic and social development abroad with a culturally sensitive approach – accepting limitations on the transference of our own economic and social culture to other nations.

WHY STRATEGIC INDEPENDENCE SHOULD NOW DISPLACE THE CURRENT AMERICAN NATIONAL SECURITY STRATEGY

The vast majority of Americans desire peace, but we differ about how to achieve it. One group prefers continuing reliance on MAD – a balance of terror that, it is hoped and believed, will compel logical leaders among our adversaries to avoid war. Another prefers that our defense be sufficiently in our own hands that we can respond successfully to irrational actions by possible adversaries.

There is no reconciling these different preferences. They demand very different approaches. We can't have the vulnerability MAD requires and the defensive security Strategic Independence promises simultaneously. So either MAD must exclude Strategic Independence (SI) – or SI must subordinate MAD. Yet, we must acknowledge that complementarity and substitution are dependent on context, and differ by adversary. MAD cannot forestall China (or for that matter, but of far less danger to us at this moment, India and Pakistan) from building ballistic missile capabilities; nor does it offer any way to reduce the toll of a nuclear exchange. Only Strategic Independence provides hope for containing these risks. Nuclear disarmament, another suggested alternative, has the disadvantages that it will make the world free for conventional war and put America – which in this scheme would also have disarmed – at risk of nuclear attack by nations that cheat on the disarmament agreements, or of attack by rogue states (as surrogates for the great powers that protect them). The goal should be SI, but where compelled we can accept MAD for cosuperpowers, and SI elsewhere.

Continuing the current American defense policy means keeping ourselves vulnerable to a nuclear attack from Russia at the present and from China in the very near future. The strategy of MAD presumes that neither Russia nor China will accept destruction at our hands as the price of an attack on us or our close allies, and by extension will deter conventional aggression even if our nonnuclear forces are drastically reduced. For the moment, this may be true of Russia, but it won't stop China from seizing Taiwan or further aggression on its borders.

We foresee a change in U.S. policy to a transition path in which we cope with the growing risk of disaster by simultaneously being self-restrained to mollify the Kremlin's and Beijing's fears, while announcing our intention to gradually build a comprehensive ballistic missile defense from ground or space and take other actions necessary to assert Strategic Independence.

The desirability of Strategic Independence to cope with low intensity destabilizing events is obvious, buttressed by the possibility of contagion.

Low-intensity conflicts can metastasize, proliferate and escalate into high intensity wars and global conflagrations. Russia's full spectrum arms modernization, China's bluster, Kim Jong Il's provocations, intervention in Dafur, flare ups between India and Pakistan all may trigger arms races, and brinksmanship of the sort that raises the ante on belligerence. And unfortunately, there is the growing risk that bilateral nuclear exchanges, could spark a chain reaction incinerating North Korea, China, India, Pakistan, Russia, and the United States. With the stakes this high, it would be unwise for America just to speak softly, when it could nip the danger in the bud by carrying a big stick.

The shift from a strategy grounded in MAD to Strategic Independence is both motivated and made possible by the rapid transition that is taking place among the world's major powers. The wider diffusion of technology ensures that more nations will acquire nuclear weapons and ballistic missiles. In short, we face more nations with more nuclear weapons and more reasons to use them. Consequently, the danger of nuclear war may soon be greater than during the Cold War.

We should seek to become a mature superpower. In this role, we would try to avoid entanglements abroad, but seek instead somewhat arm's-length relations with other powers in which we equitably engage other nations, reaping some of the advantages of power without becoming abusive. This will not make other nations love us – some will be envious, others vengeful – but we should expect to be respected. Being a mature superpower requires us to correctly perceive the new reality, to shun delusions of grandeur and corresponding obligations, and to resist Utopian schemes, from right or left, of imposing our economic and political order on the world. Within these limits we should encourage social justice and economic reform abroad. Finally, as a mature superpower we must reserve the right of self-defense, otherwise we will discover what we discovered after September 11, 2001 – that many, perhaps most, of the other nations of the world are prepared to let us be a target for terrorists and then restrain our efforts at self-defense in order to further their own national interests.

It is because it has an internally consistent approach to the extremes of our danger – to a nuclear exchange at one extreme and to terrorists attacks at the other – and flexibility to design responses to situations in between, that Strategic Independence is the preferred policy for us. Our current policy (MAD, preemption, and denial) is inflexible and inconsistent in comparison, and therefore unreasonably risky.

The desire for peace is not the exclusive property of people who engage in wishful thinking, or of those who advocate multilateralism or pacifism. We all desire peace – even us realists. And it is possible – at least large-scale peace is possible, even if small conflicts are necessary to get there. We advocate objectivity and Strategic Independence not so that we can have wars, but because we believe it is a path to peace – to more and deeper peace than is obtainable via any other course.

At the end of World War II, General of the Army George C. Marshall wrote in his report on our victory to the president and the American people as follows: "The security of the United States of America is [thankfully, again] entirely in our own hands. . . . We have tried since the birth of our nation to promote our love of peace by a display of weakness. This course has failed us utterly. . . . The world does not seriously regard the desires of the weak. Weakness presents too great a temptation to the strong . . ."[10] We concur with General Marshall's view.

Years later, George Kennan wrote in his history of American Diplomacy that the public after World War I was not ready to fully accept the Wilsonian idea of a legalistic and moralistic rule of law governing the nations of the world. Kennan wrote: "Our own national interest is all that we are really capable of knowing and understanding and the courage to recognize that if our own purposes and undertakings here at home are decent ones, unsullied by arrogance or hostility toward other people or delusions of superiority, then the pursuit of our national interest can never fail to be conducive to a better world."[11]

This is the core of the legitimacy of Strategic Independence, and it sets a very high standard for America – not the lower one which would be set by the leveling influence of a multinational approach.

CHAPTER 14: KEY POINTS

Strategic Independence involves

1. enhancing our conventional military power through the continuation of the Revolution in Military Affairs;
2. enhancing our defense capability via a missile defense initiative;
3. acting preemptively when necessary;
4. using a combination of forces to deter or defeat an antagonist, but not requiring military superiority over all possible antagonists at all times;
5. making our strategic decisions after consultation with other countries, but ceding to no other country or international body decisions about the defense of our people; and
6. acting multilaterally whenever possible.

PART SEVEN

LEADING TOWARD PEACE

FIFTEEN

The Dangers of Overreach

The public culture of America causes our leaders to find it difficult to defend ourselves in a moderate manner. Historically, we either retreat behind our ocean barriers, or we embark on crusades to remake the world. America focuses on our internal concerns, or we try to rebuild the globe in our image. This dynamic is now reemerging in our country. Our politics may soon be dominated by proponents of each: on the one side, Republicans pressing for a militarily dominant America overreaching itself by trying to remake the world; on the other side Democrats pressing for an underreaching America retreating into reduced armament and multilateralism (we will see that disarmament and multilateralism are necessarily related). Either course is the wrong reach and would spell disaster.

OVERREACH

America as a Model for the World

President George W. Bush has thrust America onto a course of extending our system broadly in the world. At his speech at commencement at the U.S. Coast Guard Academy in 2003, President Bush said, "America's national ambition is the spread of free markets, free trade, and free societies. These goals are not achieved at the expense of other nations, they are achieved for the benefit of all nations. America seeks to expand, not the borders of our country, but the realm of liberty." He quoted Woodrow Wilson to underscore the point: Bush quoted from Woodrow Wilson: "President Woodrow Wilson said, 'America has a spiritual energy in her which no other nation can contribute to the liberation of mankind.'"

The president's appeal to the crusading spirit of America is widely popular because it reflects a strong element of our public culture. Americans believe that the world is going our way, that evil-doers obstruct constructive developments, and that the United States should straighten the situation out. John Updike described the conviction concisely in his novel *Villages*, "The world was full of destruction and evil, and only the United States . . . could put it right."[1]

The president and his supporters seem to have unlimited ambition in this regard. Those who support the president's goal of spreading democracy do it enthusiastically. For example, Charles Krauthammer wrote, "We cannot democratize the world overnight, and therefore . . . we must proceed sequentially."[2] We must proceed sequentially to democratize the world! Thought of without reference to the merits of the goal, but simply as the objective of a nation state to remake the world in its own image, this is a remarkably arrogant objective. We surely wouldn't tolerate this from any other nation.

Democracy is a marvelous thing, but it works best in certain contexts, and it is a long stretch to insist that it works best in all contexts – that it is the world's political panacea.

Furthermore, it is instructive to note how far America's foreign policy has evolved from what it was during the Cold War. George Kennan defined containment, the core of our policy toward the Soviet Union, as a strictly defensive posture, specifically, "the adroit and vigilant application of counter-force at a series of constantly shifting geographical and political points, corresponding to the shifts and maneuvers of Soviet policy . . ."[3]

But the policy of the Bush administration is much more proactive – dangerously so. Containment was a difficult policy for American public culture to accept, because it lacked both the key illusions of harmonism and convergence. But it was justified by the dangers of a nuclear war with the Soviets, which forced us into a modest stance. With the apparent removal of a threat from the Russians, American policy now is again unrestrained, and becomes greatly ambitious – to remake the entire world in our image.

America's System Is Too Good to Transfer

There are major problems with America as a model for others. We as a culture are uncertain who we are, and we are at the moment in a major internal political battle about our national character. For example, Americans support the war on terror, but we are divided about why: is it to support traditional moral values, or is it to free the world for a new morality, one based on toleration of sexual preferences and gender equality?

Our version of democracy may not fit other nations for a variety of reasons. Surprisingly, in some of its aspects our system is too good for them; in others, not good enough.

There's a key reason why the American political system, with all its freedom, isn't suitable for most other societies, including Western Europe (which offers far less economic freedom than the United States). The U.S. system, because it is relatively free, continually generates challenges to itself. It permits, even encourages, development of positions of great wealth, which generates economic and political power that invites attempts to undermine the system by corruption or seizure of power. The American system has to confront and overcome these challenges every few decades (for example, during the robber baron period, the 1920s, today). Also, America's military strength, when the country is armed, sometimes throws up military leaders who challenge civilian dominance and the civilian power has to confront and overcome such challenges from time to time.

The military challenges are interesting. During the Civil War, two Union generals challenged Lincoln for leadership of the nation. General George McClellan ran for president against Lincoln in the 1864 presidential election, in the midst of the war, and lost. General Joseph Hooker told his officers that the Union needed not Lincoln but a dictator. Lincoln was informed of Hooker's comment, and when Lincoln promoted him, Lincoln wrote to him, "It was not because of this but in spite of it that I have given you the command. . . . What I now ask of you is military success, and I will risk the dictatorship."[4]

In 1920 General Pershing, victor of World War I, offered himself as a Republican candidate for president. George C. Marshall was then the general's top aide, and almost alone among those around the general, opposed a presidential bid. As summarized by his biographer, Marshall argued that "Pershing the war hero was honored; Pershing the presidential candidate was a threat to American democracy."[5]

During the Korean War, President Truman felt compelled to relieve General Douglas MacArthur of command in Korea in order to preserve, as he told the American people in a speech, civilian control of the military.

The American democracy, with all its freedom, therefore generates antitheses that challenge the system. The result is not a synthesis, but the triumph of the thesis itself. This is the genius of American democracy – that it is so strongly rooted that it overcomes significant challenges which it spawns. (At least it has overcome them up to now.)

Other countries are not so favored. American-style freedom would generate wealth that so corrupts the system that it threatens to take it over.

American-style militarism elsewhere generates an officer class that is likely to successfully seize power.

Thus, the danger is that implanting American style democracy in many situations abroad is likely to be self-defeating because the dynamics of the American-style freedom generate challenges that overcome the democracy. Further, democracies often end in dictatorships: the Weimar Republic ended in Hitler; the Provisional Republic of Russia ended in Lenin's Soviet Union; the Italian democracy ended in Mussolini (to cite only a few of numerous examples).

Hence, the Bush administration's crusade for democracy in the Muslim world could have unfortunate outcomes.

The often-cited exceptions are the success of imposed democracy in Germany and Japan following World War II. Both countries were given democratic constitutions and governments; and both have been close friends of the Western alliance since. These have been enormous successes, but both are somewhat exceptional cases. In both instances, the conversion was accomplished only after both countries had overreached greatly in geopolitical terms and had been conclusively defeated. Geopolitical ambition had been beaten out of them. Both countries were energetic, vibrant, even in key ways progressive societies that were able to mold to the Western model when there was a clear incentive to do so, and the incentive was supplied by the Soviet Union – an aggressive, alien culture, whose massive military strength and global ambitions threatened each. Absent any of these exceptional factors – the success of the Marshall Plan and NATO in Germany and of the MacArthur occupation and demilitarization in Japan – and even with them there was a failure in both Germany and Japan to transplant American-style free enterprise, as we shall see later – the success of the remaking of Germany and Japan after the war would have been far less extensive and the case in support of extending the American system internationally would not have had the apparent support of these two major experiences.

Germany has reinforced dramatically its commitment to democracy by embedding itself in the European Union. Japan is especially interesting, because it has no such close network of support by other countries, and it has its own very amoral side – demonstrated during World War II – yet deference to group norms within Japan, much changed since World War II, keeps it on track.

But although Germany and Japan have democracies that are much like those of America (though Germany's system is much less centralized than ours, and Japan's involves an Emperor and what is virtually a one-party system), neither has an American style economic culture. This is of significance because it is often argued that Japan's resurgence after World War II, like that of Western Europe, is based on the American capitalist system and American guided economic reconstruction efforts. Were this the fact, it would diminish our thesis that the American economic culture cannot easily be emulated. But, of course, the American system was not exported to either Germany or Japan. In fact, Germany today, like France, possesses a so-called European economic model that is contrasted favorably and negatively according to one's point of view, with the so-called Anglo-Saxon model. And the Japanese rejected the American economic model in favor of a communalist, large company (keiretsu)-managed export driven growth. From the American perspective, the Japanese system is intrinsically anticompetitive and discourages individual entrepreneurship. It is also protectionist. The Japanese model is widely recognized as non-American, which is why we are constantly pressuring the Japanese government to liberalize the Japanese economy. Furthermore, in Japan, American-style freedom at the end of World War II generated wealth that corrupted the political process (it remains corrupted today) and caused Japan to move quickly away from American style economic freedom.

America's System Isn't Good Enough to Transfer

The United States has both a popular culture and its traditional culture (both distinct from what we have called the public culture and the economic culture) – the pop culture is licentious; the traditional culture is almost puritan. The pop culture is the direction in which the country is moving; the adherents of the traditional culture are increasingly uncomfortable with the direction of the nation. The popular culture is showy and dominated by images offered by the entertainment world and the media generally; the traditional culture is quiet (except for some literature urging people to defend it more vigorously) and watches the popular culture with an uneasy mixture of entertained fascination (what will they do to shock us next?), and disquiet. Which is the real America? The answer, obviously, is both. We have a dual personality as a people. But what effect does this have on our suitability as models outside our own borders? Our bifurcation of culture understandably makes other countries uneasy.

Nor is our political system free of significant limitations. In the United States much of what would be considered bribery or blackmail (extortion) in other advanced democracies (in Europe and Japan) is legal. This is not a question simply of violations of the law, which occur to a greater or lesser degree in every democracy. Instead, America actually makes bribery and extortion legal. Briefly, American law now permits politicians to raise money from contributors in return for access to legislation, the so-called Pay to Play system. It also permits legislators to threaten reprisals in regulations against companies and individuals who refuse to send them the lobbyists they select (the so-called K Street strategy).[6]

Whether being legal keeps these actions from being bribery or extortion is merely a question of terminology – they're unethical and ought to be illegal. Because they are not illegal in America, there's a very good question as to how valid a model American democracy is for others.

The American system is adversarial and very weak in problem solving; lacking an effective mechanism for problem solving, it leaves many difficulties unresolved and festering for decades, sometimes leading to great tragedies, as in the flooding in New Orleans that accompanied a forecasted hurricane.[7]

People who wish to excuse American democracy these serious shortcomings refer with acceptance to the "messiness" of our political system – as if it were a positive characteristic that what is unethical is legal – and accuse those who condemn bribery and extortion in politics of being elitist. This isn't convincing at all. In the past America has sometimes had a cleaner political process – there are few eras in which it has had a dirtier one than today – and it was still American democracy. It isn't necessary to be as corrupt as we've become to be a functioning democracy.

Furthermore, our economic system has recently weakened itself as a model for others. At the center of today's American economy is a gaping hole (one of the imperfections in our economy which we identified previously as limiting the performance of the American economy below what it could be), a sort of economic ground zero, but this time completely self-inflicted – where only a few years ago stood an apparently great edifice – the temple of financial capitalism. What is often trumpeted to the world as the model for long-term growth and economic power, and has sometimes been emulated, especially in Europe via venture firms, new equity markets (especially for a brief period in Germany's Neue Market), startups and IPOs, hostile takeovers (part of a market for corporate control), a culture of investing (with millions buying equities for the first time), opening of financial markets to banks and brokerages from abroad with European banks buying American investment banks and getting American style pay for bankers and CEOs, stock options, American style imperial corporate chief executives in large corporations – all this, has now been revealed to have been largely a sham – American corporate financial performance driven by fraud, CEOs grossly overpaid for their performance, and often paid when performance was terrible, the great

stock market boom having collapsed amid prosecutions and recrimina-
tions, banks and accounting firms revealed as willing accomplices to fraud –
the American economic model looking as corrupt as third world crony
capitalism; other countries can't adopt it anyway because of differences in
national economic cultures; and even if every other nation adopted it, peace
and harmony wouldn't necessarily result. Our potential opponents would
just be strengthened a bit by having it. To promote American-style democracy and free enterprise as a route to prosperity and peace is to fall into the
trap of wishful thinking.

Finally, the trend in the social health of America has not been favorable,
so other countries might understandably be concerned about adopting our
system. For example, there is evidence of substantial social disintegration in
America:

- Since 1970, scholastic aptitude and performance scores down[8]
- Child abuse up substantially (U.S. Dept. of Health and Human Services)
- Criminal arrest of teens (14–17) up 150 percent (Bureau of Census)
- Teen suicide up 450 percent (National Center for Health Statistics)
- Illegal drug use among teenagers up substantially (National Institute on
  Drug Abuse)
- Divorce up 350 percent (Bureau of Census)
- Births to unmarried teenagers up 500 percent (Census bureau)
- Some 30 percent of American children are now born out of wedlock;
  roughly every fifth child lives in a single-parent home; and some 30 percent
  of children live in homes accepting at least one form of means-tested
  public assistance (welfare).[9]
- There is much more inequality and less redistribution in the United States
  than in most other developed nations.[10]

Reflecting on all this, an English critic of America wrote: "America is less
of a coherent and therefore exportable social and political model . . . than
it . . . suggests. The USA . . . remains an unending process, distorted by big
money and public emotion, a system tinkering with institutions . . . to make
them fit realities unforeseen. . . . It simply does not lend itself to copying."[11]
John Maynard Keynes, patron saint of modern political economics ("We're
all Keynesians now," said Herbert Stein, President Nixon's chief economist),
had this to say in summarizing modern capitalism: "Modern capitalism
is absolutely irreligious, without internal union, without much public
spirit . . . a mere congeries of possessors and pursuers [of wealth]."[12] This
didn't mean to Keynes there isn't much to admire in the Western world.
Keynes spoke of "The English tradition of humane science" – to which

perhaps we Americans can legitimately claim to stand heir, to at least some considerable degree – ". . . an extraordinary continuity of feeling . . . a tradition marked by a love of truth . . . and by an immense disinterestedness and public spirit."[13] Thus, for Keynes there was good and bad in our system; and it should not surprise any of us if others, and perhaps ourselves included, come to a similar conclusion.

BEYOND SELF-AFFIRMING SLOGANEERING

Americans should move beyond self-affirming slogans such as democracy for all to geopolitical sophistication. It follows that we must give up promoting the American system of political economy and democracy uncritically. For those interested, we should provide assistance in copying elements of our system that might work for them. There is evidence that there is considerable interest in our system, so that other countries may seek assistance from us in transplanting aspects of our political and economic systems.[14]

There is a worldwide desire for the better elements of the American system – those ideals to which we aspire even as we so often fall short of them. Recent public opinion polls outside the United States show that for all their misgivings about the United States, most nations support the democratic, free-market model that America advocates, and even embrace the tenets of globalization. Most Muslim populations expressed the view that Western-style democracy could work in their countries. (A survey conducted by the Pew Institute, called "Views of a Changing World," was released by Madeleine K. Albright, the former secretary of state who is chairwoman of the global project in the summer of 2003. The polling was done by telephone and face-to-face interviews in late April and May. In most countries, the survey involved national population samples, but others were done only in urban areas. The nonpartisan center surveyed thirty-eight thousand people in forty-four nations during the summer and fall of 2002, and followed up with interviews of sixteen thousand people in twenty nations and in the areas administered by the Palestinian Authority.)

Whatever support there is abroad for the American system, we should never attempt to impose it by force, as we are arguably doing in Iraq and Afghanistan today. Our system works well for us; but it may not work as well for others.

What does America stand for at the opening of the twenty-first century? President Bush says it stands for freedom. Yet, how is that freedom used in our country? In the words of one writer for an influential American magazine, the ideal seems to be that "life bubbled along as one big wonderful party."[15] To many people in the world, and some in America, that doesn't seem quite enough meaning for life. But it's an image portrayed to the world by our mass consumption popular culture. Perhaps it's an aspiration of most human beings – for a life of luxury and diversion, of pleasure and self-indulgence – but there are always in the world some people who because of their circumstances or their convictions, reject such a view of life. Certainly, the Puritan founders of New England would have rejected it out of hand; and had they not, the North American continent would never have become home to a nation like the United States. There were, of course, among the early English visitors to North America people who partied incessantly, including native Americans in their revels. They were unsuccessful in building enduring settlements. But their approach to life finds much more support in America today than it did among the early settlers and later pioneers of our country.

Some of our culture is strongly positive and is affirmed by large majorities of Americans today, including individual freedom, broad toleration, and racial, ethnic, and gender diversity. But other elements of our culture are highly controversial among us. We project different images abroad, and they are incompatible with each other. Interestingly, so confused are others about us, that they condemn both sides of our national personality, although, since they are opposites, one would think that other people would opt for one and reject the other.

In a time in which almost all American political discussants present themselves first and foremost as moral idealists (the politics of values, it is called), espousing principles that are supposedly above reproach, and coloring their analysis and prescriptions accordingly, we reject their approach (Pietism of the right and left) as the foundation stone of contemporary economic and security policy. Although we think idealistic values very important, we do not see sermonizing about them or trying to press them on other countries as the central element of America's defense policy. Instead, it appears that the two sides in America wish to project our internal politics onto the world stage, as if these were the key issues for the 95 percent of humanity who are not Americans. There is evidence of this all around us, not the least in books of nonfiction by Americans as they try to understand and explain to other Americans the behavior of others in the world. For example, Shana Penn has written an important book about the women who, when their men were imprisoned by the Communist authorities, led Poland to liberation in the 1980s. Yet in the book she confesses that her Polish subjects had very different understandings of the role of women in the world than did she, an American, and very different aspirations.[16]

The presumption that American concerns are the most important concerns of others and that Americans possess the solutions (although Americans don't agree among ourselves what those solutions are) constitutes the arrogance of which others in the world rightfully (in this instance) accuse our country.

We underestimate the difficulty of imitating many of our institutions abroad, including democracy, the rule of law, private enterprise, and our system of higher education. These are marvelous institutions, each shared by some of the countries of the world, but no country has them all in the size and effectiveness that we do, and they are very difficult to transplant.

Many Americans must perceive the danger that our overreach creates for us, but most turn a blind eye to it. Many see the danger, don't have a solution, but are irrationally confident that a solution will emerge. It is a form of suspended disbelief.

DEMOCRACY AS THE WELLSPRING OF PEACE

There are certain significant propositions that wishful thinking urges upon us. The most important of these is the notion of democratic peace – that democracies rarely fight one another – and so that the spread of democracy in the world will make the world more peaceful. Both the Clinton and Bush administrations voice this view as justification for trying to build democracy abroad.

"The world has a clear interest in the spread of democratic values," President George W. Bush told Americans, "because stable and free nations do not breed the ideologies of murder. They encourage the peaceful pursuit of a better life."[17]

Yet, like almost every other element of wishful thinking, this conviction is wrong. Scholars studying it have found scores of examples in history of democracies having begun wars. The United States itself is said to be the greatest attacker of other democracies – between 1898 and 1928 the United States made some thirty military interventions in Latin America against democracies of various sorts.

Conversely, it is likely that American power in the past century has prevented conflicts among democracies.[18] It is after all, say many commentators, a Pax Americana – that is, a peace in the world kept by the Americans.

None of this is to say that democracy isn't a goal in itself, and that we shouldn't support those abroad who seek it; but it is to say that promoting democracy abroad needn't be a key part of our defense strategy, and shouldn't be relied on as an alternative to defending ourselves militarily.

Many Americans seem to have a shallow notion of democracy that is part of the wishful thinking of our public culture. Political insiders are content with democracy as a multiparty system with balloting, and care much less about popular sovereignty in a more significant sense. Democracy itself sometimes seems so corrupt and usually so weak in the international setting that it is at risk of drastic failure. Churchill saw corruption as the Achilles heel of democracy because it provides weak leadership and poor policy making. America struggles against political corruption continually, so Churchill's observation seems on target.

Most Europeans can't stand observations like this, nor can most Americans. Democracy is glorious in theory, and often inept and impotent in practice, again with the current exception of the United States. In Europe, people might say, we could govern ourselves well enough by democracy like the Swiss if only we were left alone like they have been by outside powers. But, of course, they won't be left alone without the protection of a superpower – and the United States provides that protection.

The Western European democracies were crushed by dictatorships in the World War II period, and would have disappeared, except for the United States, which is the big exception to how democracies ordinarily function. The United States is the world's single militant democracy, and it protects all the others. But the United States would have likely prevailed in the great conflicts of the twentieth century even if it weren't a democracy, so the success of the United States in the international setting isn't necessarily an endorsement for democracy. Today, democracies are generally corrupt, confused, impotent and survive only because of U.S. protection.

A further danger is that democracy in the context of the poor and discontented creates ethnic hatred and global instability, and foreign aid doesn't yield development but corruption.[19] In a recent example, President Musharraf of Pakistan permitted real elections in the fall of 2002, which resulted in a huge advance for the "Islamist parties – obscurantist, intolerant and misogynist to the core, and openly preaching violence and hate."[20] Democracy is very imperfect and cannot be perfected in much of the world, (including Iraq) where nations have multiple and bitter ethnic and religious divisions. Kenneth Arrow, an American economist, demonstrated that logically a democratic society can't successfully accommodate the conflicting needs of all different kinds of people.

The first great embarrassment to the administration and the Europeans in the policy of aggressive democratization occurred in the Palestinian elections of January 2006, when a terrorist organization captured a majority of seats in the Palestinian parliament. Immediately, some European commentators took the position that the West should accept a democratic outcome, however unpalatable. Presumably, they would have argued for accepting Adolf Hitler as Chancellor of Germany after the Nazi Party won the election 1932 which placed him in that position. The Bush administration was more realistic, refusing to accept the result unless Hamas altered some of its key positions. But as that was unlikely, the risk that freely conducted elections would result in an intolerable consequence was demonstrated, and the limitations of the definition of democracy as free elections was revealed. By democracy, Americans should mean more than merely freely conducted elections – we should mean a liberal society that includes free elections.

We must therefore be careful in what we wish for other nations. We might get what we wish for, only to have it turn out very differently than we expected.

The Danger of American Overreach

There is now a significant danger of American overreach due to illusions on both sides of America's political aisle. Conservatives encourage us to build free enterprise abroad; liberals point to building democracy; the conservatives don't mind democracy that much – they say they support it; the liberals don't mind free enterprise that much – they say they support it; the result is a political consensus in which America overreaches.

Because of this confluence of ambitions between right and left our country risks falling into the danger of imperial arrogance. Our economic power translates into military power that we then transfer into cultural arrogance. It seems to many that we now exhibit the arrogance of a nineteenth-century colonial power – the notion that our culture is best and will replace others. It was exactly this chain of causality – from economic power to military power – that created the imperialistic arrogance of the nineteenth century and we have to be careful not to go where the European imperialists went: the dynamic was that economic expansion in northern Europe created military power that permitted domination of others, and power and domination generated a feeling of cultural superiority that was an arrogance still resented a half century after the end of the empires.

Wishful thinking contributes to arrogance. It has a corollary in the notion of final victory for our way of doing things – of a final peace with harmony in the world. This Utopian vision becomes a goal of our nation's leaders – for whom security and self-defense seems no longer enough. The vision of the wishful thinkers seems to be replacing the Puritans' "light on a hill" vision, in which the United States was a beacon, an example for the rest of the world. Today's vision is more ambitious: The United States is no longer simply an example, but it now seeks to impose its system and values on other countries via force or financial pressure. In the end, the vision is of a world in which all nations are brought into our house, not as elements of an empire, but as partners in a single system. The United States thus becomes a sort of secular but still missionary nation. Like our religious forebears we remain missionaries, but our message has changed from one of religion to one of democracy and free enterprise.

Coupled with our continuing uneasiness about paying a price in blood and treasure for victory in such a quest, the new vision seems to be a dangerous overreach.

How sincere is the American government about its rhetoric? The question is very important both in its implications for America's actions in the world and for the degree of support which the actions receive from the American public. The Bush administration's document "The National Security Strategy of the United States," issued by the White House in September 2002, was greeted by the media with a discussion of its advocacy of preemption. But there was much more to the document than preemption alone. As we pointed out in Chapter 3, the document is actually a full foreign policy statement of the Bush administration and includes not only preemption and military dominance, but also the intent to build a world of democracies and free enterprise economies.

But what are we to make of these broad objectives set out in the document? The sections about free markets and democracy might be merely political boilerplate, or they might be an expression of overreaching ambition to remake the world.

At some trivial level, most Americans salute the principles of free markets and democracy abroad. But to embark the United States on a serious effort via military power to clear the way for remaking much of the globe in our own image is a very serious matter indeed.

Yet President Bush continually asserts just such an ambition. This is surprising because his initial justifications for our actions in Afghanistan and Iraq were exclusively defensive – to root out the terrorists who had attacked the World Trade Center and their supporters, and to be sure we were not endangered by weapons of mass destruction that might be in the hands of the Iraqi dictator. But as these defensive goals have been advanced, even to some degree achieved, the president has, in response to urgings from some of his advisors, adopted a much more ambitious set of goals.

Speaking to the National Endowment for Democracy on November 6, 2003, the President declared: "The establishment of a free Iraq at the heart of the Middle East will be a watershed event in the global democratic revolution. . . . As long as the Middle East remains a place where freedom does not flourish, it will remain a place of stagnation, resentment and violence ready for export. . . . Therefore the United States has adopted a new policy: a forward strategy of freedom in the Middle East . . ."[21]

In a visit to England in November 2003, President Bush is reported to have insisted that "our necessary global war on terror cannot be separated from the political struggle to extend human freedom."[22] In this view he finds strong support. "The war against terror," writes Bernard Lewis, "and the quest for freedom are inextricably linked, and neither can succeed without the other."[23] But, of course, the question is why are freedom and the war against terror inextricably linked? Returning to the president's comments, why can't the global war on terror be separated from the political struggle to extend human freedom? They are two very different things: The one is a matter of defending America from attack; the other is a broad political objective.

Confusing the two is a mistake. We might win the war on terror without extending freedom; and we might find that trying to extend freedom inhibits our ability to suppress terror. After all, by freedom we usually mean something like modern western democracy, and what does democracy mean? To many Americans, democracy means not merely a manner of selecting political leaders, but a whole complex set of political attitudes and freedoms. For example, asked what should American foreign policy aim for in Iraq, Roberta Combs, the head of America's Moral Majority, and a strong supporter of President Bush, answered, "In the new country, under the new democracy, why should the official religion be Muslim? I think as Iraq becomes a democracy, there are going to be a lot of churches springing up."[24]

In the Islamic world, where religion and politics are much differently connected than in America today, such an expectation is a major change. Should America be trying to impose it by force of arms? We began with an effort to defend ourselves, and end up trying to remake the culture and politics of Iraq. Why? Because of wishful thinking that if we can make Iraq like us, conflict will disappear. It is to this notion, deeply imbedded in us, that President Bush is appealing when he transforms our mission in Iraq from defending America to building an Iraq in our own image.

According to Kenneth Pollack, a former CIA and National Security Council official, "The Middle East is in a great deal of difficulty right now, after Saddam Hussein and the U.S. invasion of Iraq. Not only do we have amess in Iraq to fix, but there is an even bigger mess out there in the larger Middle East. We're going to need to deal with that mess, too, if we are going to be able to defend our interests and our own security from the threats we now face in the region. But the situation in Iraq is entirely salvageable. . . . If we can build on the positive developments, if we can get to a position where maybe five, ten or fifteen years down the road Iraq is a stable pluralist state, then you will start to see a lot of changes in the region."[25] In fact, reports about the Syria Accountability and Lebanon Sovereignty Act, passed by our Congress and signed into law by President Bush in December 2003, indicate that it also envisions new democratic regimes in those countries.

In appearing to adopt such ambitions – to transform Iraqi society completely into a copy of our own, and then to expect a transformed Iraq to become a beacon for a similar transformation of the entire Middle East – in his own rhetoric President Bush has created for himself a dilemma. Either he is miscalculating if he thinks his expansive rhetoric is reassuring to people, and so he's undermining support for his defense position; or he's overreaching in his approach to America's role in the world. If he is not serious about his rhetoric regarding building democracy outside America, and so is concealing his real motives for the actions we're taking in the Middle East, then he is seriously overestimating the credulity of Americans, and underestimating the perceptiveness of the rank and file, and he is therefore providing much opportunity to his critics for poking fun at the Administration.

The primary task of the American government is forestalling thousands of American casualties in further terrorist attacks, insurrections that destabilize the Middle East and spark conflict along the periphery of the crescent of fire, or cause millions of American casualties in a nuclear exchange with a great power. Its task is not the achievement of a Utopian aim – such as spreading freedom and democracy around the world in the mistaken belief that remaking others in our image will secure a lasting peace.

CHAPTER 15: KEY POINTS

1. As promising as an American-style system based on market-based free enterprise economics might seem, it does not transfer well to many other countries.
2. In some respects, the American system is too good to transfer.
3. In other respects, the American system isn't good enough to transfer.
4. Democracy is not one thing but a very complicated set of activities (including elections, representative government, an independent judiciary, a capacity to periodically stave off challenges that might lead to

dictatorships), and as such has many different manifestations in the world. Not all are likely to insure peace.

5. In consequence of the above, it is a dangerous form of overreach for the United States to try to spread democracy all over the world. We should assist countries and leaders that ask our assistance, and we should encourage democratic reforms wherever possible; but we should not make this a cornerstone of our foreign policy.

SIXTEEN

The Transatlantic Trap

America has had new responsibilities thrust on it in the world and is trying to determine how best to cope with them. Europe sponsors a vision of world peace brought about by cooperation among nations to remove deprivation and oppression from the world. The notion is that the West can sponsor its values to the rest of the world – via the United Nations, international law, and international courts of justice – and they will be adopted, and that peace and prosperity will follow.

On the surface, this idealistic multilateralism seems desirable. It asserts that we should consult with our friends abroad, particularly our European allies, in determining what to do, and then act jointly with them. If we consult, and don't agree, then presumably we should consult some more until agreement is reached. If we act without the support of other nations, and over their objections, and they criticize us, then it appears that we've been arrogant and have lost the confidence and support of our allies, and that this is reprehensible.

The problem with multilateralism, however, is that it is so easily abused. Other countries often do not share our interests or concerns. When we are attacked, they express public sympathy but attempt to use the situation for their own purposes. Recognizing American economic and military power, those who would restrain the application of American power, or who oppose American initiatives, seek to force the United States into multinational forums where we are most ineffective and therefore weakest. Like an octopus, multilateralism has many arms that threaten to fasten on to us and immobilize us.

There is a difference between multilateralism in the international political arena, which is sponsored by the Western Europeans and has become a trap for us, and what our Department of Defense calls security cooperation – interaction with foreign defense establishments that allow us bases and support outside the United States. Security cooperation is important to us.

We described ourselves in the first chapter of this book as long-term economic realists. We are also George Washington–type Americans, before the advent of partisan party politics in our country. Like Washington, we have a profound distrust of European motivations. "Our detached and distant situation invites and enables us to pursue a different course . . . ," Washington told our nation in his farewell address. "Why forgo the advantages of so peculiar a situation? . . ." he asked. "Why, by intertwining our destiny with that of any part of Europe, estrange our peace and prosperity in the toils of European ambition, rivalry, interest, humor or caprice?"[1] The rhetorical questions are as compelling today as when Washington posed them – why indeed?

THE MULTILATERALIST VISION

Wishing has spread the belief that there is no longer any compelling need for nuclear weapons or strategies which involve them because the world is entering a more enlightened age in which conflicts are resolved with goodwill in an environment of universal prosperity. It is said that global free enterprise is already rendering nuclear weapons, nuclear deterrence, and perhaps even war itself obsolete. Consider the views of William Wallace, Professor of International Relations at the London School of Economics and member of the British House of Lords, who argues that patient reason and bountiful aid to the underdeveloped world will usher in an age of universal social democracy, in which the world will be like Europe, relatively prosperous and nonaggressive.[2]

Europe has had a strong pacifist component to public opinion since the massive slaughter and subsequent economic and social disruption accompanying the two world wars. After 1945, Europe rejected balance-of-power politics and instead embraced reconciliation, multilateral cooperation and integration as the principal means to safeguard peace that followed the world's most devastating conflict. Over time, Europe came to see this experience as a model of international behavior for others to follow. "The transmission of the European miracle to the rest of the world has become Europe's new mission," writes Robert Kagan. In addition, Europe is now divided and militarily weak, compared to the United States, and this situation is said to explain why Europe and America now so often see the world very differently.

"Strong powers naturally view the world differently than weaker powers. They measure risks and threats differently, they define security differently, and they have different levels of tolerance for insecurity," explains Robert Kagan.[3]

Rather than the threat of force and unilateralism, Europe believes conflicts are best resolved through peaceful diplomacy and multilateral engagement. Not war, but international opinion and UN inspections would have secured Iraq's disarmament, argue the Europeans. "Thus we arrive at what may be the most important reason for the divergence in views between Europe and the United States," Kagan writes. "America's power and its willingness to exercise that power – unilaterally if necessary – constitute a threat to Europe's new sense of mission."

We share with the Europeans what Samuel Huntington has aptly labeled "the idea of the west." It's a set of convictions that include the values of individualism, rationality (enlightened reason), economic liberty, democracy, social justice, tolerance, diversity, conflict avoidance, and an assumption that rational self-interest will eventually impel rivals to amicably resolve their conflicts. This is how many of us believe the world is, or at least how it should be, and if it isn't yet, we believe it's trending in that direction.

Multilateralists urge on America:

- nonintervention abroad except with multinational approval;
- greatly increased foreign aid;
- response with extreme reticence when insulted or attacked;
- building world government on the framework of the United Nations;
- multilateral consultation and consensus before action;
- free trade and free enterprise; and
- careful regulation of our economy in pursuit of social welfare at home.

Before the fall of the Soviet Union, the general European prescription included state ownership (that is, socialism) and economic planning. These elements have now been dropped in favor of the market as a mechanism of solving domestic and international economic woes, and democratic political governance, including on an international level via the United Nations, to provide peaceful international relations, especially by restraining the United States from acting against those who attacked us.

During the 2004 presidential campaign, Senator Kerry suggested that United States policy should meet a "global test" (articulated in the first presidential debate, September 30, 2004, by Senator John Kerry), apparently a test of acceptability to our allies or the United Nations.

Such a global test is inappropriate for several reasons. Other countries who would administer the test of our proposed policies have:

- different agendas, or
- hidden agendas (such as a role in the corrupt oil for food program sponsored by the UN for Iraq); and
- some of the key countries to whom we would turn for a test of our policies are increasingly our rivals, especially China and Russia and those in the Crescent of Fire and would respond in ways that are not to our advantage.

In consequence, we cannot expect a global test of our proposed policies by disinterested, supportive, and fair-minded foreign nations.

The European desire to bind America to European aspirations is evident in many ways. For example, in 2004 as our national elections approached, some Europeans talk about their supposed right to take part. ". . . [A]s long as the United States remains the worlds sole superpower, Americans business is anybody's business," reported Frances Stead Sellers in the *Washington Post*. Europeans propose ". . . creating a democratic global forum of elected representatives, which would offer people beyond America's borders a direct way to influence world affairs."[4]

Many thoughtful Americans support similar proposals. For example, Richard Haass calls for "effective multilateralism" in which the United States accepts limits imposed by other nations on its own actions and seeks consensus on the urgent issues of the day. Only this, he argues, can ensure the continued advance of peace and prosperity.[5]

Each of these suggestions – multilateralism, a global test, permitting some form of noncitizen participation in our elections – embodies a desire to influence American decision making, but not with American interests in mind (except to the extent that some might argue that American interests are best realized through satisfying the interests of others). Underneath each proposal is the harmonist illusion – that other nations will constrain our country for the purpose of peace and prosperity, rather than in pursuit of their own hidden agendas.

FORECASTS OF A DECLINING AMERICA

The multilateralist position is continually reinforced by pundits announcing the imminent decline of the American colossus and the emergence of a world-leading Europe. The implication of their arguments is that America must get aboard the multilateralist train or it will otherwise be left behind.

Almost a decade ago, Lester Thurow announced that the century beginning in 2000 would be the "Century of Europe." Charles Kupchan forecast a "decline of America [that will] play itself out over this decade and the next." This is because, in his view, "the United States will lose interest in playing the role of global protector of last resort," and he sees the European Union as the new global superpower.[6]

Warren Zimmerman refers to the erosion of American influence in the world, saying that "the imperial America inaugurated in 1898 . . . lasted almost exactly a century," during which time America became a "mature great power" whose influence is now in decline. He attributes our decline to weakness of the presidency vis-à-vis Congress; to limitations of our military power; to a weakening of our power, will and leadership; and finally to a backlash against us in the world.[7]

We are told that we cannot avoid being bound to the European view of the world's future. "The European way of doing will have become the world's," Mark Leonard wrote, and the United States will "inevitably be sucked into the process of integration."[8]

All this supports the European position that America is not strong enough to protect itself unilaterally; that it must nestle together with other countries in multinational forums if anything of significance, including keeping the peace, is to be done successfully in the world.

COLLECTIVE SECURITY DOESN'T WORK

At the center of the multilateralist recommendation is the concept of collective security – that a group of nations working together can forestall threats. Unfortunately, collective security doesn't work. It has an inherent flaw that is continually evidenced – virtually daily as our country attempts to deal via the United Nations with crises in the Middle East and in East Asia (including the Iraqi wars, Iranian and North Korean nuclear ambitions, the tension over Taiwan, etc.). As expressed by a leading historian, "The theory of averting the danger of war by the threat of . . . large-scale collective action requires . . . countries be willing to go to war . . . over specific issues . . . of only marginal significance to them. . . . It makes every little war into a very big one."[9] Hence, nations almost never collectively confront a challenge in a timely fashion.

U.S. presidents after World War I were driven by a popular American desire to enforce world peace through the rule of law alone. Most Americans today believe that we were merely "isolationist" during the interwar era, but the history tells us more than that. We weren't just inactive – hiding from the world. Instead, this was a time when the United States applied legal methods to prevent war. Presidents Harding, Coolidge, and Hoover all worked on arms control agreements to limit naval forces in the world. This was a process that began with the 1921 Washington Conference, which assigned tonnage ratio limits to the United States, Britain, Japan, France, and Italy, whereby the United States and Britain were given the highest amount 10, Japan 7, France and Italy 3.5 each. These naval arms control agreements culminated in a July 1930 agreement to limit a class of light cruisers and other boats that could be converted to military purposes not covered by the 1921 treaty. However, none of these treaties involved Germany, the nation whose U-boats were such a menace in the World War I era.

Rather than accumulate military force to deter war, the American people and our government continued to rely on improvements in international law. It was presumed that no nation wanted war; that all peoples sought to live in peace. In January 1929, Coolidge's Secretary of State, Frank Kellogg, building on an agreement reached at a 1928 meeting in Paris with French Prime Minister Aristide Briand, signed a pact legally binding the United States to renounce the option of a military first strike. The great powers vowed to never use war again as an instrument of foreign policy:

"The High Contracting Parties solemnly declare," read the pact, "in the names of their respective peoples that they condemn recourse to war for the solution of international controversies, and renounce it, as an instrument of national policy in their relations with one another."[10]

Parties to this pledge included all of the European Great Powers involved in World War I, as well as China and Japan. It was intended to effectively eliminate war as a possibility, and, was made part of U.S. law under President Hoover, in 1929. The United States and the League of Nations tried to use legal methods to stop the subsequent Japanese aggression. One of the legal methods used was nonrecognition. The most famous example is the Stimson Doctrine, credited to Hoover's Secretary of State, Henry Stimson. In January 1932, Stimson made a simple declaration based on the principle of sovereignty: the United States refused to recognize any territorial expansion or change in national boundaries unless that expansion or change comes about through peaceful means. This position was adopted by the League of Nations later that year.

It did nothing to avoid World War II – Japan, Italy, the Soviet Union, and Germany violated the pact at will. As a result, Stimson and the U.S. position on collective security were shown to be weak and ineffective. Legal restrictions on nations alone would not deter war, nor would they safeguard national interests. After reviewing this fact of international life, Stimson admitted that the sword was mightier than international laws that melt away in the heat of battle. It was in this context that Stimson said that without an effective military component to collective security, statesmen were left with "spears of straw and swords of ice." The effort stands as a memorial to the futility of international law based on the presumption of harmonism as a barrier to overt conflict in the world.

Is the world different in any fundamental way today? Does harmonism have a greater validity? It isn't likely. During the period between World Wars I and II, Germany, Japan, Italy, and the Soviet Union gave the lie to the harmonist assumption. Today, terrorists, North Korea, China, and Russia do the same.

The impulse of harmonism, and its consequence – a belief in the effectiveness of international law – continues. We still mislead ourselves about the effectiveness of collective security. It was not the Western alliance (NATO) that deterred Soviet aggression – it was the United States, which used the Western alliance to provide it with forward bases against the USSR. It was useful to us to have land bases in Europe to deter the Soviets from fighting a conventional war there. Although the allies were useless in most other respects, we had to work with them to save them from their own pacifism and wishful thinking (the factors that virtually destroyed the Western allies – France and Britain – before World War II), or our task of confronting the Soviets would have been a bit more difficult.

We have for reasons of international politics given much more credit to our allies than is realistic. Absent the American superpower, the Western alliance would have been ineffective against the Soviets; and without the alliance, the United States would have deterred Soviet expansion as effectively (although in different ways). We think its contribution was small, but whatever the contribution of collective security during the Cold War, our need for land bases today in theaters of potential conflict is much less important, and collective security is therefore of less significance to us.

The most significant recent example of the damage that can be done by overdependence on alliances occurred during the first Gulf War. It is now recognized that President George H. W. Bush made a disastrous error in not removing Saddam Hussein from power at the end of the war. Because he was left in power, American troops had to remain in the Gulf region, contributing to the growth of radical opposition to our presence, and ultimately requiring a second Gulf War. Yet, as President George H. W. Bush explained at the time, his agreement with our coalition partners, in the first Gulf War, was that the sole purpose of the war was the liberation of Kuwait, not the overthrown of Saddam. It was because of the insistence of our allies in the coalition that the grievous mistake of leaving Saddam in power was made. We'd have been better off without the coalition; with Strategic Independence instead.

But the advice to rely on collective security continues. Criticizing the George W. Bush administration, two experts on the international situation in Asia wrote: "Multinational organizations, and to some extend formal alliances, are regarded [by the Bush administration] as structures that inhibit the full exercise of American power. While perhaps offering advantages in the pursuit of some short-term goals, America's focus on military tools and its instinctive suspicion of multilateral institutions are out of step with politics in Asia today and contrary to long-term US interests in the region." This characterization of the American approach the writers label "realist."

They then caution the American government that Asian leaders are "organizing and building new regional institutions to avoid precisely the sort of power politics that America is practicing."[11] This is naïve. No regional institution is going to bind China as its power expands, and it is unlikely that any national leader in Asia believes that it will. Regional institutions can do some good; they will not change the nature of world powers. This is actual realism, rather than the mix of militarism and unilateralism (in tactics as well as strategy) that the authors attribute to the Bush administration.

The most active of the multinationalists in the region are smaller nations that have no illusions that the Chinese or Japanese or Americans, or perhaps even the Indians, are really constrained by regional groupings (in fact, the Chinese won't let the Americans into the southeast Asian grouping) – but think that working on multilateral initiatives can at least minimize the risk of a calamity due to misunderstanding or lack of intermediaries (the smaller nations being possible intermediaries) to communicate among the great powers in a crisis. In other words, multilateral groupings might help, though they do not really alter the major features of the international landscape. With this key caveat in mind, with strategic independence as its primary approach, the American government can safely support such limited initiatives at the multinational level.

THE LIMITS TO BEING A TEAM PLAYER

America is urged to orchestrate the formation of a new world government, perhaps building on the United Nations as a framework. One eloquent commentator contrasts "The image of a world in which the United Nations acts as the supreme political arbiter [versus] an image of a world shaped by American leadership."[12]

This is a powerful vision – America would help establish the rule of law in the world abandoning its global leadership for multinational harmony. One of the reasons that multilateralism is so attractive a position to many Americans is that it reflects key elements of American public culture. Europe sponsors these illusions on the world stage, and thereby reinforces them in our public culture. The key element involved is an ideal of global harmony attained by multinational cooperation. Both harmony and cooperation are attractive ideas, and emerge out of the wishful thinking of the American populace.

Multinationalists assert that group decision making via the United Nations is morally superior to the decision making of any nation, especially the United States, on its own. There are many people of good will who find these propositions compelling – they support the United Nations and international law and the high ideals with which the propositions are advanced. It would be a good thing if our world were close to adopting these ideals and propositions broadly and honestly.

But it is not. The institutions are deeply flawed, unable to bear the weight of the responsibilities that they are said to be ready for. The supporting and enforcement elements (like the police in a community), are not in place. The governments that support the propositions and advance the ideals are hypocritical and known to be so by their peers. It is unfortunate that international law is part of this game. According to a recent study, states (not only the United States) follow international law only when it's in their own interests.[13] In this unpleasant situation, the United States should consistently describe the UN as a debating club of rivals, worthy of no particular reverence. Any support we provide the UN should be proportional to the merit of what it is doing, not to some idealized version of this unhappy institution.

Proponents of international law in European governments are especially adept at using ideals and the people who support them for their own ulterior motives.

The American people must distinguish between declared motives and real motives of the nations who urge multilateralism on us. There is a spectrum of response along which we can choose:

Rejection	Objectivity	Acceptance

We want to be in the middle; to go from rejection (denial) about motives of others to objectivity, but not to uncritical acceptance.

If instead of objectivity, the tenets of harmonism are assumed, and harmony and cooperation are believed to support unilateralism, then the combination becomes very dangerous to America. Evidence is overwhelming that the world isn't ready for a form of global government based on a rule of law emanating from the United Nations. The United Nations today is an ineffective Security Council and an Assembly that routinely passes resolutions condemning our policies in the Middle East and which has made Syria, Sudan, and Libya members of, and Qadaffi, the dictator of Libya, the head of the United Nation's Human Rights Commission. This is not an organization in which we can be comfortable or on which we can place reliance.

The Europeans press on us a requirement for the UN's approval to be necessary before any action. The Security Council is an important locus of discussion and exchange of views. In some instances, it can be a source of security cooperation. But in many other instances, the UN would be used by rivals to frustrate our actions, advance hidden agendas or even just pick our pockets in a variety of ways. Acceptance of a requirement for approval from other countries before we act to defend ourselves (which is the situation we were urged to accept in dealing with Saddam Hussein) is merely an invitation to extortion.

Pressures are exerted on the United States continually from our supposed allies in Europe to take actions that make no sense from the point of view of our own defense. For example, the editors of the *Financial Times*, voicing what is much European opinion, urge the United States not to develop space weapons, saying "the threat from ballistic missiles remains remote." They point to "stateless terrorists" as "the most pressing and foreseeable threats."[14] Yet, they surely know that building a major weapons system (including any for space) will take a decade or so, and therefore that it must be designed for distant future challenges, not the most pressing of today. So what is the ulterior motive behind this pressure on the American government to make long-range decisions about our defense based on the crisis of the moment?

Another example involves the critical issue of eliminating North Korea's nuclear missiles. In mid-September 2005, the six countries involved in talks to get North Korea to abandon its nuclear weapons programs announced a new agreement that was allegedly a major step in this direction. But immediately it became clear that there were significant limitations to the agreement. There was a long history of flawed agreements and North Korean deception about its nuclear programs. Why then did the United States (we leave aside here the same question applied to the other powers) again endorse and give credibility to a misleading assertion of progress on this important matter? The answer is that China had presented a proposal that other countries involved had found it expedient for their own purposes to applaud. The United States was then cornered into going along – giving peace a chance, one might say. Again, wishful thinking dominates, at best, or we are fooled by the hidden agendas of other powers; and no real progress is made.

Being a multilateralist team player is a trap for us in a world in which we are the primary target of terrorists and other rivals for global power. The United States cannot be both the world's dominant power, and act multilaterally. The reason is that if we are the dominant power, we will become a target (as we are now) and must defend ourselves – we cannot allow other nations to tell us that we can't defend ourselves – either directly or indirectly. This is the great fallacy of the multilateralist position. We can only act multilaterally in terms of how to defend ourselves; never in terms of whether or not to do it; and when other countries urge on us a method that seems likely to be no defense at all, we can't accept it.

They will try to do so. During the controversy that preceded the American invasion of Iraq, Germany's foreign minister had this to say, "A world order in which the superpower decides on military strikes based only on its own national interest simply cannot work."[15] He defines our attempt to defend our country from terrorist attack – an attempt made necessary by thousands of deaths at the World Trade Center – as merely pursuit of America's "own national interest" – rather as if defending ourselves was to be equated with a concern for trade advantages. He might as well have said that the superpower (America) must accept attacks without effective response, as for it to respond effectively might inconvenience or endanger other countries. Apparently the German foreign minister thought that his country and others should, in a multinational context such as the United Nations, have the right to determine whether or not the United States was free to defend itself – after all, in his view our defending ourselves was nothing more than pursuit of national interest.

In this comment of the German foreign minister was exposed the great danger for America of the multilateralist counsel – it would cede much more than we can safely do to the determination of others. They will act in their own interests, not ours, and we will be hostage to them.

These strictures pressed on America do not correspond to the reality of European behavior, neither in their own economies (where they are strong regulators and heavy taxers) nor in their foreign relations (where they are deeply engaged in many other countries). In essence, what Europe offers us is a form of duplicity that is meant to immobilize us in favor of European interests. In private, Europeans often acknowledge this, and say they expect nothing different from us.

The counsel about coming American weakness and European strength is unconvincing for reasons set out earlier in this book. For the present, Europe lacks the economic and military strength and the political cohesion necessary to suck others into its way of doing things, although it doesn't lack the self-assurance to try. But in the longer run, should the European Union become increasingly like a nation-state, building cohesion and military strength, then it may well attempt to dictate the structure of global politics, as it did during the centuries of European imperialism.

The transatlantic trap invites America to deny some of the most evident risks in the world today. Denial isn't responsible statesmanship. America must openly confront nuclear proliferation, the Crescent of Fire, the widening gap between rich and poor nations, Russia's dangerous unpredictability, and China's rapid emergence as a military challenge – not simply presume that these sources of danger are going to disappear of their own accord in the way that harmonism and convergence do.

In a situation of long-term and dramatic economic divergence between nations and regions, in which the United States is widening the gap between its economic and military strength and that of the rest of the developed world, the strategy of the weak is to show the United States that there is no politically acceptable way for it to exercise its superiority. All talk of the sanctity of international law, the legitimacy of the United Nations, and the moral imperative of multilateralism is simply the implementation of a strategy of this sort.

The European approach to world problems is generally either a stern rebuke for bad behavior or an offer of incentives for better behavior. For example, a senior human rights envoy of the European Union to Russia issued what the *Financial Times* called "a stern rebuke over judicial standards" to Russia on September 30, 2004.[16] It's hard to believe the Russians were much affected by a stern rebuke. Quite the contrary, private discussions with Russian officials indicate that this sort of thing provides the Russians with chuckler. In response, they adopt the role of the wounded innocent ("certainly we do nothing to be criticized for"), but laugh about the matter in private. How can the Europeans who do this sort of thing seriously expect anything but ridicule?

As for incentives for better behavior, the European approach is on display in the controversy over the Iranian nuclear weapons program. Initially, the Europeans offered incentives to the Iranians to cease their program; the Iranians took the incentives and continued with their program. The Europeans protested, so the Iranians demanded more incentives.[17]

Neither terrorists, insurrectionists, rogue states, the Russians, nor the Chinese will pay any attention to this sort of moral suasion at all (although they'll accept any money the Europeans offer, without abiding by the agreements, of course), so it is dangerous for us to do so.

ALL THE WAY VIA MULTILATERALISM TO A WORLD GOVERNMENT

There is now much support in Europe and on the American left for multilateral decision making – a form of world government. Is the UN a tolerable vehicle for this? The UN wasn't put together for this, but it's all we have. If we are to contemplate full multilateral decision making – that is, world government – then we must redesign the UN or design something else.

Immediately at the end of World War II, President Harry Truman spoke at the founding of the United Nations: "We all have to recognize – no matter how great our strength – that we must deny ourselves the license to do always as we please."[18] Revisiting this speech a writer for *The Economist* complained, "The contrast with the attitude of most subsequent American governments, and especially the current one [the George W. Bush Administration] could not be more stark."[19] Yet *The Economist* ignored two factors: Truman's careful qualification of his endorsement of multilateralism – "to do *always* as we please." The United States does not and should not always act as it pleases, including now. But when it is a matter of national defense, the country must act, even if it is not supported by other countries whose agendas are quite different. In addition, there is now a long history of foolishness and futility in the United Nations against which Americans must weigh our support for multilateralism.

The confusion that characterizes European thought about the United Nations continues unabated. For example, "Why ... should Russia with a GDP smaller than the Netherlands have a permanent seat (in the United Nation's Security Council) rather than Japan ... ?" ask the editors of *The Economist*, quite seriously.[20] The answer is very simple – Russia is a fully armed nuclear power covering almost one-seventh of the landmass of the globe and should therefore be on the Security Council. The size of GDP is immaterial when the question is Russian participation in world affairs. The major point is that asking the question reveals both European myopia (they just ignore the nuclear power of Russia) and the European confusion of consumer economics with military power – they are not always synonymous. The United Nations Security Council is about war and peace, it shouldn't be another world trade organization. The confusion is of consumer economies with military strength, and of the present with the future (Russia is about to fully modernize its forces while Japan has not yet chosen its course in the future).

If we retain the United Nations in a significant role, then we must shift our position to one of multilateralism generally, for otherwise we are asserting both independence and dependence and there are certain to be different expectations of us by our allies, and when we disappoint them, there is certain to be a major controversy with our allies and more harm than would otherwise be done. Disappointed expectations embitter people and create tension and conflict. They are a sure trap to fall into, and are the result of our not having sufficiently adjusted our policy for the end of the Cold War.

This is the core of what's happening now over Iraq. The argument is being made that it was the attitude of the American government – allegedly unilateralist and arrogant – that undercut and made ineffective the efforts of the United Nations to disarm Iraq. "... the entire process of trying to avert a war through inspections and negotiations was undercut by the military buildup," wrote Richard C. Holbrooke, American ambassador to the United Nations in the Clinton Administration, "that the United States said was necessary to force Iraq to comply – a buildup that some officials later argued could not be reversed without the United States losing face. 'In retrospect, the military buildup and the diplomacy were out of sync with each other.' ... 'The policies were executed in a provocative way that alienated our friends.'"[21]

As beguiling on the surface as multilateralism is the notion of international law. "In a lawless society the only natural right is superior might."[22] We can do better than that, goes the argument. Rather than force as an arbiter of controversy, there would instead by a rule of law. That's how a modern democracy works, and so should the world. It's a compelling vision.

The core of the matter is that other nations have learned how to use the United Nations to handcuff the United States procedurally and moralistically. They claim to do this in support of justice and other such verities. More often, they do it in support of their own interests.[23] Multilateralism and international law used this way are a sham, and hold that we should be bound to them is to believe that we should sacrifice our security for an idealist fiction.

It is a mistaken notion that diplomacy is a win-win process; and that overt conflict is only win-lose. This confuses characteristics of means with characteristics of results. Diplomacy is often lose-lose when needed actions do not occur (as today, for example, in the continued diplomatic ineffectiveness in stopping nuclear proliferation) and overt conflict can be win-win when an evil is eradicated. The American Civil War, for example, was an overt conflict that put an end to a great evil, slavery, which the southern states couldn't end for themselves; in this way it was win-win. The same is true of World War II, which put an end to Nazism, which ultimately benefited both Germany and its enemies.

Similarly, it's an illusion to think that diplomacy is an expression of harmony; it often is not; it's frequently a form which conflict takes. Just as individuals can be in conflict who are not actually at blows, so nations are sometimes in conflict even when there is not war between them. Diplomacy can, when it is successful, preserve the peace; but a war can reestablish peace. They are both, in that sense, a road to peace. The advantage of diplomacy is that it is not war, and can sometimes avoid war. But the absence of war is not the absence of conflict; and in diplomacy conflict often simmers until war breaks out.

Hence, it's also an illusion to think that diplomacy is somehow different than conflict; it's different from war, but it's often simply another form of rivalry between nations. It's a mistake, therefore, to think that diplomacy provides win-win solutions, while war is always a win-lose. More often, both diplomacy and war are lose-lose for the parties engaged. Diplomacy can be a means of problem solving with an attempt to reach win-win solutions, but it need not be. And war can sometimes create an environment in which problem-solving takes over. But it is an error to associate diplomacy with problem-solving in all cases – it isn't that.

"Politics is war by other means," wrote Will and Ariel Durant in their study of world history.[24] The politics of the United Nations is no different.

MULTILATERALISM AS AN END

For some, multilateralism has become an end in itself – that is, a device, a method, has become an objective itself.

Some seem to celebrate multilateralism explicitly for failing to serve Americas interests. In this concept, multilateralism is a device by which America champions principles and norms that serve to bind itself, and this seems to them only fair, because, in this view, the United States would play by the rules it asked others to accept. This, it seems, is fair, and so the rules of the game become as important as the game itself, of which sight is lost. The game is the national security of the United States, reacting at this moment to the most serious loss of life from a foreign attack on its own soil in more than one hundred and fifty years. But of this sight has been lost. "Cooperation was contingent on the United States itself playing by the rules," wrote Lisa Martin implying that France didn't cooperate with us in suppressing terror because we didn't play by the rules of multilateralism.[25]

This is a complete reversal of the actual causality. Rather, we rejected multilateralism because France didn't cooperate in combating terror, but pursued private and hidden agendas instead.

The error is to look no deeper than methods in determining the objective of our policy. Multilateralism, like unilateralism, is only a device to other ends a device that may or may not be valuable depending on what it can accomplish to the larger ends. What does multilateralism really mean in today's environment? It means not acting without the imprimatur of the United Nations – which is only obtained by the support of China, Russia, and France. It means subordinating our own interests to theirs. Multinationalists support this. In making multilateralism an objective, its supporters risk straying into a shadowy zone in which they have become a fifth column for Americas rivals serving the interests of our rivals while pretending that they are serving America.

Multinationalists seem to glory in the notion that America should now make sacrifices to return to multilateralism. It will take time and resources to rebuild the U.S. reputation for multilateralism. It will require making concessions and accepting compromises on a wide range of issues. Thus, to get others to support us, we must give them what they want at cost to ourselves. The baby of American interests is here thrown to the multilateralist wolves, our interests are sacrificed to other nations, some of which are often hostile, and some of which are disguised as our allies, but who are allies only on a situational basis and are as often our rivals and antagonists as our friends and supporters.

"To argue that the United States should always work through the UN is to argue that China, Russia, or France should have a veto over our use of military force," wrote Stanley Michalak. "Neither the Clinton administration nor any previous administration accepted that position. Nor will any administration in the future, or any other member of the Security Council, do so. Were Taiwan to declare its independence, the last thing China would do is ask UN Security Council for permission to use military force."[26]

Amitai Etzioni noted that "Many champions of the United Nations . . . treat the organization as if it were already some kind of democratic world government. Hence, they attribute enormous importance to whether the United Nations approves of a course of action. . . . They confuse what the United Nations one day can be with the way it is . . ."[27] We are less hopeful. There is no reason to believe that the United Nations can be effectively reformed, although proposals to do so will remain part of the diplomatic game played by the nations. Nor can the United Nations be disbanded, the political consequences are too great, and there is sometimes a use for an international forum. It is a partisan forum of mostly nondemocratic societies (whatever label they wear), pursuing an agenda largely at odds with our own, while promoting a humanitarian image for cover. It should not be invested with dignity by our government, but can be used as an instrument of convenience if and when opportunity arises.

UNILATERAL PARTIAL DISARMAMENT

Wishful thinking has reached deeply into the American mentality and may in fact bring about a great divide in American politics.

For those Americans who wish to abandon assertive defense in favor of multilateralism, the force of logic will propel them to advocacy of substantial disarmament. This will be a primary alternative to Strategic Independence, impelling America toward a great choice: military dominance combined with Strategic Independence, or disarmament combined with multilateralism. Any other combinations have at their hearts a contradiction, and so will ultimately fail and be abandoned.

Briefly, to attempt Strategic Independence with disarmament is to become a reckless adventurer in the world, attempting things we cannot achieve, and challenging others we cannot defeat. To attempt multilateralism while militarily dominant is to make us a target because of our military strength, and simultaneously deprive us of an effective response by subordinating our response to the interests and concerns of others.

Multilateralism requires reduction in armaments for the same reason that military dominance requires Strategic Independence (namely, the dominant power becomes a target). Over time this intimate connection between dominance and independence, and between multilateralism and arms reduction, will become evident to everyone.

A policy in which America would largely stop being the world's sole superpower is now being proposed. We would disengage and let others police their regions of influence. The United States would reduce its commitments around the world, letting other powers maintain their own spheres of influence. "The very preponderance of American power may now make us not more secure but less secure."[28] Schwarz told an interviewer, "The tremendous power we have presents us with an opportunity to . . . somewhat disengage militarily from the world." Also, he said, "the United States has never wanted Europe to play a powerful and independent role in world politics, or

develop the kind of military capabilities it would need to police its sphere."
He argues that Europe doesn't keep house in Europe or the Middle East
because the United States doesn't want it to. Freed by the United States,
Europe would, he implies, develop the decision-making competence and
military strength to police its sphere of influence.[29]

Were we to disarm to the status of other powers, then we'd be part of
a world in which Russia, China, ourselves, France, and Britain would be
superpowers, and the rivalry of nations would return to something like that
of the early part of the twentieth century. We might be able to maintain
peace, and we might not. But we'd certainly have to make the attempt in
combination with other countries – in a frankly multilateralist way. We could
try again to be isolationist, and let others attempt to preserve the peace, as
we did early in the 1930s; and then join with others more directly, as we did
later in the 1930s, in our failed attempt to dissuade Hitler and Imperial Japan
from war. But we might not fail this time, since there is now no counterpart
for Hitler and for the Japanese militarists on the world scene.

We can be truly multilateralist, indeed, we'd have no other choice, if we
were no longer the dominant power. This used to be our tactic. After a war,
we'd disarm, signaling the world that we were no threat to any significant
power, and forcing ourselves to act with other countries (multilateralism)
or not at all (we did in fact try to work with the western European powers
in the 1930s to reduce the risk of war, despite our not being part of the
League of Nations). We could return to this approach, this time being fully
engaged in the United Nations. We could substantially reduce our military
strength and become another of the several great powers. Then we couldn't
act unilaterally and expect success, and so we'd be forced to be multilateral.
In fact, so strong is this logic – the intimate connection of multilateralism
with disarmament – that those who today advocate multilateralism will find
themselves tomorrow advocating disarmament.

The logically consistent alternative to Strategic Independence involves
three imperatives:

1. Reduce our arms to the level of other great powers – Russia, China,
   England, France – so that we won't be a target of terrorists or aggressive
   great power rivals (this occurs in part because without sole superpower
   status, we won't be pulled into all conflicts in the world);
2. Act multilaterally – so that we won't be resented; and
3. Play a constructive role in the world – so that we'll be appreciated.

Then, so goes the argument, we'll be left in peace. In a sense, the United
States would be acting as if it had become a member of the European Union,

turning to our transatlantic allies for help in deciding about major international issues, and acting without the high level of military power the United States now exercises. We would voluntarily renounce our leading role in the world, and let others play a much more significant part.

Already the Chinese have three times the troop level of our forces, and the Russians have more nuclear weapons (more than officially declared), so that, were we to disarm to the status of the European powers, then we'd become a subpower. We would be much endangered if we joined the Europeans in weakness.

The rivalry of nations would return to something like that of the early part of the twentieth century, with China and Russia in the part of Germany and Japan. We might be able to maintain peace, and we might not. But we'd certainly have to make the attempt in combination with other countries – in a frankly multilateralist way. We could try again to be isolationist, and let others try to preserve the peace, as we did early in the 1930s; and then join with others more directly, as we did later in the 1930s, in our failed attempt to dissuade Hitler and Imperial Japan from war.

The choice between these two alternatives is likely to become a critical fault line in American politics. Its fundamental cause is the collapse of the Soviet Union, which left America the world's sole superpower, and so a target and with responsibilities that it alone can shoulder. Thus, history forced us to a choice that has been very hard for our political process to recognize and articulate. But slowly it is emerging, and at this point it appears that some politicians may embrace partial disarmament and multilateralism, turning to the Europeans for support; and others, may embrace preparedness and some form of Strategic Independence.

Already the Clinton administration took a large step in the direction of partial disarmament, reducing our military forces under the banner of a peace dividend (declared at the end of the Cold War) to be directed toward domestic concerns. The result is a force structure that seems more suited to a small America than to one that is asserting dominance, and a force structure that is sorely strained by our involvement in Iraq.

Were the American public to divide closely on this issue, the unilateralist position might become untenable – that is, the country requires greater unity of purpose to be dominant than to be one of a group of powers relying very much on others. So if the controversy over which way we should go becomes too intense, then we will lack a key condition for being the world's sole superpower. Put differently, unilateralists have to win the national debate on our direction in the world by a larger margin than multilateralists if their position is to prevail. So a unilateralist presidential candidate has to make a better case; has to be more articulate and persuasive, than his or her opponent. Is this likely? The present president is having difficulty measuring up to the challenge – not of the policy he has embraced, but of persuading his countrymen and women of its correctness.

AN INDEPENDENT AMERICA

America has attempted to follow the multilateralist prescription. Secretary of State Colin Powell tried to sponsor a multilateral approach to the Iraq issue, but was undermined by the French position and by opposition of other nations partly driven by the financial incentives offered by Saddam Hussein. The core of the French position was a desire to drive a wedge between Europe and the United States in the interest of European unity. Hidden agendas of this sort make the United Nations ordinarily an impossible mechanism for multilateralism for America.

Still, we often accept a role continually being thrust on us by others, the world's policeman, making peace and keeping peace in the trouble spots of the world. We often have difficulty refusing demands to intervene in a scene of turmoil, but it must be done very sparingly, since our own interests are not directly involved, since there are usually neighboring nations who should intervene, and since too many of these involvements can stretch our forces and the attention of our leaders so much that we cannot effectively pursue our own higher priority concerns.

For us to continue to pay for military to police the world, and allow others to dictate its use, makes the United States an instrument of the interests of others. It's the worst solution for our country. And we are finding ourselves in exactly that position. Why, for example, are American troops still in Kosovo? Why doesn't the European Union take over this pacification role in its own backyard? Our continued involvement in Kosovo shows our willingness to play the international sucker.

If we chose to strengthen ourselves and avoid being victimized by others, then Strategic Independence is our best strategic posture because it leaves us in charge of the use of our own capabilities. If we disarm, then multilateralism is appropriate. But to keep armed and allow others to dictate our policy is to get the worst of both worlds – that we won't be permitted by others to defend ourselves, and yet that we make ourselves a target by our continual interventions which others will require when it's in their interests (as for example in Bosnia and Kosovo).

An America that declines the multinational fetters in which Europe wishes to bind it, need not be alone as a result. An America that adopts Strategic

Independence, and so eschews multilateralism at the highest levels of decision, will still want to act multinationally most of the time. When the United States stayed out of the League of Nations at the end of World War I, it was to preserve independence in decision but not in action. We should decide after consultation with others what it is necessary for us to do in our own defense, but we must decide independently; we should act multilaterally, via security cooperation, if at all possible. That is, we will not be bound by decisions of others, but we will act with them. The Bush administration has been ineffective in making this distinction convincing in the debate over the Second Gulf War although it has often tried to articulate it persuasively.

We could choose to be fully multinationalist, as many urge on us, ceding decision making as well as tactical cooperation to a multilateralist process. Indeed, we'd have no other choice if we were no longer the dominant power.

George Washington advised our nation to "avoid entangling alliances." The modern variant is "entangling multilateralism" including the United Nations, which is behind multiple efforts to dilute American influence but retain influence over the use of American power. For example, the United Nations now seeks to expand Security Council membership, reducing our role, a proposal that draws strong support from some American commentators.

". . . [T]he United States," wrote Walter Russell Mead, "has spent more time and energy resenting the inadequacies of the current international architecture than in leading the way to its renewal. . . . We should be moving . . . to promote the restructuring and reform of the United Nations. . . . We should be seeking . . . dynamic and flexible single-purpose and regional institutions. . . . Ideally, the United States should support the candidacies of Mexico, Brazil, Egypt, Nigeria, South Africa, India, Germany, Indonesia, and Japan to permanent, veto-wielding seats on the Security Council. . . . It would be harder to get a consensus . . . but when a consensus was achieved, it would be seen as a much more legitimate and binding expression of the global political will than anything the Security Council can now produce."[30]

It's hard to imagine a proposal more likely to lead to the further embarrassment of the United States in world politics and to handing more influence over the employment of American power to other nations. The Commissioner of the United Kingdom to the UN, commented on the British Broadcasting System on July 21, 2004, "It's silly to talk about the UN as if it had a separate existence from the great powers." Yet idealists of multilateralism do just that.

Further examples are as discouraging. The Internet is now run by a committee of private individuals under the oversight of the U.S. Department of Commerce. The UN wants to displace the United States running it. To other countries, according to press reports, "the central problem is that [the current system of Internet governance] is seen as an expression of American unilateralism," even though the United States contributes a disproportionate amount of the financial and technological support of the Internet.[31] Washington's position is the traditional American attitude, and remains valid today.

Many idealists seem able to ignore unpleasant realities that discredit their visions. This is a strong component of wishful thinking. The advocates of world government in the present context seem mindless of the corruption and authoritarianism that permeates the world's governance. Do such people really want a majority of countries composed of or pandering to Muslim fundamentalists to determine gender status? Do they want the Chinese communist party, as part of a coalition of countries seeking to limit American power, to impose its brand of democracy on America?

The UN was even used by Saddam Hussein to frustrate American efforts in the Middle East. "Russia, France and China-all permanent members of the U.N. Security Council-were the top three countries in which individuals, companies or entities received the lucrative vouchers to sell Iraqi oil. Hussein's goal was to provide financial incentives so that these nations would use their influence to help undermine the economic sanctions placed on Iraq after the 1991 war. At a minimum, Saddam wanted to divide the five permanent members and foment international public support of Iraq at the U.N. and throughout the world by a savvy public relations campaign and an extensive diplomatic effort."[32] Had Russia and France not protected Saddam from having to comply with the United Nations' resolutions, then multilateralism might have worked.

But in the current state of international ethics, how could it work? According to Paul Volker's investigation of the UN's corrupt oil-for-food program, Russia had the most companies involved followed by France. It can be no surprise that Russia and France were Saddam's strongest defenders on the UN Security Council.[33] Furthermore, French diplomat Jean-Bernard Merimee, once France's ambassador to the United Nations, has been accused by Volker of accepting substantial bribes from Saddam Hussein in the form of rights to barrels of oil under the Oil for Food scandal. In light of this, France's defense of the Iraqi dictator, its calls for multilateralism and consensus, take on a very different appearance. That France had a hidden agenda is clear; and so did other nations. It is the persistence of hidden agendas in multinational forums that make unrealistic proposals for greater reliance on multilateralism to curb global dangers and ills (such as repressive regimes).

Naïve idealism that denies the reality of corruption and self-dealing that permeates the United Nations is dangerous because it plays into the hands of our adversaries. There is however, a less naïve idealism which its supporters label aspirational realism which seeks modest improvements in the United Nations, while being cautious about potential pitfalls. Its proponent, Michael Glennon, contends that America's decision to unilaterally act in Iraq was precipitated by the de facto collapse of the UN, and argues that the UN can only be salvaged by radically reconstructing the institution so that its "laws" are consonant with the operative cultures of the international community. These laws may contain an aspirational element, but idealism cannot go beyond the bounds which invalidate the law through confusion. Glennon also maintains national will is more legitimate than that of the United Nations because the UN, like the EU, is no more than an expression of bureaucratic preferences while the will of nation states is based on popular will as expressed in democratic processes.[34]

When the UN has acted effectively (Korea in the 1950s, Iraq in the early 1990s), it has been by giving the job to the United States. The UN is powerless on its own. So what supporters of UN-based multilateralism mean by the rule of international law is that American power should be harnessed to the political decisions of the UN. This is all it can mean.

"To the principle that human dignity is dependent on the physical power of nations to defend themselves, these organizations [UN etc.] and their spokesmen inveterately prefer the quixotic quest for pan-acceptance of universal legal principles. In recent year, we have repeatedly seen the perverse effects of this disposition. Pitting the humanitarians against the very societies that have striven the hardest to abide by legal principles . . . it has aligned them instead with terrorists . . ."[35]

Strategic Independence requires that United States should cease trying to cogovern with others including the United Nations and the European Union. As a substitute, we should co-coordinate. The difference is that we are compelled to seek consensus in the first instance, risking the kind of obstructionism we encountered with Iraq, but can operate independently in the latter case. The advantage of co-coordination is that we can garner the benefit of working with others, without getting too entangled.

But if we are to assert the independence of our decision-making in international affairs, then we must be all the more careful about what we choose to do. And here there is great danger that we will go too far.

Focusing on security cooperation rather than multilateralism does not mean that our usual posture with respect to other nations is confrontation (as it was over the Iraqi issue). Instead, cooperation is desirable and often possible; but where there is an impasse which threatens our vital interests, we must be prepared to act unilaterally.

After cataloging the changing fortunes of American alliances with other countries, showing that disagreements have continually reoccurred, even with such staunch allies as Britain (over the Suez invasion by Britain in the 1950s and the Grenada invasion by America in the 1980s, for example), Dov Zakheim comments, "Does all this mean that 'there are no alliances, only interests?' Not at all. The distinction is a false one. All states have interests, and when their interests converge often enough they will form alliances. Rarely, if ever, will interests converge all of the time, over years and decades. When some aspect of those interests diverge, the ties that bind alliances might fray, but are unlikely to come apart if underlying commonalities remain intact."[36]

The United States should pursue adaptive, nonentangling engagement. America is not the only nation interested in restraining nuclear proliferation, suppressing nonstate terrorists, and coping with Russia and China, so that we will find allies for each of these purposes. We need not tie our hands further by a flawed form of multilateralism.

The United States should give no one (not an ally, not the United Nations) a veto over our national security. We should be prepared to extend the principle of cooperation, but within reasonable bounds. We must not be bound to rules the Europeans try to impose on us.

Our political leaders repeatedly must assert that the UN is only a consultative body, and sometimes provides services that we can oppose, or refuse to accept or fund. What it is that we really oppose is "stealth world governance" – the real problem we have with multilateralism. Multilateralism can be easily tamed by our president repudiating wishful thinking about it. Likewise the Administration should desanctify the UN by describing it as a forum for rivals to America, and doing so without without reproach or malice – simply being honest with the American people.

CHAPTER 16: KEY POINTS

1. Cooperating with other countries to build a better world is a central element of wishful thinking, and it is fraught with danger for America if it is taken too far.

2. Other countries have hidden agendas and often consider our attempts to defend our citizens from attack as nothing more than an expression of American self-interest.
3. Proposals to subordinate our Strategic Independence to a multilateralist approach are therefore very dangerous for us, and we should reject them.
4. To accept a multilateralist limitation on our freedom of action is to seriously underreach in the current international situation.

SEVENTEEN

The Middle Course

We are living in contentious era of probes and provocations without the ideological crispness of the Cold War. There will be a new wave of dominance seeking in various regions of the world, and clashes over the control of natural resources, especially oil. Changes will be required because of population and economic dynamics, and the resultant political dynamics – there are nations with population growth and limited resources; others with population decline and enormous resources; nations with growing economic and military power but little geopolitical influence, and others with declining economic and military power but substantial geopolitical influence.

The great challenge, therefore, is how to manage international relations so that peace is maintained among continual pressures toward conflict; and this requires a method of altering the status quo, because failure to do so simply causes pressures to build until there are explosions into conflict. The international system (e.g., the UN) today is designed to maintain the status quo and so engenders conflict; it is not a means of resolution.

America should follow a middle course in which we neither try to dominate the world via military supremacy and a utopian effort to spread our systems of politics and economics everywhere, nor look for safety in a falsely idealistic multilateralism. Our middle course involves Strategic Independence and modesty in reach and action.

ADJUSTING TO MAJOR CHANGES IN THE WORLD

" . . . Governments have an interest in preserving the current international order and thus play by the rules. Terrorists . . . want to overturn the existing order and . . . therefore . . . break the rules."[1]

This is a very clear statement of a fundamental danger, but it also reveals another problem whose significance the author misses – that governments tend to try at all cost to maintain the status quo, and so rigidify the world. Yet peace cannot be maintained in the form of an unchanging status quo, because the impact of different economic cultures is to drive the world apart – and adjustments will have to be made. Unless necessary changes can be made peacefully, attempts will be made to achieve them by force.

Adjustment to change is required by major economic and demographic changes that have been described previously in this book. Failure of the international order to adjust peacefully probably will yield open conflicts. But the international system is designed for stability, not change. The geo-political status quo (including membership in key international organizations, even national borders) cannot be maintained in the face of what are now enormous shifts in relative economic and demographic power, and the international system has no way to adjust to these changes. Maintaining the status quo is a likely recipe for war caused by frustrating growing powers. Hence, the United States should sponsor change.

But there is a paradox. The necessary changes are likely to strengthen the emerging powers, like China, so that we face the danger of strengthening our adversaries before a conflict and tempting them thereby to conflict via the opportunity.

So, if we don't make changes, there is an increased likelihood of conflict; and if we do, there is an increased likelihood of conflict. If this is an accurate reading of the situation, then conflict is virtually inevitable. The internal causal dynamics (the logic inherent in a situation) is very important; it dictates resultant events no matter what are the ephemeralities of day to day politics and international relations. The logic in the situation of rapid and significant global change in economics and demographics is conflict, and only how well we are able to sponsor necessary change will lessen the likelihood of conflict.

Change on a large scale inevitability creates tensions, reinforces rivalries and leads to conflict among nations. This is happening now. Our national leadership has two responsibilities:

- To be sure we prevail in any contest in which we get involved; and
- To try to limit the scope of conflict so that as little damage occurs as possible.

Our public culture senses the danger, but it presumes that deprivation is the principle cause of conflict and expects convergence to resolve the matter. But this is a primitive, naïve, and inadequate conceptualization – more important than economic deprivation as a cause of international conflict are the changes in demographics and national power which we've identified in this book.

Interestingly, the American business world confronted a similar challenge created by the necessity for change beginning almost a half century ago when international competition began to heighten in the American market. Survival of our companies required considerable change. To get flexibility, the business community weakened the power of the unions (a force for the industrial status quo), achieved employee relations stability (we have few strikes now), and then shifted its focus to managing change. Union strength was a casualty of the process, and business greed is blamed, but people know there's more to it than that – hence the continuing discussion in Europe about a need for acceptance of productivity enhancing reforms by unions. A similar shift of focus is needed in international relations. The UN may possibly be a casualty as the unions have been. That is, unions were a force for status quo in industry and as a time of major change came on, they declined; the UN is a force for status quo in the world, and as a time of major change comes on, its influence is likely to decline.

The challenge for the United States is to lead necessary changes within in a peaceful mode. To do that we have to objectively assess various situations and address them early with imaginative and realistic solutions, while confronting early on states that might try to bring about changes through war.

Unfortunately, there are people who are averse to facing reality. They aren't pathological, and when things become unbearable they master their aversions, but by delaying find themselves at a serious disadvantage. As a people, we find ourselves in that position because of our public culture; and we threaten to enmesh our president in the same neurotic unwillingness to face reality.

Winston Churchill condemned democracies of the 1920s and 1930s for lack of "persistence and conviction" leading to a great war beginning on a very unsatisfactory basis (note that the condemnation is dual – not just that lack of persistence and conviction led to war, but that it led to war from a position of weakness).[2] The American government today is subject to condemnation for a lack of objectivity caused by our public culture possibly leading to war on an equally unsatisfactory basis in the future. In both cases the basic failing is the inability to confront emerging antagonists while they are weak, thereby insuring a conflict when they become strong.

A significant peril is something that endangers the survival of our nation, like conquest by a foreign power and occupation by foreign troops; or to see much of the nation physically destroyed and millions dead; or to lose self-government and have liberty extinguished; or to cease to be our own masters; or to have our people dispossessed and condemned to penury and servitude. A significant danger is to experience what happened to Greece at the hands of Rome; or to Constantinople at the hands of the Turks. These are significant risks.

There loom on the horizon rival nations with the potential to do these things to the United States. Russia has the capability to level our cities with nuclear weapons (not just one or two cities, which is the potential of terrorists at their worst, but all of our cities); China is building the capability to do so.

FINDING A GRAND STRATEGY

If we are to be successful in changing the game in grand politics from one of predatory exploitation of the vulnerable – whether politically or militarily exposed – to one of problem solution, then we require a grand strategy.

Today our country has no grand strategy, though one – Strategic Independence – is knocking at our door. A key reason that we have no grand strategy is that we have trouble recognizing one. We have a concept of an objective, but not of a strategy to achieve it. We confuse the objective with a strategy. For example, there's been a consensus among our political parties and politicians that the United States is both an Asian and European power and is the keystone to security in those regions. Our objective is peace, and we recognize a responsibility that the American people are today willing to accept and that requires us to maintain certain levels of military force.

But this is not a strategy; at best it's that part of a strategy that involves an assessment of the context and an overall objective. It's simply a statement of the continuing desirability of global engagement for United States, but says nothing at all about its terms. It's therefore seriously deficient. By default, our grand strategy continues to have at its core Mutual Assured Destruction. It's via MAD that we hope to preserve peace among great powers; and peace among the great powers is our most important objective.

The core of the inadequacy of this notion at the level of grand strategy is its failure to recognize that the international context no longer permits the kind of stability the bipolar world of the Cold War permitted. How then are we to maintain stability – and if we can't, how should our objective change and what should be the means to accomplish it? A strategy must have both ends and means.

At the level not of objectives but of means, America also faces a deep confusion about missile defense – we have been told that it is necessary to counter a threat from rogue states; it follows that its target is not Russia or China, so it is natural to seek to limit the system which we build so that it doesn't disturb Russia and China. But then our logic adds a caveat – unless the intentions of Russia or China are hostile.

And this, of course, makes no sense. How is a limited NMD created solely to deal with rogue states in the Crescent of Fire and North Korea to counter Russian and Chinese weaponry, should either of those states prove hostile? It cannot.

This is a failure to think through the implications of the new global context of instability.

America faces a host of objective threats that need to be addressed.

Danger number 1 is Russia because it has so many nuclear weapons and is corrupt and unstable.

Danger number 2 is China because there is likely a fundamental conflict between our interests and theirs in Asia that cannot be resolved through trade and economic integration.

Danger number 3 is nuclear proliferation and other weapons of mass destruction.[3]

Danger number 4 is terrorism, states in the Crescent of Fire and nuclear proliferation – a witch's brew of substantial size all its own.

Danger number 5 is the general and increasing instability caused by the widening gap between countries that are growing rapidly and those that are stagnant or declining.

A grand strategy links our policies with respect to these diverse situations into a coherent whole. It would have long term elements that should be pursued both in the short-run and in the future. It is crucial to recognize that the means are different in the two time frames.

Diplomats and most politicians focus on the short term, and often think that the long-term is nothing more than a series of short terms. While discussing China Henry Kissinger observed, "Here the challenge to statecraft is to 'navigate' toward a workable formula . . . where Taiwan will not declare independence unless attacked, and the People's Republic will not attack unless Taiwan declares independence."

The worst approach would be to attempt a clear resolution of the matter. "An attempt to achieve 'a clear-cut solution will produce an explosion.'" [4]

This is certainly the proper formulation for short-term peace. But in this approach ends and means are hopelessly confused and the principal means has become an end in itself– that is, the principal means is dialogue – "navigation" – but to keep it going has become an end in itself. That is, the challenge for statecraft in Kissinger's formulation is to avoid overt conflict by keeping a process going. The process has become the objective as there is no other objective than to avoid a more unpleasant result, and dialogue does that.

Continuing dialogue as a principal means permits us to pursue our own interests vigorously, generating resentment and desperation and thereby sowing the seeds of war. This is where the short- and long-term means interfere with one another. If dialogue is both the short and long term means to peace, we will find that it becomes less and less effective until the underlying conditions are such that dialogue no longer works and we stumble into war. We need a more positive approach to the long term, one that lessens the underlying causes of conflict. The more positive approach is one offering partnership and gains to others and thereby avoiding war affirmatively, not merely by dialogue, even where it is accompanied by rejection of overt aggression ourselves. Without a positive approach for the long term, the danger is that other nations will conclude that they have less to lose by war than by peace.

There is also the danger that dialogue becomes the preferred means of those who are complacent. Satisfied with their position, they have no goal for which conflict can be risked; hence conflict is to be avoided as a goal in itself. This is true of the West today, but not of much of the rest of the world. The disproportionate rates of economic growth and the maldistribution of new technology in the world promote anarchistic conflicts and invite growing powers like China to dismember weak neighbors like Russia.

A way out of the conflict of short and long term, and of means and ends, is offered by having a clear grand strategy such as Strategic Independence and federalist pluralism. With a grand strategy we need only determine what means is most likely to secure our strategy's success.

American foreign policy should recognize that over the next quarter century Russia will weaken and shouldn't be treated as an equal; while over the same period China will strengthen and should be treated accordingly. U.S. policy must begin now to favor the transition of Russia to a reduced status and of China to our principal rival, and we must manage it well or the result will be disastrous. At the core of the danger lies that moment in history when Russia's leaders face up to the Chinese threat to Russia and the great issue for us is how to keep that confrontation from involving us. Because of our role in the world, we are likely not to be able to stand aside – we will be drawn in as we've been drawn into the broad political conflict that is raging in the Middle East. Hence, we must try to defuse the situation early.

What is America's overall foreign policy objective with respect to the other great powers, declining and emergent? We have to get our overall purpose right, or we will stumble into conflicts that might have been avoided.

Avoidance of a major war involving an exchange of nuclear missiles is the over-riding objective. Everything else is subordinate to this goal. Preventing terrorist attacks on our homeland is a moral imperative, but even it must be subordinate to the goal of preventing a nuclear holocaust. Advancing democracy and free enterprise capitalism are legitimate goals, but they also should be much subordinate to avoiding nuclear war.

RESPONDING TO RUSSIA

The first step toward responsible action is to acknowledge that Russia isn't what we wish it to be. Its leaders aren't enlightened rationalists and democrats committed to maximizing consumer welfare with generally competitive markets under a rule of law. Russian culture is a complex mix of authoritarianism and unprincipled opportunism that rejects a democratic rule of law. When the autocrat is strong, Russia tends to be a potent military superpower. When the autocrat is weak, as were Gorbachev and Yeltsin, opportunism comes to the fore. Asset-grabbing (so-called privatization), racketeering (the Russian "mafia") and countless other swindles become the order of the day.

Russia's leaders desire the advantages of Western industrial modernization as they did during the Soviet era, and seek the benefits of partial marketization, but still cling to the authoritarian martial police state. They embrace the rhetoric of liberalism and popular self-determination, while acting like autocrats. They know what should be done to achieve the ideas of the West, but what will they do? The answer for the last half millennium has been to profess Western populist ideals but act as apostles of the authoritarian martial police state, and this still seems the most likely course.

The West would do best by predicating its policies on the recognition that Russia is "abnormal;" recognizing that tsarist and communist Russia never experienced the Enlightenment, and that the Russian system poses extraordinary risks to itself and others.[5] It is more politically unstable, violence prone, predatory, and imperial than the West. Moscow will continue to modernize as it has in the past, but won't Westernize in our lifetime, nor will it play by U.S. and EU rules of international engagement.

American policy makers have been intent on attempting a partnership with Russia. A recent formulation of American policy by Thomas Graham of the National Security Council and Special Assistant to the President (Senior Director for Russian Affairs) illustrates the quixoticness of the West's approach. He talks of a strategic partnership that is making progress and urges further measures to strengthen it.[6]

America should reverse field. We have acted decisively before, most notably on the ABM Treaty, NATO enlargement, and the denuclearization of the non-Russian states of the former Soviet Union. We can build and employ the force needed to contain Russia, but the EU cannot because it is reluctant to construct, maintain, and use the military means essential for achieving its vision of a post-modern world order.[7] This asymmetry bodes ill. It seems that even if Washington and Brussels see Moscow for what it is, divergent aspirations and attitudes will make it difficult to devise comprehensive diplomatic strategies, even though well-informed commentators such as Zbigniew Brzezinski believe they can and must.[8]

If Russia develops a new generation of nuclear weapons and ballistic missiles while we are paying billions to remove nuclear triggers from its older generation of weapons, we should stop the assistance – it's doing us little or no good. And of course if the Russian leadership can't convincingly demonstrate that they are becoming democrats under a rule of law, we should guard against their irrationalism with Strategic Independence, secure in the knowledge that they can't compete with our overall defense capability.

We should not appease the Russian leadership. Only by being dry-eyed and resolute can we gradually influence Russia's culture and turn it in our direction. These prescriptions assume that we really want to integrate Russia into the new global order, and don't want to prey on its vulnerabilities by enticing Kremlin elites into accepting NATO expansion in return for "no-questions-asked" assistance. We appreciate that skilled Western policy makers can simultaneously play at many levels, but believe that where nuclear security is concerned we should restrain our power-seeking impulse, and lead by example.

RESPONDING TO CHINA

The lines for a confrontation over U.S. policy in East Asia are being drawn now. On one side the liberal establishment (with the EU as its ally) and the rapidly growing part of our business community (especially WalMart) who have investments in China – all ensconced in the public culture; on the other side the current administration, the military-industrial complex, the Japan and Taiwan-oriented part of the American business community (the old "China lobby) now estranged from the public culture; and not yet persuaded as to either view, the cautious electorate of the nation's midsection (the old Midwest) – which now holds the balance of political power in the country. The shift in American thinking about China started about five years ago when the Asian specialists suddenly abandoned Japan for China. Asian specialists are influential; for example, John Hopkins regularly arranges Congressional trips through its facilities in Nanjing. When the shift occurred five years ago, the leading force was the government funding institutions, not individual scholars, who were dumbfounded.

The first clear statement of one side of the conflicting views appeared in an editorial in the *New York Times* of May 6, 2005. "Japan: For years, the United States has urged Tokyo to cast off its postwar pacifism and play a larger role in regional defense. Japan's current prime minister, Junichiro Koizumi, is happy to oblige. But he has combined a more assertive military stance with an embrace of right-wing nationalism that offends and alarms the Asian nations that suffered wartime Japanese aggression and atrocities. His repeated visits to the Yasukuni Shrine in Tokyo have been particularly provocative; the shrine is where top Japanese war criminals are among the honored and the country's Asian conquests are celebrated."[9]

This position condemns a democratic ally of the United States (Japan) for alleging offending the communist authoritarian government of China. It is a consequence of the insistence that China isn't really authoritarian – that it's modernizing and liberalizing – and should be encouraged on that path by helpful consideration from us. Regarding Koizumi and the war memorial shrine, this is entirely pretextual by China because Koizumi is opposed to militarism.

The *Times* has picked up the Chinese line on Asian geopolitics completely, and doesn't hesitate to directly urge the United States to accommodate the Chinese reach for more power in the region. All this is fully consistent with and supported by the American public culture with its wishful thinking about convergence and harmonization.

Yet, in this environment, the Bush administration is strengthening American military forces in East Asia, ostensibly directed against North Korea, but actually against China (this is especially evident if one thinks of North Korea as a satellite or protectorate of China – which the administration for diplomatic reasons will not acknowledge). Faced with our public culture, the president shies away from being candid about the real situation – Chinese assertiveness, the increasing squeeze China is placing on Japan, the simultaneous Chinese peace offensive, North Korean militance as an expression of part of Chinese policy, and the U.S. military buildup in response – and instead says little, risking public confusion should hostilities break out.

Although our government seems uncertain which course to pursue, the Chinese have calculated, probably correctly, that our government will accommodate American business interests and so decide in China's favor.

With respect to China there are essentially three approaches being suggested for American policy, if one considers a policy to be composed of trade and security. One approach is to press trade and manage security conflicts as they arise. This approach is supported by the major nations in southeast Asia.

Goh Chok Tong, senior minister of Singapore, at a conference about southeast Asia, commented: "Great power competition and rivalry are facts of life.... It was the stability generated by American power that provided the foundation for East Asia's prosperity and development.... American power will provide the overarching strategic unity within which the interaction of Chinese, Indian and Japanese interests with American interests will be an increasingly important factor.... There are voices in the US that ... argue that it is better to deal with China now when it is relatively weak rather than after it has become strong. This is dangerously myopic. To treat China as an enemy will only arouse Chinese nationalism and make China an enemy. The rest of the region will not play this game. It is not in our interest, nor the world's. There need not be any fundamental conflict between the US and China."[10] He then refers to differences about trade and economic systems, saying they are not fundamental. Gone is any reference to great power competition and rivalry, which before he had labeled a fact of life. Here wishful thinking again engages us, and we are told that China will be an antagonist only if we are hostile – so that we are to blame for something which in reality we do not control, or perhaps even effect. It is unlikely that China's leaders are merely awaiting evidence of U.S. attitudes before deciding their policy. Our problem is to ferret out Chinese intentions, and to protect ourselves if they are hostile. Can we rely on Mr. Goh's assurances that Chinese intentions are benign?

Conflict isn't inevitable, no matter what China does. There is always acquiescence. In this sense Mr. Goh is right. And he has a point about the "The American Peace." But as we know from history this isn't enough; the peacemaker can always be challenged.

The United States should not be provocative. A national missile defense to achieve Strategic Independence allows us to be more tolerant of Chinese military modernization because it reduces the threat to us. If it is necessary to sugarcoat our efforts to defend ourselves for diplomatic purposes, then America can suggest, as it is doing, that missile defense is necessary against tactical and strategic ballistic missiles – with or without nuclear warheads – that might be delivered by Iran and Islamic fundamentalists. But this should only be done if Congress supports the ruse, and resists gutting the Chinese component of the program.

A second approach is to quarantine China both economically and militarily and to prepare to confront it militarily with a view toward the collapse of the current dictatorship.

A third approach is to press for continued development of trade, while pressing China to renounce military expansion by demonstrating its ineffectiveness. This is the course America should follow.[11]

The importance of the Iraqi wars to the honing of American large-scale military performance should not be underestimated, and is not lost on our potential rivals. The First Gulf War taught our military that large numbers of main battle tanks take too much supply to be able to go as far and as fast as needed; and similarly for masses of infantry. Hence, in the First Gulf War, the coalition deployed some seven hundred thousand troops. In the second a different coalition deployed only about 120,000. But the second was more successful than the first. In the first coalition forces stopped on the way to Baghdad and left Saddam Hussein in power, partly for political reasons (we'd promised the other coalition members that our only objective in the war was to liberate Kuwait and that had been achieved), but partly because we were unable to supply columns of tanks rushing on Baghdad. In the second war, columns of fewer tanks were followed closely by a massive supply column, going fast and very deep into the enemy heartland, and outrunning his ability to successfully resist. But we learned in that exercise that the supply columns are vulnerable to attack by irregular troops, and presumably our next conflict will see preparations made for better protection of supply columns.

The Iraqi war has had its effect on the opinions of others. America's demonstration of the reality of the Revolution in Military Affairs has persuaded the Chinese, probably among others, that China cannot win a conventional war against the United States outside mainland China. This is exactly the opposite of the military situation prevailing at the time of the Korean War (1950–1953) when we were unable to defeat Chinese Communist forces conventionally and General Douglas McArthur, commanding our forces, suggested that we employ nuclear weapons. President Harry Truman declined the suggestion, removed General McArthur for this recommendation and other reasons (including his perceived rudeness to the President), and Truman's successor, President Dwight Eisenhower, settled for a draw in Korea. Today, instead, Chinese military leadership acknowledges that it cannot win a conventional against the United States, and instead suggests that it should employ nuclear weapons. "If the Americans draw their missiles and position-guided ammunition on to the target zone on China's territory, I think we will have to respond with nuclear weapons," the official, Maj. Gen. Zhu Chenghu, said at an official briefing. "'War logic' dictates that a weaker power needs to use maximum efforts to defeat a stronger rival," he said, speaking in fluent English. "We have no capability to fight a conventional war against the United States," General Zhu said. "We can't win this kind of war."[12] As the Chinese move toward this tactical conclusion, it becomes more important that the United States seek to deny them the additional long-range nuclear missile capability they are now seeking.

A conflict between the two strands of this policy occurs when American companies want to sell to China items that have important defense implications – especially computer technology (both hardware and software). We should refuse very firmly on this, so long as China is seeking to build strategic missiles that can be targeted on us.

The third approach has an instinctive appeal to many Americans, but is viable only as part of an overall strategy of Strategic Independence. Otherwise, it is merely an invitation to an arms race – one that unfortunately is already beginning – as the Chinese attempt to develop nuclear missiles that can hit the entire mainland of the United States.

The same approach first adopted to the Soviet Union has an instinctive appeal to many in dealing with China, but here the situation is both worse and better. It's worse because China's authoritarian free enterprise makes it a more potent competitor than the Soviet Union. And it's better because the success of China's commercial sector could gradually modify its authoritarianism. Under these circumstances it is worth applying carrots and sticks. Commercial relations should be encouraged on a strictly equitable basis without appeasement, and U.S. commitment to its Asian allies should be resolute. We should develop and deploy the weapons needed to deter the Chinese from developing or using modernized nuclear weaponry. This approach may stabilize the region and make free enterprise more desirable to China than regional aggression.

The Bush Administration's national missile defense proposal announced in the spring of 2002 is justified as an initiative against rogue states, and in so defending the proposal the Administration has fallen into a trap of its own devising. To lend credence to its otherwise suspicious claim that missile defense is justified by rogue states, the proposal for national missile defense was coupled with a call to reduce America's nuclear arsenal to fifteen hundred ballistic missile warheads. Unfortunately, this would assure China reaches parity with America in strategic nuclear capability in short order, given the rate at which China is now building missiles. This would be a disastrous result for America, though, as we have pointed out previously, it might be welcomed by supporters of MAD, for whom a balance of nuclear force is a prerequisite to the careful calculation of risk and reward that MAD requires to have any hope of success. The Administration does not suggest that it favors strengthening China vis-à-vis America in the nuclear arms arena in order to preserve MAD, but it may well be twisting itself into exactly that position.

The proper objective for the United States is to so develop our offensive and defensive capability that we deter the Chinese from building additional strategic weapons capability – not that we deter them from using their capability once it is built. The distinction is crucial. MAD argues for our accepting the Chinese buildup of strategic missile capability and then count on mutually assured destruction to deter them from using it. Strategic Independence is a step ahead of MAD. It seeks to deter the Chinese from building additional strategic missile capability in the first place.

We are not advocating an arms race with the Chinese or the Russians, yet by its emphasis on retaining current American military superiority the Administration seems to have accepted the need to outbuild both Russia and China. If the United States adheres to the Bush Doctrine's emphasis on military superiority, then when the Russians initiate mass rearmament with fifth-generation weapons in 2006 (as stated in Putin's official defense reform program), all hell will break loose as we strive for the first time to race the Russians in earnest. Again, we repeat that the United States did not really engage in an arms race with the Soviet Union, but relied instead on a different configuration of arms and diplomacy to counter the Soviet buildup – and we should do the same again. Similarly, we should not race China in the building of nuclear missiles. What we should do, and what Strategic Independence means, is so configure our defense capability and diplomatic initiatives that we either dissuade the Russians and Chinese from build ups, or manage our way through the Russian's likely cycle (up and down in two decades ahead), and seek to defuse the Chinese threat via missile defense.

SHOULDER OR SHED: ARE WE SUITED TO BE A HYPERPOWER?

Americans have certain very good attitudes for our role as citizens of the world's only superpower, including a new maturity and willingness to bear the costs human and financial of our defense in a world in which we are both a leader and a target. Unfortunately, we have five very significant limitations:

- significant illusions about the world;
- media and politicians that exaggerate dangers and objectives;
- a temptation to overreach;
- an overreliance on our military; and
- a preference for inexperienced leaders.

According to a historian of the British Empire, the "most burning question of American politics is, should the United States seek to shed or shoulder the imperial load it has inherited?" By "imperial load" he doesn't mean a traditional, or colonial, empire. "The US will always be a reluctant ruler of other people."[13]

The answer to the question of shoulder or shed lies in the suitability of the American nation to leadership in the world. Are we are able to be the sole superpower, to act in leadership of the world? Have we the national characteristics to do it? The supreme issue is what role American can play successfully? This formulation of the issue may seem an error to some, who ask if the supreme issue isn't rather what role we wish to play? The question reflects the tendency to overreach in American thought – the notion is that if we chose to play a role, however ambitious, we can do it. This is a dangerous notion. We must decide what role we can play successfully and limit ourselves to that.

If we are not suited for the role of sole superpower, then the case for our substantial disarmament and retrenchment in the world is very much strengthened; and the case for Strategic Independence is thereby very much weakened.

The core of this issue is for people to set aside their preferences about the question of America's role in the world, and ask simply whether, if we chose to pursue Strategic Independence as a superpower, we could do so effectively?

America's primary strengths as it addresses its role as the sole superpower are:

- A new maturity in our commitment to the role;
- A willingness to bear the defense burden;
- A new realism about the world and its dangers; and
- A well-led, well-equipped military.

This book has already addressed our nation's strengths. It's time now to dispassionately assess its weaknesses.

The argument against the suitability of America to be a superpower (presuming that it wishes to do so) is that the political and social environment in America makes it impossible for us to be effective. There are four major indictments:

1. Lack consensus on national self-interest, lack of proportion in judgment, and lack of historical knowledge and perspective, so that we

are likely to make error after error, and perhaps never get to the right solution to any crisis;

2. Find it very difficult to withstand opposition to our leadership from abroad when that opposition is given hypocritical expression in moralistic terms (as occurred in the controversy preceding our invasion of Iraq);

3. Choose weak presidential leadership because of American party politics and a mass media continually exaggerating events and stirring up hysteria so that our leaders are continually forced to respond within a context of confusion and misinformation; and as a result, we

4. Have too short an attention span for the sorts of persistent challenges the international environment poses; see other places as simplified mirror images of ourselves; have a deep tendency to misjudge what we're doing abroad; are too insular; and too parochial for international success.

5. Have a propensity to conflate totems like trust, goodwill, love, pacifism, confidence building, administrative reform, education, technology, development, and gender equality collectively purveyed as "soft power" for real security.

OVERRELIANCE ON OUR MILITARY

The military has a significant role to play in a middle course for America, but we have a tendency to overrely on it which is very dangerous. Our media is now correctly pointing out the significance of the American military and the risk of our political leaders overusing it. "The United States alone has a military that can project force anywhere on the globe, fight and win," a reporter wrote. "America's technological advantage in warfare has become so large that, despite the ritual references to coalition forces, the Pentagon finds it more of a burden than a benefit to have allies in combat. (It demonstrated this by turning down offers of assistance for the fighting in Afghanistan. The Department of Defense's desire for assistance in peacekeeping is another issue entirely.)"[14]

The United States today has one clearly effective strategic advantage: its military. Presidents are most likely to be successful in international relations when they use it, and most likely to be unsuccessful when they do not. As a result they overuse the military, and misuse it. For example, the limitations of our execution of small scale military operations against terrorists employing high technology weapons are described in convincing detail in Sean Naylor's study of Operation Anaconda in Afghanistan.[15] The danger is that we are not as good at this as we think; and that as we give small scale antiterrorist operations a greater priority, we lessen our ability to counter and deter major powers that might become our enemy.[16]

Dana Priest, a reporter for the *Washington Post* studied the matter. "US leaders have been turning more and more to the military to solve problems that are often at their root political and economic," she concluded.[17] Ms. Priest argues that this is because the United States has allowed its civilian foreign service to decline and that its result is that the United States fails to lead the world toward peace. Her broad point about the overuse of the American military for inappropriate missions is well taken, but her inferences as to cause and consequence are both questionable. The cause is the paradox that non-state conflict merges military and political much more closely, so that the distinction she makes between a military approach and political approach is outdated. It follows that her preferred civilian political approach may be no more effective than a military approach. We must either enhance the political capability of our military (which we're doing), or the force-using capability of our diplomats, or find some way to team them.

But we're not yet doing that effectively. "The two major phases of the [Afghanistan] conflict have been considered independently," commentators report. "Specialists in military affairs study the campaign . . . largely ignoring . . . implications for the subsequent political turmoil. Students of Afghanistan's political situation, on the other hand, tend to ignore the significance of the way in which the military campaign itself was conducted. Neither approach by itself will do."[18]

Our limited success in Afghanistan is a result of our failure to more closely interconnect military and political efforts. Had we placed an Army division and a Marine combat unit or a little more in Afghanistan, we'd have been able to much better influence subsequent political developments there. Our failure to do this let Al Qaeda disperse much of its organization outside the country, forcing us to hunt them down all over the world. This was therefore "an opportunity missed," through our failure to consider the political consequences of how we took military action (that the Afghan government which followed our military success would be too weak to dismantle Al Qaeda), and the military consequences of our political actions (that because the Afghan government couldn't dismantle Al Qaeda, we'd have to put our military to chasing them down all over the world).[19]

This is the paradox of terrorist warfare – that its military tactics involve more politics than in the past. For example, when adversaries fire from churches, mosques, schools and hospitals, to attract fire in return and cause civilian casualties, then our troops have to have available countercrowd measures such as tear gas, power water hoses, rubber bullets, and so on, to respond without inflicting civilian casualties – the political nature of the challenge requires a political response.

The problem here is that the United States separates the two. War is the failure of diplomacy: "... the crushing weight of failed statescraft."[20]

But this is a false dichotomy between diplomacy and war. War is the extension of diplomacy; and diplomacy the extension of war; and neither is absolute or excludes the other, and it's a continuing and serious failure of American thinking in all areas that it makes this distinction so absolutely. Yet reality raises its head via inconsistency. The author cited here writes on her next page about "blending diplomacy and force ... " which is the opposite concept and the proper one.[21]

At the tactical level, the error is extended when a president announces in advance that he won't commit ground troops to an operation because this shows his limits and weakens bargaining. Clinton did this with respect to the Bosnia and Kosovo operations.

After our invasion the political situation in Afghanistan has deteriorated. "The reason is not that Afghanistan needs a Marshall Plan but that we pursued a military strategy detrimental to the development of a stable political order in that country." The error was to have used one side in a civil war to drive out Al Qaeda, that is, mostly non-Afghanistan foreign forces, and thereby get involved in the civil war, rather than to use our own forces.[22]

AN INAPPROPRIATE PUBLIC CULTURE

We in America often lose sight of proportion. A complex composed of media (both news and entertainment) and political leaders gives expression to our public culture. The media need excitement; politicians need attention. The result is that most situations are exaggerated out of all proportion. Lack of proportion leads to bad decisions and mistaken actions result.

Our public culture also requires us to envelope in a cloak of morality all our actions. It's not enough to defend ourselves, we have to try to remake the world as well. In a sense, we always create for ourselves a moral crusade. This is a key source of our confusion about our response to challenges in the world today – it emerges from the firm grip of wishful thinking in our public culture. The result is a problem of keeping balance among the threats we face – of prioritizing and allocating our attention and resources. The hype about terrorism is especially significant today because it threatens to blind us to other threats and to cause a perilous misallocation of our resources.

For example, careful authors today identify Islamic terrorism as our nation's principle enemy and subordinate all other foreign policy concerns to winning it.[23] This is the opposite of what is needed: a recognition that America faces much more dangerous risks than Islamic terrorism (namely nuclear war among great powers and nuclear proliferation to rogue or client states) and that if we overreach against terrorism, we will imperial ourselves greatly and unnecessarily.

Our public culture is unsuited for global responsibility, and we must overcome its dangers if we wish to be effective leaders in the world. At the moment we are able to dissuade many aggressors by our military strength, but our ability to do this is subject to a limitation – and has been so for the two hundred–plus years of our history as a nation. While improving technology and economic growth are strengthening our potential military deterrent – as much conventional as nuclear – our political culture is weakening our military. America is now widely viewed in the world as unwilling to take casualties, as relying too much on air power that is often ineffectual, and as lacking the political will for a drawn-out conflict. The consequence is that leaders in much of the world are increasingly tempted to conclude that in certain circumstances American power can be successfully defied.

"Once ... [Eleanor Roosevelt] debated with Winston Churchill the best way to keep peace in the ... world. By an Anglo-American alliance, said he; by improving living standards throughout the world, said she."[24]

Mr. Churchill and Mrs. Roosevelt each understood that they were giving very different answers, not necessarily incompatible with the other, but very possibly in conflict. In essence, Mr. Churchill thought that peace was kept by the action of the nations in combining against possible aggressors, whatever were living standards throughout the world, while Mrs. Roosevelt felt that without improvements in living standards in areas of deprivation, disruptions of the peace would necessarily occur, whatever the great power alliances that were made to try to preserve the peace.

This division reflects two different but deep convictions in our thinking that continue to this day. Churchill represents the strain of geopolitical realism in American political thinking; Mrs. Roosevelt represents the strain of economic and social wishful thinking.

Both notions play a strong role in American thinking. Fortunately they are not inconsistent with one another. The proper course for America is to adopt a policy of Strategic Independence as the keystone of our defense, to support economic growth and political freedom abroad, but to reject trying to rebuild the world in our own image, especially by the use of force and with the belief that in so doing we will assure our safety.

CHAPTER 17: KEY POINTS

We need a strategy to deal with the five key dangers we face:

1. Russia because it has so many nuclear weapons and is corrupt and unstable;
2. China because there is likely a fundamental conflict between our interests and theirs in Asia that cannot be resolved through trade and economic integration;
3. nuclear proliferation;
4. terrorism especially invoking the Crescent of Fire; and
5. general and increasing instability caused by the widening gap between nations that are growing fast economically and those that are stagnant or declining.

PART EIGHT

AMERICAN PRESIDENTIAL LEADERSHIP

W hy does America do international relations so clumsily, and why are we so unpredictable? When other countries expect us to act as a dominant power, we oftentimes don't – confusing them and risking conflict. In part the answer is that our presidents are captured by our public culture, and so fail to make proper decisions. They are captured either because they believe the tenets of the public culture, or because they are such weak leaders that, though they know it is full of illusions, they flee to the shelter of the public culture to try to raise support for their policies. In addition, America is first and foremost concerned with domestic politics and neglects international relations, so that we chose presidents ill-prepared for international responsibilities. Finally, we vest in our presidents both leadership and managerial responsibilities, and rarely do we chose as president a person who can do both. Thus, we don't select presidents who are prepared for the challenges of leading a great power in the world – who are able to master the illusions of our people. We are "... a great imperium with the outlook of a great emporium," in Victoria DeGrazia's phrase,[1] and never more so than today, with our first president who has been trained as an MBA.

EIGHTEEN

How Public Culture Inhibits Presidential Leadership

POOR CHOICES FOR PRESIDENT

Modern thought makes strong distinctions between three functions that we used to treat as one. Administration involves the application and enforcement of rules and procedures; management involves a focus on getting results accomplished and doing so in an efficient way; leadership involves energizing others via a vision of the future – it requires an objective comprehension of the situation, development of effective responses and the ability to persuasively inform the public about them. Administrators care little for getting things done (results) or for efficiency; managers require both results and efficiency in order to make profits, and are impatient with rules and procedures; leaders focus on broad directions and gathering the support of others, and care little for rules and procedures, or for daily results and efficiency. Modern societies, like modern corporations require all three functions. Few people are trained for more than one of the three functions, or are good at more than one.[1]

Today, the United States invests little administrative responsibility in our president, administration is accomplished in specialized agencies. But managerial and leadership responsibilities are combined in the president's office. The president is responsible for the functioning and budget of much of the federal government – managerial responsibilities; and also for broad direction for our society and for the gathering of public support for major initiatives, including especially military conflicts – leadership responsibilities.

It happens that President Clinton was first and foremost a leader; trained as an attorney and with a distinct ability to mobilize public support. He was neither a manager nor much interested in the elements of management. It is fitting to criticize his presidency far less for improper direction than for failure to carry out policies effectively – including especially the conflict that we later termed the war on terror.

President George W. Bush was trained as a manager at a time in the history of the Harvard Business School before it distinguished between leadership and management and at a time it confused good management with effective leadership. He has strong managerial skills, including the ability to set goals and timetables, to select effective subordinates (with conspicuous cronyist lapses), and to delegate responsibilities to them. But he lacks key leadership skills, including the ability to articulate effectively a long-term vision (including understanding the interrelationships of complex events) and to energize others around it. In consequence, in order to obtain public support, he makes recourse to the public culture – not to lead the people, but to embrace what they already believe.

Our nation needs presidents who are effective at both management and leadership; and it rarely gets them. Instead, the American political process selects inexperienced presidents and the nation's public culture then ties their hands in foreign policy. The result is weak presidential leadership in peace and war. Given the dangers we now face in the world, this pattern of behavior of the American electorate is likely to be self-defeating.

WEAK PRESIDENTIAL LEADERSHIP

U.S. presidential leadership is often in the wrong direction, or if in the right direction, is often ineffective. Our presidents are often victims of public culture – they fall for naive idealism. Our leaders are gullible to public culture and need to be trained to be more self aware. Like our public culture, they confuse ends and means, making means become ends in themselves. Democracy and free enterprise are ends to human happiness; not ends in themselves. Multilateralism is a method toward our defense, not a goal in itself. By adopting democracy, free enterprise and multilateralism as ends, we are in fact thinking wishfully – believing that these means will necessarily end in the more important real ends – happiness and peace. This is not certain. There are many kinds and meanings of democracy – they are not all benevolent; there are many forms and kinds of free enterprise – our own is full of imperfections; there are different forms of multilateralism – one that is full of hidden agendas is not to our advantage. But our public culture endorses them all uncritically.

Historically, America has faced great challenges from abroad with poor presidential leadership. We have often prevailed over foreign enemies in spite of weak leadership because of the energy and determination of our people and the failings and errors of our enemies – that is, often we have less won our conflicts than our enemies have lost. Victorious via whatever cause, we have incurred huge costs for victory – unnecessary costs, had we had better leadership. There is always the danger that in the future our good fortune and the incompetence of our enemies may not continue. Because our position in the world grows ever greater and the risks we face are now escalating quickly, it becomes more and more important that we chose leaders to match our role in the world.

Our history is full of potential disasters into which our leadership has led us, and from which only the enormous energy of our people has rescued us. We need to do better today in selecting leaders for our world role; but paradoxically, we have more opportunity now, because of our military dominance, to choose leaders recklessly, than ever before. If we do so, the consequences could call into question our very survival. Evidence in previous chapters is that the American people have been maturing in our attitudes toward the world; but our leadership isn't maturing as quickly as our people.

We Americans are proud of our history and of the great conflicts in which we've engaged and from which we've emerged victorious. It is somewhat disorienting, therefore, to take a critical look at our experience during these conflicts and conclude that we've made many significant errors from which we need to learn as we enter a period of world history in which our performance as an international leader is more important than ever before. If we perform well, there will not be a record of great conflicts and costly but glorious victories, because great wars will have been avoided.

Americans also admire their leaders, the presidents who have led us through great conflicts to victory. It is therefore discomfiting as well to have to admit that upon close inspection leadership was often inept and more costly than necessary to our nation in lives and treasure.

But disconcerting though it may be, the fact is that our nation has made significant errors in the past and our leadership has been often inept, and from an objective consideration of our limitations much is to be learned and gained for the future.

What is most striking in today's environment is to recognize that American presidents were unable to persuade Americans into essential use of preemptive force, adequate war preparation, and timely intervention in the twentieth century, when they were much needed. Either the presidents didn't try, or they were ineffective as leaders. The record as it was presented in the previous chapter is very strong.

The United States tried to stay out of World War I so that it didn't tip the balance against war, and without our weight on the Allied side, Germany thought it could overpower its European rivals, and so World War I was fought. Ultimately we had to enter the war to enable the western powers to prevail, but by then the world was different and far more dangerous than before. By the time we entered the war to bring it to a successful conclusion, the Red coup d'etat was taking place in Russia, and Germany was beginning its tragic journey via defeat to the Hitler nightmare.

President Woodrow Wilson was unable to get our country into the League of Nations as a way to engage us in early responses to war threats. In part as a result, but not for this reason alone, the League was ineffectual in heading off the Fascist challenge.

President Franklin Roosevelt and Adolf Hitler took power in their respective countries almost simultaneously. Hitler embarked on rearmament and a course to world war. Half way around the globe Japanese militarists did the same. FDR didn't or couldn't get the United States to intervene early to stop Japan or Germany short of World War II. Nor did he prepare.

In each instance, the United States finally entered the world wars – and determined the outcomes. The sad truth is that both wars could have been avoided had we thrown our weight into the scales earlier. Our inaction and lack of preparation for war – well known to both our friends and enemies abroad, and we made no significant effort to hide it – had led the aggressors to the incorrect conclusion that we would not fight, and that if we did, we'd be ineffectual. This is one of the fundamental reasons the wars occurred, and a different approach by the United States would have avoided both.

Looked at in this way, the great wars of the twentieth century share a common feature: each began and grew largely because America failed in its responsibility to be prepared for war and to enter early enough to dissuade our ultimate enemies from full-scale war.

We are justly proud of Presidents Wilson and Franklin Roosevelt for leading us to victory in great wars. But victory alone should not be the sole criteria of greatness in presidential leadership – not when success is bought at too great a cost. We lost 116,000 killed in the avoidable first world war and 292,131 killed in the even more avoidable second world war. Neither Wilson (who became president before the first world war, promising the people not to get us into war, and thereby making it almost certain that the war would occur and we'd ultimately be involved at high cost) nor FDR (who for more than six years watched Nazi power grow, ineffective in stopping it, until World War II began) was an effective enough leader of the American people to avoid either war.

There is more. FDR's flirtation with Stalin probably helped bring on the Korean War in which we lost some fifty-four thousand dead; and John Kennedy's inexperience lead us into the Vietnam conflict in which we ultimately lost some fifty-eight thousand dead.

This is not a record of presidential leadership that ought to be admired, or ought to be our standard going forward.

THE GEOPOLITICS OF PRESIDENTIAL PERSONALITIES

Harry Truman

Presidents often find it very difficult to master the expectations of the public culture and retreat into its illusions in order to build support for whatever they do. Thus, they take actions based on geopolitical realities, as best they understand or, if captured by the public culture, misunderstand them, then wrap the actions in a rationale drawn from the public culture. Too often, they then have tied their hands for future policy, or they are caught in the deception and destroyed.

Harry Truman is an excellent example. He entered the presidency on Franklin Roosevelt's death thoroughly unprepared. He'd been vice president for only a few months, and FDR had not included him in any of the wartime deliberations and decision making. Truman decided to use the atomic bomb on Japan in order to avoid an invasion which was expected to cost as many American soldier's lives as had already been lost in the entire second world war up to that point. But in the years following the war, there emerged great objections to his use of the bomb. Non-Americans who never did care about the potential loss of American lives attacked the use of the bomb, and so did many Americans who, as years passed, forgot the situation in the war in summer, 1945, and were increasingly upset by the horror caused by the bombs.

Truman, unable to justify his action by appeal to the military realities of the time, appealed instead to the public culture. He defended his use of the bombs as part of a struggle of free people's against tyranny, and he threatened to use them again in the same cause (the Truman Doctrine).

In fairness, given his lack of preparation for the job, Truman avoided many major errors, and he initiated the containment policy that in the end permitted us to wait out the collapse of the Soviet Empire while avoiding a full-scale nuclear war.

John F. Kennedy as "a Little Boy"

Early in his presidency, John F. Kennedy met with Nikita Khrushchev, the leader of the Soviet Union, at a summit in Vienna in 1961. At the time George Kennan was horrified by how unprepared for the encounter President Kennedy was. We learned in 2003 from Soviet archives what the American people didn't know then, but JFK knew and didn't share with us – that the Soviet premier was contemptuous of America's young president. Khrushchev called Kennedy "a little boy," adding he "can neither stand up to the American public nor can he lead them."[2]

Midway through his talks with Khrushchev in June 1961, Kennedy complained to his top advisors that Khrushchev was treating him like a "little boy," a reference in part to the endless lectures from Khrushchev. Ambassador Charles Bohlen was concerned that Kennedy failed to steer Khrushchev away from debates over the merits of communism versus capitalism, failing to discuss test bans and arms control. Ambassador George Kennan stated forcefully that Kennedy was overmatched. According to Kennedy's biographer, Robert Dallek, "Kennan thought that Khrushchev had tied the president in knots and that Kennedy appeared hesitant and overwhelmed."[3] Michael Beschloss and Richard Reeves are both cited by Dallek with the same reading of this events and Kennan's consternation with Kennedy and his lack of fitness to negotiate with Khrushchev.

After having been bullied by the Soviet dictator during their first summit, John Kennedy turned to *New York Times* reporter Scotty Reston and said, "Now we have a problem making our power credible, and Vietnam is the place."[4] For more than a decade after, this was the single constant in that awful war – three American presidents (Kennedy, Johnson, and Nixon) each found it necessary to demonstrate to the Soviets and the Chinese evidence of our resolve and the credibility of our power.

Perhaps the American people would have understood had President Kennedy told them that this was the reason for the war; but he didn't. Instead, he created a rationale for our involvement that was fully within the spirit of our public culture. Our government expressed a desire to see the Vietnamese people have a strong country in which there was religious freedom, especially for the Catholic Church, from the atheism of the Communist north, and some form of popular government. Thus, JFK justified a geopolitical necessity by trying to give it a rationale within the public culture, drawing on our belief in harmonism and convergence – the Vietnamese wanted to be like us, democratic, religious, the president argued, and we would assist them.

Vietnam

The origin of America's role as a major contestant in the Vietnam War lay in President Kennedy's need to appear strong and formidable to a tough old Soviet dictator, himself a veteran of the Nazi invasion of Russia during World War II, a war brutal beyond the imagination of most Americans. Vietnam was a war made necessary through the selection by the American people of a young and inexperienced president. The Vietnam War was not about Vietnam, nor about the domino theory, nor was it merely an error of U.S. strategy – it was part and parcel of the Cold War, which had begun almost two decades earlier. Vietnam was the theatre in which President Kennedy chose to demonstrate American resolution to the Soviets.

In some peculiar way, despite our embarrassment in Vietnam (which can also be described as loss of the war), the demonstration succeeded. Much was learned about maintaining our national credibility during the Vietnam War, in particular that America could demonstrate its power in other areas of the world and could stalemate its adversaries even while engaged in a draining conflict, and could emerge in the long-run stronger for the experience – in contrast, for example, to the very different experience of the Soviet Union after its withdrawal from the Afghan War. If the Afghan War were the Soviet Union's Vietnam, as several commentators have suggested, then the outcomes for the USSR and the United States were very different. After Vietnam, the United States took steps to reinvigorate our military via an extensive training effort focused on line officers at the unit level which brought the American Army back from the chaos and degeneration of the Vietnam War to the far more effective military we have today.[5] In contrast, the USSR collapsed soon after the end of its Afghan war. Thus, Vietnam allowed the United States to demonstrate its ability to conduct a major hot war in Vietnam without weakening in the Cold War; and its ability to recover from a significant setback in Vietnam by establishing a stronger military within a relatively short time. The Soviet experience with their Afghan war was, as we have said the opposite. The country was led by an inexperienced president into a war made necessary only by his inexperience; and two further presidents were unable to extract us without a final embarrassing defeat. But our country's resilience quickly overcame its poor leadership, emerging stronger than before.

THE CUBAN MISSILE CRISIS

Unfortunately, JFK's escalation of the conflict in Vietnam was not itself enough to alter Khrushchev's opinion of the American president or to give the USSR pause in its testing (engagement) of the young American. A great challenge to President Kennedy came in Cuba, where the Soviets tried to install nuclear-armed missiles only ninety miles from American shores. President Kennedy resisted. At the height of tensions over Cuba in 1962, newly available Soviet archives show, members of the Soviet leadership were expecting an order to attack the United States but at the last minute Khrushchev put on the brakes. "The thing is," Khrushchev told them, "we do not want to unleash a war. We wanted to scare, to rein in, America." Khrushchev added, "The tragedy is that they may attack and we will answer. It may end up in a huge war."

Fortunately it didn't because Khrushchev backed down, but the challenges to and responses of national leaders, even when the lives of millions are at stake, are perhaps nowhere in American history better illustrated than in Khrushchev's show of contempt for John F. Kennedy. There is an important footnote to this story that indicates that history might have had a different ending. Having demonstrated to Khrushchev his resolve in the Cuban missile crisis, John Kennedy no longer had need of a war in Vietnam for that purpose. Hence, it is probably true, as Kennedy's defenders insist, that he was preparing to withdraw from the Vietnam conflict in the fall of 1963 when he was assassinated. For a variety of reasons his successor, Lyndon Johnson, decided not to withdraw but to escalate the war in Vietnam.

As Khrushchev's behavior demonstrates, the geopolitical challenge to America is a very personal challenge at the level of the president. Today, just as in JFK's time, America is perpetually being probed by our enemies, and also by our friends, to see if we are vulnerable. "Testing" of this nature is the very heart of international relations – not the sort of coping with misunderstandings so often depicted in our public culture (part of what we label "harmonism"). We are tested by the leaders of other countries because of their ambitions and our strength. Our response to these tests is much of what determines success or failure in our foreign policy. Probing is complex, unceasing, and poorly reported to the public when it is reported the nature of what is occurring is often disguised by disinformation and lies. The sort of elbowing between American and the Chinese that is now continual is a good example of this (see Chapter 10). The consequences of a failure by our leaders to manage wisely our response to probes can be catastrophic. Vietnam is perhaps the foremost example of poor management by our presidents (three in a row) to foreign probes. Harry Truman's response to Stalin's probe (through his North Korean satellite) in the Korean War is a foremost example of wise presidential management.

Some foreign leaders are far cleverer than others in dealing with American presidents. Stalin was surprisingly adept. He never bearded the American lion like Hitler, Tojo, and Saddam did – each of whom paid with their positions and two with their lives (Saddam may yet). Saddam wasn't clever. He tried to have the first president Bush assassinated, and then he mocked the second president Bush – a president inexperienced in global politics, unlike his father, and one who therefore had to prove himself. George W. Bush responded. Why? Among the other reasons previously elaborated President Bush felt he had to respond, not merely to a personal insult (as a person might at a cocktail party) because that would have been no more than a matter of injured pride, but because as president he represents and symbolizes America, so that in mocking him, Saddam was mocking our nation, and to permit him to do so was to invite further attacks on our people.

In a revealing comment to a television reporter, a high White House aide once explained the background of our attack on Iraq in 2003 as partially the need to get rid of a tin-hat dictator – Saddam Hussein – who kept mocking the President of the United States. This pointed to a real cause of the war – that the Arab world was beginning to believe that America could be attacked physically (for example, as in the attack on the USS *Cole* in Yemen and on the World Trade Center) and it would not respond – so that America had to establish credibility again. The matter was deeply personal, but Bush did not view it as a personal agenda. President Bush in his official capacity is the foremost representative of the United States; hence, he had to uphold its reputation in the world – just as did President Kennedy. If a president allows himself to be mocked and doesn't respond effectively, then he invites attacks by rivals who underestimate resolve. This was a factor in the origin of our second war in Iraq, and it is very similar to the origin of our first war there. The first war was the result of Saddam bearding the American lion by seizing Kuwait. The second war was the result of Saddam bearding the American lion by disregarding American-sponsored UN resolutions (and also by congratulating the attackers of the World Trade Center). The success of the invasion of Iraq in 2003 helped establish the credentials of another inexperienced president whom the American people had elected to lead them. Iraq happened to be the location where broader issues were fought out – most importantly one in which America demonstrated to China that it was not a paper tiger – that the revolution in military affairs – prematurely oversold during the First Gulf war – was now in fact a stunning reality.

Finally, the American lion demonstrated to the Arab world that it could not be bearded incessantly without grave danger to those who dared to do so.

Or at least so it must seem to the Bush administration. But though it may seem that such a response is necessary, should we consider that it may have set an unappealing precedent? If America can be provoked into attack in part by insults and mockery, as happened to Iraq, then our adversaries have been provided with a tool with which to manipulate us. If our rivals are smart (which they are), they'll get several small countries to insult us at once from all corners of the globe so a major power can finish us off while our troops are elsewhere. Thus, when and why we strike has to be made clear to the American people and the world by an American president.

DOMESTIC FOCUS IN LEADERSHIP SELECTION

Often our leaders create crises that they then have to muddle through, often doing the country considerable damage. Recent administrations of both parties have managed to take an international police problem – that of the ambitions of Iraq's petty dictator – and turn it into a global political crisis, always blaming, of course, others. And they have taken another international police problem, that of North Korea's nuclear ambitions, and are turning it into a global political crisis. These things happen because our presidents didn't understand history and geopolitics well enough to understand how other countries are likely to react to our actions, although it is usually completely predictable; instead they are caught up in the illusions of our public culture.

The Iraqi crisis has its roots in incompetent leadership in America and Europe – it developed as a result of a black comedy of errors and misapprehensions. The result is that although Saddam had the weakest hand to play, for a long while he did the best. By the tone of the political uproar that preceded our invasion of Iraq, many Americans would have preferred to attack France rather than Iraq. It was high farce.

In our case, some of the problem is that America can't effectively be the sole superpower in the world, and yet elect its president essentially on domestic issues. Yet this is what we still try to do, confusing ourselves by thinking that because of our current power, the world is safer, and therefore that we can indulge ever more fully our own domestic concerns and disputes. The opposite is the case – with greater responsibility in the world comes greater attention to it, and the key in a representative democracy such as ours is that the nation's leadership be prepared to lead it in the world. Yet this is not so in America, and this is one of the dreadful ironies of the present that might undermine our position in the world quickly.

Our electorate is increasingly ill prepared to select a president for our global responsibilities. Americans as a group are becoming more insular. We travel less abroad, in large part due to fears acerbated by the 9/11 attacks; we watch fewer foreign films; we read far fewer books in translation from foreign languages than we did years ago.[6] Probably it is true that Americans aren't interested, and it is in part because of the vast size of the United States, our separation by oceans from the rest of the world, and our country's wealth.

WEAK LEADERSHIP IN FOREIGN AFFAIRS

Given their lack of preparation, it should be no surprise that most American presidents don't excel in foreign affairs. They rarely achieve anything in that sphere, except to avoid disaster, and they regularly do their political prospects and their reputations harm.

Our criticism of the performance of American presidents may seem harsh. The most plausible defense of our presidents in foreign policy is that they are not so much ill prepared and ineffective, as that they are responding to particular limitations of democracy itself, and so cannot be expected to perform better. It is argued that democracies generally, and that of America in particular, suffer from short-sightedness and are often captured by special interests. Thus, it would be concluded, that American presidents must be expected to behave in foreign relations with a short-sightedness and lack of independence of action (that is, that our foreign relations are tied to the concerns of special interests) that reflect basic characteristics of our democracy. There is merit in this view, but it doesn't excuse our presidents, but rather deepens the indictment by recognizing the failures we cite and simply trying to excuse them. It is a very limited use of the notion of leadership to excuse a president from effective performance of his or her key responsibility (to conduct the nation's foreign affairs) on the grounds that the president must follow, not lead, the public opinion.

In Chapter 6, we examined the view of Americans from abroad. An aspect of that topic is significant here.

What do foreigners think about American presidential leadership?

Generally, they think it isn't very good.

Seen from abroad, American leadership is poorly educated, unevenly cultured, and globally inexperienced, as are its citizens. "American power" must seem an oxymoron given the lack of American leadership in foreign policy affairs, for such power should be the result of strong and effective leadership. In fact, "American power" is not the result of American leadership, but of something far different – American power grows out of the initiative, energy and effectiveness of the broad mass of the American people, free to pursue their own interests on a large geographic scale with many resources at their disposal.

America has rarely, if ever, had leadership to match her people. The freedom and energy of our people are released by historical and legal and political factors that together constitute the American economic and political cultures and that together generate great economic and military power, but usually corrupt and ineffective leadership.

That our system does not produce strong presidential leadership has been noticed abroad, where observers frequently comment on it. So it is that many American presidents are simply not appreciated outside our country, our current president being one of the most dramatic such cases. About our system Winston S. Churchill was right, it's the worst, except all the others – implicitly it cannot be justified on absolute standards of measurement. And about our system Plato was most profound – democracy doesn't ordinarily choose good leaders.

Perhaps the most cogent comment comes from a leftist English historian whose critical assessment of American leadership is not invalidated simply because he is our opponent – rather, he says what much of the rest of the world believes: "The United States . . . is a country that is geared to operate with mediocrities, because it has to, and it has been rich and powerful enough to do so. . . . The problem is that . . . its political system is geared to the ambitions and reactions of New Hampshire primaries and provincial protectionism, that it has no idea what to do with its power . . . "[7]

MISJUDGING FOREIGN LEADERS

After meeting him for the first time in 2001, President George W. Bush said he had looked into Mr. Putin's eyes, got "a sense of his soul," and liked what he saw.

Bush is not the first Western leader to so assess a foreign dignitary, but sometimes these assessments are tragically wrong. In 1938 British Prime Minister Neville Chamberlain traveled to the European continent to meet Hitler in hopes of preserving peace. He returned to Britain reassuring the people of his country that "I got the impression that here was a man [Hitler] who could be relied upon when he had given his word."[8] Chamberlain was dead wrong – Hitler was not a man of his word. Further, Hitler saw Chamberlain a bit differently; he referred to him as a "small worm." The result of Chamberlain's misassessment was a strengthened Hitler and a much longer and more difficult World War II.

In the midst of World War II, American President Franklin Roosevelt met with Soviet dictator Joseph Stalin to forge an alliance to crush Nazi Germany. A key strategic issue was how closely America should cooperate with the communist state and to what degree we should support or resist its expansion. Roosevelt summarized his attitude toward the answer to this crucial issue in a very personal assessment: "I think," he pronounced, "we can trust Uncle Joe (Stalin)." Unfortunately, we couldn't, and the outcome was the Cold War against a vastly strengthened Soviet Union.

Western leaders have a tendency to think that the leaders of other nations are simply politicians like themselves. Our leaders expect the good will on our side to be answered by the other side with good will, unless we ourselves do something to undermine it. This is the harmonist illusion; it is a retreat into denial of objective reality (what foreign leaders are often really like), though one that is usually very popular at the time with the broad electorates, who, as we saw above, are addicted to wishful thinking.

President Bush has publicly assessed Russian President Vladimir Putin in similar terms to those that Chamberlain applied to Hitler and FDR to Stalin. Will Bush turn out to be more accurate than his predecessors? Does President Putin of Russia deserve such a strong positive endorsement from President Bush?

Asked by a reporter in the fall of 2003 if he regretted any part of the KGB's history, Putin replied, "No, of course not. . . . There was absolutely nothing that I could be ashamed of." The KGB was the Soviet secret police, in which Putin spent most of his career before being selected by Boris Yeltsin to follow him as president of Russia. Nothing to be ashamed of in the KGB or in his own career in it? Astonishing! The KGB ran the labor camps – the Gulag; stifled dissent in Soviet Russia by vigorous repression. Nothing at all to be ashamed of!

But Putin also told the reporter: "The totalitarian regime brought the country to a national catastrophe and to the collapse of the Soviet Union. . . . We firmly stand on the path of development of democracy and of a market economy."[9]

The two comments are very much at odds with each other. The KGB of which he was proud, was the key instrument of the regime he now condemns as a failure.

Why would an American president say he'd looked into this man's soul and liked what he saw? Perhaps because in the intensely personal interaction of great power politics our president was inexperienced, and he sought through a personal relationship to do quickly what could only be done realistically through implementing a consistent policy and by continuing education and persuasion – that is, to bring President Putin into the sort of friendly and cooperative relationship with America that President Bush seems to believe is the ideal state of international relations.

American presidents are often naïve and impatient in foreign affairs (although the example above of Britain's Neville Chamberlain shows that they are not alone). Inexperienced and untested, pressured to quickly establish themselves among world leaders, they rely too much on personal assessments for which they lack adequate preparation and they are often themselves underestimated by their foreign counterparts. Underestimated, they feel they have no alternative but to act in exaggerated fashion to establish their credibility – and for this America pays a substantial price.

AMERICAN PRESIDENTS' QUESTIONABLE SKILLS AT WAR

Our presidents also have not been very effective war leaders. They meddle too much in military affairs; they are not good at selecting top military leaders; they find it difficult to set clear strategic objectives; they demonize our opponents, which encourages our people and our military to underestimate them; and they idealize our allies which lends strength to those who are often our next antagonists. This is a harsh judgment; and it may seem to be contradicted on its face by the many wars in which we have been victorious. How, if our presidential leadership is so poor in wartime, have we won so many wars? But though these wars were won, they were won at excessive costs, including sometimes sacrificing the basic objectives of the war. For example, the Civil War ended slavery, but not racial discrimination that preserved much of the most unfortunate aspects of slavery; World War I did not make the world safe for democracy, and it was not a war to end wars, as President Wilson had famously promised, but led instead to World War II; the second world war ended with a new conflict, the Cold War, that was even more dangerous than the war against Germany and Japan; and the Vietnam War ended in an embarrassing debacle. Each war cost tens of thousands of lives, and Chapter 14 demonstrates that the worst wars could probably have been almost entirely avoided by taking preemptive action, had there been better presidential leadership.

President Wilson

Woodrow Wilson took us into a war he had promised to avoid when it wasn't really necessary, and we were so ill prepared that tens of thousands of

Americans were killed unnecessarily. Then he lost the peace; outmaneuvered by the leaders of our allies who fashioned a very different kind of peace than he had hoped.

President Franklin Roosevelt

FDR has much to answer for: both World War II and the Holocaust. History seems to have forgotten that FDR took office at the same time as Hitler. FDR was leader of the country that, under Wilson's leadership, had tipped the balance to victory for the allies in World War I, and then sought to dictate the peace. America had lost the peace, allowing Britain and France to dictate a retributive treaty and then failing to join the system of multilateral defense we had urged on the world, the League of Nations – but America was still potentially the greatest power in the world. Yet America stood aside while Hitler built German power, and FDR permitted France and Britain to appease the Nazis. FDR failed to assert American power against Hitler, and he bears considerable personal responsibility as a result. This is so whether he didn't try to stop the Nazis in time, or whether he tried and failed because he couldn't lead our nation well enough to accomplish his objective. He was either indifferent or ineffective in dealing with the greatest leadership challenge of his era (which was to avoid a second world war, not to win it when it was underway), and neither speaks well for him as a national leader. FDR was, of course, not alone in failing to confront Hitler in a timely fashion. There were many lesser political figures of the time who acted vigorously to keep America from confronting Hitler when it could have been done easily, and they bear a great responsibility also – but FDR was the president, and his responsibility is correspondingly greater.

World War II began when Hitler invaded Poland in 1939, an action made possible by his alliance with the Soviets. The two dictators then divided the country. Stalin refused pleas for an alliance with the Western powers, France and England, leaving Hitler free to overrun France and threaten England. After the war he is said to have commented, "With Germany, we could have been invincible."[10] In cooperation with Hitler, Stalin apparently envisioned dividing the British and French empires and relegating the United States to insignificance. It might have happened. Instead, Hitler betrayed his partner by invading the Soviet Union in 1941 – something that so surprised Stalin that when first informed of the invasion, he ordered Soviet officials to contact Hitler to tell him about it, certain that Hitler hadn't been involved and would stop any border incidents.

But during the eight years of Franklin Roosevelt's first two terms as president, this enormous menace to America of Nazi Germany and Soviet Russia, and then of Germany and Japan had grown without effective counteraction by America. This record is hardly one of successful leadership by the American president.

Our country came very close to losing World War II. Let General of the Army George Marshall describe the situation: "In those hours [of the summer of 1942] Germany and Japan came so close to complete domination of the world that we do not yet realize how thin the thread of Allied survival had been stretched. . . . The crisis had come and gone at Stalingrad and El Alamein [after the summer of 1942] before this Nation was able to gather sufficient resources to participate in the fight in a determining manner."[11] Thus, the war had been a very close run thing, and we had not been determinative in it. We were just lucky it turned out well, and owed our luck to the courage and efforts of the Russians and the British. This is the strongest possible condemnation of the effectiveness of the Roosevelt administration before the war.

There were great men in the period, including George Marshall, George Patton, and George Taylor. They won the war. FDR was a more limited person who thought he could trust Stalin; Eisenhower was a more limited person who prolonged the war by six months and allowed the Russians to capture Berlin and much very valuable German military technology (jets and missiles and submarines in particular).

President Truman

Truman and General McArthur allowed themselves to be surprised by Chinese intervention in the second phase of the Korean War. Truman left office in large part due to his failure to succeed in the war, leaving to his successor, Dwight Eisenhower, the task of achieving an end to the fighting. Fifty years later, one still cannot say a secure peace has yet been achieved.

President Kennedy

John F. Kennedy led the United States both into a failed conflict in Cuba – which was carried out by surrogates at the Bay of Pigs and was a very embarrassing defeat for America – and the beginnings of the tragic conflict in Vietnam. The best that can be said for JFK is that had he lived, he might have cut our losses in Vietnam by withdrawing.

President Johnson

Lyndon Johnson by his conduct of the Vietnam War ruined his reputation, his political legacy (domestic economic reform), and, ultimately, his health.

President Nixon

President Nixon inherited the Vietnam War from his predecessors and spent almost four years trying to disentangle us from it, costing thousands of additional lives, and ending in our last troops being chased out of Saigon by the victorious communists.

President Carter

We've not had large wars in recent years, but that is not an indication that presidential leadership in foreign affairs has improved. President Carter was unable even to handle a challenge from Iran.

President Reagan

President Reagan stumbled badly over the management responsibility of his office. He began by talking geopolitics candidly to the American people. In 1983, he said, "The Soviet-Cuban militarization of Grenada, in short, can only be seen as power projection into the region. And it is in this important economic and strategic area that we're trying to help the Governments of El Salvador, Costa Rica, Honduras, and others in their struggles for democracy against guerrillas supported through Cuba and Nicaragua. These pictures only tell a small part of the story. I wish I could show you more without compromising our most sensitive intelligence sources and methods. But the Soviet Union is also supporting Cuban military forces in Angola and Ethiopia. They have bases in Ethiopia and South Yemen, near the Persian Gulf oil fields. They've taken over the port that we built at Cam Ranh Bay in Vietnam. And now for the first time in history, the Soviet Navy is a force to be reckoned with in the South Pacific."[12] Here was a president talking geopolitical realities to the American people without couching them in the comforting idealism of the public culture. But it all ended in the political disaster of the Iran-Contra scandal and the President's apology for it. In 1987, President Reagan commented on the scandal: "Once I realized I hadn't been fully informed, I sought to find the answers. Some of the answers I don't like. As the Tower board reported, and as I said last March, our original initiative rapidly got all tangled up in the sale of arms, and the sale of arms got tangled up with hostages. Secretary Shultz and Secretary Weinberger both predicted that the American people would immediately assume this whole plan was an arms-for-hostages deal and nothing more. Well, unfortunately, their predictions were right. As I said to you in March, I let my preoccupation with the hostages intrude into areas where it didn't belong. The image – the reality – of Americans in chains, deprived of their freedom and families so far from home, burdened my thoughts. And this was a mistake. My fellow Americans, I've thought long and often about how to explain to you what I intended to accomplish, but I respect you too much to make excuses. The fact of the matter is that there's nothing I can say that will make the situation right. I was stubborn in my pursuit of a policy that went astray."[13] Here Reagan admits candidly to a failure of management – a failure of too much delegation and too little oversight.

President Bush, Senior

George Herbert Walker Bush failed to explain how his demonization of Saddam Hussein during the first Iraqi war related to his objective to liberate Kuwait but leave Saddam in power in Iraq as a barrier to Iranian ambitions in the region; so when he failed to depose Saddam Hussein, he left the American people frustrated and his own reputation in tatters. More than any other president in American history, Bush the elder managed to snatch political defeat from military victory.

President Clinton

Bill Clinton struggled continually between an idealistic romanticism and realism. A recent biographer wrote, "One of the continuing dramas of [Bill Clinton's] presidency was the contest between competing strains of romance and realism in the Clinton character. The romantic in Clinton was a politician of florid imagination who viewed himself on history's stage in a line of heroic presidents who left large imprints on their times. . . . The realist in Clinton was an accommodator who accepted political limits and tried to work within them. . . . All presidents must react to circumstances and play the hand they are dealt. The greatest presidents, however, manage simultaneously to create their own circumstances – to impose their own values and purposes on the age."[14] In our terminology, the greatest presidents master the illusions of the public.

Clinton failed to capitalize on the most momentous opportunity in our lifetimes, the chance to help Russia make a real break from autocracy to democracy and from a state managed economy to free enterprise. There was possibly a chance for this to occur, because the potential was welling up within Russia itself, not being imposed from abroad. At best, the chance of a successful transition in Russia was very small (to expect it to have occurred on its own is a fallacy, as we saw in Chapter 8), but our actions made it virtually certain that the transition would fail. The failure is finally being acknowledged by the principal participants on behalf of the West. For example, in December 2002, a story was first reported in Pravda, which said in an accompanying editorial comment: "I told you so!" The story reported an admission by the World Bank that it had mishandled the attempted transition of Russia from communism to free enterprise. The administration was not unaware that things were going wrong. Late in his administration, Clinton instructed the U.S. Ambassador to Moscow to stop reporting the bleak truth even in secret dispatches because it could be used against the administration. Clinton's was a very serious failure, and now that Russia is rearming, means that the United States blew the opportunity presented by the collapse of the Soviet Union and the end of the Cold War. How did this happen? In large part it occurred because of inadequate presidential leadership.

Grading President George W. Bush

How well is President Bush fulfilling the challenge that we've just posed for the American president? The standard assessments of American presidential leadership and policy are inadequate for two reasons:

- First, because they do not consider modern distinctions between management and leadership, and so confuse the two; and
- Second, because they are infected with the same kinds of rationalizations – those of the public culture – that cause the problem in the first place.

We must therefore access the record differently. Are President Bush and his key advisors masters of illusions, so that the American strategy makes sense if it can be decoded from the confusion of the public culture? Or do they pursue an approach primarily within the conceptual confines of public culture but give it a rhetorical gloss that is sufficient to mislead us?

Bush entered his presidency more favorably disposed to a strong defense than his predecessor. But he had no comprehensive understanding of the array of threats we describe and its sequencing. Until 9/11, his policies differed little from Clinton's. Rhetoric aside, he was thoroughly entangled with Europe and the UN in engagement with the rest of the world. The attacks on the World Trade Center provided an opportunity to the president to reconceptualize the threat array, but Bush did so only with respect to terrorism, and even there remains muddled about how to handle the Middle East. He supports a national missile defense, but doesn't see the deeper links with other aspects of strategy, and hasn't adjusted the program accordingly. In short, he is deficient in what his father called "the vision thing" and has no overall strategy. Thus, if we use the perspective of objective assessment of threat to refocus the assessment of the president, then the record is one of response to the terror shock, but nothing more.

During his presidency, George W. Bush made a remarkable about face on certain matters critical to effective American defense policy – matters about which he had been quite eloquent when criticizing the Clinton Administration during the 2000 election campaign. In effect, Bush sought the Presidency on opposite grounds from those in which he conducted defense policy himself. "I don't think our troops ought to be used for what's called nation-building," he said in the second presidential debate in 2000. "I think our troops ought to be used to fight and win war."[15] By 2005, he was engaged in nation-building in both Iraq and Afghanistan and using our troops for exactly that.

Also, during the 2000 campaign Bush argued that Clinton (and thereby Al Gore, Clinton's vice president)had failed to set priorities for the use of America's military might and "unless a president sets his own priorities, his priorities will be set by others – by adversaries, or the crisis of the moment, live on CNN."[16] By 2005, he had turned his own priorities completely around. Instead of dealing with the emerging threats from China and Russia, he had defined our conflict with terrorists as "as great a danger to our national interests as strong states" – a statement that on its face is absurd. Perhaps he meant that conflict with terrorists and the weak states that sometimes support them could also cause a danger to our national interests, as could strong states. But to say that the terrorist threat was comparable to that posed by the Russian nuclear missile array or the Chinese military buildup was to reveal a major confusion of priorities.

What had caused the shift? It was the need of the president to get support for his interventions in Iraq and Afghanistan by appeal to the public culture – to the notion that other countries can be improved and made peaceful by being made into something like ourselves – the self-affirming missionary impulse of America. He, like other presidents before him had failed to persuade the American people that defending them alone was sufficient reason for actions abroad, and to gain broader support had adopted instead the illusions which so mislead them. In doing so he had brought the country into a military and political bog and had lost leverage in what should be higher priority situations. He had employed exaggeration and hype, appealed to the public culture, and drifted into positions he knew in advance were mistaken – using our military for nation-building and letting the media (via the public culture) set his priorities.

This assessment must of necessity be tentative since it is based on limited information and perspective. We do not know yet how far success as it occurs is due to good fortune – the serendipitous consequence of expediency after expediency – as opposed to mastery of the situation; nor how far failure as it occurs is due to lack of mastery as opposed to bad fortune.

Much of what Bush tried to do is right for America. We should be independent in our strategy making, not tied to supposed allies who have hidden agendas. But, much of the way he approached the doing of it was very clumsy. The administration's frequent disregard of diplomatic niceties was needlessly insulting to other countries. Others deserve respect and attention, even if we don't agree with them. The Bush administration seemed to confuse two things – what it was doing and how it was doing it – which are separate and ought to be dealt with separately. Because we are a rival of another country does not mean we should be hostile; because we do not agree with them does not mean we should ignore or insult them; because we are going a different direction does not mean we should be antagonistic; because we must take strong actions does not mean we should be abrasive. Quite the contrary. The more forceful our actions, the more diplomatic should be our presentation.

Strategic independence means that we should minimize multilateralism in strategy, but embrace it in tactics. This does not relegate consultation with others to a lesser role. How we do something is as important as what we do. Strategy is no more important than tactics, and no less so. But strategy is especially vulnerable to perversion by others with hidden agendas. We should be objective about other countries motives and behavior, consult primarily ourselves with regard to our interests and defense strategy, and deal politely and honestly with all but our most violent adversaries in how we go about our purposes.

The president has in recent years increasingly imbedded his rhetoric about America's engagement with the world in the language of our public culture. In his speech at commencement activities of the U.S. Coast Guard Academy in 2003, President Bush quoted President Wilson. "President Woodrow Wilson said, 'America has a spiritual energy in her which no other nation can contribute to the liberation of mankind.'" Bush then added, "America's national ambition is the spread of free markets, free trade, and free societies. These goals are not achieved at the expense of other nations, they are achieved for the benefit of all nations. America seeks to expand, not the borders of our country, but the realm of liberty."

At his second inaugural address given on January 20, 2005, President Bush told our nation, "We are led, by events and common sense, to one conclusion: The survival of liberty in our land increasingly depends on the success of liberty in other lands. The best hope for peace in our world is the expansion of freedom in all the world."

Yet, the president was almost certainly not led by events and common sense to this very debatable conclusion, but rather was led to it by the illusions of our public culture. And when President Bush says such things as he did at his news conference on March 3, 2005: "Preventing another terrorist attack on America is the greatest challenge of our time," we are challenged as to what to make of it. The statement is on its face absurd: there are far greater challenges to America than preventing another terrorist attack – challenges of the environment, of medical science, of murderous crime (in America twenty times as many people are murdered in a single year as the number dead in the World Trade Center attack), of a nuclear conflict with a major power such as Russia or China. The president's statement is therefore merely playing to the public culture. But how are we to know if such statements are merely part of managing the illusions of the public or instead show that the President shares those illusions?

Secretary of State Condoleezza Rice suggests that the Administration believes its own rhetoric. "...the most serious threats to our security now emerge within states not between them," she commented on July 29, 2005, in a reference to terrorists. This statement, as our analysis later in this book shows, is either wrong, or it is a statement only about the immediate future. But if it is only about the immediate future, then the Secretary of State and the administration generally are failing in their duty to prepare the American people for what lies beyond. Preparation is critical because both political and military preparations must begin now for the next in a sequence of threats that we describe in the following chapter, since the time lags are so substantial.[17]

Do the president and the Secretary of State believe their rhetoric? We cannot know, but we hope that they are merely attempting to manage illusions and do not share them.

It appears to us that the actual current strategy of the United States is a close cousin to the course of Strategic Independence which we advocate later in this book, and that its political expression is expansive democracy. In other words, President Bush is pursuing a strategy designed to preserve American interests in a dramatically changing world by lessening our reliance on outdated alliances, and thereby disentangling ourselves from alliances just as urged upon us by our first President, George Washington, and simultaneously encouraging the world to make needed adjustments to changing configurations of national power. Furthermore, the President is clothing this strategy in rhetoric that engages support even within the context of the national wishful thinking that is parent to our public culture.

The merit of the president's approach arises from two causes:

1. The end of the Cold War and the increasing obsolescence of the U.S. alliance with Western Europe; and
2. The dramatic changes in national power (economic, political and military) that are occurring in the world. As the world changes, relationships among nations are strained and power equations must change (perhaps including some borders).

In this environment, the United States best defends itself and facilitates necessary change by acting independently. Alliances become primarily tactical and expedient – coalitions of the willing. The United States is right to break free of European entanglements which are the real remaining chains of twentieth century conflicts. The future of much of the globe is going forward without the Western Europeans who try to hang on to declining power and influence in the world via limited military power, intermediate economic power and unlimited sanctimonious hypocrisy which they confuse with moral influence. The western Europeans have their fifth column in the United States, and its political expression is in our public culture.

Strategic Independence should replace Mutual Assured Destruction, MAD, as the cornerstone of our nuclear policy. When Secretary of State John Foster Dulles mentioned "massive retaliation" at a meeting of the Council on Foreign Relations in January 1954, the possibility of all-out, full-scale nuclear war with the Soviet Union or a Soviet satellite became a more frightening specter looming over the world scene. In 1964, Secretary of Defense Robert McNamara modified the massive retaliation policy when he coined the term, Assured Destruction, to which his critics prefixed Mutual, thereby giving the world Mutual Assured Destruction – MAD. MAD relies on the economic concept of the law of diminishing returns – no one would launch a nuclear attack on America, McNamara reasoned, fearing an American nuclear counterattack, or series of counter attacks, had the potential to escalate to massive retaliation. Even so, MAD means that we are always on the brink of nuclear destruction if our nuclear deterrence policy fails to prevent a nuclear first strike. Strategic Independence offers a possible defense short of nuclear retaliation.

President George W. Bush deserves praise for seeing beyond the universal application of MAD. In 2002 at West Point he said:

> For much of the last century, America's defense relied on the Cold War doctrines of deterrence and containment. In some cases those strategies still apply. But new threats also require new thinking. Deterrence, the promise of massive retaliation against nations, means nothing against shadowy terrorist networks with no nation or citizens to defend. Containment is not possible when unbalanced dictators with weapons of mass destruction can deliver those weapons on missiles or secretly provide them to terrorist allies.[18]

Is President Bush a master of illusion? Certainly, if American policy in the Middle East succeeds, he will be thought to be so. By contrast, success could be merely the result of internal factors like those that caused the collapse of the Soviet Union should something of that nature occur in Syria and/or Egypt. What is more important is how a master of illusion should proceed amid the causal ambiguity.

There is a danger that President Bush, Secretary of State Condoleezza Rice, and Secretary of Defense Donald Rumsfeld aren't masters of illusion, but that they see only part of the picture because they are ensnared by various delusions of the public culture. They have excessive faith in democracy and free enterprise and in building other nations on such a foundation. Excessive faith leads them to adopt policies that are counterproductive to containing terrorists and insurrectionaries in Iraq and compromise American geostrategic autonomy by trying to accomplish too much (and thereby needing too much assistance from abroad). It is possible to commend Rice's toughness on German reunification early in her career without believing that she is a paragon of the art of objective strategy today.

President Bush in his first administration learned how to more effectively master the illusions of the public culture. Historically, his learning is very similar to that of President Abraham Lincoln during the first two years of the Civil War, leading to the freeing of the slaves in January, 1863, as an act to gain political support for the war. President Bush's recent embrace of democracy as a goal for American military action in Iraq serves a similar purpose – to rally moral sentiment behind acts of defense. But it may lead us to a dangerous overreach in which we try to impose on the world our system in the belief that our illusions about the world are true.

These comments make the limitations of the neoconservative and liberal worldviews clear. Most of our politicians are blissfully unaware of public culture in all its dimensions, although they operate in it, like fish who live in water but do not know it; they don't appreciate the Federalist nuance of the American way when applied to other nations (that is, that we seek not a particular form of government abroad but accept any of a number that offer us no threat); and they lack a grasp of the reconfiguration of global wealth and power and the stresses and needs for change it is generating in the world body politic. Without knowledge in each of these two critical areas, our leaders cannot create effective strategies and cannot master the illusions of our collective life.

DON'T RELY ON ADVISORS

In general, American presidents are not very good at foreign affairs and they are poor war leaders. Can personal deficiencies be made up by reliance on advisors?

Many of us excuse presidential lack of preparation for global and wartime leadership by insisting that good advisors will fill gaps in a president's knowledge and experience. So the excuse is often offered in conversations among voters that though a favored candidate has few or no qualifications for running the foreign and defense policy of America, he or she can get good advisors who'll make up for the candidate's deficiency. But this is an illusion. Carried to its logical extreme, as the voters sometimes seem to do, the absurd result of such reliance is that the voters shouldn't care who is elected because whoever is president can get good advisors!

Many Americans have taken the notion from business that a good executive can manage anything – including businesses he or she doesn't understand – by picking good subordinates. There is merit to this because the tasks of both president and corporate chief executive officer are much the same:

- Both are answerable to constituencies;
- Both desire to placate stakeholders of various kinds;
- Both have to defend their rights against assault from domestic and foreign sources;
- Both must seek to balance short- and long-run considerations;
- Neither can do all he or she promises, but must instead make accommodations continually;
- Both are constrained by the need for coalition building;
- The president is supposed to abide by the will of the electorate, and the CEO by the will of the shareholders, but both in practice have substantial discretion and power;

- Both must chose subordinates to carry out their purposes; and
- Interestingly, the formal mathematical structure of the objective each faces is the same (to maximize a utility function subject to constraints).

The president's task is more complex, because the organization (the United States) is larger and includes more diverse interests than a corporation, but the leadership task is essentially the same.

The leadership task itself cannot be delegated, including the choosing of advisors. In consequence, a president, like a CEO, with large gaps in his or her knowledge and experience won't know when to get an advisor (instead choosing to make the decisions on his or her own) or won't be able to choose well. It isn't enough for presidents to get good advisors. They still make crucial decision, they still choose the advisors, and they determine what is acceptable performance by the advisors – presidents have to have personal knowledge, experience, and judgment. When they don't, bad things happen. The advisors picked are often themselves devotees of the public culture. At worst, presidents pick not well-qualified advisors but political hacks from whom nothing can be expected but loyalty.

It's a myth that good advisors can make up for a lack of preparation of the leader – because the president chooses advisors and if the president is ignorant or prejudiced, the advisor is likely to be also; and because an advisor provides advice, and the president must decide whether or not to accept it and what to do with it. The only situation in which an advisor is able to surmount these limitations of his or her role is when the president virtually delegates to the advisor the running of key aspects of U.S. policy. This sometimes happens; but more often the president insists on being in on the decisions, often actually making them, and his or her limitations become the source of errors and failures in our approach to the rest of the globe.

The most tragic example involves President Lyndon B. Johnson and the Vietnam War. Lyndon Johnson. The war was under way when Johnson became president. The Kennedy Administration hawks, military advisors, and the foreign policy establishment, all convinced LBJ to continue prosecuting the war, rather than take Option 1 that McNamara gave him in 1966, which was to cut our losses and get out of Vietnam.[19]

In early 1965, Vice President Hubert Humphrey stated that he disagreed with National Security Advisor McGeorge Bundy's recommendation for a torrent of bombing in the north. Bundy had just paid a visit to Vietnam and made that recommendation in response to what he saw. But, rather than keep Humphrey involved in these meetings, LBJ banished Humphrey from all war planning meetings for at least a year for opposing the bombing idea.

There are only two exceptions to the lamentable record of presidential ill-preparation and consequent missteps during most of the twentieth century; one is understandable, the other somewhat of a surprise. The commonality is that both had substantial personal experience in dealing with our foreign foes before entering the White House. They were Eisenhower and Reagan.

That Eisenhower is an exception is obvious – he had years of experience in the American military abroad; the leadership of the western powers in the war against Nazi Germany; close contact at top level with our Soviet allies, and then rivals. His experience carried us successfully through eight of the early years of the Cold War, ending the Korean War and avoiding conflicts from such incidents as that of our U2 spy plane that was shot down over the Soviet Union.

The surprise is Ronald Reagan, whose career had been as a Hollywood actor, then governor of California, and who would seem to have had no experience in foreign affairs. But the appearance was misleading. Reagan had extensive experience in battling Soviet agents in the almost subterranean political conflicts that embroiled American unions in the early Cold War period. Reagan is the only American president to have been president of a trade union, and was in that position at a time when the communists sought to capture American trade unions as part of the fifth column movement they sponsored in every Western democracy. For many nights anti –communist trade unionists in America stayed up late to keep communist groups from seizing control of union meetings after others had tired and gone home in order to push their radical agendas (a favorite tactic of small, well-disciplined minorities). Many noncommunist trade unionists worried that they would be murdered. Reagan had these experiences.[20] To the great benefit of Americans since, noncommunist leaders prevailed in most American unions, and Ronald Reagan was one of them. When he became President of the United States, he knew his adversary. He understood the significance of this experience to his own preparation for the American presidency, and he gives it clear prominence in his autobiography. His biographers, however, failed to understand its significance, writing instead about an old political controversy – the Congressional hearings of the 1950s about communist influence in Hollywood, in which Reagan was caught up.[21] Thus, his biographers missed one of the most important and most closely contested political struggles of the Cold War – the battle for control of American unions – and they miss the significance of Reagan's role in it both for him and for the nation.

With his background of fighting the communists in union halls, Reagan was well prepared to meet Soviet leaders on a larger battlefield of the cold war.

There was no major war during his presidency – no major test of his mettle by Soviet leaders who would otherwise have been tempted to underestimate him – and during his presidency the Soviet Union began to crack apart.

Clinton was poorly prepared for the presidency in its foreign policy aspects. But he was the luckiest of all our presidents – entering the White House just after Soviet Union had collapsed and there was no great power to challenge him.

Perhaps there is some mitigation for Clinton to be found in the circumstances of being president today. "I can't think; I can't act," Clinton complained while in office. "I can't do anything but go to fund raisers and shake hands. I can't focus on a thing except the next fund raiser."[22]

A political cartoon described the situation rather well early in Bush's presidency. In it, President Bush has one arm stuck in a bees nest labeled the "middle east," another arm has a snake wound round it labeled "Iran," one foot is painfully stepping on a porcupine labeled "North Korea," and the other foot is caught in a vise labeled "Iraq." Uncle Sam is watching the president and says to him, "Considering that you're not a foreign policy kind of guy, Mr. President, you've picked things up quickly."[23]

To look hard at the American presidency and the people who've occupied it is not to be overly critical, and it's not to imply that other countries have done better. For example, here's what a historian has to say about Nikita Khruschev:

Nikita Sergeyevich Khrushchev was the unquestioned leader of the Soviet Union from 1957 to 1964. In this fairly short span, he managed to provoke two major international crises, survive a coup (a second toppled him), order two disastrous economic overhauls, and hold erratic confrontations with nearly everyone in sight – the Chinese leadership, President Kennedy and Vice President Nixon, the neo-Stalinists in his Presidium, and the Russian intellectuals in his midst.[24]

This was the man with whom John Kennedy had to deal. Perhaps it is no surprise that a result was the Vietnam War.

THE GREATEST PRESIDENTIAL CHALLENGES

To assess the challenge to the American presidency in our time, we should revisit the major challenges of our past. We'll find that they were surmounted only in part.

In 1860, newly elected President Abraham Lincoln faced the situation that there was a great evil, slavery, in the country but the electorate was very divided about whether or not it ought to be disposed. Probably a majority didn't want to end slavery. So Lincoln took the position that slavery was a great evil but that his duty was only to preserve the union, not end slavery, and he initiated the Civil War on that issue. He continued to educate the country against slavery, but to refuse to act against it, until, late in 1862, the conditions were ripe to move against slavery, and he did then act to begin its abolition.

Lincoln had political genius, and it shouldn't be unexpected that a successful politician is good at his or her trade.[25] But political genius is at best only a part of a presidential leadership. In fact, it may be a great shortcoming of democracy that the skills needed to attain office are impediments to performing an effective leadership role. We often recognize this in private discussion when we say that a president is still campaigning and hasn't realized that he or she has been elected and now has to govern. Lincoln was an effective politician; yet his campaigning for office helped lead the country into a war that might have been avoided; and his frequent blunders in office made that war the most costly in lives we have ever had, exceeding greatly even World War II. For example, with the crisis of the Civil War at hand, in the months immediately proceeding Gettysburg and the Siege of Vicksburg, and over the bitter personal objections of his top commanders in the field, "Lincoln was still making military appointments as political favors," filling the Union Army with unqualified commanders who cost the nation much in blood and treasure because of their incompetence.[26] This is not to say that there wasn't much to admire in Lincoln – there was, and some of it is cited in this book; but the overall record was more destructive and bloody than necessary. Interestingly, many of the same people who today denounce the use of even moderate force in political affairs continue to praise Lincoln for what was unparalleled, in American history at least, resort to force in a political dispute. Apparently the slavery of African Americans was a sufficient evil to justify massive bloodshed; why isn't the indiscriminate murder of thousands of American citizens by Islamic terrorists sufficient to justify moderate bloodshed? Judgments that violence is justified in one circumstance and not another are political – not historical nor even, in the broader scope (that is, divorced from political convictions), objective.

FDR's situation paralleled Lincoln's in 1933 when he took office. In Germany a great evil was emerging. Hitler was coming into power, and although FDR opposed Nazism he didn't act against it because of isolationist sentiment in America. Our country was not prepared militarily to act, because although it was one of the victorious powers of World War I and party to the Versailles treaty that had ended the war, we had disarmed after the war and retreated into internal considerations. FDR recognized the danger, but the American public wasn't ready to act, didn't see the need, and was stuck in isolationism and the Depression. So for almost a decade FDR maneuvered in support of the other western democracies without being able to tip the balance against Hitler. In April 1939, in an especially significant incident, FDR sent a telegram to Hitler asking him to guarantee the territorial integrity of twenty small nations in Europe and the Mideast. Hitler read the telegram in a mocking voice to the Reichstag (Germany's parliament), amid thunderous laughter from the Nazis who were the audience – an insult that FDR waited a chance to repay.[27] In 1941, the Japanese attacked Pearl Harbor causing Hitler to declare war on the United States, and finally FDR had his opportunity to destroy Nazism with the American people standing united behind him.

This is how the story of these two momentous periods in our history is ordinarily told. But there is more to both stories. Lincoln's initial failure to persuade Americans to end slavery meant that the war was fought for two years without abolition as its goal, and was almost lost in the process. And FDR's inability to persuade the American people to rebuff German and Japanese militarism early in the career of both meant that a great war had to be fought and won.

"The first duty of a statesman," FDR told the American people in one of his first speeches as president, "is to educate."[28] In so saying, FDR positioned education ahead of other possible priorities including preserving the peace and defending our nation. Yet FDR understood that preserving peace and defending America depended on knowledgeable voters, who will support a president's leadership or not, and who will ultimately elect the next president and thus set the course of American foreign policy. It took FDR years to educate Americans sufficiently to the danger of the Nazis and the Japanese militarists to rouse us to their destruction, and even then he required the assistance of the Japanese through their attack on Pearl Harbor.

Today, there is as great presidential challenge – this time it is to define America's place in the world so as to avoid the worst possible consequences of Islamic extremism in the Middle East and across the Crescent of Fire, Russian instability, Chinese nationalism, and the dangerous persuasiveness of the leaders of the European Union.

There is, however, a major difference. In the case of both Lincoln and FDR the challenge was to pull the American people into a military effort sufficient to destroy the enemy. Today, the challenges are more subtly political and the threats we confront are less well defined than slavery and Nazism. More, not less, judgment in foreign affairs is required, ironically at a time when the selections our country is making for president seem to be going toward ever more inexperience. Without the necessary judgment, our presidents are captives of our public culture, and prone to dangerous error in how we engage the world.

CHAPTER 18: KEY POINTS

1. America has generally had poor presidential leadership in matters of our relations with the rest of the world.
2. Our presidents have
   - Failed to take effective preventive action to avoid great wars we were later drawn into;
   - Got us into smaller wars that led only to stalemate and sometimes defeat;
   - Romanticized foreign dictators; and
   - Set us on unnecessary moralistic crusades with large costs in lives and treasures, and almost all unsuccessful.
3. A key reason for the poor showing of American presidents on the world stage is that they are victims of our public culture – either because they believe its tenets, or because they are such weak leaders that they have to appeal to it in order to gain public support. In part, our presidents are victims of public culture because we select presidents primarily on the basis of domestic concerns, and our selections have little experience in world affairs, and have to be trained on the job; they simply don't know enough to master the public culture.
4. A lack of judgment in a president cannot be made up by advisors.

NINETEEN

Choosing a Great President

A great irony of the American political process – one can almost say the internal contradiction in it that threatens to make a failure of the whole thing – is that the Constitution grants the president power primarily in foreign affairs, while he or she is elected primarily on domestic issues. Put into a nutshell – as an old saw says – in domestic matters the president proposes and the Congress disposes; in foreign affairs the Congress proposes and the president disposes! But the choice of a president presumes exactly the opposite. The result is that we get a president ill-equipped for his or her foreign policy responsibilities, and frustrated by his or her lack of power in domestic matters. In the preceding chapter, we've seen the unfortunate result of this inconsistency. A key challenge today is whether the American people in their new maturity can overcome this limitation of our political tradition.

A LEADERSHIP DEFICIENCY

According to a report from a conference in the fall of 2003 of leading special- ists on international relations in Asia: America appears even to its regional allies to be a difficult and often unpredictable power. We are said to be erratic and unpredictable, adding a major element of instability to the world. Some panelists characterized the United States approach to security issues in post–Cold War Asia as seeking to maintain an environment of stability and friendly relations, but doing so with ad hoc methods and on the basis of American primacy, with little effort to establish supporting institutions or a viable balance of power structure.[1]

The Russians have a concept of correlation of force – strength weighted by credibility of use of force. Russia and China can use force – both are authoritarian governments in which electoral politics play no significant role. Their governments are able to use force both internally and externally as they desire without concern for reaction at home. The EU and Japan are in very different situations. The countries of the EU possess military force, but the various nations are both unable to coordinate effectively and their democratic electorates are largely pacifist in orientation. Japan lacks a military large enough and well-enough equipped with nuclear weapons to apply force credibly, its constitution largely eschews force, and its electorate is as pacifist as that of Europe. So the EU and Japan can be bluffed by the authoritarian powers if they wish to do so. In recent years, China has bluffed Japan on an increasing scale.

The United States lies somewhere between the two groups of the great powers. It is the most strongly armed of all; it is also democratic and has a substantial body of opinion that is very reluctant to use force. Sometimes America responds to provocation with force; sometimes it does not. We did not respond significantly to attacks on the Marine barracks in Lebanon; or to the attack on the USS *Cole* in Yemen. But when essentially the same adversaries attacked the World Trade Center, we responded with great force. Saddam must have been extremely surprised when after a decade of hesitation, the United States suddenly attacked Iraq and deposed him, giving as a public rationale weapons of mass destruction that he did not possess.

The United States is erratic and has been so. It actions can't be predicted. Hence, there is always a significant likelihood of misassessment of U.S. reaction by other nations, and therefore a risk of stumbling into war. When other countries expect us to act as a dominant power, we oftentimes don't, and confuse them. Why are we so unpredictable? Because we are first and foremost focused on our domestic politics and therefore our international relations are simply those of a commercial society which pays only small attention to international relations except with respect to trade, other than to hope on faith that relations between countries will not interrupt trade. Commercialism is a major contributor to our public culture – it is one of two dominant roots of convergence and harmonism – the other is our Christian-humanistic idealism.

Whatever its roots; however it is explained, the unpredictability of U.S. action in the world is a failure of presidential leadership. Our presidents have been largely unable to discover and act on the political, economic and military facts of life in the outside world. Most have been content to accept the illusions of our public culture – harmonism and convergence – as premises of how they view the world. As a consequence, our leadership has ignored the implications of the reconfiguration of global wealth and power, which is transforming the world's security situation. Hence, events that are largely predictable, surprise us. We have no context in which to decide how to react. This makes the responses of our presidents dangerously erratic and no other nation can predict when we might quit ignoring unpleasant realities and suddenly lash out with military force.

Indeed, under President Clinton there was a real danger that our leadership, confused by reliance on illusions, was veering toward the kind of nuclear and conventional disarmament, which in short order could make China and Russia bipolar supreme powers.

Under Bush, the danger has been almost the opposite – that we will seriously overreach our strength in an attempt to rebuild much of the world in our own economic, political and social image. If we do so overstretch, then we will not have left the power to surmount large challenges from Russia, China, or in the distant future, from a united Europe.

We've not made much headway in defusing this ominous situation because our leadership has been inadequate to the challenge. Political leadership has been weakened by a failure of intellect which causes it to accept public culture; and by an unwillingness to trust the public with honest information about our goals and strategies so that the public culture does not adapt to the real world.

We will stumble into global conflict if our leadership deficit continues. To avoid such a result, American leaders must grasp the significance of the reconfiguration of global wealth and power and recognize that Russia's and China's rulers aren't predictable on the basis of the illusions of our public culture, and tailor America's international security strategy accordingly.

America's security environment, that seems clear when looking at the current situation with the rose colored glasses of wishful thinking and convergence, looks completely different when global economic trends are factored into the equations. Russia seems eternally weak from the first perspective, and dangerous in various ways from the second. China seems a manageable rival from the first and a greatly destabilizing factor from the second. The war on terror seems the most important thing from the first perspective and distinctly subordinate in significance from the second. Thus, we are getting our priorities wrong and not addressing the most significant dangers. If we let them grow, they beget tragedies.

Americans should now be able to recognize the signals of oncoming disaster having already failed to do so twice in the twentieth century, resulting in our fighting two world wars.

Furthermore, today's dangers should be addressed immediately – only by changing course now we can reduce the threat to us and to our children. Yet it is difficult to achieve a change of policy to meet dangers foreseen in the future, because national security policy in our country is the result of political infighting with little serious attention paid to devising a security strategy for averting conflict and stabilizing peace. We react, but are rarely proactive.

Any American president will have to focus on antiterrorism, insurrectionaries in the Middle East, and Muslim fundamentalist extremism in the Crescent of Fire, currently. But the practical test of successful foreign policy is how we leverage a security strategy built around antiterrorism into one that is effective in dealing with the broader foreseeable sequence of unfolding threat arrays which we have identified in previous chapters.

PREPARATION FOR THE PRESIDENCY

Living and working in our country is probably sufficient preparation for a person to lead on domestic issues if he or she is elected president. Just being around and involved provides familiarity. It may also be helpful if he or she also has some executive experience in government.

But foreign relations are very different. A person doesn't learn about that from just hanging around in our country. Quite the contrary. Just hanging around in America promotes a myopic perspective that the rest of the world must be like us, and most of it isn't. This is a source of many problems in our foreign policy.

A good presidential candidate needs to have had experience in the issues, challenges and dynamics of global politics. How is it to be gained? First-hand experience abroad and in the State Department, Defense Department, intelligence agencies and even the White House are very valuable, but if the experience is in lower-level positions, not much of the actual interplay of global politics is experienced. So it must be obtained vicariously. The continual study of history is a great source, but a person must be a critical student, so that he is careful to avoid interpretations of history that place harmonism and convergence at its heart. History often is confused with gripping story telling, so he must be careful of the mythology of history created by too sympathetic biographers, by national champions, and by partisan narrators.

To handle foreign policy a person needs both preparation and experience – both experience working abroad and preparation through courses and reading on history, diplomacy, foreign cultures, and so on. But there is little such preparation for Americans, even most otherwise well-educated Americans, such as the graduates of our better universities.

As Bernard Lewis, one of our most knowledgeable historians of Islamic culture and Professor Emeritus at Princeton commented, "the general level of historical knowledge in American society is abysmally low."[2] Presidents Clinton and George W. Bush were accurate reflections of our electorate in this regard when they entered office. For example, it was reliably reported at the time that when President Clinton went to Normandy for the fiftieth anniversary of the D-Day invasion, he had to be tutored about World War II, even as to which nations had been the combatants and on which sides.

To a large degree we have isolated ourselves from the rest of the world by our vanity. "Starting in the 1970s," a student of political thought reports, " ... scholarship focused on ... 'microhistory' ... the ... repercussions of race, class, gender and ethnicity.... Given their relentless preoccupation with the inequities of American life, contemporary Americanists now write and teach about the United States from the 'inside.' ... regularly called upon America ... to 'come home,' and to focus on the country's domestic troubles.... The ... obsession with American social history has coincided with ... distain for political, military, diplomatic, and intellectual history, fields which require some knowledge of issues and trends [abroad].... As a result, too little attention is now paid ... to how life in the United States is affected by the decisions and policies made by foreign leaders ... "[3]

Because foreign matters are becoming more and more important to America, as it becomes more a target and assumes more responsibilities abroad – our presidents must be better prepared for these responsibilities. But in a great inconsistency, or paradox, they're not!

We've been choosing presidents from the ranks of our states' governors, and being governor of a state is not adequate preparation for leading the world's most significant power. Look at the recent record: Jimmy Carter had been governor of Georgia; Ronald Reagan of California; Bill Clinton of Arkansas; George W. Bush of Texas. The record wasn't much different early in the century. Woodrow Wilson had been governor of New Jersey and FDR of New York. Wilson had little foreign experience, which perhaps contributed to the mess he made of the peace negotiations at the end of World War I. He also opted for the idealism of the public culture, and was completely unable to deliver what he'd promised the world. FDR, though he'd been governor of New York before becoming president, had also had experience in the Department of the Navy in Washington, which makes even more perplexing his failure to deal with the rise of Hitler short of World War II. Yet he also embraced the idealism of the public culture, embracing Stalin as a way of pretending that idealism was merited, an action that almost certainly contributed to the dangers of the Cold War.

So firmly have American presidents like Wilson and Franklin Roosevelt grasped on to the idealism of popular culture to build support for war, that one almost wonders if Americans can be trusted to defend their countries without motives based in illusion.

Governorships are ordinarily not a good place to look for presidential candidates with foreign experience. Nor do our presidential candidates ordinarily prepare themselves effectively for the mission. The problem with a governor with presidential aspirations is that he or she is so busy running for president that he or she lacks the time to prepare to be president – except in the most superficial ways – learning the names of countries, the names of some of the more important foreign leaders; being briefed on simple answers to complex policy issues; and even gaining a tiny vocabulary about history. So for our recent presidents it's been on the job training, with, therefore, of significant and costly challenges from abroad.

QUALIFICATIONS FOR THE PRESIDENCY

What criteria should we be using in light of our global position to select a president, in addition to our concerns about a candidate's position on domestic issues? We should look for depth of experience and demonstrated personal qualifications.

Experience

A candidate for president should have:

- helped form domestic coalitions that have positively impacted US foreign policies;
- proposed and passed in Congress a wide range of viable legislative initiatives that impact foreign relations;
- an appreciation of the special interests (including those of the outsourcing federal bureaucacies) that affect our policies abroad and how to overcome them when necessary;
- the flexibility to lead under the constraints supplied by interest groups and the Congress;
- the honesty needed to use experience for the public good, without being beguiled or corrupted; and
- an ability to rise above platitudes in addressing issues of national security.

Because our presidents need better grounding in the international and defense aspects of their responsibilities, and the morning intelligence briefing is too short-sighted to meet the need, there should be a supplementary tutorial mechanism for either elected presidents or major party candidates for the office, including:

1. A briefing or education meeting for every presidential candidate about the public culture, the real situation, and how objectivity can be attained. The purpose is to provide a basket of knowledge to the president that is different than politics requires; and so it must be nonpartisan in its design and delivery. Ideally the briefings should come from a professional organization that monitors the world constantly and which is not identified with either party.

2. There should be an office of longer-term planning in the White House that assists the president with issues of international relations and defense policy. Part of the function of this office should be to advise the president on handling the press on these issues so that he can better confront the public culture. A president is likely to get better in performance by knowing what to do and how to do it; the objective is to assist the president in mastering the public culture.

DEMONSTRATED PERSONAL QUALIFICATIONS

A person who is well qualified for the presidency can come from any walk of life, but must necessarily have accomplished more than the garden variety of political and business leadership. His or her record of accomplishment should have demonstrated certain personal qualifications. Core character qualifications involve those that are obvious and apply to domestic as well as foreign policy leadership, including integrity, courage, and so on, so they need not be listed here. Instead, below are qualities a president should not have (although they are qualities that often make a successful politician at the state level). What a person who is our president should not be is:

- short-sighted, because many leaders of other nations or even terrorist groups act with long time horizons in mind – this is especially difficult to achieve in the United States because of our four-year presidential election cycle;
- superficial in thought and action, because international relations are often conducted with layer on layer of disguise and motivation;
- befuddled by the conflicting elements of public culture, so that he or she is unable to chart a consistent course and to change it when necessary; and
- beguiled by flattery or cunning by domestic and foreign adversaries, because to many abroad the American presidency seems to be handed

by our voters to people who are not prepared for it and who are on what is essentially a ego trip, inviting flattery or cunning as a device to beguile them.

Let us turn now to the positive mode. A president should encourage criticism and is always open to bad news, thereby insuring that s/he will always have all of the important information necessary to decision making.

A president should understand history – it doesn't always allow us to avoid errors, but it helps make them evident to us early. Probably, rigorous history studies should be a requirement for a presidential candidate! So should a thorough knowledge of the current international situation. Having to train presidents on the job is very dangerous.

The value of history is that it provides context to know what the intentions of others are and can permit us to predict their behavior (for example, presidents should know that a division in ideology, say between Iraq and Al Qaeda, does not mean they won't work together against us, like Hitler and Stalin did against Poland), understand other nations' fundamental interests and behavior patterns of their leadership; and get corrected the misinformation provided by the press as it pursues on a day-to-day basis its penchant for sensationalism, simplicity, and hysteria. Being truthful with, rather than stereotyping and antagonizing the media is likely to bring more constructive results, even if a president can only tell them a small amount.

Another part of the solution is leadership with courage. A president ought to ask us to act with courage, not whine about our losses. Here is what Winston Churchill said during the German Blitz on London in 1940, "The people should be accustomed to treat air raids as a matter of ordinary routine . . . as if they were no more than thunderstorms." Some forty thousand Londoners died during these "thunderstorms," but the British never panicked and surrendered as Hitler expected them to do.

A role of leadership is to never lose sight of the long term, always exploiting short-term events for long-term gain. Lyndon Johnson lacked this quality, and the result was the continuing Vietnam War.

The economy played a role, but not the major role, in George H. W. Bush's defeat and Clinton's election. The major role was played by Bush's inability to capitalize on his success in Iraq, and by the recognition of the American people that with the collapse of the Soviet Union we no longer needed a president who could stand up to the Soviets, so an inexperienced politician of Clinton's background – with his contempt for the military and his lack of interest and knowledge in world affairs – suddenly became acceptable as president – because the risk of world conflagration had so much declined.

There is also much to be said for the selection of a person who is not primarily a politician – as Eisenhower and Reagan were. It's important to note that two of the greatest leaders of democracy of our era were people of such strong character. Gandhi and Churchill (interestingly, political opponents themselves) shared a commitment to personal, physical work, as a key element of their common touch and common sense – Gandhi spun thread, and Churchill built walls. Here is Churchill describing his work: "At Chartwell . . . I built with my own hands a large part of two cottages and extensive kitchen-garden walls . . . " And, again, Captain Pim, who was sent to look after the War Room at the Admiralty in London after Churchill returned as First Lord of the Admiralty at the outset of World War II in 1939, encountered Churchill in the room. Churchill asked, "Who are you?" "I've been ordered to look after your war room," replied Captain Pim. "Right!" Churchill exclaimed, "get to the other end of this carpet and we'll roll it up together."[4]

Experience and demonstrated personal qualifications are very important, but insufficient. What is crucial to America's security today is the capacity of a president to execute properly the nation's approach to its defense. This means that the ability of a president to implement Strategic Independence is now the highest qualification for office. This requires that a president see through the layers of deceit that characterize the relationships among nations, and have the courage to act in the nation's interests even at some political cost. Generally, however, our politicians are far better at rousing speeches and high ideals than at accomplishing a task – even the defense of our nation – quickly, efficiently, and fully. As we've seen, effective implementation has almost always been a shortcoming of our presidents, and it's what we should be looking for in our candidates via experience and demonstrated personal qualifications.

CHAPTER 19: KEY POINTS

1. America has a history of ultimate success in conflict abroad, but it has been at much greater risk and cost than if we had had better presidential leadership.
2. Great presidential leadership involves
   - Keeping America safe at reasonable cost in lives by avoiding great wars; and
   - Leading and educating our people about other countries and how their actions affect us, so that he or she has support in the steps necessary to avoid great conflicts.

3. Choosing great presidents requires us to select people who have experience in foreign affairs and demonstrated accomplishments in that arena. This is more important to America's survival today than ever before, because the challenges we now face and will face in the future are increasingly complex and dangerous.

TWENTY

Master of Illusions

The heart of this book is the question: How can our leaders deal with an electorate whose heads are full of illusions?

Our public culture is a major contributor to making the United States unpredictable and consequently an agent of instability in the world. This is because an American president ordinarily fears the political consequences of being candid with the American people about our objectives when what he tells them is in conflict with deeply held illusions.

How much truth can the American people take? Our public culture is driven by wishful thinking by the public and results in illusions which our politicians and media embrace in order to curry our favor. There would appear to be no prospect within this dynamic for a more candid presidency.

Our conclusion about the reality of the United Nations and what it means for American policy is precisely the sort of hard truth that our country begs from our president but that so contradicts the illusions of our public culture that it is very difficult for the president to respond honestly. Do we really want to know about the reality of the UN and can we accept it?

The difficult issues arise when the answer is no – when we cling tenaciously, as we often do, to the illusions of our public culture. In that case, what should the president do? Should he follow the illusions, dignify the UN and treat it as a leading force in the world – that is, should our president become captive to our public culture and lead the United States into what he recognizes to be dangerous grounds? Alternatively, should he tell the nation the truth and try to survive what is likely to be a firestorm of denunciation fueled by the public culture. Finally, can he find another course by which he demonstrates himself to be a master of our illusions?

Since September 11, 2001, the American public has gained a new dimension of maturity. The world is recognized to be more dangerous than our public culture suggests; so that a window is opened for our president to be more honest with our people than before. But the window is not very broad, and the resilience of the public culture is very strong. Can the opportunity be seized?

Unfortunately, many of our leaders do not seem to realize the subtle shift that new maturity has brought, and instead of explaining the true motives of American action abroad, continue to mislead us with half-truths and overly moralistic messages.

A STRONG TIDE OF TRUTH

In the majority in our country today are the members of the baby boom generation, crucially shaped by the experience of Vietnam and retaining a profound distrust of presidential authority. Although recognizing that in today's threatening global environment a president must act, sometimes plunging the nation into overt conflict, they mistrust his or her motives and insist on being fully informed. They want to know exactly how the president makes a decision in favor of conflict, and why he makes it. Otherwise, they will not support the president. And because the great strength of America lies in the energy and initiative of our people, failure to gain public support is often fatal to even the proper policies.[1] The new maturity of Americans means that we are prepared to do things that we didn't do in the past because we thought they could be avoided. The continuing suspicion of Americans means that for our leaders to be successful, they must do these things in a way that gains public confidence, both more open and more honest than in the past.

This is no different fundamentally from any human action – that there are always two things about which we must be concerned – what is done and how it is done. The wrong thing done the right way (although this may seem an oxymoron) will fail; the right thing done the wrong way will also fail. We argue in this book that the right thing for America in the world is a policy of Strategic Independence, and the right way to do it is with much more honesty about motives and much more openness about the basis of decisions than is common today in diplomacy and presidential leadership.

Strategic Independence is the freedom to defend our nation effectively without being deflected by the hidden agendas of other nations. This is very different from strategic overreach – the attempt to remake the world in our own image – that has always been a great temptation to American leaders and is almost certain to end again in frustration and tragedy.

As American public culture matures it is going to become increasingly difficult to pull the wool over the eyes of the American people, and presidents who miss this trend will see their policies frustrated.

But this is very hard for presidents and presidential candidates to recognize. Honesty is not natural to politicians, especially when bad news is involved. The easier path is to exaggerate or misrepresent to gain immediate public support for the required action.

The temptation in politics to resort to what are believed to be popular motives and conceal real ones is very strong. But in a more mature America, a president who succumbs to the temptation is likely to forfeit the trust of the American people.

But there's more to the case for dissembling than this. In the international arena, a great power, such as America, acting in its own interests, alarms the rest of the world, and so it seems that diplomacy requires that it disguise its motives. This happens even when we are only seeking our own protection. For example, when we put troops in Saudi Arabia, then in Afghanistan, then in Iraq, we thoroughly alarmed both other governments in the region and the Russians – all of who distrust our motives even if self-defense is one of them. As Paul Kennedy has argued, great powers collapse in part because their power forces the rest of the world to organize against them.[2] To avoid this natural tendency, he implies, a great power needs to find an ideological reason that can command wide support outside its borders to justify its use of force.

When the incentive to get immediate support can be combined with an opportunity to discomfort the domestic political opposition, and when foreign governments that might be hostile can be placated as well, then the temptation to dissemble may become overwhelming. Sometimes, a president simply can't help himself.

Underneath the expediency that leads to clumsy deceptions about motives is an underlying belief that most people are stupid and can't make informed decisions if given the truth. But it is exactly this sort of consideration – ones that support dissembling about motives – that undermines support among our people for our government, because contrived causes are rarely convincing to many people. Rationalizations for dishonesty significantly underestimate the American people and show that an administration fails to recognize our new maturity.

In the case of the Second Gulf War, the connection of the invasion of Iraq to the war on terror was seemingly difficult for the Bush administration to make, and efforts to do so did not provide immediate broad public support. But danger from possible Iraqi weapons of mass destruction aroused immediate support in America, and even abroad, although other reasons intervened to generate opposition. Furthermore, because the Administration's opposition comes from the political left, it was thought that an idealistic motive with a liberal slant could be very effective in helping to split what was likely to be ideologically based opposition to the war. Hence, the administration offered the invasion of Iraq as an attempt to liberate women and religious minorities. The administration was thus able to combine an immediate threat from weapons of mass destruction with liberal idealism to both generate support and confuse opposition.

There was a strong element of deception in all this – because the threat from weapons of mass destruction was exaggerated; because the administration was not really acting for the objective of liberating Iraq's women and religious minorities and because the administration's real objectives – in the battle against Islamic terror and in the large power rivalry of geopolitics – were not being truthfully acknowledged. To couch America's true motives for invading Iraq in the cloak of eliminating weapons of mass destruction, when they're not to be found; and of liberating women when the administration has done little to indicate that it cares about women's rights and American women know it; was likely to be ridiculed and ineffective, and that's what happened. Clumsy efforts at concealing true motives are a key reason why presidents fail to gain full public support for foreign policy.

Presidential deception about motives for war has been common. In what is perhaps the best known example in American history, President McKinley wanted to seize Spanish colonies in the Pacific to secure a sea-route to China. At the time, coal-powered ships needed a series of coaling stations to cross the Pacific. McKinley justified the Spanish-American War as a way to liberate Cubans and Filipinos from Spanish tyranny. Today we know better and now think of President McKinley as a racist and the victim of manipulation by Hearst's newspaper empire. So today McKinley's reputation is in tatters.

The trouble with following today the historic pattern of global politics and the current incentives to dissemble about motives is that with the current attitude of the American people, it is almost certain to boomerang on an administration. This is in large part due to the rising sophistication of communications technology – which arguably is why Clinton was impeached (tried but not convicted) for sexual misconduct in office while Kennedy was given a free pass. If voters feel they've been had – and there are many technologies today that allow them to discover – then anger mounts and supports erodes. Such deception is exactly the reason why people come to distrust their presidents – because when he isn't telling the truth, it becomes obvious.

TRUTH USED TO BE THE FIRST CASUALTY OF WAR

Although the Bush administration stumbled in its justification of the reasons for the war, it has been remarkably open in its conduct of the war.

It is widely held that truth is the first casualty of war – but not this time in Iraq. Instead there was a strong tide of truth. There were reporters with American troops at the front lines in Iraq (so-called embedded reporters) and, although their stories were sometimes held up and sometimes censored, there was much more up to the minute and accurate news from the battle front than ever before. A British Broadcasting Company study showed that reporters embedded with American and British forces in Iraq provided more balanced news coverage than the traditional news system. The finding is particularly interesting as the BBC was no friend of the war in Iraq.[3]

Reports were also coming from the other side, not just propaganda, although that too, but the reports of professional news correspondents. At a key moment in the war, when the Iraqi government was insisting to reporters that American troops were far from Baghdad, reporters looked out on the streets in front of their hotels, saw American tanks, and asked the Iraqi information minister how he could expect them to believe what their eyesight denied.

This incident was reminiscent of a similar one, although reporters played no role. In 1940 while Hitler still sought an agreement with Stalin, the Soviet foreign minister, Vyacheslav Molotov, visited Berlin. During a discussion, Hitler's foreign minister told him that the English, with whom Germany was already at war, were finished. Just then an air raid began. "Then whose," asked Molotov, "bombers are those above, and whose bombs?" The answer, as Molotov well knew, was that they were English bombers and English bombs falling on Berlin. The Soviets would not accept the Nazi assertions that England was finished when their own senses told them otherwise.

Similarly, in 2003, reporters in Baghdad, like Molotov in Berlin, refused to accept the assurances of Iraqi ministers of state about a supposedly ineffective enemy (Britain in 1940 and the United States in 2003) when their eyes and ears told them otherwise.

The openness in 2003 became even more surprising after the war. President Bush had justified the American invasion of Iraq largely on the grounds that Iraq had or was developing weapons of mass destruction. So when American forces overran the country, people in America and elsewhere wanted to see the weapons. But they were not found. That they were not found was a matter of some considerable political embarrassment to the president, and many people suspected that there would be false reports that weapons had been found, or at least an embargo on the almost daily news that they had not been found. If truth were always a casualty of war, here it would certainly be.

Yet nothing of the sort happened. The reports continued that the administration had failed to find the weapons on which it has laid so much importance; and the embarrassment continued. The administration didn't provide or permit the reporting of the whole truth, and certainly there were also falsehoods and rumors (rather that nothing but the truth), but there was a lot of truth nonetheless, and certainly more than in the past and more than many of us expected this time. Many people are very cynical about governments and politicians in this sort of situation, yet the administration seems to have been very straight about this. It's surprising – why is it happening this way?

The answer is in large part that the American people are more mature. Truth didn't undermine the support of the American people for the president or the administration. It lessened support when the president was suspected of misleading us about the causes of the war; it forced the president to spend time trying to bolster his case; but it didn't cripple our policy.

The administration seems to have understood that our people are now more mature, and can handle unpleasant news, whether about casualties or about errors we've made; perhaps even about being mislead. The administration appears to have calculated that not many people care strongly enough about the existence or not of weapons of mass destruction to punish the president politically. No one will admit to wanting to put Saddam back in power, if anyone does.

Rather than undermining the president, the truth only embarrassed him somewhat, and the embarrassment the truth brought to the president allowed observers like the authors of this book to insist that the president would have been better advised to tell the American people his full motivation for invading Iraq, rather than a somewhat contrived explanation which didn't stand up in the light of postwar discovery (or lack thereof).

It is always easy in government to think of reasons why the truth could be harmful to our country's interests, and to use that as a rationale for not being truthful. Sometimes the argument has merit, as when we try to disguise the identity of our intelligence agents. But often the argument is used to suppress information that would be embarrassing to those in power, rather than dangerous to those serving the country. The opinion of many diplomats and experts in international affairs seems based on contempt for the intelligence of the American voter, and so the presumption that information should be withheld or falsified. This is an error. Although there is room for differences about how much might be revealed, there is little room for differences about whether or not what is said should be truth or not. It should be truth; a key reason for this conclusion today is that since Vietnam, presidents are deeply distrusted by many of our people, so that reinforcing mistrust by dishonesty undermines the president's support and power. The only exception to the practicality of truth is when there is a tactical, short-term reason to mislead an adversary in order to protect our troops or agents (as in a planted story to mislead an enemy).

Honesty is thus a practical as well as ethical issue; it's a vehicle for amassing support. In order for presidents to be effective, they need the support of the people. Our history provides examples of major failures in foreign policy because the president couldn't get the support of the people. In retrospect, it seems that this was largely because the president had failed to be honest with the people about the world situation and the reason for actions we were taking (or worse, the need for actions we were not taking). Gaining the support and trust of the people is the key to getting things done in America; it is the ultimate source of power in a democracy. Tens of thousands of Americans might not have died in combat, had our presidents leveled with the American people about the real situations they faced. Had the people known the real reasons, a debate might have been encouraged that would have flushed out any shortcomings of the president's strategy, allowing him to perfect it by taking advantage of the collective intelligence. America's great strength has never been her leadership – not in government nor in business – but always the imagination and energy of her people. This is the strength of a free people – our leaders know it, but don't really believe it or act on it. But for intelligence and creativity to be harnessed, a leader must clearly state his or her objectives. Communications are not merely a game, or merely part of a game – they are essential to success in our county.

People resist calls to action when the reasons don't make sense, which is something the president is learning about his Iraq policy. But as we've said above, the culprit is not too much honesty (that is, permitting the public to know that no weapons of mass destruction were found), but too little.

There is a paradox in this. Modern means of communications and psychological manipulation are continuing to strengthen the hands of propagandists. In consequence, there is a temptation to use propaganda just as our opponents do. But for us to go that direction risks our becoming lost in a wilderness of disinformation to the point of befuddlement.

The Bush administration is due a compliment for the greater degree of honest information than in the past that it has shared with the American people. But it hasn't gone far enough.

The American people are asking is there any way to get a president who cares enough about our country to tell the truth, or has high enough ethical standards to put politics behind, not before, the nation's welfare? Or even understands the practical utility of honesty in building and retaining support from the American people?

But truth, important as it is, is not enough. We want more than truth from our president – we want effective action that will defend our country. A president mired in illusions who is truthful about his mistaken policies is not much to be preferred to one who isn't truthful. There is danger that we now find ourselves in that situation – with a president who is being honest about his motivations, but who is mistaken in them. There is strong evidence that the Bush administration is sincere in its desire to implant Western-style democracy in the Middle East, just as was Woodrow Wilson sincere in his desire to build a League of Nations that would make the world safe for democracy, and Franklin Roosevelt was sincere in his desire to build a United Nations that would cause the Soviet Union to champion the goals of the Atlantic Charter. Sincerity did not justify naïve idealism that ended in each instance in either disaster or a serious risk of war.

Unfortunately, the Bush administration is demonstrating the same sort of naïve idealism about America's role in the world as did Wilson and Franklin Roosevelt, and is as sincere about it. Were it not the case, then the Bush administration would have to be preparing the American people for a long period of conflict of one sort or another on the Crescent of Fire. If the administration were simply using democracy and free enterprise as a tactic in the conflict, then it should be preparing our population at home for the problematic nature of the task in the Middle East, and building support for staying the course. But aside from some almost perfunctory lines in his speeches, the president seems to believe this isn't necessary. This is the same blunder made in our transition strategy for the former USSR – to imply that convergence guarantees a fairly direct transition abroad to our sort of society.

GEORGE W. BUSH AND OUR PUBLIC CULTURE

"The Presidency is the focus for the most intense and persistent emotions in the American polity," James Barber told us. ". . . The President is one man trying to do a job – a picture . . . understandable to the mass of people . . ."[4] This presidential obligation is made much more difficult by our public culture that now departs in its key elements so much from the reality of the situations with which the president must deal.

The president has been kept well informed as to the thinking of the public, and therefore has been continually confronted with its dependence on the illusions of the public culture. Bush studied marketing at Harvard Business School, but he has advanced far beyond his teachers, and so are politicians generally far ahead of business executives in effective marketing today.

A recent hot topic in business marketing is collaborative customer relations marketing, but political candidates of the same party have shared poll information, and thereby done collaborative customer-relations marketing for years with increasing sophistication and skill.[5]

The president has monitored the electorate (his customers) continually via polls, measuring customer attitudes and desires. He has continually adjusted the product (policies and actions) provided by the White House and its presentation via media and advertising to the perceived wants of voters.

America does not have a well-educated and informed population in matters of national security, and that is partly a cause of the wishful thinking that drives our illusions, but is also very much a result of them. "The ordinary man" H. G. Wells told us decades ago, "thinks as little about political matters as he can, and stops thinking about them as soon as possible.... The modern citizen must be informed first, then consulted. Before he can vote, he must hear the evidence; before he can decide, he must know. It is not by setting up polling-booths, but by setting up schools and making literature and knowledge and news universally accessible that the way is opened ... to the willingly cooperative state that is the modern ideal."[6]

Frequently, polls provide contradictory data about America's values and beliefs. However, a greater concern is that this has less to do with the measurement device – the survey, survey-taker – and more to do with the person answering the questions in the poll. "Sometimes collective preferences [measured by polls] seem to represent something like the will of the people, but frequently they do not.... In the final analysis the primary culprit is not any inherent shortcoming in the methods of survey research. Rather it is the limited degree of knowledge held by ordinary citizens about public affairs and the tendency for some kinds of people to be better informed than others."[7] The confusion is related to the way that Americans are miseducated into being superficial, an aspect of our public culture.

Presidents usually muddle messages for most issues, but, on a central issue, they try to be clear. Yet, in recent years, we've seen confusion of rationales and of objectives for key actions emanating from the president.

President Bush presented the war on terror is as the central issue of his Administration; why then was his message about it so muddled?

There are several reasons, involving:

1. An encounter with public culture, in which the president sought a way to justify his actions in a popular mode, but also tried to be candid, and the two conflicted;

2. The erroneous conviction fostered by the public culture that things are better than they are (the harmonist fallacy), so that sacrifices were not necessary;

3. Failure to develop a clear strategy for the United States – instead groping toward it in a mist of confusion, as is case with most American presidents;

4. Difficulty seeing the future and therefore connecting what was being done in the present to what was needed ahead; and

5. Difficulty integrating what was going on in one part of the world with what was occurring in another, combined with a growing realization that the interconnections are in fact crucial.

The result of these factors was confusion in the president's mind about what he was doing and as a result, an inability to articulate it clearly. Hence, it should not be surprising that President Bush in some instances failed to provide the clear message so central to leadership since the public culture makes it so difficult to be candid about objectives and methods.

The situation was not improved by the Bush public relations offensive for democracy initiated in 2005, because it embedded the administration's position too deeply in our public culture and thereby created fissures of inconsistency in the Administration's policy. Initially, the PR offensive was a great success, because:

1. It abandoned and replaced the fiasco of the justification of the invasion of Iraq because of weapons of mass destruction;

2. Tactically, it put the Europeans and Democrats in a tough spot (because they don't want to oppose exporting democracy) and so for a while took the heat off the Administration on Iraq; and

3. Strategically, it nudged the rest of the world toward a posture which left the United States dominant because only the United States can combine a modern democracy (which it invented) with superpower effectiveness (via enough national unity to do something effective). In part, this is because of the strength provided by the U.S. economic culture. "Democracies don't wage aggressive wars against democracies" means that all but the United States are too divided and pacifist to do so – even to defend themselves effectively. So if all other countries are pushed or pulled to the U.S. democratic model, they will all be ineffective. This was perhaps the deep meaning behind Bush's offensive for democracy.

This criticism of President George W. Bush is a deep one – that he has not accomplished the necessary big things – Russia is beginning to remilitarize; China is modernizing its military and becoming more nationalistically belligerent; so called rogue states are building nuclear weapons and none of these things are being successfully countered. He has been unable to provide leadership that matches resources with the significance of the threats we face, because he's been caught in the web of exaggeration and illusions that are our public culture and cannot bring a proper perspective to the issues he has confronted.

A TACTICAL RESPONSE VERSUS A STRATEGIC OBJECTIVE

Suppose that the Administration hasn't been serious about bringing democracy to the Arab world, in the sense that it doesn't actually believe that it is possible, even if desirable. What then might be the actual strategy? It might be, and if so is a much more sensible strategy, to seize the strategic center of the Middle East and use it against our opponents (Syria, Iran, and various terrorist organizations). By such an action, we disconcert our enemies (including Syria, the Palestinian terrorists, and the Iranians – to say nothing of our rivals, the French, Germans, Russians, and Chinese).

Seeking a plan for victory in the Iraq War is misguided. What we want is containment of insurrection and terror in the Middle East and Crescent of Fire without provoking a nuclear conflict with another major power. It's possible to achieve these purposes without an end of the war in Iraq – because Iraq may slide into civil war even though the power of the terrorists is broken in the international context, which is our main objective. Again, led by muddle-headed politicians and an always confused media, we find ourselves way off the mark in our strategic thinking, focusing on Iraq and losing sight of the overall objectives of our defense policy.

What happens in Iraq isn't as important as what happens around Iraq. But Iraq is the key to what happens around it – it is the strategic center of the region (though not its strongest or richest country). Metaphorically, it is the high ground that dominates the Mid-eastern battlefield. So to seize it was an effective move. "With the American imperium encroaching menacingly on Iran's frontiers," students of the Middle East tell us, "Khamenei [for eighteen years the leader of Iran], one of the country's most hawkish thinkers, is being forced to lean toward the pragmatists on some issues."[8] This is very important because Iran is increasingly dangerous. "Protected by its nuclear umbrella, Iran will be able to promote terror, undermine pro-Western governments, and transfer its nuclear know-how to other recalcitrant states – all with near-impunity."[9] To justify the seizure of Iraq by reference to weapons of mass destruction was merely a political device that backfired.

There is certainly a consideration about oil in our involvement in the Middle East. There is much discussion that if the United States were less dependent on Middle Eastern oil, we could avoid involvement in the turmoil of the region. There is truth in this. At this point, however, there is no likely other source of sufficient oil for ourselves or the other major nations of the world. Russia is the hope of many. "Bush Sr. made the landmark deal between the United States and Saudi Arabia that was the basis of U.S.-OPEC 'cooperation' for two decades up to 2001, said Chris Weafer, chief strategist at Alfa Bank and an adviser to OPEC. Weafer speculated that Bush could have come to Moscow to help build new ties and 'help get U.S. companies directly involved in big oil and gas projects – especially ahead of Chinese or Indian companies.'"[10] However, Russia holds 5 percent of the world's proven oil reserves; Saudi holds 25 percent. The "most important energy relationship . . . is the only one that has really mattered for more than half a century: the one between Saudi Arabia and America."[11] Until the United States is much less dependent on oil than it is now, this is a key element of the geopolitical equation and explains in part why we have seized a key strategic position in the Middle East, in part in order to defend Iraq's neighbors, the Saudis.

The administration is thus far unable to craft a consistent energy policy, although the president is eloquently insisting that the nation's dependence on foreign oil is a serious security problem. The price of oil is not a market price – it is a price set by a cartel of nations of which we are not a member and the price is a political decision, not an economic one. We have chosen to accept it; it is not given us by market forces. We have lacked a credible policy to move away from dependence, but we have allowed a cartel to create economic havoc in the world while pouring money into the coffers of regimes in the Middle East that are not always our friends. The administration condemns the situation but takes no steps to end it that are commensurate with the scale of the problem.

In addition, if we must fight large numbers of terrorists somewhere, it is certainly better for us to be fighting them in Iraq than in the United States itself. In the same way that there had to be killing grounds for the Nazi faithful – there being no other way to end the horrors they sponsored – and these were best on their soil and not ours, there must now be places to eliminate the terrorists.

Such an action by a great power (the invasion of Iraq as part of a strategy reaching far beyond the borders of Iraq itself and involving broad geopolitical objectives) is difficult or impossible to justify within the popular culture. Therefore, without making many attempts to explain what is really happening (there were some early on – for example, when the administration said that every country that supported the terrorists was a potential target for us), the administration abandoned the effort and retreated (its proponents would say "progressed") into a much more politically effective posture dictated by the public culture – one that focused on bringing democracy to the Middle East.

The great danger is that in having finally discovered a successful formulation of its foreign policy within the public culture, so that it briefly cowed its critics and mobilized its friends, the administration (like all other administrations before it) was inclined to begin to believe its own rhetoric (to "drink the Kool-Aid" in the language of the venture capital community, which often faces a similar danger of deluding itself about the quality of its investments) and so lose its objectivity about fitting solution to problem. An extensive criticism of the instability arising out of a modern form of fascist-like movement in Ecuador, Peru, and Bolivia notes the danger that popular elections pose in this situation and ends with the comment: "Despite all this, as demonstrated in Ecuador in 2002 and in Bolivia in 2003, Washington is either preoccupied or paralyzed by an unrealistic belief in some kind of inevitability of democracy everywhere – whether in Peru, Bolivia, or Iraq. The consequences are as dangerous whatever the cause."[12]

In the process of shifting ground, Bush may have been captured by the public culture. He defended democracy everywhere in all conditions, which is a form of overreach. Speaking in Riga, Latvia, on May 7, 2005, the president said: "We will not repeat the mistakes of other generations, appeasing or excusing tyranny, and sacrificing freedom in the vain pursuit of stability. We have learned our lesson; no one's liberty is expendable. In the long run, our security and true stability depend on the freedom of others."[13]

Writing about the centuries' long effort of the Greeks after Alexander's conquests to root Greek culture into the Middle East, Will Durant observed that it didn't work. "The masses . . . continued to speak their native tongues, to pursue their long-accustomed ways, and to worship their . . . gods. . . . There was no such fusion of races and cultures as Alexander had dreamed of; there were Greeks and Greek civilization on the top, and a medley of Asiatic peoples and cultures underneath. . . . Oriental monarchy proved more powerful than Greek democracy, and finally impressed its form upon the West . . . the Asiatic theory of the divine right of kings passed down through Rome and Constantinople into modern

Europe.... The Greeks offered the East philosophy, the East offered Greece religion; religion won..."[14]

It is this history of which the Bush Administration remained apparently ignorant. Seeking to graft American style political liberty into the Middle East generally, starting with Iraq, they soon came face to face with reality in other countries of the region, and modifying their high rhetoric of spreading democracy, they quickly began to sound like hypocrites. President Bush declared in his second inaugural that "It is the policy of the United States to seek and support the growth of democratic movements and institutions in every nation and culture, with the ultimate goal of ending tyranny in our world.... All who live in tyranny and hopelessness can know: the United States will not ignore your oppression, or excuse your oppressors. When you stand for your liberty, we will stand with you." After that declaration, the president repeatedly supported dictators, normalizing relations with Muammar Qadhafi of Libya, congratulating President Murabak of Egypt on a rigged election, supporting the Saudi monarchy, and fumbling the restoration of Lebanese democracy. Similarly, the Administration has shifted its concern in Russia from democracy to oil. "Since it no longer considers relations with Moscow to be a priority, the United States no longer intends to emphasize issues related to democracy in Russia – thus giving the Kremlin carte blanche in any policies that don't affect American interests."[15] By these actions, President Bush made a mockery of his own policy for all the world to see. No one made him adopt the extension of democracy as the keystone of American foreign policy, and no one made him make a mockery of it. The president did it himself.[16]

These actions add to the impression that President Bush hid behind the public culture to try to get public support for his actions abroad; that he acted in ways inconsistent with his pretensions; that he was unable to pursue a consistent policy; and that he appointed as key subordinates people who were unable to cause him to do better. It was a classic failure of leadership – a retreat into demagoguery and inconsistency of policy.

Our role in Iraq should not be to determine its future or to make it work successfully as a state. It is only to make sure that it doesn't fall into the hands of people who are our enemy and attack us directly or via surrogates from it. We should get out when it is not in enemy hands. Whether or not the consequence is a viable state or a civil war is for the Iraqis, not us, to determine.

To continue our presence in Iraq may very well be an error. The tactics of the weaker (in direct confrontation) will often be decoy, demoralize, and destroy. These were the tactics of the Mongols when their armies, less numerous than those of their foes and less heavily armed, swept over Asia and Europe in the thirteenth century.[17] They are the tactics, adopted to a different technological setting, of al-Queda now. They are successful when the stronger side falls for them, which was very common during Genghis Khan's time, and it is up to us to determine for our time.

Our effort in Iraq is to find the small percentage of insurrectionaries in Iraq or terrorists flooding into Iraq who truly wish to attack us. Using military forces to go from home to home to look for terrorists is probably not going to yield the desired result. Moreover, by rooting through the vast majority who are not our enemies, we are upsetting the status quo, potentially destabilizing it and adding to our opponents. This is the basic paradox of guerrilla (or terrorist) warfare – that in trying to root the minority who are militants out of the overall population, a foreign power (ourselves in this instance) risks alienating the majority, and so worsening its situation. The militants count on this happening.

A GAME PLAYED WITH OTHER PEOPLE'S LIVES

Grand politics, the way it's played by dictators like Hitler, Stalin, Mao, and Saddam Hussein, is a game played with other people's lives. It's a distasteful, immoral game to most of us, and the Western democracies have spent much effort trying to keep out of the game – always unsuccessfully as successive wars have demonstrated, until now.

Some people are very confused about this. They continue to favor reliance on diplomacy to an extent that it is a lot like the strategy labeled appeasement before World War II, and that degenerated into strengthening aggressors for war. They offer "incentives" to states such as Iran and North Korea, to stop their nuclear weapons programs. Already, those states understand the game – they both ask for incentives and then cheat on their commitments, just as such governments have always done.

But the new strategy now available to America, Strategic Independence, refuses to play the game of grand politics with dictators and police states: that's the beauty of it. Far from objecting to America's Strategic Independence, people all over the world who find the old sort of grand politics, particularly in its form of real politik, should welcome it as the first opportunity in centuries to break out of a distasteful and immoral game.

Strategic Independence can be integrated into America's engagement with the world. Recent administrations have been groping toward this strategy. There is a way out of the old and discredited game of international power politics; the way involves greater Strategic Independence for the United States.

The multilateral arrangements of the Cold War are now dissolving. Germany and France are seeking to define a path for Europe that is independent of our country, and the historic German suspicion of America – born in two world wars – is now reasserting itself and merging with a French rivalry with America that hasn't wavered significantly in more than two hundred years. With China surging and American protection of Japan less certain than in the past, Japan is beginning to assert a more independent tone as well.

Cooperation with other countries is possible and desirable, indeed it is essential in carrying out many military operations abroad. But, we must be able to go it alone whenever there is an impasse with potential allies on a matter which we believe threatens our vital interests. We shouldn't give anyone a veto over our national security. We are prepared to extend the principle of cooperation, but only within bounds we consider reasonable. We shouldn't accept the rules the Europeans try to impose on us. In behaving in this way, we believe the president has been correct.

The Chinese position is for good statesmen to be like bamboo, bending when they have to, but never breaking. It is a good simile for us.

"Every story of Presidential decision-making is really two stories, according to a scholar of the presidency, "an outer one in which a rational man calculates and an inner one in which an emotional man feels."[18] Yet we cannot afford to depend on emotional responses by presidents little experienced in international relations. Instead, "it is absolutely essential, in order to have intelligence at all, for a system to have flexible, nonbrittle common sense that can handle unexpected situations in a fluid, natural way, bringing to bear whatever it happens to know."[19] It is exactly flexible common sense that Strategic Independence brings to American national security policy.

THE NEXT STEPS

We have been concerned in this book with American presidential leadership and the public culture as it affects our ability to deal effectively with the central risks faced by America. "My most solemn duty," President George W. Bush told our nation in his second inaugural speech on January 20, 2005, "is to protect this nation and its people from further attacks and emerging threats." How is that to be done?

The primary task of our leadership at this time is to act to avoid foreseeable dangers if at all possible. To do so, we must never lose sight of them. We must judge every action we take (including antiterrorist activities) in light of these looming dangers; and we must do nothing to limit our ability to address the greater dangers.

We do not do this effectively by striving to have good relations with the other great powers. Ambition and interest always take precedence over relations. This is the great fallacy of many proposals for improving the international atmosphere for peace. It's nice to have good relations but not crucial. Good relations with a potential challenger are valueless when it comes to deflecting a challenge. Nor do we protect ourselves from great dangers by overreaching with respect to more modest ones now.

This is the fallacy of the Bush initiatives in Iraq. To the extent that Iraq demonstrates the effectiveness of our military and its new weapons, it suggests caution to Russia and China and their client states, a good result; to the extent that our involvement in Iraq goes beyond this and suggests to our potential rivals that we are overstretched or unable to distinguish what is important from what is illusion, then the Iraq adventure is counterproductive. Our current effort at democracy-building in Iraq is high risk; our public should be informed that we are gambling. If we fail, if Iraq culture is resistant to democracy, we have to revert to a different position, and this will be much easier if the Administration has prepared for it.

The first task of a master of illusion is to recognize that idealism can be retained for some purposes but must be strictly limited to appropriate uses. Masters of Illusion understanding this in the current context will recognize that we confront a sequence of unfolding challenges – the Crescent of Fire, Russia, China, and the EU – that can be dealt with best using a composite strategy of Strategic Independence and global federalism with only a veneer of democratic free enterprise. Masters of Illusion understand all the interdependences, and continuously make proposals to adjust programs and expenditures to maximize American social welfare and national security. Masters of Illusions aren't totalitarians or sci-fi planners. They don't fool themselves into believing in micro-management of the world. But with a grasp of the big picture they have the capacity to navigate the shoals of engagement much more effectively than their predecessors.

This realization is the most important point in this book. Our nation is ensnared by public cultural blinders, and cannot be free unless it sees through the snare.

Many people have failed to attain this insight because they accept the public culture and base their arguments on approved partial truisms. This gets them somewhere, but never far enough. They can justify positions that are grounded in the public culture by claiming a need to deceive, both Americans and others; but since they don't have a stratified realist strategy, a fact proven by the internal contradictions of their policies, they are merely deceiving themselves. We call for more candor, hoping that our leaders will then emerge from the hiding of deception into a more forthright statement of realistic strategies.

The inability of the vast majority to see through public culture is partly a failure of individual intellect. But it is also conditioned by socialization, especially the inadequacies of our educational system and the media. The best solution is for a cultural revolution where as individuals and a nation we understand the ways in which we deceive ourselves, and develop antidotes. The media, and miseducation make this difficult, which is why it is imperative for public intellectuals to sound the alarm, and preach the need for masters of illusion committed to the values of democratic free enterprise but not to the illusions of the public culture.

What are the most important things an American president could achieve for our security? They are five in number:

1. Define the United States geopolitical goals in non-rhetorical terms, outside the public culture (that is, not as building democracies in the world but in the terms of long-term economic realism); the best context for this is our concept of a pluralist, diverse world, rather than a messianic search for democracies everywhere, motivated by the strictures of our public culture;

2. Articulate and pursue Strategic Independence – a major challenge for the President is to sell Strategic Independence to the American people in the face of the predisposition against it created by our public culture. Americans don't want to face the reality of threats (harmonism and convergence both deny them). But unless the reality of threats is accepted, then there is no reason for a response such as Strategic Independence envisions. And within Strategic Independence lies with crucial importance the need for an effective national missile defense in some form, to which opposition within the public culture is intense – to build such a defense contradicts the strong denial of danger which is at the heart of our public culture. Here is a direct test of a president's ability to show himself or herself master of our illusions, and one that will confront the next several of our presidents;

3. Join Strategic Independence with the concept of Global Federalism (not insider sovereign World Government masquerading under the banner of globalization), which accepts cultural diversity as a rationale for not imposing our way of life on everyone else, while supporting international cooperation. Strategic Independence is not only for

self-defense, but to diminish nuclear risk. It also provides support for an intrinsically multicultural world – one in which there is neither harmonism nor the expectation of convergence. It is against the acceptance of a truly multicultural world that the assumptions of harmonism and convergence, the key elements of our public culture, stand most evidently as illusions – for the world is multicultural; it is not benign; and it is not evolving toward a state in which everyone else is just like us in America;

4. Promote a less commercial, less sensationalistic media in which honest information is available; and

5. Achieve certain key improvements in our strategic positioning:
   - Break our dependence on imported oil – because that frees us from the Middle Eastern cauldron with all its interactions with every other major country in the world (the EU, China, Russia, Japan);
   - Forestall the building of China's ballistic missile capability to hit the United States; and
   - Forestall the Russians building the next generation of nuclear missile capability.

Unfortunately, although items 2 and 3 above are the most important of all to the longer-term security of the American people – as only Russia and China are likely in the next several decades to have the military capacity to destroy our homeland (isolated nuclear attacks by terrorists or by rogue states, although awful to contemplate, are a much smaller order of threat) – we certainly can't deter Russia and probably not China from this course if they determine to build new nuclear capability, and our best option in that case is to achieve a solo ballistic missile defense capability.

6. Deal with nuclear proliferation in an effective manner. Graham Allison has urged in recent articles and books the three Nos: "The centerpiece of a serious campaign to prevent nuclear terrorism is a strategy based on the three no's (no loose nukes, no new nascent nukes, and no new nuclear weapons sites) should be denying terrorists access to weapons and their components. After all, no nuclear weapons or material means no nuclear terrorism; it's that simple." Ashton Carter has pointed out in conversations that plutonium and uranium used in atomic bombs do not themselves give off much radiation (until detonated). They cannot be easily detected, therefore, when in shipment. In consequence, the most effective means of avoiding nuclear attack by terrorists are those advocated by Allison. The effort must rely on avoidance rather than detection.[20]

Politics defines a major issue as a conflict of domestic and defense programs. But this isn't really the case. The United States may need more resources for defense with its new role in the world, but it isn't really a matter of dollars. A nation needs more dollars, the less effective leadership it has, because without good leadership there is a huge amount of waste. Priorities aren't correctly identified, and money is wasted going in many directions at once.

Joe Nye observed that presidential leadership means pointing out that the U.S. economy can afford both domestic and international security if Americans are willing to pay for them. Without such leadership, the American ability to convert potential power into actual influence is diminished. A leader who wants to maintain American power must follow a strategy that rebuilds the domestic bases of American strength while also investing resources to maintain international influence.[21]

Good leadership gets the balance right between defense and domestic needs; between different weapons systems; between the old and the new in military affairs; and between the different armed services. Bad leadership tries to do it all, or puts too much money in the wrong places.

Economic divergence, driven by culture and systems in the decades ahead will be a double-edged sword. It will foment discord, but simultaneously create power asymmetries allowing America to unilaterally suppress conflict for the common good. Masters of illusion should seize the opportunity to do more than bribe, appease, stall, engage, sanction and cast spells with dreams of democracy, free enterprise, globalism, peace and harmony. They should weave Strategic Independence into the mix of instruments employed to keep the lid on the caldron of discord, aggression, and irrationalism, adjusting the mix to suit the circumstances.

In general, we require presidents who can choreograph the global social ballet to achieve a safe and prosperous world. This means, first and foremost, that they must be able to master the illusions of our public culture so that they can objectively assess the world situation and communicate their decisions persuasively to our people.

THE KEY ARGUMENTS OF THIS BOOK

1. From the standpoint of national security what needs to be done by the United States is:
   • Recognize the likely threat sequence – terrorism, Russia, China, Europe – and allocate to each its proper priority as the threats mature.

- Respond to each threat via Strategic Independence. Strategic Independence doesn't require a crash program or crusade. We can do it subtly with discreet persistence.
- Reform our public culture by disavowing wishful thinking and recognizing its distorting influence on our attitudes toward the United Nations, the European Union and multilateralism.

2. We ourselves are the enemy of our survival and we can save ourselves by recognizing it and rectifying our misperceptions.

3. America's most immediate foreign engagement is containing insurrection and terror in the Middle East and the Crescent of Fire, but it is not the most important challenge we face. Our most important challenge remains what it has been for sixty years: to avoid a nuclear exchange between great powers. Terrorists and insurrectionaries can kill thousands; great powers can kill hundreds of millions. World War II, for example, killed some sixty million people worldwide, almost all before the advent of nuclear weapons. A nuclear war today would kill many more. America must not lose sight of this highest priority item as it wages the war on terror.

4. Since the Soviet Union's collapse, the United States has failed to secure a complete and lasting peace, and we now find ourselves facing vortexes of danger, including as great a nuclear threat as before the end of the Cold War due to nuclear modernization in China and Russia and to nuclear proliferation in India, Pakistan, North Korea, and Iran.

5. The international situation is now becoming destabilized by major changes in the fate of the great powers, in particular Russia's decline and China's rise. Reconfiguration of national wealth and power doesn't deterministically generate conflict, but historical examples show that the process frequently does culminate in war. Critics may counter that the evidence taken from history doesn't include modern developments such as the asserted end of the age of nationalism, or the possibility of a harmonious global community. This is true, so far as it goes, but an end to nationalism is hard to reconcile with today's resurgent Chinese nationalism, and a harmonious global community is hard to reconcile with Russian great power chauvinism and with the radical Islamist concept of Ummah.

6. By 2010, Russia will choose to remilitarize and will be building fifth-generation nuclear capability. Russia will become a catalyst for global conflict and war as it begins rearming to redress its economic failures and thereby triggers an arms spiral in Asia, and beyond.

7. Thereafter, Russia is likely to invite Chinese aggression when its inferior economic system disintegrates under the weight of its military burden.

8. Meanwhile, China will be enlarging and modernizing its nuclear missile capability and by 2020 will emerge as a much more effective rival to America and our allies (especially in Taiwan and Japan) than it now is. The most dangerous part of the globe during the first quarter of the twenty-first century will be Asia. China's aspirations will create flashpoints around its borders.

9. American presidential leadership is historically weak in foreign affairs – with the result of unnecessarily costly wars – so we need to select presidents better qualified to handle these matters.

10. Our leaders face great temptation to overreach in our engagement with the world, due to our illusions and the inexperience of our leaders. We're doing it again now.

11. Due to terrorist attacks and preemptive war the American people are maturing in their attitudes toward our foreign involvements. We are able now to consider more frankly our role in the world. We are not aggressive, nor are we imperialist, but we do insist on defending ourselves.

12. For almost two centuries, America tried to stay out of foreign conflicts, but we were often dragged into distant wars. Now the growth of our economic and military power has made us a target for both terrorists and for the rivalry of large nations.

13. All around us the world is being driven to conflict by power seeking and the different economic experience of nations. This is especially significant in the Middle East, the Far East, and in the environs of the old Soviet Union.

14. A major driver of potential conflict among the great powers is the struggle for power and wealth among nations – belying the rhetoric of economic harmonization. Divergent national economic cultures and different rates of economic growth over a long period acerbate tensions and create conflict.

15. National economies are growing at different long-term rates with major impacts on national power. Differential growth arises from varying national economic cultures rooted in a variety of historical, geographic, cultural, social, and ideological forces. The United States and China are destined to be tomorrow's dominant powers, while other nations underperform economically. This is leading to a rivalry among many nations for international

influence that is more likely to end in overt conflict than in peaceful transition.

16. Economic forces underlie national rivalries, power, and ambitions. Economic deprivation is one of many economic factors involved. But in fact, growing economic power – like China's – is as much a potential cause of conflict as falling economic power – like Russia's – or grinding poverty – like much of Africa's.

17. America has a moral duty to help the world prosper, but because prosperity is as much a danger to world peace as is poverty, promoting economic development in poverty-stricken regions can make only a limited contribution to our national security.

18. A wealthy or poor economy, on its own, does not create a threat. Economic changes, such as growing wealth or declining fortunes don't, in themselves, create a threat either; but they must be closely monitored because the country's reaction to its good or bad fortune may indeed become a threat: for example, Russia's economic decline isn't a threat in and of itself, but if Russia panics and rearms that is a different story. Economic changes may serve as catalysts for threats or may magnify a threat, as is the case with China. China's nationalism has posed a threat for many years; but its growing economic power is giving its government better means with which to pursue its ambitions.

19. An important part of American policy must be to encourage Russia and China to Westernize their economies and governance, and to abandon military modernization along an authoritarian trajectory, which is where both – contrary to much reporting and comments by our media and political leadership – are now headed. We cannot expect this to work overnight, if it works at all; nor can it be successful without a credible American defense capability. If a policy of encouragement toward peaceful direction is to have any success at all, it must be followed with patience and without great expectations.

20. American foreign policy must be overhauled in order to avoid major wars. For America to provide effective leadership toward this objective there must be far more realism about the world in which we live and a greater willingness to take action on our own initiative.

21. America needs a transition path to cope with the growing risk of nuclear war – a path that simultaneously places restraints on our aggressiveness in the world's economic and political interplay to mollify our adversaries' fears, while utilizing our technological and economic strength to deter potential breakers of the peace. A major opportunity for a more active defense for America – going beyond

the balance of terror concept of deterrence – is to develop space-based defensive systems.

22. The coming resurgence of Russian power, the enlargement and modernization of Chinese nuclear missile capability, and nuclear proliferation mean that in order to maintain peace, the United States is being forced to abandon the strategy of balance of power that characterized the Cold War and instead seek to attain independence in its strategic positioning. It is important that this evolution be carefully thought through in order that a predictable policy replace today's confusion of purposes and means.

23. The old bipolar world of MAD has disappeared with nuclear proliferation. We can't trust our past allies any more (a coalition always decays when the threat that called it into being disappears). We should abandon multilateralism for Strategic Independence.

24. Strategic Independence involves enhancing our military power via continuing the revolution in military affairs and adding significant additional defense capabilities, such as space-based systems or national missile defense via earth-based interceptors, should they become technically possible and economically efficient.

25. Political leaders in our country don't ignore critical issues of these sorts, but they currently address them with policies so restricted by their own limited knowledge and experience, by partisan blinders, and public misperceptions that they make significant errors.

26. Wishful thinking causes us to underestimate danger and to overestimate our strength, thereby tempting us to overreach abroad through trying to export, with the help of force, our economic and political culture.

27. Wishful thinkers on both sides of the political aisle are now pressing us toward overreach abroad.

28. America's economic and political systems work for us; some of our systems may work for others; much of it will work for no one else. Many Americans believe, because of the convergence illusion, that if we can distribute our system around the world, then we will be far more secure. It's a hard lesson that our culture and our political economy are not likely models for others.

29. We need some humility about this. What is required is a form of limited engagement with the world. America should advocate democratic free enterprise, but without bribes disguised as foreign aid, and we should caution other nations that they have the responsibility for themselves.

30. Rather than being a core part of our defense policy, rebuilding Iraq and other nations into a copy of the United States is a huge diversion of focus from our national security and probably a blind alley in terms of results.

31. American presidential leadership is historically weak in foreign affairs, so we need to select presidents better qualified to handle these matters. If we are to survive the challenges of the coming years, then the American people need to begin to select presidents to a far greater degree than in our recent history on the basis of experience and capability in foreign relations.

32. American presidents need to a far greater degree than in our recent history be honest with the American people about our objectives in matters of war and peace. The increasing maturity of the American people about such issues means that they both expect and can handle such candor. Presidential dishonesty about motives threatens to undermine public support for needed changes in our policies abroad.

33. Politicians in America need to avoid taking actions under the umbrella of national defense that are motivated by moralistic reasons. All objectives should be based on the practicality of the country's survival. We should limit the use of force to the purpose of protecting ourselves – never employing our military might to impose ideological religious, democratic or economic standards on others. If we do so, we risk transforming ourselves into imperialists, confusing ourselves about our objectives, losing our focus, and stumbling into the very large conflicts that we are trying to avoid.

34. Our leaders need to break free of our public culture to act in accordance with objective assessments of the threats we face.

BRIEF KEY POINTS OF THIS BOOK

- Americans have a new maturity born in terrorist attacks and preemptive wars.
- Our political leadership is not recognizing this and is not dealing honestly with the American people.
- Instead, our political leadership is deceiving us about motives and intentions, believing that will increase public support. It won't, but instead the opposite as the deceptions become clear.
- We face several serious threats, only one of which is terrorism. A remilitarized Russia and a nationalist China with modernized nuclear weapons are both significant challenges to us.

- The old strategy of deterrence against nuclear war – Mutual Assured Destruction (MAD) – no longer is reliable in a world of multiple nuclear powers.
- Nor can we rely on other countries to help defend us.
- America is overreaching to the terrorist threat by trying to remake the world in its own image.
- It's an illusion to expect that we can remake the world into American-type democracies with free enterprise economies; and it's an illusion to think that if we did, peace would certainly follow. Economic development can lessen human tensions; but it also can supply to an aggressive power the sinews of war. We should support economic and political development abroad but not make it part of our defense strategy nor ever impose our system by force.
- Instead, the United States needs to focus on defense and return to an older strategy of national defense, one in which we rely primarily on ourselves – Strategic Independence.
- We have great strengths as well for the role of superpower. Our economy is the world's strongest and is very likely to remain so; the energy of our people is unmatched; our technology leads the world; at the moment we have the world's most effective military; and we have a new maturity in addressing issues of global concern.
- We also face significant impediments to success in the role of sole super-power, which we must assess realistically. Our limitations include a serious tendency to overreach in our engagement with the rest of the world – a tendency driven by illusions about the world that also cause us to wish to deny certain dangerous realities – and a propensity to choose as our leaders people with insufficient experience in global affairs. We need to abandon our illusions and ground our leadership choices on a more sub-stantial foundation if we are to survive the challenges ahead.
- We must recognize that self-defense is a higher ethical imperative than moralistic utopian yearnings.

Notes

Preface

1. Alfred Marshall, quoted in John Maynard Keynes, *Essays in Biography*, edited by Geoffrey Keynes, New York: W. W. Norton, 1951, p. 204.

Chapter 1: A World Wounded

1. Neustadt, Richard E, "Presidency and Legislation: The Growth of Central Clearance," *American Political Science Review* 48 (September 1954), 641–71; "Presidency and Legislation: Planning the Presidency's Program," *American Political Science Review* 49 (December 1955): 980–1021; "Approaches to Staffing the Presidency," *American Political Science Review* 57 (December 1963), 855–63; and *Presidential Power and the Modern Presidents: The Politics of Leadership from Roosevelt to Reagan*, New York: Free Press, 1990. See also Terry M. Moe and William G. Howell, "Unilateral Action and Presidential Power: A Theory," *Presidential Studies Quarterly* (December 1, 1999); William G. Howell, *Power without Persuasion: The Politics of Direct Presidential Action* by William G. Howell, Princeton University Press, 2003; Kenneth R. Mayer, *With the Stroke of a Pen: Executive Orders and Presidential Power*, Princeton University Press, 2001; Andrew Rudalevige, *Managing the President's Program: Presidential Leadership and Legislative Policy Formulation*, Prinction University Press, 2002; Andrew Rudalevige, "The Structure of Leadership: Presidents, Hierarchies, and Information Flow," *Presidential Studies Quarterly* (June 1, 2005); Charles M. Cameron, Randall Calver, and Thrainn Eggertsson, *Veto Bargaining: Presidents and the Politics of Negative Power*, Cambridge University Press, 2000; William G. Howell and Kenneth R. Mayer, "The Last One Hundred Days," *Presidential Studies Quarterly*, vol. 35, no. 3 (September 1, 2005); William G. Howell, "Unilateral Powers: A Brief Overview," *Presidential Studies Quarterly*, vol. 35, no. 3 (September 1, 2005); and Kenneth R. Mayer, "By Order of the President: The Use & Abuse of Executive Direct Power," *Presidential Studies Quarterly*, vol. 33, no. 1 (March 1, 2003).
2. There exists a voluminous literture on this topic as it applies to business, although most writers distinguish only between management and leadership. For a full

discussion, see D. Quinn Mills, *Leadership: How to Lead – How to Live*, Waltham, MA: MindEdge Press, 2005 and D. Quinn Mills, *Principles of Management*, Waltham, MA: MindEdge Press, 2005.

3. Samuel Kernal, Going Public: New Strategies of Presidential Leadership, CQPress, 3rd edition, 1997, pp. 12 and 20. See also Andrew Rudalevige, *The New Imperial Presidency: Renewing Presidential Power after Watergate*, University of Michigan Press, 2005; Charles M. Cameron, "Studying the Polarized Presidency," Presidential Studies Quarterly, v. 32, n. 4 (December 1, 2002), pp. 647–63; and Charles Cameron, John S. Lapinski, and Charles R. Riemann, "Testing Formal Theories of Political Rhetoric," *Journal of Politics*, vol. 62, no. 1 (February 1, 2000), pp. 187–205.

4. George C. Edwards, III, *On Deaf Ears: The Limits of the Bully Pulpit*. New Haven, CT: Yale University Press, 2003, pp. 241 and 6, respectively.

5. Anatol Lieven, "The Modern Limits of Democracy," *The Financial Times*, January 12, 2005, p. 13.

6. Nicholas J. Spykman, *America's Strategy in World Politics*, Yale, 1942, pp. 446 and 460.

7. Jawaharlal Nehru, *Glimpses of World History: Being Further Letters to his Daughter Written in Prison*. New York: The John Day Company, 1942, p. 232.

8. See, for example, United States, National Intelligence Council, *Mapping the Global Future . . . the 2020 Project*, 2004.

9. G. John Ikenberry, "Review of United Nations Secretary General's High-Level Panel on Threats, Challenges and Change, *A More Secure World: Our Shared Responsibility*, 2004," *Foreign Affairs*, vol. 84, no. 3, May/June, 2005, p. 131.

10. William E. Odom and Robert Dujarric, *America's Inadvertent Empire*, New Haven: Yale University Press, 2003.

11. Thomas de Zengotita, "Believing Whatever," *The Chronicle of Higher Education Review*, November 11, 2005, p. B14; and *Mediated: How the Media Shapes Your World and the Way You Live in It*, Bloomsbury, 2005.

12. Thomas Babington Macaulay, *The History of England: James II*, London: Longman, Brown, Green, and Longmans, 1856, p. 282.

Chapter 2: Long-Term Economic Realism

1. David Pryce-Jones, "Jews, Arabs and French Diplomacy," *Commentary*, May, 2005, pp. 27–53.

2. See Roger Phillipe, *The American Enemy: the History of French Anti-Americanism*. Chicago: University of Chicago Press, 2004.

3. Arthur Waldron, "A Korean Solution?" *Commentary*, 119, 6, June, 2005, p. 63.

4. Stephen Blank, "Outsourcing Korea," Strategic Studies Institute, US Army War College Carlisle Barracks, PA 17013, August 2005.

5. Robert B. Laughlin, "Reinventing Physics," *Chronicle of Higher Education Review*, February 11, 2005, p. B7.

6. Henry A. Kissinger, "America's Assignment," *Newsweek*, November 8, 2004, p. 38.

7. Quoted in Joshua Muravchik, "The Case Against the UN," *Commentary*, November 2004, p. 36.

8. FDR's opposition to colonialism and its impact in contributing greatly to the demise of the European colonial empires (and thereby to French animosity to the United States) is described in Gerhard L. Weinberg, *Visions of Victory: The Hopes of Eight World War II Leaders*, New York: Cambridge University Press, 2005, pp. 191–195.

9. Paul Johnson, *A History of the American People*, New York: HarperCollins, 1998, p. 229.

10. David McCullough, *1776*. New York: Simon and Schuster, 2005, p. 40.

11. Joseph Ellis, *His Excellency, George Washington*, New York, Alfred A. Knopf, 2004, pp. 234–236.

12. An observation attributed to Daniel Patrick Moynihan in James Q. Wilson, "Islam and Freedom," *Commentary*, December, 2004, p. 24.

13. J. F. C. Fuller, *A Military History of the Western World*, vol. 3, p. 364.

14. See John Yoo, "A United Iraq – What's the Point?" *Los Angeles Times*, August 25, 2005.

15. Plato, *Republic*. New York: Vintage Books, 1963, Book III, 389–390, p. 86.

16. Daniel Yankelovich and Isabella Furth, "The Role of Colleges in an Era of Mistrust," *Chronicle of Higher Education, The Chronicle Review*, September 16, 2005, p. B10.

Chapter 3: "Smooth Comforts False" – The Illusions That Confuse Us

1. Terry Teachout, "Culture in the Age of Blogging," *Commentary*, 119, 6, June, 2005, p. 40.

2. Daniel Druckman, "Nationalism, Patriotism, and Group Loyalty: A Social Psychological Perspective," in *Mershon International Studies Review*, vol. 38, no. 1 (April 1994), 43–68.

3. Williamson Murray and Allan R. Millett, *A War to be Won: Fighting the Second World War*, Cambridge, Mass.: Harvard University Press, 2000, p. 1.

4. Robert D. Kaplan, "Euphorias of Hatred," *Atlantic Monthly*, 291, 4, May, 2003, p. 44.

5. Wendell L. Willkie, *One World*, New York: Simon and Schuster, 1943.

6. Speros Vryonis Jr., *The Mechanism of Catastrophe: The Turkish Pogrom of September 6–7, 1955, and the Destruction of the Greek Community of Istanbul*, Greekworks.com, 2005; and "Causes of Catastrophe," *The Economist*, August 27, 2005, p. 67.

7. Jeffrey Sachs, quoted by Kirk Johnson, "A Cockeyed Optimist Professes the Dismal Science," *The New York Times*, April 25, 2002, p. A32. See also Jeffrey Sachs, *The End of Poverty: Economic Possibilities for Our Time*, New York: Penguin, 2005.

8. Richard Haass, *The Opportunity: America's Moment to Alter History's Course*, New York: Public Affairs, 2005.

9. Bill Clinton, "This Conference Will not be like so Many Before it," *The Financial Times*, September 16, 2005, p. 15.

10. Andrew Wheatcroft, *Infidels: A History of the Conflict Between Christendom and Islam*, New York: Random House, 2005.

11. Thomas Friedman, *The World is Flat: A Brief History of the Twenty-First Century*, New York: Farrar, Straus and Giroux, 2005.

12. Walter Russell Mead, *Power, Terror, Peace and War: America's Grand Strategy in a World at Risk*, New York: Knopf, 2004, p. 192.

13. Merle Goldman, *From Comrade to Citizen: The Struggle for Political Rights in China*, Cambridge: Harvard University Press, 2005.

14. Robert D. Kaplan, "The Lawless Frontier," *Atlantic Monthly*, September 2000, pp. 66–80; the quotations in our text are from pages 63, 76, and 80 respectively.

15. Jeff Madrick, "Grim Facts on Global Poverty," *The New York Times*, August 7, 2003.

16. Mark Leonard, "China's Long and Winding Road," *The Financial Times*, July 9–10, 2005, pp. W1 and W2.

17. "Who Wins in the New Economy?" *The Wall Street Journal*, June 27, 2000, p. B1. No author given.

18. John Micklewait and Adrian Wooldridge, *A Future Perfect: The Challenge and Hidden Promise of Globalization*, New York: Times Books, 2000.

19. "Democratic Realism: The Third Way," *The New Democrat Blueprint*, "The National Security Issue," Winter, 2000, pp. 6–13, at p. 9. Some even assert that free trade is an effective means for achieving nuclear disarmament. See C. Fred Bergsten, "Globalizing Free Trade," *Foreign Affairs*, vol. 75, no. 3 May/June 1996, pp. 105–121.

20. Stephen M. Walt, "Two Cheers for Clinton's Foreign Policy," *Foreign Affairs*, 79, 2, March–April, 2000, pp. 63–79.

21. *Foreign Affairs*, March–April, 2000. This is from the abstract in the issue contents, p. iii.

22. John Rawls, *Justice as Fairness: A Restatement*, Cambridge, MA: Harvard University Press, 2001, pp. 25–26; see also Rawls, *A Theory of Justice*, Cambridge, MA: Harvard University Press, 1971.

23. Edward Folliard, "Oral History Interview with Edward Folliard, White House Correspondent for the Washington Post, 1923–1967," Harry S. Truman Presidential Library, August 20, 1970, available at http://www.trumanlibrary.org/oralhist/folliard.html.

24. Mark Taylor, "What Derrida Really Meant," *The New York Times*, October 14, 2004. The concept of public culture elaborated here provides a framework for systematically identifying not only what has been left out, but what has been distorted, as a first step toward scientifically sorting out the truth, and formulating effective national policy.

25. Cf. Samuel Huntington, "The West: Unique, Not Universal," *Foreign Affairs*, vol. 75, no. 6, November/December 1996, pp. 28–46.

26. See Abram Bergson, "A Reformulation of Certain Aspects of Welfare Economics," *Quarterly Journal of Economics*, 52 (1), February 1938, pp. 310–334. Bergson, "The Concept of Social Welfare," *Quarterly Journal of Economics*, 68 (2), May, 1954, pp. 233–252, Bergson, "Social Choice and Welfare Economics under Representative Government," *Journal of Public Economics*, 6 (3), October, 1976, pp. 171–190. Kenneth Arrow, *Social Choice and Individual Values*, 2nd ed., Wiley, New York, 1963. Paul Samuelson, "Bergsonian Welfare Economics," in Steven Rosefielde, ed., *Economic Welfare and the Economics of Soviet Socialism*, Cambridge, Cambridge University Press, 1981, pp. 223–266.

27. James Kurth, "America and the West," *Foreign Policy Research Institute*, Watch on the West, http://www.fpri.org, vol. 5, no. 7, September 2004. "Today's

postmodern Europe is very unlike the old, high-modern Europe that lasted well into the 1960s . . . But today's America is also different. . . . Not only is there now a postmodern American elite that is different from the modern-American elite of the past century, but there is the Bush administration, which in important ways is different from them both . . . the concept of the West was always unstable and will not survive as a viable basis for U.S.-European relations. . . . European elites wish to promote a new kind of universalism, in particular an ideology centered upon the ideas of humanitarianism and cosmopolitanism. . . . The new European ideology not only required the overthrow of old conservative ideas, but the old Marxist ideology as well. . . . The old Marxism was too bound up with the industrial working-class, hierarchical organizations, and collectivist values to fit the new Leftism-it was too modern, rather than postmodern. NB. Kurth's characterization refers only to a revised credo, not hidden agendas and public cultural implementation.

28. Barbara Ehrenreich, "The New Macho: Feminism," *The New York Times*, July 29, 2004. "So here in one word is my new counter-terrorism strategy for Kerry: feminism. . . . So John and John: Announce plans to pour dollars into girl's education in places like Pakistan. . . . If you want to beat Osama, you've got to start listening to Carmen (bin Laden)."

29. Michael Ledeen, "The 9/11 Vision," *National Review Online*, July 23, 2004. http://www.nationalreview.com The National Commission on Terrorist Attacks Upon the United States suggests that "state sponsors were somehow beside the point; the commission focus is entirely on terrorist groups. This is an odd position, given all the evidence of deep involvement of countries like Iran, Syria, and Iraq. . . . It pretends to criticize Congress, but only discusses sins of omission – insufficient oversight. . . . Worse still, the report calls for even more money for intelligence, and an entirely new layer of bureaucracy, the effect of which would be far greater centralization of the whole process. . . . In short, we should strive for competitive intelligence. . . . Reuel Gerecht has taught us, no bureaucratic fix can possibly undo the terrible damage wrought by more than 30 years of restrictions and the consequent culture of risk avoidance and long-distance spy craft." Cf. Philip Shenon, "Correcting the Record on September 11, in Great Detail," *The New York Times*, July 25, 2004.

30. Huntington, "The West: Unique, Not Universal."

31. Paul Krugman, "Triumph of the Trivial," *The New York Times*, July 30, 2004. "I've been reading 60 day's worth of transcripts from the places four out of five Americans cite as where they usually get their news. . . . I couldn't even find a clear statement that Mr. Kerry wants to roll back recent high-income tax cuts and use the money to cover most of the uninsured. When reports mentioned the Kerry plan at all, it was usually horse race analysis – how it's playing, not what's in it. . . . There are two issues here, trivialization and bias." John Horgan, "Do Genes Influence Behavior? Why We Want to Think They Do," *The Chronicle of Higher Education*, November 26, 2004, pp. B12–B13. "The source of the extensive coverage given to false science isn't merely that it is sensational, but that the chosen misinformation is responsive to our wishes – to what we want to hear."

32. John R. Zaller, *The Nature and Origins of Mass Opinion*, Cambridge University Press, New York, 1992. "Beginning in the middle of the 20th century people were

concerned that media with new propaganda techniques (pioneered by Goebbels for Hitler and by Stalin) would control all opinion (see George Orwell's 1984); but research after the Second World War suggested that the media was much less effective. More recent research has reestablished "a healthy respect for what the media and politicians who use it, can accomplish." p. 7. ". . . the public responds to elite-supplied information and leadership cues. How could it be otherwise in a world in which events are ambiguous and in which the public must regularly have opinions about matters that are, to use Lippman's phrase . . . 'out of reach, out of sight, out of mind.'?" p. 311. Cf. Scott L. Althaus, *Collective Preferences in Democratic Politics: Opinion Surveys and the Will of the People*, Cambridge University Press, New York, 2003. Kathleen Hall Jamieson, and Paul Waldman, *The Press Effect: Politicians, Journalists, and the Stories that Shape the Political Work*, Oxford University Press, New York, 2003. Robert Jervis, "Security Studies: Ideas, Policy, and Politics," in Edward Mansfield and Richard Sesson, eds., *The Evolution of Political Knowledge*, Ohio State University Press, Columbus, 2004.

33. Zaller, *The Nature and Origins of Mass Opinion*. "First . . . citizens vary in their habitual attention to politics and hence in their exposure to political information and argumentation in the media. . . . Second . . . people are able to reach critically to the arguments they encounter only to the extent that they are knowledgeable about political affairs. . . . Third . . . citizens typically carry around in their heads fixed attitudes on every issue . . . rather they construct 'opinion statements' on the fly as they confront each new issue. Fourth . . . in constructing their opinion statements, people make greatest use of ideas that are . . . at the 'top of the head.'" p. 1. ". . . Interaction between political awareness and political pre-dispositions is fundamental to the process by which citizens use information . . . to form opinions . . . individuals do not possess true attitudes . . ." p. 308.

34. During the 2004 election campaign for example, CBS broadcast an expose on George Bush Jr.'s National Guard service concocted by a Democratic activist to besmirch the record, and improve John Kerry's electoral prospects. See William Safire, "First Find the Forger," *New York Times*, September 22, 2004. Also, it should be noted that public culture isn't the only factor degrading the effectiveness of American democracy and free enterprise. They are also impaired by psychological and emotional disorders, as well as individual role playing that conflates persona with personality. Also, Zaller, *The Nature and Origin of Opinion*, writes, "The information that reaches the public is never a full record of important events and development in the world. It is, rather a highly selective and stereotyped view of what has taken place. . . . (The public) requires news presentations that are short, simple, and highly thematic – in a word stereotyped." p. 7.

Chapter 4: Towers of Illusions: Dysfunctional Behaviors

1. Brian Bremner, et al. "Why Japan and China are Squaring Off," *Business Week*, April 25, 2005, p. 57.

2. Daniel Byman and Matthew Waxman, *The Dynamics of Coercion: American Foreign Policy and the Limits of Military Might*, New York: Cambridge University Press, 2002, p. xi.

3. Byman and Waxman, p. 229.
4. Daniel Bell, *Dissent*, 1961, quoted in Mark Gerson, *The Neoconservative Vision: From the Cold War to the Culture Wars*, Lanham, MD: Madison Books, 1996.
5. *CNN*, 1/29/05.
6. Mead, *Power, Terror, Peace and War*, p. 7 and p. 191.
7. Paul Johnson, *History of the American People*, p. 449.
8. Richard Brookhiser, "Close Up: The Mind of George W. Bush," *Atlantic Monthly*, April 2003, p. 68.
9. Brookhiser, "Close Up: The Mind of George W. Bush," p. 69.
10. Michael J. Mandel, et al. "How War Will Reshape the Economy," *Business Week*, April 14, 2003, p. 32.
11. Rudy Rummel, Professor Emeritus of Political Science, http://freedomspeace. blogspot.com/2005/12/reevaluating-colonial-democide.html.
12. Peggy Noonan, *The Wall Street Journal*, June 11, 2003, p. 8.
13. Bruce Berkowitz, *The New Face of War*, New York: Free Press, 2003, p. 17.
14. Condoleezza Rice, "US to Have Military Superiority Because It Is 'Very Special,'" *Agence Presse France*, September 26, 2002.
15. Allen S. Weiner, "Law, Just War, and the International Fight Against Terrorism: Is it War?" CDRLL Working Papers, no. 47, 2005. The working paper is ultimately for a forthcoming edited volume called "Intervention, Terrorism, and Torture: Challenges to Just War Theory in the 21st Century."
16. Richard W. Stevenson, "President Makes It Clear: Phrase Is 'War on Terror,'" *The New York Times*, August 4, 2005.
17. Jan Ting, "Immigration and National Security," Foreign Policy Research Institute, September 9, 2005, from fpri@fpri.org.
18. Berkowitz, *The New Face of War*, p. 143.
19. Winston S. Churchill, *The World Crisis*, vol. 2, New York: Charles Schribners, 1923, p. 454.
20. Winston S. Churchill, *The Age of Revolution*, New York: Dodd and Mead, 1957, p. 4.
21. Gennady Petrov, "Was the Game Worth the Cost? It's hard to Pick a Clean Winner in Ukraine," *Johnson's Russia List*, Number 21, January 14, 2005.
22. See, for example, C. J. Chivers, "How Top Spies in Ukraine Changed the Nation's Path," *The New York Times*, January 17, 2005.
23. Gerhard L. Weinberg, *A World at Arms: A Global History of World War II*, Cambridge: Cambridge University Press, second edition, 2005, p. 831.
24. Jonathan Steele, "Orange revolution oligarchs reveal their true colours: The high hopes for Ukraine after Yushchenko took power are being dashed as rival elites squabble over spoils," *The Guardian*, in *Johnson's Russia List*, #9267, 14 October 2005, #21, October 13, 2005.
25. Steven Lee Myers, "News Analysis: A Tug of War Over Ukraine," *The New York Times*, November 24, 2004.
26. There is no assurance that an optimal functioning, scientific, public culture will always identify the best course. A genius may be right against the informed electorate. Masters of illusion may sometimes be forced to play god, uncongenial as this may be to the idea of the west.

27. Thomas Frank, "Why They Won," *The New York Times*, November 5, 2004, speculates on how Republicans have beguiled the "forgotten man." Paul Krugman sounds the alarm that the "New Deal" is under siege in "No Surrender," *The New York Times*, November 5, 2004, and David Brooks, "The Values-Vote Myth," *The New York Times*, November 6, 2004, challenges the importance of identity politics. But none attempt to consider how their critiques can be mapped into optimal national policy strategies.

Chapter 5: Mythomaniacs: The Sources of Our Illusions

1. Steven A. LeBlanc, "Prehistory of Warfare," *Archaeology*, May–June, 2003, p. 25; see also, LeBlanc, *Constant Battles*, New York: St. Martin's Press, 2003.
2. Robyn Meredith, "Reunification, Chinese Style," *Forbes*, October 28, 2002, p. 194.
3. Keynes, *Essays in Biography*, p. 77.
4. Michael A. Ledeen, "Angrier and Angrier," *National Review Online*, August 25, 2003.
5. Michael A. Ledeen, "The Peace Trap," *National Review Online*, August 27, 2003.
6. See Robert Patterson, *Dereliction of Duty*, Washington, DC: Regnery, 2003, pp. 53 and 57.
7. Committee on Presidential Debates, First Bush-Kerry Presidential Debate, University of Miami, Coral Gables, FL, September 30, 2004, transcript available at http://www.debates.org/pages/trans2004a.html.
8. Alexis de Tocqueville, *Democracy in America*, Translated, edited, and with an Introduction by Harvey C. Mansfield and Delba Winthrop. Chicago: University of Chicago Press, 2000, Volume 1, Part One, Chapter 3, "Social State of Anglo-Americans," p. 51.
9. Mike France, "Is There a Market for the Middle?," *Business Week*, November 29, 2004, pp. 111–112.
10. Jamieson and Waldman, pp. xi–xvii
11. Jamieson and Waldman, p. 170.
12. V. O. Key, Jr., *Public Opinion and American Democracy*, New York: Knopf, 1961, p. 395.
13. Zaller, *The Nature and Origins of Mass Opinion*, p. 319.
14. Jamieson and Waldman, p. 172.
15. C. Edwin Baker, *Media, Markets and Democracy*, New York: Cambridge University Press, 2002, pp. 290–291.
16. William L. Shirer, *20th Century Journey: A Memoir of the Life and Times*, Volume III, *A Native's Return*, 1945–1988, New York: Bantam Nonfiction, 1992, pp. 112–113.
17. David Halbertsam, *The Powers That Be*, New York: Alfred A. Knopf, 1979, p. 146.
18. John C. Waugh, *Reelecting Lincoln: The Battle for the 1864 Presidency*, New York: Crown, 1997.
19. Stephen Skowronek, *The Politics Presidents Make*, Cambridge, MA: Harvard University Press, 1997.
20. Zell Miller, "George Bush vs. the Naïve Nine," *The Wall Street Journal*, November 3, 2003, p. A14.

21. Thomas L. Friedman, "The Chant Not Heard," *The New York Times*, November 30, 2003.

Chapter 6: Champions of Freedom or Imperialists: How We're Perceived

1. Hugo Lindgren, "The Way We Live Now," *The New York Times Magazine*, August 31, 2003, in which he points out that tawdry behavior of athletes is so strong, an audience attraction in the sports news that it is now the subject of fictional programs by sports networks.
2. See Anthony DeCurtis, "Rufus Wainwright Journeys to 'Gay Hell' and Back," *The New York Times*, August 31, 2003, in which Wainwright in an interview describes a life of drugs and sex that he resists only because it threatens to end his song-writing.
3. Christopher Marquis, "World's View of U.S. Sours After Iraq War, Poll Finds," *The New York Times*, June 4, 2003.
4. *The Chronicle of Higher Education*, October 2, 2003.
5. E. H. Carr, "The Twenty Years' Crisis," quoted by John J. Mearsheimer, *The Tragedy of Great Power Politics*, New York: W. W. Norton, 2001, p. 26.
6. Adam Clymer, "World Survey Says Negative Views of U.S. Are Rising," *The New York Times*, December 5, 2002.
7. Seymour Martin Lipset, *American Exceptionalism*, New York: W. W. Norton, 1966, p. 63.
8. John J. Mearsheimer, *The Tragedy of Great Power Politics*, New York: W. W. Norton, 2001.
9. Andrey A. Piontkovsky, "The Pillars of International Security: Traditions Challenged," *Johnson's Russia List*, no. 7258, Article 18, July 21, 2003.
10. Quoted in Ed Cray, *General of the Army: George C. Marshall*, New York: Simon and Schuster, 1990, p. 82.
11. David McCullough, *John Adams*, New York: Simon and Schuster, 2001, p. 395.
12. Richard Rorty, "American Pride, American Shame," *The Chronicle of Higher Education*, The Chronicle Review, January 31, 2002, p. B10.
13. Richard J. Whalen, "Imperialism . . . ," *Across the Board*, March/April, 2003, p. 75. These comments come in a review of Andrew J. Bacevich's *American Empire: The Realities and Consequences of U.S. Diplomacy*, Cambridge, MA: Harvard University Press, 2002.
14. Dana Priest, *The Mission*, New York: W.W. Norton, 2003, p. 13.
15. Andrew J. Bacevich, *American Empire*, p. 244.
16. Jedediah Purdy, Being America. On *C-Span* March 9, 2003.
17. Gore Vidal, quoted in Niall Ferguson, "America: An Empire in Denial," *The Chronicle of Higher Education Review*, March 28, 2003, p. B7.
18. Chalmers Johnson, quoted in Ferguson, "America: An Empire in Denial," p. B7. See also Chalmers Johnson, *The Sorrows of Empire: Militarism, Secrecy and the End of the Republic*, New York: Metropolitan Books, 2004.
19. Bacevich, *American Empire*, pp. 2–3.
20. Bacevich, *American Empire*, p. 6.
21. Ferguson, "America: An Empire in Denial," p. B10.
22. Ferguson, "America: An Empire in Denial," p. B8.

23. See Joshua Muravchik, "The New Gloomsayers," *Commentary*, June, 2003, p. 25.
24. Charles A. Beard, *Giddy Minds and Foreign Quarrels*, New York: The MacMillan Co., 1939, p. 87.

Chapter 7: We're Different Now

1. Robin Toner, "Trust in the Military Heightens Among Baby Boomers' Children," *The New York Times*, May 27, 2003.
2. Toner, "Trust in the Military Heightens Among Baby Boomers' Children." See also, David C. King, et al. *The Generation of Trust: How the U.S. Military Has Regained the Public's Confidence Since Vietnam*, Washington, DC: The American Enterprise Institute for Public Policy Research, 2002.
3. Quoted in Ed Cray, *General of the Army: George C. Marshall*, New York: Simon and Schuster, 1990, p. 77.
4. Peter Bergen, *The Osama bin Laden I Know: An Oral History*, New York: The Free Press, 2006, pp. 75–76.

Chapter 8: The Economic Roots of American Power

1. Keynes, *Essays in Biography*, p. 144.
2. Gerard Baker, "America's Economy Takes on All Comers," *The Financial Times*, November 6, 2003, p. 13.
3. Paul Kennedy, *The Rise and Fall of the Great Powers*, New York: Random House, 1987.
4. Murray Weidenbaum, "The Economics of Defense Spending," Foreign Policy Research Institute, E-Notes, February 14, 2006.
5. *Wall Street Journal*, July 3, 2000, p. 1. According to the American Psychologist 26 percent of Americans reported in 1996 that they were on the verge of a nervous breakdown.
6. Steven Rosefielde, *Comparative Economic Systems: Culture, Wealth and Power in the 21st Century*, available from: Oxford, Blackwell, 2002, in English and from MGIMO in Russian (2004).
7. A. Gary Shilling, "Broken China," *Forbes*, May 12, 2003, p. 156.
8. Subramanian Swamy, "Financial System Constraints in China and India," *SCMS Journal of Indian Management*, October–December, 2005, pp. 5–17.
9. Steven Rosefielde, *Russia in the 21st Century: Prodigal Superpower*, Cambridge: Cambridge University Press, 2005.
10. See D. Quinn Mills, *Labor, Government and Inflation*, Chicago: University of Chicago Press, 1975.
11. Jeanne Whalen, "Putin's Speech is Grim on State of Russia," *The Wall Street Journal*, July 10, 2000, p. A22.
12. Prime Minister Mikhail Kasyanov has been accused of demanding a 2 percent bribe on the government contracts he controls. *Daily Yomiuri*, July 8, 2000.
13. Paul Krugman, "The Myth of Asia's Miracle," *Foreign Affairs*, vol. 73, no. 6 November/December 1994, pp. 62–79.
14. Philippe Debroux, *Human Resource Management in Japan: Changes and Uncertainties*, Aldershot: Ashgate, 2003.

15. "Social Solidarity," *The Economist*, July 22, 2000, p. 49

16. Howard Banks, "Walls Around Europe," *Forbes*, May 15, 2000, p. 158.

17. Paul Johnson, "The Anti-Semitic Disease," *Commentary*, 119, 6, June, 2005, p. 36.

Chapter 9: Economic Disparities Among Nations

1. Angus Maddison, *The World Economy: Historical Statistics*, OECD, Paris, 2003, pp. 219. The figure for Chad was $445.

2. Steven Rosefielde, *Comparative Economic Systems, Culture, Wealth and Power in the 21st Century*, Oxford: Blackwell, 2002, pp. 145–148.

3. Steven Rosefielde, "The Riddle of Postwar Russian Economic Growth: Statistics Lied and Were Misconstrued," *Europe-Asia Studies*, vol. 55, no. 3, 2003, pp. 469–481.

4. Maddison, *The World Economy*, p. 185. Sano's misgivings were expressed to Rosefielde in the summer of 2003.

5. Maddison, *The World Economy*, p. 185.

6. Maddison's estimates show American and the twelve major West European living standards growing respectively at 1.7 and 1.6 percent per annum 1990–2001, with the American advantage widening thereafter. Ibid., pp. 65 and 89. Per capita GDP in Germany, France and Italy grew at only a 1.4 percent annual rate. For figures on the subperiod 2001–2004, see Martin Wolf, "Outpaced: Why are the big Eurozone Countries and Japan Doing Worse than English-speaking Nations?" *The Financial Times*, January 13, 2005, p. 13.

7. Angus Maddison, *Chinese Economic Performance in the Long Run*, Development Center Studies, OECD, Paris, 1998. Maddison, "Measuring the Performance of a Communist Command Economy: An Assessment of the CIA Estimates for the USSR," *Review of Income and Wealth*, September, 1998.

8. United Nations, *Human Development Report, 2003*, New York: Oxford University Press, 2003.

Chapter 10: Geopolitical Aspirations of the Nations

1. Claudia Dreyfus, "The World of Doctor K," *Modern Maturity*, July–August, 2001, p. 25.

2. James Kynge and Richard McGregor, "China replaces its 'five principles' with foreign policy pragmatism," *The Financial Times*, February 24, 2003, p. 4.

3. David Shambaugh, *Modernizing China's Military*, Berkeley: University of California Press, 2002, p. 5.

4. Shambaugh, *Modernizing China's Military*, p. 85.

5. Shambaugh, *Modernizing China's Military*, p. 5.

6. Shambaugh, *Modernizing China's Military*, p. 5.

7. Shambaugh, *Modernizing China's Military*, p. 6.

8. Benjamin Fulford, "The Dragon and the Bear," *Forbes*, March 17, 2003, pp. 74 and 76.

9. Shambaugh, *Modernizing China's Military*, p. xx.

10. Warren Zimmerman, *First Great Triumph*, New York: Farrar, Strauss, Giroux, 2002, p. 33.

11. Mark L. Clifford, "Is China Bound to Explode?" *Business Week*, May 5, 2003, pp. 17 and 19, reviewing Ross Terrill, *The New Chinese Empire*, New York: Basic Books, 2003.
12. Arthur Waldron, letter in *Commentary*, 116, 5, December, 2003, p. 14.
13. "Beijing Boldly Goes," *The Financial Times*, October 16, 2003, p. 14.
14. Suisheng Zhao, *A Nation-State by Construction: Dynamics of Modern Chinese Nationalism*, Stanford University Press, 2004.
15. Yasheng Huang, "China's Strength Begins at Home," *The Financial Times*, June 2, 2005, p. 15.
16. Arthur Waldron, "Hong Kong and the Future of Freedom," *Commentary*, September 2003, p. 21.
17. *Chronicle of Higher Education*, October 31, 2003.
18. Gordon Chang, *The Coming Collapse of China*, New York: Random House, July 31, 2001.
19. Jim Yardley, "Issue in China: Labor Camps That Operate Outside the Courts," *The New York Times*, May 9, 2005, online.
20. *Time*, June 27, 2005, p. 13.
21. Shizhong Chen, "Where in China are Your Dolls and Toys Made?" *Falun Gong Human Rights Newsletter*, Issue 16, October 2005.
22. See also, Mure Dickie, "Chinese Dissident Attacks Yahoo over Jailing of Journalist," *Financial Times*, October 18, 2005, p. 2.
23. Peter C. Perdue, *China Marches West: The Qing Conquest of Central Eurasia*, Cambridge, MA: Harvard University Press, 2005.
24. Keith Bradsher, "China Economy Rising at Pace to Rival U.S.," *The New York Times*, June 28, 2005.
25. Qin Jize, "Japan's 'China Threat' Remarks Provoke China," *China Daily*, December 23, 2005.
26. Victor Mallet, "Strait Ahead? China's Military Buildup Prompts Fears of an Attack on Taiwan," *The Financial Times*, April 7, 2005, p. 11.
27. The Carnegie Institution, *Proliferation Brief*, vol. 5, N. 8, April 30, 2002.
28. Shambaugh, *Modernizing China's Military*, p. 6.
29. From a TV interview with David Shambaugh.
30. Shambaugh, *Modernizing China's Military*, p. 4.
31. Shambaugh, *Modernizing China's Military*, p. 90.
32. Shambaugh, *Modernizing China's Military*, p. 91.
33. Shambaugh, *Modernizing China's Military*, p. 92.
34. Shambaugh, *Modernizing China's Military*, p. 243.
35. Shambaugh, *Modernizing China's Military*, p. 329.
36. Shambaugh, *Modernizing China's Military*, p. 329.
37. David Cohen, "Speakers Give Contrasting Views of Academic Caliber of Australia's Foreign-Student Market," *The Chronicle of Higher Education*, October 17, 2005.
38. "Steve Ballmer on Microsoft's Future," *Business Week*, December 1, 2003, p. 72 and 74.
39. Marcus Franda, *China and India Online: Information Technology Politics and Diplomacy in the World's Two Largest Nations*, Lanham, MD: Rowman and Littlefield, 2002, p. 2; and Marcus Franda, *Launching Into Cyberspace: Internet*

Development ande Politics if Five World Regions, Boulder, CO: Lynne Reiner, 2002.

40. Chris Buckley, "Rapid Growth of China's Huawei Has Its High-Tech Rivals on Guard," *The New York Times*, October 6, 2003.

41. "China Tested New Missile," *The Straits Times*, June 24, 2005, p. 9.

42. Wang Zheng, "US Congress Calls for Sacking of Chinese General," *The Epoch Times*, July 25, 2005, http://www.theepochtimes.com/news/5–7–25/30545.html.

43. Kenneth Lieberthal, "Preventing a War over Taiwan," *Foreign Affairs*, 84, 2 March/April, 2005, p. 61.

44. John J. Mearsheimer, *The Tragedy of Great Power Politics*, New York: W. W. Norton, 2001, pp. 4 and 402.

45. *BBC World News*, April 25, 2005, 5:05 A.M.

46. Janusz Bugajski, *Cold Peace: Russia's New Imperialism*, New York: Praeger, 2004.

47. Philip Stevens, "The West Pays a Heavy Price . . . ," *The Financial Times*, October 14, 2005, p. 15.

48. "Putin Power: The West Should Stop Pretending that Russia is a Free Democracy," *The Economist*, editorial, October 11, 2003, p. 15.

49. Nina Khrushcheva, "The Two Faces of Vladimir Putin" *Johnson's Russia List*, no. 9208, Article 5, July 22, 2005.

50. Alexander Yakovlev, *A Century of Violence in Soviet Russia*, New Haven, CT: Yale University Press, 2002, pp. x–xi.

51. Steven Rosefielde and Stefan Hedlund, *Russia After 1984: Wrestling with Westernization*, Cambridge: Cambridge University Press, 2007. The term authoritarian martial police state describes the system's defining attributes without implying an immutable ideal type, or the impossibility of transition. The word recombinant resonates with the concept of "smuta" as interpreted by Valery Solovey, an historian who works at the Gorbachev Foundation. See "Russia on the Eve of a Time of Troubles," http://www.postindustrial.net/doc/free/Solovey2004.12.doc. Times of trouble are periods of changed societal traditions, often allowing yesterday's enemies to become today's friends, but the collapse of state power doesn't last. Smuta are an intrinsic aspect of the Muscovite phenomenon, and a mechanism for its perpetuation. Putin he claims from this perspective may either represent a move toward authoritarian restoration, or toward further breakdown and chaos. Paul Goble, "Window on Eurasia: Toward a General Theory of Russian "Smuta," *Johnson's Russia List*, no. 9226, Article 13, August 18, 2005.

52. Mancur Olson, *Power and Prosperity: Outgrowing Capitalist and Communist Dictatorships*, New York: Basic Books, 2000.

53. Stefan Hedlund, *Russian Path Dependence*, London: Routledge, 2005.

54. Marshall Goldman, "Putin and the Oligarchs," *Foreign Affairs*, vol. 83, no. 6, (November/December 2004), pp. 33–44. The term command describes the power to decree (ukaz), without implying nano-direction through the party, military, secret police and state bureaucracy.

55. Ekho Moskvy news agency, Moscow, in Russian 0659 gmt January 21, 2006, BBC Monitoring, *Johnson's Russia List* 2006–#19, January 21, 2006.

56. Steven Rosefielde, *Russia in the 21st Century: The Prodigal Superpower*, Cambridge: Cambridge University Press, 2005.

57. "Interview With Minister of Defense Sergei Ivanov," *Argumenty i Fakty*, no. 13, March 30, 2005, p. 3, Retrieved from Lexis-Nexis and cited in Stephen J. Blank, "Potemkin's Treadmill: Russian Military Modernization," U.S. Army War College, August, 2005.

58. Martin Sieff, "Ballistic Missile Defense: Old Russian ICBMs still work," *Johnson's Russia List*, no. 9267, October 14, 2005.

59. Keir Lieber and Daryl Press, "The Rise of U.S. Nuclear Primacy," *Foreign Affairs*, vol. 85, no. 2 (March/April, 2006), pp. 42–54. Russian Defense Minister Sergei Ivanov announced that weapons outlays would increase fifty percent in 2006. See *Johnson's Russia Test*, no. 82, Article 16, "Defense Minister: Russia will spend 50% more on weapons in 2006 than in 2005," April 6, 2006. If Robert Norris and Hans Kristensen, "Russian Nuclear Forces 2006." *Johnson's Russia Test*, no. 83, Article 28 April 7, 2006.

60. Heinrich Vogel, "Europe and Russia: A partnership without a Vision," *Johnson's Russia List*, February 12, 2006, 2006–40, no. 30, February 10, 2006.

61. Alec Stone Sweet, *The Judicial Construction of Europe*, Oxford: Oxford University Press, 2004.

62. Quentin Peel, "Europe's Best Hope for Credibility is to Grow," *The Financial Times*, June 2, 2005, p. 15.

63. George Melloan, "Europe's Ambitious Bid for a More Perfect Union," *The Wall Street Journal*, June 17, 2003, p. A 17.

64. See Steven S. Rosefielde, book review, *Slavic Review*, vol. 65, no. 2, summer 2006, pp. 395-96, of Jakob Hedenskog, Vilhelm Konnander, Bertil Nygren, Ingmar Oldberg and Christer Pursiainen, editors, *Russia as a Great Power*, New York: Routledge, 2005.

65. William Safire, "Baudelaire's Bird," *The New York Times*, September 10, 2003.

66. Loukas Tsouklais, *What Kind of Europe?* Oxford: Oxford University Press, 2003.

67. Robert Kagan, "Power and Weakness," *Policy Review Online*, Heritage Foundation, Summer 2003.

68. Tony Judt, *Postwar: A History of Europe Since 1945*, New York: Penguin Press, 2005, p. 8.

69. Christine Ollivier, "French Nuclear Response to Terrorism." Associated Press, January 20, 2006.

70. John Redwood, *Superpower Struggles: Mighty America, Faltering Europe, Rising Asia*, London: Palgrave Macmillan, 2005.

71. Angus Maddison, *The World Economy: Historical Statistics*, pp. 64–65.

72. Philip Stephens, "Europe's Defense Plans are Worth Fighting for," *The Financial Times*, October 17, 2003, p. 15.

73. Craig Smith, "A New European Keeps a Wary Eye on America," *The New York Times*, August 9, 2003.

Chapter 11: A Witch's Brew of Troubles: The Next Big Wars

1. George C. Marshall. *The Winning of the War in Europe and the Pacific: Biennial Report of the Chief of Staff of the United States Army, July 1, 1943 to June 30, 1945, to the Secretary of War,* New York: Published for the War Department by Simon and Schuster, 1945, p. 102.

2. Demetri Sevastopulo, "Russia Urges US to Avoid Space Arms Race," *The Financial Times*, May 19, 2005, p. 2.

3. Norman Stone, *The Eastern Front: 1914–1917*, London: Hodder and Stoughton, 1975, pp. 58 and 59.

4. Steven Mosher, *Hegemon: China's Plan to Dominate Asia and the World*, San Francisco: Encounter Books, 2000.

5. Julian Cooper, "The Russian Military Industrial Complex: Current Problems and Future Prospects," conference on "Russia's Future Potential," House of Estates, Helsinki, Finland, March 23, 2001.

6. "Defense Minister: Russia Will Spend 50% More on Weapons in 2006 Than in 2005," *Johnson's Russia List*, no. 82, article16, April 6, 2006.

7. Will and Ariel Durant, *The Age of Louis IV*, New York: Simon and Schuster, 1963, p. 25.

8. Pavel Felgenhauer, "Putin Dreaming of Empire," *Moscow Times*, December 2, 2003, reprinted in *Johnson's Russia List*, no. 7449, December 3, 2003.

9. David E. Sanger, "Asia's Splits Deepen Korea Crisis," *The New York Times*, December 29, 2002, pp. 4–1 and 4–10 at 4–1.

10. Steven Blank, "Central Asia and the Transformation of Asia's Strategic Geography," U.S. Army War College, January, 2003.

11. Druckman, "Nationalism, Patriotism, and Group Loyalty," pp. 55–56.

12. See Joseph Cirincione, "Nuclear Cave-In," http://list.carnegieendowment.org/t/63011/39741/42590/0/, March 2, 2006.

13. Alexander M. Haig, Jr. "Lessons of the Forgotten War," *Foreign Policy Research Institute*, online, August 14, 2003, citing William Taubman, *Khrushchev: The Man and His Era*, New York: W. W. Norton, 2003.

14. Fritz W. Ermarth, "National Intelligence on War Scare of 1983," in *Johnson's Russia List*, no. 7449, December 3, 2003.

15. Peter Pry, *War Scare: Russia and America on the Nuclear Brink*, Westport, CI: Praeger, 1999.

16. Bill Gertz, *Betrayal*, Regnery, Washington, DC, 1999.

17. "China, America and Japan," *The Economist*, March 17, 2001, p. 22.

18. Avery Goldstein, *Deterrence and Security in the 21st Century: China, Britain, France and the Enduring Legacy of the Nuclear Revolution*, Palo Alto: Stanford University Press, 2000.

19. Steven Blank, "Central Asia and the Transformation of Asia's Strategic Geography," US Army War College, January 2003.

20. Claudia J. Kennedy, *Generally Speaking*, New York: Warner Books, 2001, p. 289.

21. John J. Mearsheimer, *The Tragedy of Great Power Politics*, New York: W. W. Norton, 2001, p. 25.

Chapter 12: The Middle East

1. Yoni Fighel, Institute for Counter-Terrorism, "An Introduction to Terrorism: Definitions, Groups, Approaches," and "Strategic Overview of the Global and Middle Eastern Terrorism," Tel Aviv University, Israel, Monday May 30, 2005. Fighel considers terrorism primarily a tool for achieving political goals through media manipulation. He desires to clarify the special criminality of terrorist attacks on civilians in international law. On nineteenth-century Russian

terrorisms see Anna Geifman, *Thou Shalt Kill: Revolutionary Terrorism in Russia*, Princeton, NJ, Princeton University Press, 1996. Bruce Hoffman, *Inside Terrorism*, New York: Columbia University Press, 1999. Ralph Peters, *Beyond Terror: Strategy in a Changing World*, Mechanicsburg, PA, Stackpole Books, 2002. Mark Juergensmeyer, *Terror in the Mind of God: The Global Rise of Religious Violence*, Berkeley: University of California Press, 2003. *La Mort Sera Votre Dieu: Du Nihilisme Russe au Terrorisme Islamiste*, La Table Ronde: Paris, 2005.

2. Fighel, "An Introduction to Terrorism."

3. Robert Baer, *See No Evil: The True Story of a Ground Soldier in the CIA's War on Terrorism*, New York: Crown, 2002. Rachel Ehrenfeld, *Funding Evil: How Terrorism is Finance and How to Stop It*, New York: Basic Books, 2003. Benjamin Netanyahu, *How Democracies Can Defeat Domestic and International Terrorism*, *Diane Publishing*, 1995.

4. Isaiah (Judean Kingdom 8 BCE) prophesies the "End of Days." The manuscript is included in the Dead Sea Scrolls. Christopher Reuter, *My Life Is a Weapon: A Modern History of Suicide Bombing*, Princeton, NJ, Princeton University Press, 2004. See also Debra Zedalis, *Female Suicide Bombers*, University Press of the Pacific, 2004. This is now available online at http://www.carlisele.army.mil/ssi/pdffiles/PUB408.pdf.

5. Brian Michael Jenkins, *The Study of Terrorism: Definitional Problems*, Santa Monica, CA: RAND, 1980; Hoffman, *Inside Terrorism*, especially Chapter 1. A comprehensive discussion of terrorism is found in Alex P. Schmid, *Political Terrorism: A New Guide to Actors, Authors, Concepts, Data Bases, Theories, and Literature*, Royal Netherlands Academy of Arts and Sciences, 1988.

6. Steven R. Weisman, "Rice Challenges Saudi Arabia and Egypt on Democracy Issues," *The New York Times*, June 20, 2005.

7. A religious group that mixed Buddhist and Hindu beliefs, based in Japan. Om means universe, shin truth, ri reason, and kyo faith. It had nine thousand members in Japan and forty thousand worldwide in 1995. After changing its name to Aleph in 2000, membership has declined to fifteen hundred. The groups founder Shoko Asahara attacked a Tokyo subway station with saran gas in 1995 for reasons which remain obscure. http://en.wikipedia.org/wiki/Aum_Shinrikyo. Haruki Murakami, *Underground: The Tokyo Gas Attack and the Japanese Psyche*, New York: Vintage, 2001. Sean O'Callaghan, *The Informer*, 1999. Eli Karmon, "NBC Terrorism and Aum Shinrikyo," Tel Aviv University, May 31, 2005.

8. Nicholas Eberstadt, "Behind the Veil of a Public Health Crisis: HIV/AIDS in the Muslim World," *American Enterprise Institute*, June 8, 2005. Reuven Paz, PRISM (Project for the Research of Islamist Movements), "Islamic Fundamentalist Terrorism," and "Hamas, Islamic Jihad and the Islamic Movement in Israel," Tel Aviv University, Israel, May 30, 2005.

9. David Victor and Nadejda Victor, "Axis of Oil?" *Foreign Affairs*, vol. 82, no. 2, March/April 2003, pp. 47–61.

10. Samuel Huntington, *The Clash of Civilizations and the Remaking of World Order*, New York: Simon and Schuster, 1996; also Huntington, "The West: Unique, Not Universal."

11. Bernard Lewis, *What Went Wrong, The Clash Between Islam and Modernity in the Middle East*, New York: Perennial, 2002. Rohan Gunaratna, *Inside Al Qaeda-Global Network of Terror*, New York: Columbia University Press, 2002.

12. Paz, "Islamic Fundamentalist Terrorism." Modern Islamists use the term "The Islamic/Muslim Ummah" to refer to all the people in the lands and countries where predominantly Muslims reside, where the khilafah state once ruled. They include non-Muslim minorities. http://en.wikipedia.org/wiki/Ummah.

13. Paz, "Islamic Fundamentalist Terrorism." Paz contends that fundamentalists see themselves as victims of a worldwide Jewish conspiracy based in free masonry, extending to the construction of the Suez Canal, the destruction of the Ottoman empire, the founding of Israel and the communist incursions into Islamic lands. These themes are echoed by Dr. Marouf Bakhit, the Jordanian ambassador to Israel, in a lecture, at Tel Aviv University, May 30, 2005, in which the Arab world was portrayed as the hapless victim of western imperialism.

14. Karl Marx, *The Grundrisse*, New York: Harper Torchbooks, 1971; Marx, and Friedrich Engels, *The Communist Manifesto*, Baltimore: Pelican Books, 1972; and *The Economic and Philosophic Manuscripts of 1844*, New York International Publishers, 1971.

15. David Menashri, "Iran Following the Fall of Saddam Hussein," Dan Panorama Hotel, Tel Aviv, Friday June 3, 2005.

16. Caliph is the term or title for the Islamic leader of the Ummah, or community of Islam. It is an Anglicized/Latinized version of the Arabic word khalifah, which means "successor", that is, successor to the prophet Muhammad. http:en//wikipedia.org/wiki/Caliph Jonathan Schanzer, *Al-Qaeda's Armies*, 2004. Alan Krueger and David Laitin, "Mis-underestimating Terrorism," *Foreign Affairs*, vol. 83, no. 5, September/October 2004, pp. 8–13.

17. Lewis, *What Went Wrong?* Michael Rubin, "Islamists Are Intrinsically Anti-Democratic," *American Enterprise Institute*, June 3, 2005. http:www.aei.org/publication22611.

18. Angus Maddison, *The World Economy: Historical Statistics*, OECD, Paris, 2003, Table 8b. Cf. Table 8.4.

19. Maddison, *The World Economy*, Table 6c, Table 8–3.

20. Maddison, *The World Economy*, Table 5c.

21. Maddison, *The World Economy*, Table 5c.

22. Maddison, *The World Economy*, Table 5b, and Table 8.3.

23. Angus Maddison, *Growth and Interaction in the World Economy: The Roots of Modernity*, AEI Press, 2005.

24. Mark Oppenheimer, "The Sixties' Surprising Legacy: Changing our Notions of the Possible, *The Chronicle of Higher Education*, October 3, 2003, p. B11. See also Mark Oppenheimer, *Knocking on Heaven's Door: American Religion in the Age of Counterculture*, New Haven: Yale University Press, 2003.

25. Dana Priest, *The Mission*, New York: W. W. Norton, 2003, p. 14.

26. Amy Chua, *World on Fire: How Exporting Free Market Democracy Breeds Ethnic Hatred and Global Instability*, New York: Doubleday, 2003.

27. Alston Chase, *Harvard and the Unabomber: The Education of an American Terrorist*, New York: W. W. Norton, 2003, p. 369.

28. Chase, *Harvard and the Unabomber*, pp. 29–30.

29. Alan B. Krueger and Jitka Maleckova, "Seeking the Roots of Terrorism," *Chronicle of Higher Education*, June 6, 2003, p. B11.

30. Scott Atran, "Who Wants to be a Martyr?" *The New York Times*, May 5, 2003, p. A27.
31. Joshua Muravchik, "Listening to Arabs," *Commentary*, 116, 5, December, 2003, p. 32.
32. Claude Berrebi, cited in Alan B. Krueger, "Cash Rewards and Poverty Alone do not Explain Terrorism," *The New York Times*, May 29, 2003, p. C2.
33. Michael Radu, "The Futile Search for the 'Root Causes' of Terrorism," *Foreign Policy Research Institute, E-Notes*, May 4, 2002.
34. Katherine Zoepf, "About 40 Students of Syrian University Reportedly Were Arrested and Tortured," *Chronicle of Higher Education*, May 9, 2005, online.
35. http://www.cnn.com/2005/WORLD/meast/06/21/lebanon.blast.
36. Christopher Henzel, "The Origins of al Qaeda's Ideology: Implications for US Strategy," *Parameters*, Spring 2005, pp. 69–80.
37. See for an update on the situation in Saudi Arabia, Sherifa Zuhur, "Saudi Arabia: Islamic Threat, Political Reform, and the Global War on Terror," US Army War College, March 2005.
38. A list of terrorist attacks by Islamic militants against the United States before September 11, 2001, is included in Allen S. Weiner, "Law, Just War, and the International Fight Against Terrorism: Is it War?" CDRLL Working Papers, no. 47, 2005. The working paper is ultimately for a forthcoming edited volume called "Intervention, Terrorism, and Torture: Challenges to Just War Theory in the 21st Century."
39. Bernard Lewis, *The Crisis of Islam*, London: Orion Publishing, 2003, pp. 48 and 125.
40. Lewis, *The Crisis of Islam*.
41. Louise Richardson, "The Terrorist Weapon of Choice," *The Financial Times*, July 2/3, 2005, p. W4, reviewing Diego Gambretta, editor, *Making Sense of Suicide Missions*, New York: Oxford University Press, 2005, and Anne Marie Oliver and Paul Steinberg, *The Road to Martyrs' Square: A Journey into the World of the Suicide Bomber*, New York: Oxford University Press, 2005.
42. Fred Halliday, *The Middle East in International Relations: Power, Politics and Ideology*, Cambridge University Press, 2004.
43. Thomas L. Friedman, "A Saudi-Israelis Deal," *The New York Times*, November 13, 2003.
44. Philip Stevens, "The Reality and Rhetoric of America's Unlearnt Lessons," *The Financial Times*, November 7, 2003, p. 15.
45. Dr. Marouf Bakhit, Jordanian ambassador to Israel blamed all Muslim conflict with the West on the Israel-Palestine dispute. Tel Aviv University, May 30, 2005.
46. A significant segment of the Israeli electorate has always rejected the notion that the Palestinians will be content with half a loaf.
47. Dennis Ross, "The Middle East Predicament," *Foreign Affairs*, vol. 84, no. 1, January/February, 2005, pp. 61–74.
48. David Menashri, "Iran Following the Fall of Saddam Hussein," Richard Bernstein, "Iran Said to Admit Tests on Path to Atom Arms," *The New York Times*, June 16, 2005. Joseph Cirincione, Jon Wolfstahl, and Miriam Rajkumar, *Deadly Arsenals: Nuclear, Biological and Chemical Threats*, second edition, Carnegie Endowment of International Peace, 2005.

49. Daniel Benjamin and Steven Simon, *The Age of Sacred Terror: Radical Islam's War Against America*, New York: Random House, 2002.

50. Dr. Marouf Bakhit, Jordan ambassador to Israel asserted that a compromise might be worked out along the lines proposed by President William Jefferson Clinton, limiting return solely to former residents, not their descendants. Yasser Arafat rejected the suggestion. Tel Aviv University, May 30, 2005.

51. There were 8.5 million Palestinians worldwide in 2000, up from 1.6 million in 1948. 4.1 million are in Israel/Palestine, 3.7 million elsewhere in the Middle East, and North Africa and 700 thousand in other countries. Sergio DellaPergola, "Demography in Israel/Palestine: Trends, Prospects, Policy Implications," IUSSP XXIV General Population Conference, Salvador de Bahia, August 2001, Table 3, p. 7. (Http:"www.uissp.org/Brasil 2001/s60/s64_02_frllsprthols.pdf). An expanded version of the paper was published in the *American Jewish Year Book*, vol. 103, 2003. Medium demographic forecasts indicate that the Palestine population in the West Bank and Gaza could nearly quadruple from 3 to 11.6 million by 2050. See Table 8, p. 17.

52. CIA, *World Fact Book*. www.cia.gov/cia/publications/factbook/geos/is.htm UN partitioned Palestine into two states after Britain withdrew from its mandate in 1948, but Palestinians rejected the solution. Subsequently, the Israelis defeated the Arabs in the 1967 and 1973 wars. On April 25, 1982, Israel withdrew from the Sinai pursuant to the 1979 Israel-Egypt Peace Treaty. On September 13, 1993 Israel and the Palestinians signed a Declaration of Principles (the Oslo Accords) guiding an interim period of Palestinian self-rule. Outstanding disputes were settled October 26, 1994 in the Israel-Jordan Treaty of Peace. On May 25, 2000, Israel unilaterally withdrew from Lebanon, which it occupied since 1982. In keeping with the framework established at the Madrid Conference October 1991, bilateral negotiations between Israel and Palestinian representatives, and Syria were conducted to achieve a permanent settlement. On June 24, 2002, President Bush laid out a roadmap for resolving the Israel-Palestine conflict, which envisions a two-state solution. However, progress has been impeded by violence stemming from the intifada begun in September 2000. The conflict may have reached a turning point with the election of Mahmud Abbas on January 2005, following Yasser Arafat's death in November 2004. Akiva Eldar, "Moratinos Document: The Peace that Almost Was at Taba," *Ha'aretz*, February 14, 2002. The Ehud Barak administration held negotiations in Taba Egypt for thirteen months, continuing Bill Clinton's failed Camp David settlement talks of 2000. The talks failed, but there are differing interpretations about the cause.

53. CIA, *World Fact Book*, UN Resolution of 1948.

54. Hamas is interpreting Sharon's withdrawal plan as a victory for the intifada, and the organization is widely expected to continue the terrorist war after Israeli withdrawal. Captured Hamas weapons on display at the Sirkin Air Force Base, Israel are primitive, suggesting either that interdiction in the Philadelphia corridor has been effective, or that outsiders aren't providing advanced armaments. Once Israel withdraws from Gaza, the combat effectiveness of Hamas could increase substantially.

55. Bennett Zimmerman, Roberta Seid, and Michael Wise, with Ambassador Yoram Ettinger, and a larger team: "West Bank/Gaza Demography Study: The

1.5 Million Population Gap." First issued at an American Enterprise Institute press conference in January, 2005. See http://www.pademographics.com or http://www.aei.org, or e-mail Zimmerman (ben@pademographics.com) or Ettinger (ram@pademographics.com).
56. Natan Sharansky, Prime Minister's Office, Jerusalem, June 2, 2005. Sharansky criticizes Sharon for not implanting democracy and free enterprise in the Gaza strip prior to withdrawal. Cf. Natan Sharansky (Anatoly Shcharansky), *The Case for Democracy: The Power of Freedom to Overcome Tyranny & Terror*, New York: Public Affairs, 2004. Newt Gingrich, "Defeat of Terror, Not Roadmap Diplomacy, Will Bring Peace," *American Enterprise Institute*, June 16, 2005.
57. Sergio DellaPergola, "Demography in Israel/Palestine: Trends, Prospects, Policy Implications, IUSSP XXIV General Population Conference, Salvador de Bahia, August 2001, p. 22 (E-mail: sergioa@huji.ac.il). The issue of homelands, Diaspora and ethnic compositions is complex. Table 8.1n shows that legal entitlement is murky, and coexistence fragile. Cf. Elia Zureik, "Demography and Transfer: Israel's Road to Nowhere," *Third World Quarterly*, vol. 24, no. 4, August 2003, pp. 619–630.

Table 11.1n. *Population in Palestine West of the Jordan River, by Religious Groups, 1st Century to 2000. Rough Estimates, Thousands.*

Year	Jews	Christians	Muslims	Total
First half 1st century C.E.	Majority	–	–	
5th Century	Minority	Majority	–	
End 12th Century	Minority	Minority	Majority	225+
14 century	Minority	Minority	Majority	225
After Black Death	Minority	Minority	Majority	150
1533–39	5	6	15	157
1690–91	2	11	219	232
1800	7	22	246	275
1890	43	57	432	532
1914	94	70	525	689
1922	84	71	589	752
1931	175	89	760	1,033
1947	630	143	1,181	1,970
1960	1,911	85	1,090	3,111
1967	2,374	102	1,204	3,716
1975	2,959	116	1,447	4,568
1985	3,517	149	2,166	5,908
1995	4,522	191	3,241	8,112
2000	4,969	217	3,891	9,310

Source: Sergio DellaPergola, "Demography in Israel/Palestine: Trends, Prospects, Policy Implications, IUSSP XXIV General Population Conference, Salvador de Bahia, August 2001.

58. Palestinians would have a small majority in a combined Israeli-Palestinian state including the West Bank by 2005 unless there were gerrymandering. See Sergio DellaPergola, "Demography in Israel/Palestine: Trends, Prospects, Policy Implications," IUSSP XXIV General Population Conference, Salvador de Bahia, August 2001, p. 17.

59. Lewis, *The Crisis of Islam*, p. xxiii.

60. Richard Wolin, "Are Suicide Bombings Morally Defensible?" *The Chronicle of Higher Education*, October 24, 2003, p. B13.

61. Former Deputy Undersecretary of Defense John A. Shaw, cited in Kenneth R. Timmerman. "Ex-Official: Russia Moved Saddam's WMD," NewsMax.com, February 19, 2006.

62. George W. Bush, "Address to the United Nations General Assembly," September 12, 2002, available at http://www.whitehouse.gov/news/releases/2002/09/20020912–1.html.

63. Stephen F. Hayes, "Case Closed," *The Weekly Standard*, 009, 11, 11/24/2003, citing the U.S. government's secret memo detailing cooperation between Saddam Hussein and Osama bin Laden.

64. Robert J. Lieber, "The Neoconservative-Conspiracy Theory: Pure Myth," *The Chronicle of Higher Education*, May 2, 2003, p. B14.

65. Thomas L. Friedman, "Because We Could," *The New York Times*, June 4, 2003, p. A31.

66. Lewis, *The Crisis of Islam*, p. 47.

67. Christopher Caldwell, "A War Between Strategists and Humanists," *The Financial Times*, June 7–8, 2003, p. 7.

68. "Secret Weapons," an editorial, *The Economist*, May 31, 2003, p. 12.

69. Richard Pells, "America: Lost in Translation," *The Chronicle of Higher Education, The Chronicle Review*, October 14, 2005.

70. "Birth of a Bush Doctrine," *The Economist*, March 1, 2003, pp. 28–29, citing Bush speech of February 26 to the American Enterprise Institute.

71. Anthony Shadid, *Night Draws Near: Iraq's People in the Shadow of America's War*, New York: Henry Holt, 2005.

72. Larry Diamond, *Squandered Victory: The American Occupation and the Bungled Effort to Bring Democracy to Iraq*, New York: Times Book, 2005; and David L. Phillips, *Losing Iraq: Inside the Postwar Reconstruction Fiasco*, Boulder, CO: as Westview Press, 2005.

73. H. G. Wells, *The Outline of History*, Garden City, NY, Garden City Books, 1920, p. 849.

74. Niall Ferguson, "Stalin's Intelligence," *Johnson's Russia List*, no. 9175, Article 26, June 12, 2005. ". . . before the invasion of Iraq, inaccurate assessments about Saddam Hussein's military capabilities were acted upon. The world would be a different place today if . . ." this intelligence had been ignored. "And thousands of Americans might still be alive."

75. Paz, "Islamic Fundamentalist Terrorism." Ned Walker, "Islam and Post-Soviet Russia: Territory and Contested Space," *Eurasian Geography and Economics*, vol. 4, May 2005. On November 2003, President Vladimir Putin asserted that there are twenty million Muslims in Russia, a figure that Walker believes is exaggerated.

76. Xiaojie Xu, "The Oil and Gas Links Between Central Asia and China: a Geopolitical Perspective, *OPEC Review*, vol. 23, no. 1, March 1999, p. 33. Fredrick Staar and Svante Cornell, "The Baku-Tiblisi-Celyhan Pipeline," Uppsala University, Central Asia-Caucasus Institute, 2005. http://www.silkroadstudies.org/BTC.html.

77. Dirk Barreveld, *Terrorism in the Philippines: The Bloody Trail of Abu Sayyaf, Bin Laden's East Asian Connection*, 2001. Eli Karmon, "Overview of South-East Asian Terrorism," Tel Aviv University, May 31, 2005.

78. Nicholas Kristof, "Sudan's Policy of Systematic Rape," *International Herald Tribune*, June 6, 2005, p. 8. "All countries have rapes, of course. But here in the refugee shantytowns of Dafur, the horrific stories that young women whisper are not a random criminality but of a systematic campaign of rape to terrorize civilians and drive them from 'Arab lands' – a policy of rape."

79. Recruitment for the Jihad in the Netherlands – From Incident to Trend, 2002 (available online at http://www.aivd.nl/contents/pages/2285/recrutimentbw.pdf). Cecilia Wikstrom, "EU Fails to Curb Terrorism Within its Borders," *International Herald Tribune*, June 6, 2005.

80. Paul Berman, *Terror and Liberalism*, New York: W.W. Norton, 2004. Martin Kramer, *Ivory Towers on Sand: The Failure of Middle Eastern Studies in America*, Washington, DC, Washington Institute for Near East Policy, 2001.

81. One proposal to accomplish this, rejected by prime minister Ariel Sharon, known as the Geneva Accord (unofficial document drafted by peace activists) calls for the renunciation of the refugee right to return, Israeli retention of the largest settlement blocks(but ceding Ariel), and Palestinian control of the Temple Mount (Haram al-Sharif). But only 31 percent of Palestinians favor it, with 51 percent opposed. See "The Geneva Accord," *Journal of Palestine Studies*, Winter 2004, vol. 33, no. 2, pp. 81–101. Cf. Ross, "The Middle East Predicament."

82. Judith Miller, et al., *Germs: Biological Weapons and America's Secret War*, New York: Simon & Schuster, 2001.

83. George Lopez and David Cortright, "Containing Iraq: Sanctions Worked," *Foreign Affairs*, vol. 84, no. 4, July/August 2004, pp. 90–103. Michael Knights, ed., *Operation Iraqi Freedom and the New Iraq: Insights and Forecasts*, Washington, DC: The Washington Institute of Near East Policy, 2004.

Chapter 13: Strategic Independence: An Ounce of Prevention

1. Andre Malraux, *Anti-Memoirs*, New York: Holt, Rhinehart, 1968.

2. George Herbert Walker Bush, *All the Best: My Life in Letters and Other Writings*, New York: Scribner, 1999, pp. 460–461.

3. "Bush's Nuclear Umbrella," *The Economist*, May 5, 2001, pp. 13–14.

4. Hui Zhang, "Act Now To Stop a Space Arms Race," *The Financial Times*, June 10, 2005, p. 13.

5. Bronwen Maddox, "Iran Exposes Flaws in a Pact Rooted in Past," *The London Times*, November 4, 2003.

6. Donald H. Rumsfeld, "Toward 21st Century Deterrence," *The Wall Street Journal*, June 27, 2001, p. A16.

7. Peter Harcher, "George Bush...," *Australian Financial Review*, July 28–29, 2001, p. 23.

8. *The Economist*, July 21, 2001, p. 9.

9. David Sanger, "US to Tell China It Will Not Object to Missile Buildup," *The New York Times*, September 1, 2001.

10. David E. Sanger, "U.S. Restates Its Stand on Missiles in China," *The New York Times*, Sept 5, 2001, p. A3.

11. "The National Security Strategy of the United States," available at http://www.whitehouse.gov/nsc/nss.html.

12. "National Security Strategy of the United States," http://www.whitehouse.gov/nsc/nss.html.

13. Avery Goldstein, *Deterrence and Security in the 21st Century: China, Britain, France, and the Enduring Legacy of the Nuclear Revolution*, Palo Alto: Stanford University Press, 2000; and Donald Kagan and Fred Kagan, *While America Sleeps*, New York: St. Marin's Press, 2000.

14. Donald Rumsfeld, "Transforming the Military," *Foreign Affairs*, vol. 81, no. 3, May/June 2002, pp. 20–32.

15. The first reference to the principles of Strategic Independence – one which influenced the the new doctrine of the Bush Administration for the geopolitical strategy of the United States – is found in Steven Rosefielde, "Economic Foundations of Russian Military Modernization," in Michael Crutcher, ed., *The Russian Armed Forces at the Dawn of the Millennium*, U.S. Army War College, December 2000, pp. 99–114. Pages 108–109 elaborate the concept of Strategic Independence.

16. Ian Kershaw, *Hitler: Nemesis*, New York: W. W. Norton, 2000, p. 123.

17. John Costello, *The Pacific War: 1941–1945*, New York: Quill, 1982, pp. 55–56.

18. Richard Miniter, *Shadow War: The Untold Story of How Bush is Winning the War on Terror*, Washington, DC, Regnery, 2004, pp. 58–59.

19. National Security Directive-9 (NSPD-9). On April 1, 2004, the White House released part of this otherwise classified document.

20. Winston S. Churchill, *A History of the English Speaking Peoples*, Volume 3, New York: Dodd, Mead and Company, 1957, pp. 314–315.

21. Winston S. Churchill, "My Grandfather Invented Iraq," *The Wall Street Journal*, March 10, 2003, p. A18.

22. Edward Radzinsky, *Stalin*, Translated by H. T. Willetts: New York: Anchor Books/Doubleday, 1996.

Chapter 14: America as Mature Superpower

1. Thomas Cantaloube and Henri Vernet, "Chirac vs. Bush: The Other War," cited in Glenn Kessler, "France was Ready to Send Troops to Iraq," *The Washington Post*, October 6, 2004, p. 18.

2. Andrew F. Krepinevich, Jr., "A New War Demands A New Military," *The Wall Street Journal*, September 10, 2002, p. A 12.

3. *Ibid.*

4. Stephen Biddle, *Military Power: Explaining Victory and Defeat in Modern Battle*, Princeton, NJ: Princeton University Press, 2004, p. x.

5. Biddle, *Military Power*, p. 2.
6. Biddle, *Military Power*, p. 3.
7. Michael P. Noonan, "When Less is More: The Transformation of American Expeditionary Land Power in Europe," *Foreign Policy Research Institute (FPRI), E-Note*, May 24, 2005. See also, Michael P. Noonan, "Reform Overdue: The Geopolitics of American Redeployment," *FPRI E-Note*, August 23, 2004.
8. Wesley Clark, *Winning Modern Wars*. New York: Public Affairs, 2003.
9. Marshall, *The Winning of the War in Europe and the Pacific*, p. 5.
10. Marshall, *The Winning of the War in Europe and the Pacific*, pp. 1 and 6.
11. George F. Kennan, *American Diplomacy, 1900–1950*. Chicago, University of Chicago Press, 1951, pp. 100–101.

Chapter 15: The Dangers of Overreach

1. John Updike, *Villages*, New York: Knopf, 2004, p. 14.
2. Charles Krauthammer, "The Neoconservative Convergence," *Commentary*, vol. 20, no. 1, July–August, 2005, p. 25.
3. George Kennan (Mr. X), "The Sources of Soviet Conduct," *Foreign Affairs*, July 1947.
4. Bruce Catton, *Never Call Retreat*, New York: Doubleday, 1965, p. 64.
5. Ed Cray, *General of the Army: George C. Marshall*, New York: Simon & Schuster, 1990, p. 92.
6. Juliet Eilperin, "Pay to Play," and "Getting a Seat at the Table," *The Washington Post*, August 3, 2003, based in part by a report by Democracy 21, a public interest group.
7. The Western Behaviorial Science Institute conducted an interesting online discussion of the limitations of American democracy in October, 2005; its content is available at http://www.wbsi.org.
8. College Entrance Examination Board.
9. Nicholas Eberstadt, "White Families Are in Trouble, Too," *Dallas News*, August 21, 2005.
10. Edward L. Glaeser, "Inequality" Harvard University, Kennedy School of Government, KSG Working Paper no. RWP05-056, March, 2006.
11. Eric Hobsbawm, "Only in America," *The Chronicle of Higher Education*, p. B7–B9, at page B9.
12. John Maynard Keynes, "A Short View of Russia (1925)," in *Essays in Persuasion*, New York: Norton, 1963, pp. 306–307.
13. Keynes, *Essays in Biography*, p. 101.
14. See Morton H. Halperin, Joseph T. Siegle, and Michael M. Weinstein, ed., *The Democracy Advantage: How Democracies Promote Prosperity and Peace*, New York: Routledge, 2004.
15. Elizabeth Lambert, "The Magic of Oliver Messel," *Architechtural Digest*, August 2002, p. 153.
16. Shana Penn, *Solidarity's Secret: The Women Who Defeated Communism in Poland*, Ann Arbor: University of Michigan Press, 2005. See also a book review of *Solidarity's Secret*, "Brave Women, But Not Sisters," *The Economist*, July 30, 2005, p. 76.

17. President George W. Bush speech to the American Enterprise Institute, February 26, 2003, *The New York Times*, February 27, 2003, p. 8.
18. David Glenn, "Political Scientists Debate Concept of 'Democratic Peace,'" *Chronicle of Higher Education*, September 2, 2003.
19. Chua, *World on Fire*, especially pages 287 and 288.
20. Alex Alexiev, "The Pakistani Time Bomb," *Commentary*, March 2003, p. 47.
21. George W. Bush, "President Bush Discusses Freedom in Iraq and Middle East," Remarks at the 20th Anniversary of the National Endowment for Democracy, United States Chamber of Commerce, Washington, D.C., November 6, 2003, available at http://www.whitehouse.gov/news/releases/2003/11/20031106-2.html.
22. William Safire, "Together They Stand," *The New York Times*, November 17, 2003.
23. Bernard Lewis, "Democracy and the Enemies of Freedom," *The Wall Street Journal*, December 22, 2003, p. A9.
24. Deborah Solomon, "A New Moral Majority?" *The New York Times*, November 16, 2003.
25. Kenneth M. Pollack, "America and the Middle East After Saddam," *Foreign Policy Research Institute WIRE*, Volume 12, Number 1, January, 2004.

Chapter 16: The Transatlantic Trap

1. George Washington, "Farewell Address," 1796.
2. William Wallace, "Europe, the Necessary Partner," *Foreign Affairs*, 81, 3, May/June 2001, pp. 16–34.
3. Robert Kagan, *Of Paradise and Power*, New York: Alfred A. Knopf, 2003.
4. Frances Stead Sellers, "A World Wishing to Cast a Vote," *The Washington Post*, November 21, 2004, p. 33.
5. Richard Haass, *The Opportunity: America's Moment to Alter History's Course*, New York: Public Affairs, 2005.
6. Charles A. Kupchan, *The End of an American Era: US Foreign Policy and Geopolitics of the 21ˢᵗ Century*, New York: Knopf, 2002.
7. Warren Zimmerman, *First Great Triumph*, New York: Farrar, Giroux, Straus, 2002, pp. 500–503.
8. Mark Leonard, *Why Europe Will Run the 21ˢᵗ Century*, Fourth Estate, 2004.
9. Weinberg, *A World at Arms*, 2005, p. 24.
10. Kellogg-Briand Pact, available at http://www.yale.edu/lawweb/avalon/imt/kbpact.html.
11. Eric Heginbotham and Christopher P. Twomey, "America's Bismarckian Asia Policy," *Current History*, 104, 683 (September 2005), p. 243.
12. Joshua Muravchik, "The Case Against the UN," *Commentary*, November 2004, p. 42.
13. Jack L. Goldsmith and Eric A. Posner, *The Limits of International Law*, Oxford: Oxford University Press, 2005.
14. "Space Weapons – Costly, Unnecessary," *The Financial Times*, May 23, 2005, p. 14.

15. Joschka Fischer, German Foreign Minister, quoted in Hugh Williamson, "Germany to Oppose 'New US World Order,'" *The Financial Times*, March 25, 2003, p. 5.
16. Andrew Jack, "Russia Faces Stern Rebuke . . . ," *The Financial Times*, October 1, 2004, p. 2.
17. Kenneth M. Pollock, *The Persian Puzzle: The Conflict Between Iran and America*, New York: Random House, 2004.
18. Stephen Schlesinger, *Act of Creation: The Founding of the United Nations*, Boulder, CO: Westview Press, 2003.
19. "The United Nations: Flags of Convenience," *The Economist*, September 13, 2003, pp. 76–77.
20. "Binding the Colossus," *The Economist*, November 22, 2003, pp. 25–26.
21. Steven R. Weisman, "A Long, Winding Road to a Diplomatic Dead End," *The New York Times*, March 17, 2003, p. 1ff.
22. Will and Ariel Durant, *The Age of Louis XIV*, New York: Simon and Schuster, 1963, p. 582.
23. Michael Glennon, "Why the Security Council Failed," *Foreign Affairs*, 82, 3, May/June 2003, pp. 16–35.
24. Will and Ariel Durant, *The Age of Louis XIV*, New York: Simon and Schuster, 1963, p. 326.
25. Lisa M. Martin, Self-Binding, *Harvard Magazine*, September–October, 2004, pp. 33–36.
26. Stanley Michalak, "The UN at 60," E-Notes, Foreign Policy Research Institute, October 20, 2005.
27. Amitai Etzioni, *From Empire to Community: A New Approach to International Relations*, New York: Palgrave Macmillan, 2004, p. 201.
28. Benjamin Schwarz and Christopher Lane, "A New Grand Strategy," *Atlantic Monthly*, January 2002.
29. Jesse Walker, "What Next for U.S. Foreign Policy," *Reason*, June 2003, p. 27.
30. Mead, *Power, Terror, Peace and War*, p. 202.
31. "World V web," *The Economist*, November 20, 2004, p. 66.
32. Robin Wright and Colum Lynch, "Hussein Used Oil to Dilute Sanctions" *Washington Post*, October 7, 2004, p. 1.
33. Walter Hoge, "UN to detail . . ." *The New York Times*, October 27, 2005.
34. Glennon, "Why the Security Council Failed."
35. Andrew C. McCarthy, "The End of the Right of Self-Defense?" *Commentary*, November 2004, p. 25.
36. Dov S. Zakheim, "What Makes Alliances Tick?" *Foreign Policy Research Institute*, October 1, 2004.

Chapter 17: The Middle Course

1. Berkowitz, *The New Face of War*, pp. 21–22.
2. Churchill, *The Gathering Storm*, p. 16.
3. Ashton Carter, "How to Counter WMD," *Foreign Affairs*, vol. 83, no. 5 (September/October 2004), pp. 72–85.

4. Henry Kissinger, quoted in "The Long View," *Harvard Magazine*, 102, 5, May–June, 2000, p. 84.

5. Andrei Shleifer and Daniel Treisman, "A Normal Country," *Foreign Affairs*, March/April, 2004, pp. 20–38. Andrei Shleifer, *A Normal Country: Russia After Communism*, Harvard University Press, Cambridge, MA, 2005; Steven Rosefielde, "Russia: An Abnormal country," *The European Journal of Comparative Ecomomics*, vol. 2, no. 1, 2005, pp. 3_16. Steven Rosefielde, "Premature Deaths: Russia's Radical Economic Transition in Soviet Perspective," *Europe–Asia Studies*, vol. 53, no. 8, 2001, Table 4, p. 1164.

6. Thomas Graham, "AEI (American Enterprise Institute) Conference Remarks," reported in *Johnson's Russia List*, no. 9270, Article 2, October 14, 2005. Cf. Henry Kissinger, Lawrence Summers, Charles Kupchan, *Renewing the Atlantic Partnership: Independent Task Force Report*, Council on Foreign Relations, 2004. Condoleezza Rice, Stephen Hadley and Robert Zelikow, *The National Security Strategy of the United States, National Security Council*, September 17, 2002.

7. European Union, *A Secure Europe in a Better World European Security Strategy*, Brussels, December 12, 2003.

8. Ingemar Dorfer, *America's Grand Strategy: Implications for Sweden*, FOI, Stockholm, FOI-R-1630-5, August 2003; Dorfer, "US Grand Strategy and Northern Europe," in *European Union– The US: The New Partnership*, Strategic Studies Institute Conference, Krakow, Poland, December 2–3, 2005. Zbigniew Brzezinski, *The Choice: Global Domination or Global Leadership*, Basic Books, 2004, p. 220.

9. *The New York Times*, editorial, May 6, 2005.

10. Goh Chok Tong, quoted in the *Asian Wall Street Journal*, June 10, 2005, p. A 7.

11. Robert D. Kaplan, "How We Would Fight China," *The Atlantic Monthly*, June 2005, pp. 49–64.

12. Joseph Kahn, "Chinese General Threatens Use of A-Bombs if U.S. Intrudes," *The New York Times*, July 15, 2005.

13. Ferguson, "America: An Empire in Denial," pp. B9 and 10.

14. Daniel Benjamin, "Military Revival After the Vietnam Trauma," *The New York Times*, August 15, 2003.

15. Sean Naylor, *Not a Good Day to Die: The Untold Story of Operation Anaconda*, New York: Berkeley Books, 2005.

16. See, for example, Mark Helprin, "'They are All So Wrong,'" *Wall Street Journal*, September 9, 2005.

17. Priest, *The Mission*. p. 11

18. Frederick W. Kagan, "Did We Fail in Afghanistan?" *Commentary*, March, 2003, pp. 39–45, at p. 40.

19. Frederick W. Kagan, "Did We Fail in Afghanistan?" pp. 39–45, at p. 44.

20. Priest, *The Mission*, p. 53.

21. Priest, *The Mission*.

22. See Frederick W. Hagen, letter to the editors, *Commentary*, June 2003, p. 10.

23. David Frum and Richard Perle, *An End to Evil: How to Win the War on Terror*, New York: Random House, 2003.

24. William Manchester, *The Glory and the Dream*, Boston: Little, Brown, 1973, p. 111.

Chapter 18: How Public Culture Inhibits Presidential Leadership

1. Victoria De Grazia, *Irresistible Empire: America's Advance Through Twentieth Century Europe*, Harvard University Press, 2005. There exists a voluminous literature on this topic as it applies to business, although most writers distinguish only between management and leadership. For a full discussion see D. Quinn Mills, *How to Lead – How to Live*, Waltham, MA: MindEdge Press, 2005 and D. Quinn Mills, *Principles of Management*, Waltham, MA: MindEdge Press, 2005.
2. Quoted from *The London Times* in *Johnson's Russia List*, no. 7330, Article 5, September 19, 2003.
3. Robert Dallek, *An Unfinished Life: John. F. Kennedy, 1917–1963*, Boston: Little, Brown and Co., 2003, p. 408.
4. A. J. Langguth, *Our Vietnam*, (New York: Simon and Schuster, 2000), p. 136.
5. See James Kitfield, *Prodigal Soldiers: How the Generation of Officers Born of Vietnam Revolutionized the American Style of War*, New York: Simon & Schuster, 1995. See also, Douglas A. Macgregor, *Transformation Under Fire: Revolutionizing How America Fights*, Westport, CT: Praeger, 2003.
6. Stephen Kinzer, "America Yawns at Foreign Fiction," *The New York Times*, July 26, 2003.
7. Hobsbawm, "Only in America," pp. B7–B9 at B9.
8. Kershaw, *Hitler: Nemesis*, p. 61.
9. Steven Lee Myers, "Putin's Democratic Present Fights his KGB Past," *The New York Times*, October 9, 2003.
10. "Hitler and Stalin," documentary film, broadcast 1/15/06.
11. Marshall, *The Winning of the War in Europe in Europe and the Pacific*, pp. 1 and 4.
12. Ronald Reagan, "Address to the Nation on National Security (Star Wars – SDI Speech)," March 23, 1983, available at the Reagan Presidential Library web site at http://www.reagan.utexas.edu/archives/speeches/1983/32383d.html.
13. Ronald Reagan, "Address to the Nation on the Iran Arms and Contra Aid Controversy and Administration Goals," August 12, 1987, available at http://www.reagan.utexas.edu/archives/speeches/1987/081287d.html.
14. John F. Harris, *The Survivor: Bill Clinton in the White House*, New York: Random House, 2005, p. 429.
15. "The Second 2000 Gore-Bush Presidential Debate," at http://www.debates.org/pages/trans2000b.html.
16. George W. Bush, "A Distinctly American Internationalism," Ronald Reagan Presidential Library, Simi Valley, California, November 19, 1999), at http://www.mtholoyoke.edu/acad/intrel/bush/wspeech.htm. See also J. Peter Pham, "Hesitant Home Repair or Successful Restoration? Foreign Policymaking in the George W. Bush Administration, The Conflict in Liberia, and the Case for Humanitarian Non-Intervention," in G. Hastedt and A. Eksterowicz, eds.,

The President and Foreign Policy, Nova Science Publishers, Inc., 2005, Chapter 7, pp. 99–113.

17. Secretary of State Condoleezza Rice with Senator Richard Lugar, "On the U.S. Department of State and the Challenges of the 21st Century," United States Department of State, The Benjamin Franklin Room, Washington, DC, July 29, 2005.

18. George W. Bush, "West Point Commencement Speech," in *America and the World: Debating the New Shape of International Politics* (A Foreign Affairs Book), New York–Council on Foreign Relations: W. W. Norton & Co., 2002, p. 367.

19. Walter Issacson and Evan Thomas. *The Wise Men*, New York: Simon and Schuster, 1986.

20. Ronald Reagan, *An American Life*, New York: Simon & Schuster, 1990, pp. 105–110.

21. Lou Cannon, *President Reagan: The Role of a Lifetime*, New York: Simon & Schuster, 1991, pp. 283–284.

22. Clinton to Dick Morris, quoted in Paul Johnson, "The Rogue in the White House," *Esquire*, June, 1997, p. 66.

23. *The Economist*, June 14, 2003, p. 9.

24. Robert Conquest, *Hoover Digest*, Summer 2003.

25. Doris K. Goodwin, *Team of Rivals: The Political Genius of Abraham Lincoln*, New York: Simon & Schuster, 2005.

26. Charles Bracelen Flood, *Grant and Sherman*, New York: Farrar, Straus and Giroux, 2005, p. 173.

27. Kershaw, *Hitler: Nemesis*, p. 189.

28. Franklin Delano Roosevelt, Speech at the Commonwealth Club, Chicago, 1932.

Chapter 19: Choosing a Great President

1. Jacques deLisle, "Asia's Shifting Strategic Landscape: Long-Term Trends and the Impact of 9/11," *Foreign Policy Research Institute E-Notes*, November 26, 2003.

2. Lewis, *The Crisis of Islam*, p. xvii.

3. Richard Pells, "American Historians Would Do Well to Get Out of the Country," *The Chronicle of Higher Education*, June 20, 2003, pp. B7–B9.

4. Jack LeVien and John Lord, *Winston Churchill: The Valiant Years*, New York: Random House, 1962.

Chapter 20: Master of Illusions

1. D. Quinn Mills, *Not Like Our Parents: How the Baby Boom Generation is Changing America*, New York: William Morrow and Co., 1987.

2. Kennedy, *The Rise and Fall of the Great Powers*.

3. Tim Burt, "Embedded Reporters Gave 'More Balanced War Coverage,'" *The Financial Times*, November 6, 2003, p. 6.

4. James David Barber, *The Presidential Character*, Englewood Cliffs, NJ: Prentice Hall, 1972, pp. 4 and 5.
5. See D. Quinn Mills, et al., *Collaborative Customer Relations Marketing*, New York: Springer, 2003.
6. Wells, *The Outline of History*, pp. 664 and 587–588, respectively.
7. Scott L. Althaus, *Collective Preferences in Democratic Politics: Opinion Surveys and the Will of the People*, New York: Cambridge University Press, 2003, pp. 9–10.
8. Kenneth Pollack and Ray Takeyh, "Taking on Tehran," *Foreign Affairs*, 84, 2 March/April, 2005, p. 24.
9. Michael B. Oren, "Bomb Shelter," *Commentary*, February 2005, p. 79.
10. Catherine Belton, "Bodman Pushes Energy Dialogue," *Moscow Times*, May, 25, 2005, *Johnson's Russia List*, no. 9159, Article 16, May 25, 2005.
11. Vijay V. Vaitheeswaran, "Axis of Oil," *The Wall Street Journal*, May 23, 2005, p. A14.
12. Michael Radu, "Andean Storm Troopers," *Foreign Policy Research Institute*, *E-Notes*, May 4, 2005.
13. George W. Bush, "Discussion of Freedom and Democracy in Latvia," May 7, 2005, available at http://www.whitehouse.gov/news/releases/2005/05/20050507–8.html.
14. Durant, *The Life of Greece*, pp. 577–578.
15. Dmitri Sidorov, "The United States Chooses between Russian oil and Russian Democracy Introducing the Bush Administration's New Policy on Russia," *Kommersant*, October 17, 2005, in *Johnson's Russia List*, no. 9269, Article 1, October 17, 2005.
16. Michael Rubin, "Who Killed the Bush Doctrine?" Haaretz, American Enterprise Institute, September 30, 2005.
17. Jack Weatherford, *Genghis Khan*, New York; Random House, 2004.
18. James David Barber, *The Presidential Character*, Englewood Cliffs, NJ: Prentice Hall, 1972, p. 7.
19. J. Haugeland, "Farewell to GOFAI," in P. Baumgartner and S. Payr, eds., *Speaking Minds: Interviews with Twenty Eminent Cognitive Scientists*, Princeton: Princeton University Press, 1995, p. 105.
20. Graham Allison, "How to Stop Nuclear Terror," *Foreign Affairs*, January/February 2004, p. 69.
21. Joseph Nye, *Bound to Lead*, Chicago: University of Chicago Press, 1990, p. 228.

Glossary

convergence

An hypothesis that the world's disparate political and economic systems are destined to converge to a common type, most often assumed to be some ideal form of just democratic free enterprise. The notion has been fashionable since the 1950s, and implies that living standards of poor nations will rise to the level of rich countries because of technology transfer and superior profit opportunities, and that once convergence is achieved there won't be a subsequent reconfiguration of global wealth and power. This assumes that the economic potential of all systems are the same, or that globalization will make them so.

crescent of fire

A swarth of Muslim lands stretching in an arc from Morocco to Indonesia driven by Islamic fundamentalist ferment, and prone to terrorism and insurrection internally and across its periphery. If the fundamentalists have their way, the crescent of fire will become a pan-Islamic theocratic empire called the Ummah.

democracy

Any of a variety of political regimes that try to achieve popular sovereignty through balloting and representative institutions. In American public culture, democracy often is associated with the notion that the people's will is infallible, allowing wishful thinkers to misinfer that balloting is enough to assure that every democratized nation will be a good neighbor.

engagement

In contemporary international politics, a term used to describe the process in which rivals peacefully press their special interests, with the hidden premise that this is the best, failsafe approach to maximizing American national security.

harmonism	A belief that there exists an ideal situation in which all human conflicts are reconcilable (for example, Marx's full communism). In international relations, harmonism is the insistence that if threats are placated they will be resolved by reason, or even divine intervention.
idea of the west	The Enlightenment idea that democratic free enterprise, or social democracy, is the most rational and therefore the best way to organize society. Harmonists extend the concept by inferring that if the idea of the West is best, it is also ineluctable.
leadership	A social function distinct from administration and management, in which the leader is charged with charting strategic policy and implementation rather than being mired in daily operations. At the American presidential level, this entails piercing public cultural illusion, educating the public without pandering to wishful thinking, and ensuring that policies are implemented by Congress and an often recalcitrant bureaucracy.
multilateralism	In contemporary political discourse, a process of multi-party engagement, in which majority opinion is thought to limit American national security policy properly, even though others are self-interested or hostile. The concept is a variant of democratic harmonism applied to international relations that potentially makes the majority opinion of despots binding on individual popular democracies. Proponents claim that multilateralism is better than strategic independence.
mutual assured destruction (MAD)	A strategic nuclear doctrine claiming that war between superpowers is preventable if both sides have sufficient numbers of nuclear weapons to obliterate each other, even if one party attempts a first strike. The concept first advocated by U.S. Defense Secretary Robert McNamara became official American doctrine in the 1960s and was modified into a countervailance concept in James Carter's presidential directive 59 on July 25, 1980, in which the notion of annihilating the leadership replaced destroying the population of an antagonist. Adopting MAD precluded efforts to attain strategic independence, which may have been appropriate at a time when the Soviet Union could build enough offensive weapons to thwart ballistic missile defense. The doctrine has now been rendered partially obsolete by nuclear proliferation, and by America's superior technology and weapons production potential.

nation-building	In public policy, the notion that it is possible, desirable, and cost-effective to transform less developed nations into free enterprise democracies through a process of modernization (technology transfer), and democratization without being thwarted by entrenched and hostile cultural forces. Nation-building was thought to be a principal engine of convergence, but this is belied statistically by the widening gap between rich and poor states.
public culture	patchwork of beliefs, platitudes, and attitudes akin to a collective mind that allows policy makers to build consensus on bi- or nonpartisan wishful thinking. American public culture approves partisan debate, tolerates distortion and attitude management by the media, business, and government, and conceals latent conflicts to promote tranquility and forge consensus on the basis of shared wishful thinking. American public culture has the virtue of protecting democracy but the defect of making us purblind, especially concerning national security and foreign relations. It is akin to ideology, but far more subtle.
reconfiguration of global wealth and power	A change in the predominant postwar pattern of wealth and power relations among nations. The facts of reconfiguration belie simpler characterizations of convergence and diverge embraced alternatively by free enterprisers and Marxists. Reconfiguration is driven by differences in the performance potential of rival economic systems.
regime change	A change of government, but not culture or political economy, that doesn't infringe national sovereignty. Regime change is often preferable to nation-building from the standpoint of maximizing American national security.
rule of law	In economics, the notion that a just society empowers individuals to maximize utility restricted only by voluntarily negotiated, and state-enforced contracts instead of having outcomes dictated by nondemocratic authorities (the rule of men). It is indispensable for any well-functioning democratic free enterprise society. Although this is widely understood by professionals, harmonists don't hesitate to assume that economies governed by the rule of men are efficient enough to assure convergence.
rule of men	In economics, the principle of dictation by the powerful, as distinct from voluntarily negotiated transactions enforced by the rule of law. From a political perspective,

Westerners scorn tyrants, but harmonists often contend that this doesn't matter if authoritarians pay lipservice to balloting and markets.

social democracy   A variant of the idea of the West in which a socially concerned state manages an otherwise free economy through democratic means to promote social justice. The model is often referred to as the welfare state. Social democracy is the cornerstone of the European Union. It is a source of Europe's ethical appeal, and the cause of its material inferiority creating a conflict between its aspirations and abilities that is increasing roiling transatlantic relations.

strategic independence   A conscious policy to determine for ourselves the best programs for maximizing American national security without tying our hands with obsolete doctrines such as mutual assured destruction, or needlessly appeasing third parties, whether they declare themselves friends or foes.

structural militarization   Term used to describe a productive system with a large embedded military-industrial sector capable of persuading government leaders to provide sufficient resources to deal with worst-case security threats.

superpower   Preeminent nuclear states. During the Cold War, America and the Soviet Union were considered superpowers because they possessed more than 90 percent of the planet's nuclear weapons, and were said to have rough strategic parity. Some analysts insist that America today is the only superpower because of its economic superiority. Contrary to a great deal of nonsense, Russia has a larger strategic nuclear capability today than America. The numbers in the public domain are official arms control figures, which bore no resemblance to reality during Soviet times, and continue to be disinformational.

terrorism   The employment of violence to intimidate civilian or military adversaries, and to wreak vengeance. It can be used by anyone from the uniformed military to guerrillas, insurrectionaries, and civilians. It can serve as a tool of domestic repression (Stalin's Great Terror), or as a weapon against foreigners. In contemporary political discourse, a sharp distinction is made among the filial categories of common criminality, terror, and war in order to establish appropriate rules of engagement. But the boundaries are more illusive than legal formalists are willing to acknowledge. Terror isn't really an "ism." It is a tactic, and its contemporary importance lies wholly in the willingness of Islamic fundamentalists and insurrectionaries to employ violence against civilian noncombatants of various descriptions in the Ummah, Israel, Russia, China, and the West.

ummah

In contemporary political usage, a pan-Islamic theocratic state under construction that seeks to restore the governing order of the first Caliphate. Advocates such as Osama bin Laden hope to use the concept to found a mighty empire, armed with nuclear weapons that can recapture territories and assets lost to infidels and revive past glories.

vortexes of danger

A concept stressing the possibility that conflicts between two rivals may spiral into regional or global cataclysms. The danger necessitates the formulation of national security strategies addressing vortexes rather than short-sighted piecemeal conflict management.

war on terrorism

The Bush administration's term for America's campaign to counter the threat of Islamic fundamentalist, and insurrectionary attacks on U.S. civilians and assets at home and abroad through enhanced security, pre-emption, and surgical strikes against hostiles, and war against states that support them. The term is a misnomer because from a juridical standpoint we cannot be at war with nonstate actors, and our countermeasures aren't directed at terrorists generally, but at Islamic fundamentalists capable of employing weapons of mass destruction and insurrectionaries seeking to cause havoc in the Middle East, and related targets of opportunity. The formulation seeks to mobilize support for worthy self-defensive measures disapproved by our public culture by equating it with people's fears about Islamist violence. The approach is shortsighted because it blurs perceptions of the Ummahist menace, conceals more serious perils, and prevents America from devising an optimal national security policy that minimizes dangers from all quarters.

westernization

The adoption of the ideals of the West including economic liberty, democracy, social justice, tolerance, diversity, and conflict avoidance by developing and transitioning economies. Westernization is a more demanding concept than modernization, which only entails adopting Western technologies. Harmonists conflate modernization with westernization, a sleight of hand that allows them to blind themselves to the Russian, Chinese, and Ummahist perils.

wishful thinking   A proclivity of American public culture to avoid overtly
                          acknowledging and grappling with complex problems
                          by pretending they don't exist, or supposing that they
                          can be easily solved with panaceas approved by public
                          culture.

Bibliography

Abrams, Irwin and Wang Gungwu. *The Iraq War and Its Consequences: Thoughts of Nobel Peace Laureates and Eminent Scholars.* Cambridge, MA: Harvard University Press, 2003.

Allison, Graham. *Nuclear Terrorism: The Ultimate Preventable Catastrophe.* New York: Times Books, 2004.

Alterman, Eric. *When President's Lie.* New York: Viking, 2004.

Althaus, Scott L. *Collective Preferences in Democratic Politics: Opinion Surveys and the Will of the People,* New York: Cambridge University Press, 2003.

Ambrose, Stephen. *Eisenhower: Volume II: The President.* New York: Simon and Shuster, 1984.

Anderson, Brian C. *South Park Conservatives: The Revolt Against Liberal Media Bias.* New York: Regnery, 2005.

Anderson, Fred and Andrew Cayton. *The Dominion of War: Empire and Liberty in North America, 1500–2000.* New York: Viking, 2005.

Andrews, David M., ed. *The Atlantic Alliance Under Stress: US-European Relations After Iraq.* Cambridge: Cambridge University Press, 2005.

Angell, Norman. *The Great Illusion: A Study of the Relation of Military Power in Nations to Their Economic and Social Advantage.* London: Heinemann, 1911.

Arrow, Kenneth. *Social Choice and Individual Values, 2nd ed.* Wiley: New York, 1963.

Ash, Timothy Garton. *Free World: Why a Crisis of the West Reveals the Opportunity of Our Time.* New York: Random House, 2004.

Audoin-Rouzeau and Annette Becker. *Understanding the Great War,* translated by Catherine Temerson, New York: Hill and Wang, 2002.

Bacevich, Andrew J. *American Empire.* Cambridge, MA: Harvard University Press, 2002.

Baer, Robert. *See No Evil: The True Story of a Ground Soldier in the CIA's War on Terrorism.* New York: Crown, 2002.

Baker, C. Edwin. *Media, Markets and Democracy.* New York: Cambridge University Press, 2002.

Barreveld, Dirk. *Terrorism in the Philippines: The Bloody Trail of Abu Sayyaf, Bin Laden's East Asian Connection,* New York: Writers Club Press, 2001.

Beach, Derek: *The Dynamics of European Integration: Why and When the EU Institutions Matter.* London: Palgrave Macmillan, 2005.

Baily, Martin Neil and Jack Funk Kirkegaard. *Transforming the European Economy.* Washington, DC: Institute for International Economics, 2004.

Bamford, James. *A Pretext for War: 9/11, Iraq, and the Abuse of America's Intelligence Agencies.* New York: Doubleday, 2003.

Barber, James David. *The Presidential Character.* Englewood Cliffs, NJ: Prentice Hall, 1972.

Barnett, Thomas P. M. *The Pentagon's New Map.* New York: Putnam, 2004.

Baumgartner, P. and S. Payr, eds. *Speaking Minds: Interviews with Twenty Eminent Cognitive Scientists.* Princeton: Princeton University Press, 1995.

Beard, Charles. *Giddy Minds and Foreign Quarrels.* New York, 1939.

Benjamin, Daniel and Steven Simon. *The Age of Sacred Terror: Radical Islam's War Against America,* New York: Random House, 2002.

Bennett, James C. *The Anglosphere Challenge.* New York: Rowman and Littlefield, 2004.

Bergen, Peter. *The Osama bin Laden I Know: An Oral History.* New York: The Free Press, 2006.

Berkowitz, Bruce. *The New Face of War.* New York: Free Press, 2003.

Berman, Paul. *Terror and Liberalism.* New York: W. W. Norton, 2004.

Biddle, Stephen. *Military Power: Explaining Victory and Defeat in Modern Battle.* Princeton: Princeton University Press, 2004.

Black, Conrad. *Franklin Delano Roosevelt: Champion of Freedom.* New York: Public Affairs Press, 2003.

Bobbitt, Philip. *The Shield of Achilles: War, Peace and the Course of History.* New York: Alfred A. Knopf, 2002.

Bodansky, Yossef. *Secret History of the Iraqi War.* New York: Harper Collins, 2003.

Brands, H. W. *Woodrow Wilson.* New York: Times Books, 2003.

Brzezinski, Zbigniew. *The Choice: Global Domination or Global Leadership.* New York: Basic Books, 2002.

Brzezinski, Zbignew. *The Grand Chessboard: American Primacy and Its Geostrategic Imperatives.* New York: Basic Books, 1998.

Bugajski, Janusz. *Cold Peace: Russia's New Imperialism.* New York: Praeger, 2004.

Burns, James MacGregor. *Roosevelt: The Soldier of Freedom,* New York: Harcourt, Brace, Jovanovich, 1970.

Busch, Nathan E. *No End in Sight: The Continuing Menace of Nuclear Proliferation.* Lexington: University of Kentucky Press, 2004.

Bush, George Herbert Walker. *All the Best: My Life in Letters and Other Writings.* New York: Scribner, 1999.

Byman, Daniel and Matthew Waxman. *The Dynamics of Coercion: American Foreign Policy and the Limits of Military Might.* New York: Cambridge University Press, 2002.

Cameron, Charles M., Randall Calver, and Thrainn Eggerttsson, *Veto Bargaining: Presidents and the Politics of Negative Power.* Cambridge: Cambridge University Press, 2000.

Catton, Bruce. *Never Call Retreat.* New York: Doubleday, 1965.

Canes-Wrone, Brandice. *Who Leads Whom: Presidents Policy and the Public.* Chicago: University of Chicago Press, 2006.

Cannon, Lou. *President Reagan: The Role of a Lifetime.* New York: Simon & Schuster, 1991.

Carter, Ashton B., and William J. Perry. *Preventive Defense: A New Security Strategy for America.* Russian Edition. Washington, DC: Brookings Institution, 2003.

Chang, Gordon. *The Coming Collapse of China.* New York: Random House, 2001.

Charles Bracelen Flood, *Grant and Sherman,* New York: Farrar, Straus and Giroux, 2005.

Chase, Alston. *Harvard and the Unabomber: The Education of an American Terrorist.* New York: W. W. Norton, 2003.

Chomsky, Noam. *Hegemony or Survival: America's Quest for Global Dominance.* New York: Henry Holt, 2003.

Chura, Amy. *World on Fire: How Exporting Free Market Democracy Breeds ethnic Hatred and Global Insecurity.* New York: Doubleday, 2002.

Churchill, Winston S. *The Age of Revolution: A History of the English Speaking Peoples,* vol. 3. New York: Dodd, Mead and Co., 1957.

Cirincione, Joseph, Jon Wolfstahl, and Miriam Rajkumar. *Deadly Arsenals: Nuclear, Biological and Chemical Threats.* Second edition, Washington, DC: Carnegie Endowment of International Peace, 2005.

Clarke, Jonathan and Stefan Halper. *America Alone: Neoconservatives and the Global Order.* New York: Cambridge University Press, 2004.

Clark, Wesley. *Winning Modern Wars: Iraq, Terrorism and the American Empire.* New York: Perseus Books, 2003.

Clarke, Richard D. *Against All Enemies: Inside America's War on Terror.* New York: Free Press, 2003.

Clinton, William Jefferson (Bill). *My Life.* New York: Knopf, 2004.

Coll, Steve. *Ghost Wars: The Secret History of the CIA, Afghanistan, and Bin Laden from the Soviet Invasion to September 10, 2001.* New York: Penguin Press, 2004.

Cook, Haruko Taya and Theodore F. Cook. *Japan at War: An Oral History.* New York: The New Press (Norton), 1992.

Costello, John. *The Pacific War: 1941–1945.* New York: Quill, 1982.

Cranston, Alan. *The Sovereignty Revolution,* Stanford: Stanford University Press, 2004.

Cray, Ed. *General of the Army: George C. Marshall.* New York: Simon and Schuster, 1990.

Cullen, L. M. *A History of Japan 1582–1941.* New York: Cambridge University Press, 2002.

Daalder, Ivo and James M. Lindsay. *America Unbound: The Bush Revolution in Foreign Policy.* Washington, DC: Brookings, 2003.

Dallek, Robert. *An Unfinished Life: John. F. Kennedy, 1917–1963.* New York: Oxford University Press, 2003.

Dallek, Robert. *FDR and American Foreign Policy.* New York: Oxford University Press, 1995.

Dallek, Robert. *Flawed Giant: Lyndon Johnson and his Times.* New York: Oxford University Press, 1998.

Davis, Kenneth S. *FDR: The War President, 1940–1943.* New York: Random House, 1960.

Dawson, Joseph G. ed., *Commanders in Chief: Presidential Leadership.* Lawrence, KS: University of Kansas Press, 1993.

Debroux, Philippe. *Human Resource Management in Japan: Changes and Uncertainties.* Ashgate, Aldershot, 2003.

De Grazia, Victor. *Irresistible Empire: America's Advance through Twentieth Century Europe.* Cambridge, MA: Harvard University Press, 2005.

DeLong-Bas, Natana J. *Wahhabi Islam.* New York: Oxford University Press, 2003.

de Tocqueville, Alexis. *Democracy in America.* Translated, edited, and with an Introduction by Harvey C. Mansfield and Delba Winthrop. Chicago: University of Chicago Press, 2000.

De Zengotita, Thomas. *Mediated: How the Media Shapes Your World and the Way You Live in It.* New York: Bloomsbury, 2005.

Diamond, Jared. *Collapse: How Societies Choose to Fail or Succeed.* New York: Viking, 2004.

Diamond, Larry. *Squandered Victory: The American Occupation and the Bungled Effort to Bring Democracy to Iraq.* New York: Times Books/Henry Holt, 2005.

Dionne, E. J. *Why Americans Hate Politics.* New York: Simon and Schuster, 1991.

Dorfer, Ingemar. *America's Grand Strategy: Implications for Sweden,* FOI, Stockholm, FOI-R-1630-5, August, 2003.

Dorrien, Gary. *Imperial Designs: Neoconservatives and the New Pax America.* New York: Routledge, 2004.

Durant, Will. *The Life of Greece.* New York: Simon and Schuster, 1939.

Durant, Will. *Caesar and Christ.* New York: Simon and Schuster, 1944.

Durant, Will. *The Life of Greece.* New York: Simon and Schuster, 1997.

Durant, Will and Ariel. *The Age of Louis XIV.* New York: Simon and Schuster, 1963.

Edwards, George C. *On Deaf Ears: The Limits of the Bully Pulpit.* New Haven: Yale University Press, 2003.

Ehrenfeld, Rachel. *Funding Evil: How Terrorism is Finance and How to Stop It.* New York: Basic Books, 2003.

Ellings, Richard J., Aaron Friedberg, ed. *Fragility and Crisis: Strategic Asia.* Seattle: National Bureau of Asian Research, 2003.

Ellis, Joseph J. *American Sphinx: The Character of Thomas Jefferson.* New York: Alfred A. Knopf, 1997.

Eland, Ivan. *The Empire Has No Clothes: U.S. Foreign Policy Exposed.* New York: The Independent Institute, 2004.

Ellis, Joseph J. *His Excellency George Washington.* New York: Alfred A. Knopf, 2004.

Englund, Steven. *Napoleon: A Political Life.* New York: Scribner, 2003.

Etzioni, Amitai. *From Empire to Community: A New Approach to International Relations.* New York: Palgrave Macmillan, 2004.

European Union. *A Secure Europe in a Better World European Security Strategy.* Brussels, December 12, 2003.

Fairbank, John King and Merle Goldman. *China: A New History, Second Enlarged Edition.* Cambridge, MA: Harvard University Press, 2005.

Farago, Ladilas. *Patton: Ordeal and Triumph.* New York: Dell, 1962.

Feldman, Noah. *What We Owe Iraq.* Princeton: Princeton University Press, 2004.

Ferguson, Niall. *Colossus: The Price of America's Empire.* New York: Penguin, 2003.

Ferguson, Niall. *Empire: The Rise and Demise of the British World Order and the Lessons for Global Power.* New York: Basic Books, 2001.

Fishman, Ted C. *CHINA Inc.* New York: Schribners, 2004.

Flood, Charles Bracelen. *Grant and Sherman.* New York: Farrar, Straus and Giroux, 2005.

Fornieri, Joseph R. *Abraham Lincoln's Political Faith.* Chicago: Northern Illinois University Press, 2003.

Fortescue, J. W. *A History of the British Army.* London: Macmillan, 1912, volume 1.

Franda, Marcus. *China and India Online: Information Technology Politics and Diplomacy in the World's Two Largest Nations.* Lanham, MD: Rowman and Littlefield, 2002.

Franda, Marcus. *Launching Into Cyberspace: Internet Development ande Politics if Five World Regions.* Boulder, CO: Lynne Reiner, 2002.

Friedman, Thomas. *The Lexus and the Olive Tree.* New York: Farrar Straus and Giroux, 1999.

Friedman, Thomas. *The World Is Flat.* New York: Farrar Straus and Giroux, 2005.

Fromkin, David. *Europe's Last Summer: Who Started the Great War in 1914?* New York: Alfred A. Knopf, 2004.

Frum, David and Richard Perle. *An End to Evil: How to Win the War on Terror.* New York: Random House, 2003.

Fukuyama, Francis. *The End of History and The Last Man.* New York: The Free Press, 1992.

Fukuyama, Francis. *State-Building: Governance and World Order in the 21st Century.* Ithaca, NY: Cornell University Press, 2004.

Fuller, J. F. C. *A Military History of the Western World, Vol. 3.* New York: Funk and Wagnalls, 1955.

Gaddis, John. *The US and the End of the Cold War.* New York: Oxford University Press, 1992.

Gaddis, John. *Surprise, Security and the American Experience.* Cambridge, MA: Harvard University Press, 2004.

Gambretta, Diego, ed. *Making Sense of Suicide Missions.* New York: Oxford University Press, 2005.

Geifman, Anna. *Thou Shalt Kill: Revolutionary Terrorism in Russia.* Princeton, NJ: Princeton University Press, 1996.

Geifman, Anna and Rodolphe Lachat. *La Mort Sera Votre Dieu: Du Nihilisme Russe au Terrorisme Islamiste.* La Table Ronde: Paris, 2005.

Gellately, Robert and Ben Kiernan. ed. *The Specter of Genocide: Mass Murder in Historical Perspective.* New York: Cambridge University Press, 2003.

Gerges, Fawaz. *The Far Enemy: Jihadish Ideology and the War on Terror.* New Haven: Yale University Press, 2006.

Gerson, Mark. *The Neoconservative Vision.* New York: Madison Books, 1996.

Gertz, Bill. *Betrayal.* Washinton, DC: Regenery, 1999.

Gilley, Bruce. *China's Democratic Future: How Will It Happen, Where Will It Lead?* New York: Columbia University Press, 2004.

Goldman, Merle. *From Comrade to Citizen: The Struggle for Political Rights in China.* Cambridge, MA: Harvard University Press, 2005.

Goldsmith, Jack L. and Eric A. Posner. *The Limits of International Law*. Oxford: Oxford University Press, 2005.

Goldstein, Avery. *Deterrence and Security in the Twenty-First Century: China, Britain, France and the Enduring Legacy of the Nuclear Revolution*. Palo Alto: Stanford, 2000.

Goldstein, Joshua S. *The Real Price of War: How You Pay for the War on Terror*. New York: NYU Press, 2004.

Goodwin, Doris K. *Team of Rivals: The Political Genius of Abraham Lincoln*. New York: Simon and Schuster, 2005.

Gordon, John Steele. *An Empire of Wealth: The Epic History of American Economic Power*. New York: HarperCollins, 2004.

Gordon, Philip H. and Jeremy Shapiro. *Allies at War: America, Europe and the Crisis over Iraq*. New York: McGraw-Hill, 2004.

Gould, Lewis L. *Grand Old Party: A History of the Republicans*. New York: Random House, 2003.

Gould, Lewis L. *The Modern American Presidency*. Lawrence: University of Kansas Press, 2003.

Gray, Colin S. *The Sheriff: America's Defense of the New World Order*. Lexington: University of Kentucky Press, 2003.

Gunaratna, Rohan. *Inside Al Qaeda-Global Network of Terror*. New York: Columbia University Press, 2002.

Habeck, Mary R. *Knowing the Enemy: Jihadist Ideology and the War on Terror*. New Haven: Yale University Press, 2006.

Halbertsam, David. *The Powers That Be*. New York: Alfred A. Knopf, 1979, p. 146.

Halliday, Fred. *The Middle East in International Relations: Power, Politics and Ideology*. New York: Cambridge University Press, 2004.

Halperin, Morton H., Joseph T. Siegle, and Michael M. Weinstein. *The Democracy Advantage: How Democracies Promote Prosperity and Peace*. New York: Routledge, 2004.

Hart, Gary. *The Fourth Power: An Essay Concerning a Grand Strategy for the United States in the 21st Century*. New York: Oxford University Press, 2004.

Hardt, Michael and Antonio Negri. *Empire*. New York: Penguin Press, 2000.

Hardt, Michael and Antonio Negri. *Multitude: War and Democracy in the Age of Empire*. New York: Penguin Press, 2004.

Haass, Richard N. *The Opportunity: America's Moment to Alter History's Course*. New York: Public Affairs, 2005.

Harris John F. *The Survivor: Bill Clinton in the White House*. New York: Random House, 2005.

Hashim, Ahmed S. *Insurgency and Counter-Insurgency in Iraq*. Ithaca: Cornell University Press, 2005.

Hastings, Max. *Armageddon: The Battle for Germany, 1944–1945*. New York: Knopf, 2003.

Hedenskog, Jakob, Vilhelm Konnander, Bertil Nygren, Ingmar Oldberg and Christer Pursiainen, editors. *Russia as a Great Power*. New York: Routledge, 2005.

Hedlund, Stefan. *Russian Path Dependence*. London: Routledge, 2005.

Held, David. *Global Covenant: The Social Democratic Alternative to the Washington Consensus.* Cambridge: Polity, 2004.

Hentz, James J., editor. *The Obligations of Empire.* Lexington: University of Kentucky Press, 2004.

Hersh, Seymour R. *Chain of Command: The Road from 9/11 to Abu Ghraib.* New York: HarperCollins, 2004.

Hoffman, Bruce. *Inside Terrorism.* New York: Columbia University Press, 1999.

Hoffmann, Stanley with Frederic Bozo, *Gulliver Unbound: America's Imperial Temptation and the War in Iraq.* Lanham, MD: Rowman and Littlefield, 2004.

Hollander, Paul, ed. *Understanding Anti-Americanism.* Chicago: Ivan R. Dee, 2004.

Holt, Michael. *The Fate of Their Country: Politicians, Slavery Extension, and the Coming of the Civil War.* New York: Farrar, Straus and Giroux, 2004.

Honderich, Ted. *After the Terror.* Edinburgh: Edinburgh University Press, 2002.

Horowitz, David. *Unholy Alliance: Radical Islam and the American Left.* Washington, DC: Regnery, 2003.

Howell, William G. *Power without Persuasion: The Politics of Direct Presidential Action.* Princeton, NJ: Princeton University Press, 2003.

Howorth, Jolyon and John Keeler, editors. *Defending Europe: The EU, NATO and the Quest for European Autonomy.* London: Palgrave Macmillan, 2005.

Huntington, Samuel. *The Clash of Civilizations and the Remaking of World Order.* New York: Simon and Schuster, 1996.

Issacson, Walter and Evan Thomas. *The Wise Men.* New York: Simon and Schuster, 1986.

Jamieson, Kathleen Hall and Paul Waldman. *The Press Effect: Politicians, Journalists, and the Stories that Shape the Political World,* New York: Oxford University Press, 2003.

Jacobs, Lawrence R. and Robert Y. Shapiro. *Politicians Don't Pander: Political Manipulation and the Loss of Democratic Responsiveness.* Chicago: University of Chicago Press, 2000.

Johnson, Chalmers. *The Sorrows of Empire: Militarism, Secrecy and the End of the Republic.* New York: Metropolitan Books, 2004.

Johnson, Paul. *A History of the American People.* New York: Harpers, 1997.

Judis, John B. *The Folly of Empire: What George W. Bush Could Learn from Theodore Roosevelt and Woodrow Wilson.* New York: Scribner, 2003.

Judt, Tony. *Postwar: A History of Europe Since 1945.* New York: Penguin Press, 2005.

Ka Zeng. *Trade Threats, Trade Wars: Bargaining, Retaliation and American Coercive Diplomacy.* Ann Arbor: University of Michigan Press, 2004.

Kagan, Robert. *Of Paradise and Power: American and Europe in the New World Order.* New York: Knopf, 2003.

Keegan, John. *Intelligence in War.* New York: Knopf, 2003.

Kennedy, Claudia J. *Generally Speaking.* New York: Warner Books, 2001.

Kennan, George F. *American Diplomacy, 1900–1950.* Chicago, University of Chicago Press, 1951.

Kennedy, Paul. *The Rise and Fall of the Great Powers.* New York: Random House, 1987.

Kepel, Gilles. *The War for Muslim Minds: Islam and the West.* Cambridge: Belknap Press, 2004.

Kernal, Samuel. *Going Public: New Strategies of Presidential Leadership.* Third edition. Washington, DC: CQ Press, 1997.

Kershaw, Ian. *Hitler: Nemesis.* New York: W. W. Norton, 2000.

Keynes, John Maynard. *Essays in Biography,* edited by Geoffrey Keynes. New York: W. W. Norton, 1951.

Key, V. O., Jr. *Public Opinion and American Democracy.* New York: Knopf, 1961.

King, David C. *The Generation of Trust: How the U.S. Military Has Regained the Public's Confidence Since Vietnam.* Washington, DC: The American Enterprise Institute for Public Policy Research, 2002.

Kissinger, Henry, Lawrence Summers, and Charles Kupchan, *Renewing the Atlantic Partnership: Independent Task Force Report,* New York: Council on Foreign Relations, 2004.

Kitfield, James. *Prodigal Soldiers: How the Generation of Officers Born of Vietnam Revolutionized the American Style of War.* New York: Simon & Schuster, 1995.

Klare, Michael T. *Blood and Oil: The Dangers and Consequences of America's Growing Petroleum Dependence.* New York: Metropolitan Books, 2004.

Knights, Michael. *Operation Iraqi Freedom and the New Iraq: Insights and Forecasts.* Washington, DC: The Washington Institute of Near East Policy, 2004.

Kramer, Martin. *Ivory Towers on Sand: The Failure of Middle Eastern Studies in America.* Washington, DC: Washington Institute for Near East Policy, 2001.

Krugman, Paul. *The Great Unraveling: Losing Our Way in the New Century.* New York: W. W. Norton, 2003.

Krugman, Paul. *Peddling Prosperity: Economic Sense and Nonsense in the Age of Diminished Expectations.* New York: W. W. Norton, 1994.

Kuper, Leo. *Genocide: It's Political Use in the Twentieth Century.* New Haven: Yale University Press, 1982.

Kupchan, Charles A. *The End of an American Era: US Foreign Policy and Geopolitics of the Twenty-first Century.* New York: Knopf, 2002.

Kupchan, Charles. *Renewing the Atlantic Partnership: Independent Task Force Report.* New York: Council on Foreign Relations, 2004.

Lake, Anthony. *Six Nightmares: Real Threats in a Dangerous World and How Americans Can Meet Them.* Boston: Little,Brown and Co., 2000.

Lal, Deepak. *In Praise of Empire: Globalization and Order.* New York: Palgrave Macmillan, 2004.

Langguth, A. J. *Our Vietnam.* New York: Simon and Schuster, 2000.

Lapidas, Ira M. *A History of Islamic Societies.* New York: Cambridge University Press, 2002.

LeBlanc, Steven A. *Constant Battles.* New York: St. Martin's Press, 2003.

Leff, Laurel. *Buried by the Times: The Holocaust and America's Most Important Newspaper.* Cambridge: Cambridge University Press, 2004.

Leonard, Mark. *Why Europe Will Run the 21st Century.* New York: Fourth Estate, 2004.

LeVien, Jack, and John Lord, *Winston Churchill: The Valiant Years.* New York: Random House, 1962.

Levi, Michael A. and Michael E. O'Hanlon. *The Future of Arms Control.* Washington, DC: Brookings Institution Press, 2005.

Lewis, Bernard. *What Went Wrong, The Clash Between Islam and Modernity in the Middle East.* New York: Perennial, 2002.

Lewis, Bernard. *What Went Wrong?* New York: Perennial, 2003.

Lewis, Bernard. *The Crisis of Islam.* London: Orion, 2003.

Lieven, Anatol. *America Right or Wrong: An Anatomy of American Nationalism.* Oxford: Oxford University Press, 2004.

Lilley, James. *China Hands.* New York: Perseus, 2004.

Lipset, Seymour Martin. *American Exceptionalism.* New York: W. W. Norton, 1966.

Lord, Carnes. *The Modern Prince: What Modern Leaders Need to Know Now.* New Haven: Yale University Press, 2003.

Lovins, Amory B. et al., *Winning the Oil Endgame: Innovations for Profits, Jobs and Security.* Snowmass, CO: Rocky Mountain Institute, 2004.

Macaulay, Thomas Babington. *The History of England,* Volume 1. London: Longman, Brown, Green and Longmans, 1856.

Maddison, Angus. *Chinese Economic Performance in the Long Run.* Development. Center Studies, OECD, Paris, 1998.

Maddison, Angus. *Growth and Interaction in the World Economy: The Roots of Modernity.* Washington, DC: AEI Press, 2005.

Maddison, Angus. *The World Economy: Historical Statistics.* Geneva: OECD, 2003.

Malraux, Andre. *Anti-Memoirs.* New York: Holt, Rhinehart, 1968.

Manchester, William. *American Caesar: Douglas MacArthur.* Boston: Little, Brown, 1978.

Manchester, William. *The Glory and the Dream.* Boston: Little, Brown, 1973.

Mandelbaum, Michael. *The Case for Goliath: How America Acts as the World's Government in the 21st Century.* New York: Public Affairs Press, 2004.

Mann, James. *The Rise of the Vulcans: The History of Bush's War Cabinet.* New York: Viking, 2004.

Martin, Andrew and George Ross, editors. *Euros and Europeans: Monetary Integration and the European Model of Society.* New York: Cambridge University Press, 2004.

Marshall, George W. *The Winning of the War in Europe and the Pacific: Biennial Report of the Chief of Staff of the United States Army, July 1, 1943 to June 30, 1945, to the Secretary of War.* New York: Published for the War Department by Simon and Schuster, 1945.

Marx, Karl and Friedrich Engels. *The Communist Manifesto,* Pelican Books, Baltimore, 1972.

Marx, Karl. *The Grundrisse.* New York: Harper Torchbooks, 1971.

Mayer, Kenneth R. *With the Stroke of a Pen: Executive Orders and Presidential Power.* Princeton, NJ: Princeton University Press, 2001.

McAdams, Dan P. *The Redemptive Self: Stories Americans Live By.* New York: Oxford University Press, 2005.

McCullough, David. *John Adams.* New York: Simon and Schuester, 2001.

McCullough, David. 1776. New York: Simon and Schuster, 2005.

Macgregor, Douglas A. *Transformation Under Fire: Revolutionizing How America Fights.* Westport, CT: Praeger, 2003.

Mead, Walter Russell. *Power, Terror, Peace and War: America's Grand Strategy in a World at Risk.* New York: Knopf, 2004.

Mearsheimer, John J. *The Tragedy of Great Power Politics*. New York: W. W. Norton, 2001.

Micklewait, John and Adrian Wooldridge. *A Future Perfect: The Challenge and Hidden Promise of Globalization*. New York: Times Books, 2000.

Miller, John J. and Mark Molesky. *Our Oldest Enemy: A History of America's Disastrous Relationship with France*. New York: Doubleday, 2004.

Miller, Judith et al. *Germs: Biological Weapons and America's Secret War*. New York: Simon & Schuster, 2001.

Mills, D. Quinn et al. *Collaborative Customer Relations Marketing*. New York: Springer, 2003.

Mills, D. Quinn. *Labor, Government and Inflation*. Chicago: University of Chicago, 1975.

Mills, D. Quinn. *Leadership: How to Lead – How to Live*. Waltham, MA: MindEdge Press, 2005.

Mills, D. Quinn. *Not Like Our Parents: How the Baby Boom Generation is Changing America*. New York: William Morrow and Co., 1987.

Mills, D. Quinn. *Principles of Management*. Waltham, MA: MindEdge Press, 2005.

Miniter, Richard. *Shadow War: The Untold Story of How Bush is Winning the War on Terror*. Washington, DC: Regnery, 2004.

Morris, Edmund. *Theodore Rex*. New York: Random House, 2001.

Morrow, John H. Jr. *The Great War: An Imperial History*. New York: Routledge, 2003.

Mosher, Steven. *Hegemon: China's Plan to Dominate Asia and the World*. San Francisco: Encounter Books, 2000.

Moynihan, Daniel Patrick. *Coping: Essays on the Practice of Government*. New York: Random House, 1973.

Mueller, John. *War, Presidents and Public Opinion*. New York: Wiley, 1992.

Murray, Williamson and Allan R. Millett. *A War to be Won: Fighting the Second World War*. Cambridge, MA: Harvard University Press, 2000.

Murakami, Haruki. *Underground: The Tokyo Gas Attack and the Japanese Psych*. New York: Vintage, 2001.

Naftali, Timothy. *Blind Spot: The Secret History of American Counterterrorism*. New York: Basic Books, 2004.

Napoleoni, Loretta. *Modern Jihad*. Sterling, VA: Pluto Press, 2003.

National Academy. *Making the Nation Safer: The Role of Science and Technology in Countering Terrorism*. Washington, DC: the National Academies Press. 2002.

National Commission on Terrorist Attacks Upon the United States. *The 9/11 Commission Report: Final Report*. New York: W. W. Norton, 2003.

Naylor, Sean. *Not a Good Day to Die: The Untold Story of Operation Anaconda*. New York: Berkeley Books, 2005.

Nehru, Jawaharlal. *Glimpses of World History: Being Further Letters to his Daughter Written in Prison*, New York: The John Day Company, 1942.

Netanyahu, Benjamin. *Fighting Terrorism: How Democracies Can Defeat Domestic and International Terrorism*. New York: Farrar, Straus and Giroux, 2001.

Neustadt, Richard E. *Presidential Power and the Modern Presidents: The Politics of Leadership from Roosevelt to Reagan*. New York: Free Press, 1990.

Nye, Joseph S. *Bound to Lead: The Changing Nature of American Power*. Chicago: University of Chicago Press, 1990.

Nye, Joseph S. *The Paradox of American Power: Why the World's Only Superpower Can't Go it Alone*. Oxford: Oxford University Press, 2002.

Nye, Joseph S. *Soft Power: The Means to Success in World Politics*. New York: Public Affairs, 2003.

O'Dell, Peter R. *Why Carbon Fuels Will Dominate the 21st Century's Global Energy Economy*. Multi-Science Publishing, 2004.

Odum, William E. and Robert Dujarric. *America's Inadvertent Empire*. New Haven: Yale University Press, 2003.

Oliver, Anne Marie and Paul Steinberg. *The Road to Martyrs' Square: A Journey into the World of the Suicide Bomber*. New York: Oxford University Press, 2005.

Olson, Mancur. *Power and Prosperity: Outgrowing Capitalist and Communist Dictatorships*. New York: Basic Books, 2000.

Olsen, Mancur. *The Rise and Decline of Nations: Economic Growth, Stagflation and Social Rigidities*. New Haven: Yale University Press, 1982.

Oppenheimer, Mark. *Knocking on Heaven's Door: American Religion in the Age of Counterculture*. New Haven: Yale University Press, 2003.

Patterson, Robert. *Dereliction of Duty*. Washington: Regnery, 2003.

Paul, T. V., James J. Wirtz and Michel Fortmann, editors. *Balance of Power*. Palo Alto: Stanford University Press, 2004.

Perdue, Peter C. *China Marches West: The Qing Conquest of Central Eurasia*. Cambridge, MA: Harvard University Press, 2005.

Perkins, John. *Confessions of an Economic Hit Man*. San Francisco: Berrett-Koehler, 2004.

Peters, Ralph. *Beyond Terror: Strategy in a Changing World*. Stackpole, 2002.

Phillipe, Roger. *The American Enemy: the History of French Anti-Americanism*. Chicago: University of Chicago Press, 2004.

Phillips, David L. *Losing Iraq: Inside the Postwar Reconstruction Fiasco*. Boulder, CO: Westview Press, 2005.

Phillips, Kevin. *William McKinley*. New York: Times Books, 2003.

Plato. *The Republic*. New York: Vintage Books, 1965.

Plutarch. *The Rise and Fall of Athens*. Baltimore: Penguin Books, 1964.

Pollack, Kenneth M. *The Persian Puzzle: The Conflict Between Iran and America*. New York: Random House, 2004.

Power, Samantha. *"A Problem from Hell": American and the Age of Genocide*. New York: Basic Books, 2002.

Prestowitz, Clyde. *Rogue Nation: American Unilateralism and the Failure of Good Intentions*. New York: Basic Books, 2003.

Priest, Dana. *The Mission*. New York: W. W. Norton, 2003.

Pry, Peter Vincent. *War Scare*. New York: Greenwood, 1999.

Puddington, Arch. *Lane Kirkland*. New York: Wiley, 2005.

Rabkin, Jeremy A. *The Case for Sovereignty: Why the World Should Welcome American Independence*. Washington, DC: AEI Press, 2004.

Rawls, John. *A Theory of Justice*, Cambridge, MA: Harvard University Press, 1971.

Rawls, John. *Justice as Fairness: A Restatement*. Cambridge, MA: Harvard University Press, 2001.

Redwood, John. *Superpower Struggles: Mighty America, Faltering Europe, Rising Asia.* London: Palgrave Macmillan, 2005.

Reid, T. R. *The United States of Europe: The New Superpower and the End of American Supremacy.* London: Penguin, 2004.

Remini, Robert V. *Andrew Jackson and the Course of American Democracy, 1833–1845, Vol. 3.* New York: Harper and Row, 1984.

Reuter, Christopher. *My Life Is a Weapon: A Modern History of Suicide Bombing.* Princeton, NJ: Princeton University Press, 2004.

Rice, Condoleezza, Stephen Hadley, and Robert Zelikow, *The National Security Strategy of the United States, National Security Council.* September 17, 2002.

Ricks, Thomas E. *Fiasco: The American Military Adventure in Iraq.* New York: Penguin Press, 2006.

Rifkin, Jeremy. *The European Dream.* London: Penguin, 2004.

Roberts, Paul. *The End of Oil: On the Edge of a Perilous New World.* New York: Houghton Mifflin, 2004.

Robin, Corey. *Fear: The History of a Political Idea.* Oxford: Oxford University Press, 2004.

Roger, Phillipe. *The American Enemy: the History of French Anti-Americanism.* Chicago: University of Chicago Press, 2004.

Rosefielde, Steven. *Comparative Economic Systems: Culture, Wealth and Power in the 21st Century.* Oxford: Blackwell, 2002.

Rosefielde, Steven. *Russia in the 21st Century: Prodigal Superpower.* Cambridge: Cambridge University Press, 2005.

Rosefielde, Steven. *Russian Economics: From Lenin to Putin.* Oxford: Blackwell, 2006.

Rosefielde, Steven, and Stefan Hedlund, *Russia After 1984: Wrestling with Westernization.* Cambridge: Cambridge University Press, 2007.

Ross, Andrew and Kristin Ross, editors. *Anti-Americanism.* New York: NYU Press, 2004.

Ross, Dennis. *The Missing Peace: The Inside Story of the Fight for Middle East Peace.* New York: Farrar, Strauss & Giroux, 2004.

Roy, Olivier. *Globalised Islam.* New York: Columbia University Press, 2004.

Rudalevige, Andrew. *Managing the President's Program: Presidential Leadership and Legislative Policy Formulation.* Princeton, NJ: Princeton University Press, 2002.

Rudalevige, Andrew. *The New Imperial Presidency: Renewing Presidential Power after Watergate.* Ann Arbor: University of Michigan Press, 2005.

Sachs, Jeffrey. *The End of Poverty: Economic Possibilities for Our Time,* New York: Penguin, 2005.

Sageman, Marc. *Understanding Terror Networks.* Philadelphia: University of Pennsylvania Press, 2004.

Said, Edward W. *From Oslo To Iraq And The Road Map.* New York: Pantheon, 2004.

Sakwa, Richard. *Putin: Russia's Choices.* New York: Rutledge, 2004.

Sapir, Andre et al. *An Agenda for a Growing Europe: The Sapir Report.* New York: Oxford University Press, 2004.

Schlesinger, Stephen. *Act of Creation: The Founding of the United Nations.* Boulder, CO: Westview Press, 2003.

Scheuer, Michall. *Imperial Hubris: Why the West is Losing the War on Terror.* New York: Brassey, 2003.

Schmid, Alex P. *Political Terrorism: A New Guide to Actors, Authors, Concepts, Data Bases, Theories, and Literature.* Amsterdam: Royal Netherlands Academy of Arts and Sciences, 1988.

Service, Robert. *Stalin.* New York: Macmillan, 2004.

Shadid, Anthony. *Night Draws Near: Iraq's People in the Shadow of America's War.* New York: Henry Holt, 2005.

Shambaugh, David. *Modernizing China's Military.* Berkeley: University of California Press, 2003.

Sharansky, Natan. *The Case for Democracy: The Power of Freedom to Overcome Tyranny & Terror.* New York: Public Affairs, 2004.

Shenkar, Oded. *The Chinese Century.* New York: Pearson/Wharton School, 2005.

Shirer, William L. *20th Century Journey: A Memoir of the Life and Times, Volume III, A Native's Return, 1945–1988.* New York: Bantam Nonfiction, 1992.

Shleifer, Andrei. *A Normal Country: Russia After Communism.* Cambridge, MA: Harvard University Press, 2005.

Shogan, Robert. *The Riddle of Power: Presidential Leadership.* New York: Dutton, 1991.

Skidelsby, Robert. *John Maynard Keynes,* volume 3. New York: Viking, 2001.

Skowronek, Stephen. *The Politics Presidents Make.* Cambridge, MA: Harvard University Press, 1997.

Smith, Jean Edward. *Grant.* New York: Simon and Shuster, 2001.

Soros, George. *The Bubble of American Supremacy: Correcting the Misuse of American Power.* New York: Public Affairs, 2002.

Spykman, Nicholas J. *America's Strategy in World Politics.* New Haven: Yale University Press, 1942.

Stelzer, Irwin, ed. *Neoconservatism.* New York: Atlantic Books, 2004.

Stern, Jessica. *Terror in the Name of God: Why Religious Militants Kill.* New York: Eco, 2003.

Stevenson, David. *Cataclysm: The First World War as Political Tragedy.* New York: Basic Books, 2004.

Stone, Norman. *The Eastern Front: 1914–1917,* London: Hodder and Stoughton. 1975.

Strachan, Hugh. *The First World War.* New York: Viking, 2004.

Sweet, Alec Stone. *The Judicial Construction of Europe.* Oxford: Oxford University Press, 2004.

Taliaferro, Jeffrey W. *Balancing Risks: Great Power Intervention in the Periphery.* Ithaca, NY: Cornell University Press, 2004.

Terrill, Ross. *The New Chinese Empire.* New York: Basic Books, 2003.

Thatcher, Margaret. *The Downing Street Years.* New York: Harper, Collins, 1993.

Timmerman, Kenneth R. *The French Betrayal of America.* New York: Crown Forum, 2004.

Tsouklais, Loukas. *What Kind of Europe?* Oxford: Oxford University Press, 2003.

Tuchman, Barbara. *Stilwell and the American Experience in China, 1911–1945,* New York: Macmillan, 1971.

Turque, Bill. *Inventing Al Gore: A Biography.* Boston: Houghton-Mifflin, 2000.

Turner, Edward Raymond. *Europe Since 1789.* New York: Doubleday, 1925,

Unger, Craig. *House of Bush, House of Saud.* New York: Scribner, 2004.

United Nations. Human Development Report, Oxford: Oxford University Press 1995.

United Nations. Human Development Report, Oxford: Oxford University Press, 1998.

United Nations, Secretary General. *A More Secure World: Our Shared Responsibility.* New York: United Nations, 2004.

United States, National Intelligence Council. Mapping the Global Future, The 2000 Project, Washington, DC: NIC, 2004.

Valentino, Benjamin A. *Final Solutions: Mass Killing and Genocide in the 20th Century.* Ithaca, NY: Cornell University Press, 2004.

Vryonis, Speros Jr. *The Mechanism of Catastrophe: The Turkish Pogrom of September 6–7, 1955, and the Destruction of the Greek Community of Istanbul.* Greekworks.com, 2005.

Walt, Stephen M. *Taming American Power: The Global Response to U.S. Primacy.* New York: Norton, 2005.

Walzer, Michael. *Arguing About War.* New Haven: Yale University Press, 2004.

Waugh, John C. *Reelecting Lincoln: The Battle for the 1864 Presidency.* New York: Crown, 1997.

Weinberg, Gerhard L. *A World at Arms: A Global History of World War II.* New York: Cambridge University Press, second edition, 2005.

Weinberg, Gerhard L. *Visions of Victory: The Hopes of Eight World War II Leaders.* New York: Cambridge University Press, 2005.

Weitz, Eric D. *A Century of Genocide.* Princeton: Princeton University Press, 2003.

Wells, H. G. *The Outline of History,* Garden City, NY: Garden City Books, 1920.

Wheatcroft, Andrew. *Infidels: A History of the Conflict between Christendom and Islam.* New York: Random House, 2005.

William G. Howell. *Power without Persuasion: The Politics of Direct Presidential Action* Princeton, NJ: Princeton University Press, 2003.

Willkie, Wendell L. *One World.* New York: Simon & Schuster, 1943.

Wilson, Joseph. *The Politics of Truth: Inside the Lies that led to War and Betrayed my Wife's CIA Identity.* New York: Carroll and Graf, 2004.

Winterbotham, F. W. *The Nazi Connection.* New York: Dell, 1978.

Witcover, Jules. *Party of the People: A History of the Democrats.* New York: Random House, 2003.

Wolf, Charles, Anil Bamezai, K. C. Yeh and Benjamin Zycher. *Asian Economic Trends and Their Security Implications.* Santa Monica: Rand, 2000.

Wolf, Charles, K. C. Yeh, Anil Banzai, Donald Henry and Michael Kennedy. *Long Term Economic and Military Trends, 1994–2015: The United States and Asia.* Santa Monica: Rand, 1995.

Woodward, Bob. *Plan of Attack.* New York: Simon & Schuster, 2004.

Woodward, Bob. *Bush at War.* New York: Simon & Schuster, 2002.

Yakovlev, Alexander. *A Century of Violence in Soviet Russia.* New Haven: Yale University Press, 2002.

Ye-or, Bat. *Eurabia: The Euro-Arab Axis.* Madison, NJ: Fairleigh Dickinson Press, 2004.

Zaller, John R. *The Nature and Origins of Mass Opinion.* New York: Cambridge University Press, 1992.
Zedalis, Debra. *Female Suicide Bombers.* Stockton, CA: University Press of the Pacific, 2004.
Zhao, Suisheng. *A Nation-State by Construction: Dynamics of Modern Chinese Nationalism.* Stanford: Stanford University Press, 2004.
Zimmerman, Warren. *First Great Triumph.* New York: Farrar, Strauss, Girous, 2002.

There is a large literature of presidential studies that the authors use and cite when developing our own perspective. Among the most important of the scholarly studies are those of presidential leadership generally (including Joseph G. Dawson, ed., *Commanders in Chief: Presidential Leadership,* Lawrence, KS: University of Kansas Press, 1993; and Robert Shogan, *The Riddle of Power: Presidential Leadership,* New York: Dutton, 1991) and of the presidencies of Andrew Jackson (in particular Robert Remini's three volume biography), Abraham Lincoln (in particular John Waugh's *Reelecting Lincoln*), Theodore Roosevelt (in particular Warren Zimmerman's *First Great Triumph*), Woodrow Wilson, Franklin Delano Roosevelt (including Conrad Black's recent biography), Harry Truman, and the subsequent presidents to the current time (including Bill Clinton's autobiography). Other useful studies include those of presidential decision making in periods of crisis and of wartime. This is a literature to which the most recent contributions have been those of Bob Woodward, writing in a reportorial fashion about the Bush administration's efforts in Afghanistan and Iraq.

Index

2004 Presidential campaign, 89, 90
  endorsement of military preemption
    in, 103
Abizaid, John (U.S. General)
Able Archer, 252–54
ABM treaty, 308–09, 314. *See also* nuclear
    conflict, threat of
Afghanistan, 125, 247, 299, 324, 424
  and the war against the Soviets, 411
  Operation Anaconda in, 398
  U.S. invasion of,
  worsening political situation in,
    398–400
After the Terror (Honderich), 287
Al Qaeda, 125, 324, 399, 400, 443, 460.
    See also bin Laden, Osama; Muslim
    terrorism
All the King's Men (Warren), 15
Allison, Graham, 464
American public
  and distrust of president in, 260,
    446–49, 451
  and electing a suitable president, 406,
    414
  and increased support of military,
    119–20, 122–23
  need for geopolitical sophistication in,
    350–52, 414

new maturity of, 99,117–23,129, 261,
    324, 396, 407, 436, 446–48, 451
  self-image of, 103–08
American style democracy and free
    enterprise, transplanting abroad,
    17
  and Bush's public relations offensive
    for, 455
  and instability, 353
  and need for geopolitical
    sophistication about, 350–52
  and public culture, 457–60
  Bush's policy for in Iraq, 97–99,
    288–98, 354–57, 453, 457–60
  Germany as example of, 346–47
  Japan as example of, 346–47
  need to reject idea of, 401
  reasons why not good enough to
    transfer, 347–50
  reasons why too good to transfer,
    344–47
  wishful thinking about, 349
Andropov, Yuri, 252
Arafat, Yasser, 29, 264
Arrow, Kenneth, 353
Asia, vortexes of danger in, 244–48
Atlantic Monthly, The (magazine), 69
Aznar, Jose Maria, 221

Barber, James, 453
Bell, Daniel, 67
Bergson, Abram, 60
Berkowitz, Bruce, 74
Biddle, Stephen, 335
bin Laden, Osama, 24
    and failure of U.S. to locate, 295, 323
    fatwa of, 275–77
    understanding of U.S. flaws by, 129
Blair, Tony, 58, 224
Blank, Stephen, 19, 215
Bohlen, Charles, 410
Bolivia, 458
Brezhnev, Colonel, 253
Britain, 20. *See also* Blair, Tony; European
    Union
    and preemption against Napoleon,
    328
    and the EU, 225–27
Brown, Harold, 333
Brown, John, 69
Bugajski, Janusz, 204
Burke, Donald S., 321
Bush, George H.W., 308
    and assassination attempt by Hussein,
    413
    and poor war leadership of, 422
Bush, George W. and the Bush
    administration
    and Iraq as test, 124–26
    and Iraq invasion as response to
    Hussein's provocations, 413–14
    and misjudgement on Putin,
    416–18
    and mistake of labeling terrorism
    defense as war, 285
    and NMD against China, 395–96
    and policy of transplanting
    democracy, 288–98, 354–57

and public culture, 97–99, 453–56
and public culture's influence on Iraq
    policy, 456–60
and public relations offensive for
    democracy, 455
and reliance on foreign oil, 457
and roadmap for Israeli-Palestinian
    conflict, 283, 284
and strengths and weakness of
    preemption in Iraq, 329–30
and the Bush Doctrine, 316–18
and the National Security Strategy of
    the United States, xviii, 316, 317,
    355
and WMD as justification for Iraq
    invasion, 327, 450–51, 455, 457
assessment of ability to master
    illusions of public culture, 423–29
candor of, 450–51, 452, 455
deception of, 448–49
ineffective leadership of, 406, 456, 459
media distortion of, 94, 95, 96
on Russia, 206

Camus, Phillipe, 162
candor, need for in U.S. presidents, 30–32,
    261, 414, 421, 438, 446–53, 463
    about China, 392
    about coming threats, 300
    and Bush, 327, 450–51, 452, 455
    and NMD, 313
    and the UN, 382
    and weapons of mass destruction, 327
Carter, Ashton, 464
Carter, Jimmy, poor leadership of in Iran
    hostage situation, 421
Castro, Fidel, 251
casualties
    and Kosovo, 335–36

difference in scale between WWII and post 9/11, 237

myth of war without, 335–36

unwillingness of U.S. to take, 401

Chamberlain, Neville, misjudgment of Hitler by, 416

China

and Falun Gong, 192

and hidden motivations in response to Iraqi invasion, 127

and relations with Japan, 244–48, 437

and Taiwan, 245

and technology, 197–99

military of, 3, 195–02

nationalism in, 14, 185, 188–95, 245, 393, 456

need for candor about, 392

nuclear capabilities of, 12, 195–97, 254–57, 391–96

repression in, 3, 191–94

rivalry with U.S. 185–88

versus Russia, 389

wishful thinking about, 393

Chinese economy and economic culture, 142–46, 438

and fallacy of convergence, 189

and harmonism, 190

Chua, Amy, 272

Churchill, Winston, 75, 108, 225, 386, 401, 416

CIA, xxi, 61, 92, 148, 181, 206, 209, 214, 253, 254, 324, 483n7, 488n3, 491n52, 491n53, 511, 522

Civil War, 20, 223, 294, 373, 418, 428, 432–33

civilians, terrorist justifications for violence against, 288

Clarke, Richard, 324

Clinton, Bill and the Clinton administration, 46, 193

and disarmament, 377, 438

and failure to locate bin Laden, 323

and Kosovo, 400

and national missile defense, 311, 314

and wishful thinking, 89

failure in helping Russia transition to market economy, 422–23

impeachment of, 449

ineffective management of, 405

poor preparation for international relations of, 432

Cold War, 417, 418

containment policy during, 344

nuclear threats during, 251

Combs, Roberta, 356

communalism, in Japanese economic culture, 153–61

conflict, threat of to U.S. *See* by specific wars; international conflict, threat of; Iraq; Muslim terrorism; nuclear conflict, threat of; terrorism, threat of; U.S. military

convergence, 11, 47–52, 257, 344, 392, 437, 438. *See also* by specific country; global economies and economic cultures

and China, 189

defined, 41

unjustified optimism of, 52–55

wishful thinking about, 84

corporatism, in the European economy, 162–68

Crescent of Fire, *See* Middle East; Muslim terrorism

Cuban missile crisis, 251–52, 412

and JFK, 420

Dallek, Robert, 410

dangers, to U.S. *See* by specific wars;
    international conflict, threat of;
    Iraq; Muslim terrorism; nuclear
    conflict, threat of; terrorism, threat
    of; U.S. military

de Tocqueville, Alexis, 91

defense, of U.S. *See* strategic
    independence; U.S. national
    security and security policy

DeGrazia, VIctoria, 403

Deng Xiaoping, 144–45, 150, 186. *See also*
    China; Chinese economy and
    economic culture

Derrida, Jacques, 59

diplomacy, versus war, 372–73, 400. *See
    also* international relations and
    geopolitics; multilateralism

distortion, in American public culture,
    76–80

Dujarric, Robert, 14

Dulles, John Foster, 427

Durant, Ariel, 373

Durant, Will, 82, 373, 458

Economist, The (magazine), 66, 207, 291
    and the US attitude toward the UN,
        371
    on national missile defense, 312, 314

Ecuador, 458

Eisenhower, Dwight, 394, 420
    as exception to record of poor
        presidential leadership, 431

Ellis, Joseph, 26

England. *See* Britain

Ermarth, Fritz, 253

Etzioni, Amitai, 374

European Union
    and Britain, 225–27
    and exploitation of Iraq, 218–22, 260

and incentives for stopping nuclear
    programs, 370
    and multilateralism, 359–62
    approach to world problems by,
        370–71
    nation-building in, 218–25
    rivalry with U.S., 246
    threat from Muslim terrorism to, 299
    wishful thinking of, 224, 360

European Union economy and economic
    culture, 161–68
    corporatism in, 162–68

Fallon, Andrew (U.S. Admiral), 196

Falun Gong, repression of in China, 192

federalism, 25, 218, 221, 226, 429.
        See also European Union,
        nation-building in
    and strategic independence, 15, 389,
        462, 463

Ferrero-Waldner, Benita, 77

Financial Times, The (magazine), 188

Foreign Affairs (magazine), 53

foreign relations. *See* international
    relations and geopolitics

France
    and hidden agendas over Iraq, 127
    and the food for oil scandal,
        380–81
    hidden agendas of, 374, 378, 380

Freud, Sigmund, 121

Friedman, Thomas, 98
    on 9/11, 279

Gaidar, Yegor

Gates, Bill, 190

Gaviard, Jean Patrick (French General),
        332

George Bush's Unfinished Asian Agenda
    (article, Hathaway), 19

Germany
and hidden agendas over Iraq, 127
as example of transplanted
demoocracy, 346–47
Glennon, Michael, 381
global economies and economic cultures,
438. *See also* by specific country;
convergence
different results between, 140–42
divergence of, xvii, 13, 24, 55, 170–84,
240, 257, 258, 370, 429, 437, 438,
465
Goh Chok Tong, 393
Gorbachev, Mikhail, 208, 209, 390
Grenada, 421
successful U.S. preemption against, 328

Haass, Richard, 46, 362
Halberstam, David, 95
harmonism, 11, 42–47, 344, 392, 437, 454
abour foreign leaders, 417
about international law, 365
about non-Western economic
systems, 210
and China, 190
and illusions about economic
progress, 84
defined, 41
illusions about hidden agendas of
other nations, 362
unjustified optimism of, 52–55
Hathaway, Robert M., 19
Heginbotham, Eric, 64
Henry IV (Shakespeare), 37
Hitler, Adolf, 322, 323, 408
and failure of FDR to confront, 419
and misjudgement of by
Chamberlain, 416
failure to react to, 322, 326
underestimating of Britain by, 246

Holbrooke, Richard C., 372
Honderich, Ted, 287–88
honesty, need for in U.S. Presidents. *See*
candor, need for in U.S. Presidents
Hong Kong, 188
Hooker, Joseph (U.S. General), 345
Hu Jintao, 19. *See also* China
Huntington, Samuel, 361
Hussein, Saddam, 29, 300
and attempt to assassinate Bush
Senior, 413
and mocking of U.S. presidents,
413
and the food for oil scandal, 380–81
failure to depose, 394, 422
hype, in American public culture, 68–75

imperialism, accusations of U.S. 111–16
international conflict, threat of. *See also*
Iraq; Muslim terrorism; nuclear
conflict, threat of; terrorism,
threat of
and international law, 365
and Iran, 456
and Japan, 152
and Kosovo as example of myth of war
without casualties, 335–36
and poor war leadership by U.S.
presidents, 418–29
and promoting democracy, 352–54
and sequence of threats, xvii, 7, 10, 23,
33, 236, 439, 462
and Taiwan, 195, 199–03, 245
and the Cuban missile crisis, 251–52
and U.S. military response to, 336–37
and U.S./Chinese rivalry, 185–88
and Ukraine, 246
between democracies, 352–54
European approach to, 370–71. *See*
also multilateralism

international conflict (*cont.*)

    from Asian vortex of danger, 244–46

    from China, 246–48, 300

    from disruption of oil supply, 240,
        245

    from reconfiguration of global wealth
        and power, xvii, 13, 24, 55, 240,
        257, 258, 429, 437, 438, 465

    from rogue states, 222

    from Russia, 215–18, 240–44, 300

    from the great powers, 12–15, 235–39,
        389, 436–39

    from US/EU rivalry, 246

    over Japanese shipping lanes, 188, 203,
        245, 257

international relations and geopolitics,
        18–20. *See also* by specific country;
        international conflict, threat of;
        Iraq

    and Able Archer, 252–54

    and accusations of U.S. imperialism,
        111–16

    and Britain, 227

    and changes in international order,
        27–29

    and Chinese/Japanese rivalries in,
        244–48

    and diplomacy versus war, 372–73

    and dispute over 2004 Ukrainian
        elections, 76–79

    and erraticness of U.S. in, 438

    and EU approach to world problems,
        370–71

    and international view of U.S.
        presidency, 415–16

    and Kosovo as example of myth of war
        without casualties, 335–36

    and misappraisals of foreign leaders
        by U.S. presidents, 416–18

    and multilateralism, 359–63, 366–71

    and nation building in EU, 218–25,
        227–28

    and North Korea, 414

    and polling, 106

    and role of strategic independence,
        460–61

    and Russia as emerging superpower,
        204

    and Russian remilitarization, 215–18,
        240–44

    and suitabilty of U.S. as sole
        superpower, 396–98

    and Taiwan, 199–03, 245

    and testing of U.S. presidents, 410–14

    and the ABM treaty, 308, 309, 314

    and the Cuban missile crisis, 251–52

    and the Iran-Contra scandal, 422

    and the Israeli-Palestinian conflict,
        279–85

    and U.S. leadership, 259–62

    and U.S./Chinese rivalry, 185–88

    and US/EU rivalry, 246

    and use of international law
        post–WWI by U.S. presidents,
        363–65

    and weak leadership by U.S.
        presidents, 409–29, 436–39

    aspects of great U.S. presidential
        leadership in,

    exploitation of Iraqi war by major
        powers, 126–27

    inconsistency in U.S. 129

    overemphasis on relationships in,
        66–67

    power rivalries in, 246–48

    simplification of, 64–65

    successful preemptions in, 328

Iran, 247

    and Carter's poor leadership in
        hostage situation, 421

and incentives for ceasing nuclear
program of, 370, 460
and the Iran-Contra scandal, 422
danger of, 456
nuclear capabilities of, 240, 267, 300
Iraq, 29, 262
accuracy of reports from, 449–50
and Bush's policy of democracy for,
97–99, 288–98, 355–57, 453,
457–60
and geopolitical rivalries as factor in,
290–91
and strengths and weakness of
preemption in, 329–30
and terrorism, 459–60
and WMD as justification for, 327,
450–51, 455, 457
as demonstration of U.S. military
effectiveness, 124–26, 332, 394,
413, 462
as example of myth of war with no
casualties, 335–36
changing international opinion on,
109–11
deception about motives for by Bush,
448–49
errors of strategy in, 459–60
exploitation of by major powers,
126–27, 218–22, 260
guerrilla war in, 294, 297
invasion of as response to Hussein's
provocations, 413–14
number of casualties in, 237
polls on,
reasons for U.S. invasion of, 288–91
roots of in weak leadership in U.S. and
Europe, 414
Islamic fundamentalism. *See* bin Laden,
Osama; Middle East; Muslim
terrorism

isolationism, 377
and strategic independence, 307, 308
Israel
and the Israeli-Palestinian conflict,
279–85
as U.S. ally,
falling fertility rates in, 284
small margin of error for survival of,
282

Jamieson, Kathleen Hall, 93
Japan
and relations with China, 244–48, 437
as example of transplanted
demoocracy, 346–47
atomic bombing of, 409–10
nuclear capabilities of, 152
risk from, 437
shipping lanes of, 188, 203, 245, 257
Japanese economy and economic culture,
152–61
as communally managed market
system, 153–61, 167
as shame-based culture, 153, 157
Johnson, Lyndon, 31, 329
and poor war leadership in Vietnam,
421, 430
Johnson, Paul, 26
journalists. *See* media

Kagan, Robert, 360, 361
Kaplan, Robert, 50
Kennan, George, 340, 344, 410
Kennedy, John F., 252, 329
and Khrushchev, 410, 412
and poor leadership in Vietnam, 409,
410–11, 420
and public culture, 410
and the Cuban missile crisis, 420
Kennedy, Paul, 134, 208, 238, 448

Kerry, John, 89, 361

Key, V.O., 94

Keynes, John Maynard, 85, 349

Khamenei, Ayatollah Ali, 456

Khrushchev, Nikita, 197, 251, 252
  and JFK, 410, 412
  poor leadership of, 432

Kissinger, Henry, 21, 185, 388

Kohut, Andrew, 106

Korean War, 20, 122, 394
  and poor leadership in by Truman,
    420
  number of casualties in, 409

Kosovo conflict, 378, 400
  and myth of war without casualties,
    335–36

Krauthammer, Charles, 344

Krugman, Paul, 152

Kupchan, Charles, 363

Laughlin, Robert, 20

League of Nations, 224, 379, 408, 419,
    453

Ledeen, Michael, 87, 88

Leonard, Mark, 363

Lewis, Bernard, 356, 440

Liang Hong, 194

Lieven, Anatol, 8

Lincoln, Abraham, 96, 345, 428,
    432–33

Macaulay, Thomas Babington, 16

MAD (mutually assured destruction),
    203, 248–51, 307
  and Able Archer, 252–54
  and the Cuban missile crisis, 251–52
  inadequacy of, 316, 319, 337, 338–39,
    427–28
  inadequacy of against Chinese,
    395–96

Malraux, Andre, 305

Mao Zedong, 305

Marine barracks in Lebanon, attack on,
    286, 437

Marshall, Alfred, xix, 133

Marshall, George C. (U.S. General), 122,
    337, 340, 345, 420

Marshall, Will, 53

Martin, Lisa, 374

Masahiko Aoki, 153

McArthur, Douglas (U.S. General), 394,
    420

McClellan, George (U.S. General), 345

McKinley, William, 449

McNamara, Robert, 427

Mead, Walter Russell, 379

Mearsheimer, John, 203, 261

media
  and accuracy of news from Iraq,
    449–50
  and China, 188–89
  and distortion about Bush, 95, 96
  and distortion over 2004 Ukrainian
    elections, 77–80
  commercialism in, 95–96
  reinforcement of public culture by, 15,
    91–96

Men Honghua, 196

Merimee, Jean-Bernard, 380

Michalak, Stanley, 374

Middle East, 20, 98, 293, 453, 458, 459
  and Bush's policy of democracy for,
    355–57
  and national missile defense, 311,
    314
  and public opinion on feasibility of
    democracy working in, 350
  and the Israeli-Palestinian conflict,
    279–85
  economy of, 267–69
  illusions about, 266, 282, 299
  infeasibility of *Ummah* in, 267

political battle for control of, 279

strategic repositioning of as real
motive for Iraq, 456, 457

Miller, Zell, 98

Mills, John Stuart, 50

Miniter, Richard, 324

Molotov, Vyacheslav, 450

multilateralism, 359–63

and disarmamant, 375–78

and strategic independence, 305–06,
425, 461

and U.S. decline, 362–63

and unworkability of collective
security, 363–66

hidden agendas in, 372, 406, 425

trap of for U.S. 366–71

wishful thinking about, 375

Musharraf, Pervez (President of
Pakistan), 353

Muslim terrorism, 267–70

and fatwa of bin Laden, 275–77

and Iraq, 459–60

and poverty, 270–75

and Russia, 270, 299

and the EU, 299

and the Israeli-Palestinian conflict,
279–85

and U.S. as enemy of, 298–99

causes of, 270

justifications for, 288

pre 9/11 terrorist attacks on U.S. 277

threat of, 299–300, 400

mutual assured destruction. *See* MAD

Myth of Asia's Miracle, The (article,
Krugman), 152

mythomaniacs, in American public
culture, 82

Napoleon, successful preemption against,
328

Naylor, Sean, 398

New Jersey Solidarity, 287

New Orleans, flooding of, 348

New York Times, The (newspaper), 79,
315, 392

Nixon, Richard, 31

poor war leadership in Vietnam by,
421

NMD (National Missile Defense),
254–57, 307

and rogue states as justification for,
313–15

and the Clinton administration, 311,
314

and the Reagan administration, 311

as defense against nuclear
proliferation, 308–16

as deterrent to China's nuclear
build-up, 393, 395–96

need for candor about, 313

North Korea, 19, 247, 311, 368, 392

and incentives for ceasing nuclear
program of, 460

nuclear capabilities of, 240, 245, 414

nuclear conflict, threat of, 254–62

and failure of U.S. preemption,
328–29

and incentives for ceasing of nuclear
weapons programs, 370, 460

and Japan, 152

and military response to, 336–37

and NMD as defense against, 254–57,
308–16

and strategic independence as defense
against, 336–39, 427–28

and the ABM treaty, 308, 309, 314

and U.S. leadership's response to,
259–62

avoiding as overriding objective in
U.S. policy, 389

during the Cold War, 251. *See also*
Able Archer; Cuban missile crisis

nuclear conflict, threat of (*cont.*)
from China, 12, 185, 195–97, 254–57, 391–96
from Iran, 240, 267, 300, 370, 456, 460
from North Korea, 240, 245, 267, 460
from Russia, 12, 240, 390–91
future challenges, 254
unpredictability of, 254
Nye, Joe, 465

Odum, William, 14
oil, 188, 245, 248, 384, 464
danger of disruption in supply of, 240
in Russia, 457, 459
reliance on foreign, 457
Olson, Mancur, 213
On Liberty (Mills), 50
overreach, 135
in Iraq, 98, 99, 354–57
of the Bush Doctrine, 317–18

Pakistan, 353
economy of, 50
nuclear capabilities of, 267
Palestine
and the Israeli-Palestinian conflict, 279–85
Pareto, 60, 61
partisan politics, and reinforcement of public culture, 88–91
Pearl Harbor, 322, 326
Penn, Shana, 351
Perry, Bill, 333
Pershing, John J. (U.S. General), 345
Plato, 30
Pliyev, Issa, 251
Pollack, Kenneth, 356
polling, dangers of, 106
Polybius, 14
poverty, and Muslim terrorism, 270–75

Powell, Colin, 378
Powers That Be, The (Halberstam), 95
preemption, 408
against Napoleon, 328
and nuclear threats from Soviet Union, 328–29
and possibility of avoiding WWII, 322–23, 325–26, 330
and trust between President and citizens, 326–27
calculating risks of, 326–27
examples of successful, 328
failure to preempt Riad bombing, 320, 321
role of in strategic independence, 320–21
September 11, 2001 and, 323–26, 330
strengths and weakness of Iraq invasion, 329–30
Presidency, U.S. *See* U.S. presidency and political leadership
Priest, Dana, 399
Pry, Peter Vincent, 254
Pryce-Jones, David, 18
public culture, 454. *See also* American public; convergence; harmonism; wishful thinking
and diffculty of accepting containment policy, 344
and fatal flaw of perception in of U.S. superiority, 128–29
and influence on Bush's Iraq policy, 456–60
and President Bush, 97–99, 423–29, 453–56
and President Kennedy, 410
and President Truman, 409
and romanticizing of Stalin, 57–58
and the American credo, 59–61

and the U.S. military, 334
and the Vietnam War, 410
and U.S. presidents need to master
    illusions of, 3–17, 414, 435, 465
and U.S. security policy, 3–17, 96–99,
    317, 343, 400–01, 421, 465
commercialism in, 95–96, 437
distortion of reality by, 10–12, 37–2,
    76–80, 453
dysfunctional behaviors in, 11, 63–81
See also hype; simplification;
    distortion
either/or construct in, 65–66
hype in, 68–75
illusions about Middle East in, 266,
    282, 299
illusions about Russia in, 204–07, 215,
    243
morality in, 98, 99, 400
mythomaniacs in, 82
naivety in, 64–65
persistence of illusions in, 55–58
reinforcement of by media, 15, 91–96
reinforcement of by partisan politics,
    88–91
self-image in, 103–08
simplification in, 64–68
versus pop culture, 8
Putin, Vladimir, 110, 149, 150, 151, 204,
    215, 242
    and misjudgement of by Bush,
        416–18
    and remilitarization, 215
    authoritarian regime of, 173, 204, 206,
        207, 209, 210, 211, 213, 215, 216

Rawls, John, 56
Reagan, Ronald and the Reagan
    administration, 421–22
    and Able Archer, 252
    and candor about the Iran Contra
        affair, 422
    and Grenada, 328, 421
    and national missile defense, 311
    and Reagan as exception to poor
        Presidential leadership, 431–32
Revlon, Charles, 16
revolution in military affairs (RMA). *See
    under* U.S. military
Rice, Condoleezza, 71, 110, 266, 316, 426,
    428
Richardson, Louise, 279
RMA (revolution in military affairs). *See
    under* U.S. military
rogue states
    as argument for NMD, 395–96
    as justification for national missile
        defense, 313–15
    threat from, 222
Roosevelt, Eleanor, 401
Roosevelt, Franklin Delano, 45, 408, 409,
    433–34
    and failure to confront Hitler, 419
    misjudging of Stalin, 417
    naive idealism of, 453
    poor war leadership of in WWII,
        419–20
Roosevelt, Theodore, 297
Rumsfeld, 494n6, 495n14
Rumsfeld, Donald, 110, 290, 293, 313,
    318, 428
Russia. *See also* Gorbachev, Mikhail;
        Putin, Vladimir; Soviet Union;
        Yeltsin, Boris
    American illusions about, 204–07
    and dispute with U.S. over 2004
        elections in Ukraine, 76–79
    and hidden motivations over response
        to Iraqi invasion, 127
    and oil, 457

Russia (*cont.*)
    as emerging superpower, 204, 240–44
    declining population of, 217
    false democracy of, 212–14
    nuclear capabilities of, 12, 240, 242
    nuclear threats from, 390–91
    remilitarization of, 214–18, 236,
        240–44, 456
    threat of Muslim terrorism to, 270,
        299

Russian economy and economic culture,
    149–51
    and failure to transition to market
        economy, 3, 149–50, 207–12, 318,
        422–23
    and remilitarization, 214–16
    as authoritarian managed market
        system, 149–51, 207–12
    misappropriation of assets in, 208–10,
        390
    subjugation in, 214
    weakness of, 14, 240, 242, 438

Sachs, Jeffrey, 46
Samuelson, Paul, 60
Saudi Arabia, and potential preemption
    of Riad bombing, 320, 321
Schwarz, Benjamin, 375
Sealer, John R., 94
Second Gulf War. *See* Iraq
Sellers, Frances Stead, 362
Seneca, 43
September 11th, 2001, 415
    changes in U.S. from, 22, 117–23
    changing international opinion on,
        109, 110
    effect on U.S. security policy, 124–26,
        237, 264, 318
    failure to preempt, 323–26, 330

    hysteria after, 69
    number of casualties in, 237
    pre-9/11 terrorist attacks, 277
Shakespeare, William, 37
Shambaugh, David, 186
Sharon, Ariel, 284–85
Shashi Tharoor, 21
Shirer, William R., 95
Shlykov, Vitaly, 204, 253
Shultz, George, 422
Sieff, Martin, 216
simplification, in American public
    culture, 64–68
    dangerous consequences of, 68
Skowronek, Stephen, 97
Soviet Union. *See also* Gorbachev,
    Mikhail; Lenin, Vladimir;
    Krushchev, Nikita; Putin,
    Vladimir; Russia; Stalin, Joseph;
    Yeltsin, Boris
    and Able Archer, 252–54
    and failure of U.S. preemption of
        nuclear threats from, 328–29
    and the Afghan War, 411
    and the Cuban missile crisis, 251–52
    and U.S. policy of containment, 344
    dissolution of, 207–12
    economy of, 147–49
Spanish-American War, deception about
    motives for, 449
Stalin, Joseph, 57–58, 189, 329, 409, 417
Stimson Doctrine, 364
Stimson, Henry, 364, 365
strategic independence, 4, 15, 16, 25–27,
    55. *See also* U.S. national security
    and security policy
    and China, 203
    and disarmament, 375–77
    and global federalism, 15, 389, 462,
        463

and isolationism, 307, 308

and military supremacy, 319

and multilateralism, 17, 305–06, 425, 461

and NMD, 203, 308–16

and recognizing limits of transplanting American system, 337

and role of UN in, 381

and Russia, 391

and the Bush Doctrine, 316–18

as defense against nuclear threats, 336–39, 427–28

as deterrent to China's nuclear build up, 393, 395–96

core of, 306

earning of, 307

need for in U.S. defense policy, 14, 17, 338–40, 401, 447, 460–61

objections to, 319–20, 337

opportunity for assertion of, 318–20

preemption in, 320–21

role of UN in, 381

superpowers. *See also* China; European Union; international relations and geopolitics; Japan; Russia

and suitability of U.S. as sole, 396–98

Taiwan, 188, 247, 388

and China, 191, 195

and risk of conflict over, 195, 245

Tang Ben (Professor at Claremont Institute), 201

Taylor, Mark, 59

Terrill, Ross, 188

terrorism, threat of, 240. *See also* Muslim terrorism

against civilians, 288

and military response to, 336–37

need for reprioritization of, 12, 237, 259–60, 264–67, 301, 390, 399, 400, 438

paradox of terrorism, 399–400, 460

use of by Nazi's,

versus greater threat from the great powers, 235–38

The Nature and Origins of Mass Opinion (Sealer), 94

Thurow, Lester, 363

Truman, Harry, 345, 371, 394

and atomic bombing of Japan, 409–10

and poor leadership in the Korean War, 420

and public culture, 409–10

U.S. economy and economic culture. *See also* American style democracy and free enterprise, transplanting abroad

corruption in, 348–49

success of, 16, 133–40, 168

U.S. military

and attack on Marine barracks in Lebanon, 286, 437

and attack on USS Cole, 286, 437

and Iraq as demonstration of effectiveness of, 124–26, 332, 462

and myth of war without casualties, 335–36

and need for full range response to multiple threats, 336–37

and public culture, 334

and RMA (revolution in military affairs), 196, 247, 333–35, 340, 394, 413

and support of by Americans post-9/11, 119–20

challenges to civilian dominance from, 345–46

U.S. military (*cont.*)
  changing attitudes to, 122–23
  danger of over reliance on, 398–400
  effectiveness of, 332–33
  errors of strategy in Afghanistan,
    398–400
  goal of supremacy for, 319
  improved leadership in, 333
  need for full range to respond to
    multiple threats, 336–37

U.S. national security and security policy.
    See also by specific war;
    international conflict, threat of;
    Iraq; Middle East; Muslim
    terrorism; nuclear conflict, threat
    of; terrorism, threat of; U.S.
    military
  and containment during the Cold
    War, 344
  and dangers of polling, 106
  and harmonism, 42–47
  and inability to locate bin Laden, 295
  and Israel as ally,
  and mistake of labeling terrorism
    defense as war, 285
  and need for strategic independence,
    14, 340, 447, 460–61. *See also*
    strategic independence
  and nuclear threat from China,
    391–96
  and nuclear threats from Russia,
    390–91
  and poor war leadership by U.S.
    presidents, 418–29
  and public culture, 3–17, 96–99, 317,
    343, 400–01, 421, 432–35
  and reliance on foreign oil, 457
  and rivalry with China, 185–88,
    199–03

and Russia, 204
and Russian remilitarization, 215–18,
  240–44
and successful preemption in
  Grenada, 328
and suitability of U.S. as sole
  superpower, 396–98
and Taiwan, 199–03, 245
and the ABM treaty, 308, 309, 314
and the Bush Doctrine, 316–18
and the Soviet Union, 344
and threat of nuclear war. *See* MAD;
  NMD; nuclear conflict, threat of
and transplanting democracy. *See*
  American style democracy and free
  enterpise, transplanting abroad
and trap of multilateralism for, 366–71
and unworkability of collective
  security, 363–66
and vortexes of danger, 18–20
and wishful thinking, 84–88, 438
aspects of great presidential leadership
  on,
changes in after September 11th,
  124–26, 318
changes in from WWI through
  Vietnam, 121–24
coming threats to, 22–25, 336–37
either/or construct in, 65–66
erraticness of, 438
impact of international rivalries on,
  246–48
inconsistency in, 129
leadership in response to threats to,
  259–62
mature superpower as goal in, 129,
  339
need for independence in, 15
See also multilateralism; strategic
  independence

need for objectivity in, 20–21

need for presidential candor about
motives in, 446–53

need for reprioritization of terrorism
in, 12, 237, 259–60, 264–67, 301,
390, 399, 400, 438

presidential deception about motives
of, 446–53

unjustified optimism in, 52–55

weak presidential leadership in,
409–14, 436–39

U.S. presidency and political leadership.
See also by specific president

and deception about motives, 446–53

and distrust of by public, 260, 446–49,
451

and governorship as poor preparation
for, 440–41

and misappraisals of foreign leaders
by, 416–18

and national security, 432–35, 465

and need for managerial and
leadership skills in, 405–06

and need to master illusions of public
culture, 3–17, 262, 422, 435, 465

and overreliance on advisors, 429–32

and public culture, 88–91, 96–99, 414,
465

and response to geopolitical threats,
239, 259–62

and testing of by foreign leaders,
410–14

and use of international law
post–WWI, 363–65

and weak leadership in, 436–39

and weakness in international affairs,
409–18

and wishful thinking towards Soviet
Union, 206–07

aspects of great leadership,

criteria for electing, 406, 414, 444

international view of, 415–16

military challenges to, 345–46

need for candor in, 17, 30–32, 261,
313, 327, 382, 392, 414, 421, 438,
446–49, 463

need for recognition of maturity, 129

poor war leadership of, 406–09,
418–29

preparation for, 439–41

Ukraine
and dispute over 2004 elections in,
76–79

and threat of conflict over, 246

Ummah (pan-Muslim theocracy)
infeasibility of, 267

United Nations, 12, 371–75
food for oil scandal of, 380–81

need for candor about, 382

United States
accusations of imperialism of, 111–16

and Able Archer, 252–54

and dispute with Russia over 2004
elections in Ukraine, 76–79

and flooding of New Orleans, 348

and rivalry with China, 185–88

and suitabilty of as sole superpower,
396–98

and the Cuban missile crisis, 251–52

changes since September 11th, 22

mature superpower as goal for, 129

pop versus traditional culture in, 347

See also public culture and American
public

pre-9/11 terrorist attacks on, 277

rivalry with EU, 246

social disintegration in, 349

Updike, John, 344

USS *Cole*, attack on, 286, 437

USSR. *See* Russia; Soviet Union

Vietnam, 333

Vietnam War, 20, 122, 410–11, 418
  and changes in defense policy after, 124
  and poor leadership by Johnson, 421, 430
  and poor leadership by Kennedy, 409, 420
  and poor leadership by Nixon, 421
  and public culture, 410
  failure to win hearts and minds in, 292, 293
  number of casualties in, 409

Villages (Updike), 344
Volker, Paul, 380
vortexes of danger, 13, 19

Waldron, Arthur, 188
Wallace, William, 360
Walt, Stephen, 53
war on terror, 12, 264, 265, 266, 291, 297, 300, 307, 438, 454
  Clinton's ineffectiveness in, 406
  need to reduce funding in, 262
war, threat of. *See* by specific war;
    international conflict, threat of;
    Iraq; nuclear conflict, threat of;
    U.S. military
Warren, Robert Penn, 15
Washington, George, 360, 379, 427
  Farewell Address of, 26, 360
Weafer, Chris, 457
weapons of mass destruction, 97, 264, 266, 293, 437
  as justification for Iraq invasion, 327, 450–51, 455, 457
Weinberger, Caspar, 252, 253, 422
Weiner, Allen, 72
Wells, H.G., 454
Wheatcroft, Andrew, 47

Willkie, Wendell, 45
Wilson, Woodrow, 235, 343, 408
  naive idealism of, 453
  poor war leadership of, 418
wishful thinking, 89, 417
  about China, 191, 393
  about democracy, 266
  about multilateralism, 375
  about transplanting of American system abroad, 349
  about world peace, 406
  and American public, 83–84
  and dictatorships, 84–86
  and national security, 438
  and self-deception in foreign policy, 84–86
  and the Israeli-Palestinian conflict, 283
  and U.S. security policy, 86–88
  European, 360
Woodward, Bob,
world peace
  wishful thinking about, 83, 406
World War I, 20, 235, 363–65, 408, 418
  number of casualties in, 408
World War II, 20, 235, 292, 373, 408, 418
  and Truman's decision to use the atomic bomb, 409–10
  failure to preempt, 322–23, 325–26, 330
  number of casualties in, 237, 408
  poor war leadership in by FDR, 419–20

Yakovlev, Alexander, 212
Yeltsin, Boris, 150, 208, 209, 210, 390

Zakheim, Dov, 382
Zhu Chenghu (Chinese General), 201, 394
Zimmerman, Warren, 363